■ ■ ■

BETWEEN WORLDS

■ ■ ■

BETWEEN WORLDS

A Reader, Rhetoric, and Handbook

Second Edition

SUSAN BACHMANN
El Camino College

MELINDA BARTH
El Camino College

An imprint of Addison Wesley Longman, Inc.

New York • Reading, Massachusetts • Menlo Park, California • Harlow, England
Don Mills, Ontario • Sydney • Mexico City • Madrid • Amsterdam

Publishing Partner: Anne E. Smith
Development Manager: Patricia A. Rossi
Developmental Editor: Lynn Walterick
Marketing Manager: Ann Stypuloski
Project Coordination and Text Design: York Production Services
Cover Designer: Lili Schwartz
Full Service Production Manager: Valerie Zaborski
Manufacturing Manager: Hilda Koparanian
Electronic Page Makeup: York Production Services
Printer and Binder: Maple-Vail Book Manufacturing Group
Cover Printer: The Lehigh Press, Inc.
Cover Art: The glass spheres on the cover, photographed by Claire Garoutte, are the work of Seattle glass artist Dale Chihuly. They are up to 42 inches in diameter and are called "Niijima Floats" (1992) after the island near Tokyo where glassblowers once made balls for Japanese fishermen to keep their nets afloat. Mr. Chihuly recalls that when he was a child, he found the fishermen's floats on the beaches near his home in Tacoma, Washington.

Library of Congress Cataloging-in-Publication Data
Between worlds: a reader, rhetoric, and handbook/[compiled by]
Susan Bachmann, Melinda Barth.
p. cm.
Includes bibliographical references and index.
ISBN 0-321-01195-3
1. College readers. 2. English language—Rhetoric. 3. English language—Grammar—Handbooks, manuals, etc. I. Bachmann, Susan. II. Barth, Melinda.
PE1417.B43 1997 96-52582
808′.0427–dc21 CIP

ISBN 0-321-01195-3

1234567890–MA–00999897

Again, to the men in our lives:
Ron, Dylan, and Evan Barth
and
Walter, Ryan, and Adam Gajewski

Contents

■ ■ ■

Preface

■ ■ ■

Between Worlds, Second Edition, remains a reader, rhetoric, and handbook that offers students and instructors essential materials to support their writing courses. A diverse reader with thematically arranged selections includes writing prompts that encourage students to write about each reading in isolation as well as in relation to other texts. A concise rhetoric and handbook follow the reader. They are designed to help students through every aspect of the writing process and through some of the most common writing assignments, including the research paper. Although each section of this textbook can be used independently, both instructor and student will find the cross-referencing of material between the reader and the rhetoric an advantage for teaching and learning.

Since the publication of the first edition, we have received overwhelming support for combining three texts within one cover, for our selection of provocative readings, and for the cross-referencing of these readings with meaningful assignments and accessible rhetorical instruction. This edition retains our successes and includes some exciting changes and additions.

NEW READINGS AND MORE VARIED TOPICS

New selections revitalize each of the existing chapters to reflect the conflicting realms—the "between worlds"—in which most of us live. Like us, the individuals in these readings are caught between balancing the burdens of work and school, satisfying family obligations and meeting personal needs, and defining self while relating with others. New topics feature paired readings to show divergent views about protecting the environment, living online, interpreting history, and evaluating a popular television program. Additional new readings complement the existing themes of family pressures and expectations, gender and culture identification, self-images and perceptions, and value choices.

NEW VOICES AND FAVORITE VOICES

This edition continues to include writers favored by students and instructors: Ellen Goodman, Anne Tyler, Noel Perrin, Warren Farrell, Barbara Ehrenreich, Joyce Carol Oates, Sharon Olds, Gary Soto, Brent Staples, Tony Cade Bambara, Marge Piercy and Gloria Naylor. Important voices, new to this edition, include Martin Luther King, Jr., Seamus Heaney, Michael Ventura, Michael Dorris, Wendell Berry, Jay McInerney, Elayne Rapping, Cliff Stoll, Nicholas Negroponte, Jane Tompkins, Barbara Kafka, Gloria Anzaldúa, and Dorothy Noyes.

NEW READING QUESTIONS AND WRITING ASSIGNMENTS

Each of the readings is followed by "Thinking About the Text" questions so that students can examine the content of the work before class discussion. "Writing from the Text" sections provide students with writing topics for the individual work. In "Connecting with Other Texts," both the new and retained readings are linked thematically within each chapter and throughout the book. These assignments encourage students to examine multiple perspectives critically and then use diverse materials to support their points in papers.

NEW GENRES

Diverse forms, styles, and techniques are reflected in the readings in this edition. In addition to the standard academic essay exemplified in both short, focused pieces and longer, more complex forms, the readings include editorials and commentaries, expository essays, explicit arguments, descriptive narratives, reviews, a letter, four short stories, and six poems.

NEW ADDITIONS TO THE RHETORIC

A new section on summary writing teaches how to write a summary and examines a student model. A new section on poetry analysis demystifies that writing assignment and includes a student model and discussion of it. Because we recognize that writing is a discovery process, we continue to emphasize numerous prewriting strategies; practical advice for considering audience; ideas about arrangement, outlining, drafting, and revision; and tips for constructing and revising the thesis. Throughout the rhetoric we show that writing is not a step-by-step process; it involves concurrent and recursive activities.

An expanded section on audience provides analysis of a writer's strategy in an argument essay. Additional practice exercises are included throughout.

NEW MATERIALS ON RESEARCH AND ELECTRONIC SOURCES

Updated MLA guidelines are illustrated and discussed as well as APA documentation forms. This edition includes a section on using and abusing electronic sources as well as on documenting them. Because so much of the research process has become computer-based, we also include a glossary of computer-related terms to help novices shuttle between the world of books and the newer world of cyberspace.

NEW HANDBOOK ENTRIES

The handbook remains compact because it is designed to empower students but not overwhelm them. We focus on the most common errors—the "terrible ten"—that persistently appear in student writing. A list of margin symbols is included to help students interpret their instructors' comments. We have added new examples and new entries to the alphabetical list of troublesome words that many writers confuse or misuse.

ACKNOWLEDGMENTS

This textbook could never have been written without the help of many people who have been particularly supportive and generous with their time as we worked on this book. Two superb librarians, Judy Harris and Eileen Wakiji, have given us enough information on computers to save us from looking foolish in front of our students. We are especially grateful to Rïse Daniels and Bill Bachmann for their talented teamwork on this book and for putting aside their own projects when we needed their expertise. We are grateful to Ernest Hankamer, Professor of Philosophy at the University of Maryland, for his timely and incisive introductory remarks and definitions for Jane Tompkins' essay. Over the years, colleagues at El Camino College, Marymount College, the State University of New York at Buffalo, the University of Wisconsin at Madison, the University of Illinois at Champaign, and California State University at Dominguez Hills have shared teaching strategies and writing ideas that inspired portions of this book. One of those colleagues, Devon Hodges, Professor of English at George Mason University, asked her students to critique our first edition, and those evaluations helped shape this edition. Shannon Paaske and Salma Jetha worked energetically to help us meet our deadline, and we are pleased that some of our other students—Chris Thomas, Bruce Halling, Tim Hogan, and Jennifer Tabaldo—also became published writers with the printing of this text. Our students merit hearty applause.

Special thanks must go to a number of fine reviewers who brought insights from their teaching to improve our efforts in creating this text. We wish to thank these supportive critics: Marilyn Anderson, El Camino College; Roy K. Bird, University of Alaska, Fairbanks; Cheryl Glenn, Oregon State University; Christine Hult, Utah State University; Maurice Hunt, Baylor University; Susan M. Hunter, Kennesaw State University; David A. Jolliffe, DePaul University; Phyllis Kiernan, Jefferson Community College; Bill Lamb, Johnson County Community College; Sarah Liggett, Louisiana State University, Lisa J. McClure, Southern Illinoise University,; Brian Monahan, Westchester Community College; Rolf Norgaard, University of Colorado; Cathy Powers Dice, University of Memphis; Mary Prindiville, University of Wisconsin, Green Bay; Glenda Richter, Grossmont College; and Mary Lynn West, Spokane Community College.

We are grateful to our friends at Longman (formerly HarperCollins): Patricia A. Rossi, Development Manager, who was immediately and continuously enthusiastic about our project; Anne E. Smith, Publishing Partner, whose phone calls cheered and supported us; and Lynn Walterick, our extraordinarily well-read development editor, who fortified us to revise and improve this book.

Finally, we want to try to thank the men in our lives who lived *Between Worlds* with us. Walter and Ron rescued us from computer chaos and kept our children from feeling that they had been banished to another world. Ryan and Adam and Dylan and Evan helped as well—sometimes with hugs, often with humor, and occasionally by simply disappearing! Other family members and friends sent us relevant articles, offered their help, and understood when we turned down invitations and did not answer letters or phone calls. They all believed this project was worth their being temporarily "displaced" . . . and we applaud their willingness to live "between worlds" with us.

Susan Bachmann
Melinda Barth

I

THE READER

■ ■ ■

The readings in this text have been chosen to reflect the interests of college students like you, who are juggling school and work as well as balancing social lives and family expectations. The selections have been arranged thematically into five chapters. These chapters describe the multiple worlds that all of us live in and the tensions that pull us between the realms of generations, genders, cultures, perceptions, and values. We chose these readings to stimulate your thinking so that you can write meaningful essays—the goal of your composition course.

Each chapter contains many essays, some short stories, and a poem or two, all arranged to parallel or contrast with each other. After each reading, you will find a section called "Thinking About the Text." These questions were designed for you to use as a study review before class and for small-group discussions during class. We follow these questions with "Writing from the Text," a section of writing assignments that spring from the readings and from your own experience. Your instructor may assign these topics, or they can be used for practice writing in a journal. You will find help for writing these assignments in the rhetoric portion of this text.

A third section, "Connecting with Other Texts," will help you if your instructor asks you to compare two or more readings in this book. Some assignments in this section will encourage you to find extra material in the library; these assignments can be used if your instructor assigns a paper that requires research. You will find instruction on how to write research papers of various lengths in the rhetoric portion of this text.

Some of the authors in this book are caught between generations and, like you, are trying to understand themselves in relation to parents and grandparents. And just as you are examining the roles that define your gender, many of these authors argue for a reexamination of those roles that limit the lives of people of both sexes. Whether you are a newcomer to the United States, a second- or third-generation American, or a settled citizen, you may find that these writers describe what you have experienced living between cultures. Your perception of who you are inevitably is colored by others' images of you. Yet your desire to be perceived as an individual, rather than a stereotype, is also the experience of many college students and of the authors who write about being between perceptions. The selections in Chapter 5 encourage you to think about your values—something you probably have done more seriously since you started college. You may want to examine the ideas of the authors in this last chapter to reassess your own convictions.

1

Between Generations

■ ■ ■

In our opening essay, Ellen Goodman quotes André Malraux's belief that without family the individual "alone in the world, trembles with the cold." The family often nurtures its members and tolerates differences and failings that friends and lovers cannot accept. If you have a strong bond with a grandparent, you will value Eric Marcus' essay and appreciate the friendship and understanding he gains when his grandmother accepts who he is. The narrator in Seamus Heaney's poem respects his father and grandfather but comes to an acceptance of how he differs from them.

The differences between generations can be both instructive and humorous, as you will see in the short stories by Anne Tyler and Toni Cade Bambara and the essay by Dorothy Noyes. But as you may realize from your own experiences and observations, people also tremble with fear or anxiety even within the family unit. Both Michael Ventura and John Leonard illustrate in their essays that family members sometimes are forced to turn from one another. Michael Dorris provides frightening statistical evidence of the results of mothers who unwittingly have turned from their unborn children. The writers in this chapter show the family as a source of both nurturing and trembling.

Your awareness of gaps between generations, as well as a deeper sense of family connection, may inspire your own writing. The essays, short stories, and poems in this chapter attest to the will of the human spirit to mitigate family tension, to smile at some of the chaos, and to survive and thrive from one generation to the next.

THANKSGIVING
Ellen Goodman

A journalist who has worked for *Newsweek*, CBS, NBC, and a number of metropolitan newspapers, Ellen Goodman (b. 1941) has written a widely syndicated column from her home paper, the *Boston Globe*, since 1967. Goodman won the Pulitzer Prize in 1980 for distinguished commentary. Her subject matter is diverse, and her responses are entertaining. As Diane McWhorter of the *Washington Journalism Review* has said, Goodman "attacks controversies from abortion to housework to Alexander Solzhenitsyn with the combined grace and grit of a paratrooper." Goodman's own comment about her work is that she writes about "more important questions than the average columnist." She asserts that it is "much more important to look at the underlying values by which this country exists . . . the vast social changes in the way men and women lead their lives and deal with each other, [and] about children" than to write about the "trivia," such as politics, that other columnists write about. The essay included here, on the importance of family in our lives, is characteristic of Goodman's concerns. The piece was first published in the *Boston Globe* in 1980.

1 Soon they will be together again, all the people who travel between their own lives and each other's. The package tour of the season will lure them this week to the family table. By Thursday, feast day, family day, Thanksgiving day, Americans who value individualism like no other people will collect around a million tables in a ritual of belonging.

2 They will assemble their families the way they assemble dinner: each one bearing a personality as different as cranberry sauce and pumpkin pie. For one dinner they will cook for each other, fuss for each other, feed each other and argue with each other. They will nod at their common heritage, the craziness and caring of other generations. They will measure their common legacy . . . the children.

3 All these complex cells, these men and women, old and young, with different dreams and disappointments will give homage again to the group they are a part of and apart from: their family. Families and individuals. The "we" and the "I." As good Americans we all travel between these two ideals. We take value trips from the great American notion of individualism to the great American vision of family. We wear out our tires driving back and forth, using speed to shorten the distance between these two principles.

4 There has always been some pavement between a person and a family. From the first moment we recognize that we are separate we begin to wrestle with aloneness and togetherness. Here and now these conflicts are especially acute. We are, after all, raised in families . . . to be individuals. This double message follows us through life. We are taught

about the freedom of the "I" and the safety of the "we." The loneliness of the "I" and the intrusiveness of the "we." The selfishness of the "I" and the burdens of the "we."

We are taught what André Malraux said: "Without a family, man, 5
alone in the world, trembles with the cold." And taught what he said another day: "The denial of the supreme importance of the mind's development accounts for many revolts against the family." In theory, the world rewards "the supreme importance" of the individual, the ego. We think alone, inside our heads. We write music and literature with an enlarged sense of self. We are graded and paid, hired and fired, on our own merit. The rank individualism is both exciting and cruel. Here is where the fittest survive.

The family, on the other hand, at its best, works very differently. We 6
don't have to achieve to be accepted by our families. We just have to be. Our membership is not based on credentials but on birth. As Malraux put it, "A friend loves you for your intelligence, a mistress for your charm, but your family's love is unreasoning: You were born into it and of its flesh and blood."

The family is formed not for the survival of the fittest but for the 7
weakest. It is not an economic unit but an emotional one. This is not the place where people ruthlessly compete with each other but where they work for each other. Its business is taking care, and when it works, it is not callous but kind.

There are fewer heroes, fewer stars in family life. While the world may 8
glorify the self, the family asks us, at one time or another, to submerge it. While the world may abandon us, the family promises, at one time or another, to protect us. So we commute daily, weekly, yearly between one world and another. Between a life as a family member that can be nurturing or smothering. Between life as an individual that can free us or flatten us. We vacillate between two separate sets of demands and possibilities.

The people who will gather around this table Thursday live in both of 9
these worlds, a part of and apart from each other. With any luck the territory they travel from one to another can be a fertile one, rich with care and space. It can be a place where the "I" and the "we" interact. On this day at least, they will bring to each other something both special and something to be shared: these separate selves.

THINKING ABOUT THE TEXT

1. What is the central contradiction or paradox that Goodman expresses in "Thanksgiving" about Americans coming together for this yearly celebration?

2. In what ways are we "raised in families . . . to be individuals"? In what way is the family also the center of "revolt," as André Malraux might express it?

3. On what principle is our membership in the family based, according to Goodman? On what does she insist it is *not* based?

WRITING FROM THE TEXT

1. Describe some unique aspect of yourself that has developed because you were "raised" or nurtured by your family.

2. Goodman writes that on Thanksgiving, people who "live in both worlds"—the world of the individual and the family world—meet and "interact." Write a descriptive scene of your family life and let the account *show* the interaction of the "I" and the "we." Discover a focus point about your being "a part of" and your being "apart from" your family as you develop your narrative. Conclude with that focus expressed as a thesis.

3. Write a brief analysis of a family that you know, focusing on the non-merger of individuals and the failure to create a family life.

4. Consider one of Goodman's statements, such as "We are . . . raised in families . . . to be individuals," or "We don't have to achieve to be accepted by our families. We just have to be." Show how one of these statements is or is not valid for defining your family life.

CONNECTING WITH OTHER TEXTS

1. Use any of the positive depictions of family life in *Between Worlds,* including "Ignorance Is Not Bliss" (p. 14), "Digging" (p. 21), "Proper Care and Maintenance" (p. 170), or "Like Mexicans" (p. 188) to write an essay that focuses on the nurturing elements of family life. Use the texts for examples and specific support.

2. Use any of the *Between Worlds* depictions of troubles in families, including "The Ties That Bind" (p. 7), "The Only Child" (p. 11)," "Fetal Alcohol Syndrome" (p. 23), "Your Place Is Empty" (p. 27), or "Where Are You Going, Where Have You Been?" (p. 101) to focus on the problems in family life. Use the texts for examples and specific support.

■ THE TIES THAT BIND

Michael Ventura

Born in New York in 1945, Michael Ventura has lived the last eighteen years in the Los Angeles area. He has earned his living as a writer since 1974 and has published six books and hundreds of essays and articles. Ventura attributes his abilities not to his two years of college but to the "two excellent teachers in high school who had the skill" to help him hone his craft. Further, he reads extensively and has "always been around intelligent people who read a lot." His most recent books include two novels, *The Death of Frank Sinatra* (1996) and *The Zoo Where You're Fed to God* (1994), as well as a collection of essays, *Letters at 3 a.m.* (1993). The powerful essay that follows appeared in the *Los Angeles Times* on April 14, 1996.

Americans don't like to think of themselves as belonging to others. That is not a democratic idea. We are the country that invented self-invention. We like to believe we can be anything we choose—even if this means choosing what we define as family. 1

When being introduced, we rarely use family names anymore. Just a generation ago, even in California, it would have been rude for a friend to introduce me as anything other than "Mr. Ventura"—a name that comes, in my case, from a small village near Palermo, Italy, and carries with it the history of that place. Until recently, the name you met the world with wasn't merely your own, it was also that of your ancestors—your bloodline walked with you into the world. A new acquaintance had to ask permission to address you by your Christian instead of your family name. The asking and giving of this permission was considered an important stage in the ritual of friendship. 2

Now, with family denigrated in importance, you are usually introduced by an unattached first name, a name that doesn't speak of where you came from or who your ancestors were. In social intercourse, your past is abandoned. It helps reinforce the illusion that all we have to do to leave our family is to leave home. 3

But what if the Unabomber is your brother? 4

What if you're David Kaczynski, and you have good reason to suspect that your older brother, Theodore, has wounded or maimed 23 people, killed three and has even threatened to blow up airplanes—airplanes that could be carrying children? Then, the new ways fade and the old ties become excruciatingly real—in the name of your family, you must face what your brother has not: the innocence of the dead. Your brother, your blood, flesh of your flesh, could be the person killing people who in no way have merited such a death. It has become a family affair—and we all know how unreasonable family affairs can be. 5

6 To be David Kaczynski is to be faced with a moral dilemma both terrifying and unavoidable: Do you or do you not give up your brother? Either way, you live the rest of your life under the shadow of a guilt that no one but you can gauge or bear. If you rat on him, you will be part of the mechanism by which your brother may eventually be executed; if you don't and he kills again, that blood will be on your hands. Either way, you, too, become a killer.

7 This is the kind of situation the word "tragic" was invented to describe—for tragedy occurs when the stakes are life and death, and every available choice is devastating.

8 If you are David Kaczynski, then you are thrust face to face with a truth that our contemporary discussions of family avoid: As members of a family, we are inextricably involved with each other, no matter how far we go to avoid that involvement. The very lengths some go to distance themselves from their families testify to the power of family bonds.

9 For whether we're speaking of "family values," the disappearance of the nuclear family or the emergence of the single-parent family; whether we're discussing the legitimacy of "a family of friends" or of gay families—our arguments tend to be technical, legal, bloodless. As a culture, we seem to have forgotten what David Kaczynski has been forced to remember: To be family is to be inextricably implicated in the moral choices of our kin.

10 No psychologist can talk us out of the bone-deep feeling that if my brother kills, something in me is a killer; if my brother goes insane, something in me may be mad; if my sister dies, something in me dies; if my sister deserts her family, something in me may be a deserter. The only way not to feel this is to harden our hearts. And again, the extent to which we must toughen ourselves against some family members measures the depth of the bond.

11 The Kaczynski family teaches us that this is true no matter how great the estrangement of a family member. No one could have been more estranged from his people than Ted Kaczynski. He lived more than a thousand miles from his brother and mother, without a telephone, in a tiny shack in the wilderness. Apparently, he didn't even read most of their letters, because he demanded that if they were writing of an emergency, they should underline the stamp with red ink. Clearly, those are the only letters he felt obligated to read. His family sent him such a letter when his father committed suicide (because of cancer) in 1990. Ted wrote back in anger, saying the death of his father did not constitute an emergency. This is estrangement with a vengeance.

Yet, the moral dilemma that Ted's brother felt brought them close— 12
no matter how much distance was between them. David had to do something or nothing, and either choice would steep them in guilt. For we may have the same choice with a friend or a lover; we may suspect them of terrible things, and have to choose silence or action. But who is so soulless as to claim that the guilt in such cases has a different weight? Who, reading of the Kaczynskis doesn't feel some shock that David turned in his brother? And isn't that shock the true indication of what we really think of family—as opposed to what our superficial beliefs may be?

We may believe David was justified, but this is different from be- 13
lieving he was right. There was no way for David to be entirely right. In this tragic situation, any choice he made was bound to be part wrong, bound to make him guilty, in his own eyes and ours. Not that we blame him. In a sense, he acted on our behalf. Still, we do not trust him. No one will ever wholly trust someone who turned in his own brother.

And, it is likely he will never wholly trust himself again. 14

Reportedly, David tried to save his brother by striking a deal with 15
the FBI that he would only give his information if Ted didn't get the death penalty, if convicted. It was a desperate ploy. An intelligent man, David must have known that once he told anything, he'd have to tell everything. If he didn't, he could be charged with obstruction of justice, or even arrested as an accessory. When the FBI refused to deal, David gave his information anyway. Thus, he is his brother's saddest victim. For whether or not Ted Kaczynski is the Unabomber (and that's for a jury to decide), David has turned in his brother. Nothing can change that. And, in the process, he has taught us how, in spite of all our rationalizations, family still has the power to entangle us, to enmesh us in one another's fates.

The Kaczynskis have shown us that a brother, a father, a sister, a 16
mother, can mark us even from afar—and change our lives utterly.

Not long ago, I had dinner with my brother, Vincent, for the first 17
time in years. We live 3,000 miles apart, and we're both obsessed with our work and our lives, so we see each other rarely. How good it was to sit across a table and look into one another's eyes. We lifted our wine glasses, clinked them, and I said, "Blood on blood, Vinnie."

"Blood on blood, Mike," my brother answered. 18

We both knew where those words came from: Bruce Springsteen's 19
"Highway Patrolman" on the "Nebraska" album: "Me an' Frankie, laughin' and drinkin'/ Nothing feels better than blood on blood." The song tells of a cop whose life is ruined when he lets his brother escape from a murder scene. "When it's your brother, sometimes you look the other way," Springsteen sings.

20 Sometimes you can't, as David Kaczynski couldn't. The power of family is the power to force us to such choices. Most are lucky enough not to be put to that test, but still that power is implicit in the family bond. What happens to my brother in some sense happens to me. No amount of rhetoric can erase that, no matter how far apart we live, or how well we hide.

THINKING ABOUT THE TEXT

1. From the introduction on, the writer's strategy is to expose key myths and "superficial beliefs" about the family and family bonds. What are these myths?
2. What does Ventura believe is "a truth that our contemporary discussions of family avoid"? Find the varied restatements of this truth in the essay. Is this repetition effective or redundant? Why?
3. How does the Kaczynski case support Ventura's thesis? Discuss Ted Kaczynski's "estrangement" from the family.
4. Why might some people think that David Kaczynski was "justified" in turning in his brother but not necessarily "right" to do it? Do you agree?
5. How does Ventura's experience with his own brother relate to the Kaczynskis' experience? Did you find the reference to Bruce Springsteen's "Highway Patrolman" useful or distracting? Explain.

WRITING FROM THE TEXT

1. Write an essay arguing that David Kaczynski was either right or wrong to alert the FBI to his suspicions about his brother. You might consider the distinction that Ventura makes between being justified and being right. Is this a valid distinction?
2. Ventura claims, "No psychologist can talk us out of the bone-deep feeling that if my brother kills, something in me is a killer; if my brother goes insane, something in me may be mad . . . ." Using the Kaczynski case as well as experiences of your own, write an essay supporting or refuting this assumption.

CONNECTING WITH OTHER TEXTS

1. Read "The Only Child" (p. 11) and then write an essay comparing and contrasting the different roles, responsibilities, and sense of guilt that David Kaczynski and John Leonard may experience concerning their brothers.

2. Using "Why Johnny Can't Disobey" (p. 277) and Ventura's essay, write an analysis of David Kaczynski's decision to speak out rather than be silent about his brother's possible guilt.
3. Research additional news articles about David Kaczynski's decision to identify his brother as a Unabomber suspect, and write an essay analyzing the character traits of either brother. (See character analysis, pp. 436–443.)

■ THE ONLY CHILD
John Leonard

After studying at Harvard University and Berkeley, where he received his B.A. in 1962, John Leonard (b. 1939) worked as a book reviewer, a producer of dramas and literature programs, a publicity writer, a staff writer for the *New York Times*, and a cultural critic for *Variety*. Leonard intends his writing to ask moral questions: How do you want your children to grow up? What do you think is decent and fair? Who are your friends, and why? His work included here, from *Private Lives in the Imperial City* (1976), probes family tensions and concerns.

He is big. He always has been, over six feet, with that slump of the shoulders and tuck in the neck big men in the country often affect, as if to apologize for being above the democratic norm in size. (In high school and at college he played varsity basketball. In high school he was senior class president.) And he looks healthy enough, blue-eyed behind his beard, like a trapper or a mountain man, acquainted with silences. He also grins a lot. 1

Odd, then, to have noticed earlier—at the house, when he took off his shabby coat to play Ping-Pong—that the white arms were unmuscled. The coat may have been a comment. This, after all, is southern California, where every man is an artist, an advertiser of himself; where every surface is painted and every object potted; where even the statues seem to wear socks. The entire population ambles, in polyesters, toward a Taco Bell. To wear a brown shabby cloth coat in southern California is to admit something. 2

So he hasn't been getting much exercise. Nor would the children have elected him president of any class. At the house they avoided him. Or, since he was too big to be avoided entirely, they treated his presence as a kind of odor to pass through hurriedly, to be safe on the other side. They behaved like cats. Of course, he ignored them. But I think they were up to more than just protecting themselves from his lack of curiosity. Children are expert readers of grins. 3

4 His grin is intermittent. The dimples twitch on and off; between them, teeth are bared; above them, the blue eyes disappear in a wince. This grin isn't connected to any humor the children know about. It may be a tic. It could also be a function of some metronome made on Mars. It registers inappropriate intervals. We aren't listening to the same music.

5 This is the man who introduced me to the mysteries of mathematical science, the man I could never beat at chess, the man who wrote haiku and played with computers. Now there is static in his head, as though the mind had drifted off its signal during sleep. He has an attention span of about thirty seconds.

6 I am to take him back to where he lives, in the car I have rented in order to pretend to be a Californian. We are headed for a rooming house in one of the beach cities along a coast of off-ramps and oil wells. It is a rooming house that thinks of itself as Spanish. The ruined-hacienda look requires a patio, a palm tree and several miles of corrugated tile. He does not expect me to come up to his room, but I insist. I have brought along a six-pack of beer.

7 The room is a slum, and it stinks. It is wall-to-wall beer cans, hundreds of them, under a film of ash. He lights cigarettes and leaves them burning on the windowsill or the edge of the dresser or the lip of the sink, while he thinks of something else—Gupta sculpture, maybe, or the Sephiroth Tree of the Kabbalah. The sink is filthy, and so is the toilet. Holes have been burnt in the sheet on the bed, where he sits. He likes to crush the beer cans after he has emptied them, then toss them aside.

8 He tells me that he is making a statement, that this room is a statement, that the landlord will understand the meaning of his statement. In a week or so, according to the pattern, they will evict him, and someone will find him another room, which he will turn into another statement, with the help of the welfare checks he receives on account of his disability, which is the static in his head.

9 There are no books, no newspapers or magazines, no pictures on the wall. There is a television set, which he watches all day long while drinking beer and smoking cigarettes. I am sufficiently familiar with the literature on schizophrenia to realize that this room is a statement he is making about himself. I am also sufficiently familiar with his history to understand that, along with his contempt for himself, there is an abiding arrogance. He refuses medication. They can't make him take it, any more than they can keep him in a hospital. He has harmed no one. One night, in one of these rooms, he will set himself on fire.

He talks. Or blurts: scraps from Oriental philosophers—Lao-tzu, I think—puns, incantations, obscenities, names from the past. There are conspiracies; I am part of one of them. He grins, winces, slumps, is suddenly tired, wants me to get out almost as much as I want to get out, seems to have lapsed in a permanent parenthesis. Anyway, I have a busy schedule. 10

Well, speed kills slowly, and he fiddled too much with the oxygen flow to his brain. He wanted ecstasy and revelation, the way we grew up wanting a bicycle, a car, a girlfriend. These belonged to us by right, as middle-class Americans. So, then, did salvation belong to us by right. I would like to thank Timothy Leary and all the other sports of the 1960s who helped make this bad trip possible. I wish R. D. Laing would explain to me, once again and slowly, how madness is a proof of grace. "The greatest magician," said Novalis, "would be the one who would cast over himself a spell so complete that he would take his own phantasmagorias as autonomous appearances." 11

One goes back to the rented car and pretending to be a Californian as, perhaps, one had been pretending to be a brother. It is odd, at my age, suddenly to have become an only child. 12

THINKING ABOUT THE TEXT

1. Discuss how each telling detail about Leonard's brother provides a glimpse of his early promise. Then explain how these same details now underscore his sad transformation.
2. Why does Leonard's brother feel his life-style and room are "making a statement"? What type of "statement" does the author feel his brother is making?
3. In this autobiographical essay, Leonard, a New Yorker, can only "pretend to be a Californian." Find details that illustrate what California represents for him.
4. Who or what does Leonard seem to blame for his brother's experimentation with drugs? Why? What is Leonard's implied thesis?
5. Discuss all possible meanings of the title. Why does Leonard wait until the end to focus on it?

WRITING ABOUT THE TEXT

1. Write an essay contrasting Leonard's recollection of his brother before he took drugs with his perception of him now.
2. If drug addiction or mental illness has plagued any members of your own family, write an essay that illustrates an important insight you have learned from this experience.

3. Find a photograph that shows you with one or more of your siblings. Write an analysis of your relationship with your brother and/or sister based on the dynamics that you perceive in the photograph.

CONNECTING WITH OTHER TEXTS

1. Read "The Ties That Bind" (p. 7) and show how Ventura's and Leonard's experiences link and where they diverge.
2. Using "The Only Child," "Thanksgiving" (p. 4), "Ignorance Is Not Bliss" (below), or "Your Place Is Empty" (p. 27), write an essay describing and analyzing the positive and negative aspects of family members reuniting and discovering how they have changed.

■ IGNORANCE IS NOT BLISS

Eric Marcus

A graduate of Vassar and Columbia, Eric Marcus (b. 1958) is a journalist who has published articles and book reviews on a variety of subjects. His books include *Making History: The Struggle for Gay and Lesbian Equal Rights, 1945–1990; Is It a Choice? Answers to 300 of the Most Frequently Asked Questions About Gays and Lesbians;* and *Why Suicide? Answers to 200 of the Most Frequently Asked Questions About Suicide, Attempted Suicide, and Assisted Suicide* (1996). He coauthored *Breaking the Surface,* the autobiography of Olympic diver and gold-medalist Greg Louganis. Marcus is a former producer of "Good Morning, America" and "CBS This Morning." The essay included here originally appeared in *Newsweek,* "My Turn," July 5, 1993.

1 Sam Nunn didn't need to hold Senate hearings to come up with his "don't ask, don't tell" solution for handling gays in the military. If he'd asked me, I could have told him this was exactly the policy some of my relatives suggested years ago when I informed them that I planned to tell my grandmother that I was gay. They said, "She's old, it'll kill her. You'll destroy her image of you. If she doesn't ask, why tell?"

2 Don't ask, don't tell made a lot of sense to these relatives because it sounded like an easy solution. For them, it was. If I didn't say anything to my grandmother, they wouldn't have to deal with her upset over the truth about her grandson. But for me, "not telling" was an exhausting nightmare, because it meant withholding everything that

could possibly give me away and living in fear of being found out. At the same time, I didn't want to cause Grandma pain by telling her I was gay, so I was easily persuaded to continue the charade.

If I hadn't been close to my grandmother, or saw her once a year, hiding the truth would have been relatively easy. But we'd had a special relationship since she cared for me as a child when my mother was ill, and we visited often, so lying to her was especially difficult. 3

I started hiding the truth from everyone in 1965, when I had my first crush. That was in second grade and his name was Hugh. No one told me, but I knew I shouldn't tell anyone about it, not even Hugh. I don't know how I knew that liking another boy was something to hide, but I did, so I kept it a secret. 4

I fell in love for the first time when I was 17. It was a wondrous experience, but I didn't dare tell anyone, especially my family, because telling them about Bob would have given me away. I couldn't explain to them that for the first time in my life I felt like a normal human being. 5

By the time I was an adult, I'd stopped lying to my immediate family, with the exception of my grandmother, and told them that I was gay. I was a second-rate liar so I was lucky that Grandma was the only person in my life around whom I had to be something I wasn't. I can't imagine what it's like for gays and lesbians in the military to hide the truth from the men and women with whom they serve. The fear of exposure must be extraordinary, especially because exposure would mean the end of their careers. For me, the only risk was losing Grandma's love. 6

Hiding the truth from her grew ever more challenging in the years that followed. I couldn't tell her about the man I then shared my life with. I couldn't talk about my friends who had AIDS because she would have wondered why I knew so many ill men. I couldn't tell her that I volunteered for a gay peer-counseling center. I couldn't talk to her about the political issues that most interested me because she would have wondered why I had such passionate feelings about gay rights. Eventually I couldn't even tell her about all of my work, because some of my writing was on gay issues. In the end, all we had left to talk about was the weather. 7

If being gay were only what I did behind closed doors, there would have been plenty of my life left over to share with my grandmother. But my life as a gay man isn't something that takes place only in the privacy of my bedroom. It affects who my friends are, whom I choose to share my life with, the work I do, the organizations I belong to, the magazines I read, where I vacation and what I talk about. I know it's the same for heterosexuals because their sexual orientation affects everything, from a 8 choice of senior-prom date and the finger on which they wear their wedding band to the birth announcements they send and every emotion they feel.

9 So the reality of the "don't ask, don't tell" solution for dealing with my grandmother and for dealing with gays in the military means having to lie about or hide almost every aspect of your life. It's not nearly as simple as just not saying, "I'm gay."

10 After years of "protecting" my grandmother I decided it was time to stop lying. In the worst case, I figured she might reject me, although that seemed unlikely. But whatever the outcome, I could not pretend anymore. Some might think that was selfish on my part, but I'd had enough of the "don't tell" policy, which had forced me into a life of deceit. I also hoped that by telling her the truth, we could build a relationship based on honesty, a possibility that was worth the risk.

11 The actual telling was far less terrifying than all the anticipation. While my grandmother cried plenty, my family was wrong, because the truth didn't kill her. In the five years since, Grandma and I have talked a lot about the realities of my life and the lives of my gay and lesbian friends. She's read many articles and a few books, including mine. She's surprised us by how quickly she's set aside her myths and misconceptions.

12 Grandma and I are far closer than we ever were. Last fall we even spent a week together in Paris for her birthday. And these days, we have plenty to talk about, including the gays in the military issue.

13 A few months ago, Grandma traveled with me to Lafayette College, Pa., where I was invited to give a speech on the history of the gay civil-rights movement. After my talk, several students took us to dinner. As I conversed with the young women across the table from me, I overheard my grandmother talking to the student sitting next to her. She told him he was right to tell his parents he was gay, that with time and his help they would adjust. She said, "Don't underestimate their ability to change."

14 I wish Sam Nunn had called my grandmother to testify before his Senate committee. He and the other senators, as well as Defense Secretary Les Aspin and the president, could do far worse than listen to her advice.

THINKING ABOUT THE TEXT

1. What are the expressed reasons Eric Marcus didn't tell his grandmother he is gay? What do you imagine his unexpressed concerns might be?

2. What parts of his life could Marcus not talk about with his grandmother? Why was this secret a problem for him?
3. Why does Marcus believe that the "don't ask, don't tell" policy is not a solution for gays in the military?
4. What does Marcus show about his grandmother to illustrate her understanding and acceptance of his sexual identity?

WRITING FROM THE TEXT

1. Write an essay telling about a time that you feared a family member's response to some revelation about you—something you had done, a choice you made, or one of your beliefs or values. Show the responses to your revealing this truth.
2. On the basis of your own or a friend's experience in telling some important truth, argue for or against revealing the truth to others.
3. Write an analysis of your own or a friend's sexual orientation to support Marcus' view that one's sexual identity influences one's choice of friends and leisure activities.

CONNECTING WITH OTHER TEXTS

1. In "Women: Invisible Cages" (p. 80), Brigid Brophy describes the subtle pressure society puts on women and men to limit their choices. Use Brophy's essay as a starting point and compare the restrictions she describes with those discussed by Marcus. Structure your paper as a comparison and/or contrast study (p. 402) or problem analysis (p. 427), whichever seems best to you.
2. Compare the values and behavior exhibited by Marcus with those described by Cooper Thompson in "A New Vision of Masculinity" (p. 63). In your essay, analyze the values and try to come to some insightful conclusions.

■ SENIOR-TEENER, A NEW HYBRID

Dorothy Noyes

Honored with countless awards for her work in advertising, child-rearing, health, world hunger, and the environment, Dorothy Noyes (b. 1906) earned two masters degrees from Yale University when she was 60 and her Ph.D. at age 70. She has published articles in the *New York Times* and numerous magazines and journals and has written two books, *Your Child: Step by Step Toward Maturity* (1960) and *Environmental Hazards to Young Children* (1985). At age 80 she was invited by the President of Brown University to work as a consultant and researcher on world hunger in developed countries. Currently writing her memoirs for publication, Noyes explains, "I started out as a kid wanting to be a reporter and learn the facts. Now I'm interested in the inner me, in my feelings, and my writing is more lyrical." The following essay originally appeared in *Newsweek*, "My Turn," September 5, 1994.

1 Come next May, there's no denying the fact that I'll have racked up 89 years as an inhabitant of planet earth. One glance and you'd know I'm a Senior. The hair on my head is white, and although my face is not overly lined, it's obvious that I'm past 50 or 60 or even 70. While I work at standing erect, my shoulders slouch a bit. And, despite regular swim sessions and frequent brisk walks, I have difficulty hiding my protruding belly. But the *inner* me, the *emotional* me, is so frequently a Teener. I feel much as I did 75 years ago: alone, tremulous and fearful about my future.

2 Were Charles Darwin to arise from the dead, I'd say to him, "There's a new subspecies abroad today, sir." And I'd tell him about its evolution during the latter part of the 20th century when humankind—particularly womankind—was living longer and longer in an amazing state of physical health. But I'd have to come clean as to the emotional downside: the sense of queasiness that from time to time overtakes an otherwise reasonably fit body. For today I'm often jittery and "out of it" as in long-ago days—no special boyfriend or agemates. Three husbands have predeceased me, and my longtime female intimates have also made their final exits.

3 At the start of my adolescence, my self-confidence was on the low side. Because I was born a southpaw, conventional wisdom forced me to learn to write with the "right" hand. Even now, my friends' exhortations to "type, don't write" can be amusing but far from uplifting. That I was clumsy was dinned into me time and again. Well, I still feel clumsy.

4 Transplant shock also took its toll. When I was 12, and for the next several years, we lived in cities in three different states. This meant four high schools. I've never succeeded in blocking out the memory of that sense of desolation when I was 13½ and a sophomore in Montclair High School in New Jersey—far from the kids I knew as a freshman in Evanston, Ill. That unforgettable moment when I saw the spot on my white skirt: I was a child no longer. How to blot it out? Where to go?

5 This is somewhat comparable to one of Seniors' embarrassing problems: the need for protective garments to cope with the unexpected lack of control over failing body parts. While Senior and Teener are not *look*-alikes, they're so often *act*-alikes.

6 Obviously, the female bodily changes of Teener and Senior are not the same. Teener's route is onward and upward, though it doesn't always seem so to her as she deplores some of the external blemishes. For Se-

nior it's mostly downhill, obliged as she is to spend more and more time in body-repair shops to compensate for eyes and ears and other organs that malfunction. Our commonality lies in our need to face up to the inevitable biologic changes with equanimity—to learn the art of self-mastery, of peaceful acceptance of the inevitable and of our own self-worth as the life cycle spirals on. Living comfortably with one's own body with its limitations and defects is no easy assignment.

One of our most difficult challenges comes from the outside world. 7
It's another factor that makes our struggle to mature so alike: coping with those numerous unsympathetic, contemptuous and sometimes outright hostile others. Like those folk who accuse Teeners of being too self-absorbed, irresponsible, sex-driven, booze-drinking, "no good"; and for those who look upon Seniors with much disdain, not as national treasures.

Virtually from the first moment last spring when I was introduced to 8
the about-to-be 15-year-old stepdaughter of my godson, I remembered how, long ago, I cherished the companionship of an elderly spinster who paid special attention to insecure young me. This probably prompted me to issue a spur-of-the-moment invitation to Christine. She seemed ecstatic at the thought of spending part of a holiday weekend with me. All during the first day as we meandered through Central Park and again at dinner and at the dance theater, I was struck by her apparent maturity—fascinated as she was in studying people's faces. "What do you suppose they're thinking about, Dorothy?" But this confidence—this absorption with others—was not to last. Christine was pondering her trip home the next day: alone in a taxi and the crowd at Penn Station! She hated to bother me, but would I mind coming along as a pal, just in case . . . ? Of course I went. Her scary moment of panic came when she couldn't find the platform for the train's departure. (I experience comparable panicky self-doubt when I'm under pressure.)

In the early '60s, when Doubleday was about to publish my first 9
book, there was great discussion as to the title of this parental "how to" guide. It was understandable that it should be called "Your Child," based as it was in part on my syndicated newspaper column with that title. The big question was: should we add "from birth to maturity"? Not *to* maturity, I insisted, but rather *toward* maturity. For who knows when maturity has been reached? And, besides, what kind of maturity are we thinking about?

For Teener, maturity means graduation from kid-dom—the search 10
for personhood in her own right, the freedom to find her own worth and her own place. For Senior, maturity means greater acceptance of waning physical powers and the ability to continue to grow in understanding

and, yes, in wisdom—to accept death as a part of life. Neither Teener nor Senior can control biological maturity, but each can have much effect over psychological and philosophical maturity.

11 Many times, the Teener part of this hybrid is thrown by what she feels must be grasped to gain self-mastery and to appreciate what life is all about. So, too, the Senior is frequently nonplussed by how much more there is to discover about our universe. And time is running short—gotta crowd in as much as possible as fast as possible! Each of us must deal with continuing bodily changes and our reactions to them as well as with our changing relationships with our fellow earthlings. Both of us long for many of those Others to appreciate what seems to be the professional consensus that Teeners and Seniors both are almost *over*endowed with heartfelt compassion for all humankind.

THINKING ABOUT THE TEXT

1. The pairing of seniors and "Teeners" may not seem obvious at first, so the writer needs to explain what they have in common despite their obvious dissimilarities. List the ways that seniors and teeners are "act-alikes."
2. Noyes' supporting examples are drawn mostly from her own experience and observations. Illustrate these and evaluate their effectiveness. Did you think that Noyes needed to use any research to support her points?
3. Considering the reference to Darwin, how does Noyes justify redefining seniors as a "new subspecies" or a hybrid? Although these terms imply an improvement, what is the "emotional downside" to being a "Senior-Teener"?

WRITING FROM THE TEXT

1. Using details from Noyes' essay and your own observations, write a comparison and contrast of seniors and "teeners" that supports a strong assertion or thesis.
2. At the end of her essay, Noyes claims that "Teeners and Seniors both are almost *over*endowed with heartfelt compassion for all humankind." Write an analysis of Noyes' ability to show compassion for seniors *and* teens without slipping into self-pity. You may want to analyze her lighthearted but sensitive tone, her empathy for teens, and her ability to smile at herself.

CONNECTING WITH OTHER TEXTS

1. With Noyes' essay as your starting point, analyze life as a "Senior-Teener" and draw additional support from Mrs. Ardavi in "Your Place Is Empty" (p. 27) and from Hazel Peoples in "My Man Bovanne" (p. 46). How do these characters reflect some of the concerns, insecurities, and strengths of teens and how are they unlike teens?
2. Use Noyes' description of the "Teener" to analyze Connie in "Where Are You Going, Where Have You Been?" (p. 101). In what ways does Connie exemplify Dorothy Noyes' description of a teenager? In what ways is Connie different?

DIGGING

Seamus Heaney

A native of Northern Ireland, Seamus Heaney (b. 1939) is at home in Dublin as well as at Harvard University, where he teaches. Heaney is recognized as one of Ireland's finest living poets, and since receiving the Nobel Prize for Literature in 1995, he has been one of Ireland's most famous poets. Critic Blake Morrison describes Heaney as a rare poet, one who is "rated highly by critics and academics yet popular with the common reader." At boarding school, where he was sent when he was eleven, Heaney read poets like Robert Frost who created poetry from their local environments. Heaney learned to value his childhood experience, which he says he once "considered archaic and irrelevant to 'the modern world.'" Do you see any of Heaney's initial ambivalence about his past reflected in this early poem from *Death of a Naturalist?*

Between my finger and my thumb
The squat pen rests; snug as a gun.

Under my window, a clean rasping sound
When the spade sinks into gravelly ground:
My father, digging. I look down

Till his straining rump among the flowerbeds
Bends low, comes up twenty years away
Stooping in rhythm through potato drills
Where he was digging.

The coarse boot nestled on the lug, the shaft
Against the inside knee was levered firmly.

He rooted out tall tops, buried the bright edge deep
To scatter new potatoes that we picked
Loving their cool hardness in our hands.

By God, the old man could handle a spade.
Just like his old man.

My grandfather cut more turf in a day
Than any other man on Toner's bog.
Once I carried him milk in a bottle
Corked sloppily with paper. He straightened up
To drink it, then fell to right away
Nicking and slicing neatly, heaving sods
Over his shoulder, going down and down
For the good turf. Digging.

The cold smell of potato mould, the squelch and slap
Of soggy peat, the curt cuts of an edge
Through living roots awaken in my head.
But I've no spade to follow men like them.

Between my finger and my thumb
The squat pen rests.
I'll dig with it.

THINKING ABOUT THE TEXT

1. The speaker in the poem seems to have a pen in his hand when he is interrupted by a sound under his window. What thoughts are triggered by that sound?
2. How are the activities of the three men in this poem—the narrator, his father, and his grandfather—comparable? Use the text of the poem and your own thoughts to list as many comparisons as you can.
3. The narrator expresses pride in his father's and his grandfather's success in their jobs, but he decides to follow a career that uses a different tool. Which lines show the speaker's pride in the work of his father and grandfather? Which lines in the poem show his decision and the reasons for it?
4. In what specific ways does the title of the poem link all three generations?

WRITING FROM THE TEXT

1. Copy all of the definitions of the words *dig* and *digging* and write an analysis of the poem that shows how knowing these definitions contributes to an understanding of the poem.
2. Write an essay that illustrates how the negative images in the poem help the narrator to decide not to follow his father's and his grandfather's choice of work. (See p. 444 for a definition and discussion of image.)
3. Write an essay that shows a specific moment in your life when you realized that you would not follow the paths of your family members. (See p. 388 for a discussion of showing in a narrative.)

CONNECTING WITH OTHER TEXTS

1. In Seamus Heaney's poem, the narrator-son has an epiphany, or moment of realization, and decides to depart from family tradition. In Eric Marcus' "Ignorance Is Not Bliss," the author also departs from his family's expectations by telling his grandmother of his sexual identity. Using details from both works, write an essay that focuses on the importance and difficulty of revealing a choice that deviates from family expectations.
2. Darnell, in "Proper Care and Maintenance" (p. 170), has an epiphany that helps him determine how to gain work. Compare or contrast his moment of sudden insight with the epiphany of the narrator in "Digging." (See pp. 402–413 for how to write a comparison–contrast paper.)

■ FETAL ALCOHOL SYNDROME: A NATIONAL PERSPECTIVE

Michael Dorris

A Native American who has written widely on Native American culture, Michael Dorris (1945–1997) writes both nonfiction and fiction for adults and young readers. Dorris and his wife, Louise Erdrich, collaborated on the novel *The Crown of Columbus* (1991), an Indian perspective on the Columbus Quincentenary. Dorris may be best known for *The Broken Cord* (1989), his extensively researched book about fetal alcohol syndrome and his personal story of his adopted son, who suffered severe physical and mental impairment as a result of his biological mother's heavy drinking during her pregnancy. The book has been described as a memoir but also as a love story and a study of a public health issue. The essay reprinted here first appeared in *Newsweek* in 1990.

1 At the time I adopted my oldest son, Abel, in 1971, I knew that his birth mother had been a heavy drinker, but even the medical textbooks in those days stated that exposure to alcohol could not damage a developing fetus. I knew that Abel had been born small and premature, had "failed to thrive," and was an initially slow learner, but for ten years as a single parent I convinced myself that nurture, a stimulating environment, and love could open up life to my little boy.

2 It wasn't true. At the University of Washington and elsewhere, biochemists and psychologists now confirm that for some women even moderate doses of prenatal exposure to alcohol can permanently stunt a human being's potential. According to the U.S. surgeon general, *no* level of ethanol is guaranteed to be "safe."

3 My grown son has a full range of physical disorders: seizures; curvature of the spine; poor coordination, sight, and hearing. But his most disabling legacy has to do with his impaired ability to reason. Fetal alcohol syndrome (FAS) victims are known for their poor judgment, their impulsiveness, their persistent confusions over handling money, telling time, and in distinguishing right from wrong.

4 Since the publication of *The Broken Cord* last August, I have received an outpouring of wrenching letters from literally hundreds of readers—rural and urban, religious and agnostic, of all ethnic and economic backgrounds—who share experiences of heartache, grief, and frustration uncannily identical to my wife's and mine. Their sons, daughters, or grandchildren have been repeatedly misdiagnosed with the same amorphous labels: retarded, sociopathic, attention-deficit, unteachable troublemakers.

5 A majority of full-blown FAS victims are adopted or in state care, but many children who are less drastically impaired (i.e., with fetal alcohol effect [FAE]) remain with their natural parents. Depending on the term of pregnancy in which the harmful drinking occurred, these individuals may look perfectly healthy and test in the normal range for intelligence, yet by early adolescence they show unmistakable signs of comprehension problems or uncontrollable rage. It is currently estimated that in the United States some eight thousand babies are born annually with full FAS and another sixty-five thousand with a degree of FAE. Nothing will ever restore them to the people they might otherwise have been.

6 And it seems that's far less than the half of it. An additional three hundred thousand babies prenatally bombarded with illegal drugs will be born in this country in 1990. Recent studies indicate that crack cocaine, if smoked during pregnancy, causes learning deficits in offspring similar to those caused by alcohol. The "first generation" of children

from the 1980s' crack epidemic is about to enter public school, and these children are consistently described as "remorseless," "without a conscience," and passive, apparently lacking that essential empathy, that motivation toward cooperation, upon which a peaceful and harmonious classroom—and society—so depends.

No curriculum or training program has so far proven to be com- 7
pletely effective for people with this totally preventable affliction, and a Los Angeles pilot education project costs taxpayers $15,000 a year per pupil. However, the price of doing nothing, of ignoring the issue, is beyond measure.

Nothing like crack—a baby shower gift of choice in certain popula- 8
tions because it is reputed to speed and ease labor—has occurred before. According to one survey, upwards of 11 percent of all U.S. infants in 1988 tested positive for cocaine or alcohol the first time their blood was drawn. A New York City Health Department official estimated that births to drug-abusing mothers had increased there by about 3,000 percent in the past ten years.

Why? Some explanations have to do with a paucity of available ser- 9
vices and support. Too many fathers regard their baby's health as solely their partner's concern. Only one residential treatment program specifically for chemically dependent pregnant women exists in New York City, where the State Assembly Committee on Alcoholism and Drug Abuse estimates that "twelve thousand babies will be born addicted . . . in 1989, and the number of children in foster care has doubled in two years from twenty-seven thousand in 1987 to more than fifty thousand today, mainly because of parental drug abuse." The system has broken down. Sixteen percent of all American mothers have had insufficient prenatal medical attention—increasing to 33 percent for unmarried or teenage mothers, 30 percent for Hispanic women, and 27 percent for black women.

At last, thanks to a 1989 act of Congress, liquor bottle labels must in- 10
clude a warning, and signs posted in many bars proclaim the hazards of alcohol to unborn children. But what happens when public education doesn't work as a deterrent, when a pregnant woman herself is a victim of FAS or prenatal crack and therefore cannot understand the long-term disastrous consequences for the life of another resulting from what she drinks or inhales? It isn't that these women don't love the *idea* of their babies. They just can't foresee the cruel realities.

The conflict of competing rights—of protecting immediate civil 11
liberty versus avoiding future civil strife—is incredibly complex, with no unambiguously right or easy answers, but as a nation it's uncon-

scionable to delay the debate. If we close our eyes we condemn children not yet even conceived to existences of sorrow and deprivation governed by prison, victimization, and premature death.

12 My wife and I think of these tragedies as we wait for our son to have brain surgery that may reduce the intensity of his seizures, though not eliminate them. At twenty-two, despite all of our efforts and his best intentions, he remains forever unable to live independently, to manage a paycheck, or to follow the plot of a TV sitcom, and we worry about the very fabric of society when hundreds of thousands of others with problems similar to his or worse become teenagers, become adults, beyond the year 2000.

THINKING ABOUT THE TEXT

1. What are the specific symptoms of fetal alchohol syndrome, or FAS? What are the characteristics of the child born with FAE, or fetal alcohol effect?
2. Besides citing the specific symptoms of this problem, how does Michael Dorris convince his reader of the severity of the problem?
3. What does Dorris mean when he identifies the problem as the ideological conflict of "protecting immediate civil liberty versus avoiding future civil strife"? What do you infer to be Dorris' position?
4. What is Michael Dorris' rhetorical strategy in beginning and ending his essay by referring to his son? What is the effect of the first sentence in the second paragraph: "It wasn't true"?
5. This essay first appeared in *Newsweek.* Why do you think it even more important to print this essay in a college text?

WRITING FROM THE TEXT

1. Write an essay in which you argue that because "*no* level of ethanol is guaranteed to be 'safe,'" legislation should be passed that prohibits pregnant women from drinking alcohol. Use the data in "Fetal Alcohol Syndrome" to argue your case.
2. Write an essay from the point of view that education, not legislation, must be the way to alter the number of FAS and FAE births. Use the statistics in Michael Dorris' essay to argue your points.
3. Write an essay to persuade a reader that pregnant women should not drink. Use data from Michael Dorris' essay as well as information and experience you may have to convince your reader.

CONNECTING WITH OTHER TEXTS

1. Write an essay comparing Michael Dorris' description of his son's symptoms with John Leonard's description of his brother's problems in "The Only Child" (p. 11). How do the sources of these problems contrast?
2. If you read Michael Dorris' collected essays in *Paper Trail,* and we recommend that you do, you will learn in "The Power of Love" (pp. 111–117) that Abel died after being hit by a car while he was crossing a street at night. Use that essay, "Fetal Alcohol Syndrome: A Parent's Perspective" (pp. 82–102 in *Paper Trail*), and "Fetal Alcohol Syndrome: A National Perspective" from this text to write an essay that discusses the tragedies of FAS.
3. The causes, symptoms, and treatments related to fetal alcohol syndrome would be an interesting subject for a major research paper. Consider this topic if you are assigned such a paper.

■ YOUR PLACE IS EMPTY

Anne Tyler

Known to many as the author of *The Accidental Tourist,* Anne Tyler (b. 1941) is a critically acclaimed writer of many other novels and of short fiction. She grew up in a number of Quaker communities in the Midwest and the South. It was this "setting-apart situation" and her attempt "to fit into the outside world" that helped mold Tyler into a writer. "I don't talk well," she writes. "For me, writing something down was the only road out." A theme that runs through Tyler's work is that people cannot fully communicate with one another, and the sorrow that results creates a melancholy world in which people try to reach and love each other. Tyler lives with her Iranian-born husband and their two daughters. The following story first appeared in *The New Yorker* in 1976.

Early in October, Hassan Ardavi invited his mother to come from Iran for a visit. His mother accepted immediately. It wasn't clear how long the visit was to last. Hassan's wife thought three months would be a good length of time. Hassan himself had planned on six months, and said so in his letter of invitation. But his mother felt that after such a long trip six months would be too short, and she was counting on staying a year. Hassan's little girl, who wasn't yet two, had no idea of time at all. She was told that her grandmother was coming but she soon forgot about it. 1

Hassan's wife was named Elizabeth, not an easy word for Iranians to pronounce. She would have been recognized as American the world over—a blond, pretty girl with long bones and an ungraceful 2 way of walking. One of her strong points was an ability to pick up foreign languages, and before her mother-in-law's arrival she bought a textbook and taught herself Persian. "*Salaam aleikum*," she told the mirror every morning. Her daughter watched, startled, from her place on the potty-chair. Elizabeth ran through possible situations in her mind and looked up the words for them. "Would you like more tea? Do you take sugar?" At suppertime she spoke Persian to her husband, who looked amused at the new tone she gave his language, with her flat, factual American voice. He wrote his mother and told her Elizabeth had a surprise for her.

3 Their house was a three-story brick Colonial, but only the first two stories were in use. Now they cleared the third of its trunks and china barrels and *National Geographics*, and they moved in a few pieces of furniture. Elizabeth sewed flowered curtains for the window. She was unusually careful with them; to a foreign mother-in-law, fine seams might matter. Also, Hassan bought a pocket compass, which he placed in the top dresser drawer. "For her prayers," he said. She'll want to face Mecca. She prays three times a day."

4 "But which direction is Mecca from here?" Elizabeth asked.

5 Hassan only shrugged. He had never said the prayers himself, not even as a child. His earliest memory was of tickling the soles of his mother's feet while she prayed steadfastly on; everyone knew it was forbidden to pause once you'd started.

6 Mrs. Ardavi felt nervous about the descent from the plane. She inched down the staircase sideways, one hand tight on the railing, the other clutching her shawl. It was night, and cold. The air seemed curiously opaque. She arrived on solid ground and stood collecting herself—a small, stocky woman in black, with a kerchief over her smooth gray hair. She held her back very straight, as if she had just had her feelings hurt. In picturing this moment she had always thought Hassan would be waiting beside the plane, but there was no sign of him. Blue lights dotted the darkness behind her, an angular terminal loomed ahead, and an official was herding the passengers toward a plate-glass door. She followed, entangled in a web of meaningless sounds such as those you might hear in a fever dream.

7 Immigration. Baggage Claims. Customs. To all she spread her hands and beamed and shrugged, showing she spoke no English. Meanwhile her fellow-passengers waved to a blur of faces beyond a glass wall. It seemed they all knew people here; she was the only one who didn't. She had issued from the plane like a newborn baby, speechless and friendless. And the customs official didn't seem pleased with her. She had brought too many gifts. She had stuffed her bags with them, discarding

all but the most necessary pieces of her clothing so that she would have more room. There were silver tea sets and gold jewelry for her daughter-in-law, and for her granddaughter a doll dressed in the complicated costume of a nomad tribe, an embroidered sheepskin vest, and two religious medals on chains—one a disc inscribed with the name of Allah, the other a tiny gold Koran, with a very effective prayer for long life folded up within it. The customs official sifted gold through his fingers like sand and frowned at the Koran. "Have I done something wrong?" she asked. But of course he didn't understand her. Though you'd think, really, that if he would just *listen* hard enough, just meet her eyes once . . . it was a very simple language, there was no reason why it shouldn't come through to him.

For Hassan, she'd brought food. She had gathered all his favorite 8
foods and put them in a drawstring bag embroidered with peacocks. When the official opened the bag he said something under his breath and called another man over. Together they unwrapped tiny newspaper packets and sniffed at various herbs. "Sumac," she told them. "Powder of lemons. *Shambahleh*." They gazed at her blankly. They untied a small cloth sack and rummaged through the *kashk* she had brought for soup. It rolled beneath their fingers and across the counter—hard white balls of yogurt curd, stuck with bits of sheep hair and manure. Some peasant had labored for hours to make that *kashk*. Mrs. Ardavi picked up one piece and replaced it firmly in the sack. Maybe the official understood her meaning: she was running out of patience. He threw up his hands. He slid her belongings down the counter. She was free to go.

Free to go where? 9

Dazed and stumbling, a pyramid of knobby parcels and bags, scraps 10
of velvet and brocade and tapestry, she made her way to the glass wall. A door opened out of nowhere and a stranger blocked her path. "Khanom Jun," he said. It was a name that only her children would use, but she passed him blindly and he had to touch her arm before she would look up.

He had put on weight. She didn't know him. The last time she'd 11
seen him he was a thin, stoop-shouldered medical student disappearing into an Air France jet without a backward glance. "Khanom Jun, it's me," this stranger said, but she went on searching his face with cloudy eyes. No doubt he was a bearer of bad news. Was that it? A recurrent dream had warned her that she would never see her son again—that he would die on his way to the airport, or had already been dead for months but no one wanted to break the news; some second or third cousin in America had continued signing Hassan's name to his cheerful,

anonymous letters. Now here was this man with graying hair and a thick mustache, his clothes American but his face Iranian, his eyes sadly familiar, as if they belonged to someone else. "Don't you believe me?" he said. He kissed her on both cheeks. It was his smell she recognized first—a pleasantly bitter, herblike smell that brought her the image of Hassan as a child, reaching thin arms around her neck. "It's you, Hassan," she said, and then she started crying against his gray tweed shoulder.

12 They were quiet during the long drive home. Once she reached over to touch his face, having wanted to do so for miles. None of the out-of-focus snapshots he'd sent had prepared her for the way he had aged. "How long has it been?" she asked. "Twelve years?" But both of them knew to the day how long it had been. All those letters of hers: "My dear Hassan, ten years now and still your place is empty." "Eleven years and still . . ."

13 Hassan squinted through the windshield at the oncoming headlights. His mother started fretting over her kerchief, which she knew she ought not to have worn. She'd been told so by her youngest sister, who had been to America twice. "It marks you," her sister had said. But that square of silk was the last, shrunken reminder of the veil she used to hide beneath, before the previous Shah had banished such things. At her age, how could she expose herself? And then her teeth; her teeth were a problem too. Her youngest sister had said, "You ought to get dentures made, I'm sure there aren't three whole teeth in your head." But Mrs. Ardavi was scared of dentists. Now she covered her mouth with one hand and looked sideways at Hassan, though so far he hadn't seemed to notice. He was busy maneuvering his car into the right-hand lane.

14 This silence was the last thing she had expected. For weeks she'd been saving up stray bits of gossip, weaving together the family stories she would tell him. There were three hundred people in her family—most of them related to each other in three or four different ways, all leading intricate and scandalous lives she had planned to discuss in detail, but instead she stared sadly out the window. You'd think Hassan would ask. You'd think they could have a better conversation than this, after such a long time. Disappointment made her cross, and now she stubbornly refused to speak even when she saw something she wanted to comment on, some imposing building or unfamiliar brand of car sliding past her into the darkness.

15 By the time they arrived it was nearly midnight. None of the houses were lit but Hassan's—worn brick, older than she would have expected. "Here we are," said Hassan. The competence with which he parked the

car, fitting it neatly into a small space by the curb, put him firmly on the other side of the fence, the American side. She would have to face her daughter-in-law alone. As they climbed the front steps she whispered, "How do you say it again?"

"Say what?" Hassan asked. 16

"Her name. Lizabet?" 17

"Elizabeth. Like Elizabeth Taylor. *You* know." 18

"Yes, yes, of course," said his mother. Then she lifted her chin, hold- 19
ing tight to the straps of her purse.

Elizabeth was wearing bluejeans and a pair of fluffy slippers. Her 20
hair was blond as corn silk, cut short and straight, and her face had the grave, sleepy look of a child's. As soon as she had opened the door she said, "*Salaam aleikum.*" Mrs. Ardavi, overcome with relief at the Persian greeting, threw her arms around her and kissed both cheeks. Then they led her into the living room, which looked comfortable but a little too plain. The furniture was straight-edged, the rugs uninteresting, though the curtains had a nice figured pattern that caught her eye. In one corner sat a shiny red kiddie car complete with license plates. "Is that the child's?" she asked. "Hilary's?" She hesitated over the name. "Could I see her?"

"*Now?*" said Hassan. 21

But Elizabeth told him, "That's all right." (Women understood 22
these things.) She beckoned to her mother-in-law. They climbed the stairs together, up to the second floor, into a little room that smelled of milk and rubber and talcum powder, smells she would know anywhere. Even in the half-light from the hallway, she could tell that Hilary was beautiful. She had black, tumbling hair, long black lashes, and skin of a tone they called wheat-colored, lighter than Hassan's. "There," said Elizabeth. "Thank you," said Mrs. Ardavi. Her voice was formal, but this was her first grandchild and it took her a moment to recover herself. Then they stepped back into the hallway. "I brought her some medals," she whispered. "I hope you don't mind."

"Medals?" said Elizabeth. She repeated the word anxiously, mispro- 23
nouncing it.

"Only an Allah and a Koran, both very tiny. You'll hardly know 24
they're there. I'm not used to seeing a child without a medal. It worries me."

Automatically her fingers traced a chain around her neck, ending in 25
the hollow of her collarbone. Elizabeth nodded, looking relieved. "*Oh* yes. Medals," she said.

"Is that all right?" 26

"Yes, of course." 27

28 Mrs. Ardavi took heart. "Hassan laughs," she said. "He doesn't believe in these things. But when he left I put a prayer in his suitcase pocket, and you see he's been protected. Now if Hilary wore a medal, I could sleep nights."

29 "Of course," Elizabeth said again.

30 When they re-entered the living room, Mrs. Ardavi was smiling, and she kissed Hassan on the top of his head before she sat down.

31 American days were tightly scheduled, divided not into morning and afternoon but into 9:00, 9:30, and so forth, each half hour possessing its own set activity. It was marvellous. Mrs. Ardavi wrote her sisters: "They're more organized here. My daughter-in-law never wastes a minute." How terrible, her sisters wrote back. They were all in Teheran, drinking cup after cup of tea and idly guessing who might come and visit. "No, you misunderstand," Mrs. Ardavi protested. "I like it this way. I'm fitting in wonderfully." And to her youngest sister she wrote, "You'd think I was American. No one guesses otherwise." This wasn't true, of course, but she hoped it would be true in the future.

32 Hassan was a doctor. He worked long hours, from six in the morning until six at night. While she was still washing for her morning prayers she could hear him tiptoe down the stairs and out the front door. His car would start up, a distant rumble far below her, and from her bathroom window she could watch it swing out from beneath a tatter of red leaves and round the corner and disappear. Then she would sigh and return to her sink. Before prayers she had to wash her face, her hands, and the soles of her feet. She had to draw her wet fingers down the part in her hair. After that she returned to her room, where she swathed herself tightly in her long black veil and knelt on a beaded velvet prayer mat. East was where the window was, curtained by chintz and misted over. On the east wall she hung a lithograph of the Caliph Ali and a color snapshot of her third son, Babak, whose marriage she had arranged just a few months before this visit. If Babak hadn't married, she never could have come. He was the youngest, spoiled by being the only son at home. It had taken her three years to find a wife for him. (One was too modern, one too lazy, one so perfect she had been suspicious.) But finally the proper girl had turned up, modest and well-mannered and sufficiently wide of hip, and Mrs. Ardavi and the bridal couple had settled in a fine new house on the outskirts of Teheran. Now every time she prayed, she added a word of thanks that at last she had a home for her old age. After that, she unwound her veil and laid it carefully in a drawer. From another drawer she took thick cotton stockings and elastic garters; she stuffed her swollen feet into open-toed vinyl sandals. Unless she was going out, she wore a housecoat. It amazed her how wasteful Americans were with their clothing.

Downstairs, Elizabeth would have started her tea and buttered a 33
piece of toast for her. Elizabeth and Hilary ate bacon and eggs, but bacon of course was unclean and Mrs. Ardavi never accepted any. Nor had it even been offered to her, except once, jokingly, by Hassan. The distinctive, smoky smell rose to meet her as she descended the stairs. "What does it taste like?" she always asked. She was dying to know. But Elizabeth's vocabulary didn't cover the taste of bacon; she only said it was salty and then laughed and gave up. They had learned very early to travel a well-worn conversational path, avoiding the dead ends caused by unfamiliar words. "Did you sleep well?" Elizabeth always asked in her funny, childish accent, and Mrs. Ardavi answered, "So-so." Then they would turn and watch Hilary, who sat on a booster seat eating scrambled eggs, a thin chain of Persian gold crossing the back of her neck. Conversation was easier, or even unnecessary, as long as Hilary was there.

In the mornings Elizabeth cleaned house. Mrs. Ardavi used that 34
time for letter writing. She had dozens of letters to write, to all her aunts and uncles and her thirteen sisters. (Her father had had three wives, and a surprising number of children even for that day and age.) Then there was Babak. His wife was in her second month of pregnancy, so Mrs. Ardavi wrote long accounts of the American child-rearing methods. "There are some things I don't agree with," she wrote. "They let Hilary play outdoors by herself, with not even a servant to keep an eye on her." Then she would trail off and gaze thoughtfully at Hilary, who sat on the floor watching a television program called "Captain Kangaroo."

Mrs. Ardavi's own childhood had been murky and grim. From the 35
age of nine she was wrapped in a veil, one corner of it clenched in her teeth to hide her face whenever she appeared on the streets. Her father, a respected man high up in public life, used to chase servant girls through the halls and trap them, giggling, in vacant bedrooms. At the age of ten she was forced to watch her mother bleed to death in childbirth, and when she screamed the midwife had struck her across the face and held her down till she had properly kissed her mother goodbye. There seemed no connection at all between her and this little overalled American. At times, when Hilary had one of her temper tantrums, Mrs. Ardavi waited in horror for Elizabeth to slap her and then, when no slap came, felt a mixture of relief and anger. "In Iran—" she would begin, and if Hassan was there he always said, "But this is not Iran, remember?"

After lunch Hilary took a nap, and Mrs. Ardavi went upstairs to say 36
her noontime prayers and take a nap as well. Then she might do a little laundry in her bathtub. Laundry was a problem here. Although she liked Elizabeth, the fact was that the girl was a Christian, and therefore unclean; it would never do to have a Christian wash a Moslem's clothes.

The automatic dryer was also unclean, having contained, at some point, a Christian's underwear. So she had to ask Hassan to buy her a drying rack. It came unassembled. Elizabeth put it together for her, stick by stick, and then Mrs. Ardavi held it under her shower and rinsed it off, hoping that would be enough to remove any taint. The Koran didn't cover this sort of situation.

37 When Hilary was up from her nap they walked her to the park—Elizabeth in her eternal bluejeans and Mrs. Ardavi in her kerchief and shawl, taking short painful steps in small shoes that bulged over her bunions. They still hadn't seen to her teeth, although by now Hassan had noticed them. She was hoping he might forget about the dentist, but then she saw him remembering every time she laughed and revealed her five brown teeth set wide apart.

38 At the park she laughed a great deal. It was her only way of communicating with the other women. They sat on the benches ringing the playground, and while Elizabeth translated their questions Mrs. Ardavi laughed and nodded at them over and over. "They want to know if you like it here," Elizabeth said. Mrs. Ardavi answered at length, but Elizabeth's translation was very short. Then gradually the other women forgot her, and conversation rattled on while she sat silent and watched each speaker's lips. The few recognizable words—"telephone," "television," "radio"—gave her the impression that American conversations were largely technical, even among women. Their gestures were wide and slow, disproving her youngest sister's statement that in America everyone was in a hurry. On the contrary, these women were dreamlike, moving singly or in twos across wide flat spaces beneath white November skies when they departed.

39 Later, at home, Mrs. Ardavi would say, "The red-haired girl, is she pregnant? She looked it, I thought. Is the fat girl happy in her marriage?" She asked with some urgency, plucking Elizabeth's sleeve when she was slow to answer. People's private lives fascinated her. On Saturday trips to the supermarket she liked to single out some interesting stranger. "What's the matter with that *jerky*-moving man? That girl, is she one of your dark-skinned people?" Elizabeth answered too softly, and never seemed to follow Mrs. Ardavi's pointing finger.

40 Supper was difficult; Mrs. Ardavi didn't like American food. Even when Elizabeth made something Iranian, it had an American taste to it—the vegetables still faintly crisp, the onions transparent rather than nicely blackened. "Vegetables not thoroughly cooked retain a certain acidity," Mrs. Ardavi said, laying down her fork. "This is a cause of constipation and stomach aches. At night I often have heartburn. It's been

three full days since I moved my bowels." Elizabeth merely bent over her plate, offering no symptoms of her own in return. Hassan said, "At the table, Khanom? At the table?"

Eventually she decided to cook supper herself. Over Elizabeth's 41
protests she began at three every afternoon, filling the house with the smell of dillweed and arranging pots on counters and cabinets and finally, when there was no more space, on the floor. She squatted on the floor with her skirt tucked between her knees and stirred great bowls of minced greens while behind her, on the gas range, four different pots of food bubbled and steamed. The kitchen was becoming more homelike, she thought. A bowl of yogurt brewed beside the stove, a kettle of rice soaked in the sink, and the top of the dishwasher was curlicued with the yellow dye from saffron. In one corner sat the pudding pan, black on the bottom from the times she had cooked down sugar to make a sweet for her intestines. "Now, this is your rest period," she always told Elizabeth. "Come to the table in three hours and be surprised." But Elizabeth only hovered around the kitchen, disturbing the serene, steam-filled air with clatter and slams as she put away pots, or pacing between stove and sink, her arms folded across her chest. At supper she ate little; Mrs. Ardavi wondered how Americans got so tall on such small suppers. Hassan, on the other hand, had second and third helpings. "I must be gaining five pounds a week," he said. "None of my clothes fit."

"That's good to hear," said his mother. And Elizabeth added some- 42
thing but in English, which Hassan answered in English also. Often now they broke into English for paragraphs at a time—Elizabeth speaking softly, looking at her plate, and Hassan answering at length and sometimes reaching across the table to cover her hand.

At night, after her evening prayers, Mrs. Ardavi watched television 43
on the living-room couch. She brought her veil downstairs and wrapped it around her to keep the drafts away. Her shoes lay on the rug beneath her, and scattered down the length of the couch were her knitting bag, her sack of burned sugar, her magnifying glass, and *My First Golden Dictionary*. Elizabeth read novels in an easy chair, and Hassan watched TV so that he could translate the difficult parts of the plot. Not that Mrs. Ardavi had much trouble. American plots were easy to guess at, particularly the Westerns. And when the program was boring—a documentary or a special news feature—she could pass the time by talking to Hassan. "Your cousin Farah wrote," she said. "Do you remember her? A homely girl, too dark. She's getting a divorce and in my opinion it's fortunate; he's from a lower class. Do you remember Farah?"

44 Hassan only grunted, his eyes on the screen. He was interested in American politics. So was she, for that matter. She had wept for President Kennedy, and carried Jackie's picture in her purse. But these news programs were long and dry, and if Hassan wouldn't talk she was forced to turn at last to her *Golden Dictionary*.

45 In her childhood, she had been taught by expensive foreign tutors. Her mind was her great gift, the compensation for a large, plain face and a stocky figure. But now what she had learned seemed lost, forgotten utterly or fogged by years, so that Hassan gave a snort whenever she told him some fact that she had dredged up from her memory. It seemed that everything she studied now had to penetrate through a great thick layer before it reached her mind. "Tonk you," she practiced. "Tonk you. Tonk you." "Thank you," Hassan corrected her. He pointed out useful words in her dictionary—grocery-store words, household words—but she grew impatient with their woodenness. What she wanted was the language to display her personality, her famous courtesy, and her magical intuition about the inside lives of other people. Nightly she learned "salt," "bread," "spoon," but with an inner sense of dullness, and every morning when she woke her English was once again confined to "thank you" and "NBC."

46 Elizabeth, meanwhile, read on, finishing one book and reaching for the next without even glancing up. Hassan chewed a thumbnail and watched a senator. He shouldn't be disturbed, of course, but time after time his mother felt the silence and the whispery turning of pages stretching her nerves until she had to speak. "Hassan?"

47 "Hmm."

48 "My chest seems tight. I'm sure a cold is coming on. Don't you have a tonic?"

49 "No," said Hassan.

50 He dispensed medicines all day; he listened to complaints. Common sense told her to stop, but she persisted, encouraged by some demon that wouldn't let her tongue lie still. "Don't you have some syrup? What about that liquid you gave me for constipation? Would that help?"

51 "No, it wouldn't," said Hassan.

52 He drove her on, somehow. The less he gave, the more she had to ask. "Well, aspirin? Vitamins?" Until Hassan said, "Will you just let me *watch?*" Then she could lapse into silence again, or even gather up the clutter of her belongings and bid the two of them good night.

53 She slept badly. Often she lay awake for hours, fingering the edge of the sheet and staring at the ceiling. Memories crowded in on her, old grievances and fears, injustices that had never been righted. For the first

time in years she thought of her husband, a gentle, weak man given to surprising outbursts of temper. She hadn't loved him when she married him, and at his death from a liver ailment six years later her main feeling had been resentment. Was it fair to be widowed so young, while other women were supported and protected? She had moved from her husband's home back to the old family estate, where five of her sisters still lived. There she had stayed till Babak's wedding, drinking tea all day with her sisters and pulling the strings by which the rest of the family was attached. Marriages were arranged, funerals attended, childbirth discussed in fine detail; servants' disputes were settled, and feuds patched up and then restarted. Her husband's face had quickly faded, leaving only a vacant spot in her mind. But now she could see him so clearly—a wasted figure on his deathbed, beard untrimmed, turban coming loose, eyes imploring her for something more than an absent-minded pat on the cheek as she passed through his room on her way to check the children.

She saw the thin faces of her three small boys as they sat on the rug 54
eating rice. Hassan was the stubborn, mischievous one, with perpetual scabs on his knees. Babak was the cuddly one. Ali was the oldest, who had caused so much worry—weak, like his father, demanding, but capable of turning suddenly charming. Four years ago he had died of a brain hemorrhage, slumping over a dinner table in faraway Shirāz, where he'd gone to be free of his wife, who was also his double first cousin. Ever since he was born he had disturbed his mother's sleep, first because she worried over what he would amount to and now, after his death, because she lay awake listing all she had done wrong with him. She had been too lenient. No, too harsh. There was no telling. Mistakes she had made floated on the ceiling like ghosts—allowances she'd made when she knew she shouldn't have, protections he had not deserved, blows which perhaps he had not deserved either.

She would have liked to talk to Hassan about it, but any time she 55
tried he changed the subject. Maybe he was angry about the way he had heard of Ali's death. It was customary to break such news gradually. She had started a series of tactful letters, beginning by saying that Ali was seriously ill when in truth he was already buried. Something in the letter had given her away—perhaps her plans for a rest cure by the seaside, which she never would have considered if she'd had an ailing son at home. Hassan had telephoned overseas, taking three nights to reach her. "Tell me what's wrong," he said. "I know there's something." When her tears kept her from answering, he asked, "Is he dead?" His voice sounded angry, but that might have been due to a poor connection. And when he hung up, cutting her off before she could say all she

wanted, she thought, I should have told him straight out. I had forgotten that about him. Now when she spoke of Ali he listened politely, with his face frozen. She would have told him anything, all about the death and burial and that witch of a wife throwing herself, too late, into the grave; but Hassan never asked.

56 Death was moving in on her. Oh, not on her personally (the women in her family lived a century or longer, burying the men one by one) but on everybody around her, all the cousins and uncles and brothers-in-law. No sooner had she laid away her mourning clothes than it was time to bring them out again. Recently she had begun to feel she would outlive her two other sons as well, and she fought off sleep because of the dreams it brought—Babak lying stiff and cold in his grave, Hassan crumpled over in some dark American alley. Terrifying images would zoom at her out of the night. In the end she had to wrap herself in her veil and sleep instead on the Persian rug, which had the dusty smell of home and was, anyway, more comfortable than her unsteady foreign mattress.

57 At Christmas time, Hassan and Elizabeth gave Mrs. Ardavi a brightly colored American dress with short sleeves. She wore it to an Iranian party, even leaving off her kerchief in a sudden fit of daring. Everyone commented on how nice she looked. "Really you fit right in," a girl told her. "May I write to my mother about you? She was over here for a year and a half and never once stepped out of the house without her kerchief." Mrs. Ardavi beamed. It was true she would never have associated with these people at home—children of civil servants and bank clerks, newly rich now they'd finished medical school. The wives called their husbands "Doctor" even in direct address. But still it felt good to be speaking so much Persian; her tongue nearly ran away with her. "I see you're expecting a baby," she said to one of the wives. "Is it your first? I could tell by your eyes. Now don't be nervous. I had three myself; my mother had seven and never felt a pain in her life. She would squat down to serve my father's breakfast and 'Eh?' she would say. 'Aga Jun, it's the baby!' and there it would be on the floor between her feet, waiting for her to cut the cord and finish pouring the tea." She neglected to mention how her mother had died. All her natural tact came back to her, her gift with words and her knowledge of how to hold an audience. She bubbled and sparkled like a girl, and her face fell when it was time to go home.

58 After the party, she spent two or three days noticing more keenly than ever the loss of her language, and talking more feverishly when Hassan came home in the evening. This business of being a foreigner was something changeable. Boundaries kept shifting, and sometimes it

was she who was the foreigner but other times Elizabeth, or even Hassan. (Wasn't it true, she often wondered, that there was a greater distance between men and women than between Americans and Iranians, or even *Eskimos* and Iranians?) Hassan was the foreigner when she and Elizabeth conspired to hide a miniature Koran in his glove compartment; he would have laughed at them. "You see," she told Elizabeth, "I know there's nothing to it, but it makes me feel better. When my sons were born I took them all to the bath attendant to have their blood let. People say it brings long life. I know that's superstition, but whenever afterward I saw those ridges down their backs I felt safe. Don't you understand?" And Elizabeth said, "Of course." She smuggled the Koran into the car herself, and hid it beneath the Texaco maps. Hassan saw nothing.

59 Hilary was a foreigner forever. She dodged her grandmother's yearning hands, and when the grownups spoke Persian she fretted and misbehaved and pulled on Elizabeth's sleeve. Mrs. Ardavi had to remind herself constantly not to kiss the child too much, not to reach out for a hug, not to offer her lap. In this country people kept more separate. They kept so separate that at times she felt hurt. They tried to be so subtle, so undemonstrative. She would never understand this place.

60 In January they took her to a dentist, who made clucking noises when he looked in her mouth. "What does he say?" she asked. "Tell me the worst." But Hassan was talking in a low voice to Elizabeth, and he waved her aside. They seemed to be having a misunderstanding of some sort. "What does he *say*, Hassan?"

61 "Just a minute."

62 She craned around in the high-backed chair, fighting off the dentist's little mirror. "I have to know," she told Hassan.

63 "He says your teeth are terrible. They have to be extracted and the gums surgically smoothed. He wants to know if you'll be here for another few months; he can't schedule you till later."

64 A cold lump of fear swelled in her stomach. Unfortunately she *would* be here; it had only been three months so far and she was planning to stay a year. So she had to watch numbly while her life was signed away, whole strings of appointments made, and little white cards filled out. And Hassan didn't even look sympathetic. He was still involved in whatever this argument was with Elizabeth. The two of them failed to notice how her hands were shaking.

65 It snowed all of January, the worst snow they had had in years. When she came downstairs in the mornings she found the kitchen icy cold, crisscrossed by drafts. "The sort of cold enters your bones," she told

Elizabeth. "I'm sure to fall sick." Elizabeth only nodded. Some mornings now her face was pale and puffy, as if she had a secret worry, but Mrs. Ardavi had learned that it was better not to ask about it.

66 Early in February there was a sudden warm spell. Snow melted and all the trees dripped in the sunshine. "We're going for a walk," Elizabeth said, and Mrs. Ardavi said, "I'll come too." In spite of the warmth, she toiled upstairs for her woolen shawl. She didn't like to take chances. And she worried over Hilary's bare ears. "Won't she catch cold?" she asked. "I think we should cover her head."

67 "She'll be all right," said Elizabeth, and then shut her face in a certain stubborn way she had.

68 In the park, Elizabeth and Hilary made snowballs from the last of the snow and threw them at each other, narrowly missing Mrs. Ardavi, who stood watching with her arms folded and her hands tucked in her sleeves.

69 The next morning, something was wrong with Hilary. She sat at the breakfast table and cried steadily, refusing all food. "Now, now," her grandmother said, "won't you tell old Ka Jun what's wrong?" But when she came close Hilary screamed louder. By noon she was worse. Elizabeth called Hassan, and he came home immediately and laid a hand on Hilary's forehead and said she should go to the pediatrician. He drove them there himself. "It's her ears, I'm sure of it," Mrs. Ardavi said in the waiting room. For some reason Hassan grew angry. "Do you always know better than the experts?" he asked her. "What are we coming to the doctor for? We could have talked to you and saved the trip." His mother lowered her eyes and examined her purse straps. She understood that he was anxious, but all the same her feelings were hurt and when they rose to go into the office she stayed behind.

70 Later Hassan came back and sat down again. "There's an infection in her middle ear," he told her. "The doctor's going to give her a shot of penicillin." His mother nodded, careful not to annoy him by reminding him she had thought as much. Then Hilary started crying. She must be getting her shot now. Mrs. Ardavi herself was terrified of needles, and she sat gripping her purse until her fingers turned white, staring around the waiting room, which seemed pathetically cheerful, with its worn wooden toys and nursery-school paintings. Her own ear ached in sympathy. She thought of a time when she had boxed Ali's ears too hard and he had wept all that day and gone to sleep sucking his thumb.

71 While Hassan was there she was careful not to say anything, but the following morning at breakfast she said, "Elizabeth dear, do you remember that walk we took day before yesterday?"

"Yes," said Elizabeth. She was squeezing oranges for Hilary, who'd 72
grown cheerful again and was eating a huge breakfast.

"Remember I said Hilary should wear a hat? Now you see you 73
should have been more careful. Because of you she fell sick; she could
have died. Do you see that now?"

"No," said Elizabeth. 74

Was her Persian that scanty? Lately it seemed to have shrunk and 75
hardened, like a stale piece of bread. Mrs. Ardavi sighed and tried again.
"Without a hat, you see—" she began. But Elizabeth had set down her
orange, picked up Hilary, and walked out of the room. Mrs. Ardavi
stared after her, wondering if she'd said something wrong.

For the rest of the day, Elizabeth was busy in her room. She was 76
cleaning out bureaus and closets. A couple of times Mrs. Ardavi advanced as far as the doorway, where she stood awkwardly watching. Hilary sat on the floor playing with a discarded perfume bottle. Everything, it seemed, was about to be thrown away—buttonless blouses and
stretched-out sweaters, stockings and combs and empty lipstick tubes.
"Could I be of any help?" Mrs. Ardavi asked, but Elizabeth said, "Oh,
no. Thank you very much." Her voice was cheerful. Yet when Hassan
came home he went upstairs and stayed a long time, and the door remained shut behind him.

Supper that night was an especially fine stew, Hassan's favorite ever 77
since childhood, but he didn't say a word about it. He hardly spoke at
all, in fact. Then later, when Elizabeth was upstairs putting Hilary to
bed, he said, "Khanom Jun, I want to talk to you."

"Yes, Hassan," she said, laying aside her knitting. She was fright- 78
ened by his seriousness, the black weight of his mustache, and her own
father's deep black eyes. But what had she done? She knotted her hands
and looked up at him, swallowing.

"I understand you've been interfering," he said. 79

"I, Hassan?" 80

"Elizabeth isn't the kind you can do that with. And she's raising the 81
child just fine on her own."

"Well, of course she is," said his mother. "Did I ever say other- 82
wise?"

"Show it, then. Don't offer criticisms." 83

"Very well," she said. She picked up her knitting and began count- 84
ing stitches, as if she'd forgotten the conversation entirely. But that
evening she was unusually quiet, and at nine o'clock she excused herself
to go to bed. "So early?" Hassan asked.

"I'm tired," she told him, and left with her back very straight. 85

86 Her room surrounded her like a nest. She had built up layers of herself on every surface—tapestries and bits of lace and lengths of paisley. The bureau was covered with gilt-framed pictures of the saints, and snapshots of her sisters at family gatherings. On the windowsill were little plants in orange and aqua plastic pots—her favorite American colors. Her bedside table held bottles of medicine, ivory prayer beads, and a tiny brick of holy earth. The rest of the house was bare and shiny, impersonal; this room was as comforting as her shawl.

87 Still, she didn't sleep well. Ghosts rose up again, tugging at her thoughts. Why did things turn out so badly for her? Her father had preferred her brothers, a fact that crushed her even after all these years. Her husband had had three children by her and then complained that she was cold. And what comfort were children? If she had stayed in Iran any longer Babak would have asked her to move; she'd seen it coming. There'd been some disrespect creeping into his bride's behavior, some unwillingness to take advice, which Babak had overlooked even when his mother pointed it out to him. And Hassan was worse—always so stubborn, much too independent. She had offered him anything if he would just stay in Iran but he had said no; he was set on leaving her. And he had flatly refused to take along his cousin Shora as his wife, though everyone pointed out how lonely he would be. He was so anxious to break away, to get *going*, to come to this hardhearted country and take up with a Christian girl. Oh, she should have laughed when he left, and saved her tears for someone more deserving. She never should have come here, she never should have asked anything of him again. When finally she went to sleep it seemed that her eyes remained open, burning large and dry beneath her lids.

88 In the morning she had a toothache. She could hardly walk for the pain. It was only Friday (the first of her dental appointments was for Monday), but the dentist made time for her during the afternoon and pulled the tooth. Elizabeth said it wouldn't hurt, but it did. Elizabeth treated it as something insignificant, merely a small break in her schedule, which required the hiring of a babysitter. She wouldn't even call Hassan home from work. "What could he do?" she asked.

89 So when Hassan returned that evening it was all a surprise to him—the sight of his mother with a bloody cotton cylinder hanging out over her lower lip like a long tooth. "What *happened* to you?" he asked. To make it worse, Hilary was screaming and had been all afternoon. Mrs. Ardavi put her hands over her ears, wincing. "Will you make that child hush?" Hassan told Elizabeth. "I think we should get my mother to bed." He guided her toward the stairs, and she allowed herself to lean on him.

"It's mainly my heart," she said. "You know how scared I am of dentists." When he had folded back her bedspread and helped her to lie down she closed her eyes gratefully, resting one arm across her forehead. Even the comfort of hot tea was denied her; she had to stay on cold foods for twelve hours. Hassan fixed her a glass of ice water. He was very considerate, she thought. He seemed as shaken at the sight of her as Hilary had been. All during the evening he kept coming to check on her, and twice in the night she heard him climbing the stairs to listen at her door. When she moaned he called, "Are you awake?"

"Of course," she said. 90

"Can I get you anything?" 91

"No, no." 92

In the morning she descended the stairs with slow, groping feet, 93
keeping a tight hold on the railing. "It was a very hard night," she said. "At four my gum started throbbing. Is that normal? I think these American pain pills are constipating. Maybe a little prune juice would restore my regularity."

"I'll get it," Hassan said. "You sit down. Did you take the milk of mag- 94
nesia?"

"Oh, yes, but I'm afraid it wasn't enough," she said. 95

Elizabeth handed Hassan a platter of bacon, not looking at him. 96

After breakfast, while Hassan and his mother were still sitting over 97
their tea, Elizabeth started cleaning the kitchen. She made quite a bit of noise. She sorted the silverware and then went through a tangle of utensils, discarding bent spatulas and rusty tongs. "May I help?" asked Mrs. Ardavi. Elizabeth shook her head. She seemed to have these fits of throwing things away. Now she was standing on the counter to take everything from the upper cabinets—crackers, cereals, half-empty bottles of spices. On the very top shelf was a flowered tin confectioner's box with Persian lettering on it, forgotten since the day Mrs. Ardavi had brought it. "My!" said Mrs. Ardavi. "Won't Hilary be surprised!" Elizabeth pried the lid off. Out flew a cloud of insects, grayish-brown with V-shaped wings. They brushed past Elizabeth's face and fluttered through her hair and swarmed toward the ceiling, where they dimmed the light fixture. Elizabeth flung the box as far from her as possible and climbed down from the counter. "Goodness!" said Mrs. Ardavi. "Why, *we* have those at home!" Hassan lowered his teacup. Mixed nuts and dried currants rolled every which way on the floor; more insects swung toward the ceiling. Elizabeth sat on the nearest chair and buried her head in her hands. "Elizabeth?" said Hassan.

98 But she wouldn't look at him. In the end she simply rose and went upstairs, shutting the bedroom door with a gentle, definite click, which they heard all the way down in the kitchen because they were listening so hard.

99 "Excuse me," Hassan said to his mother.

100 She nodded and stared into her tea.

101 After he was gone she went to find Hilary, and she set her on her knee, babbling various folk rhymes to her while straining her ears toward the silence overhead. But Hilary squirmed off her lap and went to play with a truck. Then Hassan came downstairs again. He didn't say a word about Elizabeth.

102 On the following day, when Mrs. Ardavi's tooth was better, she and Hassan had a little talk upstairs in her room. They were very polite with each other. Hassan asked his mother how long they could hope for her to stay. His mother said she hadn't really thought about it. Hassan said that in America it was the custom to have house guests for three months only. After that they moved to a separate apartment nearby, which he'd be glad to provide for her as soon as he could find one, maybe next week. "Ah, an apartment," said his mother, looking impressed. But she had never lived alone a day in her life, and so after a suitable pause she said that she would hate to put him to so much expense. "Especially," she said, "when I'm going in such a short time anyway, since I'm homesick for my sisters."

103 "Well, then," said Hassan.

104 At supper that night, Hassan announced that his mother was missing her sisters and would like to leave. Elizabeth lowered her glass. "Leave?" she said.

105 Mrs. Ardavi said, "And Babak's wife, of course, will be asking for me when the baby arrives."

106 "Well . . . but what about the dentist? You were supposed to start your appointments on Monday."

107 "It's not important," Mrs. Ardavi said.

108 "But we set up all those—"

109 "There are plenty of dentists she can see at home," Hassan told Elizabeth. "We have dentists in Iran, for God's sake. Do you imagine we're barbarians?"

110 "No," Elizabeth said.

111 On the evening of the third of March, Hassan drove his mother to the airport. He was worrying about the road, which was slippery after a snowfall. He couldn't find much to say to his mother. And once they

had arrived, he deliberately kept the conversation to trivia—the verifying of tickets, checking of departure times, weighing of baggage. Her baggage was fourteen pounds overweight. It didn't make sense; all she had were her clothes and a few small gifts for her sisters. "Why is it so heavy?" Hassan asked. "What have you got in there?" But his mother only said, "I don't know," and straightened her shawl, looking elsewhere. Hassan bent to open a tooled-leather suitcase. Inside he found three empty urn-shaped wine bottles, the permanent-press sheets from her bed, and a sample box of detergent that had come in yesterday's mail. "Listen," said Hassan, "do you know how much I'd have to pay to fly these things over? What's the matter with you?"

"I wanted to show my sisters," his mother said. 112

"Well, forget it. Now, what else have you got?" 113

But something about her—the vague, childlike eyes set upon some 114
faraway object—made him give in. He opened no more bags. He even regretted his sharpness, and when her flight was announced he hugged her closely and kissed the top of her head. "Go with God," he said.

"Goodbye, Hassan." 115

She set off down the corridor by herself, straggling behind a line of 116
businessmen. They all wore hats. His mother wore her scarf, and of all the travelers she alone, securely kerchiefed and shawled, setting her small shoes resolutely on the gleaming tiles, seemed undeniably a foreigner.

THINKING ABOUT THE TEXT

1. Discuss Mrs. Ardavi's effort to adjust to American culture. Where do you see her making a genuine effort, and where do you see her clinging to her own customs?

2. At first, Elizabeth tries hard to make her mother-in-law feel at home. Discuss her efforts; then specify the signs that Elizabeth is feeling stressed by Mrs. Ardavi's prolonged stay.

3. Mrs. Ardavi notes, "Boundaries kept shifting, and sometimes it was she who was the foreigner but other times Elizabeth, or even Hassan." Point out scenes where each seems the foreigner and explain why.

4. Discuss scenes where Mrs. Ardavi is "interfering." Explain each from her perspective and then from Hassan's or Elizabeth's.

5. In what ways does the title relate to the story?

WRITING FROM THE TEXT

1. Write an essay comparing Mrs. Ardavi's beliefs and behaviors with Elizabeth's. What are the barriers between them, and which are hardest to resolve? What is Hassan's role in their relationship? Focus on an assertion or thesis you can prove about the key differences or bonds between them.
2. Rather than portraying Mrs. Ardavi as a stereotypical mother-in-law, Tyler helps us understand her as a complex and rich human, caught between worlds. Consider Mrs. Ardavi's upbringing and past as well as her current predicament in a new culture and write an analysis of her character. (See the character analysis section, pp. 436–443.)
3. Write an essay focusing on an experience when you felt "undeniably a foreigner." As Tyler suggests, this alienation may happen in your own environment or your own home, as it does to Hassan and Elizabeth. Include examples that illustrate the alienation you felt.

CONNECTING WITH OTHER TEXTS

1. Using this story and any two other readings in this text, write an essay analyzing the pressure and demands of parenting. Suggested readings from this text include "Fetal Alcohol Syndrome" (p. 23), "My Man Bovanne" (p. 46), "Like Mexicans" (p. 188), "Coke" (p. 249), and "Proper Care and Maintenance" (p. 170).
2. Intercultural marriages bring an added complexity to family relationships. Research a specific Islamic custom or belief that relates to this story (e.g., arranged marriages, Christians as unclean, the wearing of medals, or carrying the Koran) and explain its origin and significance.

■ MY MAN BOVANNE

Toni Cade Bambara

A civil rights activist, college professor, editor, and author of short stories, a novel, and screenplays, Toni Cade Bambara (1939–1996) also directed recreation in the psychiatry department of a metropolitan hospital. During the 1960s, Bambara became involved in urban political and cultural activities, an interest that appears in the author's work. In the *New York Times Book Review,* C. D. B. Bryan wrote that "Bambara tells . . . more about being black through her quiet, proud, silly, tender, hip, acute, loving stories than any amount of literary polemicizing could hope to do. She writes about love: a love for one's family, one's friends, one's race, one's neighborhood, and it is the sort of love that comes with maturity and inner peace." The short story included here was first published in *Gorilla, My Love* in 1971.

Blind people got a hummin jones if you notice. Which is understandable completely once you been around one and notice what no eyes will force you into to see people, and you get past the first time, which seems to come out of nowhere, and it's like you in church again with fat-chest ladies and old gents gruntin a hum low in the throat to whatever the preacher be saying. Shakey Bee bottom lip all swole up with Sweet Peach and me explainin how come the sweet-potato bread was a dollar-quarter this time stead of dollar regular and he say uh hunh he understand, then he break into this *thizzin* kind of hum which is quiet, but fiercesome just the same, if you ain't ready for it. Which I wasn't. But I got used to it and the onliest time I had to say somethin bout it was when we was playin checkers on the stoop one time and he commenst to hummin quite churchy seem to me. So I says, "Look here Shakey Bee, I can't beat you and Jesus too." He stop. 1

So that's how come I asked My Man Bovanne to dance. He ain't my man mind you, just a nice ole gent from the block that we all know cause he fixes things and the kids like him. Or used to fore Black Power got hold their minds and mess em around till they can't be civil to ole folks. So we at this benefit for my niece's cousin who's runnin for somethin with this Black party somethin or other behind her. And I press up close to dance with Bovanne who blind and I'm hummin and he hummin, chest to chest like talkin. Not jammin my breasts into the man. Wasn't bout tits. Was bout vibrations. And he dug it and asked me what color dress I had on and how my hair was fixed and how I was doin without a man, not nosy but nice-like, and who was at this affair and was the canapés dainty-stingy or healthy enough to get hold of proper. Comfy and cheery is what I'm tryin to get across. Touch talkin like the heel of the hand on the tambourine or on a drum. 2

But right away Joe Lee come up on us and frown for dancin so close to the man. My own son who knows what kind of *warm* I am about; and don't grown men call me long distance and in the middle of the night for a little Mama comfort? But he frown. Which ain't right since Bovanne can't see and defend himself. Just a nice old man who fixes toasters and busted irons and bicycles and things and changes the lock on my door when my men friends get messy. Nice man. Which is not why they invited him. Grass roots you see. Me and Sister Taylor and the woman who does heads at Mamies and the man from the barber shop, we all there on account of we grass roots. And I ain't never been souther than 3

Brooklyn Battery and no more country than the window box on my fire escape. And just yesterday my kids tellin me to take them countrified rags off my head and be cool. And now can't get Black enough to suit em. So everybody passin sayin My Man Bovanne. Big deal, keep steppin and don't even stop a minute to get the man a drink or one of them cute sandwiches or tell him what's goin on. And him standin there with a smile ready case someone do speak he want to be ready. So that's how come I pull him on the dance floor and we dance squeezin past the tables and chairs and all them coats and people standin round up in each other face talkin bout this and that but got no use for this blind man who mostly fixed skates and skooters for all these folks when they was just kids. So I'm pressed up close and we touch talkin with the hum. And here come my daughter cuttin her eye at me like she do when she tell me about my "apolitical" self like I got hoof and mouf disease and there ain't no hope at all. And I don't pay her no mind and just look up in Bovanne shadow face and tell him his stomach like a drum and he laugh. Laugh real loud. And here come my youngest. Task, with a tap on my elbow like he the third grade monitor and I'm cuttin up on the line to assembly.

4 "I was just talkin on the drums," I explained when they hauled me into the kitchen. I figured drums was my best defense. They can get ready for drums what with all this heritage business. And Bovanne stomach just like that drum Task give me when he come back from Africa. You just touch it and it hum thizzm, thizzm. So I stuck to the drum story. "Just drummin that's all."

5 "Mama, what are you talkin about?"

6 "She had too much to drink," say Elo to Task cause she don't hardly say nuthin to me direct no more since that ugly argument about my wigs.

7 "Look here Mama," say Task, the gentle one. "We just tryin to pull your coat. You were makin a spectacle of yourself out there dancing like that."

8 "Dancin like what?"

9 Task run a hand over his left ear like his father for the world and his father before that.

10 "Like a bitch in heat," say Elo.

11 "Well uhh, I was goin to say like one of them sex-starved ladies gettin on in years and not too discriminating. Know what I mean?"

12 I don't answer cause I'll cry. Terrible thing when your own children talk to you like that. Pullin me out the party and hustlin me into some stranger's kitchen in the back of a bar just like the damn police. And

ain't like I'm old old. I can still wear me some sleeveless dresses without the meat hangin off my arm. And I keep up with some thangs through my kids. Who ain't kids no more. To hear them tell it. So I don't say nuthin.

"Dancin with that tom," say Elo to Joe Lee, who leanin on the folks' freezer. "His feet can smell a cracker a mile away and go into their shuffle number post haste. And them eyes. He could be a little considerate and put on some shades. Who wants to look into them blown-out fuses that—" 13

"Is this what they call the generation gap?" I say. 14

"Generation gap," spits Elo, like I suggested castor oil and fricassee possum in the milk-shakes or somethin. "That's a white concept for a white phenomenon. There's no generation gap among Black people. We are a col—" 15

"Yeh, well never mind," says Joe Lee. "The point is Mama . . . well, it's pride. You embarrass yourself and us too dancin like that." 16

"I wasn't shame." Then nobody say nuthin. Them standin there in they pretty clothes with drinks in they hands and gangin up on me, and me in the third-degree chair and nary a olive to my name. Felt just like the police got hold to me. 17

"First of all," Task say, holdin up his hand and tickin off the offenses, "the dress. Now that dress is too short, Mama, and too low-cut for a woman your age. And Tamu's going to make a speech tonight to kick off the campaign and will be introducin you and expecting you to organize the council of elders—" 18

"Me? Didn nobody ask me nuthin. You mean Nisi? She change her name?" 19

"Well, Norton was supposed to tell you about it. Nisi wants to introduce you and then encourage the older folks to form a Council of the Elders to act as an advisory—" 20

"And you going to be standing there with your boobs out and that wig on your head and that hem up to your ass. And people'll say, 'Ain't that the horny bitch that was grindin with the blind dude?'" 21

"Elo, be cool a minute," say Task, gettin to the next finger. "And then there's the drinkin. Mama, you know you can't drink cause next thing you know you be laughin loud and carryin on," and he grab another finger for the loudness. "And then there's the dancin. You been tattooed on the man for four records straight and slow draggin even on the fast numbers. How you think that look for a woman your age?" 22

"What's my age?" 23

"What?" 24

25 "I'm axin you all a simple question. You keep talkin bout what's proper for a woman my age. How old am I anyhow?" And Joe Lee slams his eyes shut and squinches up his face to figure. And Task run a hand over his ear and stare into his glass like the ice cubes goin calculate for him. And Elo just starin at the top of my head like she goin rip the wig off any minute now.

26 "Is your hair braided up under that thing? If so, why don't you take it off? You always did do a neat cornroll."

27 "Uh huh," cause I'm thinkin how she couldn't undo her hair fast enough talking bout cornroll so countrified. None of which was the subject. "How old, I say?"

28 "Sixtee-one or—"

29 "You a damn lie Joe Lee Peoples."

30 "And that's another thing," say Task on the fingers.

31 "You know what you all can kiss," I say, gettin up and brushin the wrinkles out my lap.

32 "Oh, Mama," Elo say, puttin a hand on my shoulder like she hasn't done since she left home and the hand landin light and not sure it supposed to be there. Which hurt me to my heart. Cause this was the child in our happiness fore Mr. Peoples die. And I carried that child strapped to my chest till she was nearly two. We was close is what I'm trying to tell you. Cause it was more me in the child than the others. And even after Task it was the girlchild I covered in the night and wept over for no reason at all less it was she was a chub-chub like me and not very pretty, but a warm child. And how did things get to this, that she can't put a sure hand on me and say Mama we love you and care about you and you entitled to enjoy yourself cause you a good woman?

33 "And then there's Reverend Trent," say Task, glancin from left to right like they hatchin a plot and just now lettin me in on it. "You were suppose to be talkin with him tonight, Mama, about giving us his basement for campaign headquarters and—"

34 "Didn nobody tell me nuthin. If grass roots mean you kept in the dark I can't use it. I really can't. And Reven Trent a fool anyway the way he tore into the widow man up there on Edgecomb cause he wouldn't take in three of them foster children and the woman not even comfy in the ground yet and the man's mind messed up and—"

35 "Look here," say Task. "What we need is a family conference so we can get all this stuff cleared up and laid out on the table. In the meantime I think we better get back into the other room and tend to business. And in the meantime, Mama, see if you can't get to Reverend Trent and—"

"You want me to belly rub with the Reven, that it?" 36

"Oh damn," Elo say and go through the swingin door. 37

"We'll talk about all this at dinner. How's tomorrow night, Joe 38
Lee?" While Joe Lee being self-important I'm wonderin who's doin the cookin and how come no body ax me if I'm free and do I get a corsage and things like that. Then Joe nod that it's O.K. and he go through the swingin door and just a little hubbub come through from the other room. Then Task smile his smile, lookin just like his daddy and he leave. And it just me in this stranger's kitchen, which was a mess I wouldn't never let my kitchen look like. Poison you just to look at the pots. Then the door swing the other way and it's My Man Bovanne standin there sayin Miss Hazel but lookin at the deep fry and then at the steam table, and most surprised when I come up on him from the other direction and take him on out of there. Pass the folks pushin up towards the stage where Nisi and some other people settin and ready to talk, and folks gettin to the last of the sandwiches and the booze fore they settle down in one spot and listen serious. And I'm thinkin bout tellin Bovanne what a lovely long dress Nisi got on and the earrings and her hair piled up in a cone and the people bout to hear how we all gettin screwed and gotta form our own party and everybody there listenin and lookin. But instead I just haul the man on out of there, and Joe Lee and his wife look at me like I'm terrible, but they ain't said boo to the man yet. Cause he blind and old and don't nobody there need him since they grown up and don't need they skates fixed no more.

"Where we goin, Miss Hazel?" Him knowin all the time. 39

"First we gonna buy you some dark sunglasses. Then you comin 40
with me to the supermarket so I can pick up tomorrow's dinner, which is goin to be a grand thing proper and you invited. Then we goin to my house."

"That be fine. I surely would like to rest my feet." Bein cute, but 41
you got to let men play out they little show, blind or not. So he chat on bout how tired he is and how he appreciate me takin him in hand this way. And I'm thinkin I'll have him change the lock on my door first thing. Then I'll give the man a nice warm bath with jasmine leaves in the water and a little Epsom salt on the sponge to do his back. And then a good rubdown with rose water and olive oil. Then a cup of lemon tea with a taste in it. And a little talcum, some of that fancy stuff Nisi mother sent over last Christmas. And then a massage, a good face massage round the forehead which is the worryin part. Cause you gots to take care of the older folks. And let them know they

still needed to run the mimeo machine and keep the spark plugs clean and fix the mailboxes for folks who might help us get the breakfast program goin, and the school for the little kids and the campaign and all. Cause old folks is the nation. That what Nisi was sayin and I mean to do my part.

42 "I imagine you are a very pretty woman, Miss Hazel."

43 "I surely am," I say just like the hussy my daughter always say I was.

THINKING ABOUT THE TEXT

1. Who is the narrator of this story? What specific facts do you learn about her? What can you infer about her?
2. What are the conflicts in this story? In what ways are they typical of most "generation gaps," and in what ways are they unique to this family? Which conflicts do you imagine are related to the time period (1960–1970) in which this short story is set?
3. Ironic situations are those that are contrary to expectation. Discuss the ironic aspects of this story.
4. This story is entertaining, but it also instructs. If this short story were an essay, what might its *thesis* be?

WRITING FROM THE TEXT

1. Write about a time when one of your parents or one of your children embarrassed you. How did you respond? Create the scene so that your reader sees your experience. What did you learn?
2. Write an analysis of Hazel Peoples' children that uses facts and specific details from the short story for support.

CONNECTING WITH OTHER TEXTS

1. Write an essay comparing traits that Hazel Peoples exemplifies with those that Dorothy Noyes describes about herself in "Senior-Teener: A New Hybrid" (p. 17).
2. Research the Black Power movement of the 1960s and 1970s and write a paper describing the characteristics of the movement

that are reflected in this story. You might consider these aspects: goals of the movement, characteristics of dress and hair style, language of the movement, the role of churches in Black communities, and other characteristics you discover in your research that Bambara shows in her fiction.

3. Read Toni Cade Bambara's short story "The Lesson," also from *Gorilla, My Love,* and write a character analysis of Sylvia. For a character analysis of Hazel Peoples, see p. 439.

2

Between Genders

■ ■ ■

As you can imagine, if women and men were completely satisfied with their lives, this chapter of readings probably would be quite different. Essays would show that gender conflicts were issues of the past, poems would celebrate gender equality, and memoirs would attest to universal self-acceptance.

But as the work in this chapter reveals, many lives are still riddled with tensions related to gender. The women's movements of the last four decades have helped to identify and address these tensions, and the men's movement of the last decade has raised questions that also disturb the status quo. Some individuals embrace this disturbance, others fear it, and many feel caught in between. You and your friends may be in the process of exploring or resolving some of the same gender issues that the writers in this chapter discuss.

All of the writers show how stereotypes circumscribe the actions and thinking of women and men. Both Amy Gross and Noel Perrin argue the advantages of androgyny as they expose the limitations of the "macho" male. Traditional male roles and behaviors also are the sources of problems analyzed by Cooper Thompson. In one essay, Armin Brott criticizes the negative depictions of men in children's books. In another essay, Warren Farrell analyzes the burden placed on men to be "success objects." Social conditioning encourages men to pursue stereotypical goals. You may have noticed the results of this conditioning in your father or uncle if not yet in your brother or yourself. You will find ideas in these essays to help you consider choices and understand what you have observed.

Clearly, women do not escape the stereotyping that limits behavior and self-acceptance. Brigid Brophy believes that women exist in "invisible cages" that thwart their vital participation in life, and Marge Piercy illustrates the specific myths that keep women confined. We believe that you will find these writers addressing problems that you also have considered in the last few years. Finally, several of our writers explore a problem that affects both genders:

violence against women. This problem is discussed in analytical essays and a short story by contemporary writers Ellen Sweet, Ellen Goodman, Barbara Ehrenreich, and Joyce Carol Oates.

You undoubtedly have found that gender problems are central concerns, showing up in such diverse places as the lyrics of popular music and the feature articles of newspapers and magazines. In this chapter our writers explore these concerns and suggest choices that may interest you. These authors reexamine gender roles, expose myths, and pose solutions that may help both sexes reach accord between genders.

THE APPEAL OF THE ANDROGYNOUS MAN

Amy Gross

An honors graduate with a degree in zoology from Connecticut College for Women, Amy Gross (b. 1942) has been a writer for *Glamour* and a writer and editor for *Mademoiselle, Vogue,* and *Mirabella* magazines. She is currently editorial director with *Elle* magazine. The essay included here first appeared in *Mademoiselle* in 1976.

James Dean was my first androgynous man. I figured I could talk to him. He was anguished and I was 12, so we had a lot in common. With only a few exceptions, all the men I have liked or loved have been a certain kind of man: a kind who doesn't play football or watch the games on Sunday, who doesn't tell dirty jokes featuring broads or chicks, who is not contemptuous of conversations that are philosophically speculative, introspective, or otherwise foolish according to the other kind of man. He is more self-amused, less inflated, more quirky, vulnerable and responsive than the other sort (the other sort, I'm visualizing as the guys on TV who advertise deodorant in the locker room). He is more like me than the other sort. He is what social scientists and feminists would call androgynous: having the characteristics of both male and female. 1

Now the first thing I want you to know about the androgynous man is that he is neither effeminate nor hermaphroditic. All his primary and secondary sexual characteristics are in order and I would say he's all-man, but that is just what he is not. He is more than all-man. 2

The merely all-man man, for one thing, never walks to the grocery store unless the little woman is away visiting her mother with the kids, or is in the hospital having a kid, or there is no little woman. All-man men don't know how to shop in a grocery store unless it is to buy a 6-pack and some pretzels. Their ideas of nutrition expand beyond a 6-pack and pretzels only to take in steak, potatoes, scotch or rye whiskey, 3 and maybe a wad of cake or apple pie. All-men men have absolutely no taste in food, art, books, movies, theatre, dance, how to live, what are good questions, what is funny, or anything else I care about. It's not exactly that the all-man's man is an uncouth illiterate. He may be educated, well-mannered, and on a first-name basis with fine wines. One all-man man I knew was a handsome individual who gave the impression of being gentle, affectionate, and sensitive. He sat and ate dinner one night while I was doing something endearingly feminine at the sink. At one point, he mutely held up his glass to indicate in a primitive, even ape-like, way his need for a refill. This was in 1967, before Women's Liberation. Even so, I was disturbed. Not enough to break the glass over his handsome head, not even enough to mutely indicate the whereabouts of the refrigerator, but enough to remember that moment in all its revelatory clarity. No androgynous man would ever brutishly expect to be waited on without even a "please." (With a "please," maybe.)

4 The brute happened to be a doctor—not a hard hat—and, to all appearances, couth. But he had bought the whole superman package, complete with that fragile beast, the male ego. The androgynous man arrives with a male ego too, but his is not as imperialistic. It doesn't invade every area of his life and person. Most activities and thoughts have nothing to do with masculinity or femininity. The androgynous man knows this. The all-man man doesn't. He must keep a constant guard against anything even vaguely feminine (*i.e.*, "sissy") rising up in him. It must be a terrible strain.

5 Male chauvinism is an irritation, but the real problem I have with the all-man man is that it's hard for me to talk to him. He's alien to me, and for this I'm at least half to blame. As his interests have not carried him into the sissy, mine have never taken me very far into the typically masculine terrains of sports, business and finance, politics, cars, boats and machines. But blame or no blame, the reality is that it is almost as difficult for me to connect with him as it would be to link up with an Arab shepherd or Bolivian sandalmaker. There's a similar culture gap.

6 It seems to me that the most masculine men usually end up with the most feminine women. Maybe they like extreme polarity. I like polarity myself, but the poles have to be within earshot. As I've implied, I'm very big on talking. I fall in love for at least three hours with anyone who engages me in a real conversation. I'd rather a man point out a paragraph in a book—wanting to share it with me—than bring me flowers. I'd rather a man ask what I think than tell me I look pretty. (Women who are very pretty and accustomed to hearing that they are

pretty may feel differently.) My experience is that all-man men read books I don't want to see paragraphs of, and don't really give a damn what I or any woman would think about most issues so long as she looks pretty. They have a very limited use for women. I suspect they don't really like us. The androgynous man likes women as much or as little as he likes anyone.

Another difference between the all-man man and the androgynous man is that the first is not a star in the creativity department. If your image of the creative male accessorizes him with a beret, smock and artist's palette, you will not believe the all-man man has been seriously shortchanged. But if you allow as how creativity is a talent for freedom, associated with imagination, wit, empathy, unpredictability, and receptivity to new impressions and connections, then you will certainly pity the dull, thick-skinned, rigid fellow in whom creativity sets no fires. 7

Nor is the all-man man so hot when it comes to sensitivity. He may be true-blue in the trenches, but if you are troubled, you'd be wasting your time trying to milk comfort from the all-man man. 8

This is not blind prejudice. It is enlightened prejudice. My biases were confirmed recently by a psychologist named Sandra Lipsetz Bem, a professor at Stanford University. She brought to attention the fact that high masculinity in males (and high femininity in females) has been "consistently correlated with lower overall intelligence and lower creativity." Another psychologist, Donald W. MacKinnon, director of the Institute of Personality Assessment and Research at the University of California in Berkeley, found that "creative males give more expression to the feminine side of their nature than do less creative men. . . . [They] score relatively high on femininity, and this despite the fact that, as a group, they do not present an effeminate appearance or give evidence of increased homosexual interests or experiences. Their elevated scores on femininity indicate rather an openness to their feelings and emotions, a sensitive intellect and understanding self-awareness and wide-ranging interests including many which in the American culture are thought of as more feminine 9

Dr. Bem ran a series of experiments on college students who had been categorized as masculine, feminine, or androgynous. In three tests of the degree of nurturance—warmth and caring—the masculine men scored painfully low (painfully for anyone stuck with a masculine man, that is). In one of those experiments, all the students were asked to listen to a "troubled talker"—a person who was not neurotic but simply lonely, supposedly new in town and feeling like an outsider. The masculine men were the least supportive, responsive or humane. "They 10 lacked the ability to express warmth, playfulness and concern," Bem concluded. (She's giving them the benefit of the doubt. It's possible the masculine men didn't express those qualities because they didn't possess them.)

11 The androgynous man, on the other hand, having been run through the same carnival of tests, "performs spectacularly. He shuns no behavior just because our culture happens to label it as female and his competence crosses both the instrumental (getting the job done, the problem solved) and the expressive (showing a concern for the welfare of others, the harmony of the group) domains. Thus, he stands firm in his opinion, he cuddles kittens and bounces babies and he has a sympathetic ear for someone in distress."

12 Well, a great mind, a sensitive and warm personality are fine in their place, but you are perhaps skeptical of the gut appeal of the androgynous man. As a friend, maybe, you'd like an androgynous man. For a sexual partner, though, you'd prefer a jock. There's no arguing chemistry, but consider the jock for a moment. He competes on the field, whatever his field is, and bed is just one more field to him: another opportunity to perform, another fray. Sensuality is for him candy to be doled out as lure. It is a ration whose flow is cut off at the exact point when it has served its purpose—namely, to elicit your willingness to work out on the field with him.

13 Highly masculine men need to believe their sexual appetite is far greater than a woman's (than a nice woman's). To them, females must be seduced: Seduction is a euphemism for a power play, a con job. It pits man against woman (or woman against man). The jock believes he must win you over, incite your body to rebel against your better judgment: in other words—conquer you.

14 The androgynous man is not your opponent but your teammate. He does not seduce: he invites. Sensuality is a pleasure for him. He's not quite so goal-oriented. And to conclude, I think I need only remind you here of his greater imagination, his wit and empathy, his unpredictability, and his receptivity to new impressions and connections.

THINKING ABOUT THE TEXT

1. Before actually defining androgyny, Amy Gross describes the characteristics of men she likes and those whom she does not like. What are those contrasting characteristics that she cites throughout her essay?
2. How does Gross' second paragraph function to answer her reader's unexpressed comment about androgyny?

3. Gross cites a Stanford University psychologist's experiment with masculinity and femininity. What were the discoveries of that experiment? What conclusions do you draw from the findings?
4. Gross anticipates the reader's response to her description of the androgynous man as one who lacks "gut appeal." How does she argue for the sex appeal of the androgynous man? Is she convincing?

WRITING FROM THE TEXT

1. Write an essay in which you contrast two males that you know—one "all-man man" and one androgynous man. Be *specific* in your contrasting descriptions.
2. Use Gross' essay as a model for your essay celebrating the virtues of the woman you will define and describe as more than the "all-female female"—the androgynous woman.

CONNECTING WITH OTHER TEXTS

1. Connect Gross' concept of the androgynous man with Perrin's points in his essay (below). Write an extended definition of androgyny and give examples from both essays as well as your own awareness and experience to support your definition.
2. Compare Gross' concept of the ideal man with the concepts that Cooper Thompson advocates in "A New Vision of Masculinity" (p. 63).

■ THE ANDROGYNOUS MAN

Noel Perrin

An English professor at Dartmouth College, Noel Perrin (b. 1927) has written both scholarly and personal essays, many of which have been published in *The New Yorker.* A number of his essays have been collected and published in book form, especially those about his experiences as a part-time farmer in Vermont. Perrin's account of his discovery of and preference for androgyny, included here, was first published in the *New York Times Magazine* in 1984.

The summer I was 16, I took a train from New York to Steamboat Springs, Colorado, where I was going to be assistant horse wrangler at a camp. The trip took three days, and since I was much too shy to talk to strangers, I had quite a lot of time for reading. I read all of *Gone With the* 1

Wind. I read all the interesting articles in a couple of magazines I had, and then I went back and read all the dull stuff. I also took all the quizzes, a thing of which magazines were even fuller then than now.

2 The one that held my undivided attention was called "How Masculine/Feminine Are You?" It consisted of a large number of inkblots. The reader was supposed to decide which of four objects each blot most resembled. The choices might be a cloud, a steam engine, a caterpillar and a sofa.

3 When I finished the test, I was shocked to find that I was barely masculine at all. On a scale of 1 to 10, I was about 1.2. Me, the horse wrangler? (And not just wrangler, either. That summer, I had to skin a couple of horses that died—the camp owner wanted the hides.)

4 The results of that test were so terrifying to me that for the first time in my life I did a piece of original analysis. Having unlimited time on the train, I looked at the "masculine" answers over and over, trying to find what it was that distinguished real men from people like me—and eventually I discovered two very simple patterns. It was "masculine" to think the blots looked like man-made objects, and "feminine" to think they looked like natural objects. It was masculine to think they looked like things capable of causing harm, and feminine to think of innocent things.

5 Even at 16, I had the sense to see that the compilers of the test were using rather limited criteria—maleness and femaleness are both more complicated than *that*—and I breathed a huge sigh of relief. I wasn't necessarily a wimp, after all.

6 That the test did reveal something other than the superficiality of its makers I realized only many years later. What it revealed was that there is a large class of men and women both, to which I belong, who are essentially androgynous. That doesn't mean we're gay, or low in the appropriate hormones, or uncomfortable performing the jobs traditionally assigned our sexes. (A few years after that summer, I was leading troops in combat and, unfashionable as it now is to admit this, having a very good time. War is exciting. What a pity the 20th century went and spoiled it with high-tech weapons.)

7 What it does mean to be spiritually androgynous is a kind of freedom. Men who are all-male, or he-man, or 100 percent red-blooded Americans, have a little biological set that causes them to be attracted to physical power, and probably also to dominance. Maybe even to watching football. I don't say this to criticize them. Completely masculine men are quite often wonderful people: good husbands, good (though sometimes overwhelming) fathers, good members of society. Furthermore, they are often so unself-consciously at ease in the world

that other men seek to imitate them. They just aren't as free as us androgynes. They pretty nearly have to be what they are; we have a range of choices open.

The sad part is that many of us never discover that. Men who are not 100 percent red-blooded Americans—say, those who are only 75 percent red-blooded—often fail to notice their freedom. They are too busy trying to copy the he-men ever to realize that men, like women, come in a wide variety of acceptable types. Why this frantic imitation? My answer is mere speculation, but not casual. I have speculated on this for a long time. 8

Partly they're just envious of the he-man's unconscious ease. Mostly they're terrified of finding that there may be something wrong with them deep down, some weakness at the heart. To avoid discovering that, they spend their lives acting out the role that the he-man naturally lives. Sad. 9

One thing that men owe to the women's movement is that this kind of failure is less common than it used to be. In releasing themselves from the single ideal of the dependent woman, women have more or less incidentally released a lot of men from the single ideal of the dominant male. The one mistake the feminists have made, I think, is in supposing that *all* men need this release, or that the world would be a better place if all men achieved it. It wouldn't. It would just be duller. 10

So far I have been pretty vague about just what the freedom of the androgynous man is. Obviously it varies with the case. In the case I know best, my own, I can be quite specific. It has freed me most as a parent. I am, among other things, a fairly good natural mother. I like the nurturing role. It makes me feel good to see a child eat—and it turns me to mush to see a 4-year-old holding a glass with both small hands, in order to drink. I even enjoyed sewing patches on the knees of my daughter Amy's Dr. Dentons when she was at the crawling stage. All that pleasure I would have lost if I had made myself stick to the notion of the paternal role that I started with. 11

Or take a smaller and rather ridiculous example. I feel free to kiss cats. Until recently it never occurred to me that I would want to, though my daughters have been doing it all their lives. But my elder daughter is now 22, and in London. Of course, I get to look after her cat while she is gone. He's a big, handsome farm cat named Petrushka, very unsentimental, though used from kittenhood to being kissed on the top of the head by Elizabeth. I've gotten very fond of him (he's the adventurous kind of cat who likes to climb hills with you), and one night I simply felt like kissing him on the top of the head, and did. Why did no one tell me sooner how silky cat fur is? 12

13 Then there's my relation to cars. I am completely unembarrassed by my inability to diagnose even minor problems in whatever object I happen to be driving, and don't have to make some insider's remark to mechanics to try to establish that I, too, am a "Man With His Machine."

14 The same ease extends to household maintenance. I do it, of course. Service people are expensive. But for the last decade my house has functioned better than it used to because I've had the aid of a volume called "Home Repairs Any Woman Can Do," which is pitched just right for people at my technical level. As a youth, I'd as soon have touched such a book as I would have become a transvestite. Even though common sense says there is really nothing sexual whatsoever about fixing sinks.

15 Or take public emotion. All my life I have easily been moved by certain kinds of voices. The actress Siobhan McKenna's, to take a notable case. Give her an emotional scene in a play, and within 10 words my eyes are full of tears. In boyhood, my great dread was that someone might notice. I struggled manfully, you might say, to suppress this weakness. Now, of course, I don't see it as a weakness at all, but as a kind of fulfillment. I even suspect that the true he-men feel the same way, or one kind of them does, at least, and it's only the poor imitators who have to struggle to repress themselves.

16 Let me come back to the inkblots, with their assumption that masculine equates with machinery and science, and feminine with art and nature. I have no idea whether the right pronoun for God is He, She or It. But this I'm pretty sure of. If God could somehow be induced to take that test, God would not come out macho, and not feminismo, either, but right in the middle. Fellow androgynes, it's a nice thought.

THINKING ABOUT THE TEXT

1. How does the magazine test reinforce stereotypes of masculine and feminine?
2. In what ways might Perrin be perceived as "all-male"?
3. According to Perrin, what are the strengths and limitations of the he-man? What does Perrin feel is so sad about those who try to imitate he-men?
4. How does Perrin define androgyny? In what specific ways has it liberated him?

WRITING FROM THE TEXT

1. Perrin notes that as a youth he would not have touched a book like "Home Repairs Any Woman Can Do" and would not have let anyone see him cry. Write an essay about certain behaviors or actions that you might have avoided or hidden in the past because of a fear of seeming not masculine or feminine enough.
2. Considering Perrin's article, write an essay describing "the androgynous female." Show us how she differs from the "all-female" woman.
3. Write an essay arguing that it is easier for either males or females to be androgynous in our society. Support this with specific examples and illustrations.
4. Write a critique of Perrin's essay from the perspective of a he-man or an "all-female" woman.

CONNECTING WITH OTHER TEXTS

1. Using specific details from Perrin's essay as well as from "Men as Success Objects" (p. 75), write about the pressures on a male to find an identity of his own.
2. Although both Noel Perrin and Amy Gross (p. 55) underscore the advantages of the androgynous man, the tone, word choices, and approaches of their essays are distinct. Write an essay comparing and contrasting the two.

■ A NEW VISION OF MASCULINITY

Cooper Thompson

A coordinator of the Campaign to End Homophobia, Cooper Thompson is a contributor to *Changing Men*, a publication that is committed to examining and making significant changes in men's lives. Thompson conducts workshops on changing perceptions of men's socialization, and he has developed antisexist curricula for schools. The essay reprinted here first appeared in *Changing Men* in 1985.

I was once asked by a teacher in a suburban high school to give a guest presentation on male roles. She hoped that I might help her deal with four boys who exercised extraordinary control over the other boys 1 in the class. Using ridicule and their status as physically imposing athletes, these four wrestlers had succeeded in stifling the participation of the other boys, who were reluctant to make comments in class discussions.

2 As a class we talked about the ways in which boys got status in that school and how they got put-down by others. I was told that the most humiliating putdown was being called a "fag." The list of behaviors which could elicit ridicule filled two large chalkboards, and it was detailed and comprehensive; I got the sense that a boy in this school had to conform to rigid, narrow standards of masculinity to avoid being called a fag. I, too, felt this pressure and became very conscious of my mannerisms in front of the group. Partly from exasperation, I decided to test the seriousness of these assertions. Since one of the four boys had some streaks of pink in his shirt, and since he had told me that wearing pink was grounds for being called a fag, I told him that I thought he was a fag. Instead of laughing, he said, "I'm going to kill you."

3 Such is the stereotypic definition of strength that is associated with masculinity. But it is a very limited definition of strength, one based on dominance and control and acquired through the humiliation and degradation of others.

4 Contrast this with a view of strength offered by Pam McAllister in her introduction to *Reweaving the Web of Life:*

> The "Strength" card in my Tarot deck depicts, not a warrior going off to battle with his armor and his mighty sword, but a woman stroking a lion. The woman has not slain the lion nor maced it, not netted it, nor has she put on it a muzzle or a leash. And though the lion clearly has teeth and long sharp claws, the woman is not hiding, nor has she sought a protector, nor has she grown muscles. She doesn't appear to be talking to the lion, nor flattering it, nor tossing it fresh meat to distract its hungry jaws.
>
> The woman on the "Strength" card wears a flowing white dress and a garland of flowers. With one hand she cups the lion's jaws, with the other she caresses its nose. The lion on the card has big yellow eyes and a long red tongue curling out of its mouth. One paw is lifted and the mane falls in thick red curls across its broad torso. The woman. The lion. Together they depict strength.

5 This image of strength stands in direct contrast to the strength embodied in the actions of the four wrestlers. The collective strength of the woman and the lion is a strength unknown in a system of traditional male values. Other human qualities are equally foreign to a traditional conception of masculinity. In workshops I've offered on the male role

stereotype, teachers and other school personnel easily generate lists of attitudes and behaviors which boys typically seem to not learn. Included in this list are being supportive and nurturant, accepting one's vulnerability and being able to ask for help, valuing women and "women's work," understanding and expressing emotions (except for anger), the ability to empathize with and empower other people, and learning to resolve conflict in non-aggressive, non-competitive ways.

All of this should come as no surprise. Traditional definitions of masculinity include attributes such as independence, pride, resiliency, self-control, and physical strength. This is precisely the image of the Marlboro man, and to some extent, these are desirable attributes for boys and girls. But masculinity goes beyond these qualities to stress competitiveness, toughness, aggressiveness, and power. In this context, threats to one's status, however small, cannot be avoided or taken lightly. If a boy is called a fag, it means that he is perceived as weak or timid—and therefore not masculine enough for his peers. There is enormous pressure for him to fight back. Not being tough at these moments only proves the allegation. 6

Violence is learned not just as a way for boys to defend allegations that they are feminized, but as an effective, appropriate way for them to normally behave. In "The Civic Advocacy of Violence" Wayne Ewing clearly states: 7

> I used to think that we simply tolerated and permitted male abusiveness in our society. I have now come to understand rather, that we *advocate* physical violence. Violence is presented as effective. Violence is taught as the normal, appropriate and necessary behavior of power and control. Analyses which interweave advocacy of male violence with "SuperBowl Culture" have never been refuted. Civic expectations—translated into professionalism, financial commitments, city planning for recreational space, the raising of male children for competitive sport, the corporate ethics of business ownership of athletic teams, profiteering on entertainment—all result in the monument of the National Football League, symbol and reality at once of the advocacy of violence.

Ultimately, violence is the tool which maintains what I believe are the two most critical socializing forces in a boy's life: *homophobia,* the hatred of gay men (who are stereotyped as feminine) or those men believed to be gay, as well as the fear of being perceived as gay; and *misogyny,* the hatred of women. The two forces are targeted at different classes of victims, but they are really just the flip sides of the same coin. Homophobia is the hatred of feminine qualities in men while misogyny 8 is the hatred of feminine qualities in women. The boy who is called a fag is the target of other boys' homophobia as well as the victim of his own homophobia. While the overt message is the absolute need to avoid being feminized, the implication is that females—and all that they traditionally represent—are contemptible. The United States Marines have a philosophy which conveniently combines homophobia and misogyny in the belief that "When you want to create a group of male killers, you kill 'the woman' in them."

9 The pressures of homophobia and misogyny in boys' lives have been poignantly demonstrated to me each time that I have repeated a simple yet provocative activity with students. I ask them to answer the question, "If you woke up tomorrow and discovered that you were the opposite sex from the one you are now, how would you and your life be different?" Girls consistently indicate that there are clear advantages to being a boy—from increased independence and career opportunities to decreased risks of physical and sexual assault—and eagerly answer the question. But boys often express disgust at this possibility and even refuse sometimes to answer the question. In her reports of a broadbased survey using this question, Alice Baumgartner reports the following responses as typical of boys: "If I were a girl, I'd be stupid and weak as a string;" "I would have to wear make-up, cook, be a mother, and yuckky stuff like that;" "I would have to hate snakes. Everything would be miserable;" "If I were a girl, I'd kill myself."

10 The costs associated with a traditional view of masculinity are enormous, and the damage occurs at both personal and societal levels. The belief that a boy should be tough (aggressive, competitive, and daring) can create emotional pain for him. While a few boys experience short-term success for their toughness, there is little security in the long run. Instead, it leads to a series of challenges which few, if any, boys ultimately win. There is no security in being at the top when so many other boys are competing for the same status. Toughness also leads to increased chances of stress, physical injury, and even early death. It is considered manly to take extreme physical risks and voluntarily engage in combative, hostile activities.

11 The flip side of toughness—nurturance—is not a quality perceived as masculine and thus not valued. Because of this, boys and men experience a greater emotional distance from other people and fewer opportunities to participate in meaningful interpersonal relationships. Studies consistently show that fathers spend very small amounts of time interacting with their children. In addition, men report that they seldom

have intimate relationships with other men, reflecting their homophobia. They are afraid of getting too close and don't know how to take down the walls that they have built between themselves.

As boys grow older and accept adult roles, the larger social costs of masculinity clearly emerge. Most women experience male resistance to an expansion of women's roles; one of the assumptions of traditional masculinity is the belief that women should be subordinate to men. The consequence is that men are often not willing to accept females as equal, competent partners in personal and professional settings. Whether the setting is a sexual relationship, the family, the streets, or the battlefield, men are continuously engaged in efforts to dominate. Statistics on child abuse consistently indicate that the vast majority of abusers are men, and that there is no "typical" abuser. Rape may be the fastest growing crime in the United States. And it is men, regardless of nationality, who provoke and sustain war. In short, traditional masculinity is life threatening. 12

Masculinity, like many other human traits, is determined by both biological and environmental factors. While some believe that biological factors are significant in shaping some masculine behavior, there is undeniable evidence that cultural and environmental factors are strong enough to override biological impulses. What is it, then, that we should be teaching boys about being a man in a modern world? 13

- Boys must learn to accept their vulnerability, learn to express a range of emotions such as fear and sadness, and learn to ask for help and support in appropriate situations.
- Boys must learn to be gentle, nurturant, cooperative, and communicative, and in particular, learn non-violent means of resolving conflicts.
- Boys must learn to accept those attitudes and behaviors which have traditionally been labeled feminine as necessary for full human development—thereby reducing homophobia and misogyny. This is tantamount to teaching boys to love other boys and girls.

Certain qualities like courage, physical strength, and independence, which are traditionally associated with masculinity, are indeed positive qualities for males, provided that they are not manifested in obsessive ways nor used to exploit or dominate others. It is not necessary to completely disregard or unlearn what is traditionally called masculine. I believe, however, that the three areas above are crucial for developing a broader view of masculinity, one which is healthier for all life. 14

15 These three areas are equally crucial for reducing aggressive, violent behavior among boys and men. Males must learn to cherish life for the sake of their *own* wholeness as human beings, not just *for* their children, friends, and lovers. If males were more nurturant, they would be less likely to hurt those they love.

16 Leonard Eron, writing in the *American Psychologist*, puts the issue of unlearning aggression and learning nurturance in clear-cut terms:

> Socialization is crucial in determining levels of aggression. No matter how aggression is measured or observed, as a group males always score higher than females. But this is not true for all girls. There are some girls who seem to have been socialized like boys who are just as aggressive as boys. Just as some females can learn to be aggressive, so males can learn *not* to be aggressive. If we want to reduce the level of aggression in society, we should also discourage boys from aggression very early on in life and reward them too for other behaviors; in other words, we should socialize boys more like girls, and they should be encouraged to develop socially positive qualities such as tenderness, cooperation, and aesthetic appreciation. The level of individual aggression in society will be reduced only when male adolescents and young adults, as a result of socialization, subscribe to the same standards of behavior as have been traditionally encouraged for women.

17 Where will this change in socialization occur? In his first few years, much of a boy's learning about masculinity comes from the influences of parents, siblings and images of masculinity such as those found on television. Massive efforts will be needed to make changes here. But at older ages, school curriculum and the school environment provide powerful reinforcing images of traditional masculinity. This reinforcement occurs through a variety of channels, including curriculum content, role modeling, and extracurricular activities, especially competitive sports.

18 School athletics are a microcosm of the socialization of male values. While participation in competitive activities can be enjoyable and healthy, it too easily becomes a lesson in the need for toughness, invulnerability, and dominance. Athletes learn to ignore their own injuries and pain and instead try to injure and inflict pain on others in their attempts to win, regardless of the cost to themselves or their opponents. Yet the lessons learned in athletics are believed to be vital for full and complete masculine development, and as a model for problem-solving in other areas of life.

In addition to encouraging traditional male values, schools provide too few experiences in nurturance, cooperation, negotiation, non-violent conflict resolution, and strategies for empathizing with and empowering others. Schools should become places where boys have the opportunity to learn these skills; clearly, they won't learn them on the street, from peers, or on television. 19

Despite the pressure on men to display their masculinity in traditional ways, there are examples of men and boys who are changing. "Fathering" is one example of a positive change. In recent years, there has been a popular emphasis on child-care activities, with men becoming more involved in providing care to children, both professionally and as fathers. This is a clear shift from the more traditional view that child rearing should be delegated to women and is not an appropriate activity for men. 20

For all the male resistance it has generated, the Women's Liberation Movement has at least provided a stimulus for some men to accept women as equal partners in most areas of life. These are the men who have chosen to learn and grow from women's experiences and together with women are creating new norms for relationships. Popular literature and research on male sex roles are expanding, reflecting a wider interest in masculinity. Weekly news magazines such as *Time* and *Newsweek* have run major stories on the "new masculinity," suggesting that positive changes are taking place in the home and in the workplace. Small groups of men scattered around the country have organized against pornography, battering and sexual assault. Finally, there is the National Organization for Changing Men which has a pro-feminist, pro-gay, pro-"new man" agenda, and its ranks are slowly growing. 21

In schools where I have worked with teachers, they report that years of efforts to enhance educational opportunities for girls have also had some positive effects on boys. The boys seem more tolerant of girls' participation in co-ed sports activities and in traditionally male shops and courses. They seem to have a greater respect for the accomplishments of women through women's contributions to literature and history. Among elementary school-aged males, the expression of vulnerable feelings is gaining acceptance. In general, however, there has been far too little attention paid to redirecting male role development. 22

I think back to the four wrestlers and the stifling culture of masculinity in which they live. If schools were to radically alter this culture and substitute for it a new vision of masculinity, what would that look 23 like? In this environment, boys would express a full range of behaviors and emotions without fear of being chastised. They would be permitted and encouraged to cry, to be afraid, to show joy, and to express love in a gentle fashion. Extreme concern for career goals would be replaced by a consideration of one's need for recreation, health, and meaningful work. Older boys would be encouraged to tutor and play with younger students. Moreover, boys would receive as much recognition for artistic talents as they do for athletics, and, in general, they would value leisure-time, recreational activities as highly as competitive sports.

24 In a system where maleness and femaleness were equally valued, boys might no longer feel that they have to "prove" themselves to other boys; they would simply accept the worth of each person and value those differences. Boys would realize that it is permissible to admit failure. In addition, they would seek out opportunities to learn from girls and women. Emotional support would become commonplace, and it would no longer be seen as just the role of the female to provide the support. Relationships between boys and girls would no longer be based on limited roles, but instead would become expressions of two individuals learning from and supporting one another. Relationships between boys would reflect their care for one another rather than their mutual fear and distrust.

25 Aggressive styles of resolving conflicts would be the exception rather than the norm. Girls would feel welcome in activities dominated by boys, knowing that they were safe from the threat of being sexually harassed. Boys would no longer boast of beating up another boy or of how much they "got off" of a girl the night before. In fact, the boys would be as outraged as the girls at rape or other violent crimes in the community. Finally, boys would become active in efforts to stop nuclear proliferation and all other forms of military violence, following the examples set by activist women.

26 The development of a new conception of masculinity based on this vision is an ambitious task, but one which is essential for the health and safety of both men and women. The survival of our society may rest on the degree to which we are able to teach men to cherish life.

THINKING ABOUT THE TEXT

1. What are the stereotypical definitions of masculinity that are revealed in this essay as being prevalent in our culture?
2. According to the essay, what are the attitudes and behaviors that males in our culture seem not to learn?

3. How does the author—and Wayne Ewing, whom he quotes in the essay—believe men learn violence?
4. How does the author support his view that homophobia and misogyny are "the two most critical socializing forces in a boy's life"?
5. What are the costs for the individual and for society of males being reared with traditional views of masculinity?
6. What does Thompson believe we should be teaching boys instead of the traditional behaviors of masculinity? How does the author think this new socialization will occur?
7. Why does Thompson include the ideas of so many other writers, psychologists, and educators and specifically quote them in his short essay? What is his rhetorical strategy?

WRITING FROM THE TEXT

1. Thompson's essay was written over a decade ago. Argue that his vision of masculinity is no longer new and that as we approach the twenty-first century, men have been socialized to the behavior Thompson advocates. Cite specific examples from your experience and reading as you describe in a well-focused essay the predominant traits of males today.
2. Argue that Thompson's essay presents a vision of masculinity that has yet to be achieved. In your essay, contrast his list of ideal behavior and character traits for males with conditions that you have observed.
3. Consider specific examples from the school curriculum that you have experienced, the influences of your parents and those of your friends, and media images of masculinity to write an essay to support or refute Thompson's views of how men are reared in our culture.
4. Write a descriptive analysis of an ideal elementary and secondary curriculum that would foster positive qualities in males. Be specific in describing actual courses and methods to achieve the ideal.

CONNECTING WITH OTHER TEXTS

1. Compare the ideas in "The Appeal of the Androgynous Man" (p. 55) and "The Androgynous Man" (p. 59) with Thompson's ideas to write an analysis of what these three authors consider ideal male personality and behavior traits.

2. Write an essay that argues that Warren Farrell's description of "men as success objects" (p. 75) would be outmoded if Thompson's "new vision of masculinity" were achieved.
3. Brigid Brophy argues (p. 80) that both women and men are trapped in "invisible cages" that limit choices and encourage particular personality traits. In an essay that starts with a summary of Brophy's points, argue that socializing men to Thompson's standards would also get women and men out of their invisible cages.
4. In her study of date rape (p. 89), Ellen Sweet describes some attitudes that males have about rape. Write an essay in which you argue that those attitudes would change if men were socialized to Thompson's ideal.

NOT ALL MEN ARE SLY FOXES

Armin A. Brott

Armin A. Brott (b. 1958) started studying the Russian language at San Francisco State University and continued his studies at the American Graduate School of International Management, from which he received his M.B.A. He has worked as a commodities trader and is currently writing and consulting on business opportunities in Russia. Brott avoided all writing courses in college and believes that his parents' insistence on his reading has contributed to his ability to write. His advice is: "Find an issue and do a lot of research on it. Knowing how to use the library is vital to success." The research for this "My Turn" essay for *Newsweek* was done in the young children's section of the library. The essay was published June 1, 1992.

1 If you thought your child's bookshelves were finally free of openly (and not so openly) discriminatory materials, you'd better check again. In recent years groups of concerned parents have persuaded textbook publishers to portray more accurately the roles that women and minorities play in shaping our country's history and culture. "Little Black Sambo" has all but disappeared from library and bookstore shelves; feminist fairy tales by such authors as Jack Zipes have, in many homes, replaced the more traditional (and obviously sexist) fairy tales. Richard Scarry, one of the most popular children's writers, has reissued new versions of some of his classics; now female animals are pictured doing the same jobs as male animals. Even the terminology has changed: males and females are referred to as mail "carriers" or "firefighters."

2 There is, however, one very large group whose portrayal continues to follow the same stereotypical lines as always: fathers. The evolution of children's literature didn't end with "Goodnight Moon" and "Char-

lotte's Web." My local public library, for example, previews 203 new children's picture books (for the under-5 set) each *month*. Many of these books make a very conscious effort to take women characters out of the kitchen and the nursery and give them professional jobs and responsibilities.

Despite this shift, mothers are by and large still shown as the primary caregivers and, more important, as the primary nurturers of their children. Men in these books—if they're shown at all—still come home late after work and participate in the child rearing by bouncing baby around for five minutes before putting the child to bed. 3

In one of my 2-year-old daughter's favorite books, "Mother Goose and the Sly Fox," "retold" by Chris Conover, a single mother (Mother Goose) of seven tiny goslings is pitted against (and naturally outwits) the sly Fox. Fox, a neglectful and presumably unemployed single father, lives with his filthy, hungry pups in a grimy hovel littered with the bones of their previous meals. Mother Goose, a successful entrepreneur with a thriving lace business, still finds time to serve her goslings homemade soup in pretty porcelain cups. The story is funny and the illustrations marvelous, but the unwritten message is that women take better care of their kids and men have nothing else to do but hunt down and kill innocent, law-abiding geese. 4

The majority of other children's classics perpetuate the same negative stereotypes of fathers. Once in a great while, people complain about "Babar's" colonialist slant (little jungle-dweller finds happiness in the big city and brings civilization—and fine clothes—to his backward village). But I've never heard anyone ask why, after his mother is killed by the evil hunter, Babar is automatically an "orphan." Why can he find comfort only in the arms of another female? Why do Arthur's and Celeste's mothers come alone to the city to fetch their children? Don't the fathers care? Do they even have fathers? I need my answers ready for when my daughter asks. 5

I recently spent an entire day on the children's floor of the local library trying to find out whether these same negative stereotypes are found in the more recent classics-to-be. The librarian gave me a list of the 20 most popular contemporary picture books and I read every one of them. Of the 20, seven don't mention a parent at all. Of the remaining 13, four portray fathers as much less loving and caring than mothers. In "Little Gorilla," we are told that the little gorilla's "mother loves him" and we see Mama gorilla giving her little one a warm hug. On the next page we're also told that his "father loves him," but in the illustration, father and son aren't even touching. Six of the remaining nine books 6 mention or portray mothers as the only parent, and only three of the 20 have what could be considered "equal" treatment of mothers and fathers.

7 The same negative stereotypes also show up in literature aimed at the *parents* of small children. In "What to Expect the First Year," the authors answer almost every question the parents of a newborn or toddler could have in the first year of their child's life. They are meticulous in alternating between references to boys and girls. At the same time, they refer almost exclusively to "mother" or "mommy." Men, and their feelings about parenting, are relegated to a nine-page chapter just before the recipe section.

8 Unfortunately, it's still true that, in our society, women do the bulk of the child care, and that thanks to men abandoning their families, there are too many single mothers out there. Nevertheless, to say that portraying fathers as unnurturing or completely absent is simply "a reflection of reality" is unacceptable. If children's literature only reflected reality, it would be like prime-time TV and we'd have books filled with child abusers, wife beaters and criminals.

9 Young children believe what they hear—especially from a parent figure. And since, for the first few years of a child's life, adults select the reading material, children's literature should be held to a high standard. Ignoring men who share equally in raising their children, and continuing to show nothing but part-time or no-time fathers is only going to create yet another generation of men who have been told since boyhood—albeit subtly—that mothers are the truer parents and that fathers play, at best, a secondary role in the home. We've taken major steps to root out discrimination in what our children read. Let's finish the job.

THINKING ABOUT THE TEXT

1. What are the specific stereotypes that Brott objects to in children's stories? What support does Brott have for his thesis?
2. What are the consequences of parenting books minimizing a father's role in child rearing?

WRITING FROM THE TEXT

1. Write an essay in which you argue from your memory of the books that you heard or read in your childhood that Brott is right or wrong in his depiction of fathers in young children's literature. You will need specific references to literature to support your view.

2. Is Brott arguing for censorship of children's literature so that only politically correct depictions of women and men are allowed? Argue one way or the other in your essay.

CONNECTING WITH OTHER TEXTS

1. In his essay "Men as Success Objects" (below), Warren Farrell also notes that men are often maliciously depicted in popular culture. Besides greeting cards, self-help books, and children's literature, where else are men or fathers maligned? Using the work of both Brott and Farrell, write an essay with the intent of describing the specific examples you cite and of proposing reform or discussing the consequences.
2. In "A New Vision of Masculinity" (p. 63), Cooper Thompson advocates an educational system that teaches men to have more nurturing traits. Write an essay that argues that men reared within Thompson's system will not be the "sly foxes" caricaturized in children's books.
3. Repeat Brott's reading experience in your library with the intention of learning how *mothers* are depicted in young children's books. Write an essay like Brott's to present your findings.

■ MEN AS SUCCESS OBJECTS

Warren Farrell

Educated at Montclair State College, UCLA, and New York University, Warren Farrell (b. 1943) has both taught and written in a variety of fields: political science, public administration, sociology, and psychology. He is currently a free-lance writer whose books treat some of the issues of the men's movement. *The Liberated Man* (1974) examines why feminism is so important to men, and *Why Men Are the Way They Are* (1986) looks at a number of gender-related issues. His most recent book is *The Myth of Male Power* (1993). The article printed here first appeared in *Family Therapy Networker* in 1988.

For thousands of years, marriages were about economic security and survival. Let's call this Stage I in our culture's conception of marriage. Beginning in the 1950s, marriages became focused on personal fulfillment and we entered into the era of the Stage II relationship. In Stage II, love was redefined to include listening to each other, joint parenting, 1 sexual fulfillment, and shared decision making. As a result, many traditional marriages consummated in Stage I failed under the new Stage II expectations. Thus we had the great surge of divorces beginning in the '60s.

2 The increasing incidence of divorce altered the fundamental relationship between women, men, and the workplace. Before divorce became common, most women's income came from men, so discrimination in favor of a woman's husband benefited her. But, as the divorce rate mushroomed, the same discrimination often hurt her. Before divorce became a common expectation, we had two types of inequality—women's experience of unequal rights in the workplace and men's experience of unequal responsibility for succeeding in the workplace. To find a woman to love him, a man had to "make his mark" in the world. As women increasingly had to provide for themselves economically, we confined our examination of inequality between the sexes to inequality in the workplace. What was ignored was the effect of inequality in the homeplace. Also ignored was a man's feeling that no woman would love him if he volunteered to be a full-time house-husband instead of a full-time provider. As a result, we falsely assumed that the experience of inequality was confined to women.

3 Because divorces led to a change in the pressures on women (should she *become* a doctor, marry a doctor, or have a career and marry a doctor?), that change became "news" and her new juggling act got attention in the media. Because the underlying pressures on men did not change (women still married men who earned more than they did), the pressure on men to succeed did not change, and, therefore, received no attention. With all the focus on discrimination against women, few understood the sexism directed against men.

4 The feminist perspective on relationships has become like fluoride in water—we drink it without being aware of its presence. The complaints about men, the idea that "men are jerks," have become so integrated into our unconscious that even advertisers have caught on. After analyzing 1,000 commercials in 1987, researcher Fred Hayward found that when an ad called for a negative portrayal in a male-female interaction, an astonishing 100 percent of the time the "bad guy" was the man.

5 This anti-male bias isn't confined to TV commercials. A sampling of the cards in the "Love and Friendship" section of a greeting card store revealed these gems:

6 "If they can send one man to the moon, why can't they send them all?"

7 "When you unzip a man's pants . . . his brains fall out."

"If we can make penicillin out of moldy cheese . . . maybe we can 8
make men out of the low-lifes in this town."

A visit to the bookstore turns up titles like *No Good Men*. Imagine 9
No Good Women or *No Good Jews*. And what do the following titles have in common? *Men Who Can't Love; Men Who Hate Women and the Women Who Love Them; Smart Women/Foolish Choices; Successful Women, Angry Men: Peter Pan Syndrome*.

Feminism-as-fluoride has left us acknowledging the working mother 10
("Superwoman") without even being aware of the working father. It is by now well recognized that, even among men who do more housework or more childcare than their wives, almost never does the man truly share the 24-hour-a-day psychological responsibility of ministering to everyone's needs, egos, and schedules.

But it is not so widely recognized that, despite the impact feminism 11
has had on the contemporary family, almost every father still retains 24-hour-a-day psychological responsibility for the family's financial well-being. Even women who earn more than their husbands tell me that they know their husbands would support their decision to earn as much or as little as they wish. If a woman marries a successful man, then she knows she will have an option to work or not, but not an obligation. Almost all men see bringing home a healthy salary as an obligation, not an option.

A woman today has three options: 12

Option 1: Full-time career.
Option 2: Full-time family.
Option 3: Some combination of career and family.

A man sees himself as having three "slightly different" options: 13

Option 1: Work full time.
Option 2: Work full time.
Option 3: Work full time.

The U.S. Bureau of the Census explains that full-time working 14
males work an average of eight hours more per week on their jobs than full-time working females.

Since many women now earn substantial incomes, doesn't this re- 15
lieve the pressure on men to be a wallet? No. Why? Because successful women do exactly what less-successful women do—"marry up," that is, marry a man whose income is greater than her own. According to statistics, if a woman cannot marry up or marry someone with a high wage-earning potential, she does not marry at all. Therefore, a man often reflexively backs away from a woman he's attracted to when he discovers

she's more successful than he is because he senses he's only setting himself up for rejection. Ultimately, she'll dump him for a more successful man. She may sleep with him, or live with him, but not marry him unless she spots "potential." Thus, of top female executives, 85 percent don't get married; the remaining 15 percent almost all marry up. Even successful women have not relaxed the pressure on men to succeed.

16 Ask a girl in junior high or high school about the boy whom she would "absolutely love" to ask her out to the prom and chances are almost 100 percent that she would tell you her fantasy boy is *both* good-looking *and* successful (a jock or student leader, or someone who "has potential"). Ask a boy whom he would absolutely love to ask out to the prom and chances are almost 100 percent his fantasy girl is good-looking. Only about 25 percent will also be interested in a girl's strong career potential (or her being a top female jock). His invisible curriculum, then, taught him that being good-looking is not enough to attract a good-looking girl—he must be successful *in addition* to being good-looking. This was his experience of inequality: "Good-looking boy does not equal good-looking girl." Why are boys willing to consider themselves unequal to girls' attention until they hit their heads against 21 other boys on a football field?

17 In part, the answer is because boys are addicted. In all cultures, boys are addicted to the images of beautiful women. And in American culture this is enormously magnified. Boys are exposed to the images of beautiful women about 10 million times per year via television, billboards, magazines, etc. In the process, the naturally beautiful girl becomes a *genetic celebrity*. Boys become addicted to the image of the quasi-anorexic female. To be the equal of this genetic celebrity, the adolescent boy must become an *earned celebrity* (by performing, paying on dates, etc.). Until he is an earned celebrity, he feels like a groupie trying to get a celebrity's attention.

18 Is there an invisible curriculum for girls and boys growing up? Yes. For girls, "If you want to have your choice among boys, you had better be beautiful." For boys, it's "You had better be handsome *and* successful." If a boy wants a romantic relationship with a girl he must not only be successful and perform, he must pay and pursue—risk sexual rejection. Girls think of the three Ps—performing, paying, and pursuing—as male power. Boys see the three Ps as what they must do to earn their way to female love and sexuality. They see these not as power, but as compensations for powerlessness. This is the adolescent male's experience of inequality.

THINKING ABOUT THE TEXT

1. How do Farrell's historical descriptions of marriage relate to the point of his essay? What is the cause-and-effect relationship that he describes?
2. What inequalities does Farrell perceive for both genders, and how are the inequalities relevant to the men's movement? What is Farrell's thesis?
3. According to Farrell, how are men depicted in popular culture? What has the culture failed to address?
4. How do men's and women's options for making a living compare? Do you agree with Farrell's perceptions? What *is* the "invisible curriculum"? Does he overlook anything in his reasoning?
5. How does each gender's perceptions of a desirable date influence the perception of power or powerlessness that each gender has?

WRITING FROM THE TEXT

1. Interview male and female acquaintances of your age to find out whether adults' views of the desirable date or mate are consistent with the views Farrell cites for junior high and high school students. Write an essay to present your views.
2. Who has more options in the dating/mating and work worlds—women or men? Support your assertion with *specific* examples.
3. A psychological/sociological study that was done twenty years ago determined that, generally, women felt limited by what they were *allowed* to do and men felt limited by what they felt *required* to do. After discussing this perception with friends, write an essay to show what the genders feel in the last decade of the twentieth century.

CONNECTING WITH OTHER TEXTS

1. Write an analysis of the "invisible curriculum" for women and men using the essay by Brigid Brophy, "Women: Invisible Cages" (p. 80), with Farrell's work to support your points.
2. Do some research to learn more about the main grievances of the men who are in the men's movement. Write a paper in which you focus on the concerns of the movement. Incorporate the ideas of Cooper Thompson (p. 63).

WOMEN: INVISIBLE CAGES

Brigid Brophy

An Anglo-Irish social critic who acknowledged her desire to promote a better world, Brigid Brophy (1929–1995) wrote novels, essays, short stories, plays, and criticism. In spite of the fact that she published widely, Brophy insisted that she did not like to write. Asked during an interview what she most admired in men, Brophy replied, "Beauty." And in women? "Emancipation from domesticity." The essay printed here is from *Don't Never Forget: Collected Views and Reviews, 1963.* The problems that Brophy discusses in this essay, which was published more than thirty years ago, are still relevant issues of the women's and men's movements today.

1 All right, nobody's disputing it. Women are free. At least, they *look* free. They even feel free. But in reality women in the western, industrialised world today are like the animals in a modern zoo. There are no bars. It appears that cages have been abolished. Yet in practice women are still kept in their place just as firmly as the animals are kept in their enclosures. The barriers which keep them in now are invisible.

2 It is about forty years since the pioneer feminists, several of whom were men, raised such a rumpus by rattling the cage bars—or created such a conspicuous nuisance by chaining themselves to them—that society was at last obliged to pay attention. The result was that the bars were uprooted, the cage thrown open: whereupon the majority of the women who had been held captive decided they would rather stay inside anyway.

3 To be more precise, they *thought* they decided; and society, which can with perfect truth point out "Look, no bars," *thought* it was giving them the choice. There are no laws and very little discrimination to prevent western, industrialised women from voting, being voted for or entering the professions. If there are still comparatively few women lawyers and engineers, let alone women presidents of the United States, what are women to conclude except that this is the result either of their own free choice or of something inherent in female nature?

4 Many of them do draw just this conclusion. They have come back to the old argument of the anti-feminists, many of whom were women, that women are unfit by nature for life outside the cage. And in letting this old wheel come full cycle women have fallen victim to one of the most insidious and ingenious confidence tricks ever perpetrated.

5 In point of fact, neither female nature nor women's individual free choice has been put to the test. As American Negroes have discovered, to be officially free is by no means the same as being actually and

psychologically free. A society as adept as ours has become at propaganda—whether political or commercial—should know that "persuasion," which means the art of launching myths and artificially inducing inhibitions, is every bit as effective as force of law. No doubt the reason society eventually agreed to abolish its anti-women laws was that it had become confident of commanding a battery of hidden dissuaders which would do the job just as well. Cage bars are clumsy methods of control, which excite the more rebellious personalities inside to rattle them. Modern society, like the modern zoo, has contrived to get rid of the bars without altering the fact of imprisonment. All the zoo architect needs to do is run a zone of hot or cold air, whichever the animal concerned cannot tolerate, round the cage where the bars used to be. Human animals are not less sensitive to social climate.

The ingenious point about the new-model zoo is that it deceives 6
both sides of the invisible barrier. Not only can the animal not see how it is imprisoned; the visitor's conscience is relieved of the unkindness of keeping animals shut up. He can say "Look, no bars round the animals," just as society can say "Look, no laws restricting women" even while it keeps women rigidly in place by zones of fierce social pressure.

There is, however, one great difference. A woman, being a thinking 7
animal, may actually be more distressed because the bars of her cage cannot be seen. What relieves society's conscience may afflict hers. Unable to perceive what is holding her back, she may accuse herself and her whole sex of craven timidity because women have not jumped at what has the appearance of an offer of freedom. Evidently quite a lot of women have succumbed to guilt of this sort, since in recent years quite an industry has arisen to assuage it. Comforting voices make the air as thick and reassuring as cotton wool while they explain that there is nothing shameful in not wanting a career, that to be intellectually unadventurous is no sin, that taking care of home and family may be personally "fulfilling" and socially valuable.

This is an argument without a flaw: except that it is addressed ex- 8
clusively to women. Address it to both sexes and instantly it becomes progressive and humane. As it stands, it is merely antiwoman prejudice revamped.

That many women would be happier not pursuing careers or intel- 9
lectual adventures is only part of the truth. The whole truth is that many *people* would be. If society had the clear sight to assure men as well as women that there is no shame in preferring to stay non-competitively and non-aggressively at home, many masculine neuroses and ulcers

would be avoided, and many children would enjoy the benefit of being brought up by a father with a talent for the job instead of by a mother with no talent for it but a sense of guilt about the lack.

10 But society does nothing so sensible. Blindly it goes on insisting on the tradition that men are the ones who go out to work and adventure—an arrangement which simply throws talent away. All the home-making talent which happens to be born inside male bodies is wasted; and our businesses and governments are staffed quite largely by people whose aptitude for the work consists solely of their being what is, by tradition, the right sex for it.

11 The pressures society exerts to drive men out of the house are very nearly as irrational and unjust as those by which it keeps women in. The mistake of the early reformers was to assume that men were emancipated already and that therefore reform need ask only for the emancipation of women. What we ought to do now is go right back to scratch and demand the emancipation of both sexes. It is only because men are not free themselves that they have found it necessary to cheat women by the deception which makes them appear free when they are not.

12 The zones of hot and cold air which society uses to perpetuate its uneconomic and unreasonable state of affairs are the simplest and most effective conceivable. Society is playing on our sexual vanity. Just as the sexual regions are the most vulnerable part of the body, sexuality is the most vulnerable part of the Ego. Tell a man that he is not a real man, or a woman that she is not one hundred per cent woman and you are threatening both with not being attractive to the opposite sex. No one can bear not to be attractive to the opposite sex. That is the climate which the human animal cannot tolerate.

13 So society has us all at its mercy. It has only to murmur to the man that staying at home is a feminine characteristic, and he will be out of the house like a bullet. It has only to suggest to the woman that logic and reason are the province of the masculine mind, whereas "intuition" and "feeling" are the female *forte*, and she will throw her physics text-books out of the window, barricade herself into the house and give herself up to having wishy-washy poetical feelings while she arranges the flowers.

14 She will, incidentally, take care that her feelings *are* wishy-washy. She has been persuaded that to have cogent feelings, of the kind which really do go into great poems (most of which are by men), would make her an unfeminine woman, a woman who imitates men. In point of fact, she would not be imitating men as such, most of whom have never written a line of great poetry, but poets, most of whom so far happen to be

men. But the bad logic passes muster with her because part of the mythology she has swallowed ingeniously informs her that logic is not her *forte*.

Should a woman's talent or intelligence be so irrepressible that she 15
insists on producing cogent works of art or watertight meshes of argument, she will be said to have "a mind like a man's." This is simply current idiom; translated, it means "a good mind." The use of the idiom contributes to an apparently watertight proof that all good minds are masculine, since whenever they occur in women they are described as "like a man's."

What is more, this habit of thought actually contributes to perpetu- 16
ating a state of affairs where most good minds really do belong to men. It is difficult for a woman to *want* to be intelligent when she has been told that to be so will make her like a man. She inclines to think an intelligence would be as unbecoming to her as a moustache; and many women have tried in furtive privacy to disembarrass themselves of intellect as though it were facial hair.

Discouraged from growing "a mind like a man's," women are en- 17
couraged to have thoughts and feelings of a specifically feminine tone. For society is cunning enough not to place its whole reliance on threatening women with blasts of icy air. It also flatters them with a zone of hot air. The most deceptive and cynical of its blandishments is the notion that women have some specifically feminine contribution to make to culture. Unfortunately, as culture had already been shaped and largely built up by men before the invitation was issued, this leaves women little to do. Culture consists of reasoned thought and works of art composed of cogent feeling and imagination. There is only one way to be reasonable, and that is to reason correctly; and the only kind of art which is any good is good art. If women are to eschew reason and artistic imagination in favour of "intuition" and "feeling," it is pretty clear what is meant. "Intuition" is just a polite name for bad reasoning, and "feeling" for bad art.

In reality, the whole idea of a specifically feminine—or, for the 18
matter of that, masculine—contribution to culture is a contradiction of culture. A contribution to culture is not something which could not have been made by the other sex—it is something which could not have been made by any other *person*. Equally, the notion that anyone, of either sex, can create good art out of simple feeling, untempered by discipline, is a philistine one. The arts are a sphere where women seem to have done well; but really they have done *too* well—too well for the good of the arts. Instead of women sharing the esteem which ought to

belong to artists, art is becoming smeared with femininity. We are approaching a philistine state of affairs where the arts are something which it is nice for women to take up in their spare time—men having slammed out of the house to get on with society's "serious" business, like making money, administering the country and running the professions.

19 In that "serious" sphere it is still rare to encounter a woman. A man sentenced to prison would probably feel his punishment was redoubled by indignity if he were to be sentenced by a woman judge under a law drafted by a woman legislator—and if, on admission, he were to be examined by a woman prison doctor. If such a thing happened every day, it would be no indignity but the natural course of events. It has never been given the chance to become the natural course of events and never will be so long as women remain persuaded it would be unnatural of them to want it.

20 So brilliantly has society contrived to terrorise women with this threat that certain behaviour is unnatural and unwomanly that it has left them no time to consider—or even sheerly observe—what womanly nature really is. For centuries arrant superstitions were accepted as natural law. The physiological fact that only women can secrete milk for feeding babies was extended into the pure myth that it was women's business to cook for and wait on the entire family. The kitchen became woman's "natural" place because, for the first few months of her baby's life, the nursery really was. To this day a woman may suspect that she is unfeminine if she can discover in herself no aptitude or liking for cooking. Fright has thrown her into such a muddle that she confuses having no taste for cookery with having no breasts, and conversely assumes that nature has endowed the human female with a special handiness with frying pans.

21 Even psycho-analysis, which in general has been the greatest benefactor of civilisation since the wheel, has unwittingly reinforced the terrorisation campaign. The trouble was that it brought with it from its origin in medical therapy a criterion of normality instead of rationality. On sheer statistics every pioneer, genius and social reformer, including the first woman who demanded to be let out of the kitchen and into the polling booth, is abnormal, along with every lunatic and eccentric. What distinguishes the genius from the lunatic is that the genius' abnormality is justifiable by reason or aesthetics. If a woman who is irked by confinement to the kitchen merely looks round to see what other women are doing and finds they are accepting their kitchens, she may well conclude that she is

abnormal and had better enlist her psycho-analyst's help towards "living with" her kitchen. What she ought to ask is whether it is rational for women to be kept to the kitchen, and whether nature really does insist on that in the way it insists women have breasts. And in a far-reaching sense to ask that question is much more normal and natural than learning to "live with" the handicap of women's inferior social status. The normal and natural thing for human beings is not to tolerate handicaps but to reform society and to circumvent or supplement nature. We don't learn to live minus a leg; we devise an artificial limb.

That, indeed, is the crux of the matter. Not only are the distinc- 22
tions we draw between male nature and female nature largely arbitrary and often pure superstition: they are completely beside the point. They ignore the essence of *human* nature. The important question is not whether women are or are not less logical by nature than men, but whether education, effort and the abolition of our illogical social pressures can improve on nature and make them (and, incidentally, men as well) *more* logical. What distinguishes human from any other animal nature is its ability to be unnatural. Logic and art are not natural or instinctive activities; but our nature includes a propensity to acquire them. It is not natural for the human body to orbit the earth; but the human mind has a natural adventurousness which enables it to invent machines whereby the body can do so. There is, in sober fact, no such creature as a natural man. Go as far back as they will, the archaeologists cannot come on a wild man in his natural habitat. At his most primitive, he has already constructed himself an artificial habitat, and decorated it not by a standardised instinctual method, as birds build nests, but by individualised—that is, abnormal—works of art or magic. And in doing so he is not limited by the fingers nature gave him; he has extended their versatility by making tools.

Civilisation consists not necessarily in defying nature but in making 23
it possible for us to do so if we judge it desirable. The higher we can lift our noses from the grindstone of nature, the wider the area we have of choice; and the more choices we have freely made, the more individualised we are. We are at our most civilised when nature does not dictate to us, as it does to animals and peasants, but when we can opt to fall in with it or better it. If modern civilisation has invented methods of education which make it possible for men to feed babies and for women to think logically, we are betraying civilisation itself if we do not set both sexes free to make a free choice.

THINKING ABOUT THE TEXT

1. What are the specific points of Brophy's comparisons between the modern zoo without bars and what has happened to women?
2. In what ways does Brophy argue for emancipation of both women and men?
3. How do our stereotypical views of gender and our clichés of language perpetuate the problems that Brophy discusses?
4. In spite of her title, what is Brophy advocating in her essay?

WRITING FROM THE TEXT

1. Write an essay in which you describe the "invisible cages" in which women are kept. In addition to your own points, use and appropriately document Brophy's points in your essay.
2. Compare the "invisible cages" of women *and* men.
3. Write an essay in which you focus on the "zone[s] of hot or cold air" that keep adventurous women "in their place."
4. Interview some men with the specific goal of learning whether any of them would stay at home if they had mates who earned enough money to support the family. What are your subjects' responses to the idea of being househusbands? How many would find staying at home ego threatening? Is Brophy right or wrong? Write an essay using your collected material for specific support.

CONNECTING WITH OTHER TEXTS

1. Warren Farrell's view in "Men as Success Objects" (p. 75) is that men are required to be successful because the hidden agenda expects attractive dates and mates to be successful. How does Farrell's essay complement Brophy's? Write an essay from your own perspective, using these essays for support.
2. Use this essay and Marge Piercy's poem "A Work of Artifice" (p. 87) to write an essay that shows the restrictions that are placed on women. Use these works for support of your point.
3. Brophy concludes her essay with the thought that "the more choices we have freely made, the more individualised we are." Write an analysis of the problems facing women and/or men in your generation. Propose a way that either or both genders can become free. Any of the material in this chapter will be useful to your analysis, but the work of Brophy, Thompson, Perrin, and Farrell will be especially helpful in describing the problems that each gender faces.

■ A WORK OF ARTIFICE

Marge Piercy

Educated at the University of Michigan and Northwestern University, Marge Piercy (b. 1936) has served as a visiting lecturer, writer in residence, and professor at many universities in the United States. She has won many prizes, awards, and honors for her novels, short stories, plays, and essays. Of her work, Piercy says, "I have been particularly although not exclusively concerned with the choices open to—or perceived to be open to—women of various eras, races, and classes. I am one of the few contemporary American novelists consciously and constantly preoccupied with social class and the economic underpinnings of decision and consequence." The following poem is from *Circles on the Water* (published in 1969), one of Piercy's many collections of poetry. Her most recent, *Mars and Her Children: Poems,* was published in 1992.

The bonsai tree
in the attractive pot
could have grown eighty feet tall
on the side of a mountain
till split by lightning.
But a gardener
carefully pruned it.
It is nine inches high.
Every day as he
whittles back the branches
the gardener croons,
It is your nature
to be small and cozy
domestic and weak;
how lucky, little tree,
to have a pot to grow in.
With living creatures
one must begin very early
to dwarf their growth:
the bound feet,
the crippled brain,
the hair in curlers,
the hands you
love to touch.

THINKING ABOUT THE TEXT

1. According to the poem, how is a bonsai tree created and maintained?

2. What are the comparisons between the creation and care of a bonsai and the creation and care of a woman? Do you object to the art of bonsai? How do you feel about what happens to women?
3. Look up the word *artifice* in a dictionary and copy all of the definitions listed for the word. In what ways is each meaning of the word useful to Piercy in conveying the point of her poem? What *is* her point?

WRITING FROM THE TEXT

1. Write an essay in which you explain how Marge Piercy's title contains perfect word choice for conveying the theme of the poem. You will want to examine the multiple definitions of the word *artifice* as part of your analysis.
2. Write an essay analyzing the ways that women are "crooned" to and the resultant "cozy" and "weak" ways that they are kept. Show your attitude or stance toward this situation in your essay.

CONNECTING WITH OTHER TEXTS

1. Look up information about the art of bonsai in an encyclopedia or gardening text in your school or local library or on the Internet. Write an essay about the goals of this art form and summarize the process of maintaining a bonsai plant.
2. In an essay, explain how the history of keeping women "small and cozy / domestic and weak" has been opposed in recent years. Use specific examples of the presence of women in professional, business, or academic worlds to argue that "the crippled brain" is a metaphor of the past.
3. Write an essay comparing Marge Piercy's perception about what happens to women in "A Work of Artifice" to the insights about women in Kim Edwards' essay "In Rooms of Women" (p. 130).
4. Piercy's gardener has moved the tree, which might have grown to "eighty feet tall," to an "attractive pot" where it will stay "small and cozy." Brigid Brophy, in "Women: Invisible Cages" (p. 80), also describes forces that keep women domestic. Write an essay analyzing these forces. Is the agent always a *man* with an overt plan?

■ DATE RAPE

Ellen Sweet

A graduate of Smith University with a master's degree in teaching from Yale, Ellen Sweet (b. 1942) worked as a senior editor for *Ms.* magazine where her special interest was in health-related issues. Formerly an executive editor for *New Choices* magazine, Sweet is now Director of Communications at the Vera Institute of Justice, an organization committed to improving systems of justice and services for victims.

> It was the beginning of spring break when I was a junior. I was in good spirits and had been out to dinner with an old friend. We returned to his college [dorm]. There were some seniors on the ground floor, drinking beer, playing bridge. I'm an avid player, so we joined them, joked around a lot. One of them, John, wasn't playing, but he was interested in the game. I found him attractive. We talked, and it turned out we had a mutual friend, shared experiences. It was getting late, and my friend had gone up to bed, so John offered to see me safely home. We took our time, sat outside talking for a while. Then he said we could get inside one of the most beautiful campus buildings, which was usually locked at night. I went with him. Once we were inside, he kissed me. I didn't resist, I was excited. He kissed me again. But when he tried for more, I said no. He just grew completely silent. I couldn't get him to talk to me any more. He pinned me down and ripped off my pants. *I couldn't believe it was happening to me* . . . 1

Let's call this Yale graduate Judy. Her experience and her disbelief, as she describes them, are not unique. Gretchen, another student victim of date rape (or acquaintance rape, as it is also called), had known for five years the man who invited her to an isolated vacation cabin and then raped her. "I considered him my best friend," she says on a Stanford University videotape used in discussions of the problem. "I couldn't believe it. *I couldn't believe it was actually happening to me*." 2

Such denial, the inability to believe that someone they know could have raped them, is a common reaction of victims of date rape, say psychologists and counselors who have researched the topic and treated these women. In fact, so much silence surrounds this kind of crime that many women are not even aware that they have been raped. In one study, Mary P. Koss, a psychology professor at Kent State University, Ohio, asked female students if they had had sexual intercourse against their will through use of or threat of force (the minimal legal definition of rape). Of those who answered yes, only 57 percent went on to identify 3 their experience as rape. Koss also identified the other group (43 percent) as those who hadn't even acknowledged the rape to themselves.

4 "I can't believe it's happening on our campus," is usually the initial response to reports such as Koss's. She also found that one in eight women students had been raped, and another one in four were victims of attempted rape. Since only 4 percent of all those reported the attack, Koss concluded that "at least ten times more rapes occur among college students than are reflected in official crime statistics." (Rape is recognized to be the most underreported of all crimes, and date rape is among the least reported, least believed, and most difficult to prosecute, second only to spouse rape.)

5 Working independently of Koss, researchers at Auburn University, Alabama, and more recently, University of South Dakota and St. Cloud State University, Minnesota, all have found that one in five women students were raped by men they knew.

6 Koss also found a core group of highly sexually aggressive men (4.3 percent) who use physical force to compel women to have intercourse but who are unlikely to see their act as rape. These "hidden rapists" have "oversubscribed" to traditional male roles, she says. They believe that aggression is normal and that women don't really mean it when they say no to sexual advances. Such men answer "True" to statements like "most women are sly and manipulating when they want to attract a man," "a woman will only respect a man who will lay down the law to her," and "a man's got to show the woman who's boss right from the start or he'll end up henpecked."

7 In Koss's current study, one respondent who answered yes to a question about obtaining intercourse through physical force, wrote in the comment, "I didn't rape the chick, she was enjoying it and responding," and later, "I feel that sex is a very pleasant way to relieve stress. Especially when there are no strings attached."

8 "He acted like he had a right, like he *didn't believe me*," says a coed from Auburn University on a videotaped dramatization of date rape experiences. And several weeks later, when she confronts him, saying he forced her, he says no, she wanted it. "You raped me," she finally tells him. And the picture freezes on his look of incredulity.

9 Barry Burkhart, a professor of psychology at Auburn, who has also studied sexual aggression among college men, found that 10 percent had used physical force to have intercourse with a woman against her will, and a large majority admitted to various other kinds of aggression. "These are ordinary males operating in an ordinary social context," he says. "So what we conclude is that there's something wrong with that social context."

The something wrong is that our culture fosters a "rape supportive belief system," according to social psychologist Martha Burt. She thinks that "there's a large category of 'real' rapes, and a much smaller category of what our culture is willing to call a 'real' rape. The question is, how does the culture manage to write off all those other rapes?" The way it's done, says Burt, currently director of the Social Services Research Center at the Urban Institute in Washington, D.C., is by believing in a series of myths about rape, including: 10

- It didn't really happen (the woman was lying);
- Women like rape (so there's no such thing as rape);
- Yes, it happened, but no harm was done (she wasn't a virgin; she wasn't white);
- Women provoke it (men can't control themselves);
- Women deserve it anyway.

It's easy to write off date rapes with such myths, coupled with what Burt calls our culture's "adversarial sexual beliefs": the gamesmanship theory that everybody is out for what they can get, and that all sexual relationships are basically exploitive and predatory. In fact, most victims of date rape initially blame themselves for what happened, and almost none report it to campus authorities. And most academic institutions prefer to keep it that way, judging from the lack of surveys on date rape—all of which makes one wonder if they don't actually blame the victim, too. 11

As long as such attacks continue to be a "hidden" campus phenomenon, unreported and unacknowledged by many college administrators, law enforcement personnel, and students, the problem will persist. Of course, the term has become much better known in the three years since *Ms.* reported on the prevalence of experiences such as Judy's and Gretchen's. (See "Date Rape: A Campus Epidemic?" September 1982.) It has been the subject of talk shows such as "The Donahue Show" and TV dramas ("Cagney and Lacey"). But for most people it remains a contradiction in terms. "Everybody has a stake in denying that it's happening so often," says Martha Burt. "For women, it's self-protective . . . if only bad girls get raped, then I'm personally safe. For men, it's the denial that 'nice' people like them do it." 12

The fault has not entirely been that of the institutions. "Ten years ago, we were telling women to look over your shoulder when you go out at night and lock your doors," says Py Bateman, director of a nationally known rape education program in Seattle, Alternatives to Fear. The prevailing myth was that most rapes were committed by strangers in dark alleys. 13

14 "If you have to think that sixty to eighty percent of rape is by people you know—that's hard to deal with," says Sylvia Callaway, who directed the Austin, Texas, Rape Crisis Center for more than eight years before leaving last July. "No rape center in a university community would be surprised that the university is not willing to deal with the problem."

15 Statistics alone will not solve the problem of date rape, but they could help bring it out into the open. Which is why Ms. undertook the first nationwide survey on college campuses. The Ms. Magazine Campus Project on Sexual Assault, directed by Mary P. Koss at Kent State and funded by the National Center for the Prevention and Control of Rape, reached more than seven thousand students at a nationally representative sample of thirty-five schools, to find out how often, under what circumstances, and with what aftereffects a wide range of sexual assaults, including date rape, took place.

16 Preliminary results are now ready, and the information is no surprise. Participating schools were promised anonymity, but each will receive the results applying to its student body. Our hope is that the reaction of "we can't believe it's happening on our campus" will be followed by "what can we do about it—now."

17 Just how entrenched is denial of this problem today? One gauge might be the difficulty our own researchers had in persuading schools to let us on campus. For every college that approved our study, two others rejected it. Their reasons (in writing and in telephone conversations) were themselves instructive: "we don't want to get involved," "limited foreseeable benefit," "too volatile a topic," "have not had any problems in this area," "worried about publicity," "can't allow surveys in classroom," "just can't invest the time now," "would be overintrusive," "don't want to be left holding the bag if something goes wrong."

18 Several schools rejected the study on the basis that filling out the questionnaire might upset some students, and that we were not providing adequate follow-up counseling. (Researchers stayed on campus for at least a day after the distribution of the questionnaire, gave students listings of counselors or rape crisis centers to consult if anything upset them, and offered to meet with school personnel to brief them.) But isn't it less upsetting for a student to recognize and admit that she has been the victim of an acquaintance rape than to have buried the trauma of that rape deep inside herself?

19 "It's a Catch-22 situation. You want a survey to publicize a problem that has tremendous psychological implications. And the school says, 'Don't do it, because it will get people psychologically upset,'" admits John Jung, who heads the human subjects review committee at California State University/Long Beach (a school that declined our study).

One wonders just who are the "people" who will get most psycho- 20
logically upset: the students, or their parents who pay for their educations, or the administrators who are concerned about the school's image. "There may have been an episode here," said John Hose, executive assistant to the president of Brandeis University, "but there is no cause célèbre surrounding the issue. In such cases, the reaction of Student Affairs is to encourage the student to be in touch with her parents and to take legal action."

"Student Affairs" at Brandeis is headed by Rodger Crafts, who 21
moved to this post about a year ago from the University of Rhode Island. "I don't think we have a significant problem here because we have a sophisticated and intelligent group of students," said Dean Crafts. As for the University of Rhode Island, more students there are "first generation college attenders," as he put it, and therefore have "less respect" for other people. Vandalism and physical harm are more likely to occur with "lower educational levels." Respect for other people goes along with "intelligence level."

Back at the University of Rhode Island, the counseling center is 22
sponsoring a twelve-week support and therapy group this fall for male students who are coercive and abusive in their relationships with women. Even though Nancy Carlson, director of Counseling and Career Services, is enthusiastic about such programs and workshops she notes, "the awareness about date rape has been a long time coming."

Another school where administrators were the last to confront the 23
challenge to their school's self-image is Yale. Last year, two student publications reported instances of date rape on campus that surprised students, faculty, and administration. "There are no full statistics available on rape between students at Yale anywhere. . . . There is no mention of rape in the 1983–1984 Undergraduate Regulations. There is no procedure for a victim to file a formal complaint of rape with the university. But there is rape between students at Yale," wrote Sarah Oates in the *Yale Daily News*. Partly in response to such charges, current Yale undergraduate regulations now list "sexual harassment" under "offenses that are subject to disciplinary action"—but still no mention of rape.

Yale students brave enough to bring a charge of sexual harassment 24
may go before the Yale College Executive Committee, a specially convened group of faculty, administrators, and students that can impose a series of penalties, graduated in severity, culminating in expulsion. All its hearings and decisions are kept secret (but can in theory be subpoenaed in a court of law). But Michael McBride, current chair of the committee, told me that cases of date rape have come up during the past year, leading in one instance to a student being asked to "resign" from

the university, and in another, the conclusion that there was not "sufficient evidence." (In Judy's case, described at the beginning of this article, the senior she charged was penalized by being denied the privilege of graduating with his class. But she claims that after he demanded that the case be reconsidered, he was fully exonerated.) Said McBride, "What surprised me the most was how complicated these cases are. It's only one person's word against another's. It's amazing how different their perceptions can be."

25 Judy chose to take her case before the Executive Committee rather than report it to the local police, because she felt she would have complete confidentiality and quick action. Actually, there were many delays. And then, because the man she accused hired a lawyer, she was forced to hire one too. As a result, the meeting felt very much like a jury trial to her, complete with cross-examinations that challenged her truthfulness and raised excruciatingly embarrassing questions.

26 Judy's lawyer felt that such painful questions were necessary. But it seems as if the lesson feminists in the sixties and seventies worked so hard and successfully to make understood—not to blame the victim for stranger rape—is one that will have to be learned all over again in the case of acquaintance rape. Only this time, the woman who reports the rape suffers a triple victimization. Not only is she attacked and then not believed, but she carries the added burden of losing faith in her own judgment and trust in other people.

27 In a recently published study of jurors in rape trials, University of Illinois sociologist Barbara Reskin found that jurors were less likely to convict a man if the victim knew him. "Consent is the preferred rape defense and gets the highest acquittal rates," Reskin observes. "In a date rape situation, I would think the jury would assume that the woman had already accepted his invitation in a romantic sense. It would be a matter of how *much* did she consent to."

28 Personal characteristics also influence jurors, Reskin says. Those she studied couldn't imagine that certain men would commit a rape: if they were attractive, had access to sexual partners such as a girlfriend or a wife. More often than not, they'd say, "But he doesn't look like a rapist." Reskin imagines that this pattern would be "magnified in date rape, because these are men who could get a date, they're not complete losers."

29 It may turn out that solutions to the problem will turn up at places with a less genteel image to protect. Jan Strout, director of Montana State, Women's Resource Center, wonders if schools such as hers, which recognize that they are dealing with a more conservative student body and a "macho cowboy image," aren't more willing to take the first step toward acknowledging the problem. A group called Students Against

Sexual Assault was formed there two-and-a-half years ago after several students who were raped or resisted an attempted rape "went public." With men and women sharing leadership, this group is cosponsored by the Women's Resource Center and the student government.

Admitting to the problem isn't easy even when data is available, as 30
doctoral student Genny Sandberg found at the University of South Dakota. Last spring, she announced the results of a dating survey she coauthored with psychologists Tom Jackson and Patricia Petretic-Jackson. The most shocking statistic: 20 percent of the students (most from rural backgrounds and living in a rural campus setting) had been raped in a dating situation. The state board of regents couldn't believe it. "I just think that that's absolutely ridiculous," former regent Michael Rost said, according to the Brookings *Daily Register*, "I can't believe we would allow that to occur. If it is true, it's a very serious problem." Regent William Srstka agreed, "If this is true it's absolutely intolerable."

Following testimony by one of the researchers, the board changed 31
its tune. Members are now discussing how to begin a statewide education and prevention program.

An inspiring example of how an administration can be led to new 32
levels of consciousness took place at the University of Michigan earlier this year. Spurred by an article in *Metropolitan Detroit* magazine, a group of students staged a sit-in at the office of a university vice-president who had been quoted as saying that "Rape is a red flag word. . . . [The university] wants to present an image that is receptive and palatable to the potential student cohort," and also that "Rape is an issue like Alzheimer's disease or mental retardation [which] impacts on a small but sizable part of the population. . . . Perhaps it has to become a crisis that is commonly shared in order to get things done."

The students who spent the entire day in Vice-President Henry 33
Johnson's office claimed that rape had already become a crisis on their campus. They presented a list of twelve demands, ranging from a rape crisis center on campus to better lighting and installation of outdoor emergency phones. By the end of the day, Johnson had started to change his mind. Although he insisted that he had been misquoted and quoted out of context in the press, he told me that "I did not realize [before that] acquaintance rape was so much of a problem, that it was the most prevalent type of rape. There is a heightened awareness now on this campus. Whether we as a faculty and administration are as sensitive as we should be is another issue—and that will take some time."

In the meantime, members of the Michigan Student Assembly 34
Women's Issues Committee (one of the groups active in organizing the protest) took their demands before the school's board of regents. The

result: a $75,000 program for rape prevention and education on campus, directly reporting to Johnson's office. "We'll now be in a position to document the problem and to be proactive," says Johnson. Jennifer Faigel, an organizer of the protest, acknowledges a change in the administration's awareness but says the students themselves, disappointed in the amount of funding promised for the program, have already formed a group (Students Organized Against Rape) to develop programs in the dorms.

35 In just the three years since *Ms.* first reported on date rape (in 1982), several new campus organizations have sprung up and other ongoing programs have surfaced.

36 But the real measure of a school's commitment to dealing with this problem is the range of services it provides, says Mary Harvey, who did a nationwide study of exemplary rape programs for the National Center for the Prevention and Control of Rape. "It should have preventive services, crisis intervention, possibilities for long-term treatment, advocacy, and women's studies programs that educate about violence. The quality of a university's services to rape victims can be measured by the degree to which these other things are in place."

37 Minimally, rape counselors and educators feel, students need to be exposed to information about date rape as soon as they enter college. Studies show that the group most vulnerable to acquaintance rape are college freshmen, followed by high school seniors. In Koss's original survey, for example, the average age of the victim was eighteen.

38 "I'd like a program where no first-year students could finish their starting week at college without being informed about the problem of acquaintance rape," says Andrea Parrot, a lecturer in human service studies at Cornell University, who is developing a program to train students and dorm resident advisers as date rape awareness counselors. Parrot and others admit that this would be a bare minimum. Handing out a brochure to read, even conducting a workshop on the subject during the busy orientation week and counting on students voluntarily attending, needs to be followed up with sessions in dormitories or other living units. These are the most common settings for date rapes, according to a study by Parrot and Robin Lynk.

39 So how do we go about changing attitudes? And how do we do it without "setting student against student?" asks Gretchen Mieszkowski, chair of the Sexual Assault Prevention Committee at the University of Houston/Clear Lake. Chiefly a commuter campus, with a majority of married women students, Clear Lake nevertheless had seventeen acquaintance rapes reported to the local crisis hot line last year. "We had

always focused on traditional solutions like lighting and escort services at night," Mieszkowski says. "But changing lighting in the parking lot is easy; it's only money."

Many who have studied the problem of rape education believe it 40
has to begin with college-age women and men talking to each other more frankly about their beliefs and expectations about sex. Py Bateman of Alternatives to Fear thinks it has to start earlier, among teenagers, by developing rudimentary dating skills at the lower end of the sexual activity scale. "We need to learn more about holding hands than about sexual intercourse."

Bateman continues: "We've got to work on both sides. Boys don't 41
know what they want any more than girls do. The way our sexual interaction is set up is that boys are supposed to push. Their peers tell them that scoring is what counts. They're as divorced from intimacy as girls."

Gail Abarbanel of the Rape Treatment Center at Santa Monica 42
Hospital agrees. Her center conducts educational programs for schools in Los Angeles County. In a recent survey of more than five thousand teenagers, she found a high degree of misconception and lack of information about rape: "Most boys say yes to the question, 'If a girl goes back to a guy's house when she knows no one is home, is she consenting to sex?' And most boys believe that girls don't mean no when they say it."

Women clearly need to get more convincing, and men clearly need 43
to believe them more. But until that ideal time, Montana State's Jan Strout warns, "Because men have been socialized to hear yes when women say no, we have to scream it."

THINKING ABOUT THE TEXT

1. How is it possible for ambiguity to exist in defining rape? What is the social context that permits ambiguity?
2. Given the incidence of rape on college campuses, why did many schools refuse to participate in the study conducted by *Ms?* What does Ellen Sweet imply might be the reason for their reluctance to participate?
3. Is Rodger Crafts correct in saying that physical harm is more apt to occur with "lower educational levels"? Do any of the studies noted here belie that assertion?
4. According to Sweet, what inhibits women from reporting that they have been raped? How do the cases noted here support a woman's reluctance to press charges against a rapist?

5. What specifically can schools do to help prevent rapes on campus? What is the most realistic solution to the problem?

WRITING FROM THE TEXT

1. Write an essay to persuade your reader that you understand the causes of date rape, and propose a solution to the problem.
2. Write a letter to a school newspaper—your school's paper if appropriate—arguing for a rape prevention program on campus. Cite the benefits that you expect to come from such a program.

CONNECTING WITH OTHER TEXTS

1. Take one aspect of the problem of rape—the treatment of rape victims, the types of trials held to prosecute rapists, the jury response to alleged rapists, the ambiguity in some males' minds about what constitutes rape, the preventative education programs on campuses, or some other aspect of the problem that interests you—and do research to complement Sweet's essay and "When a Woman Says No" by Ellen Goodman (below).
2. Learn what has been done on your campus about rape prevention and write an analysis of your school's program. If statistics are available from your counseling or health center, use them in your paper.

■ WHEN A WOMAN SAYS NO

Ellen Goodman

A widely syndicated columnist whose home newspaper is the *Boston Globe*, Ellen Goodman (b. 1941) has won the Pulitzer Prize for her outstanding journalism. Goodman believes that she writes about issues that are more important than politics, such as the "underlying values by which this country exists . . . the vast social changes in the way men and women lead their lives and deal with each other." The essay included here, first published in the *Boston Globe* in 1984, is indicative of Goodman's concerns. You also may wish to read Ellen Goodman's essays "Thanksgiving" (p. 4) and "In America, Food for Thought" (p. 404).

1 There are a few times when, if you watch closely, you can actually see a change of public mind. This is one of those times.

For as long as I can remember, a conviction for rape depended as much on the character of the woman involved as on the action of the man. Most often the job of the defense lawyer was to prove that the woman had provoked or consented to the act, to prove that it was sex, not assault. 2

In the normal course of events the smallest blemish, misjudgment, misstep by the woman became proof that she had invited the man's attentions. Did she wear a tight sweater? Was she a "loose" woman? Was she in the wrong part of town at the wrong hour? A woman could waive her right to say no in an astonishing number of ways. 3

But in the past few weeks, in Massachusetts, three cases of multiple rape have come into court and three sets of convictions have come out of juries. These verdicts point to a sea change in attitudes. A simple definition seems to have seeped into the public consciousness. If she says no, it's rape. 4

The most famous of these cases is the New Bedford barroom rape. There, in two separate trials, juries cut through complicated testimony to decide the central issue within hours. Had the woman been drinking? Had she lied about that in testimony? Had she kissed one of the men? In the end none of these points were relevant. What mattered to the juries that found four of these six men guilty was that they had forced her. If she said no, it was rape. 5

The second of these cases involved a young woman soldier from Ft. Devens who accepted a ride with members of a rock band, the Grand Slamm. She was raped in the bus and left in a field hours later. Had she flirted with the band members? Had she told a friend that she intended to seduce one of the men? Had she boarded the bus willingly? The judge sentencing three of the men to jail said, "No longer will society accept the fact that a woman, even if she may initially act in a seductive or compromising manner, has waived her right to say no at any further time." If she said no, it was rape. 6

The third of these cases was in some ways the most notable. An Abington woman was driven from a bar to a parking lot where she was raped by four men, scratched with a knife, had her hair singed with a cigarette lighter and was left half-naked in the snow. The trial testimony showed that she previously had sex with three of the men, and with two of them in a group setting. Still, the jury was able to agree with the district attorney: "Sexual consent between a woman and a man on one occasion does not mean the man has access to her whenever it strikes his fancy." If she said no, it was rape. 7

8 Not every community, courtroom or jury today accepts this simple standard of justice. But ten years ago, five years ago, even three years ago these women might not have even dared press charges.

9 It was the change of climate that enabled, even encouraged, the women to come forward. It was the change of attitude that framed the arguments in the courtroom. It was the change of consciousness that infiltrated the jury chambers.

10 The question now is whether that change of consciousness has become part of our own day-to-day lives. In some ways rape is the brutal, repugnant extension of an ancient ritual of pursuit and capture. It isn't just rapists who refuse to take no for an answer. It isn't just rapists who believe that a woman says one thing and means another.

11 In the confusion of adolescence, in the chase of young adulthood, the sexes were often set up to persist and to resist. Many young men were taught that "no" means "try again." Many young women were allowed to excuse their sexuality only when they were "swept away," overwhelmed.

12 The confused messages, the yes-no-maybes, the overpowered heroines and overwhelming heroes, are still common to supermarket gothic novels and *Hustler* magazine. It isn't just X-rated movies that star a resistant woman who falls in love with her sexual aggressor. It isn't just pornographic cable-TV that features the woman who really "wanted it." In as spritely a sitcom as "Cheers," Sam blithely locked a coyly ambivalent Diane into his apartment.

13 I know how many steps it is from that hint of sexual pressure to the brutality of rape. I know how far it is from lessons of sexual power plays to the violence of rape. But it's time that the verdict of those juries was fully transmitted to the culture from which violence emerges. If she says no, it means no.

THINKING ABOUT THE TEXT

1. In this essay, Goodman gives a brief history of social response to rape. In the past, how did lawyers defend alleged rapists? What seems to be the present attitude toward a charge of rape?
2. Goodman gives a summary of three different rape trials. What is the logic of her arrangement of the three examples to support her thesis?
3. Beyond what is asserted in the title of Goodman's essay, what is the important point she makes?

WRITING FROM THE TEXT

1. Describe a time when the "confused messages, the yes-no-maybes" resulted in an incomplete or erroneous understanding of a point you were trying to make.
2. Write a response to Goodman's allegation that "Many young men were taught that 'no' means 'try again.'" Argue that she is correct or incorrect. Use specific examples to support your view.

CONNECTING WITH OTHER TEXTS

1. Use "Date Rape" (p. 89), "Angry Young Men" (p. 118), and "When a Woman Says No" to write an analytical essay on the causes of violence against women. What does Goodman mean about the "confused messages" in our culture? Propose a solution in your essay.
2. Read recent periodical accounts of rape trials. Is Goodman accurate in saying that there has been a "sea change" in public consciousness about rape?
3. Goodman notes that a few years ago, many women would not have dared to press rape charges. Today, sexual harassment claims have become a media topic, and women are daring to charge that they are being or have been sexually harassed. Do research to learn the history of charges of sexual harassment. Focus your paper on the changes in public consciousness and use specific examples from the reported cases to support your analysis.

■ WHERE ARE YOU GOING, WHERE HAVE YOU BEEN?

Joyce Carol Oates

A novelist, poet, playwright, editor, and critic, Joyce Carol Oates (b. 1938) also teaches English at Princeton University. Since her first collection of short stories appeared when she was 25, Oates has been averaging almost two books a year. Although she writes in a variety of genres and literary styles, Oates may be best known for her ability to write suspenseful tales and to create a sense of terror in an apparently ordinary situation, as the story included here illustrates. Oates has responded to critics' comments about the terror that permeates her work: "Uplifting endings and resolutely cheery world views are appropriate to television commercials but insulting elsewhere. It is not only wicked to pretend otherwise, it is futile." The story included here, from *The Wheel of Love*, has been widely anthologized since its first publication in 1965.

For Bob Dylan

1 Her name was Connie. She was fifteen and she had a quick nervous giggling habit of craning her neck to glance into mirrors or checking other people's faces to make sure her own was all right. Her mother, who noticed everything and knew everything and who hadn't much reason any longer to look at her own face, always scolded Connie about it. "Stop gawking at yourself, who are you? You think you're so pretty?" she would say. Connie would raise her eyebrows at these familiar complaints and look right through her mother, into a shadowy vision of herself as she was right at that moment: she knew she was pretty and that was everything. Her mother had been pretty once too, if you could believe those old snapshots in the album, but now her looks were gone and that was why she was always after Connie.

2 "Why don't you keep your room clean like your sister? How've you got your hair fixed—what the hell stinks? Hair spray? You don't see your sister using that junk."

3 Her sister June was twenty-four and still lived at home. She was a secretary in the high school Connie attended, and if that wasn't bad enough—with her in the same building—she was so plain and chunky and steady that Connie had to hear her praised all the time by her mother and her mother's sisters. June did this, June did that, she saved money and helped clean the house and cooked and Connie couldn't do a thing, her mind was all filled with trashy daydreams. Their father was away at work most of the time and when he came home he wanted supper and he read the newspaper at supper and after supper he went to bed. He didn't bother talking much to them, but around his bent head Connie's mother kept picking at her until Connie wished her mother were dead and she herself were dead and it were all over. "She makes me want to throw up sometimes," she complained to her friends. She had a high, breathless, amused voice which made everything she said sound a little forced, whether it was sincere or not.

4 There was one good thing: June went places with girlfriends of hers, girls who were just as plain and steady as she, and so when Connie wanted to do that her mother had no objections. The father of Connie's best girlfriend drove the girls the three miles to town and left them off at a shopping plaza, so that they could walk through the stores or go to a movie, and when he came to pick them up again at eleven he never bothered to ask what they had done.

5 They must have been familiar sights, walking around that shopping plaza in their shorts and flat ballerina slippers that always scuffed the sidewalk, with charm bracelets jingling on their thin wrists: they would

lean together to whisper and laugh secretly if someone passed by who amused or interested them. Connie had long dark blond hair that drew anyone's eye to it, and she wore part of it pulled up on her head and puffed out and the rest of it she let fall down her back. She wore a pullover jersey blouse that looked one way when she was at home and another way when she was away from home. Everything about her had two sides to it, one for home and one for anywhere that was not home: her walk that could be childlike and bobbing, or languid enough to make anyone think she was hearing music in her head, her mouth which was pale and smirking most of the time, but bright and pink on these evenings out, her laugh which was cynical and drawling at home—"Ha, ha, very funny"—but high-pitched and nervous anywhere else, like the jingling of the charms on her bracelet.

Sometimes they did go shopping or to a movie, but sometimes they went across the highway, ducking fast across the busy road, to a drive-in restaurant where older kids hung out. The restaurant was shaped like a big bottle, though squatter than a real bottle, and on its cap was a revolving figure of a grinning boy who held a hamburger aloft. One night in mid-summer they ran across, breathless with daring, and right away someone leaned out a car window and invited them over, but it was just a boy from high school they didn't like. It made them feel good to be able to ignore him. They went up through the maze of parked and cruising cars to the bright-lit, fly-infested restaurant, their faces pleased and expectant as if they were entering a sacred building that loomed out of the night to give them what haven and what blessing they yearned for. They sat at the counter and crossed their legs at the ankles, their thin shoulders rigid with excitement, and listened to the music that made everything so good: the music was always in the background like music at a church service, it was something to depend upon. 6

A boy named Eddie came in to talk with them. He sat backward on his stool, turning himself jerkily around in semicircles and then stopping and turning again, and after a while he asked Connie if she would like something to eat. She said she did and so she tapped her friend's arm on her way out—her friend pulled her face up into a brave droll look—and Connie said she would meet her at eleven, across the way. "I just hate to leave her like that," Connie said earnestly, but the boy said that she wouldn't be alone for long. So they went out to his car and on the way Connie couldn't help but let her eyes wander over the windshields and faces all around her, her face gleaming with a joy that had nothing to do with Eddie or even this place; it might have been the music. She drew her shoulders up and sucked in her breath with the pure 7 pleasure of being alive, and just at that moment she happened to glance at a face just a few feet from hers. It was a boy with shaggy black hair, in a convertible jalopy painted gold. He stared at her and then his lips widened into a grin. Connie slit her eyes at him and turned away, but she couldn't help glancing back and there he was still watching her. He wagged a finger and laughed and said, "Gonna get you, baby," and Connie turned away again without Eddie noticing anything.

8 She spent three hours with him, at the restaurant where they ate hamburgers and drank Cokes in wax cups that were always sweating, and then down an alley a mile or so away, and when he left her off at five to eleven only the movie house was still open at the plaza. Her girlfriend was there, talking with a boy. When Connie came up the two girls smiled at each other and Connie said, "How was the movie?" and the girl said, "*You* should know." They rode off with the girl's father, sleepy and pleased, and Connie couldn't help but look at the darkened shopping plaza with its big empty parking lot and its signs that were faded and ghostly now, and over at the drive-in restaurant where cars were still circling tirelessly. She couldn't hear the music at this distance.

9 Next morning June asked her how the movie was and Connie said, "So-so."

10 She and that girl and occasionally another girl went out several times a week that way, and the rest of the time Connie spent around the house—it was summer vacation—getting in her mother's way and thinking, dreaming, about the boys she met. But all the boys fell back and dissolved into a single face that was not even a face, but an idea, a feeling, mixed up with the urgent insistent pounding of the music and the humid night air of July. Connie's mother kept dragging her back to the daylight by finding things for her to do or saying, suddenly, "What's this about the Pettinger girl?"

11 And Connie would say nervously, "Oh, her. That dope." She always drew thick clear lines between herself and such girls, and her mother was simple and kindly enough to believe her. Her mother was so simple, Connie thought, that it was maybe cruel to fool her so much. Her mother went scuffling around the house in old bedroom slippers and complained over the telephone to one sister about the other, then the other called up and the two of them complained about the third one. If June's name was mentioned her mother's tone was approving, and if Connie's name was mentioned it was disapproving. This did not really mean she disliked Connie and actually Connie thought that her mother preferred her to June because she was prettier, but the two of them kept up a pretense of exasperation, a sense that they were tugging and struggling over some-

thing of little value to either of them. Sometimes, over coffee, they were almost friends, but something would come up—some vexation that was like a fly buzzing suddenly around their heads—and their faces went hard with contempt.

One Sunday Connie got up at eleven—none of them bothered with 12
church—and washed her hair so that it could dry all day long, in the sun. Her parents and sister were going to a barbecue at an aunt's house and Connie said no, she wasn't interested, rolling her eyes to let her mother know just what she thought of it. "Stay home alone then," her mother said sharply. Connie sat out back in a lawn chair and watched them drive away, her father quiet and bald, hunched around so that he could back the car out, her mother with a look that was still angry and not at all softened through the windshield, and in the back seat poor old June all dressed up as if she didn't know what a barbecue was, with all the running yelling kids and the flies. Connie sat with her eyes closed in the sun, dreaming and dazed with the warmth about her as if this were a kind of love, the caresses of love, and her mind slipped over onto thoughts of the boy she had been with the night before and how nice he had been, how sweet it always was, not the way someone like June would suppose but sweet, gentle, the way it was in movies and promised in songs; and when she opened her eyes she hardly knew where she was, the back yard ran off into weeds and a fence line of trees and behind it the sky was perfectly blue and still. The asbestos "ranch house" that was now three years old startled her—it looked small. She shook her head as if to get awake.

It was too hot. She went inside the house and turned on the radio 13
to drown out the quiet. She sat on the edge of her bed, barefoot, and listened for an hour and a half to a program called XYZ Sunday Jamboree, record after record of hard, fast, shrieking songs she sang along with, interspersed by exclamations from "Bobby King": "An' look here you girls at Napoleon's—Son and Charley want you to pay real close attention to this song coming up!"

And Connie paid close attention herself, bathed in a glow of slow- 14
pulsed joy that seemed to rise mysteriously out of the music itself and lay languidly about the airless little room, breathed in and breathed out with each gentle rise and fall of her chest.

After a while she heard a car coming up the drive. She sat up at 15
once, startled, because it couldn't be her father so soon. The gravel kept crunching all the way in from the road—the driveway was long—and Connie ran to the window. It was a car she didn't know. It was an open jalopy, painted a bright gold that caught the sunlight opaquely. Her

heart began to pound and her fingers snatched at her hair, checking it, and she whispered "Christ, Christ," wondering how bad she looked. The car came to a stop at the side door and the horn sounded four short taps as if this were a signal Connie knew.

16 She went into the kitchen and approached the door slowly, then hung out the screen door, her bare toes curling down off the step. There were two boys in the car and now she recognized the driver: he had shaggy, shabby black hair that looked crazy as a wig and he was grinning at her.

17 "I ain't late, am I?" he said.

18 "Who the hell do you think you are?" Connie said.

19 "Toldja I'd be out, didn't I?"

20 "I don't even know who you are."

21 She spoke sullenly, careful to show no interest or pleasure, and he spoke in a fast bright monotone. Connie looked past him to the other boy, taking her time. He had fair brown hair, with a lock that fell onto his forehead. His sideburns gave him a fierce, embarrassed look, but so far he hadn't even bothered to glance at her. Both boys wore sunglasses. The driver's glasses were metallic and mirrored everything in miniature.

22 "You wanta come for a ride?" he said.

23 Connie smirked and let her hair fall loose over one shoulder.

24 "Don'tcha like my car? New paint job," he said. "Hey."

25 "What?"

26 "You're cute."

27 She pretended to fidget, chasing flies away from the door.

28 "Don'tcha believe me, or what?" he said.

29 "Look, I don't even know who you are," Connie said in disgust.

30 "Hey, Ellie's got a radio, see. Mine's broke down." He lifted his friend's arm and showed her the little transistor the boy was holding, and now Connie began to hear the music. It was the same program that was playing inside the house.

31 "Bobby King?" she said.

32 "I listen to him all the time. I think he's great."

33 "He's kind of great," Connie said reluctantly.

34 "Listen, that guy's *great*. He knows where the action is."

35 Connie blushed a little, because the glasses made it impossible for her to see just what this boy was looking at. She couldn't decide if she liked him or if he was just a jerk, and so she dawdled in the doorway and wouldn't come down or go back inside. She said, "What's all that stuff painted on your car?"

"Can'tcha read it?" He opened the door very carefully, as if he was 36
afraid it might fall off. He slid out just as carefully, planting his feet firmly on the ground, the tiny metallic world in his glasses slowing down like gelatine hardening and in the midst of it Connie's bright green blouse. "This here is my name, to begin with," he said. ARNOLD FRIEND was written in tarlike black letters on the side, with a drawing of a round grinning face that reminded Connie of a pumpkin, except it wore sunglasses. "I wanta introduce myself, I'm Arnold Friend and that's my real name and I'm gonna be your friend, honey, and inside the car's Ellie Oscar, he's kinda shy." Ellie brought his transistor radio up to his shoulder and balanced it there. "Now these numbers are a secret code, honey," Arnold Friend explained. He read off the numbers, 33, 19, 17 and raised his eyebrows at her to see what she thought of that, but she didn't think much of it. The left rear fender had been smashed and around it was written, on the gleaming gold background: DONE BY CRAZY WOMAN DRIVER. Connie had to laugh at that. Arnold Friend was pleased at her laughter and looked up at her. "Around the other side's a lot more—you wanta come and see them?"

"No." 37

"Why not?" 38

"Why should I?" 39

"Don'tcha wanta see what's on the car? Don'tcha wanta go for a 40
ride?"

"I don't know." 41

"Why not?" 42

"I got things to do." 43

"Like what?" 44

"Things." 45

He laughed as if she had said something funny. He slapped his 46
thighs. He was standing in a strange way, leaning back against the car as if he were balancing himself. He wasn't tall, only an inch or so taller than she would be if she came down to him. Connie liked the way he was dressed, which was the way all of them dressed: tight faded jeans stuffed into black, scuffed boots, a belt that pulled his waist in and showed how lean he was, and a white pullover shirt that was a little soiled and showed the hard small muscles of his arms and shoulders. He looked as if he probably did hard work, lifting and carrying things. Even his neck looked muscular. And his face was a familiar face, somehow: the jaw and chin and cheeks slightly darkened, because he hadn't shaved for a day or two, and the nose long and hawklike, sniffing as if she were a treat he was going to gobble up and it was all a joke.

47 "Connie, you ain't telling the truth. This is your day set aside for a ride with me and you know it," he said, still laughing. The way he straightened and recovered from his fit of laughing showed that it had been all fake.

48 "How do you know what my name is?" she said suspiciously.

49 "It's Connie."

50 "Maybe and maybe not."

51 "I know my Connie," he said, wagging his finger. Now she remembered him even better, back at the restaurant, and her cheeks warmed at the thought of how she sucked in her breath just at the moment she passed him—how she must have looked at him. And he had remembered her. "Ellie and I come out here especially for you," he said. "Ellie can sit in back. How about it?"

52 "Where?"

53 "Where what?"

54 "Where're we going?"

55 He looked at her. He took off the sunglasses and she saw how pale the skin around his eyes was, like holes that were not in shadow but instead in light. His eyes were like chips of broken glass that catch the light in an amiable way. He smiled. It was as if the idea of going for a ride somewhere, to some place, was a new idea to him.

56 "Just for a ride, Connie sweetheart."

57 "I never said my name was Connie," she said.

58 "But I know what it is. I know your name and all about you, lots of things," Arnold Friend said. He had not moved yet but stood still leaning back against the side of his jalopy. "I took a special interest in you, such a pretty girl, and found out all about you like I know your parents and sister are gone somewheres and I know where and how long they're going to be gone, and I know who you were with last night, and your best girlfriend's name is Betty. Right?"

59 He spoke in a simple lilting voice, exactly as if he were reciting the words to a song. His smile assured her that everything was fine. In the car Ellie turned up the volume on his radio and did not bother to look around at them.

60 "Ellie can sit in the back seat," Arnold Friend said. He indicated his friend with a casual jerk of his chin, as if Ellie did not count and she should not bother with him.

61 "How'd you find out all that stuff?" Connie said.

62 "Listen: Betty Schultz and Tony Fitch and Jimmy Pettinger and Nancy Pettinger, he said, in a chant. Raymond Stanley and Bob Hutter—"

"Do you know all those kids?" 63

"I know everybody." 64

"Look, you're kidding. You're not from around here." 65

"Sure." 66

"But—how come we never saw you before?" 67

"Sure you saw me before," he said. He looked down at his boots, as if he were a little offended. "You just don't remember." 68

"I guess I'd remember you," Connie said. 69

"Yeah?" he looked up at this, beaming. He was pleased. He began to mark time with the music from Ellie's radio, tapping his fists lightly together. Connie looked away from his smile to the car, which was painted so bright it almost hurt her eyes to look at it. She looked at that name. ARNOLD FRIEND. And up at the front fender was an expression that was familiar—MAN THE FLYING SAUCERS. It was an expression kids had used the year before, but didn't use this year. She looked at it for a while as if the words meant something to her that she did not yet know. 70

"What're you thinking about? Huh?" Arnold Friend demanded. "Not worried about your hair blowing around in the car, are you?" 71

"No." 72

"Think I maybe can't drive good?" 73

"How do I know?" 74

"You're a hard girl to handle. How come?" he said. "Don't you know I'm your friend? Didn't you see me put my sign in the air when you walked by?" 75

"What sign?" 76

"My sign." And he drew an X in the air, leaning out toward her. They were maybe ten feet apart. After his hand fell back to his side the X was still in the air, almost visible. Connie let the screen door close and stood perfectly still inside it, listening to the music from her radio and the boy's blend together. She stared at Arnold Friend. He stood there so stiffly relaxed, pretending to be relaxed, with one hand idly on the door handle as if he were keeping himself up that way and had no intention of ever moving again. She recognized most things about him, the tight jeans that showed his thighs and buttocks and the greasy leather boots and the tight shirt, and even that slippery friendly smile of his, that sleepy dreamy smile that all the boys used to get across ideas they didn't want to put into words. She recognized all this and also the singsong way he talked, slightly mocking, kidding, but serious and a little melancholy, and she recognized the way he tapped one fist against the other in homage of the perpetual music behind him. But all these things did not come together. 77

78 She said suddenly, "Hey, how old are you?"

79 His smile faded. She could see then that he wasn't a kid, he was much older—thirty, maybe more. At this knowledge her heart began to pound faster.

80 "That's a crazy thing to ask. Can'tcha see I'm your own age?"

81 "Like hell you are."

82 "Or maybe a coupla years older, I'm eighteen."

83 "Eighteen?" she said doubtfully.

84 He grinned to reassure her and lines appeared at the corners of his mouth. His teeth were big and white. He grinned so broadly his eyes became slits and she saw how thick the lashes were, thick and black as if painted with a black tarlike material. Then he seemed to become embarrassed, abruptly, and looked over his shoulder at Ellie. "*Him*, he's crazy," he said. "Ain't he a riot, he's a nut, a real character." Ellie was still listening to the music. His sunglasses told nothing about what he was thinking. He wore a bright orange shirt unbuttoned halfway to show his chest, which was a pale, bluish chest and not muscular like Arnold Friend's. His shirt collar was turned up all around and the very tips of the collar pointed out past his chin as if they were protecting him. He was pressing the transistor radio up against his ear and sat there in a kind of daze, right in the sun.

85 "He's kinda strange," Connie said.

86 "Hey, she says you're kinda strange! Kinda strange!" Arnold Friend cried. He pounded on the car to get Ellie's attention. Ellie turned for the first time and Connie saw with shock that he wasn't a kid either—he had a fair, hairless face, cheeks reddened slightly as if the veins grew too close to the surface of his skin, the face of a forty-year-old baby. Connie felt a wave of dizziness rise in her at this sight and she stared at him as if waiting for something to change the shock of the moment, make it all right again. Ellie's lips kept shaping words, mumbling along with the words blasting in his ear.

87 "Maybe you two better go away," Connie said faintly.

88 "What? How come?" Arnold Friend cried. "We come out here to take you for a ride. It's Sunday." He had the voice of the man on the radio now. It was the same voice, Connie thought. "Don'tcha know it's Sunday all day and honey, no matter who you were with last night today you're with Arnold Friend and don't you forget it!—Maybe you better step out here," he said, and this last was in a different voice. It was a little flatter, as if the heat was finally getting to him.

89 "No. I got things to do."

90 "Hey."

91 "You two better leave."

92 "We ain't leaving until you come with us."

93 "Like hell I am—"

94 "Connie, don't fool around with me. I mean, I mean, don't fool *around*," he said, shaking his head. He laughed incredulously. He placed his sunglasses on top of his head, carefully, as if he were indeed wearing a wig, and brought the stems down behind his ears. Connie stared at him, another wave of dizziness and fear rising in her so that for a moment he wasn't even in focus but was just a blur, standing there against his gold car, and she had the idea that he had driven up the driveway all right but had come from nowhere before that and belonged nowhere and that everything about him and even about the music that was so familiar to her was only half real.

95 "If my father comes and sees you—"

96 "He ain't coming. He's at a barbecue."

97 "How do you know that?"

98 "Aunt Tillie's. Right now they're—uh—they're drinking. Sitting around," he said vaguely, squinting as if he were staring all the way to town and over to Aunt Tillie's back yard. Then the vision seemed to get clear and he nodded energetically. "Yeah. Sitting around. There's your sister in a blue dress, huh? And high heels, the poor sad bitch—nothing like you, sweetheart! And your mother's helping some fat woman with the corn, they're cleaning the corn—husking the corn—"

99 "What fat woman?" Connie cried.

100 "How do I know what fat woman, I don't know every goddam fat woman in the world!" Arnold laughed.

101 "Oh, that's Mrs. Hornby . . . Who invited her?" Connie said. She felt a little light-headed. Her breath was coming quickly.

102 "She's too fat. I don't like them fat. I like them the way you are, honey," he said, smiling sleepily at her. They stared at each other for a while, through the screen door. He said softly, "Now what you're going to do is this: you're going to come out that door. You're going to sit up front with me and Ellie's going to sit in the back, the hell with Ellie, right? This isn't Ellie's date. You're my date. I'm your lover, honey."

103 "What? You're crazy—"

104 "Yes, I'm your lover. You don't know what that is, but you will," he said. "I know that too. I know all about you. But look: it's real nice and you couldn't ask for nobody better than me, or more polite. I always keep my word. I'll tell you how it is. I'm always nice at first, the first time. I'll hold you so tight you won't think you have to try to get away or pretend anything because you'll know you can't. And I'll come inside you where it's all secret and you'll give in to me and you'll love me—"

105 "Shut up! You're crazy!" Connie said. She backed away from the door. She put her hands against her ears as if she'd heard something terrible, something not meant for her. "People don't talk like that, you're crazy," she muttered. Her heart was almost too big now for her chest and its pumping made sweat break out all over her. She looked out to see Arnold Friend pause and then take a step toward the porch lurching. He almost fell. But, like a clever drunken man, he managed to catch his balance. He wobbled in his high boots and grabbed hold of one of the porch posts.

106 "Honey?" he said. "You still listening?"

107 "Get the hell out of here!"

108 "Be nice, honey. Listen."

109 "I'm going to call the police—"

110 He wobbled again and out of the side of his mouth came a fast spat curse, an aside not meant for her to hear. But even this "Christ!" sounded forced. Then he began to smile again. She watched this smile come, awkward as if he were smiling from inside a mask. His whole face was a mask, she thought wildly, tanned down onto his throat but then running out as if he had plastered makeup on his face but had forgotten about his throat.

111 "Honey—? Listen, here's how it is. I always tell the truth and I promise you this: I ain't coming in that house after you."

112 "You better not! I'm going to call the police if you—if you don't—"

113 "Honey," he said, talking right through her voice, "honey, I'm not coming in there but you are coming out here. You know why?"

114 She was panting. The kitchen looked like a place she had never seen before, some room she had run inside but which wasn't good enough, wasn't going to help her. The kitchen window had never had a curtain, after three years, and there were dishes in the sink for her to do—probably—and if you ran your hand across the table you'd probably feel something sticky there.

115 "You listening, honey? Hey?"

116 "—going to call the police—"

117 "Soon as you touch the phone I don't need to keep my promise and can come inside. You won't want that."

118 She rushed forward and tried to lock the door. Her fingers were shaking. "But why lock it," Arnold Friend said gently, talking right into her face. "It's just a screen door. It's just nothing." One of his boots was at a strange angle, as if his foot wasn't in it. It pointed out to the left, bent at the ankle. "I mean, anybody can break through a screen door and glass and wood and iron or anything else if he needs to, anybody at

all and specially Arnold Friend. If the place got lit up with a fire honey you'd come runnin' out into my arms, right into my arms an' safe at home—like you knew I was your lover and'd stopped fooling around. I don't mind a nice shy girl but I don't like no fooling around." Part of those words were spoken with a slight rhythmic lilt, and Connie somehow recognized them—the echo of a song from last year, about a girl rushing into her boyfriend's arms and coming home again—

Connie stood barefoot on the linoleum floor, staring at him. "What 119
do you want?" she whispered.

"I want you," he said. 120

"What?" 121

"Seen you that night and thought, that's the one, yes sir. I never 122
needed to look anymore."

"But my father's coming back. He's coming to get me. I had to wash 123
my hair first—" She spoke in a dry, rapid voice, hardly raising it for him to hear.

"No, your Daddy is not coming and yes, you had to wash your hair 124
and you washed it for me. It's nice and shining and all for me. I thank you, sweetheart," he said, with a mock bow, but again he almost lost his balance. He had to bend and adjust his boots. Evidently his feet did not go all the way down; the boots must have been stuffed with something so that he would seem taller. Connie stared out at him and behind him Ellie in the car, who seemed to be looking off toward Connie's right into nothing. This Ellie said, pulling the words out of the air one after another as if he were just discovering them, "You want me to pull out the phone?"

"Shut your mouth and keep it shut," Arnold Friend said, his face red 125
from bending over or maybe from embarrassment because Connie had seen his boots. "This ain't none of your business."

"What—what are you doing? What do you want?" Connie said. "If I 126
call the police they'll get you, they'll arrest you—"

"Promise was not to come in unless you touch that phone, and I'll 127
keep that promise," he said. He resumed his erect position and tried to force his shoulders back. He sounded like a hero in a movie, declaring something important. He spoke too loudly and it was as if he were speaking to someone behind Connie. "I ain't made plans for coming in that house where I don't belong but just for you to come out to me, the way you should. Don't you know who I am?"

"You're crazy," she whispered. She backed away from the door but 128
did not want to go into another part of the house, as if this would give him permission to come through the door. "What do you . . . You're crazy, you . . ."

129 "Huh? What're you saying, honey?"

130 Her eyes darted everywhere in the kitchen. She could not remember what it was, this room.

131 "This is how it is, honey; you come out and we'll drive away, have a nice ride. But if you don't come out we're gonna wait till your people come home and then they're all going to get it."

132 "You want that telephone pulled out?" Ellie said. He held the radio away from his ear and grimaced, as if without the radio the air was too much for him.

133 "I toldja shut up, Ellie," Arnold Friend said, "you're deaf, get a hearing aid, right? Fix yourself up. This little girl's no trouble and's gonna be nice to me, so Ellie keep to yourself, this ain't your date—right? Don't hem in on me. Don't hog. Don't crush. Don't bird dog. Don't trail me," he said in a rapid meaningless voice, as if he were running through all the expressions he'd learned but was no longer sure which one of them was in style, then rushing on to new ones, making them up with his eyes closed, "Don't crawl under my fence, don't squeeze in my chipmunk hole, don't sniff my glue, suck my popsicle, keep your own greasy fingers on yourself!" He shaded his eyes and peered in at Connie, who was backed against the kitchen table. "Don't mind him honey he's just a creep. He's a dope. Right? I'm the boy for you and like I said you come out here nice like a lady and give me your hand, and nobody else gets hurt, I mean, your nice old bald-headed daddy and your mummy and your sister in her high heels. Because listen: why bring them in this?"

134 "Leave me alone," Connie whispered.

135 "Hey, you know that old woman down the road, the one with the chickens and stuff—you know her?"

136 "She's dead!"

137 "Dead? What? You know her?" Arnold Friend said.

138 "She's dead—"

139 "Don't you like her?"

140 "She's dead—she's—she isn't there anymore—"

141 "But don't you like her, I mean, you got something against her? Some grudge or something?" Then his voice dipped as if he were conscious of a rudeness. He touched the sunglasses perched on top of his head as if to make sure they were still there. "Now you be a good girl."

142 "What are you going to do?"

143 "Just two things, or maybe three," Arnold Friend said. "But I promise it won't last long and you'll like me the way you get to like people you're close to. You will. It's all over for you here, so come on out. You don't want your people in any trouble, do you?"

144 She turned and bumped against a chair or something, hurting her leg, but she ran into the back room and picked up the telephone. Something roared in her ear, a tiny roaring, and she was so sick with fear that she could do nothing but listen to it—the telephone was clammy and very heavy and her fingers groped down to the dial but were too weak to touch it. She began to scream into the phone, into the roaring. She cried out, she cried for her mother, she felt her breath start jerking back and forth in her lungs as if it were something Arnold Friend were stabbing her with again and again with no tenderness. A noisy sorrowful wailing rose all about her and she was locked inside it the way she was locked inside this house.

145 After a while she could hear again. She was sitting on the floor with her wet back against the wall.

146 Arnold Friend was saying from the door, "That's a good girl. Put the phone back."

147 She kicked the phone away from her.

148 "No, honey. Pick it up. Put it back right."

149 She picked it up and put it back. The dial tone stopped.

150 "That's a good girl. Now you come outside."

151 She was hollow with what had been fear, but what was now just an emptiness. All that screaming had blasted it out of her. She sat, one leg cramped under her, and deep inside her brain was something like a pinpoint of light that kept going and would not let her relax. She thought, I'm not going to see my mother again. She thought, I'm not going to sleep in my bed again. Her bright green blouse was all wet.

152 Arnold Friend said, in a gentle-loud voice that was like a stage voice, "The place where you came from ain't there any more, and where you had in mind to go is canceled out. This place you are now—inside your daddy's house—is nothing but a cardboard box I can knock down any time. You know that and always did know it. You hear me?"

153 She thought, I have got to think. I have to know what to do.

154 "We'll go out in a nice field, out in the country here where it smells so nice and it's sunny," Arnold Friend said. "I'll have my arms tight around you so you won't need to try to get away and I'll show you what love is like, what it does. The hell with this house! It looks solid all right," he said. He ran a fingernail down the screen and the noise did not make Connie shiver, as it would have the day before. "Now put your hand on your heart, honey. Feel that? That feels solid too, but we know better, be nice to me, be sweet like you can because what else is there for a girl like you but to be sweet and pretty and give in?—and get away before her people come back?"

155 She felt her pounding heart. Her hand seemed to enclose it. She thought for the first time in her life that it was nothing that was hers, that belonged to her, but just a pounding, living thing inside this body that wasn't really hers either.

156 "You don't want them to get hurt," Arnold Friend went on. "Now get up, honey. Get up all by yourself."

157 She stood.

158 "Now turn this way. That's right. Come over here to me—Ellie, put that away, didn't I tell you? You dope. You miserable creepy dope," Arnold Friend said. His words were not angry but only part of an incantation. The incantation was kindly. "Now come out through the kitchen to me honey, and let's see a smile, try it, you're a brave sweet little girl and now they're eating corn and hot dogs cooked to bursting over an outdoor fire, and they don't know one thing about you and never did and honey you're better than them because not a one of them would have done this for you."

159 Connie felt the linoleum under her feet; it was cool. She brushed her hair back out of her eyes. Arnold Friend let go of the post tentatively and opened his arms for her, his elbows pointing in toward each other and his wrists limp, to show that this was an embarrassed embrace and a little mocking, he didn't want to make her self-conscious.

160 She put out her hand against the screen. She watched herself push the door slowly open as if she were safe back somewhere in the other doorway, watching this body and this head of long hair moving out into the sunlight where Arnold Friend waited.

161 "My sweet little blue-eyed girl," he said, in a half-sung sigh that had nothing to do with her brown eyes but was taken up just the same by the vast sunlit reaches of the land behind him and on all sides of him, so much land that Connie had never seen before and did not recognize except to know that she was going to it.

THINKING ABOUT THE TEXT

1. Identify Connie's character traits and illustrate each. How is she a rather typical 15-year-old, and how is she unique?
2. Illustrate the various ways that Arnold Friend initially appeals to Connie.
3. Identify the numerous intimidation tactics that Friend uses to manipulate Connie.
4. Study Ellie's role in this story. How does Oates use him to illuminate Arnold Friend's character, temperament, and motives?

5. Although the ending is ambiguous, Oates has revealed that this story was based on details from actual rapes and murders committed by Charles Schmid and his accomplice John Saunders in Tucson, Arizona, during the 1960s. How do various details in the story, and particularly in the ending, suggest that a crime was going to be committed?

6. Without reducing this story to simple morals, discuss the insights (about subjects such as adolescence, parenting, role playing, manipulation, and intimidation) that we can draw from this story.

WRITING FROM THE TEXT

1. Write a character analysis (see pp. 436–443) of Arnold Friend, demonstrating how he knows and preys upon the insecurities and fantasies of a 15-year-old girl. Include details from the story to support your thesis.

2. In an essay, argue that Connie does or doesn't *choose* to go with Arnold Friend at the end. Could she have resisted more than she did? Cite specific evidence from the story to support your thesis.

3. Considering Connie's character and life-style, is Oates suggesting that Connie is to be blamed for what happened to her, or does the blame fall on Arnold Friend for taking advantage of a vulnerable 15-year-old? Write an essay to support your argument.

CONNECTING WITH OTHER TEXTS

1. Read "When a Woman Says No" (p. 98) and write an essay applying Ellen Goodman's comments to Connie's experience.

2. Read "Angry Young Men" (p. 118) and "Date Rape" (p. 89) and use ideas from these readings and from Oates' story as you consider and analyze Arnold Friend's perspective.

3. Find and read the article in *Life* magazine (March 4, 1966) about the Charles Schmid case. Then write an essay comparing the actual details of his rapes and murders with this story.

4. Joyce Chopra's 1985 feature film *Smooth Talk,* based on Oates' story, is available on video, and Oates is reported to have been pleased with this adaptation. Note the differences between the video and the story versions, and write an essay analyzing the changes that were made in the film.

ANGRY YOUNG MEN
Barbara Ehrenreich

Educated at Reed College and Rockefeller University, where she received her Ph.D., Barbara Ehrenreich (b. 1941) has worked as a staff member in New York City's Health Policy Advisory Center, and she has been an assistant professor of health sciences. As both a feminist and a health services worker, she has written to expose the male domination of the female health care system (*Complaints and Disorders: The Sexual Politics of Sickness* and *For Her Own Good: One Hundred Fifty Years of the Experts' Advice to Women*). Ehrenreich has this to say about her life and work: "My writing is motivated by my commitment to social justice. I have been involved in the anti-war movement and the women's movement and have recently been involved in the women's health movement." Ehrenreich's work appears in many national magazines, including *Ms.* and *Mother Jones.* The essay included here appeared in *New York Woman* in 1989.

1 Recall the roar of commentary that followed the murderous 1989 assault on a 28-year-old woman jogging in Central Park. Every detail of the assailants' lives was sifted for sociological significance: Were they poor? How poor? Students or dropouts? From families with two parents or one?

2 Yet weeks before the East Harlem "posse" attacked a jogger, suburbanites in nearby Long Island were shaken by two murders that were, if anything, even more inexplicably vicious than the assault in Central Park. In early March the body of 13-year-old Kelly Tinyes was found in the basement of a house just down the block from her own. She had been stabbed, strangled, and hit with a blunt instrument before being mutilated with a bayonet. A few weeks later 14-year-old Jessica Manners was discovered along the side of a road in East Setauket, strangled to death, apparently with her own bra, and possibly sexually assaulted.

3 Suspects have been apprehended. Their school friends, parents, and relatives have been interviewed. Their homes and cars have been searched, their photos published. We know who they hung out with and what they did in their spare time. But on the scale of large social meanings, these crimes don't rate. No one is demanding that we understand—or condemn—the white communities that nourished the killers. No one is debating the roots of violence in the land of malls and tract homes. In the city, apparently, crime is construed as something "socioeconomic." Out here it's merely "sick."

4 But East Setauket is not really all that far from East Harlem. If something is festering in the ghetto, something very similar is gnawing away in middle-income suburbs. A "way of life," as the cliché goes, is

coming to an end, and in its place a mean streak is opening up and swallowing everything in its path. Economists talk about "deindustrialization" and "class polarization." I think of it as the problem of the marginal men: They are black and white, Catholic and Pentecostal, rap fans and admirers of techno-pop. What they have in common is that they are going nowhere—nowhere legal, that is.

Consider the suspects in the Long Island murders. Twenty-one-year- 5
old Robert Golub, in whose basement Kelly Tinyes was killed, is described in *Newsday* as an "unemployed body-builder." When his high school friends went off to college, he stayed behind in his parents' home in Valley Stream. For a while he earned a living driving a truck for a cosmetics firm, but he lost the job, in part because of his driving record: His license has been suspended 12 times since 1985. At the time of the murder Golub had been out of work for several months, constructing a life around his weight-lifting routine and his dream of becoming an entrepreneur.

Christopher Loliscio, the suspect in the Manners case, is 19 and, 6
like Golub, lives with his parents. He has been in trouble before, charged with third-degree assault and "menacing" in an altercation that took place on the campus of the State University at Stony Brook. Loliscio does not attend college himself. He is employed as a landscaper.

The suburbs are full of young white men like Golub and Loliscio. If 7
they had been born 20 years earlier, they might have found steady work in decent-paying union jobs, married early, joined the volunteer fire department, and devoted their leisure to lawn maintenance. But the good blue-collar jobs are getting sparser, thanks to "deindustrialization." Much of what's left is likely to be marginal, low-paid work. Nationwide, the earnings of young white men dropped 18 percent between 1973 and 1986, making those at the low end of the wage scale less than desirable marriage prospects.

Landscaping, for example—a glamorous term for raking and mow- 8
ing—pays four to five dollars an hour; truck driving for a small firm is in the same range: not enough to pay for a college education, a house, or even a midsize wedding reception at the VFW hall.

And even those modest perquisites of life in the sub-yuppie class 9
have become, in some sense, "not enough." On Long Island the culture that once sustained men in blue-collar occupations is crumbling as more affluent settlers move in, filling the vacant lots with their new $750,000 homes. In my town, for example, the last five years saw the bowling alley close and the blue-collar bar turn into a pricey dining spot. Even the volunteer fire department is having trouble recruiting. The prestigious thing to join is a $500-a-year racquetball club; there's just not much respect anymore for putting out fires.

10 So the marginal man lives between two worlds—one that he aspires to and one that is dying—neither of which he can afford. Take "Rick," the 22-year-old son of family friends. His father is a machinist in an aerospace plant that hasn't hired anyone above the floor-sweeping level for years now. Not that Rick has ever shown any interest in his father's trade. For one thing, he takes too much pride in his appearance to put on the dark green, company-supplied work clothes his father has worn for the past 20 years. Rick has his own kind of uniform: pleated slacks, high-tops, Italian knit cardigans, and a $300 leather jacket, accessorized with a gold chain and earring stud.

11 To his parents, Rick is a hardworking boy for whom things just don't seem to work out. Right now he has a gig doing valet parking at a country club. The tips are good, and he loves racing around the lot in the Porsches and Lamborghinis of the stockbroker members. But the linchpin of his economic strategy is living at home, with his parents and sisters, in the same room he's occupied since third grade. This arrangement is less than ideal for his social life. Besides, Rick is a long way from being able to afford even a cramped, three-bedroom house like his family home; given the choice, he'd rather have a new Camaro anyway. So Rick's girlfriends tend to move on rapidly, looking for men who might someday have a chance in the real estate market.

12 If this were the 70's, Rick might have dropped out; he might have taken up marijuana, the Grateful Dead, and vague visions of a better world. But like so many of his contemporaries in the '80's, Rick isn't rebellious. He has no problem with "the system," which, in his mind, embraces every conceivable hustle, legal or illegal. He can't imagine demanding better jobs or a living wage when there's easy money to be made elsewhere. Two years ago he made a tidy bundle dealing coke in a local dance club, bought a $20,000 car, and smashed it up. Now he spends his evenings working as a bouncer in an illegal gambling joint—his parents still think he's out "dancing"—and is proud of the handgun he's got stowed in his glove compartment.

13 Someday Rick will use that gun, and I'll probably be the first to say—like Robert Golub's friends—"but he isn't the kind of person who would hurt *anyone*." Except that even now I can sense the danger in him. He's smart enough to know he's only a cut-rate copy of the upscale young men in GQ ads and MTV commercials whom he is trying to emulate. Viewed from Wall Street or Southampton, he's a peon, a member of the invisible underclass that parks cars, waits on tables, and is satisfied with a $5 tip and an occasional remark about the weather.

He's also proud. And there's nowhere for him to put that pride except into the politics of gesture: the macho stance, the 75-mph takeoff down the expressway, and, eventually, maybe, the drawn gun. Jobs are the liberal solution; conservatives would throw in "traditional values." But what the marginal men—from Valley Stream to Bedford-Stuyvesant—need most of all is *respect*. If they can't find that in work, or in a working-class lifestyle that is no longer honored, they'll extract it from someone weaker—a girlfriend, a random jogger, a neighbor, perhaps just any girl. They'll find a victim. 14

THINKING ABOUT THE TEXT

1. What is Ehrenreich's point in describing in detail the crimes that took place weeks before the infamous assault on the jogger in Central Park?
2. According to Ehrenreich, what is the common problem that prompts these vicious crimes?
3. What are the two worlds that the "marginal man" lives between? What are the consequences of his being marginal?
4. Do you agree with Ehrenreich's conclusion that the "marginal man" will find a victim—probably a female?

WRITING FROM THE TEXT

1. Write a character study of a "marginal man," using your own definition as well as Ehrenreich's observations.
2. Write your own analysis of the problems that influence the lifestyle and values of young men today. What can you propose to influence a positive change?

CONNECTING WITH OTHER TEXTS

1. Analyze the two essays on androgyny (p. 55 and p. 59) and "A New Vision of Masculinity" (p. 63) and relate those essays to Ehrenreich's points about angry young men. Argue that the culture that encourages a better male model (you define this) will have fewer incidents of violent crimes by men against women.

2. In what ways are the men depicted in Ellen Goodman's essay "When a Woman Says No" (p. 98) like the men described in Ehrenreich's essay? Analyze the characteristics they share. How are they different?

3. Write an essay comparing the frustrations that Farrell describes in "Men as Success Objects" (p. 75) to the points Ehrenreich makes about males' anger. Focus your essay on the causes of this anger.

3

Between Cultures

■ ■ ■

Over a million people a year come from different countries to live in the United States, and your classrooms undoubtedly reflect this diversity. After classes you may find yourself enjoying sushi or tacos, digesting cultural diversity as easily as you munch a Big Mac. Or you may find yourself perplexed by cultural pluralism, unsure of its merits. The readings in this chapter illustrate the joy and stress of living with cultural differences. As you will discover, assimilation and rejection are issues not only for immigrants but also for long-time residents of the United States who experience the psychological, political, and economic realities of living between cultures.

This chapter begins with an essay by someone like yourself, a college student, who describes the contrasts between his home and college environments. Marcus Mabry, an African American from New Jersey, writes of the discomfort he experiences traveling "between the two worlds" of poverty in the East and affluence in his life at Stanford in the West. In her poem, Gloria Anzaldúa expresses this discomfort as living in "the borderlands." Kim Edwards describes the tensions of an American living abroad and feeling isolated from the students and faculty of her school because of political differences. Even if you have not lived in a foreign country, you may have felt as though you were living in a foreign environment, and you will be able to understand her desire to be accepted.

Cultural characteristics are important because they define who we are, but they can also lead to misunderstanding and stereotyping. Judy Scales-Trent argues that instead of aggressively sorting people according to race or ethnicity, we should add "a 'multiracial' category to the next census." The treatment of Native Americans in history is a source of inquiry for Jane Tompkins, and the perverse use of the Native American in popular culture is criticized by Ward Churchill in his essay "Crimes Against Humanity." After you have read these essays, you may find yourself thinking differently about Native Americans as well as the "Indian" images that are prevalent in American life.

The stereotyping of African-American people is exposed in a poem by Sharon Olds and a short story by Susan Straight. Finally, as a humorous response to living with stereotyping, we think you will enjoy Gary Soto's amusing essay "Like Mexicans," which recounts how he went against his family's advice and fell in love with a Japanese woman.

■ LIVING IN TWO WORLDS

Marcus Mabry

After completing his B.A. in English and French literature at Stanford University, Marcus Mabry (b. 1967) also earned a B.A. in international relations and an M.A. in English—all within the four years of his scholarship agreement. Employed by *Newsweek* since 1989, he served as their Washington correspondent covering the State Department until 1994, as their Paris correspondent for two years, and currently serves as the Johannesburg bureau chief. Mabry has done free-lance writing for *Emerge* and *Black Collegiate* and held summer positions at *The Boston Globe.* He also conceived, wrote, produced, and narrated a documentary on African American families for French television. You may be interested to read Mabry's *Newsweek* essay, "No Father, and No Answers" (May 4, 1992). In this article, Mabry addresses the concerns he has had in trying to understand and to establish a relationship with his father, whom he only recently met (twenty years earlier, he left Mabry's unwed mother to raise their son without emotional or economic support). The work printed here also appeared in *Newsweek.*

1 A round, green cardboard sign hangs from a string proclaiming, "We built a proud new feeling," the slogan of a local supermarket. It is a souvenir from one of my brother's last jobs. In addition to being a bagger, he's worked at a fast-food restaurant, a gas station, a garage and a textile factory. Now, in the icy clutches of the Northeastern winter, he is unemployed. He will soon be a father. He is 19 years old.

2 In mid-December I was at Stanford, among the palm trees and weighty chores of academe. And all I wanted to do was get out. I joined the rest of the undergrads in a chorus of excitement, singing the praises of Christmas break. No classes, no midterms, no finals . . . and no freshmen! (I'm a resident assistant.) Awesome! I was looking forward to escaping. I never gave a thought to what I was escaping to.

3 Once I got home to New Jersey, reality returned. My dreaded freshmen had been replaced by unemployed relatives; badgering professors had been replaced by hard-working single mothers, and cold classrooms

by dilapidated bedrooms and kitchens. The room in which the "proud new feeling" sign hung contained the belongings of myself, my mom and my brother. But for these two weeks it was mine. They slept downstairs on couches.

Most students who travel between the universes of poverty and affluence during breaks experience similar conditions, as well as the guilt, the helplessness and, sometimes, the embarrassment associated with them. Our friends are willing to listen, but most of them are unable to imagine the pain of the impoverished lives that we see every six months. Each time I return home I feel further away from the realities of poverty in America and more ashamed that they are allowed to persist. What frightens me most is not that the American socioeconomic system permits poverty to continue, but that by participating in that system I share some of the blame. 4

Last year I lived in an on-campus apartment, with a (relatively) modern bathroom, kitchen and two bedrooms. Using summer earnings, I added some expensive prints, a potted palm and some other plants, making the place look like the more-than-humble abode of a New York City Yuppie. I gave dinner parties, even a *soirée française*. 5

For my roommate, a doctor's son, this kind of life was nothing extraordinary. But my mom was struggling to provide a life for herself and my brother. In addition to working 24-hour-a-day cases as a practical nurse, she was trying to ensure that my brother would graduate from high school and have a decent life. She knew that she had to compete for his attention with drugs and other potentially dangerous things that can look attractive to a young man when he sees no better future. 6

Living in my grandmother's house this Christmas break restored all the forgotten, and the never acknowledged, guilt. I had gone to boarding school on a full scholarship since the ninth grade, so being away from poverty was not new. But my own growing affluence has increased my distance. My friends say that I should not feel guilty: what could I do substantially for my family at this age, they ask. Even though I know that education is the right thing to do, I can't help but feel, sometimes, that I have it too good. There is no reason that I deserve security and warmth, while my brother has to cope with potential unemployment and prejudice. I, too, encounter prejudice, but it is softened by my status as a student in an affluent and intellectual community. 7

More than my sense of guilt, my sense of helplessness increases each time I return home. As my success leads me further away for longer periods of time, poverty becomes harder to conceptualize and feels that much more oppressive when I visit with it. The first night of break, I lay in our bedroom, on a couch that let out into a bed that took up the 8 whole room, except for a space heater. It was a little hard to sleep because the springs from the couch stuck through at inconvenient spots. But it would have been impossible to sleep anyway because of the groans coming from my grandmother's room next door. Only in her early 60s, she suffers from many chronic diseases and couldn't help but moan, then pray aloud, then moan, then pray aloud.

9 This wrenching of my heart was interrupted by the 3 A.M. entry of a relative who had been allowed to stay at the house despite rowdy behavior and threats toward the family in the past. As he came into the house, he slammed the door, and his heavy steps shook the second floor as he stomped into my grandmother's room to take his place, at the foot of her bed. There he slept, without blankets on a bare mattress. This was the first night. Later in the vacation, a Christmas turkey and a Christmas ham were stolen from my aunt's refrigerator on Christmas Eve. We think the thief was a relative. My mom and I decided not to exchange gifts that year because it just didn't seem festive.

10 A few days after New Year's I returned to California. The Northeast was soon hit by a blizzard. They were there, and I was here. That was the way it had to be, for now. I haven't forgotten; the ache of knowing their suffering is always there. It has to be kept deep down, or I can't find the logic in studying and partying while people, my people, are being killed by poverty. Ironically, success drives me away from those I most want to help by getting an education.

11 Somewhere in the midst of all that misery, my family has built, within me, "a proud feeling." As I travel between the two worlds it becomes harder to remember just how proud I should be—not just because of where I have come from and where I am going, but because of where they are. The fact that they survive in the world in which they live is something to be very proud of, indeed. It inspires within me a sense of tenacity and accomplishment that I hope every college graduate will someday possess.

THINKING ABOUT THE TEXT

1. Describe Mabry's university world and his role in it. Then contrast it with details from his family's home.
2. Mabry describes living "between the universes of poverty and affluence." Detail the emotional toll this takes.
3. What happens during Christmas break to restore his sense of guilt?
4. How is the supermarket sign, hanging in the bedroom, both ironic and deeply symbolic of Mabry's life between worlds?

WRITING FROM THE TEXT

1. Using details from the story, compare and contrast Mabry's "worlds." What is ironic about the impact of success on his life?

2. For Mabry, attending college has secured him a spot in a new world that is vastly different from the world of his past. Focus on your own between-worlds experience—college and home life, school and work worlds, high school and college relationships. Help the reader to see each world as vividly as Mabry's worlds; include your emotional responses, too.

3. Write about a time when you tried to escape one world and exchange it for another. How successful were you? What was the emotional toll on you?

CONNECTING WITH OTHER TEXTS

1. Analyze the between-worlds experiences described by Mabry, Edwards (p. 130), and Anzaldúa (below). How do they compare? What conclusions can you draw about the cultural tug-of-war?

2. Write a research paper examining your college's admissions and recruiting policies, scholarship programs, dropout rate, and success record for minority students. You may want to focus on what your research indicates has been the most serious obstacle to, or most successful accomplishment of, affirmative action on your campus.

■ TO LIVE IN THE BORDERLANDS MEANS YOU . . .

Gloria Anzaldúa

A poet, philosopher, and university professor, Gloria Anzaldúa (b. 1942) is a seventh-generation American who worked as a campesino—a migrant farm laborer—before she became the first person in her family to attend college. She earned her M.A. in English from the University of Texas and her Ph.D. in feminist studies from the University of California at Santa Cruz. Rebelling from what her family thought the good "Chicanita" should be, Anzaldúa says she read her way to another life and into personal freedom. Her goal in *Borderlands/La Frontera: The New Mestiza* (1987) was to show how the mestiza—a person of mixed races—"deals with space and identity." Her essay "How to Tame a Wild Tongue," in *Making Face, Making Soul/Haciendo Caras* (1990), deals with negative social attitudes toward Chicano ways of speaking. Anzaldúa has said, "Ethnic identity is twin to linguistic identity—I am my language." The connection between language and identity is apparent in this poem.

To live in the Borderlands means you
are neither hispana india negra española
ni gabacha, eres mestiza, mulata, half-breed
caught in the crossfire between camps
while carrying all five races on your back
not knowing which side to turn to, run from;

To live in the Borderlands means knowing
that the india in you, betrayed for 500 years,
is no longer speaking to you,
that mexicanas call you rajetas,
that denying the Anglo inside you
is as bad as having denied the Indian or Black;

Cuando vives en la frontera
people walk through you, the wind steals your voice,
you're a burra, buey, scapegoat,
forerunner of a new race,
half and half—both woman and man, neither—
a new gender;

To live in the Borderlands means to
put chile in the borscht,
eat whole wheat tortillas,
speak Tex-Mex with a Brooklyn accent;
be stopped by la migra at the border checkpoints;

Living in the Borderlands means you fight hard to
resist the gold elixir beckoning from the bottle,
the pull of the gun barrel,
the rope crushing the hollow of your throat;

In the Borderlands
you are the battleground
where enemies are kin to each other;
you are at home, a stranger,
the border disputes have been settled
the volley of shots have shattered the truce
you are wounded, lost in action
dead, fighting back;

To live in the Borderlands means
the mill with the razor white teeth wants to shred off
your olive-red skin, crush out the kernel, your heart

pound you pinch you roll you out
smelling like white bread but dead;

To survive the Borderlands
you must live sin fronteras
be a crossroads.

---

hispana: Hispanic, feminine form
india: Indian, feminine form
negra: Black, feminine form
española: Spaniard, feminine form
gabacha: a white person, feminine form
eres: you (familiar) are
mestiza: having mixed racial blood, feminine form
mulata: having mixed racial blood, feminine form
rajetas: coward, someone who backs out of a deal
Cuando vives en la frontera: When you live on the border
burra: female donkey, a dumb woman
buey: a stupid person, or a "jackass"
la migra: the border patrol
sin fronteras: without borders

THINKING ABOUT THE TEXT

1. Reread the poem until you can perceive the *types* of conflicts that Anzaldúa cites and that one experiences living in the borderlands.

2. Many images in the poem depict mixtures of cultures—such as the whole wheat tortilla. But the poet also describes what is missing, as the "*india*" who is "betrayed for 500 years." What does "no longer speaking to you" mean? What other images in the poem show taking away rather than mixing or combining?

3. What do the Spanish slang terms of stanza three have in common? What is the poet's purpose in using words that even native Spanish speakers would avoid using?

4. Explain the conflicts and contradictions of the images in stanzas six and seven.

5. What is the suggestion that the poet proposes "to survive" the "Borderlands"? What are the denotations and connotations of the word "crossroads"? (See pp. 443–444 for definitions of these terms.)

6. List as many reasons as you can for Anzaldúa's decision to incorporate Spanish words into her poem.

WRITING FROM THE TEXT

1. Anzaldúa's poem illustrates perfectly a between-worlds cultural conflict. But we may perceive the idea of a borderland as something other than a cultural or political concept. Write an essay in which you describe the borderland conflicts that you face in your life. You might start by defining the borderland that is central to your self-perception and then focus on particular types of conflicts you face.

2. Write a poem that uses Anzaldúa's work as a model but create images of cultural or psychological conflicts that exist in your life.

3. Write a character analysis (pp. 436–443) of someone you know who is caught "in the borderlands." Very specific and vivid examples of this person's cultural mixtures, frustrations, and conflicts will *show* your character.

4. Write an analysis of this poem (see pp. 443–452) that argues that understanding the images of borderlands is essential to understanding the insights of the poet.

5. Write an analysis of this poem by analyzing the violent images, showing how they reflect the poet's theme.

CONNECTING WITH OTHER TEXTS

1. Compare "The Bridge Poem" (p. 195) with Anzaldúa's poem. What are the comparable features of each?

2. In what ways does Anzaldúa's suggestion to survive by living "*sin fronteras*" or without borders and being "a crossroads" compare to Darnell's solution in "Proper Care and Maintenance"? Write an essay that argues that survival comes from being "a crossroads"—define this image—and then use both Anzaldúa's poem and Straight's short story for support of your thesis.

■ IN ROOMS OF WOMEN

Kim Edwards

After earning her B.A. in English at Colgate, Kim Edwards (b. 1958) earned her M.F.A. from the Iowa Writers' Workshop and then her M.A. in linguistics. She has taught English in Malaysia, Japan, and Cambodia. She is a free-lance writer of fiction and has had work published in the *Paris Review*. She won the Nelson

Algren Award for fiction in 1990. This piece, originally published as a longer essay in the *Michigan Quarterly,* evolved from her experiences teaching in Malaysia and Japan.

When I lived on the East Coast of Malaysia, I used to do aerobics over a Chinese grocery store. I went there almost every afternoon, climbed up a tunnel of concrete stairs to a narrow room infused with the perfume of hair gel and perspiration, cosmetics and worn shoes. In Malaysia, where more than half the female population drifts through the tropical days beneath layers of concealing polyester, this room was an unusual domain of women. We were relaxed here, exposed in our leotards and shorts, our determination as strong as the situation was ironic. For an hour each day we stretched and ran and sweated, devoting ourselves entirely to the care of bodies which, in the outside world, we were encouraged to hide. 1

Malaysia is a multiracial country, with Islamic Malays comprising 55% of the population. Chinese and Indians make up the rest, at 35% and 10%, respectively. Though they have shared the Malay peninsula for generations, these groups maintain distinct languages and cultural traditions. They live together in uneasy proximity, with the biggest division occurring between the Malays, who follow Islam, and the other two groups, who don't. At aerobics, though, these population demographics were reversed; only one or two of the women in that room were Malay. Their presence was an act of quiet daring. Outside, they didn't wear the polyester robes and veils. Inside, they were bold enough to appear among us in a leotard that revealed the contours of their flesh. 2

From the windows of the aerobics room we could see other Malay women as they shopped or chatted, their shiny skirts brushing their brown feet. They wore long-sleeved tunics that hung loosely to the knees, designed to hide every flux and curve of the body. On top of this most wore a *telicon,* a kind of polyester scarf that fastens beneath the chin and flows down, elbow-length, hiding the hair and curve of breasts simultaneously. Though this attire is common now, in pictures from Malaysia that are more than 15 years old, very few of the women cover their heads. Islam has been the predominant religion of the area for centuries, but traditionally it has been a gentle, even tolerant force in Malaysia, tempered by the weather and the easy-going nature of the people. In more remote villages it is still possible to see a lifestyle shaped by its quieter influence. The call to prayer comes five times a day, but little children, both boys and girls, play naked under the fruit trees. Women sit on porches, breast-feeding children. They bathe in the river together, wearing sarongs, and the most serious head-covering is a scarf 3 draped gracefully across the hair on formal occasions. There are separate spheres here, for men and for women, but the focus is less on rules and their enforcement than it is on the harmonious flow of life from one day to another.

4 By the time I went to teach in Malaysia, however, much of the country had been profoundly influenced by the Iranian revolution. The gentle religion that had thrived in the country for centuries changed rapidly as televised images of the Middle East showed a different standard of dress and practice. This growing conservatism invaded every aspect of life, but it was most immediately visible in the dress mandated for girls and women. It began with pressure for them to discard Western clothes or sarongs in favor of the shapeless polyester dresses known as the *baju kurung*. By the time I reached Malaysia, the *baju kurung* and *telicon* were commonplace, and I watched the veils grow longer, heavier, and more somber during the two years I was there. For the more radical there was *purdah*, literally *curtain*, where a veil, usually black, hides the entire face, and dark gloves protect the fingers from view. When I first went to Malaysia, it was rare to glimpse a woman in *purdah*. By the time I left, I saw them almost every other day.

5 Yet at the same time that conservative Islam was strengthening in Malaysia, the government was sending a record number of Malay students overseas to study subjects essential to a developing country. Thus, the students were caught in two opposing forces, one that dictated a life focused solely on Islam, the other that demanded they learn technology from cultures outside of Islam. The place where these two forces met was in the preparatory schools that the students attended for two years before going overseas. Here, the stated administrative goal was to provide, as much as possible, an American style of education, in hopes of reducing culture shock and gaining transfer credit. Here too the religious teachers, alarmed by what they perceived to be a decadent influence, worked hard to ensure that the students understood the terrible evil of the West. Yet belief is an insubstantial thing, difficult to pin down or measure, especially in a population of nearly a thousand students. And so it was the rules they turned to. The equation was a simple one: Those who followed the rules were virtuous, and those who did not were damned.

6 It was in one of these schools that I taught. My college was located in the East Coast of the peninsula, in the heart of the Islamic revival, and the religious teachers, or *ustaz*, were the most powerful men in the school. I'd had Malaysian students in the U.S., young women who appeared in class with tennis shoes poking out from beneath their poly-

ester robes, and I'd been assured by the people who hired me that this dress code wouldn't affect my life; that, as a Westerner, I'd be outside the rules of Islam. Moreover, though I was an English teacher, it was also part of my job to *be* American, and to expose the students to other ways of living that they would encounter when they went overseas. At the time of that interview I was teaching in a major university, with students from dozens of countries in my classes. The idea of being different didn't seem particularly intimidating. I packed my most discreet Western clothes, and expected that I'd exist with the local teachers in a state of mutual tolerance and respect.

What I didn't fully understand, before I left America, is what it 7
means to be different in a society where anything but conformity is greeted with unease. In Malaysia, as in many Asian cultures, there is an emphasis on the group over the individual. This focus is made stronger by Islam, which demands a structured and visible compliance to group norms, and which viewed my particular differences—American, non-Islamic, uncovered woman—as both evil and a threat. In a community of covered women, my short-sleeved blouses and calf-length skirts seemed suddenly immodest. The religious teachers made sure I understood this on my first day there, when they veered off the path—literally walking through mud—to avoid me. They couldn't keep the government from hiring me, but they could isolate me. They treated me as an unclean person, and the most devout students and teachers soon followed their example.

What was hardest for me, though, was the difficulty I had making 8
connections with other women. The veils that covered them were also a kind of barrier I could not seem to cross. I suppose my skin, my hair, the obvious isolation imposed on me by the *ustaz*, seemed as unnerving to them as their veils and long skirts sometimes seemed to me. Some of the women were kind, but distant. If we talked, the subject invariably came back to Islam. Others, those who were extremely devout, were visibly unfriendly. These were the women who wore thick socks with their sandals and dressed in the most somber shades of gray and brown and black. They covered even the heads of their infant daughters, and cast disapproving glances at my exposed forearms, my calves, my toes. In this atmosphere, it was more than a year before I made any women friends at school. There were never many, and I always understood that friendship with me carried risks for them. The *ustaz* and other teachers reprimanded them often for consorting with a Westerner. One of them told me this while we were at her village, sitting on the front steps eating mangos.

9 "But it isn't true," she said, thinking. "It isn't true what they say. You are not Islam. But you are good."

10 In another situation—if I'd been a Peace Corps volunteer—I might have given in, and sought a greater harmony with this community by wearing the *baju kurung*. It would have been the easiest choice—one by one, the few uncovered women at the college were folding under the pressure and donning *telicons*—and I might have done it too, despite the fact that polyester beneath a tropical sun clings like plastic to the skin. I know this is true because I wore it once. I was in a village with my friend and I wanted to make a good impression. I remember it so clearly, the polyester slipping over my head, and the feeling of claustrophobia that accompanied it. At the school, though, wearing the *baju kurung* would have served no purpose except to mislead the students about what they could expect to find in America. Already the *ustaz* spewed a mixed and misleading propaganda: America was evil, all the people were greedy and had no morals. Though I tried to keep a low profile, and to show through my actions that different ways of dressing had very little to do with a person's character, it was clear that the *ustaz* saw my clothes, and the body they revealed, as clear manifestations of Western decadence. They did their best to isolate me, and this was more insidious than simple unfriendliness. In a society which puts its emphasis on the group, isolation is the cruelest punishment of all.

11 The longer I stayed in Malaysia, and the more friends I made, the more dangerous I became. It took my friend's comment, *you are not Islam, but you are good,* to make me realize this. Islam teaches that there is only one way. That way is strict, and tolerates no deviance. By wearing Western clothes, clothes that acknowledged waist and skin, the curve of female flesh, I was suggesting that this was not so, that there was, in fact, a choice. As long as I could be isolated, cast as a symbol of decadence and evil, the implications of my dress could be contained. But as I stayed longer, made friends, committed no evil acts, it became more difficult to cast me in the black and white terms that symbols require. I was not Islam, but neither was I evil. In essence, my presence was a kind of unspoken question, and it was seen by the devout as an act of absolute aggression. From time to time—often during moments of political tension in the Islamic world—the minimal tolerance I was granted waned. At these times I was thrust out of the middle ground with all its ambiguities and became suddenly, unwillingly, polemic.

12 There were several incidents in the two years I was there, but the one that stays most significantly in my mind occurred after the Ayatollah Khomeni called for the death of Salman Rushdie. Stirred up by the

ustaz, the students made repeated denunciations—first against Rushdie himself, then the West in general, and finally against America and the three American teachers at the school. We watched this progression without reacting, but in the face of such anger, it was not enough to be silent. We were outside Islam, and our nonbelief, tolerated during calmer times, now evoked strong and emotional reactions. Even teachers who had seemed indifferent before soon joined in the general denunciation.

One day, in the worst of this, a Malay teacher who had never covered herself arrived at the college dressed in a *baju kurung* with a long black *telicon* falling over it. I remember the stir of pleasure she caused among those already covered. I remember that she passed me on the sidewalk and shot me a beatific smile. Lost, as she was, within a frame of black, I didn't recognize her at first. When I did, I understood her message immediately: *I belong, now, and I pity you, one among the damned.* She, like the more radical women in the town who donned *purdah* veils, was using her body, the negation of it, as a means of political expression. The denial of her body was a kind of aggression, and her aggression was sanctioned and supported—in this case, even demanded—by the community. 13

It is a terrible thing to hate your own body, yet in Malaysia I found that I was never far from this feeling. I was most aware of it every time I left the country, even briefly, and felt anxiety slipping from my shoulders like a heavy cloak. In Singapore I wore shorts without a stir; in Bangkok a sleeveless sundress was nothing to anyone but a sensible way of dealing with the heat. The first time it happened I was in Hong Kong, and I remember feeling light, joyously light, when the only people who followed me were the shopkeepers hoping for a sale. It is a big city, full of lovely, visible bodies. I was anonymous, and I had never felt so free. 14

In the end, of course, I left Malaysia for good. I took a job in Japan, where sometimes, at the end of a long week, I treated myself to a trip to the local hot spring. The first time I went was not long after I arrived. I remember that I felt oddly shy at the prospect of disrobing in a public area, and I realized at that moment how strongly my sense of what was appropriate had been shaped by two years in an Islamic country. Yet I made myself go. The room, at the top of an open stairway, was empty, lovely, built of pine. Moonlight flowed in through the windows and filled the wooden shelves. It was very cold. I undressed completely, as I knew was the custom, folding my clothes carefully. Wrapped in a towel, I stepped around the corner into the hot spring area. 15

16 At first I couldn't see much. Steam rose from the pool and caught the light, creating a kind of silver fog. Even with my closest friends in Malaysia, we had dressed and undressed discreetly, within sarongs, and the image of the body was never something that was shared. I still felt hesitant, standing on the smooth rocks with my towel clutched around me. Through the steam other women appeared, floating against the dark gray rocks, their bodies catching the light in a white and wavering contrast to the darkness below. They were all so different, women whose bodies plodded or strode or moved with grace, women whose breasts were rounded or sloped, pendulous or barely formed. I watched them all with appreciation, my body one among theirs, an individual collection of permutations and shapes, yet one of a set. In that spring, a foreigner and further isolated by my stumbling Japanese, I nonetheless felt a sense of community. For two years I'd carried, unwillingly, a sense of the body as something to hide, and a message that the flesh was an aggression, a sin, an evocation of the darker forces in human nature. In a Japanese hot spring, all this was washed away.

THINKING ABOUT THE TEXT

1. What are the contrasting cultural experiences that Kim Edwards had teaching abroad? What insight resulted from her hot spring experience in Japan?
2. What history of the coverings for women does Edwards give in her essay? Why didn't Edwards wear the *baju kurung?* Do you agree with her reasoning?
3. What personal discomfort did Edwards feel about her decision? Why was her decision interpreted as political?
4. Why did Edwards leave her teaching position in Malaysia? How did her experience in Japan confirm that her decision was a good one for her?

WRITING FROM THE TEXT

1. Describe a time in your life when the way that you were dressed separated you from people with whom you wanted to be friends. Describe specifically the way that you were dressed and how you think people perceived you. *Why* did people respond to you as they did? Like Edwards, see if you can come to some awareness in the process of writing about this experience.

2. Write an analysis of the compromises you have made in dressing to please yourself and at the same time to satisfy some explicit or understood societal dress code. You might contrast others' expectations with your preferred style of dress.

CONNECTING WITH OTHER TEXTS

1. Women especially, although not exclusively, receive messages about their bodies and dress throughout their lives. Many of the pieces in *Between Worlds* address or refer to this issue: "A Work of Artifice" (p. 87), "Bodily Harm" (p. 210), and "The Myth of Thin" (p. 216). Use these materials to write an analysis of one aspect of the issue of women in relation to their bodies.
2. Read Robert Heilbroner's essay "Don't Let Stereotypes Warp Your Judgments" (p. 428), and write an analysis of the problems that Edwards describes. Show in your essay that stereotyping is the source of the trouble.

■ "INDIANS": TEXTUALISM, MORALITY, AND THE PROBLEM OF HISTORY

Jane Tompkins

A Professor of English at Duke University, Jane P. Tompkins (b. 1940) is known as a literary and cultural critic. Her book *West of Everything: The Inner Life of Westerns,* published in 1992, was nominated for a Pulitzer Prize. She is currently at work on *A Life in School,* a work that she says comes from her experience as a classroom teacher and "focuses on the emotional dimensions of teaching. It describes the fear of shame, and desire for admiration and love, that motivate the behavior of both teachers and students in higher education." Tompkins also describes her current work as a relating of her attempts "over four years of experimental teaching to unsettle and reform the authoritarian patterns that molded" her and her university colleagues. According to Ernest Hankamer, Professor of Philosophy at the University of Maryland, Tompkins not only examines how Native Americans are presented in history, but also addresses one of the most critical issues of contemporary research and scholarship: Is there any such thing as objectivity and truth in the search for knowledge. Drawing on her familiarity with this challenge in the field of literature, she describes and confronts its parallel in the area of history. In a balanced and careful fashion, Tompkins makes the case for the possibility of genuine knowledge despite the realities of human ignorance and human fallibility.

1 When I was growing up in New York City, my parents used to take me to an event in Inwood Park at which Indians—real American Indians dressed in feathers and blankets—could be seen and touched by children like me. This event was always a disappointment. It was more fun to imagine that you *were* an Indian in one of the caves in Inwood Park than to shake the hand of an old man in a headdress who was not overwhelmed at the opportunity of meeting you. After staring at the Indians for a while, we would take a walk in the woods where the caves were, and once I asked my mother if the remains of a fire I had seen in one of them might have been left by the original inhabitants. After that, wandering up some stone steps cut into the side of the hill, I imagined I was a princess in a rude castle. My Indians, like my princesses, were creatures totally of the imagination, and I did not care to have any real exemplars interfering with what I already knew.

2 I already knew about Indians from having read about them in school. Over and over we were told the story of how Peter Minuit had bought Manhattan Island from the Indians for twenty-four dollars' worth of glass beads. And it was a story we didn't mind hearing because it gave us the rare pleasure of having someone to feel superior to, since the poor Indians had not known (as we eight-year-olds did) how valuable a piece of property Manhattan Island would become. Generally, much was made of the Indian presence in Manhattan; a poem in one of our readers began: "Where we walk to school today / Indian children used to play," and we were encouraged to write poetry on this topic ourselves. So I had a fairly rich relationship with Indians before I ever met the unprepossessing people in Inwood Park. I felt that I had a lot in common with them. They, too, liked animals (they were often named after animals); they, too, made mistakes—they liked the brightly colored trinkets of little value that the white men were always offering them; they were handsome, warlike, and brave and had led an exciting, romantic life in the forest long ago, a life such as I dreamed of leading myself. I felt lucky to be living in one of the places where they had definitely been. Never mind where they were or what they were doing now.

3 My story stands for the relationship most non-Indians have to the people who first populated this continent, a relationship characterized by narcissistic fantasies of freedom and adventure, of a life lived closer to nature and to spirit than the life we lead now. As Vine Deloria, Jr. has pointed out, the American Indian Movement in the early seventies couldn't get people to pay attention to what was happening to Indians who were alive in the present, so powerful was this country's infatuation with people who wore loincloths, lived in tepees, and roamed the plains

and forests long ago.[1] The present essay, like these fantasies, doesn't have much to do with actual Indians, though its subject matter is the histories of European-Indian relations in seventeenth-century New England. In a sense, my encounter with Indians as an adult doing "research" replicates the childhood one, for while I started out to learn about Indians, I ended up preoccupied with a problem of my own.

This essay enacts a particular instance of the challenge post-structuralism* poses to the study of history. In simpler language, it concerns the difference that point of view makes when people are giving accounts of events, whether at first or second hand. The problem is that if all accounts of events are determined through and through by the observer's frame of reference, then one will never know, in any given case, what really happened. 4

I encountered this problem in concrete terms while preparing to teach a course in colonial American literature. I'd set out to learn what I could about the Puritans' relations with American Indians. All I wanted was a general idea of what had happened between the English settlers and the natives in seventeenth-century New England; post-structuralism and its dilemmas were the furthest thing from my mind. I began, more or less automatically, with Perry Miller, who hardly mentions the Indians at all, then proceeded to the work of historians who had dealt exclusively with the European-Indian encounter. At first, it was a question of deciding which of these authors to believe, for it quickly became apparent that there was no unanimity on the subject. As I read on, however, I discovered that the problem was more complicated than deciding whose version of events was correct. Some of the conflicting accounts were not simply contradictory, they were completely incommensurable, in that their assumptions about what counted as a valid approach to the subject, and what the subject itself was, diverged in fundamental ways. Faced with an array of mutually irreconcilable points of view, points of view which determined what was being discussed as well as the terms of the discussion, I decided to turn to primary sources for clarification, only to discover that the primary sources reproduced the problem all over again. I found myself, in other words, in an epistemological* quandary, not only unable to decide among conflicting versions of events but also unable to believe that any such decision could, in principle, be made. It was a moral quandary as 5

[1]See Vine Deloria, Jr., *God Is Red* (New York, 1973), pp. 39–56.

***post-structuralism:** a theory of literary analysis that contends that a text has no objective or absolute meaning and therefore is open to many interpretations.

***epistemological:** concerning the origin, acquisition, nature, and criteria of knowledge (from epistemology, the theory of knowledge).

well. Knowledge of what really happened when the Europeans and the Indians first met seemed particularly important, since the result of that encounter was virtual genocide. This was the kind of past "mistake" which, presumably, we studied history in order to avoid repeating. If studying history couldn't put us in touch with actual events and their causes, then what was to prevent such atrocities from happening again?

6 For a while, I remained at this impasse. But through analyzing the process by which I had reached it, I eventually arrived at an understanding which seemed to offer a way out. This essay records the concrete experience of meeting and solving the difficulty I have just described (as an abstract problem, I thought I had solved it long ago). My purpose is not to throw new light on antifoundationalist epistemology—the solution I reached is not a new one—but to dramatize and expose the troubles antifoundationalism gets you into when you meet it, so to speak, in the road.

7 My research began with Perry Miller. Early in the preface to *Errand into the Wilderness*, while explaining how he came to write his history of the New England mind, Miller writes a sentence that stopped me dead. He says that what fascinated him as a young man about his country's history was "the massive narrative of the movement of European culture into the vacant wilderness of America."[2] "Vacant?" Miller, writing in 1956, doesn't pause over the word "vacant," but to people who read his preface thirty years later, the word is shocking. In what circumstances could someone proposing to write a history of colonial New England *not* take account of the Indian presence there?

8 The rest of Miller's preface supplies an answer to this question, if one takes the trouble to piece together its details. Miller explains that as a young man, jealous of older compatriots who had had the luck to fight in World War I, he had gone to Africa in search of adventure. "The adventures that Africa afforded," he writes, "were tawdry enough, but it became the setting for a sudden epiphany" (p. vii). "It was given to me," he writes, "disconsolate on the edge of a jungle of central Africa, to have thrust upon me the mission of expounding what I took to be the innermost propulsion of the United States, while supervising, in that barbaric tropic, the unloading of drums of case oil flowing out of the inexhaustible wilderness of America" (p. viii). Miller's picture of himself on the banks of the Congo furnishes a key to the kind of history he will

---

[2]Perry Miller, *Errand into the Wilderness* (Cambridge, Mass., 1964), p. vii; all further references will be included in the text.

write and to his mental image of a vacant wilderness; it explains why it was just here, under precisely these conditions, that he should have had his epiphany.

The fuel drums stand, in Miller's mind, for the popular misconcep- 9
tion of what this country is about. They are "tangible symbols of [America's] appalling power," a power that everyone but Miller takes for the ultimate reality (p. ix). To Miller, "the mind of man is the basic factor in human history," and he will plead, all unaccommodated as he is among the fuel drums, for the intellect—the intellect for which his fellow historians, with their chapters on "stoves or bathtubs, or tax laws," "the Wilmot Proviso" and "the chain store," "have so little respect" (p. viii, ix). His preface seethes with a hatred of the merely physical and mechanical, and this hatred, which is really a form of moral outrage, explains not only the contempt with which he mentions the stoves and bathtubs but also the nature of his experience in Africa and its relationship to the "massive narrative" he will write.

Miller's experiences in Africa are "tawdry," his tropic is barbaric be- 10
cause the jungle he stands on the edge of means nothing to him, no more, indeed something less, than the case oil. It is the nothingness of Africa that precipitates his vision. It is the barbarity of the "dark continent," the obvious (but superficial) parallelism between the jungle at Matadi and America's "vacant wilderness" that releases in Miller the desire to define and vindicate his country's cultural identity. To the young Miller, colonial Africa and colonial America are—but for the history he will bring to light—mirror images of one another. And what he fails to see in the one landscape is the same thing he overlooks in the other: the human beings who people it. As Miller stood with his back to the jungle, thinking about the role of mind in human history, his failure to see that the land into which European culture had moved was not vacant but already occupied by a varied and numerous population, is of a piece with his failure, in his portrait of himself at Matadi, to notice *who* was carrying the fuel drums he was supervising the unloading of.

The point is crucial because it suggests that what is invisible to the 11
historian in his own historical moment remains invisible when he turns his gaze to the past. It isn't that Miller didn't "see" the black men, in a literal sense, any more than it's the case that when he looked back he didn't "see" the Indians, in the sense of not realizing they were there. Rather, it's that neither the Indians nor the blacks *counted* for him, in a fundamental way. The way in which Indians can be seen but not counted is illustrated by an entry in Governor John Winthrop's journal, three hundred years before, when he recorded that there had been a

great storm with high winds "yet through God's great mercy it did no hurt, but only killed one Indian with the fall of a tree."[3] The juxtaposition suggests that Miller shared with Winthrop a certain colonial point of view, a point of view from which Indians, though present, do not finally matter.

12 A book entitled *New England Frontier: Puritans and Indians, 1620–1675*, written by Alden Vaughan and published in 1965, promised to rectify Miller's omission. In the outpouring of work on the European-Indian encounter that began in the early sixties, this book is the first major landmark, and to a neophyte it seems definitive. Vaughan acknowledges the absence of Indian sources and emphasizes his use of materials which catch the Puritans "off guard."[4] His announced conclusion that "the New England Puritans followed a remarkably humane, considerate, and just policy in their dealings with the Indians" seems supported by the scope, documentation, and methodicalness of his project (*NEF*, p. vii). The author's fair-mindedness and equanimity seem everywhere apparent, so that when he asserts "the history of interracial relations from the arrival of the Pilgrims to the outbreak of King Philip's War is a credit to the integrity of both peoples," one is positively reassured (*NEF*, p. viii).

13 But these impressions do not survive an admission that comes late in the book, when, in the course of explaining why works like Helen Hunt Jackson's *Century of Dishonor* had spread misconceptions about Puritan treatment of the Indians, Vaughan finally lays his own cards on the table.

> The root of the misunderstanding [about Puritans and Indians] . . . lie[s] in a failure to recognize the nature of the two societies that met in seventeenth century New England. One was unified, visionary, disciplined, and dynamic. The other was divided, self-satisfied, undisciplined, and static. It would be unreasonable to expect that such societies could live side by side indefinitely with no penetration of the more fragmented and passive by the more con-

[3]This passage from John Winthrop's *Journal* is excerpted by Perry Miller in his anthology *The American Puritans: Their Prose and Poetry* (Garden City, N.Y., 1956), p. 43. In his headnote to the selections from the *Journal,* Miller speaks of Winthrop's "characteristic objectivity" (p. 37).

[4]Alden T. Vaughan, *New England Frontier: Puritans and Indians, 1620–1675* (Boston, 1965), pp. vi–vii; all further references to this work, abbreviated *NEF,* will be included in the text.

> solidated and active. What resulted, then, was not—as many have held—a clash of dissimilar ways of life, but rather the expansion of one into the areas in which the other was lacking. [*NEF*, p. 323]

From our present vantage point, these remarks seem culturally bi- 14
ased to an incredible degree, not to mention inaccurate: Was Puritan society unified? If so, how does one account for its internal dissensions and obsessive need to cast out deviants? Is "unity" necessarily a positive culture trait? From what standpoint can one say that American Indians were neither disciplined nor visionary, when both these characteristics loom so large in the enthnographies? Is it an accident that ways of describing cultural strength and weakness coincide with gender stereotypes—active/passive, and so on? Why is one culture said to "penetrate" the other? Why is the "other" described in terms of "lack"?

Vaughan's fundamental categories of apprehension and judgment 15
will not withstand even the most cursory inspection. For what looked like evenhandedness when he was writing *New England Frontier* does not look that way anymore. In his introduction to *New Directions in American Intellectual History*, John Higham writes that by the end of the sixties

> the entire conceptual foundation on which [this sort of work] rested [had] crumbled away. . . . Simultaneously, in sociology, anthropology, and history, two working assumptions . . . came under withering attack: first, the assumption that societies tend to be integrated, and second, that a shared culture maintains that integration. . . . By the late 1960s all claims issued in the name of an "American mind" . . . were subject to drastic skepticism.[5]

"Clearly," Higham continues, "the sociocultural upheaval of the sixties created the occasion" for this reaction.[6] Vaughan's book, it seemed, could only have been written before the events of the sixties had sensitized scholars to questions of race and ethnicity. It came as no surprise, therefore, that ten years later there appeared a study of European-Indian relations which reflected the new awareness of social issues the sixties had engendered. And it offered an entirely different picture of the European-Indian encounter.

---

[5]John Higham, intro. to *New Directions in American Intellectual History,* ed. Higham and Paul K. Conkin (Baltimore, 1979), p. xii.
[6]Ibid.

16 Francis Jennings' *The Invasion of America* (1975) rips wide open the idea that the Puritans were humane and considerate in their dealings with the Indians. In Jennings' account, even more massively documented than Vaughan's, the early settlers lied to the Indians, stole from them, murdered them, scalped them, captured them, tortured them, raped them, sold them into slavery, confiscated their land, destroyed their crops, burned their homes, scattered their possessions, gave them alcohol, underminded their systems of belief, and infected them with diseases that wiped out ninety percent of their numbers within the first hundred years after contact.[7]

17 Jennings mounts an all-out attack on the essential decency of the Puritan leadership and their apologists in the twentieth century. The Pequot War, which previous historians had described as an attempt on the part of Massachussetts Bay to protect itself from the fiercest of the New England tribes, becomes, in Jennings' painstakingly researched account, a deliberate war of extermination, waged by whites against Indians. It starts with trumped-up charges, is carried on through a series of increasingly bloody reprisals, and ends in the massacre of scores of Indian men, women, and children, all so that Massachussetts Bay could gain political and economic control of the southern Connecticut Valley. When one reads this and then turns over the page and sees a reproduction of the Bay Colony seal, which depicts an Indian from whose mouth issue the words "Come over and help us," the effect is shattering.[8]

18 But even so powerful an argument as Jennings' did not remain unshaken by subsequent work. Reading on, I discovered that if the events of the sixties had revolutionized the study of European-Indian relations, the events of the seventies produced yet another transformation. The American Indian Movement, and in particular the founding of the Native American Rights Fund in 1971 to finance Indian litigation, and a court decision in 1975 which gave the tribes the right to seek redress for past injustices in federal court, created a climate within which histori-

---

[7]See Francis Jennings, *The Invasion of America: Indians, Colonialism, and the Cant of Conquest* (New York, 1975), pp. 3–31. Jennings writes: "The so-called settlement of America was a *re*settlement, a reoccupation of a land made waste by the diseases and demoralization introduced by the newcomers. Although the source data pertaining to populations have never been compiled, one careful scholar, Henry F. Dobyns, has provided a relatively conservative and meticulously reasoned estimate conforming to the known effects of conquest catastrophe. Dobyns has calculated a total aboriginal population for the western hemisphere within the range of 90 to 112 million, of which 10 to 12 million lived north of the Rio Grande" (p. 30).

[8]Jennings, fig. 7, p. 229; and see pp. 186–229.

ans began to focus on the Indians themselves. "Almost simultaneously," writes James Axtell, "frontier and colonial historians began to discover the necessity of considering the American natives as real determinants of history and the utility of ethnohistory as a way of ensuring parity of focus and impartiality of judgment."[9] In Miller, Indians had been simply beneath notice; in Vaughan, they belonged to an inferior culture; and in Jennings, they were the more or less innocent prey of power-hungry whites. But in the most original and provocative of the ethnohistories, Calvin Martin's *Keepers of the Game*, Indians became complicated, purposeful human beings, whose lives were spiritually motivated to a high degree.[10] Their relationship to the animals they hunted, to the natural environment, and to the whites with whom they traded became intelligible within a system of beliefs that formed the basis for an entirely new perspective on the European-Indian encounter.

Within the broader question of why European contact had such a 19
devastating effect on the Indians, Martin's specific aim is to determine why Indians participated in the fur trade which ultimately led them to the brink of annihilation. The standard answer to this question had always been that once the Indian was introduced to European guns, copper kettles, woolen blankets, and the like, he literally couldn't keep his hands off them. In order to acquire these coveted items, he decimated the animal populations on which his survival depended. In short, the Indian's motivation in participating in the fur trade was assumed to be the same as the white European's—a desire to accumulate material goods. In direct opposition to this thesis, Martin argues that the reason why Indians ruthlessly exploited their own resources had nothing to do with supply and demand, but stemmed rather from a breakdown of the cosmic worldview that tied them to the game they killed in a spiritual relationship of parity and mutual obligation.

The hunt, according to Martin, was conceived not primarily as a 20
physical activity but as a spiritual quest, in which the spirit of the hunter must overmaster the spirit of the game animal before the kill can take place. The animal, in effect, *allows* itself to be found and killed, once the hunter has mastered its spirit. The hunter prepared himself through rituals of fasting, sweating, or dreaming which reveal the identity of his prey and where he can find it. The physical act of killing is

[9]James Axtell, *The European and the Indian: Essays in the Ethnohistory of Colonial North America* (Oxford, 1981), p. viii.

[10]See Calvin Martin, *Keepers of the Game: Indian-Animal Relationships and the Fur Trade* (Berkeley and Los Angeles, 1978).

the least important element in the process. Once the animal is killed, eaten, and its parts used for clothing or implements, its remains must be disposed of in ritually prescribed fashion, or the game boss, the "keeper" of that species, will not permit more animals to be killed. The relationship between Indians and animals, then, is contractual; each side must hold up its end of the bargain, or no further transactions can occur.

21 What happened, according to Martin, was that as a result of diseases introduced into the animal population by Europeans, the game suddenly disappeared, began to act in inexplicable ways, or sickened and died in plain view, and communicated their diseases to the Indians. The Indians, consequently, believed that their compact with the animals had been broken and that the keepers of the game, the tutelary spirits of each animal species whom they had been so careful to propitiate, had betrayed them. And when missionization, wars with the Europeans, and displacement from their tribal lands had further weakened Indian society and its belief structure, the Indians, no longer restrained by religious sanctions, in effect, turned on the animals in a holy war of revenge.

22 Whether or not Martin's specific claim about the "holy war" was correct, his analysis made it clear to me that, given the Indians' understanding of economic, religious, and physical processes, an Indian account of what transpired when the European settlers arrived here would look nothing like our own. Their (potential, unwritten) history of the conflict could bear only a marginal resemblance to Eurocentric views. I began to think that the key to understanding European-Indian relations was to see them as an encounter between wholly disparate cultures, and that therefore either defending or attacking the colonists was beside the point since, given the cultural disparity between the two groups, conflict was inevitable and in large part a product of mutual misunderstanding.

23 But three years after Martin's book appeared, Shepard Krech III edited a collection of seven essays called *Indians, Animals, and the Fur Trade*, attacking Martin's entire project. Here the authors argued that we don't need an ideological or religious explanation for the fur trade. As Charles Hudson writes,

> The Southeastern Indians slaughtered deer (and were prompted to enslave and kill each other) because of their position on the outer fringes of an expanding modern world-system. . . . In the modern world-system there is a core region which establishes *economic* relations with its colonial periphery. . . . If the Indians could not produce commodities, they were on the road to cultural extinction. . . . To maximize his chances for survival, an eighteenth-century South-

> eastern Indian had to . . . live in the interior, out of range of European cattle, forestry, and agriculture. . . . He had to produce a commodity which was valuable enough to earn him some protection from English slavers.[11]

Though we are talking here about Southeastern Indians, rather than the subarctic and Northeastern tribes Martin studied, what really accounts for these divergent explanations of why Indians slaughtered the game are the assumptions that underlie them. Martin believes that the Indians acted on the basis of perceptions made available to them by their own cosmology; that is, he explains their behavior as the Indians themselves would have explained it (insofar as he can), using a logic and a set of values that are not Eurocentric but derived from within Amerindian culture. Hudson, on the other hand, insists that the Indians' own beliefs are irrelevant to an explanation of how they acted, which can only be understood, as far as he is concerned, in the terms of a Western materialist economic and political analysis. Martin and Hudson, in short, don't agree on what counts as an explanation, and this disagreement sheds light on the preceding accounts as well. From this standpoint, we can see that Vaughan, who thought that the Puritans were superior to the Indians, and Jennings, who thought the reverse, are both, like Hudson, using Eurocentric criteria of description and evaluation. While all three critics (Vaughan, Jennings, and Hudson) acknowledge that Indians and Europeans behave differently from one another, the behavior differs, as it were, within the order of the same: all three assume, though only Hudson makes the assumption explicit, that an understanding of relations between the Europeans and the Indians must be elaborated in European terms. In Martin's analysis, however, what we have are not only two different sets of behavior but two incommensurable ways of describing and assigning meaning to events. This difference at the level of explanation calls into question the possibility of obtaining any theory-independent account of interaction between Indians and Europeans. 24

At this point, dismayed and confused by the wildly divergent views of colonial history the twentieth-century historians had provided, I decided to look at some primary materials. I thought, perhaps, if I looked at some firsthand accounts and at some scholars looking at those accounts, it would be possible to decide which experts were right and 25

[11]See the essay by Charles Hudson in *Indians, Animals, and the Fur Trade: A Critique of "Keepers of the Game,"* ed. Shepard Krech III (Athens, Ga., 1981), pp. 167–69.

which were wrong by comparing their views with the evidence. Captivity narratives seemed a good place to begin, since it was logical to suppose that the records left by whites who had been captured by Indians would furnish the sort of firsthand information I wanted.

26 I began with two fascinating essays based on these materials written by the ethnohistorian James Axtell, "The White Indians of Colonial America" and "The Scholastic Philosophy of the Wilderness."[12] These essays suggest that it would have been a privilege to be captured by North American Indians and taken off to Canada to dwell in a wigwam for the rest of one's life. Axtell's reconstruction of the process by which Indians taught European captives to feel comfortable in the wilderness, first taking their shoes away and giving them moccasins, carrying the children on their backs, sharing the scanty food supply equally, ceremonially cleansing them of their old identities, giving them Indian clothes and jewelry, assiduously teaching them the Indian language, finally adopting them into their families, and even visiting them after many years if, as sometimes happened, they were restored to white society—all of this creates a compelling portrait of Indian culture and helps to explain the extraordinary attraction that Indian culture apparently exercised over Europeans.

27 But, as I had by now come to expect, this beguiling portrait of the Indians' superior humanity is called into question by other writings on Indian captivity—for example, Norman Heard's *White into Red,* whose summation of the comparative treatment of captive children east and west of the Mississippi seems to contradict some of Axtell's conclusions:

> The treatment of captive children seems to have been similar in initial stages. . . . Most children were treated brutally at the time of capture. Babies and toddlers usually were killed immediately and other small children would be dispatched during the rapid retreat to the Indian villages if they cried, failed to keep the pace, or otherwise indicated a lack of fortitude needed to become a worthy member of the tribe. Upon reaching the village, the child might face such ordeals as running the gauntlet or dancing in the center of a throng of threatening Indians. The prisoner might be so seriously injured at this time that he would no longer be acceptable for adoption.[13]

---

[12]See Axtell, "The White Indians of Colonial America" and "The Scholastic Philosophy of the Wilderness," *The European and the Indian,* pp. 168–206 and 131–67.

[13]J. Norman Heard, *White into Red: A Study of the Assimilation of White Persons Captured by Indians* (Metuchen, N.J., 1973), p. 97.

One account which Heard reprints is particularly arresting. A 28
young girl captured by the Comanches who had not been adopted into a family but used as a slave had been peculiarly mistreated. When they wanted to wake her up the family she belonged to would take a burning brand from the fire and touch it to her nose. When she was returned to her parents, the flesh of her nose was completely burned away, exposing the bone.[14]

Since the pictures drawn by Heard and Axtell were in certain re- 29
spects irreconcilable, it made sense to turn to a firsthand account to see how the Indians treated their captives in a particular instance. Mary Rowlandson's "The Soveraignty and Goodness of God," published in Boston around 1680, suggested itself because it was so widely read and had set the pattern for later narratives. Rowlandson interprets her captivity as God's punishment on her for failing to keep the Sabbath properly on several occasions. She sees everything that happens to her as a sign from God. When the Indians are kind to her, she attributes her good fortune to divine Providence; when they are cruel, she blames her captors. But beyond the question of how Rowlandson interprets events is the question of what she saw in the first place and what she considered worth reporting. The following passage, with its abrupt shifts of focus and peculiar emphases, makes it hard to see her testimony as evidence of anything other than the Puritan point of view:

> Then my heart began to fail: and I fell weeping, which was the first time to my remembrance, that I wept before them. Although I had met with so much Affliction, and my heart was many times ready to break, yet could I not shed one tear in their sight: but rather had been all this while in a maze, and like one astonished: but now I may say as, Psal. 137.1. *By the Rivers of Babylon, there we sate down; yea, we wept when we remembered Zion.* There one of them asked me, why I wept, I could hardly tell what to say: yet I answered, they would kill me: No, said he, none will hurt you. Then came one of them and gave me two spoon-fulls of Meal to comfort me, and another gave me half a pint of Pease; which was more worth than many Bushels at another time. Then I went to see King Philip, he bade me come in and sit down, and asked me whether I woold smoke it (a usual Complement nowadayes among Saints and Sinners) but this no way suited me. For though I had formerly used Tobacco, yet I had left it ever since I was first taken. It seems to be a

[14]See ibid., p. 98.

> Bait, the Devil layes to make men loose their precious time: I remember with shame, how formerly, when I had taken two or three pipes, I was presently ready for another, such a bewitching thing it is: But I thank God, he has now given me power over it; surely there are many who may be better imployed than to ly sucking a stinking Tobacco-pipe.[15]

30 Anyone who has ever tried to give up smoking has to sympathize with Rowlandson, but it is nonetheless remarkable, first, that a passage which begins with her weeping openly in front of her captors, and comparing herself to Israel in Babylon, should end with her railing against the vice of tobacco; and, second, that it has not a word to say about King Philip, the leader of the Indians who captured her and mastermind of the campaign that devastated the white population of the English colonies. The fact that Rowlandson has just been introduced to the chief of chiefs makes hardly any impression on her at all. What excites her is a moral issue which was being hotly debated in the seventeenth century: to smoke or not to smoke (Puritans frowned on it, apparently, because it wasted time and presented a fire hazard). What seem to us the peculiar emphases in Rowlandson's relation are not the result of her having *screened out* evidence she couldn't handle, but of her way of constructing the world. She saw what her seventeenth-century English Separatist* background made visible. It is when one realizes that the biases of twentieth-century historians like Vaughan or Axtell cannot be corrected for simply by consulting the primary materials, since the primary materials are constructed according to *their* authors' biases, that one begins to envy Miller his vision at Matadi. Not for what he didn't see—the Indian and the black—but for his epistemological confidence.

31 Since captivity narratives made a poor source of evidence for the nature of European-Indian relations in early New England because they were so relentlessly pietistic, my hope was that a better source of evidence might be writings designed simply to tell Englishmen what the American natives were like. These authors could be presumed to be less severely biased, since they hadn't seen their loved ones killed by Indians

[15]Mary Rowlandson, "The Soveraignty and Goodness of God, Together with the Faithfulness of His Promises Displayed; Being a Narrative of the Captivity and Restauration of Mrs. Mary Rowlandson (1676)," in *Held Captive by Indians: Selected Narratives, 1642–1836,* ed. Richard VanDerBeets (Knoxville, Tenn., 1973), pp. 57–58.

***seventeenth-century English Separatists:** pertaining to those Puritan colonists who felt that the English Reformation had been incomplete and imperfect and who believed themselves called upon to establish a new, separate, and purified church in the colonies rather than attempt any further reform of the Church of England.

or been made to endure the hardships of captivity, and because they weren't writing propaganda calculated to prove that God had delivered his chosen people from the hands of Satan's emissaries.

The problem was that these texts were written with aims no less 32
specific than those of the captivity narratives, though the aims were of a different sort. Here is a passage from William Wood's *New England's Prospect*, published in London in 1634.

> To enter into a serious discourse concerning the natural conditions of these Indians might procure admiration from the people of any civilized nations, in regard of their civility and good natures. . . . These Indians are of affable, courteous and well disposed natures, ready to communicate the best of their wealth to the mutual good of one another; . . . so . . . perspicuous is their love . . . that they are as willing to part with a mite in poverty as treasure in plenty. . . . If it were possible to recount the courtesies they have showed the English, since their first arrival in those parts, it would not only steady belief, that they are a loving people, but also win the love of those that never saw them, and wipe off that needless fear that is too deeply rooted in the conceits of many who think them envious and of such rancorous and inhumane dispositions, that they will one day make an end of their English inmates.[16]

However, in a pamphlet published twenty-one years earlier, 33
Alexander Whitaker of Virginia has this to say of the natives:

> These naked slaves . . . serve the divell for feare, after a most base manner, sacrificing sometimes (as I have heere heard) their own Children to him. . . . They live naked in bodie, as if their shame of their sinne deserved no covering: Their names are as naked as their bodie: They esteem it a virtue to lie, deceive and steale as their master the divell teacheth to them.[17]

According to Robert Berkhofer in *The White Man's Indian*, these di- 34
vergent reports can be explained by looking at the authors' motives. A favorable report like Wood's, intended to encourage new emigrants to America, naturally represented Indians as loving and courteous, civilized and generous, in order to allay the fears of prospective colonists.

---

[16]William Wood, *New England's Prospect,* ed. Vaughan (Amherst, Mass., 1977), pp. 88–89.

[17]Alexander Whitaker, *Goode Newes from Virginia* (1613), quoted in Robert F. Berkhofer, Jr., *The White Man's Indian: Images of the American Indian from Co to the Present* (New York, 1978), p. 19.

Whitaker, on the other hand, a minister who wishes to convince his readers that the Indians are in need of conversion, paints them as benighted agents of the devil. Berkhofer's commentary constantly implies that white men were to blame for having represented the Indians in the image of their own desires and needs.[18] But the evidence supplied by Rowlandson's narrative, and by the accounts left by early reporters such as Wood and Whitaker, suggests something rather different. Though it is probably true that in certain cases Europeans did consciously tamper with the evidence, in most cases there is no reason to suppose that they did not record faithfully what they saw. And what they saw was not an illusion, was not determined by selfish motives in any narrow sense, but was there by virtue of a *way* of seeing which they could no more consciously manipulate than they could choose not to have been born. At this point, it seemed to me, the ethnocentric bias of the firsthand observers invited an investigation of the cultural situation they spoke from. Karen Kupperman's *Settling with the Indians* (1980) supplied just such an analysis.

35 Kupperman argues that Englishmen inevitably looked at Indians in exactly the same way that they looked at other Englishmen. For instance, if they looked down on Indians and saw them as people to be exploited, it was not because of racial prejudice or antique notions about savagery, it was because they looked down on ordinary English men and women and saw them as subjects for exploitation as well.[19] According to Kupperman, what concerned these writers most when they described the Indians were the insignia of social class, of rank, and of prestige. Indian faces are virtually never described in the earliest accounts, but clothes and hairstyles, tattoos and jewelry, posture and skin color are. "Early modern Englishmen believed that people can create their own identity, and that therefore one communicates to the world through signals such as dress and other forms of decoration who one is, what group or category one belongs to."[20]

36 Kupperman's book marks a watershed in writings on European-Indian relations, for it reverses the strategy employed by Martin two years before. Whereas Martin had performed an ethnographic analysis of Indian cosmology in order to explain, from within, the Indians' motives for engaging in the fur trade, Kupperman performs an ethnographic

[18]See, for example, Berkhofer's discussion of the passages he quotes from Whitaker (*The White Man's Indian,* pp. 19, 20).
[19]See Karen Ordahl Kupperman, *Settling with the Indians: The Meeting of English and Indian Cultures in America, 1580–1640* (Totowa, N.J., 1980), pp. 3, 4.
[20]Ibid., p. 35.

study of seventeenth-century England in order to explain, from within, what motivated Englishmen's behavior. The sympathy and understanding that Martin, Axtell, and others extend to the Indians are extended in Kupperman's work to the English themselves. Rather than giving an account of "what happened" between Indians and Europeans, like Martin, she reconstructs the worldview that gave the experience of one group its content. With her study, scholarship on European-Indian relations comes full circle.

37 It may well seem to you at this point that, given the tremendous variation among the historical accounts, I had no choice but to end in relativism.* If the experience of encountering conflicting versions of the "same" events suggests anything certain it is that the attitude a historian takes up in relation to a given event, the way in which he or she judges and even describes "it"—and the "it" has to go in quotation marks because, depending on the perspective, that event either did or did not occur—this stance, these judgments and descriptions are a function of the historian's position in relation to the subject. Miller, standing on the banks of the Congo, couldn't see the black men he was supervising because of his background, his assumptions, values, experiences, goals. Jennings, intent on exposing the distortions introduced into the historical record by Vaughan and his predecessors stretching all the way back to Winthrop, couldn't see that Winthrop and his peers were not racists but only Englishmen who looked at other cultures in the way their own culture had taught them to see one another. The historian can never escape the limitations of his or her own position in history and so inevitably gives an account that is an extension of the circumstances from which it springs. But it seems to me that when one is confronted with this particular succession of stories, cultural and historical relativism is not a position that one can comfortably assume. The phenomena to which these histories testify—conquest, massacre, and genocide, on the one hand; torture, slavery, and murder on the other—cry out for judgment. When faced with claims and counterclaims of this magnitude one feels obligated to reach an understanding of what actually did occur. The dilemma posed by the study of European-Indian relations in early America is that the highly charged nature

---

***relativism:** the view that everything is relative, whether to a culture or to an individual. "Everything" includes not only personal values but also standards of social justice and of individual integrity. In its extreme form, relativism leads to the denial of any ultimate absolute or objective criteria of truth or behavior except itself. Thus, ironically, relativism claims to be absolutely true while denying that claim to any other point of view.

of the materials demands a moral decisiveness which the succession of conflicting accounts effectively precludes. That is the dilemma I found myself in at the end of this course of reading, and which I eventually came to resolve as follows.

38 After a while it began to seem to me that there was something wrong with the way I had formulated the problem. The statement that the materials on European-Indian relations were so highly charged that they demanded moral judgment, but that the judgment couldn't be made because all possible descriptions of what happened were biased, seemed to contain an internal contradiction. The statement implied that in order to make a moral judgment about something, you have to know something else first—namely, the facts of the case you're being called upon to judge. My complaint was that their perspectival nature would disqualify any facts I might encounter and that therefore I couldn't judge. But to say as I did that the materials I had read were "highly charged" and therefore demanded judgment suggests both that I was reacting to something real—to some facts—*and* that I had judged them. Perhaps I wasn't so much in the lurch morally or epistemologically as I had thought. If you—or I—react with horror to the story of the girl captured and enslaved by Comanches who touched a firebrand to her nose every time they wanted to wake her up, it's because we read this as a story about cruelty and suffering, and not as a story about the conventions of prisoner exchange or the economics of Comanche life. The *seeing* of the story as a cause for alarm rather than as a droll anecdote or a piece of curious information is evidence of values we already hold, of judgments already made, of facts already perceived as facts.

39 My problem presupposed that I couldn't judge because I didn't know what the facts were. All I had, or could have, was a series of different perspectives, and so nothing that would count as an authoritative source on which moral judgments could be based. But, as I have just shown, I did judge, and that is because, as I now think, I did have some facts. I seemed to accept as facts that ninety percent of the native American population of New England died after the first hundred years of contact, that tribes in eastern Canada and the northeastern United States had a compact with the game they killed, that Comanches had subjected a captive girl to casual cruelty, that King Philip smoked a pipe, and so on. It was only where different versions of the same event came into conflict that I doubted the text was a record of something real. And even then, there was no question about certain major catastrophes. I believed that four hundred Pequots were killed near Saybrook, that Winthrop was the Governor of the Massachusetts Bay

Colony when it happened, and so on. My sense that certain events, such as the Pequot War, did occur in no way reflected the indecisiveness that overtook me when I tried to choose among the various historical versions. In fact, the need I felt to make up my mind was impelled by the conviction that certain things *had* happened that shouldn't have happened. Hence it was never the case that "what happened" was completely unknowable or unavailable. It's rather that in the process of reading so many different approaches to the same phenomenon I became aware of the difference in the attitudes that informed these approaches. This awareness of the interests motivating each version cast suspicion over everything, in retrospect, and I ended by claiming that there was nothing I could know. This, I now see, was never really the case. But how did it happen?

Someone else, confronted with the same materials, could have de- 40
cided that one of these historical accounts was correct. Still another person might have decided that more evidence was needed in order to decide among them. Why did I conclude that none of the accounts was accurate because they were all produced from some particular angle of vision? Presumably there was something in my background that enabled me to see the problem in this way. That something, very likely, was post-structuralist theory. I let my discovery that Vaughan was a product of the fifties, Jennings of the sixties, Rowlandson of a Puritan world-view, and so on lead me to the conclusion that all facts are theory dependent because that conclusion was already a thinkable one for me. My inability to come up with a true account was not the product of being situated nowhere; it was the product of certitude that existed *somewhere else*, namely, in contemporary literary theory. Hence, the level at which my indecision came into play was a function of particular beliefs I held. I was never in a position of epistemological indeterminacy, I was never *en abîme*.* The idea that all accounts are perspectival seemed to give me a superior standpoint from which to view all the versions of "what happened," and to regard with sympathetic condescension any person so old-fashioned and benighted as to believe that there really was some way of arriving at the truth. But this skeptical standpoint was just as firm as any other. The fact that it was also seriously disabling—it prevented me from coming to any conclusion about what I had read—did not render it any less definite.

At this point something is beginning to show itself that has up to 41
now been hidden. The notion that all facts are only facts within a perspective has the effect of emptying statements of their content. Once I

**en abîme:* "in the abyss"

had Miller and Vaughan and Jennings, Martin and Hudson, Axtell and Heard, Rowlandson and Wood and Whitaker, and Kupperman; I had Europeans and Indians, ships and canoes, wigwams and log cabins, bows and arrows and muskets, wigs and tattoos, whisky and corn, rivers and forts, treaties and battles, fire and blood—and then suddenly all I had was a metastatement* about perspectives. The effect of bringing perspectivism to bear on history was to wipe out completely the subject matter of history. And it follows that bringing perspectivism to bear in this way on any subject matter would have a similar effect; everything is wiped out and you are left with nothing but a single idea—perspectivism itself.

42 But—and it is a crucial but—all this is true only if you believe that there is an alternative. As long as you think that there are or should be facts that exist outside of any perspective, then the notion that facts are perspectival will have this disappearing effect on whatever it touches. But if you are convinced that the alternative does not exist, that there really are no facts except as they are embedded in some particular way of seeing the world, then the argument that a set of facts derives from some particular worldview is no longer an argument against that set of facts. If all facts share this characteristic, to say that any one fact is perspectival doesn't change its factual nature in the slightest. It merely reiterates it.

43 This doesn't mean that you have to accept just anybody's facts. You can show that what someone else asserts to be a fact is false. But it does mean that you can't argue that someone else's facts are not facts *because they are only the product of a perspective*, since this will be true of the facts that you perceive as well. What this means then is that arguments about "what happened" have to proceed much as they did before post-structuralism broke in with all its talk about language-based reality and culturally produced knowledge. Reasons must be given, evidence adduced, authorities citied, analogies drawn. Being aware that all facts are motivated, believing that people are always operating inside some particular interpretive framework or other is a pertinent argument when what is under discussion is the way beliefs are grounded. But it doesn't give one any leverage on the facts of a particular case.[21]

***metastatement:** a statement about statements, i.e., analysis of the use of language. Similarly, **metadiscourse** is the discussion of the use of language.

[21]The position I've been outlining is a version of neopragmatism.* For an exposition, see *Against Theory: Literary Studies and the New Pragmatism,* ed. W. J. T. Mitchell (Chicago, 1985).

***neopragmatism:** here used to mean common sense and practicality as the criteria for truth or knowledge.

Know that it causes real pain and real suffering to real people. Know that it threatens our very survival. And know that this is just as much a crime against humanity as anything the Nazis ever did. It is likely that the indigenous people of the United States will never demand that those guilty of such criminal activity be punished for their deeds. But the least we have the right to expect—indeed, to demand—is that such practices finally be brought to a halt. 33

THINKING ABOUT THE TEXT

1. What is the history of the controversy that Churchill describes?
2. What are the specific examples that Churchill proposes for other racial and ethnic groups to parallel the team names and halftime shows that refer to Native American culture? What is the effect on the reader of his examples? What is the author's intention?
3. What are the positive responses to the controversy that Churchill cites in his essay? Why does he include these two examples?
4. What is the history of the trial of Julius Streicher, and how do facts about the Nuremberg tribunal contribute to Churchill's argument?
5. What are the crimes against the American Indian that Churchill enumerates in his essay? Why does he believe that using American Indian culture for team names, logos, mascots, and advertising perpetuates the crimes against the Native American?
6. Do you perceive any flaws in Churchill's reasoning? Are you sympathetic to his point? Do you agree with his demand for change?

WRITING FROM THE TEXT

1. Write a response to Ward Churchill that agrees with his points or argues against them. Review the suggestions for writing argument (pp. 414–416) to write a convincing paper.
2. Recall from your childhood the images of the American Indian that appeared in books, on television, and in films. Write a descriptive analysis of a few specific examples to show that Churchill is correct or incorrect in his position that popular images of the Native American are "degrading caricatures" that perpetuate the crimes against them.

CONNECTING WITH OTHER TEXTS

1. Argue that the crimes against American Indians discussed by Churchill have their origins in the historical treatments of Native Americans as discussed by Jane Tompkins (p. 137).
2. In an analytical essay, compare the images of African Americans that have disappeared from popular culture (such as Little Black Sambo and Step 'n' Fetchit) with the images of Native Americans that still permeate popular culture in the United States. What conclusion can you draw from an analysis of these images and their presence or absence in popular culture?
3. Write an analysis of recent film depictions of the Native American to argue that Hollywood has or has not moved beyond caricature in its depiction of this culture.

ON THE SUBWAY

Sharon Olds

A widely anthologized poet and recipient of numerous grants and awards for her work, Sharon Olds (b. 1942) received a B.A. from Stanford University and a Ph.D. from Columbia University. Having served as director of the creative writing program at New York University, she continues to coordinate their writing program for the disabled at Sigesmund Goldwater Memorial Hospital. Her poetry collections include *Satan Says* (1980), *The Dead and The Living* (1984), *The Father* (1992), and *The Wellspring* (1996). The poem printed here is a revised form of the one published in *The Gold Cell* (1987).

The young man and I face each other.
His feet are huge, in black sneakers
laced with white in a complex pattern like a
set of intentional scars. We are stuck on
opposite sides of the car, a couple of
molecules stuck in a rod of light
rapidly moving through darkness. He has
or my white eye imagines he has the
casual cold look of a mugger,
alert under hooded lids. He is wearing
red, like the inside of the body
exposed. I am wearing old fur, the
whole skin of an animal taken and
used. I look at his raw face,

he looks at my dark coat, and I don't
know if I am in his power—
he could take my coat so easily, my
briefcase, my life—
or if he is in my power, the way I am
living off his life, eating the steak
he may not be eating, as if I am taking
the food from his mouth. And he is black
and I am white, and without meaning or
trying to I must profit from his darkness,
the way he absorbs the murderous beams of the
nation's heart, as black cotton
absorbs the heat of the sun and holds it. There is
no way to know how easy this
white skin makes my life, this
life he could break so easily, the way I
think his back is being broken, the
rod of his soul that at birth was dark and
fluid, rich as the heart of a seedling
ready to thrust up into any available light.

THINKING ABOUT THE TEXT

1. If the speaker initially considers this encounter a face-off, in what ways does the boy seem to be intimidating? Analyze the narrator's descriptions of him.
2. Describe the narrator's appearance. Is it consistent with her inner awareness and values? Do you think the boy on the subway would be surprised to know her thoughts?
3. In what way is she in his power and he in hers? Does either one of them seem to be choosing to exercise his or her power over the other? Explain the irony here.
4. Cite phrases and images that reveal the narrator's sensitivity here. How do these contribute to the tone of the poem?
5. Find images of light versus darkness throughout, and discuss how this image pattern relates to Olds' insights about racial and economic barriers.
6. Does the poem seem hopeful or bleak? Support your interpretation with details from the poem.

WRITING FROM THE TEXT

1. List several insights that can be drawn from this poem. Then focus on any one insight and analyze how the images and tone support this insight. Cite specific details as you interpret.
2. Write an essay analyzing the various stereotypes and assumptions that are implicit in the narrator's descriptions of the boy. Then reverse the point of view and imagine the stereotypes the boy may hold in his perception of the narrator.
3. Olds focuses on a rather commonplace situation and manages to bring exceptional sensitivity to this issue. Focus on a common encounter of your own and show how it also revealed more complex issues and emotions beneath the surface.

CONNECTING WITH OTHER TEXTS

1. Using specific details from this poem and from Marcus Mabry's "Living in Two Worlds" (p. 124), show how the privileged status in each narration is a source of guilt.
2. Write an essay analyzing how stereotyping is the source of tension in "On the Subway," "Proper Care and Maintenance" (below), and "Black Men and Public Space" (p. 219). You may want to refer to Heilbroner's essay "Don't Let Stereotypes Warp Your Judgments" (p. 428).

■ PROPER CARE AND MAINTENANCE

Susan Straight

Except for the time when she did her M.F.A. work with James Baldwin at the University of Massachusetts, Susan Straight (b. 1960) has always lived in Riverside, California, a mile from the hospital where both she and her husband were born. Straight describes her community as a storytelling one: "Everyone tells stories, almost legends, about people and cars and events, and I've heard them for so many years that I wanted my stories to be on paper instead of only in the air." Her novel in stories, *Aquaboogie,* won a Milkweed National Fiction Prize. Her novel *I Been in Sorrow's Kitchen and Licked Out All the Pots* was published in 1992. True to the values of her community's oral traditions, Susan Straight is an engaging storyteller and speaker on the writing process. This short story about Darnell first appeared in the *Los Angeles Times Magazine,* June 30, 1991. Straight's novel about Darnell, *Blacker Than a Thousand Midnights,* was published in 1994. Her most recent novel is *The Gettin Place* (1996).

"See, man, I told you she was gon do it—she pimpin' you, Darnell." 1 Victor shook his head and watched Charolette hang out the window of the El Camino. "She pimpin' you big-time."

"Daddy!" she yelled, her round face bobbing furiously above the 2 door. "I want juice! In my *mouth!*"

Darnell turned away from Victor and Ronnie and the other men 3 sitting on folding chairs and boxes in the vacant lot. A blackened trash barrel breathed smoke in the early morning cool, and the pepper tree branches dangled around them. "I'm fixin' to go over my dad's," Darnell said. "He told me Sixth Avenue Baptist wants somebody to clean up that lot they got behind the church. I'll be back tomorrow, Victor."

He started toward the El Camino, and Victor called out, "Damn, 4 homey, I might be a stockbroker by then." Ronnie and the others laughed.

He put Charolette back in her car seat and she said, "*Daddy*, I hun- 5 gry. Hurry.' She watched out the window, saying, "Fire, Daddy," when they circled around the lot to the street.

"Yeah, smoke," he said, and she looked triumphant. She was almost 6 2, trying to learn about a hundred words a day. She stuck out her chin and sang to herself now, while he tried not to smile.

He hadn't wanted a baby—Brenda had surprised him. When 7 Brenda first brought her home from the hospital and laid her on a quilt in the living room, Charolette had spent hours sleeping on her stomach and Darnell had had all day to stare at her. The government funds had been cut off for seasonal firefighters. He stared at Charolette, but all he could think was that she looked like a horny toad, those rounded-flat lizards that ran past him when he was close to the fire: they'd streak out from the rocks, looking ridiculous. Charolette's belly was distended round and wide, far past her nonexistent butt, and her spindly arms and legs looked useless. He'd sat home watching this baby, impatient with the helpless crying and the way she lay on her back waving her limbs like a turned-over beetle.

Now she was old enough to talk smack, and he could jam her right 8 back—she understood. When he pulled into the driveway at his father's house, she ran inside for his mother's hot biscuits, and then she ran back to him, hollering, "Daddy, blow on it!"

"You so bad, blow on it yourself," he said, and she spit rapidly at the 9 steaming biscuit. "Yeah, right," he laughed. "Wet it up."

Darnell's mother came to the doorway in her robe. "Brenda restin'?" 10

"Sleepin' 24-7," Darnell said. "All day, except when she at work." 11

12 "That's how it is your first three months," his mother said, getting that blurry look like every woman who found out Brenda was pregnant again. "You sleep like somebody drop a rock on your chest. I remember."

13 Darnell didn't mind waking up at 6, when the curtains were just starting to hold light. Charolette called for him now. If he had a job, he had to start early anyway, before it got too hot. Brenda was a clerk for the County of Rio Seco and didn't have to go to work until 9. So Darnell left her in the warm tangle of sheets and took Charolette to his father's, where the men sat in their trucks drinking coffee before they went out. His father and Roscoe Wiley trimmed trees; Floyd King and his son Nacho hauled trash from construction sites. They all made a big deal of Charolette still in her footed sleeper, stamping from lap to lap and trying to pull dashboard knobs.

14 This morning Roscoe took her into his pickup truck and gave her a smell of his coffee. "Red Man, this girl stubborn as you," he said to Darnell's father.

15 Darnell watched Charolette poke at the glass. "Window dirty," she said.

16 "Least she look a lot better," Floyd said from his cab. "Next one gotta look like Brenda, cause this one look like Darnell spit her out his ownself."

17 Yeah. Brenda hated hearing that, Darnell thought. He remembered when the baby began to stare back at him, to crawl, and then her eyebrows grew in thick-curved like his, her teeth spaced and square like his.

18 His mother came out to the driveway for the newspaper. "Y'all need to look for a bigger place," she said. "A house, for Charolette to play in the yard. And you get a house, we can find a washer so Brenda won't drag that laundry up and down no apartment stairs."

19 "Mr. Nard rentin' out his brother's house on Pablo," Floyd called. "Got three bedrooms, and he want $625 a month.

20 "Yeah, and we can barely pay our $400 now," Darnell said.

21 "I told you get you some yards," his father said. "Steady yards, like I did."

22 "You ain't got no cleanup jobs for me next week?" Darnell said, looking at the thin chain-saw scar on his father's forearm.

23 "Yeah, Sixth Avenue Baptist wants you to do the lot—take two of you, two-day job."

24 "You gon get Victor?" Nacho said.

25 "Yeah." After Charolette, he knew he couldn't go to college for Fire Science, and he'd gotten a warehouse job, but they laid everyone off a few months later. His father had fixed up the engine on the old El Camino, which had been in the side yard since Roscoe had gotten a new truck. He lent Darnell a mower, blower, weed-whacker and rakes.

"Victor a stone alcoholic," Roscoe said. "Livin' at Jackson Park 26
now."

Nacho said, "Shoot, he taught me how to draw, back in junior high. 27
The brother was smart, too smart, started talkin' 'bout high school was boring. He just want to hang out, all day."

"He hangin' out now," Roscoe said, frowning. "All day." 28

Darnell said. "He just don't like nobody to tell him what to do. He 29
don't like to answer to nobody." He'd always watched Victor, who was five years older than he was; Victor got kicked out of school for spelling out "Superfly" in gold studs down his jeans, for outlining his fly with rhinestones. He'd quit the football team freshman year, refusing to cut off his cornrows.

"I'm tellin you, go door-to-door and get you some yards," Darnell's 30
father went on, loud. "Build up a clientele." Sophia and Paula, Darnell's younger sisters, came running out in their nightgowns to see Charolette.

"Shoot, every dude with a truck and mower runnin' around calling 31
himself a gardener," Roscoe said. "They want all these new houses gettin' built."

"Yeah, you should go see Trent," Nacho said. "He got his own busi- 32
ness, landscape design, and he live up there in Grayglen."

Floyd laughed. "With the gray men." 33

The houses were laid out in circling streets, and a sea of red-tile 34
roofs was all that showed above miles of sandy block wall. Darnell saw crews of Mexican guys building new walls at one intersection, short Indian-looking men with bowed legs and straw hats. Two white guys with thick, sun-reddened forearms watched.

Trent's street was all two-story houses and lush gardens. "A brother 35
livin' up here?" Darnell said to himself. He could tell by the yards most of these people already had gardeners. Trent was in his driveway, loading his truck with black hosing and pipes.

"Hey, Darnell," he said, and Darnell was surprised Trent remem- 36
bered the name. Trent was Victor's age. "What's up?"

"Not much," Darnell said. "I heard you were livin' large with your 37
business, and I thought maybe you had too many yards, know somebody who needs a gardener." He watched Trent count sprinkler heads.

"Man, I just do the planning and landscaping—I don't cut grass," 38
Trent said, not looking up. "I ain't into maintenance. After the irrigation, I'm gone."

"Yeah, Nacho said you went to college for this, huh?" Darnell said, 39
uncomfortable. "I just thought you might have some advice, 'cause I *been* knocked on doors, and that ain't workin'."

40 Trent clicked his spit against his teeth. "I heard you workin'" with Victor Small and Ronnie Hunter. But you gotta buy 'em some Olde English 800 to get through the day, huh?" He coiled hosing. "They scare people off."

41 Darnell folded his arms. "Yeah. Depends." So you think you better, huh, *brotha*man? Victor and Ronnie love to talk about your ass—grinnin' and skinnin' 'til you drive down the street and shake your head.

42 "Sorry I can't help you," Trent said, reaching down awkwardly into the truck bed again. "Good luck, bro."

43 "Thanks, *brotha*man," Darnell said. Threading through the streets, he watched for shaggy grass and dandelions. Had to be a few yards let go in this maze.

44 At four lawns that looked weeks overgrown, he knocked on doors, his heart beating fast, but no one answered. Another ragged one, and a woman came to the door. He said, "Hi, I'm a gardener and I wondered if you needed your yard done today or on a regular basis." He remembered his father's words, back when Darnell had been small enough to stand on cool porches and listen.

45 "I gave you five dollars yesterday," the woman said impatiently, looking back into her house, and Darnell raised his eyes. She was about 40, her lips more invisible than most white women's—no lipstick, he realized, just when she said, "I can't afford another donation."

46 "I wasn't here yesterday," Darnell said, but she was adding loudly, "I don't need anything done today."

47 "You didn't give me five dollars," he said, finally looking at her eyes, rimmed with green shadow.

48 "Oh, I'm sorry, I—your hat," she said, fingers holding her collar. "A man came by yesterday, he said he was out of work, and I—he had a hat."

49 "Yeah," Darnell said, hard. "Another Raiders fan." He walked back down the bricks, wanting to kick apart the fancy iron mailbox exactly like Trent's.

50 He drove, swerving through the streets until he found the only opening in the block walls. Where the cops? Can't they see me? He remembered getting stopped months ago, Victor and Ronnie and him driving around up here looking for yards. The cop said, "You guys have been cruising for a while, knocking on doors. You got a reason?" Victor said, "Mowers in the back, man." He didn't care who he was talking to. "Don't you have a record, didn't you do a few weeks last year?" the cop said to Victor. "What was your first clue, Sherlock?" Victor said. "Was it my big arms?"

The tires slipped on loose dirt at the corner. Yeah, our marketing 51
strategy just ain't gettin' it—door-to-door get us a sentence. If it was summer, he'd find a fire to make himself feel better, watch the flames shake up brush-covered hills, imagine himself on the line close to the roar and heat.

Three new houses were going up, and the bellied, blond construc- 52
tion workers hammering and laying brick looked up at the car. Born that way, he thought, his tongue thick and hot. Come out with hair like that, trucks with toolboxes behind the cab, stomachs already big enough—they get the job just like I can dance. Charolette's car seat rattled empty against his elbow when he scratched the tires on the asphalt, but skidding around a corner didn't make him feel any better. He looked at the crumbs crushed deep into the corduroy chair.

He'd used his Clark Kent voice one day on the phone, after he saw 53
an ad for a security guard that read, "Mature white male pref." He'd made the appointment with the cheery secretary just to see if he could, and then he threw a coffee cup against the wall; the clotted breaking sound made him feel better until he heard Charolette's high-pitched screams, like a burning animal caught in dense chaparral. "That's illegal, that ad," Brenda was yelling, and he'd yelled back, "Right, let's call our lawyer immediately, baby, we'll take this all the way to the Supreme Court."

He pressed his fingers into the crumbs, feeling cool along his shoul- 54
ders. I can't pull that act now. Driving down the hill toward the Westside, he thought about going by Jackson Park, hanging out, talking yang about anything, but he slowed at his father's street. "Daddy here!" Charolette screamed. Ain't this crazy? he thought. When he told Victor, "She my buddy now," Victor said, "You weak, nigga—you suppose to let *grown* females whip you."

She fell asleep when he drove around the old downtown section, 55
with the big historic houses and huge sloping corner lawns. He and his father had cut some of these, when Darnell was 11 and just learning to mow right.

At one old yellow house, ivy hanging over the porch, roses thick, 56
he saw three Mexican guys in the yard. Straightening Charolette's bent, lolling neck, he watched them ripping out a huge circle of ivy in the lawn, talking and chopping with machetes. Their radio blasted Mexican music, horns and swinging voices going so fast Darnell imagined them playing at 78 speed. He saw a shadow at the front screen: a gray-haired lady came out to watch the men, and he pulled away from the curb before she saw him.

57 All weekend, he kept hearing the music; he even turned the radio or TV to Mexican stations. "What are you trippin' about?" Brenda said, folding the laundry that lay in drifts all around the living room. Charolette threaded string into the wrought-iron balcony, the front door open so they could see her.

58 "Nothin'," Darnell said, listening to what he thought was an accordion.

59 "You really miss that firefightin' slave you had, huh?" Victor said when they'd been at the church lot for a few hours. "Crazy nigga loved bein' up there in the mountains with them cowboy white dudes."

60 "No, man," Darnell said. "It wasn't about the other guys. I just liked it up there." They pulled at the skeletal tumbleweeds and burned grass in the hard dirt, gathered bottles and disposable diapers. Darnell saw the rough brush where he'd dug firebreaks, the red-barked manzanita and tiny plants. Now and then he let his vision blur while he tore out weeds, and usually when he raised his head he was surprised to see cars rushing past him. But today he kept seeing the Mexican guys, their hats and laughing and music.

61 After they'd come down the long dirt road from the dump, Darnell gave Victor $50 and kept $75 for himself. He waited in front of Tony's Market, and when Victor came out with the big 40-ounce bottles of Olde English 800, he said, "I can't hang with you guys today; I got somethin' to do."

62 Victor unscrewed the cap. "Take me by Esther's, on your pop's street." He still wore his hair long and cornrowed neatly to his head, the tails stopped just at his neck. He let it go weeks before he could pay Esther to redo it, and today it was rough and clouded between the rows. "You go home to baby-bawlin', man, and I'll be chillin' out, eightballin'." He took a big swallow.

63 The next morning his father told him Mrs. Panadoukis, the doctor's wife up in Hillcrest, wanted her whole bank of ice plant cleared. When he got to Jackson Park, Darnell threw the empty car seat in the back, and Victor said, "Nigga, this the last job I want 'til next week. Don't you know black absorbs heat, man?"

64 "Shut up, Victor," Ronnie said. "You know you already broke."

65 "Hey," Victor said, "I ain't *gotta* work every day, like Darnell."

66 The ice plant had died, and the woody, tangled mesh was easy to tear from the dirt, but the piles were heavy. Ronnie and Victor took off their shirts, and Darnell remembered they didn't have anywhere to wash them. Their backs glistened in front of him. Ronnie's radio was far

away, the music thumping faintly when they clambered up the steep bank, but at lunch they unwrapped their sandwiches and turned the radio up.

"'I don't go nowhere without my jimhat,'" Victor sang along with Digital Underground. Then he said, "Yeah, my man Darnell ain't been usin' no jimmys he got another one on the way." 67

Darnell said, "Least I ain't gotta worry about AIDS—you be messin' with them strawberries." He wondered how they'd gotten that name, the desperate, ashy girls who hung out at the park doing anything with anybody for some smoke. 68

"When you need some, man, you don't care," Ronnie said. Darnell heard a scraping step on the cement, and he saw Mrs. Panadoukis, her face frozen, coming around to the back door with her purse. She looked away from them, her lips tight, and fumbled with her keys. They were silent, the music loud. 69

When she'd closed the door, Victor and Ronnie busted up. Darnell saw her held-tight cheeks. He looked at Ronnie's chest, Victor's fresh braids; he remembered the Mexican guys laughing in the ivy. The Mexican guys could be saying anything, talking dirty or yanging about the lady they were working for, but it would be in Spanish and they'd sound happy—their radio was jolly, funny, that bright quick music spangled as mariachi suits. Ronnie's radio—uh-uh. The bass was low, shuffling around her, and the drums slapped her in the face. 70

"You ready?" he said, and they went back up the bank, bending and tearing, Victor making them laugh. 71

"Darnell, you just graduated a few years ago, man, you remember Mr. Rentell, that drivin' teacher? Serious redhead, always tryin' to talk hip. He came by the park the other day, talkin' 'bout, 'Victor, is that you?' He start storyin' 'bout why was I hangin' out, couldn't I do better? I told him, 'Man, I can still drive, don't worry—let me have your car, I'll show you.'" He threw ice plant down the slope to Darnell. 72

They loaded the El Camino in the front yard. Mrs. Panadoukis had paid them, her eyes averted. Darnell thought, Sorry we don't look good. He saw a Baggie on the lawn and bent to pick it up, thinking it had dropped from the car. But someone else had put it on the grass: he saw a green flier inside and a small rock. Looking down the street, he watched a silver Toyota pickup stop for a second at each lawn. A hand threw out Baggies. He saw rakes and shovels against the cab window, mower handles in the bed. 73

"Nguyen's Oriental Gardening Service," the flier read. He spread it on his lap in the car, and Victor said, "Come on, man, it's hot." 74

75 "Let experienced Oriental Gardeners take care of your lawn and shrubs, we will mow, edge and fertilize for only $60 a month. Weekly." The note had been printed on a computer, and a picture of a bonsai tree was in the corner, with a phone number.

76 Darnell took Victor and Ronnie to the store and then to the park, hearing Mexican music and the voices of the Asian guys he remembered from school. Tim Bui and Don Nguyen—two Vietnamese guys who wanted to be homeboys, hanging out at the picnic tables with Darnell and the brothers. They tried to imitate Darnell's voice, and after a while they could dance better than some of the crew that performed at assemblies. Nguyen—that last name was like Smith in Vietnam, he remembered them explaining. "Like Johnson for niggas," Ronnie had laughed. Alone in the car, he drove to his mother's.

77 Charolette ran out to see him. His father and Roscoe were stacking wood from a pepper tree beside the house. "Y'all finish the doctor's-wife's job?"

78 "Yeah," Darnell said. "Ice plant was dead anyway."

79 "She pay you? She love to talk when she get started," his father said.

80 "She didn't get started with us," Darnell said, slipping the flier into his pocket.

81 "You pay off your crew?" Roscoe said. "You the big boss now—you take your cut?"

82 "What, you think I'm crazy?" All the way home, Charolette put the rock inside the Baggie and took it out. "Little rock?" she said. He looked at the stone—those guys were smart. The flier couldn't blow away, couldn't get wet.

83 He kept thinking of the Vietnamese kids at school, how the teacher had looked at them, but he saw Mexican faces for some reason. When he and Charolette made their weekend shopping trip, he tried not to stare. On the Westside, almost as many Mexican families lived on some streets as black families. He watched the men riding 10-speeds with plastic bags of laundry tied to the handlebars—guys, alone, leaving one to guard clothes in the Laundromat and going in a group to the store. They bought whole chickens, tortillas, chips, fruit, and he watched their faces, knowing that was where he was supposed to look to figure out what he was missing. On the street, he saw a mariachi band walking down the sidewalk with the huge guitars and glittering suits: they went into Our Lady of Guadalupe, where Darnell had gone to Catholic school.

On Monday, he drove slowly past the corners where they always 84
gathered, crowds of Mexican men waiting for daywork. And he saw the shortest, Indian-looking guys—their eyes were slanted, their hair thick and straight, their legs bowed into curves.

The men shifted and scattered when a construction truck stopped 85
at the curb, crowding around the driver. Darnell watched five guys jump in the back. Some of the disappointed ones stared at him, and he tried to recall what he could of high school Spanish. All that came to his head was "*¿Como se llama?*" and "*Hermano, hermana*"—useless stuff. He licked his lips and leaned.

"I need a guy who can speak English," he said, and three came over. 86

"I speak English, bro," a skinny, dark guy said, and Darnell knew 87
he'd been in prison by the teardrops tattooed near his eyes.

"I'll give you 10 bucks to help here, man," Darnell said. "I need two 88
dudes who know how to mow lawns, and I want them to look Oriental, you know, like those guys over there." He pointed to the short, slim men.

"He wants *los indios*," the guy said, muttering to the men. Several of 89
the Indian men gathered around him, and he brought over four with anxious faces and small, tilted eyes under thick brows. Darnell thought of Charolette's brows suddenly, how delicate they were.

"You guys can do gardening?" he asked. They nodded, and he said, 90
"But I have to be able to talk to you—who speaks English, even some?"

The youngest one, without a hat, said, "I try speak *pequeño*. My 91
brother not so much." He gestured to the older one next to him, in a baseball cap.

"Get in," Darnell said. The two men were so small compared to Vic- 92
tor and Ronnie that air still flowed through to touch his shoulders. "Where you from?"

The young one said, "Mexico." 93

"I know—I mean where in Mexico?" 94

"Osaka," he said, and Darnell frowned. Wasn't that a city in 95
Japan?—he'd heard the name. "Write it down, OK?" he said, and the guy wrote *Oaxaca* on the back of the green flier.

He watched them work at Mrs. Munson's, where his father had 96
given him the yard. Anyone could mow, and Juan, the younger one, did the front while Jose did the back. Darnell edged and helped them blow the paths clean. It took 25 minutes.

"Be back on the corner next Monday," he told them. "I think I got 97
regular work if you want it. Four bucks an hour."

Juan said, "All day?" 98

99 Darnell said, "I hope so. Where you learn English, man?"

100 "I went in college one year," Juan said. "I love English."

101 "Chill out, homey," Darnell smiled. "See you Monday."

102 He wouldn't tell Brenda what he had in mind, and when she said, "You're drivin' me crazy with that little plannin' smile and won't give up no information." Darnell just smiled it again.

103 "I gotta go see Nacho," he said. "Maybe I can make some more money."

104 "The suspense is killing me," she said, rolling her eyes, and he didn't even get angry. He went to Nacho's and said, "You the artist—can you make me a flier, one I can Xerox? I'll show you."

105 He laid out the sheet for Nacho. On it he'd written the message, and Nacho laughed. "You serious, man? You want me to print or script?"

106 "Print," Darnell said. "And put a picture in both corners—those little incense burners like you see in a Japanese garden." He thought for a minute. "Man, I hate to copy, but I bet the pine tree works."

107 He copied 300 of the sheets on light-blue paper, and then he went to the nursery for small, sparkling white rocks in bulk and bought Baggies at the store.

108 He took Charolette with him, long before dawn. She was sleepy for a few minutes, but he whispered to her, and she said, "Dark, Daddy?" He said, "We're cruisin' in the dark, baby. Watch out for trains." He remembered being angry, in a hurry, stuck behind the long trains that came through the Westside; now he tried to catch them so that she could listen in wonder to the clacking wheels and watch for the engineers.

109 "Choo-choo train!" she yelled.

110 They went to Grayglen first, Darnell driving on the wrong side of the street to drop Baggies on lawns. He pitched two onto Trent's, laughing. Charolette couldn't throw them far enough, and he gave her a pile to wreck so she wouldn't cry. "These dudes ain't even up yet, but they'll go to work soon, and then they'll find this when they get the paper," he told her.

111 "Newspaper?"

112 "You got it." They twisted through all the new streets, then went downtown and dropped more. They ended up in the university neighborhood when the sky turned gray. "We don't want nobody to see us, or we turn into pumpkins," he said, and she remembered Halloween, he could tell, because her face lit up.

113 "Cut pumpkin!" she screamed.

114 "You just like me, don't forget *nothin'*," he said, reaching over to touch her hair. "You're gonna kick some butt in school, girl."

His father laughed silly. "'Tuan's Oriental Landscape Maintenance Service,'" he read out loud to Roscoe. "Boy a damn gardener, talkin' 'bout maintenance. 'Expert Asian landscapers will mow, edge, fertilize and maintain your garden with weekly service for only $50 a month. Call now to keep your landscape beautiful.'" His father turned to him. "Who the hell is Tuan?" 115

Darnell said, "Nuh-uh—it's Juan. And Jose. If I get enough calls this week, I'm hirin' two Mexican dudes." 116

Roscoe said, "You know, he ain't crazy. They all want Mexican guys. But I don't know how you gon pull it off when they see your ugly face." 117

"They ain't gotta see me, just send the check here, to your address," Darnell said. "In case we move." His father raised his eyebrows. "And I'ma need to borrow some money, for a new mower. If this works, I'ma have to get a truck." 118

"You got the El Camino," his father said. 119

"Yeah, but I need that for my jobs. I need a used Toyota or Isuzu, for these dudes. Paint the name on the side." 120

The eyebrows went higher. "You serious, huh?" 121

"I want to call Mr. Nard about his house. Serious as a heart attack." 122

He practiced his voice in the bathroom. Brenda was at work. He tried to remember Tim Bui's words, which ones he left out, how he talked. He sat watching Oprah with the sound off, but no one called until the next day, and he was ready. A woman said, "Tuan's Landscape?" and he said, "Yes, ma'am. I can help you." 123

"Are you reliable?" 124

"Yes, ma'am, very reliable. We come every week, and do the best job." He chopped off the words carefully, his heart racing heat all the way to his ears. 125

He told Juan that they would have to comb their hair straight back, and no straw hats. He took them to K mart for white T-shirts, green pants and work boots. "And no talking, if the people are around to watch you," he said. "I don't want them to hear Spanish." 126

When he explained it as best he could, Juan frowned. "But if they say, speak to you? If they want different?" 127

"Just say like this—'Call my boss, he help you.'" 128

Juan looked at the flier closely and smiled. "I am Tuan, eh?" 129

"Maybe, man," Darnell said. "Maybe I am." 130

But he felt strange staying at home, waiting for the calls in the empty, tiny and stifling apartment. Summer—the shimmering bells passed on the sidewalk below, the Mexican popsicle guys with their carts. Darnell went to the bathroom mirror, pulled at his eyes to make 131 them long and narrow. He touched his new haircut, a fade with three lines above each ear. His father hated the razored cuts, said, "What the hell, look like a damn mower got you."

132 He stared at his face. "Homey, don'cha know me?" He'd seen Victor at a stoplight last week, near the park. Victor's eyes were half-slit and hard. "Work been *slow*, huh?"

133 "I been doin' somethin', but I got somethin' for us next week," Darnell had said. He did—his father had told someone Darnell would clean up property for the fire season.

134 He knew Nacho had told Victor about the flier, about Tuan's. He splashed water onto his face. Homey—don'cha know me? His chest was clotted with warmth when he sat on the cold edge of the bathtub. "What you gon do if somebody don't pay?" Roscoe had said.

135 "Go over there and collect."

136 "Who you—Tuan's bodyguard? His butler?" Roscoe laughed.

137 "Shit, whoever I gotta be, long as I get the cash." But he was shaking.

138 "I was just playin'," Roscoe said gently, touching his elbow. "You gon do outside jobs, get a beeper so you don't miss calls. Beepers are cheap."

139 "Yeah, and I'll look like a dope dealer," Darnell had said, turning away. "Ain't that what I'm supposed to look like anyway?"

140 He paced around the living room now, the bells fading, and he turned up the radio to pound the walls.

141 In a few weeks, he had so many yards that his father and Roscoe found a blue Toyota pickup he could buy on time. He took the El Camino to Jackson Park the next day, sweating, thinking of Victor's eyes. He'd rehearsed what he would say. Victor raised his chin half an inch when he saw Darnell. "*Brotha*man," Victor said. "What you need?"

142 "Need you guys for a job," Darnell said.

143 "Homey, don'cha know me? I'm just a nigga with an attitude."

144 "You ready?" Darnell said.

145 Victor smiled. "I heard you was hirin' illegals, man. You don't want no niggas, word is." Ronnie hovered beside him, silent.

146 "If I don't want no niggas, I better kill myself," Darnell said. "I got two Mexican guys doin' yards. Now I can do other jobs all the time. But see, Victor, man, I gotta be sweatin' every day, man, not like you. I can't wait 'til I'm in the mood.

147 "Man, you think you big shit," Victor smiled harder. "At least I ain't no strawberry."

148 Darnell breathed in through his nose. "I ain't pink." He hesitated. He had practiced this, too. "I'm just whipped, by two women. And got another one comin' to further kick my black butt. You always talkin' about Niggas ain't meant to be out in the sun, absorbin' that heat. Proper maintenance keep you from shrinkin' and fadin', man, don't you know?" He waited. "You comin'?"

149 Victor ran his hands over his braids. "I'm thirsty, man."

150 When he got home, the phone rang before he could put Charolette down. He held her giggling under his arm and said, "Tuan's Landscape Maintenance."

151 A man said, "This sounds like a really great deal. I live in the Grayglen area, and your prices are reasonable compared to others."

152 "Yes, we try to make price very cheap." He was out of breath and said, "Please, can you hold, sir?" He put Charolette down. "When you like us to start?"

153 "Well, as soon as possible," the man said. "Can you come Friday?"

154 "Yes, Friday." Everybody wanted a perfect lawn for the weekend. "We come Fridays, and you send a check to Tuan's Oriental Landscape, 2498 Picasso St. Pay by mail once a month."

155 "Picasso Street?" the man said. "Isn't that on the Westside?"

156 "Yes, sir."

157 "I thought you guys were Oriental—I bet you want to get out of a minority area like that. Pretty rough in the black neighborhood."

158 Darnell's face and neck prickled. "Yes, sir, we move soon. Very soon." After he'd hung up, he saw Charolette unfolding the towels Brenda had stacked on the couch. "Daddy talking?" She imitated his clipped voice. "We move soon, sir."

159 "You ain't gotta talk like that," he said roughly. "Leave the towels alone before I get mad." He stared at the laundry, at her round face set hard. "Let's go look at a washing machine for Mama."

160 "Move, Daddy?" she asked again, since it had bothered him when she said it the first time. When he tried to take the towels away, she said angrily, "*Move*, Daddy!" and shoved him. He pretended to fall over on his back, and then he caught her on his chest to tickle her, so she couldn't get away.

THINKING ABOUT THE TEXT

1. All short stories have conflict; if there is no conflict, there is no story. But some stories do not have an obvious protagonist/antagonist conflict. What are the conflicts in Darnell's life?

2. How does Darnell resolve his problems? How does his creating a steady source of income also embroil him in another conflict?
3. Fiction and film have negatively stereotyped African-American men. Which stereotypes does this short story counter in its portrayal of Darnell?
4. What other cultural stereotypes are understood in this story?
5. The short story is positive (it has a happy ending) and humorous in tone. How is the humor achieved?
6. What are the serious issues behind this entertaining story?

WRITING FROM THE TEXT

1. Write an analysis of Darnell's character—his values, motivations, and goals—based on inferences you can draw from the text. (See character analysis section, pp. 436–443.)
2. Write a description of the conflicts in Darnell's life. In what ways is he caught between worlds? How does he resolve his problem?
3. Write a paper that illustrates how stereotyping is the underlying cause of problems for Darnell.

CONNECTING WITH OTHER TEXTS

1. Write an essay that connects Joan Steinau Lester's essay "Passing" (p. 234) to the story of Darnell. Analyze the many ways that Darnell "passes" to solve his problems.
2. Use this short story and other essays in the text—"Living in Two Worlds" (p. 124), "Black Men and Public Space" (p. 219), and "The Atlanta Riot" (p. 224)—to write an analysis of some of the problems that African Americans face.
3. Read Robert L. Heilbroner's "Don't Let Stereotypes Warp Your Judgments" (p. 428) to argue that stereotyping is a source of the problems in "Proper Care and Maintenance."

■ WHEN THE GOVERNMENT DECIDES YOUR RACE

Judy Scales-Trent

A professor of the State University of New York at Buffalo Law School since 1984, Judy Scales-Trent (b. 1940) previously spent twelve years in Washington, D.C., practicing civil rights law. She earned her M.A. in French from Middlebury

College and her J.D. from Northwestern University. She has published *Notes of a White Black Woman: Race, Color, Community* (1995), a collection of autobiographical essays that describe her experiences living "simultaneously inside and outside of both white and black communities." She believes that it is valuable to teach about difference "only if we teach the students to see the connectedness between people where they formerly saw only disconnectedness. . . . We must help them blur the categories, turn concrete walls to powder." A version of the following essay appeared as a guest commentary in the *Los Angeles Times* on July 3, 1996.

In preparation for the next census, in the year 2000, the government is holding hearings around the country on the issue of whether it should revise its current racial categories—black, white, Asian/Pacific Islander and American Indian. 1

The government has been creating racial categories and classifying citizens by race during the census for at least a hundred years. And every 10 years it changes its mind about what those various "races" might be. For example, in 1890, there were four separate categories of African Americans. Between 1950 and 1970, Asian Indians were considered "white." Mexican Americans, too, used to be counted as "white"; today, they are in the census' only ethnic category, "Hispanic origin," which can be any race. 2

These formal changes remind us that "race" is created, then re-created over time. Now there is a move underway for allowing "multiracial" as an answer to "What is your race?" Some of those who want the "multiracial" category are calling for a march on Washington July 20, 1996 to support this change. March organizer Charles Michael Byrd says that adding this category would be a "step toward doing away with the whole concept of race." 3

This option is favored by many people who have, for example, one parent who is white and one who is black. For them it is a powerful issue of family identity. But many civil rights groups oppose this option for fear that the count of, say, black Americans will be diminished if the choice "multiracial" appears. They argue that statistical data about black Americans has been helpful for civil rights gains. 4

In my view, the debate is helpful for the whole country because it highlights our confusion about race and our bigotry. 5

I am a civil rights lawyer who has been practicing, teaching and writing about civil rights law for 25 years. Most recently, I have used my vantage point as a black American with white skin to write about how Americans create race on an ongoing basis. And I have come to the conclusion that the question of "mixed" ("multiracial") and "pure" racial groups is bizarre, because, even though the government tries 6 mightily to define who belongs in which racial category, its racial definitions make no sense. For example, the current rule states that you are black if you "have origins in any of the black racial groups of Africa"; you are white if you "have origins in any of the original [sic] white groups of Europe." Now, tell me: Who among us knows their "origins"? For if you count back in your own family, doubling the number each generation (two parents, four grandparents, eight great-grandparents, etc.) you will find 32,000 possible ancestors during the previous 15 generations alone. Do you know their "origins"? What could "pure" or "mixed" possibly mean in that context?

7 Rep. Tom Sawyer (D-Ohio), who chaired the House subcommittee that held hearings on this issue, put it this way: "We seem to have this sense of this illusion of purity, that on the one hand we act as though we know what we are talking about when we refer to notions such as race and ethnicity. I am not sure we have even the vaguest idea."

8 I disagree, however, with the notion that adding a "multiracial" category will be a "step toward doing away with the concept of race." Let's not forget that Nazi Germany created a special racial category for the children of Aryans and Jews *(Mischlinge)*, and that South Africa created the category "coloured" for those people it considered "mixed." These were not progressive acts. They were the acts of oppressive regimens trying to rationalize their oppression.

9 I also disagree with those who argue that adding the category would make civil rights gains more unlikely by reducing the count of, say, black Americans. Statistical data can help improve the lot of black Americans—but only when white Americans want this to happen; the numbers themselves have no independent power. For example, Congress can ignore—and has ignored—powerful statistics about the plight of black Americans when it sets its legislative agenda. In 1990, the DC-based Sentencing Project reported that, nationwide, one-fourth of all black men in their twenties were in the criminal justice system—either on probation, on trial, in jail, or on parole. Last fall, that same group reported that by 1995, that percentage has increased to one-third. And Congress has taken no steps to address these staggering statistics.

10 Similarly, in discrimination cases where there is strong statistical proof of discrimination, the Supreme Court can change—and has changed—how it interprets civil rights law in order to minimize the power of those statistics. For example, in *City of Richmond v. Croson*, the Supreme Court struck down a set-aside program Richmond created to help minority businesses obtain city construction contracts, despite evidence which showed that although minority groups made up half of

Richmond's population, only 0.67% of the construction contract money spent by Richmond in the preceding five years had gone to minority owned businesses. Evidence also showed that only 0.65% of the gross receipts of all businesses in this country was realized by minority businesses. Based on past Court rulings, these statistics, along with other similar evidence, should have been sufficient to justify upholding the constitutionality of the Richmond plan. But the Court changed its rules on how to interpret the Constitution in set-aside cases, and these statistics lost their force. We should not forget that one key attribute of power is the ability to change the rules to maintain that power.

The question of whether there should be a "multiracial" category brings these issues to the fore. But don't think that changing census categories will necessarily change lives. America has been changing its formal categories of race for over 100 years now, and the lives of black Americans are still very hard. The only way to improve the lives of black Americans is to address the issue that lies under the census controversy—why this country has always worked so aggressively to sort its people by race. It is clear that America creates race, then sorts by race, in order to create a hierarchy—in order to determine who is supposed to win, and who is supposed to lose. And as long as we refuse to address this underlying dynamic, the lives of those whom America puts at the bottom will remain desperately hard. 11

THINKING ABOUT THE TEXT

1. What is Scales-Trent's strategy in beginning her essay by mentioning that the government periodically changes its racial categories and creates new ones?
2. If people of mixed racial heritage are in favor of creating a category for "multiracial" descent, why are some civil rights groups opposed to this?
3. After twenty-five years of experience as a civil rights lawyer, what has Scales-Trent come to believe about the distinction between "mixed" and "pure" racial groups?
4. Why does Scales-Trent disagree that adding a "multiracial" category will be a "step toward doing away with the whole concept of race"? Why does she also disagree with those who fear that the category would threaten civil rights gains?
5. What does Scales-Trent argue is the only way to improve the lives of black Americans?

WRITING FROM THE TEXT

1. Write an analysis of Scales-Trent's argument techniques: her reliance on sound reasoning and on accurate information, her use of inoffensive language and detailed support, and her anticipation of other perspectives and possible objections.
2. Using details from Scales-Trent's essay, write an argument from the perspective of someone of mixed racial heritage and convince your peers that they should or shouldn't favor the "multiracial" category.

CONNECTING WITH OTHER TEXTS

1. Considering Scales-Trent's claim that "this country has always worked so aggressively to sort its people by race," write an argument exploring the implications of this statement. You can include supporting details from any of the following: "Living in Two Worlds" (p. 124), "Proper Care and Maintenance" (p. 170), "On the Subway" (p. 168), "Black Men and Public Space" (p. 219), and "The Atlanta Riot" (p. 224).
2. Read "Passing" (p. 234) and write an analysis of the potential impact of the "multiracial" category and concept on people who feel pressured to "pass" into the dominant race to be accepted.

LIKE MEXICANS

Gary Soto

As a child, Gary Soto (b. 1952) worked as a migrant laborer in the agricultural San Joaquin Valley of California. He went to a city college, discovered poetry, and decided he would "like to do something like this." He took university classes and began meeting other writers. He describes his wanting to write poetry as "a sort of fluke" because he came from an "illiterate family," one without books and one that did not encourage the children to read. Soto teaches in the English department at Berkeley. The essay included here was first published in *Small Faces* in 1986.

1 My grandmother gave me bad advice and good advice when I was in my early teens. For the bad advice, she said that I should become a barber because they made good money and listened to the radio all day. "Honey, they don't work como burros," she would say every time I visited her. She made the sound of donkey's braying. "Like that, honey!" For the good advice, she said that I should marry a Mexican girl. "No

Okies, hijo"—she would say—"Look, my son. He marry one and they fight every day about I don't know what and I don't know what." For her, everyone who wasn't Mexican, black, or Asian were Okies. The French were Okies, the Italians in suits were Okies. When I asked about Jews, whom I had read about, she asked for a picture. I rode home on my bicycle and returned with a calendar depicting the important races of the world. "Pues si, son Okies tambien!" she said, nodding her head. She waved the calendar away and we went to the living room where she lectured me on the virtues of the Mexican girl: first, she could cook and, second, she acted like a woman, not a man, in her husband's home. She said she would tell me about a third when I got a little older.

I asked my mother about it—becoming a barber and marrying Mexican. She was in the kitchen. Steam curled from a pot of boiling beans, the radio was on, looking as squat as a loaf of bread. "Well, if you want to be a barber—they say they make good money." She slapped a round steak with a knife, her glasses slipping down with each strike. She stopped and looked up. "If you find a good Mexican girl, marry her of course." She returned to slapping the meat and I went to the backyard where my brother and David King were sitting on the lawn feeling the inside of their cheeks. 2

"This is what girls feel like," my brother said, rubbing the inside of his cheek. David put three fingers inside his mouth and scratched. I ignored them and climbed the back fence to see my best friend, Scott, a second-generation Okie. I called him and his mother pointed to the side of the house where his bedroom was a small aluminum trailer, the kind you gawk at when they're flipped over on the freeway, wheels spinning in the air. I went around to find Scott pitching horseshoes. 3

I picked up a set of rusty ones and joined him. While we played, we talked about school and friends and record albums. The horseshoes scuffed up dirt, sometimes ringing the iron that threw out a meager shadow like a sundial. After three argued-over games, we pulled two oranges apiece from his tree and started down the alley still talking school and friends and record albums. We pulled more oranges from the alley and talked about who we would marry. "No offense, Scott," I said with an orange slice in my mouth, "but I would never marry an Okie." We walked in step, almost touching, with a sled of shadows dragging behind us. "No offense, Gary," Scott said, "but I would *never* marry a Mexican." I looked at him: a fang of orange slice showed from his munching mouth. I didn't think anything of it. He had his girl and I had mine. But our seventh-grade vision was the same: to marry, get jobs, buy cars and maybe a house if we had money left over. 4

5 We talked about our future lives until, to our surprise, we were on the downtown mall, two miles from home. We bought a bag of popcorn at Penneys and sat on a bench near the fountain watching Mexican and Okie girls pass. "That one's mine," I pointed with my chin when a girl with eyebrows arched into black rainbows ambled by. "She's cute," Scott said about a girl with yellow hair and a mouthful of gum. We dreamed aloud, our chins busy pointing out girls. We agreed that we couldn't wait to become men and lift them onto our laps.

6 But the woman I married was not Mexican but Japanese. It was a surprise to me. For years, I went about wide-eyed in my search for the brown girl in a white dress at a dance. I searched the playground at the baseball diamond. When the girls raced for grounders, their hair bounced like something that couldn't be caught. When they sat together in the lunchroom, heads pressed together, I knew they were talking about us Mexican guys. I saw them and dreamed them. I threw my face into my pillow, making up sentences that were good as in the movies.

7 But when I was twenty, I fell in love with this other girl who worried my mother, who had my grandmother asking once again to see the calendar of the Important Races of the World. I told her I had thrown it away years before. I took a much-glanced-at snapshot from my wallet. We looked at it together, in silence. Then grandma reclined in her chair, lit a cigarette, and said, "Es pretty." She blew and asked with all her worry pushed up to her forehead: "Chinese?"

8 I was in love and there was no looking back. She was the one. I told my mother who was slapping hamburger into patties. "Well, sure if you want to marry her," she said. But the more I talked, the more concerned she became. Later I began to worry. Was it all a mistake? "Marry a Mexican girl," I heard my mother say in my mind. I heard it at breakfast. I heard it over math problems, between Western Civilization and cultural geography. But then one afternoon while I was hitchhiking home from school, it struck me like a baseball in the back: my mother wanted me to marry someone of my own social class—a poor girl. I considered my fiancee, Carolyn, and she didn't look poor, though I knew she came from a family of farm workers and pull-yourself-up-by-your-bootstraps ranchers. I asked my brother, who was marrying Mexican poor that fall, if I should marry a poor girl. He screamed "Yeah" above his terrible guitar playing in his bedroom. I considered my sister who had married Mexican. Cousins were dating Mexican. Uncles were remarrying poor women. I asked Scott, who was still my best friend, and he said, "She's too good for you, so you better not."

I worried about it until Carolyn took me home to meet her parents. 9
We drove in her Plymouth until the houses gave way to farms and ranches and finally her house fifty feet from the highway. When we pulled into the drive, I panicked and begged Carolyn to make a U-turn and go back so we could talk about it over a soda. She pinched my cheek, calling me a "silly boy." I felt better, though, when I got out of the car and saw the house: the chipped paint, a cracked window, boards for a walk to the back door. There were rusting cars near the barn. A tractor with a net of spiderwebs under a mulberry. A field. A bale of barbed wire like children's scribbling leaning against an empty chicken coop. Carolyn took my hand and pulled me to my future mother-in-law who was coming out to greet us.

We had lunch: sandwiches, potato chips, and iced tea. Carolyn and 10
her mother talked mostly about neighbors and the congregation at the Japanese Methodist Church in West Fresno. Her father, who was in khaki work clothes, excused himself with a wave that was almost a salute and went outside. I heard a truck start, a dog bark, and then the truck rattle away.

Carolyn's mother offered another sandwich, but I declined with 11
a shake of my head and a smile. I looked around when I could, when I was not saying over and over that I was a college student, hinting that I could take care of her daughter. I shifted my chair. I saw newspapers piled in corners, dusty cereal boxes and vinegar bottles in corners. The wallpaper was bubbled from rain that had come in from a bad roof. Dust. Dust lay on lamp shades and window sills. These people are just like Mexicans, I thought. Poor people.

Carolyn's mother asked me through Carolyn if I would like a *sushi*. 12
A plate of black and white things were held in front of me. I took one, wide-eyed, and turned it over like a foreign coin. I was biting into one when I saw a kitten crawl up the window screen over the sink. I chewed and the kitten opened its mouth of terror as she crawled higher, wanting in to paw the leftovers from our plates. I looked at Carolyn who said that the cat was just showing off. I looked up in time to see it fall. It crawled up, then fell again.

We talked for an hour and had apple pie and coffee, slowly. Finally, 13
we got up with Carolyn taking my hand. Slightly embarrassed, I tried to pull away but her grip held me. I let her have her way as she led me down the hallway with her mother right behind me. When I opened the door, I was startled by a kitten clinging to the screen door, its mouth screaming "cat food, dog biscuits, *sushi*. . . ." I opened the door and the kitten, still holding on, whined in the language of hungry

animals. When I got into Carolyn's car, I looked back: the cat was still clinging. I asked Carolyn if it were possibly hungry, but she said the cat was being silly. She started the car, waved to her mother, and bounced us over the rain-poked drive, patting my thigh for being her lover baby. Carolyn waved again. I looked back, waving, then gawking at a window screen where there were now three kittens clawing and screaming to get in. Like Mexicans, I thought. I remembered the Molinas and how the cats clung to their screens—cats they shot down with squirt guns. On the highway, I felt happy, pleased by it all. I patted Carolyn's thigh. Her people were like Mexicans, only different.

THINKING ABOUT THE TEXT

1. What is the advice that Soto's grandmother gives him? On what is her advice based? What do you imagine would be her third point—the one she will give him when he is older?
2. What is Soto's mother's position? Why does she not seem interested in his questions?
3. How does Soto characterize his seventh-grade adolescent world? Find specific images in the text that create pictures of this time of his life.
4. What specifically does Soto see in his girlfriend's house and family that makes him comfortable? What specifically makes them "like Mexicans"?

WRITING FROM THE TEXT

1. Write about a time in your life when you feared going to a classmate's or friend's house to meet the family. Write a narrative that focuses on this experience and what you learned.
2. Write an essay in which you argue that people ought to marry within their own ethnic or racial group *or* that marrying out of one's racial or ethnic group can be advantageous. Use specific reasons to convince your reader.

CONNECTING WITH OTHER TEXTS

1. Write an essay analyzing how both Soto and the narrator of "Digging" (p. 21) deal with the expressed or self-imposed pressures of family expectations.

2. Read selections from Gary Soto's *Living Up the Street* or *Small Faces* and write an analysis of the characteristic subject matter or themes of his work.

3. Interview or find periodical interviews of racially or ethnically mixed marriages. What problems do these couples face that are different from those of other couples? Write from a thesis that you can support with specific data that you have read or collected from your interviews.

4

Between Perceptions

■ ■ ■

How we perceive ourselves is intrinsically related to our racial and ethnic roots, as well as to our gender. Our sense of self, however, goes beyond any definition of male or female, race or culture. Self-perception is often conditioned by the roles we assume—as students, workers, family members—but our self-image and how others see us may be distinct from the roles we play. You regard yourself as a college student, but when you are at home, you might be the "baby" in the family or the one diapering the baby. You know that your competence at work can gain you much-needed overtime pay, but your perception of yourself as an "A" student prompts you to cut back on hours instead. A woman who is physically disabled may not define herself as "handicapped," and a man who qualifies for affirmative action may not see himself as "disadvantaged." Perceiving oneself beyond labels or stereotypes is an essential process, as the readings in this chapter indicate.

Self-perception is complicated by others' images of us. If you feel that you are constantly trying to exist among worlds that perceive you differently, you will relate to the tensions described in our first selection. In her emphatic poem, Kate Rushin insists that she is "sick" of being the bridge or mediator for everyone she knows and of not finding "the bridge to [her] own power." This poem reflects a realization of how our ability to perceive ourselves may be thwarted by how others use us.

In their essays, Matthew Soyster, Ben Mattlin, and Jennifer Coleman fight stereotypes that threaten their self-perceptions. Their essays express the frustrations of productive individuals whose self-acceptance is threatened by other's delimiting views of them. Ted Kooser's poem shows how our perceptions of disabled people limit us.

As you may realize, eating disorders often develop from people's perception of what is attractive or their need to gain control of how they perceive themselves. In "Bodily Harm," Pamela Erens chronicles the problems of many women who have eating disorders and struggle toward self-understanding and acceptance rather than perpetuate destructive behavior. Barbara Kafka argues that it is wrong to make body size a moral issue.

To be perceived as an individual rather than a racial or ethnic stereotype may be a challenge for you or some of your friends. Fighting stereotypes can be life-threatening, as Brent Staples and Walter White reveal in their essays, or it can be uncomfortable, as Gloria Naylor and Joan Steinau Lester show in theirs.

Our perception of self is complicated by the multiple roles we play and our disparate self-images based on gender, social class, or ethnicity. Balancing how others see us with who we think we are is the condition of being between perceptions—and the basis of all of the writings in this chapter.

THE BRIDGE POEM

Kate Rushin

In addition to "millions of low-paying jobs"—in a factory, as a waitress, and as a live-in maid—Kate Rushin (b. 1951) has also worked in community theater and on radio and has participated in the artist-in-residence and poet-in-the schools program for many years. She has directed the Jefferson Park Writing Center, an adult writing project, and she has been a member of the New Words Book Store Collective, a women's bookstore, for ten years. Rushin earned an undergraduate degree from Oberlin College and has started an M.F.A. program at Brown University. Her most recent book is *The Black Back-Ups* (1993). The poem printed here was first published in *This Bridge Called My Back: Writings by Radical Women of Color* in 1983.

I've had enough
I'm sick of seeing and touching
Both sides of things
Sick of being the damn bridge for everybody

Nobody
can talk to anybody
Without me
Right?

I explain my mother to my father my father to my little sister
My little sister to my brother my brother to the White Feminists
The White Feminists to the Black Church Folks the Black Church Folks
To the ex-Hippies the ex-Hippies to the Black Separatists the
Black Separatists to the Artists the Artists to my friends' parents . . .

Then
I've got to explain myself
To everybody

I do more translating
Than the U.N.

Forget it
I'm sick of filling in your gaps
Sick of being your insurance against
The isolation of your self-imposed limitations
Sick of being the crazy at your holiday dinners
The odd one at your Sunday Brunches
I am sick of being the sole Black friend to thirty-four individual White Folks

Find another connection to the rest of the world
Find something else to make you legitimate
Find some other way to be political and hip
I will not be the bridge to your womanhood
Your manhood
Your human-ness

I'm sick of reminding you not to
Close off too tight for too long

I'm sick of mediating with your worst self
On behalf of your better selves

Sick
of having
To remind you
To breathe
Before you
Suffocate
Your own
Fool self

Forget it

Stretch or drown
Evolve or die

You see it's like this
The bridge I must be
Is the bridge to my own power
I must translate
My own fears

Mediate
My own weaknesses

I must be the bridge to nowhere
But my own true self
It's only then
I can be
Useful

THINKING ABOUT THE TEXT

1. In what specific ways does the speaker function as a "bridge"? Why is the job frustrating?
2. What can you infer about the speaker's gender, race, education, and personality? Support your inferences with information from the text.
3. What is the one bridge the speaker "must be"? In what ways does the speaker's functioning as many bridges deprive her or him of the one sought-for bridge?

WRITING FROM THE TEXT

1. Write a description of the "bridge" services that you provide in your family, social, professional, and/or personal worlds.
2. Write about a time when you were seen and used as a role or as a token member of a group. How did you feel? Let your essay *show* how you felt.
3. Write an essay arguing that all gracious people assist others by helping them connect their "human-ness" to others' "human-ness." Support your assertion with specific positive descriptions of "bridging people" that you know.

CONNECTING WITH OTHER TEXTS

1. The speaker in "The Bridge Poem" vents angry frustration at being the connecting element for one person or group to another and the token representative to make others appear "political and hip." Many readings in *Between Worlds* address the resentment people feel when they are used, when their presence is exploited by individuals or groups. Discuss this tokenism or exploitation and use "An Open Letter to Jerry Lewis" (p. 201), and "My Man Bovanne" (p. 46), to support your point.

2. Both Rushin and Gloria Anzaldúa (p. 127) describe the conflicts caused by living between diverse groups. Write an analysis of the types of tension that these two poets dramatize.

■ LIVING UNDER CIRCE'S SPELL
Matthew Soyster

A free-lance writer, journalist, and college instructor, Matthew Soyster (1954) earned a B.A. in French and Italian Literature from Stanford University and an M.A. in English and Norwegian literature from U.C. Berkeley. His work has appeared in *Newsweek, Stanford Magazine,* the *San Francisco Examiner,* and numerous other publications. Soyster has been an associate editor of *Change Magazine* and a return guest on KPFA-FM radio, discussing images of the disabled—"Monster/Victim/Hero"—in Western film, literature, and popular culture. In 1989, he organized a $10,000 benefit concert for the Multiple Sclerosis Society, and in 1991 he wrote and performed "Shape Shifter," a monologue for the premiere of the Contemporary Dance Company at a Berkeley theater. The following article appeared in the "My Turn" column of *Newsweek,* October 11, 1993.

1 "Life is brief, time's a thief." This ribbon of pop lyricism keens from an apartment-house radio into the hot afternoon air. Across the street I am sprawled in the gutter behind my minivan, bits of glass and scrap metal chewing at my knees and elbows, a cut on my hand beginning to well crimson.

2 There has been no assailant, no wound except to my psyche. I'm just a clumsy cripple whose legs buckled before he reached his wheelchair. A moment ago I yanked it from my tailgate, as I've done a thousand times. But when it spun off at a crazy angle I missed the seat and slumped to the ground.

3 Now the spasms start, shooting outward from the small of my back, forcing me prone, grinding my cheek into the asphalt. What will I look like to the first casual passerby before he catches sight of the telltale chair? A wine-soaked rummy? A hit-and-run victim? Maybe an amateur mechanic checking the rear suspension, wrong side up.

4 I'm too young and vital looking to be this helpless. I shrink from the inevitable clucking and concern. Then again, this isn't the best neighborhood. The first person to come along may simply kick me and take my wallet. No wonder I'm ambivalent about rescue, needing but not wanting to be discovered. With detachment I savor the hush of this deserted street, the symphony of birdsong in the treetops.

I am trying to remember T. S. Eliot's line about waiting without 5
hope, because hope would be hope for the wrong thing. Instead, that idiot TV commercial for the medical alarm-pager keeps ringing through my brain: "Help me. I've fallen and I can't get up."

It was only a matter of time. I've known for months that my hair's- 6
breadth maneuvering would eventually fail me. For years, in fact. When I first learned that I had multiple sclerosis I was a marathon runner and whitewater-rafting guide, a cyclist and skier, the quintessential California golden boy. Cardiovascular fitness had long since become our state religion. I lived for and through my legs.

But that's only the ad-slick surface of the California dream, the sun- 7
shine without the shadow. The town I live in is also the mecca of the disabled, the home of the Independent Living Movement, the place where broken people come to patch together their dignity and their dreams.

Yin and yang. In Berkeley, there are wheelchair users on every cor- 8
ner. Propped in sagging hospital-issue chairs. Space-age sports chairs. Motor-driven dreadnoughts. When I could still walk, I crossed the street to avoid them. What an odd tribe they seemed, with their spindly, agitated limbs, always hurtling down the avenue on some manic errand.

How could I imagine my own swift decline? A few months or years 9
passed. Soon I was relying on a cane, then crutches, and finally—after many thigh-bruising falls and a numbness so intense it turned my legs to driftwood—a wheelchair. My response to these limitations was compensation and denial. I thought I could become a disabled Olympian: wheelchair racing, tennis, rugby. I thought I could go on as before.

Wrong again. To paraphrase Tolstoy, all able-bodied people are 10
alike, but each disabled person is crippled in his own way. MS not only played havoc with my upper-body strength and agility; it clouded my mind and sapped my energy. I could totter a few steps supported at both wrists, but my days in the winter surf, high peaks and desert canyons were over.

So what is it like to spend your life forked at the waist, face-level 11
with children? The syndrome has been amply described. People see through me now, or over me. They don't see me at all. Or they fix me with that plangent, aching stare: sympathy.

They offer too much assistance, scurrying to open doors, scrambling 12
out of my way with unnecessary apologies, or they leave me no space at all, barking their shins on my foot pedals. My spirit rallies in the face of such humiliations; they have their comic aspect. What disturbs me most is not how others see me, but how I've lost my vision of myself.

13 Growing crippled is a bitch. First your body undergoes a strange enchantment: Circe's spell. Then your identity gives way. You become someone or something other, but for a long time you're not sure what that other is.

14 Along the way, I've had to give up activities and passions that define me, my safe position in society, my very sense of manhood. In our species, the pecking order is distinctly vertical. True for women. Doubly true for men. A man stands tall, stands firm, stands up for things. These are more than metaphors. The very act of sitting implies demotion. Anyone who's witnessed boardroom politics knows this much. Have a seat, barks the boss. It's not an invitation, it's an order.

15 All of this brings me back to the gutter, where I lie listening to birdsong, recognizing but not apologizing for the obstinacy that landed me here. For months my friends and family have watched my legs grow weaker. They've prodded me relentlessly to refit my van with a wheelchair lift in order to avoid just this disaster. But I've refused.

16 Twice a day at least, I've dragged my reluctant legs from beneath the steering column, hauled myself erect beside the driver's seat, inched my way down the roof rail to the rear stowage. And removed the chair by hand, standing.

17 Why have I clung to this ritual, knowing it's dangerous and futile? It's the only task I rise for anymore, in a sitting life. For a moment in the driver's doorway, I'm in control, unreliant on technology or assistance, upright. Or so I've told myself. But that moment is so fragile, the control so illusory.

18 When the time comes to change, I've said, I'll know.

19 Now I know.

20 I feel the lesson, sharp as the rap of a Zen master's stick. Lying in the hot gutter, I take a deep breath and my whole body relaxes. Tuning in to Rod Stewart's tinny wisdom from the window. Listening for a passing car or pedestrian.

21 Waiting.

THINKING ABOUT THE TEXT

1. This essay opens with the writer "sprawled in the gutter" and ends with him still "waiting" for a passing car or pedestrian to help. Analyze the effect of creating such a scene to prompt his discussion and of using the present tense (even though this event happened in the past).

2. Describe, in detail, the writer's life and his attitude about the disabled before he himself became "a clumsy cripple."

3. Soyster explains, "What disturbs me most is not how others see me, but how I've lost my vision of myself." What does he mean by this and how does his threatened self-image relate to his refusal to refit his van with a wheelchair lift?

4. Throughout this essay Soyster includes a number of allusions (incomplete references to sources outside the work): pop lyrics, Rod Stewart, the poet Rilke, the novelist Tolstoy, the myth of Circe, the Zen religion, and yin and yang. Look up these allusions in a dictionary or reader's encyclopedia and explain how each contributes to our understanding of the writer and his perspective.

WRITING FROM THE TEXT

1. Using the information that you gathered on allusions, write an essay explaining how the allusions in this essay are essential to helping us see the writer as a unique and intriguing individual and not just "a clumsy cripple."

2. Write about an event in your life that caused you to lose a vision of yourself. Dramatize your life before this crisis or event and contrast it with your current life.

CONNECTING WITH OTHER TEXTS

1. Matthew Soyster (p. 198), Ben Mattlin (p. 201), Ted Kooser (p. 205), and Shannon Paaske (p. 468) use different genres (essay, letter, poem, and research paper) to examine the attitudes that many people harbor toward the disabled. Using details from these works, write an essay supporting your own thesis about how and why people feel uneasy around the disabled—and what can be done about it.

2. Matthew Soyster (p. 198), Brent Staples (p. 219), and Jennifer Coleman (p. 207) describe how others have incorrectly stereotyped and humiliated them. Using details from any of these narratives and from "Don't Let Stereotypes Warp Your Judgment" (p. 428), write an analysis of the causes of such stereotyping and its effects on the stereotyped person and the one doing the stereotyping.

■ AN OPEN LETTER TO JERRY LEWIS

Ben Mattlin

Educated in an interdisciplinary program at Harvard University, Ben Mattlin (b. 1962) claims that his overall grades "weren't terrific," but he received his professors' high praise for his writing. After college, he therefore decided to take the chance of supporting himself for two years as a writer. Although he received his share of rejection slips, he has continued to earn a living with his writing. He has worked as a writer of in-house publications at IBM, has published articles in business and trade journals, has sold the plot for one children's cartoon, has written a novel, and is widely published as a writer of disability-related articles, including a cover story for *Television and Families* that addresses the distorted images of the disabled in television and movies. The article included here first appeared on the opinion page of the *Los Angeles Times* in 1991.

1 Dear Jerry Lewis:

2 I was born with a muscular-dystrophy-related disease, and your Labor Day telethons have always turned my stomach. I actually appeared on one in the late 1960s, as the Muscular Dystrophy Assn. poster child for the New York metropolitan area.

3 Now I am 28, a Harvard graduate, a self-employed writer, married, still in a wheelchair. I can finally formulate what I felt as a child: Despite your undoubtedly honorable intentions, you are sadly misinformed about disabilities. Moreover, you are misleading the able-bodied population while offending the rest of us.

4 You and your organization have done much good, to be sure, and I myself have benefited from your financial resources. But people with disabilities do not need or want to be characterized as objects of pity. Last year's Americans With Disabilities Act mandates our equal participation in society, including employment. What we need is to stress competence—not outmoded notions of charity.

5 Speaking of the "dystrophic child's plight," or calling disability a "curse" reinforces the offensive stereotype that we are victims. Wheelchairs are not "steel imprisonment," nor are those who use them "confined" or "bound"; they are liberating aluminum and vinyl vehicles. Similarly, phrases like "dealt a bad hand" and "got in the wrong line" are unfair. Disability is not "bad" or "wrong."

6 Other examples abound: Being dressed or fed by others is a hassle, but not an "indignity." There is no shame in needing others, no loss of dignity. Our needs are more personal and continuing than other people's—nothing to be ashamed of.

7 Saying that they are is to say our lives are somehow inferior. Is this how you feel? You have said our lives are "half"—we must learn to "do things halfway," be good at being "half a person." Even slaves in the Old South counted for three-fifths of a person.

8 Perhaps more disturbing is your use of the archaic word "cripple." While some of us have recently taken it on as a kind of hip slang among ourselves or for political purposes—much like the gay-rights group Queer Nation—this does not mean you should.

Worse still may be your ubiquitous "Jerry's Kids"—never more absurd than when followed by "of all ages." Yes, a lot of MDA's clients (not necessarily "patients") are kids, but do you know how hard it is to become, and be treated as, a self-respecting disabled adult in this society? You may argue it is a term of affection, but you wouldn't refer to your late friend Sammy Davis Jr. as your "boy." 9

What's really surprising are your inaccuracies. Your tales of disabled kids being taunted by other kids, for example, do not ring true. Most able-bodied kids whom I knew growing up couldn't wait to push my chair. They would even compete to be "chief wheeler." 10

You further allege that wheelchairs don't fit under restaurant tables, when for years they have come with "desk armrests." And what's this about their not going through metal detectors at airports? Big deal—they're metal! They go around them and are searched separately. 11

At times, you seem to understand. You talk about our right to live with dignity. What that means is access to schools and jobs, equipment like computers and vans, attendants and respect. The MDA can't be responsible for all this. But misleading people—potential employers, potential spouses, and even newly disabled people who don't know any better—only works against these goals. 12

When I was about 6 years old, I was in a full-page magazine ad for the MDA: big blue eyes peeking through blond curls. The caption read, "If I grow up, I want to be a fireman." I didn't want to be a fireman, and knew then my diagnosis called for a normal life expectancy. Confused, I decided that I wasn't really one of "them" and denied a part of my identity, my connection to the only community where I could learn to feel good about my disability. I didn't know the word "exploitation" yet. 13

I realize pity works—last year's telethon raised more money than ever before. And I know some folks think you're a saint. But I also know there were protests at last year's telethon—and will be more—asking why it has taken so long to find a cure and demanding a financial accounting. 14

Perhaps people would not be so upset if the association spoke less about finding a cure and did more to improve our lives as they are. I know MDA does buy wheelchairs and such. But what does it do to make our world more accessible and to promote employment? How many people with disabilities are employed by the organization and its corporate sponsors? 15

Don't get me wrong. Muscular dystrophy can be a killer, and we mourn our brothers and sisters who have died. Yet, despite the impression that one may get watching the telethon, we are not all terminal. And even if you whip MD, you will not end disability. It is here to stay; so are we. 16

17 Why not, this year, present active, well-adjusted disabled people—not superheroes but normal people—who nonetheless have used or could use financial assistance to achieve their goals of independent living?

18 The harm being done is considerable. A dynamic, young, educated, professional woman I know, who grew up with a disability similar to mine, says she cannot watch your telethon because it makes her want to kill herself. "Is that what people think of us?" she asks.

19 Your pity campaign is so dispiriting, so destructive, that no matter how many millions you raise, the ends do not justify the means. Why not wield your sizable influence to fight our real enemies? What truly handicaps us most are the obstacles—architectural, financial and attitudinal—erected by others.

THINKING ABOUT THE TEXT

1. What are Mattlin's objections to Jerry Lewis' Labor Day telethons?
2. How has Mattlin personally benefited from the Muscular Dystrophy Association? How has he been exploited by this same group?
3. What specific changes would Mattlin like to see in the MDA and in Lewis' telethons?

WRITING FROM THE TEXT

1. Write an essay in which you define an *ideal* televised fund-raiser. Your thesis should assert what the important elements of your program would be. Reference to Mattlin's points might be part of your support.
2. Write a letter to Mattlin showing your support for his view to have a more balanced telethon, or express your concern that he has shocked a number of sensitive, charity-supporting people into skepticism about donating money to the Muscular Dystrophy Association.

CONNECTING WITH OTHER TEXTS

1. Write an essay illustrating how Matthew Soyster (p. 198) exemplifies the life that Mattlin wants Jerry Lewis to show during his fundraisers. In your essay, contrast your perceptions of Soyster's life with the telethon images that Mattlin describes.

2. Mattlin urges Lewis to "present active, well-adjusted disabled people—not superheroes but normal people" on his program. As if in response to the disabled person's longing for role models, some advertising now features disabled people. Do research to learn something about these advertising campaigns and include an analysis of some of the specific advertisements as part of your essay.

3. Write an essay about the recent portrayals of disabled people on television and in films. Use descriptive analysis of your examples to show your reader that some portrayals are better than others.

THE BLIND ALWAYS COME AS SUCH A SURPRISE

Ted Kooser

Described by a critic as "an authentic poet of the American people," Ted Kooser (b. 1939) is also a marketing executive for Lincoln Benefit insurance company. Kooser has won national recognition, including the Society for Midlands Authors Prize for the best book of poetry of 1980 (*Sure Signs*). His poems often present vivid details and startling images of ordinary life, as does the poem reprinted here from *Sure Signs*. Asked what advice he would give college writers, Kooser repeats E.B. White's suggestion: "Simplify, Simplify, Simplify."

The blind always come as such a surprise,
suddenly filling an elevator
with a great white porcupine of canes,
or coming down upon us in a noisy crowd
like the eye of a hurricane.
The dashboards of cars stopped at crosswalks
and the shoes of commuters on trains
are covered with sentences
struck down in mid-flight by the canes of the blind.
Each of them changes our lives,
tapping across the bright circles of our ambitions
like cracks traversing the favorite china.

THINKING ABOUT THE TEXT

1. This poem is written from the point of view of someone who encounters a blind person. What is the poet's predominant point about how people with sight feel when a blind person appears?

2. The poet describes the blind person coming into four public areas. What are these places and what are the specific effects of the blind person's presence?

3. List your responses to the following vivid images and figures of speech by asking yourself what pictures or sounds the poet intends and what associations you can make with each word. Your analysis of these images will help you to understand the specific points that the poet is making beyond his general point.

   - a great white porcupine of canes
   - like the eye of a hurricane
   - The dashboards . . . and the shoes . . . covered with sentences struck down mid-flight
   - the bright circles of our ambitions
   - like cracks traversing the favorite china

WRITING FROM THE TEXT

1. Write an essay that shows that an analysis of the images in this poem helps us understand the poet's theme. (See pp. 443–452 for a discussion of how to write poetry analysis.)

2. Write an essay in which you discuss how you feel when you meet a disabled person. Do any of Kooser's images reflect some of your responses? Integrate an interpretation of Kooser's images into your discussion.

3. If you are disabled, what is your response to Kooser's poem? Write an essay that describes your feelings about how people respond to you.

CONNECTING WITH OTHER TEXTS

1. In "Living Under Circe's Spell" (p. 198), Matthew Soyster notes that people see through him or over him or don't see him at all. Write an essay that integrates Soyster's experiences with disabled people before he had MS and then later as a disabled person and Ted Kooser's descriptions of people's responses to the blind in this poem. Is your goal in your essay to inspire change in people's attitudes and behavior or to describe the existing conditions, or do you have yet another goal?

2. In "An Open Letter to Jerry Lewis" (p. 201), Ben Mattlin chastises Jerry Lewis for evoking pity to gain cash for the Muscular Dystrophy Association. Kooser, too, seems to want to evoke

something other than pity for blind people. What? Write an essay exploring what both Kooser and Mattlin suggest are natural and possibly more constructive responses to disabled people than mere pity.

DISCRIMINATION AT LARGE

Jennifer A. Coleman

A graduate of Boston College Law School, Jennifer A. Coleman (b. 1959) is a discrimination and civil rights lawyer in Buffalo, New York. Coleman wrote the essay printed here after seeing the film *Jurassic Park:* "The only bad person in the film is fat, and I'm tired of the stereotyping—which nobody objects to—that makes heavy people objects of ridicule and contempt." In addition to writing legal briefs, pleadings, letters, and a law review article, Coleman teaches constitutional law at Canisius College in Buffalo. The essay printed below first appeared in *Newsweek,* "My Turn," August 2, 1993.

Fat is the last preserve for unexamined bigotry. Fat people are lampooned without remorse or apology on television, by newspaper columnists, in cartoons, you name it. The overweight are viewed as suffering from moral turpitude and villainy, and since we are at fault for our condition, no tolerance is due. All fat people are "outed" by their appearance. 1

Weight-motivated assaults occur daily and are committed by people who would die before uttering anti-gay slogans or racial epithets. Yet these same people don't hesitate to scream "move your fat ass" when we cross in front of them. 2

Since the time I first ventured out to play with the neighborhood kids, I was told over and over that I was lazy and disgusting. Strangers, adults, classmates offered gratuitous comments with such frequency and urgency that I started to believe them. Much later I needed to prove it wasn't so. I began a regimen of swimming, cycling and jogging that put all but the most compulsive to shame. I ate only cottage cheese, brown rice, fake butter and steamed everything. I really believed I could infiltrate the ranks of the nonfat and thereby establish my worth. 3

I would prove that I was not just a slob, a blimp, a pig. I would finally escape the unsolicited remarks of strangers ranging from the "polite"—"You would really be pretty if you lost weight"—to the hostile ("Lose weight, you fat slob"). Of course, sometimes more subtle commentary sufficed: oinking, mooing, staring, laughing and pointing. Simulating a fog-horn was also popular. 4

5 My acute exercise phase had many positive points. I was mingling with my obsessively athletic peers. My pulse was as low as anyones, my cholesterol levels in the basement, my respiration barely detectable. I could swap stats from my last physical with anyone. Except for weight. No matter how hard I tried to run, swim or cycle away from it, my weight found me. Oh sure, I lost weight (never enough) and it inevitably tracked me down and adhered to me more tenaciously than ever. I lived and breathed "Eat to win," "Feel the burn." But in the end I was fit and still fat.

6 I learned that by societal, moral, ethical, soap-operatical, vegetable, political definition, it was impossible to be both fit and fat. Along the way to that knowledge, what I got for my trouble was to be hit with objects from moving cars because I dared to ride my bike in public, and to be mocked by diners at outdoor cafés who trumpeted like a herd of elephants as I jogged by. Incredibly, it was not uncommon for one of them to shout: "Lose some weight, you pig." Go figure.

7 It was confusing for awhile. How was it I was still lazy, weak, despised, a slug and a cow if I exercised every waking minute? This confusion persisted until I finally realized: it didn't matter what I did. I was and always would be the object of sport, derision, antipathy and hostility so long as I stayed in my body. I immediately signed up for a body transplant. I am still waiting for a donor.

8 Until then, I am more settled because I have learned the hard way what thin people have known for years. There simply are some things that fat people must never do. Like: riding a bike ("Hey lady, where's the seat?"), eating in a public place ("No dessert for me, I don't want to look like her"). And the most unforgivable crime: wearing a bathing suit in public ("Whale on the beach!").

9 Things are less confusing now that I know that the nonfat are superior to me, regardless of their personal habits, health, personalities, cholesterol levels or the time they log on the couch. And, as obviously superior to me as they are, it is their destiny to remark on my inferiority regardless of who I'm with, whether they know me, whether it hurts my feelings. I finally understand that the thin have a divine mandate to steal self-esteem from fat people, who have no right to it in the first place.

10 Fat people aren't really jolly. Sometimes we act that way so you will leave us alone. We pay a price for this. But at least we get to hang on to what self-respect we smuggled out of grade school and adolescence.

11 Hating fat people is not inborn; it has to be nurtured and developed. Fortunately, it's taught from the moment most of us are able to walk and speak. We learn it through Saturday-morning cartoons, prime-

time TV and movies. Have you ever seen a fat person in a movie who wasn't evil, disgusting, pathetic or lampooned? Santa Claus doesn't count.

Kids catch on early to be sensitive to the feelings of gay, black, disabled, elderly and speech-impaired people. At the same time, they learn that fat people are fair game. That we are always available for their personal amusement. 12

The media, legal system, parents, teachers and peers respond to most types of intolerance with outrage and protest. Kids hear that employers can be sued for discriminating, that political careers can be destroyed and baseball owners can lose their teams as a consequence of racism, sexism or almost any other "ism." 13

But the fat kid is taught that she deserves to be mocked. She is not OK. Only if she loses weight will she be OK. Other kids see the response and incorporate the message. Small wonder some (usually girls) get it into their heads that they can never be thin enough. 14

I know a lot about prejudice, even though I am a white, middle-class, professional woman. The worst discrimination I have suffered because of my gender is nothing compared to what I experience daily because of my weight. I am sick of it. The jokes and attitudes are as wrong and damaging as any racial or ethnic slur. The passive acceptance of this inexcusable behavior is sometimes worse than the initial assault. Some offensive remarks can be excused as the shortcomings of jackasses. But the tacit acceptance of their conduct by mainstream America tells the fat person that the intolerance is understandable and acceptable. Well it isn't. 15

THINKING ABOUT THE TEXT

1. Jennifer Coleman's focus is evident from the first paragraph of her essay. After you have read the entire essay, what do you assume is her thesis or complete assertion?
2. What is the author's personal history, and how does knowing her background contribute to your understanding of her point?
3. *Are* the jokes and slurs about overweight people "as wrong and damaging as any racial or ethnic slur"?
4. Examine Coleman's word choice in this essay. Which words and expressions specifically contribute to her making her point powerfully?
5. What are *your* feelings as you read the comments that people have made to and about Coleman?

WRITING FROM THE TEXT

1. Write an essay arguing that discrimination against the overweight is "as wrong and damaging as any racial or ethnic slur." You will want to anticipate and counter the objection that people don't *have* to be overweight.
2. Describe the character traits, habits, and values of an overweight person you know. Let the description in your essay *show* what kinds of discrimination and problems your subject has faced.

CONNECTING WITH OTHER TEXTS

1. Body image is a particular preoccupation for many women and, according to Barbara Kafka (p. 216), the world associates a thin, fit body with personal virtue. Write an essay that argues that Jennifer Coleman has virtues that we admire even though she is not thin.
2. Write an essay that argues that the people who make rude comments to Coleman expose their own "petty prejudices" as defined and described by Victoria Sackett (p. 269).
3. Use Heilbroner's essay on stereotyping (p. 428) as a definitive starting point for a descriptive essay on the discrimination that overweight people experience. You might contrast specific stereotypical depictions of overweight people in films and on television with an overweight person you know.

■ BODILY HARM

Pamela Erens

A 1985 graduate of Yale University, Pamela Erens (b. 1963) has worked as an editor and staff writer for *Connecticut Magazine,* and her reviews and articles have appeared in many magazines and newspapers. In addition to writing fiction, Erens currently is an editor at *Glamour* magazine. The essay included here was first published in *Ms.* in 1985, when Erens interned there the summer after her graduation.

1 "Before I'd even heard of bulimia," said Gloria, "I happened to read an article in *People* magazine on Cherry Boone—how she'd used laxatives and vomiting to control her weight. I thought: Wow, what a great idea! I was sure that I would never lose control of my habit."

Recent media attention to the binge-purge and self-starvation dis- 2
orders known as bulimia and anorexia—often detailing gruesome particulars of women's eating behavior—may have exacerbated this serious problem on college campuses. But why would a woman who reads an article on eating disorders want to copy what she reads? Ruth Striegel-Moore, Ph.D., director of Yale University's Eating Disorders Clinic, suggests that eating disorders may be a way to be like other "special" women and at the same time strive to outdo them. "The pursuit of thinness is a way for women to compete with each other, a way that avoids being threatening to men," says Striegel-Moore. Eating disorders as a perverse sort of rivalry? In Carol's freshman year at SUNY-Binghamton, a roommate showed her how to make herself throw up. "Barf buddies" are notorious on many college campuses, especially in sororities and among sports teams. Eating disorders as negative bonding? Even self-help groups on campus can degenerate into the kinds of competitiveness and negative reinforcement that are among the roots of eating disorders in the first place.

This is not another article on how women do it. It is an article on 3
how and why some women stopped. The decision to get help is not always an easy one. The shame and secrecy surrounding most eating disorders and the fear of being labeled "sick" may keep a woman from admitting even to herself that her behavior is hurting her. "We're not weirdos," says Nancy Gengler, a recovered bulimic and number two U.S. squash champion, who asked that I use her real name because "so much of this illness has to do with secrecy and embarrassment." In the first stages of therapy, says Nancy, much of getting better was a result of building up the strength to (literally) "sweat out" the desire to binge and to endure the discomfort of having overeaten rather than throwing up. "I learned to accept such 'failures' and moreover, that they would not make me fat. . . ."

Secret shame or college fad, eating disorders among college women 4
are growing at an alarming rate: in a recent study at Wellesley College, more than half the women on campus felt they needed help to correct destructive eating patterns. These included bingeing, chronic dieting, and "aerobic nervosa," the excessive use of exercise to maintain one's body ideal—in most women, invariably five to 10 pounds less than whatever she currently weighs.

Why now? Wasn't the Women's Movement supposed to free 5
women to be any body size, to explore the full range of creative and emotional possibilities. Instead, women in epidemic numbers are developing symptoms that make them feel hopeless about the future, deplet-

ing the energy they have for schoolwork and other activities, and if serious enough, send them right back home or into the infantilizing condition of hospitalization. What has gone wrong?

6 For Brenda, college meant the freedom to question her mother's values about sex. But when she abandoned her mothers guidelines, "I went to the other extreme. I couldn't set limits about sex, food, or anything else." The pressure on college women to appear successful and in control, to know what they want among the myriad new choices they are offered, is severe. So much so that many choose internal havoc over external imperfection. Naomi, a bulimic student at Ohio State University, said she would rather be alcoholic like her father than overweight like her mother because "fat is something you can see."

7 One reason college women hesitate to enter therapy, says Stephen Zimmer, director of the Center for the Study of Anorexia and Bulimia in New York City, is that the eating disorder has become a coping mechanism. It allows the person to function when she feels rotten inside. "In the first session," says Zimmer, "I tell my patients: 'I'm not going to try to take your eating behavior away from you. Until you find something that works better, you get to keep it.' Their relief is immense."

8 Brenda at first did not even tell the counselor whom she was seeing that she was bulimic. She started therapy because of a series of affairs with abusive men. As Brenda developed the sense that she had a right to say no to harmful relationships and to make demands on others, her inability to say no to food also disappeared.

9 However, if a woman is vomiting three times a day, she may be unable to concentrate on long-term therapy. Behavioral therapy, which directly addresses the learned habit of bingeing and purging, is a more immediate alternative. For eight years, Marlene Boskind White, Ph.D., and her husband, William White, Jr., Ph.D., ran weekend workshops for bulimic women at Cornell University, usually as an adjunct to other forms of therapy. The sessions included nutritional counseling, developing techniques of dealing with binge "triggers," feminist consciousness-raising, and examining the hidden "payoffs" that keep a woman from changing her eating behavior. Boskind-White and White report that a follow-up of 300 women they had treated one to three years earlier showed that 70 percent had entirely stopped purging and drastically reduced their bingeing.

10 Group therapy (an increasingly popular resource on college campuses) may be the first time a woman realizes she is not alone with her problem. Rebecca Axelrod, who was bulimic throughout college, and now counsels

bulimics herself, found that joining the Cornell workshop and meeting other bulimic women defused many of her fears about herself: "I saw ten other women who were not mentally ill, not unable to function," Axelrod says. She remembers the moment when she understood the meaning of her bingeing and purging. "Saturday afternoon, Marlene took the women off alone, and we discussed the 'superwoman syndrome'—that attempt to be the perfect friend, lover, hostess, student . . . and perfect-looking. And bingeing, I saw, was my form of *defiance*. But if you're living life as the perfect woman, you won't cuss, you won't get drunk or laid or drive too fast. No, in the privacy of your own room you'll eat yourself out of house and home. But how dare you be defiant? And so you punish yourself by throwing it up."

But "groups can fall into a cycle I call 'bigger and badder,'" says Axelrod. "It starts when one person comes in and says, 'I feel terrible, I binged yesterday.' Somebody else says: 'Oh, that's okay, so did I.' Then a third person says: 'That's nothing, did you know I . . .' Pretty soon everyone is lending support to the binge instead of to the woman who needs ways of coping with it." 11

However, Axelrod feels that there is much potential for women to help one another. She encourages bulimics to ask for help from their friends, saying that while she herself was initially frightened that being open about her bulimia would alienate her friends, most were very supportive. "The important thing," says Axelrod, "is to be specific about what you need. Don't say: 'Be there for me.' Tell a friend exactly what she can do: for instance, not to urge you to go out for pizza if you tell her you're feeling vulnerable. And rely on three friends, not one." 12

One of the most important strategies in treating eating disorders, says Dr. Lee Combrinck-Graham of the newly opened Renfrew Center for anorectics and bulimics in Philadelphia, is breaking old patterns. Renfrew is a residential center that houses patients for between three weeks and two months, a period that can give women with eating disorders a respite from repetitive and destructive habits that are reinforced by the college environment. But Renfrew is not a "retreat"; its residents work hard. They participate in therapy workshops, take seminars in assertiveness-training and women's issues, and even participate in "new attitude" cooking classes. Dr. Combrinck-Graham stresses that therapy itself has often become a "pattern" for women who come to Renfrew. . . . Many of Renfrew's patients, says Dr. Combrinck-Graham, can say exactly what's "wrong" with them and why, yet are still unable to control their eating habits. Renfrew combines a philosophy that recovery is the patient's responsibility—she sets her own goals and contracts for as 13 much supervision as she needs—with innovative art and movement therapy that may bypass some of the rationalizations that block the progress of "talking" therapies.

14 Women who live close to home and whose parents are not separated may want to try family therapy. Family therapy considers the family itself, not the daughter with an eating disorder, to be the "patient." Often, the daughter has taken on the role of diverting attention from unacknowledged conflicts within the family. Family therapists behave somewhat like manic stage managers, interrupting and quizzing various members of a family, orchestrating confrontations in an attempt to expose and demolish old, rigid patterns of relating. Ideally, family therapy benefits all the members of the family. Carol, the student at SUNY-Binghamton, said that family therapy revealed how unhappy her mother was as a homemaker in a traditional Italian family.

15 Situations like Carol's are at the heart of today's epidemic of eating disorders, argues Kim Chernin in her book *The Hungry Self: Women, Eating, and Identity*. Chernin claims that today's college woman is the heir of a particular cultural moment that turns her hunger for identity into an uncontrollable urge for bodily nourishment. Young women of an earlier generation were educated to have children and remain in the home, yet our culture devalued the work they did there. Later, the Women's Movement opened up vast new emotional and career possibilities, and many daughters, on the verge of achieving their mother's suppressed dreams, are struck by panic and guilt.

16 Carol agreed: "I would try to push my mother to take classes, but my father was always against it. I was a good student, but how could I keep on getting smarter than my mother? When I was young, we'd been like one person. I wanted to be a homemaker because she was one. But when I got older, I said to myself: 'This woman has no life. She never leaves the house except to get groceries. And she's miserable.' I wanted to stop growing up, and then she would always be able to lead me and guide me." According to Chernin, an eating disorder may be a way to postpone or put an end to one's development, one's need to choose, the possibility of surpassing one's mother. In a world hostile to the values of closeness and nurturance women learn from and associate with the mother-daughter relationship, an eating disorder can disguise a desire to return to the "nourishment" of that early bond.

17 And why do the daughter's problems focus around food? As Chernin reminds us, originally with her milk, the mother *is* food. Femininity itself has historically been associated with food gathering and preparation. Food—eating it, throwing it up—can become a powerful

means of expressing aspects of the mother's life or of traditionally defined femininity that the daughter is trying to ingest or reject. And relationships with other women later in life can replicate this early pattern: food mediates hostility and love.

Whatever forms of therapy prove most helpful for women with eating disorders, it is clear that therapy is only half the battle. The Stone Center for Developmental Services and Studies at Wellesley College recognizes the need for early prevention and is preparing a film for adolescents that will feature women and health professionals speaking about the uses and abuses of food in our culture. Janet Surrey, Ph.D., a research associate at the center, stresses the need to educate girls in the 10- to 15-year-old age bracket—66 percent of whom already diet—about the psychological, physical, and reproductive danger of dieting and excessive thinness. Nutritional counseling is another imperative. But to Kim Chernin, our first priority is outreach centers and school programs that will provide developmental counseling and feminist consciousness-raising for this crucial pre-high school group. If women could learn early on to confront their conflicts over their right to development, the use of power, and their place in a still male-dominated world, there might no longer be a need for the "silent language" of eating disorders. 18

THINKING ABOUT THE TEXT

1. According to Erens, how has popular press coverage of eating disorders exacerbated the problem?
2. According to Rebecca Axelrod, who is quoted in Erens' review, how does the "superwoman syndrome" contribute to the problem of recognizing and treating eating disorders?
3. How can group therapy sessions, frequently joined by people with eating disorders, actually complicate the treatment?
4. What is Kim Chernin's perception of one cause of eating disorders?
5. What is proposed to stop the increasing number of young women with eating disorders?

WRITING FROM THE TEXT

1. Do you think that women compete with each other by pursuing thinness? Do you think women bond in an effort to achieve thinness? Write an essay in which you describe and analyze the eating patterns of women you know.

2. Argue that the cause of eating disorders is not based in the mother–daughter relationship but in the superthin images in advertising. Cite and *describe* specific examples of advertising to support your views.

CONNECTING WITH OTHER TEXTS

1. Pamela Erens, Jennifer Coleman (p. 207), and Rachel Krell (p. 358) describe the kinds of harm that can be done to women who try to conform to a standardized concept of beauty. In an analysis essay, examine the problem by connecting the ideas expressed by these three writers.
2. This article, published in 1985, gives a good review of eating problems, but new information may provide increased or different insights. Use Erens' essay as a model, but use more current material to analyze the problem of eating disorders.
3. Read Kim Chernin's 1981 study of eating disorders, *The Obsession,* or at least read Chapter 9. In this chapter, Chernin argues that males' preference for "little girls" contributes to eating disorders in women. Chernin cites films such as *Taxi Driver, Manhattan,* and *The Little Girl Who Lives Down the Lane* as evidence. Argue to support or refute Chernin's point about males' preference for "little girls" with your own evidence.
4. Read the chapter called "Hunger" in Naomi Wolf's *The Beauty Myth,* published in 1991. Analyze the support she offers for her thesis: "Women must claim anorexia as political damage done to us by a social order that considers our destruction insignificant because of what we are—less. We should identify it as Jews identify the death camps, as homosexuals identify AIDS: as a disgrace that is not our own, but that of an inhumane social order. . . . To be anorexic or bulimic *is* to be a political prisoner" (208).

THE MYTH OF THIN

Barbara Kafka

A frequent guest on television and radio programs and a consultant to restaurants, Barbara Kafka (b. 1933) was a cooking instructor with the late James Beard. The author of numerous cookbooks, including *The Microwave Gourmet,* Kafka is also a contributor to *Family Circle, Food and Wine, Eating Well,* and *Vogue.* Kafka writes a monthly opinion page for *Gourmet* magazine, where this essay originally appeared in May 1996.

No woman can be too rich or too thin. This simple maxim often attributed to the late duchess of Windsor neatly encapsulates much of the odd spirit of our times. Being thin is touted as such a virtue that leptin, a recently discovered hormone that may cause rapid weight loss, has been greeted as a possible godsend. In today's world we do not hear that we can never be too loyal, too hardworking, or too honest. The shallowness of Wallis Simpson's alleged assertion stands in stark contrast to the soul-searching of Socrates and the intellectual questing of Freud. Spenser's *Faerie Queene* and Bunyan's *Pilgrim's Progress*, let alone the writings of Horatio Alger and Saint Thomas Aquinas, have all been left in the past. 1

The problem with such a reductive view is that some people actually attempt to live by it. I myself have fantasies of slipping, sylphlike, into narrow designer clothes. Consequently, I have been on a diet for the better—or worse—part of my life. Being rich wouldn't be bad either, but that won't happen unless the proverbial unknown relative dies suddenly in some distant land, leaving me millions of dollars. 2

But I'm fortunate in that I realize these *are* fantasies and have not let them ruin my existence. I am not waiting for some fictional ship to come in, and I can still enjoy a robust meal of roast beef accompanied by a fine Burgundy. Many less fortunate have deprived themselves of pleasure in life and even made themselves ill by struggling to fulfill unfulfillable dreams of thinness and wealth. 3

Where did we go off the track? When did eating butter become a sin, and a little bit of extra flesh tacky, if not repellent? All religions have their fast days and their ascetic injunctions, and gluttony is one of Christianity's seven deadly sins. However, until quite recently, most people had a problem getting *enough* to eat. In the Calvinist scheme of things, wealth was a symbol of probable salvation and high morals, and corpulence a sign of wealth and well-being. 4

Today the opposite is true. We have shifted to thinness as our new mark of virtue. The corollary is that being fat—or even only somewhat overweight—is bad because it implies a lack of moral fiber. 5

The point about virtue and its antithesis, sin, is that virtue is always a thing of the few and sin a thing of the multitude. If leptin—which has been tested in mice but not yet in humans—works, has no adverse effects, and is affordable (considering that it might require frequent, lifelong injections), what would it do to our current preconceptions? If fat is seen as a sort of disease that is readily remedied, what will we use for external indicators of salvation once everybody is thin? 6

7 Our obsession with thinness is also fueled by health concerns. It is true that in this country we have more overweight people than ever before, and that, in many cases, being overweight correlates with an increased risk of heart and coronary artery disease. These ailments, however, may have as much to do with our increasingly sedentary way of life and our high-fat diets as with excess poundage. And the associated risk of colon cancer may be more of a dietary problem—too much fat and a lack of fiber—than a weight problem.

8 The real concern, then, is not that we weigh too much, but that we neither exercise enough nor eat well. Exercise is necessary for strong bones and both cardiovascular and pulmonary health. A balanced diet without a lot of fat can also help the body avoid many diseases. We should surely stop paying so much attention to weight per se. Simply being thin is not enough. It is actually hazardous if those who get (or already are) thin think they are automatically healthy and thus free from paying attention to their overall life-style. Thinness can be pure vainglory.

9 I congratulate Dr. Jeffrey Friedman, a molecular geneticist at New York City's Rockefeller University, for his discovery of leptin, because I cannot help but feel that overweight people who use it might be released from guilt and be more easily able to change their exercise and eating patterns. Nevertheless, even if leptin proves to be a proverbial "magic bullet," we should *not* turn away from a healthy diet and regular exercise. Let's turn instead from judging the book by its cover—whether that book is someone else's or our own autobiography. Health is not a moral issue, nor should weight be.

THINKING ABOUT THE TEXT

1. According to Kafka, what is wrong with the emphasis that our culture places on being thin?
2. What do you infer to be Kafka's thesis? How does the discovery of leptin influence Kafka's point in this essay?
3. Kafka acknowledges that being overweight often correlates with high-risk diseases. But what does Kafka believe is more important than the "obsession with thinness"?
4. Kafka begins her essay with a maxim and then refers to Socrates, Freud, Spenser, Bunyan, Horatio Alger, and Saint Thomas Aquinas. What is her rheorical strategy in employing these allusions?

5. Is your immediate response to agree or disagree with Kafka? Will your response be conditioned by whether or not you have been on a diet "for the better—or worse—part of [your] life"?

WRITING FROM THE TEXT

1. Respond to Kafka's essay by arguing that she is right, that people are too obsessed with thinness rather than health, and that being thin is inappropriately recognized as being virtuous. Use your personal experience and the experience of your family and friends to support your view.
2. Respond to Kafka's essay by arguing that she is wrong—that people are not sufficiently concerned about extra fat, that risk of disease correlates with being overweight, and that is why being thin is desirable. You will need scientific medical data to support your points.
3. Kafka asks what we will use for evidence of virtue in people when everybody is thin because leptin is available as a "magic bullet." Answer her question in an essay that focuses on what the new moral standards will be in judging people. Your essay might be seriously utopian or fancifully satirical.

CONNECTING WITH OTHER TEXTS

1. Use both Barbara Kafka's essay and Jennifer Coleman's essay "Discrimination at Large" p. (207) to argue that "health is not a moral issue, nor should weight be."
2. Use Pamela Erens' essay "Bodily Harm" (p. 210) as well as Kafka's to argue that the obsession with thinness is ruining the lives of many people. In addition to the experiences cited by Erens, use your own experiences and observations for support.
3. You will find information about eating disorders and women's preoccupation with being thin in Naomi Wolf's book *The Beauty Myth.* Write an analysis of our culture's emphasis on thinness in light of the information you gain from Wolf's and Kafka's texts.

BLACK MEN AND PUBLIC SPACE

Brent Staples

After earning his Ph.D. in psychology from the University of Chicago, Brent Staples (b. 1951) worked at the *Chicago Sun-Times* and wrote for other periodicals. Currently, he is employed as an editorial writer for the *New York Times.*

His memoir, *Parallel Time: Growing Up in Black and White,* was published in 1994. The essay included here was first published in the September 1986 issue of *Ms.* magazine as one article in a section on men's perspectives.

1 My first victim was a woman—white, well dressed, probably in her early twenties. I came upon her late one evening on a deserted street in Hyde Park, a relatively affluent neighborhood in an otherwise mean, impoverished section of Chicago. As I swung onto the avenue behind her, there seemed to be a discreet, uninflammatory distance between us. Not so. She cast back a worried glance. To her, the youngish black man—a broad six feet two inches with a beard and billowing hair, both hands shoved into the pockets of a bulky military jacket—seemed menacingly close. After a few more quick glimpses, she picked up her pace and was soon running in earnest. Within seconds she disappeared into a cross street.

2 That was more than a decade ago. I was twenty-two years old, a graduate student newly arrived at the University of Chicago. It was in the echo of that terrified womans footfalls that I first began to know the unwieldy inheritance I'd come into—the ability to alter public space in ugly ways. It was clear that she thought herself the quarry of a mugger, a rapist, or worse. Suffering a bout of insomnia, however, I was stalking sleep, not defenseless wayfarers. As a softy who is scarcely able to take a knife to a raw chicken—let alone hold it to a person's throat—I was surprised, embarrassed, and dismayed all at once. Her flight made me feel like an accomplice in tyranny. It also made it clear that I was indistinguishable from the muggers who occasionally seeped into the area from the surrounding ghetto. That first encounter, and those that followed, signified that a vast, unnerving gulf lay between nighttime pedestrians—particularly women—and me. And I soon gathered that being perceived as dangerous is a hazard in itself. I only needed to turn a corner into a dicey situation, or crowd some frightened, armed person in a foyer somewhere, or make an errant move after being pulled over by a policeman. Where fear and weapons meet—and they often do in urban America—there is always the possibility of death.

3 In that first year, my first away from my hometown, I was to become thoroughly familiar with the language of fear. At dark, shadowy intersections in Chicago, I could cross in front of a car stopped at a traffic light and elicit the *thunk, thunk, thunk, thunk* of the driver—black, white, male, or female—hammering down the door locks. On less traveled streets after dark, I grew accustomed to but never comfortable with people who crossed to the other side of the street rather than pass me.

Then there were the standard unpleasantries with police, doormen, bouncers, cab drivers, and others whose business it is to screen out troublesome individuals *before* there is any nastiness.

I moved to New York nearly two years ago and I have remained an avid night walker. In central Manhattan, the near-constant crowd cover minimizes tense one-on-one street encounters. Elsewhere—visiting friends in SoHo, where sidewalks are narrow and tightly spaced buildings shut out the sky—things can get very taut indeed. 4

Black men have a firm place in New York mugging literature. Norman Podhoretz in his famed (or infamous) 1963 essay, "My Negro Problem—And Ours," recalls growing up in terror of black males, they "were tougher than we were, more ruthless," he writes—and as an adult on the Upper West Side of Manhattan, he continues, he cannot constrain his nervousness when he meets black men on certain streets. Similarly, a decade later, the essayist and novelist Edward Hoagland extols a New York where once "Negro bitterness bore down mainly on other Negroes." Where some see mere panhandlers, Hoagland sees "a mugger who is clearly screwing up his nerve to do more than just *ask* for money." But Hoagland has "the New Yorker's quick-hunch posture for broken-field maneuvering," and the bad guy swerves away. 5

I often witness that "hunch posture," from women after dark on the warrenlike streets of Brooklyn where I live. They seem to set their faces on neutral and, with their purse straps strung across their chests bandolier style, they forge ahead as though bracing themselves against being tackled. I understand, of course, that the danger they perceive is not a hallucination. Women are particularly vulnerable to street violence, and young black males are drastically overrepresented among the perpetrators of that violence. Yet these truths are no solace against the kind of alienation that comes of being ever the suspect, against being set apart, a fearsome entity with whom pedestrians avoid making eye contact. 6

It is not altogether clear to me how I reached the ripe old age of twenty-two without being conscious of the lethality nighttime pedestrians attributed to me. Perhaps it was because in Chester, Pennsylvania, the small, angry industrial town where I came of age in the 1960s, I was scarcely noticeable against a backdrop of gang warfare, street knifings, and murders. I grew up one of the good boys, had perhaps a half-dozen fist fights. In retrospect, my shyness of combat has clear sources. 7

Many things go into the making of a young thug. One of those things is the consummation of the male romance with the power to intimidate. An infant discovers that random flailings send the baby bottle 8 flying out of the crib and crashing to the floor. Delighted, the joyful babe repeats those motions again and again, seeking to duplicate the feat. Just so, I recall the points at which some of my boyhood friends were finally seduced by the perception of themselves as tough guys. When a mark cowered and surrendered his money without resistance, myth and reality merged—and paid off. It is, after all, only manly to embrace the power to frighten and intimidate. We, as men, are not supposed to give an inch of our lane on the highway; we are to seize the fighter's edge in work and in play and even in love; we are to be valiant in the face of hostile forces.

9 Unfortunately, poor and powerless young men seem to take all this nonsense literally. As a boy, I saw countless tough guys locked away; I have since buried several, too. They were babies, really—a teenage cousin, a brother of twenty-two, a childhood friend in his mid-twenties—all gone down in episodes of bravado played out in the streets. I came to doubt the virtues of intimidation early on. I chose, perhaps even unconsciously, to remain a shadow—timid, but a survivor.

10 The fearsomeness mistakenly attributed to me in public places often has a perilous flavor. The most frightening of these confusions occurred in the late 1970s and early 1980s when I worked as a journalist in Chicago. One day, rushing into the office of a magazine I was writing for with a deadline story in hand, I was mistaken for a burglar. The office manager called security and, with an ad hoc posse, pursued me through the labyrinthine halls, nearly to my editor's door. I had no way of proving who I was. I could only move briskly toward the company of someone who knew me.

11 Another time I was on assignment for a local paper and killing time before an interview. I entered a jewelry store on the city's affluent Near North Side. The proprietor excused herself and returned with an enormous red Doberman pinscher straining at the end of a leash. She stood, the dog extended toward me, silent to my questions, her eyes bulging nearly out of her head. I took a cursory look around, nodded, and bade her good night. Relatively speaking, however, I never fared as badly as another black male journalist. He went to nearby Waukegan, Illinois, a couple of summers ago to work on a story about a murderer who was born there. Mistaking the reporter for the killer, police hauled him from his car at gunpoint and but for his press credentials would probably have tried to book him. Such episodes are not uncommon. Black men trade tales like this all the time.

12 In "My Negro Problem—And Ours," Podhoretz writes that the hatred he feels for blacks makes itself known to him through a variety of avenues—one being his discomfort with that "special brand of paranoid

touchiness" to which he says blacks are prone. No doubt he is speaking here of black men. In time, I learned to smother the rage I felt at so often being taken for a criminal. Not to do so would surely have led to madness—via that special "paranoid touchiness" that so annoyed Podhoretz at the time he wrote the essay.

I began to take precautions to make myself less threatening. I move 13
about with care, particularly late in the evening. I give a wide berth to nervous people on subway platforms during the wee hours, particularly when I have exchanged business clothes for jeans. If I happen to be entering a building behind some people who appear skittish, I may walk by, letting them clear the lobby before I return, so as not to seem to be following them. I have been calm and extremely congenial on those rare occasions when I've been pulled over by the police.

And on late-evening constitutionals along streets less traveled by, I 14
employ what has proved to be an excellent tension-reducing measure: I whistle melodies from Beethoven and Vivaldi and the more popular classical composers. Even steely New Yorkers hunching toward nighttime destinations seem to relax, and occasionally they even join in the tune. Virtually everybody seems to sense that a mugger wouldn't be warbling bright, sunny selections from Vivaldi's *Four Seasons*. It is my equivalent of the cowbell that hikers wear when they know they are in bear country.

THINKING ABOUT THE TEXT

1. What is the effect on the reader of Staples' opening paragraph? How does it function to underscore the point of his essay?
2. In what places is Staples' effect on people related to his being Black? Where is his maleness and/or stature a threat? Which aspect of his physiology does Staples believe is most threatening?
3. How has Staples adjusted his life to make himself less intimidating?

WRITING FROM THE TEXT

1. Write about a time when you unwittingly threatened someone. Describe the occasion using Staples' essay as a model, so that your reader can see and *hear* ("thunk, thunk, thunk, thunk") the scene.
2. Write an essay in which you describe the problems of being stereotyped as a member of a group which threatens. What, if anything, have you done to counter or handle the dangerously charged or uncomfortable environment?

3. Write an essay describing the problem of being threatened by a group or a member of a group that you perceive as intimidating. What have you done to avoid feeling intimidated or threatened?

CONNECTING WITH OTHER TEXTS

1. Read "Passing" (p. 234) and argue that Brent Staples' history, attitudes, and behavior demonstrate that his strategies for "passing" are techniques required for survival.
2. Find periodical articles that feature the stories of African Americans or Hispanics who have been stereotyped by the police, store clerks, or doormen as muggers, criminals, or gang members. Write an essay that uses the specific examples in the articles for support.

■ THE ATLANTA RIOT

Walter White

Born one of seven children to an Atlanta, Georgia, letter carrier and former teacher, the blond, blue-eyed son of light-skinned Black parents observed that people treated him in different ways, depending on what they assumed about his racial identity. An essayist, novelist, and autobiographer, Walter White (1893–1955) is noted for his portrayals of middle-class African Americans and the effects of racism on their lives. He is known for his early (1920–1950) studies of civil rights movements, and he gained a reputation as an undercover investigator and writer revealing the identity of participants in mob violence. The essay included here was published in 1948 in *A Man Called White.*

1 There were nine light-skinned Negroes in my family: mother, father, five sisters, an older brother, George, and myself. The house in which I discovered what it meant to be a Negro was located on Houston Street, three blocks from the Candler Building, Atlanta's first skyscraper, which bore the name of the ex-drug clerk who had become a millionaire from the sale of Coca-Cola. Below us lived none but Negroes; toward town all but a very few were white. Ours was an eight-room, two-story frame house which stood out in its surroundings not because of its opulence but by contrast with the drabness and unpaintedness of the other dwellings in a deteriorating neighborhood.

2 Only Father kept his house painted, the picket fence repaired, the board fence separating our place from those on either side whitewashed, the grass neatly trimmed, and flower beds abloom. Mother's

passion for neatness was even more pronounced and it seemed to me that I was always the victim of her determination to see no single blade of grass longer than the others or any one of the pickets in the front fence less shiny with paint than its mates. This spic-and-spanness became increasingly apparent as the rest of the neighborhood became more down-at-heel, and resulted, as we were to learn, in sullen envy among some of our white neighbors. It was the violent expression of that resentment against a Negro family neater than themselves which set the pattern of our lives.

3 On a day in September 1906, when I was thirteen, we were taught that there is no isolation from life. The unseasonably oppressive heat of an Indian summer day hung like a steaming blanket over Atlanta. My sisters and I had casually commented upon the unusual quietness. It seemed to stay Mother's volubility and reduced Father, who was more taciturn, to monosyllables. But, as I remember it, no other sense of impending trouble impinged upon our consciousness.

4 I had read the inflammatory headlines in the *Atlanta News* and the more restrained ones in the *Atlanta Constitution* which reported alleged rapes and other crimes committed by Negroes. But these were so standard and familiar that they made—as I look back on it now—little impression. The stories were more frequent, however, and consisted of eight-column streamers instead of the usual two- or four-column ones.

5 Father was a mail collector. His tour of duty was from three to eleven P.M. He made his rounds in a little cart into which one climbed from a step in the rear. I used to drive the cart for him from two until seven, leaving him at the point nearest our home on Houston Street, to return home either for study or sleep. That day Father decided that I should not go with him. I appealed to Mother, who thought it might be all right, provided Father sent me home before dark because, she said, "I don't think they would dare start anything before nightfall." Father told me as we made the rounds that ominous rumors of a race riot that night were sweeping the town. . . .

6 During the afternoon preceding the riot little bands of sullen evil-looking men talked excitedly on street corners all over downtown Atlanta. Around seven o'clock my father and I were driving toward a mail box at the corner of Peachtree and Houston Streets when there came from near-by Pryor Street a roar the like of which I had never heard before, but which sent a sensation of mingled fear and excitement coursing through my body. I asked permission of Father to go and see what the trouble was. He bluntly ordered me to stay in the cart. A little later we drove down Atlanta's main business thoroughfare, Peachtree Street.

Again we heard the terrifying cries, this time near at hand and coming toward us. We saw a lame Negro bootblack from Herndon's barber shop pathetically trying to outrun a mob of whites. Less than a hundred yards from us the chase ended. We saw clubs and fists descending to the accompaniment of savage shouting and cursing. Suddenly a voice cried, "There goes another nigger!" Its work done, the mob went after new prey. The body with the withered foot lay dead in a pool of blood on the street.

7 Father's apprehension and mine steadily increased during the evening, although the fact that our skins were white kept us from attack. Another circumstance favored us—the mob had not yet grown violent enough to attack United States government property. But I could see Father's relief when he punched the time clock at eleven P.M. and got into the cart to go home. He wanted to go the back way down Forsyth Street, but I begged him, in my childish excitement and ignorance, to drive down Marietta to Five Points, the heart of Atlanta's business district, where the crowds were densest and the yells loudest. No sooner had we turned into Marietta Street, however, than we saw careening toward us an undertaker's barouche. Crouched in the rear of the vehicle were three Negroes clinging to the sides of the carriage as it lunged and swerved. On the driver's seat crouched a white man, the reins held taut in his left hand. A huge whip was gripped in his right. Alternately he lashed the horses and, without looking backward, swung the whip in savage swoops in the faces of members of the mob as they lunged at the carriage determined to seize the three Negroes.

8 There was no time for us to get out of its path, so sudden and swift was the appearance of the vehicle. The hub cap of the right rear wheel of the barouche hit the right side of our much lighter wagon. Father and I instinctively threw our weight and kept the cart from turning completely over. Our mare was a Texas mustang which, frightened by the sudden blow, lunged in the air as Father clung to the reins. Good fortune was with us. The cart settled back on its four wheels as Father said in a voice which brooked no dissent, "We are going home the back way and not down Marietta."

9 But again on Pryor Street we heard the cry of the mob. Close to us and in our direction ran a stout and elderly woman who cooked at a downtown white hotel. Fifty yards behind, a mob which filled the street from curb to curb was closing in. Father handed the reins to me and, though he was of slight stature, reached down and lifted the woman into the cart. I did not need to be told to lash the mare to the fastest speed she could muster.

The church bells tolled the next morning for Sunday service. But 10
no one in Atlanta believed for a moment that the hatred and lust for blood had been appeased. Like skulls on a cannibal's hut the hats and caps of victims of the mob the night before had been hung on the iron hooks of telegraph poles. None could tell whether each hat represented a dead Negro. But we knew that some of those who had worn hats would never again wear any.

Later in the afternoon friends of my father's came to warn of more 11
trouble that night. They told us that plans had been perfected for a mob to form on Peachtree Street just after nightfall to march down Houston Street to what the white people called "Darktown," three blocks or so below our house, to "clean out the niggers." There had never been a firearm in our house before that day. Father was reluctant even in those circumstances to violate the law, but he at last gave in at Mother's insistence.

We turned out the lights, as did all our neighbors. No one removed 12
his clothes or thought of sleep. Apprehension was tangible. We could almost touch its cold and clammy surface. Toward midnight the unnatural quiet was broken by a roar that grew steadily in volume. Even today I grow tense in remembering it.

Father told Mother to take my sisters, the youngest of them only 13
six, to the rear of the house, which offered more protection from stones and bullets. My brother George was away, so Father and I, the only males in the house, took our places at the front windows. The windows opened on a porch along the front side of the house, which in turn gave onto a narrow lawn that sloped down to the street and a picket fence. There was a crash as Negroes smashed the street lamp at the corner of Houston and Piedmont Avenue down the street. In a very few minutes the vanguard of the mob, some of them bearing torches, appeared. A voice which we recognized as that of the son of the grocer with whom we had traded for many years yelled, "That's where that nigger mail carrier lives! Let's burn it down! It's too nice for a nigger to live in!" In the eerie light Father turned his drawn face toward me. In a voice as quiet as though he were asking me to pass him the sugar at the breakfast table, he said, "Son, don't shoot until the first man puts his foot on the lawn and then—don't you miss!"

In the flickering light the mob swayed, paused, and began to flow 14
toward us. In that instant there opened within me a great awareness; I knew then who I was. I was a Negro, a human being with an invisible pigmentation which marked me a person to be hunted, hanged, abused, discriminated against, kept in poverty and ignorance, in order that

those whose skin was white would have readily at hand a proof of their superiority, a proof patent and inclusive, accessible to the moron and the idiot as well as to the wise man and the genius. No matter how low a white man fell, he could always hold fast to the smug conviction that he was superior to two-thirds of the world's population, for those two-thirds were not white.

15 It made no difference how intelligent or talented my millions of brothers and I were, or how virtuously we lived. A curse like that of Judas was upon us, a mark of degradation fashioned with heavenly authority. There were white men who said Negroes had no souls, and who proved it by the Bible. Some of these now were approaching us, intent upon burning our house.

16 Theirs was a world of contrasts in values: superior and inferior, profit and loss, cooperative and noncooperative, civilized and aboriginal, white and black. If you were on the wrong end of the comparison, if you were inferior, if you were noncooperative, if you were aboriginal, if you were black, then you were marked for excision, expulsion, or extinction. I was a Negro; I was therefore that part of history which opposed the good, the just, and the enlightened. I was a Persian, falling before the hordes of Alexander. I was a Carthaginian, extinguished by the Legions of Rome. I was a Frenchman at Waterloo, an Anglo-Saxon at Hastings, a Confederate at Vicksburg. I was defeated, wherever and whenever there was a defeat.

17 Yet as a boy there in the darkness amid the tightening fright, I knew the inexplicable thing—that my skin was as white as the skin of those who were coming at me.

18 The mob moved toward the lawn. I tried to aim my gun, wondering what it would feel like to kill a man. Suddenly there was a volley of shots. The mob hesitated, stopped. Some friends of my father's had barricaded themselves in a two-story brick building just below our house. It was they who had fired. Some of the mobsmen, still bloodthirsty, shouted, "Let's go get the nigger." Others, afraid now for their safety, held back. Our friends, noting the hesitation, fired another volley. The mob broke and retreated up Houston Street.

19 In the quiet that followed I put my gun aside and tried to relax. But a tension different from anything I had ever known possessed me. I was gripped by the knowledge of my identity, and in the depths of my soul I was vaguely aware that I was glad of it. I was sick with loathing for the hatred which had flared before me that night and come so close to making me a killer; but I was glad I was not one of those who hated; I was glad I was not one of those made sick and murderous by pride. I was glad

I was not one of those whose story is in the history of the world, a record of bloodshed, rapine, and pillage. I was glad my mind and spirit were part of the races that had not fully awakened, and who therefore still had before them the opportunity to write a record of virtue as a memorandum to Armageddon.

20 It was all just a feeling then, inarticulate and melancholy, yet reassuring in the way that death and sleep are reassuring, and I have clung to it now for nearly half a century.

THINKING ABOUT THE TEXT

1. In the opening paragraph, White focuses on specific details about his house and its location: "Below us lived none but Negroes; toward town all but a very few were white." List other details about White's house. Then discuss the significance of the house and its location in terms of Walter White's own racial "stance" in the beginning of the story.
2. Why do Walter and his father feel less threatened than other Blacks when they are driving around town that afternoon? Discuss how they become increasingly involved in incidents involving other Blacks: the lame bootblack, the three Blacks in the barouche, and the elderly cook.
3. Discuss different areas of this essay where White creates tension and builds suspense.
4. After the father hands his son a gun and the mob is moving toward them, White freezes the action for three more paragraphs and shares an epiphany (an illuminating insight) with us. Even though he has stopped time, how does he manage to hold the reader's interest? Explain all key aspects of his realization.
5. How does White's newfound identity transcend race? Considering the trauma he has been through, why is he "glad" at the end?

WRITING FROM THE TEXT

1. Write an essay analyzing how Walter White matures and changes because of this episode. Support your claims with specific illustrations from this essay.
2. In an essay, convince your reader that White's use of narration (his storytelling) helps or hinders our understanding of the actual Atlanta riots and their place in the history of humankind.

3. Analyze an episode in your own life when you could no longer remain neutral about an issue or remain on the fence, straddling two opposed worlds. What prompted your change, and how did this new position affect you?
4. If you have ever been involved in a mob encounter, write about your experience as it relates to and contrasts with White's.

CONNECTING WITH OTHER TEXTS

1. Write a paper analyzing how White's depiction of the white mob relates to "In Groups We Shrink" (p. 274) and "Why Johnny Can't Disobey" (p. 277).
2. Focusing on White's essay as well as on works by Staples (p. 219), Naylor (p. 230), Olds (p. 168), or Straight (p. 170), develop an essay focusing on how difficult it is for Blacks in this culture to avoid being stereotyped.
3. Research newspaper reports of events leading up to and including the actual riots in Atlanta in 1906. Relate your findings to Walter White's account.

■ MOMMY, WHAT DOES "NIGGER" MEAN?

Gloria Naylor

Before starting college, Gloria Naylor (b. 1950) worked as a missionary for Jehovah's Witnesses for seven years and as a hotel telephone operator for four years. Naylor's writing career started after her graduation from the City University of New York, with a B.A., in 1981. She earned an M.A. from Yale in 1983. She has been a writer in residence at many universities and a cultural exchange lecturer to India. Naylor has said, "I wanted to become a writer because I felt that my presence as a Black woman and my perspective as a woman in general had been underrepresented in American literature." Naylor is the author of the novels *The Women of Brewster Place, Linden Hills, Mama Day,* and *Bailey's Cafe.* In her work, Naylor shows how the economic and social realities of Black lives profoundly influence and limit human beings. The essay printed here appeared in the *New York Times* in 1986.

1 Language is the subject. It is the written form with which I've managed to keep the wolf away from the door and, in diaries, to keep my sanity. In spite of this, I consider the written word inferior to the spoken, and much of the frustration experienced by novelists is the aware-

ness that whatever we manage to capture in even the most transcendent passages falls far short of the richness of life. Dialogue achieves its power in the dynamics of a fleeting moment of sight, sound, smell and touch.

I'm not going to enter the debate here about whether it is language that shapes reality or vice versa. That battle is doomed to be waged whenever we seek intermittent reprieve from the chicken and egg dispute. I will simply take the position that the spoken word, like the written word, amounts to a nonsensical arrangement of sounds or letters without a consensus that assigns "meaning." And building from the meanings of what we hear, we order reality. Words themselves are innocuous; it is the consensus that gives them true power. 2

I remember the first time I heard the word nigger. In my third-grade class, our math tests were being passed down the rows, and as I handed the papers to a little boy in back of me, I remarked that once again he had received a much lower mark than I did. He snatched his test from me and spit out that word. Had he called me a nymphomaniac or a necrophiliac, I couldn't have been more puzzled. I didn't know what a nigger was, but I knew that whatever it meant, it was something he shouldn't have called me. This was verified when I raised my hand, and in a loud voice repeated what he had said and watched the teacher scold him for using a "bad" word. I was later to go home and ask the inevitable question that every black parent must face—"Mommy, what does 'nigger' mean?" 3

And what exactly did it mean? Thinking back, I realize that this could not have been the first time the word was used in my presence. I was part of a large extended family that had migrated from the rural South after World War II and formed a close-knit network that gravitated around my maternal grandparents. Their ground-floor apartment in one of the buildings they owned in Harlem was a weekend mecca for my immediate family, along with countless aunts, uncles and cousins who brought along assorted friends. It was a bustling and open house with assorted neighbors and tenants popping in and out to exchange bits of gossip, pick up an old quarrel or referee the ongoing checkers game in which my grandmother cheated shamelessly. They were all there to let down their hair and put up their feet after a week of labor in the factories, laundries and shipyards of New York. 4

Amid the clamor, which could reach deafening proportions—two or three conversations going on simultaneously, punctuated by the sound of a baby's crying somewhere in the back rooms or out on the street—there was still a rigid set of rules about what was said and how. 5

Older children were sent out of the living room when it was time to get into the juicy details about "you-know-who" up on the third floor who had gone and gotten herself "p-r-e-g-n-a-n-t!" But my parents, knowing that I could spell well beyond my years, always demanded that I follow the others out to play. Beyond sexual misconduct and death, everything else was considered harmless for our young ears. And so among the anecdotes of the triumphs and disappointments in the various workings of their lives, the word nigger was used in my presence, but it was set within contexts and inflections that caused it to register in my mind as something else.

6 In the singular, the word was always applied to a man who had distinguished himself in some situation that brought their approval for his strength, intelligence or drive:

7 "Did Johnny really do that?"

8 "I'm telling you, that nigger pulled in $6,000 of overtime last year. Said he got enough for a down payment on a house."

9 When used with a possessive adjective by a woman—"my nigger"—it became a term of endearment for husband or boyfriend. But it could be more than just a term applied to a man. In their mouths it became the pure essence of manhood—a disembodied force that channeled their past history of struggle and present survival against the odds into a victorious statement of being: "Yeah, that old foreman found out quick enough—you don't mess with a nigger."

10 In the plural, it became a description of some group within the community that had overstepped the bounds of decency as my family defined it: Parents who neglected their children, a drunken couple who fought in public, people who simply refused to look for work, those with excessively dirty mouths or unkempt households were all "trifling niggers." This particular circle could forgive hard times, unemployment, the occasional bout of depression—they had gone through all of that themselves—but the unforgivable sin was lack of self-respect.

11 A woman could never be a "nigger" in the singular, with its connotation of confirming worth. The noun girl was its closest equivalent in that sense, but only when used in direct address and regardless of the gender doing the addressing. "Girl" was a token of respect for a woman. The one-syllable word was drawn out to sound like three in recognition of the extra ounce of wit, nerve or daring that the woman had shown in the situation under discussion.

12 "G-i-r-l, stop. You mean you said that to his face?"

13 But if the word was used in a third-person reference or shortened so that it almost snapped out of the mouth, it always involved some element of communal disapproval. And age became an important factor in

these exchanges. It was only between individuals of the same generation, or from an older person to a younger (but never the other way around), that "girl" would be considered a compliment.

I don't agree with the argument that use of the word nigger at this social stratum of the black community was an internalization of racism. The dynamics were the exact opposite: the people in my grandmother's living room took a word that whites used to signify worthlessness or degradation and rendered it impotent. Gathering there together, they transformed "nigger" to signify the varied and complex human beings they knew themselves to be. If the word was to disappear totally from the mouths of even the most liberal of white society, no one in that room was naïve enough to believe it would disappear from white minds. Meeting the word head-on, they proved it had absolutely nothing to do with the way they were determined to live their lives. 14

So there must have been dozens of times that the word "nigger" was spoken in front of me before I reached the third grade. But I didn't "hear" it until it was said by a small pair of lips that had already learned it could be a way to humiliate me. That was the word I went home and asked my mother about. And since she knew that I had to grow up in America, she took me in her lap and explained. 15

THINKING ABOUT THE TEXT

1. What does Naylor express about the merits of written and spoken language?
2. What gives words meaning, according to Naylor? Think about an example from your own use of language to support her view.
3. How does Naylor's brief narration of her childhood family relationships and patterns prepare the reader for her defining the word *nigger?*
4. What awareness do you gain or have confirmed in print about the use of the words *nigger* and *girl* both inside and outside of the Black culture?

WRITING FROM THE TEXT

1. Discuss a word that has dynamics or meaning based on the consensus of a culture rather than, or in addition to, its dictionary definition.

2. Describe the events that contributed to your understanding the full implications or dynamics of a word or phrase used to describe you. You might think about apparently innocuous terms such as *student, middle child,* or *employee* or a potentially more volatile term such as *tourist, Chicano,* or *foreign student.*

CONNECTING WITH OTHER TEXTS

1. In Naylor's essay, in "An Open Letter to Jerry Lewis" (p. 201) and "To Live in the Borderlands Means You . . . " (p. 127), the authors show that the words that are chosen to describe an individual play an important role in self-perception. Write an essay that shows how a term such as *cripple, mestiza,* or *kid* can take on a pejorative consensus that harms the individual, as when a non-Black uses the term *nigger.*
2. In "Discrimination at Large" (p. 207), Jennifer Coleman quotes a number of harsh words that people use to describe her. She believes that people who would never use ethnic slurs passively accept the denigrating terms that are used on overweight people. In an essay, compare and/or contrast the effects of people using denigrating terms such as *nigger* and *pig.* Show in your essay the ways that language exacerbates discrimination.

PASSING

Joan Steinau Lester

With her doctorate in multicultural education, Joan Steinau Lester (b. 1940) conducts workshops and seminars on diversity issues. She regularly writes syndicated commentaries for the *San Francisco Examiner,* and her articles have appeared in *USA Today,* the *Los Angeles Times,* and the *Chicago Tribune.* Lester was a cofounder and the Executive Director of Equity Institute, a national firm helping public and private corporations to address complex diversity issues. She has been featured on national radio talk shows and TV programs, including "Donahue," and her newest book is entitled *Taking Charge: Every Woman's Action Guide to Personal, Political and Professional Success* (1996). Her personal life reflects her commitment to diversity. As a white teenager, she became involved in the civil rights movement, later married a Black man "when it was still illegal in twenty-seven of these United States to do so," and then "did the next worst thing a white woman could do in that situation—had children." She relates how, years later, after a divorce, "I chose as my life partner a person to whom it is still illegal to be married—a woman, with whom I've been lucky enough to be partners ever since." This essay is an excerpt from Chapter 2 of *The Future of White Men and Other Diversity Dilemmas* (1994) and has been edited with permission of the author.

All of us have developed different ways of coping with the stereotyping of our group and of ourselves. Most of us face some stereotype, whether it's based on our class ("trash" or "snob"), our ethnicity ("drunken Irish"), or some other way in which our group is regarded as inferior. 1

We all try to live free of the stereotypes attached to us. Sometimes we do that by making ourselves as different as we can from the image. We try not to act "too Italian" or "too Indian," "too Jewish" or "too Asian." Many African-Americans, for example, have told me that they were never allowed to eat watermelon as children because that would reinforce a demeaning image. A more extreme coping strategy has been simply to "pass" into the dominant group, as people frequently do with age and with sexual orientation. Because this happens in plenty of situations, intentionally or not, passing is an issue for most targeted groups. 2

Blacks in the South used to be able to get into "white only" movie theaters by dressing as Africans or by talking with an "African" accent. My ex-husband did this as a young man in Nashville, Tennessee. On Saturday afternoons, he and his friends would wrap turbans around their heads, "talk African," and pass on into the theater. What a mix of emotions he must have felt: delight at outsmarting the whites, fury at having to practice the deception in order to see a movie, confusion about why this was necessary. Looking back through the lens of the current "don't ask, don't tell" military policy, I wonder if the theater personnel were really fooled or if they found the disguise an acceptable way of preserving legal segregation and still getting their revenue. 3

Passing has been an issue for African-Americans ever since there has been oppression, and the rape of African and then African-American women created children who were sometimes light-skinned enough to pass. Why not pass and get all the benefits accorded to the dominant group? Why pass and deny a portion of one's heritage, one's reality? Why live a lie? Tens of thousands of African-American families have been ripped apart over this issue. 4

Some mostly white families have been torn, too. A European-American client, Ethan, described how he felt the need to pass his family off as all-white to his new wife's bigoted parents. He removed from his home and office pictures of his African-American nephew—the son of his sister and her African-American husband—precipitating a wrenching family rift which lasted for years. 5

6 Passing. Jews could be in the country club, or the neighborhood, or star in movies if they just changed their names and, in some cases, their noses. In my uncle's case, the name change was from Steinau to Walker. In my friend Loel's case, during his childhood his parents changed the family name from Greenberg to Greene.

7 Gays can officially be in the Catholic Church if they don't "practice" their gayness. (Is the fear that practice will make perfect?) Lesbians and gays can often remain in the family if they don't say that their "roommate" of twenty years is their life partner. Everyone knows, but no one acknowledges. That is the unspoken agreement.

8 There have been passing women, too—women who have sometimes passed as men to get a job, to be Pope, to walk a street in safety, to roam the world and have adventures, or to live with a female lover.

9 So long as there are two classes of people—those with significantly greater and lesser social power—some members of the latter group will try to pass, unobserved, into the former. Why not? There is such a cost to self. But so long as the split exists, the edges will continually need to be defined. For who is in, and who is out?

10 Some people in targeted groups may choose to pass because they consider passing a matter of survival. For others, passing comes naturally because they don't fit the stereotype of the targeted group. Either way, all passing people are invisible and, if they wish to be seen, need to "come out" about their heritage, sexual orientation, or age when they meet someone. This is a common experience for light-skinned Latinos/Latinas and Blacks and for millions of people with many sorts of mixed heritage.

11 Who is Black? Are my children Black, with one European-American parent and one African-American parent (who himself has African, Cherokee, and German ancestors)? In the United States, anyone with any acknowledged African ancestry is generally considered Black, and the infamous "one thirty-second" statutes supported that consideration. The first census in the United States listed three categories of "race": white, slave, and other.

12 And who is "white"? This designation seems to be a fiction created during slavery times to distinguish "us" from "them." Most European-Americans have been considered "white" unless they are Southern Europeans. Carlos, a friend of mine from Spain, married Mercedes, a Puerto Rican woman, and thus became "Hispanic" rather than "European." Latinos/Latinas have long presented a problem for neat racial classifications. Often they are "white" —or Black—until they open their mouths to speak. Then their language puts them into a different classification.

Their mere existence defies racial categories. Afro-Caribbeans may identify with Latinos yet be considered Black in the United States.

There are huge variations in the racial-ethnic histories of 13
Latinos/Latinas depending on their country of origin as well as their own family background. A seminar participant told us this story. His father, Miguel Rodriguez, had come from Spain as a young man. He moved to California where he wanted to marry his sweetheart, an Irish-American woman whose mother refused consent. "People will think you are Mexican. Unless you change your name you cannot marry my daughter," she said. So Miguel Rodriguez changed his name to Michael Ryan, selecting the name of the Irish bishop in his adopted hometown. He didn't tell his children this story until they were in high school. The children had been told by their Irish-American grandmother that their other grandparents, who spoke only Spanish, were "Black Irish."

The same week I heard this story, another man I have known for 14
years, whom I have always considered a British sort of fellow with a British sort of name—John Pembroke—told me that his mother is Puerto Rican, he lived with his grandparents as a child in Puerto Rico, and once he grew up he deliberately passed as Anglo. Only now, as a man of sixty, has he decided to relearn Spanish and reconnect with his island relatives.

Passing. Asian-Americans have variously been considered "white," 15
"Asian," and "other," depending on the political vagaries of the moment. In Boston in the 1960s, the School Board changed Asian-Americans back and forth from "white" to "people of color" several times within a year, as the need for various numbers shifted.

Passing. Who is Jewish? Is a Unitarian who knows Yiddish a Jew? 16
Jewish law says anyone whose mother is Jewish is a Jew. Nazi Germany's definition was similar to that for determining U.S. Blacks: anyone with any traceable Jewish ancestry is Jewish. You could convert to become a Jew, but you couldn't convert out.

And who is gay? Is the person who reads a gay magazine gay? A per- 17
son who has one same-sex encounter? Six? Ten? What about an affair? "Don't ask, don't tell" is just the latest version of passing. It is a bitter pill that will continue to be litigated and otherwise contested as policy because passing is such a painful experience and because being lesbian or gay is defined by much more than moments in bed, as is being heterosexual.

Being heterosexual involves particular rituals, like weddings, cer- 18
tain social events in mixed-gender couples, and having a heterosexual outlook on life, in which boy inevitably meets girl. Being gay involves

other rituals, like telling coming-out stories and having a different perspective on sex roles, on family, on politics. Being "in the life" is an attitude as well as a behavior. That's why gays and lesbians are so often visible. It's something wonderful and self-confident in the walk of a woman, something sweet in the look of a man. These attitudes are not easily hidden, yet people try to hide them.

19 Many people in the United States are passing, consciously or inadvertently, hiding their class, ethnicity, or some other aspect of themselves. There are many communities in hiding, driven underground by shame and fear. Part of the process of creating a diverse present is the reclaiming of ourselves—the Native American great-grandmother, the Jewish cousins and African-American nephew, the lesbian "maiden" aunts—acknowledging who we really are in all of our multilayered complexities.

THINKING ABOUT THE TEXT

1. What is Lester's implicit definition of "passing"? What are some of the reasons why people feel compelled to "pass"?
2. According to Lester, how did Blacks in the South get into "white only" movie theaters? What were the "mix of emotions" that her ex-husband must have felt at having to "pass" like this?
3. Lester describes some Jews and people of other nationalities who have changed their names, and even their noses, to belong to country clubs, live in certain neighborhoods, and star in movies. What is the story she narrates about Miguel Rodriguez and his name change?
4. What are some examples that Lester offers of the ways that gays feel compelled to "pass"? Why does she feel that "don't ask, don't tell" is "a bitter pill" for gays?
5. What are the "costs" or disadvantages of "passing"? Consider some examples that Lester offers. How do you feel about the price of "passing"?
6. By the end of Lester's essay, we get a sense of how widespread "passing" is. Name the different *types* of groups and people who have felt compelled to "pass."
7. According to the biographical information and the anecdotes Lester includes in this essay, what are some reasons that she has personal knowledge of the pressures to "pass"?

WRITING FROM THE TEXT

1. Write an essay defining "passing" and examine the motives, advantages and disadvantages, and range of examples that Lester offers. Include your own experiences and observations as well.

2. Using examples from Lester's essay and from your own experiences, study the causes and effects on the individual, family, particular groups, and a community of people who are forced to "pass" rather than live freely with their identity.

3. Dramatize episodes in your own life when you or your family members and friends felt pressured to "pass." Analyze the mixed feelings you may have experienced. If you could redo these experiences, would you change any of the choices you made?

CONNECTING WITH OTHER TEXTS

1. Using ideas from Lester's essay and from "Ignorance Is Not Bliss" by Eric Marcus (p. 14), write an argument supporting or refuting the "don't ask, don't tell" policy in the military and in many groups or organizations within our society.

2. Lester notes that many Latinos/Latinas have been classified as "'white'—or Black—until they open their mouths to speak" (p. 236). Using ideas from Lester's essay, from your own experiences, and from the work of Gloria Anzaldúa (p. 127) or Gloria Naylor (p. 230), analyze the positive and negative aspects of preserving one's native language.

3. Many of our authors describe experiences of "passing" or refusing to "pass." You may want to focus on race or ethnicity as you write an analysis of the pressures and price of "passing" or of refusing to "pass." If you focus on issues involving *race,* consider the writings by White (p. 224), Staples (p. 219), Mabry (p. 124), Straight (p. 170), Rushin (p. 195), Scales-Trent (p. 184), Bambara (p. 46), Olds (p. 168), Naylor (p. 230), and/or King (p. 295). If you focus on *ethnicity,* consider writings by Tyler (p. 27), Anzaldúa (p. 127), Soto (p. 188), Seilsopour (p. 408), Churchill (p. 159), and/or Tompkins (p. 137). Depending on your thesis, you may want to include writings about both race *and* ethnicity.

5

Between Values

■ ■ ■

This final chapter of readings is necessarily a culmination of the other chapters because our age, gender, roots, and self-perceptions all influence what we value. This chapter invites you to think about the environment, the media, group dynamics, and the problem of maintaining your individualism in a social context.

Wendell Berry and Patricia Hynes prompt us to consider the consequences of our actions and encourage us to "walk softly on this earth." American products and culture—whether Coke, television programs, or our favorite gripes—are treated in poems and essays by Philip Dacey, Elayne Rapping, Jay McInerney, and Victoria Sackett. Robert Moog argues that we need to improve the quality of products made in the United States rather than blindly "buying American." Cliff Stoll and Nicholas Negroponte debate the values of "online living."

Living in any society requires us to balance social pressures and individual needs. Carol Tavris argues that "in groups we shrink" from right actions that we would not hesitate to take as individuals, and Sarah McCarthy analyzes the sources of group conformity. Martin Luther King, Jr. shows how the individual must appropriately deal with oppression.

■ WASTE
Wendell Berry

A prolific poet, novelist, and essayist, Wendell Berry (b. 1934) reflects his strong agrarian and preservationist values in all of his work. His poetry and essays stem from his concern for his native Kentucky, but they have been widely published in national literary and popular periodicals such as the *Nation, New Directions Annual,* and the *Chelsea Review.* Berry has been the recipient of Guggenheim and Rockefeller grants. The essay included here, from *What Are People For?* (1990), is characteristic of Berry's conviction that our values must include protection of the earth.

As a country person, I often feel that I am on the bottom end of the waste problem. I live on the Kentucky River about ten miles from its entrance into the Ohio. The Kentucky, in many ways a lovely river, receives an abundance of pollution from the Eastern Kentucky coal mines and the central Kentucky cities. When the river rises, it carries a continuous raft of cans, bottles, plastic jugs, chunks of styrofoam, and other imperishable trash. After the floods subside, I, like many other farmers, must pick up the trash before I can use my bottomland fields. I have seen the Ohio, whose name (*Oyo* in Iroquois) means "beautiful river," so choked with this manufactured filth that an ant could crawl dryfooted from Kentucky to Indiana. The air of both river valleys is seriously polluted. Our roadsides and roadside fields lie under a constant precipitation of cans, bottles, the plastic-ware of fast food joints, soiled plastic diapers, and sometimes whole bags of garbage. In our county we now have a "sanitary landfill" which daily receives, in addition to our local production, fifty to sixty large truckloads of garbage from Pennsylvania, New Jersey, and New York. 1

Moreover, a close inspection of our countryside would reveal, strewn over it from one end to the other, thousands of derelict and worthless automobiles, house trailers, refrigerators, stoves, freezers, washing machines, and dryers; as well as thousands of unregulated dumps in hollows and sink holes, on streambanks and roadsides, filled not only with "disposable" containers but also with broken toasters, television sets, toys of all kinds, furniture, lamps, stereos, radios, scales, coffee makers, mixers, blenders, corn poppers, hair dryers, and microwave ovens. Much of our waste problem is to be accounted for by the intentional flimsiness and unrepairability of the labor-savers and gadgets that we have become addicted to. 2

Of course, my sometime impression that I live on the receiving end of this problem is false, for country people contribute their full share. The truth is that we Americans, all of us, have become a kind of human 3 trash, living our lives in the midst of a ubiquitous damned mess of which we are at once the victims and the perpetrators. We are all unwilling victims, perhaps; and some of us even are unwilling perpetrators, but we must count ourselves among the guilty nonetheless. In my household we produce much of our own food and try to do without as many frivolous "necessities" as possible—and yet, like everyone else, we must shop, and when we shop we must bring home a load of plastic, aluminum, and glass containers designed to be thrown away, and "appliances" designed to wear out quickly and be thrown away.

4 I confess that I am angry at the manufacturers who make these things. There are days when I would be delighted if certain corporation executives could somehow be obliged to eat their products. I know of no good reason why these containers and all other forms of manufactured "waste"—solid, liquid, toxic, or whatever—should not be outlawed. There is no sense and no sanity in objecting to the desecration of the flag while tolerating and justifying and encouraging as a daily business the desecration of the country for which it stands.

5 But our waste problem is not the fault only of producers. It is the fault of an economy that is wasteful from top to bottom—a symbiosis of an unlimited greed at the top and a lazy, passive, and self-indulgent consumptiveness at the bottom—and all of us are involved in it. If we wish to correct this economy, we must be careful to understand and to demonstrate how much waste of human life is involved in our waste of the material goods of Creation. For example, much of the litter that now defaces our country is fairly directly caused by the massive secession or exclusion of most of our people from active participation in the food economy. We have made a social ideal of minimal involvement in the growing and cooking of food. This is one of the dearest "liberations" of our affluence. Nevertheless, the more dependent we become on the *industries* of eating and drinking, the more waste we are going to produce. The mess that surrounds us, then, must be understood not just as a problem in itself but as a symptom of a greater and graver problem: the centralization of our economy, the gathering of the productive property and power into fewer and fewer hands, and the consequent destruction, everywhere, of the local economies of household, neighborhood, and community.

6 This is the source of our unemployment problem, and I am not talking just about the unemployment of eligible members of the "labor force." I mean also the unemployment of children and old people, who, in viable household and local economies, would have work to do by which they would be useful to themselves and to others. The ecological damage of centralization and waste is thus inextricably involved with human damage. For we have, as a result, not only a desecrated, ugly, and dangerous

country in which to live until we are in some manner poisoned by it, and a constant and now generally accepted problem of unemployed or unemployable workers, but also classrooms full of children who lack the experience and discipline of fundamental human tasks, and various institutions full of still capable old people who are useless and lonely.

I think that we must learn to see the trash on our streets and roadsides, in our rivers, and in our woods and fields, not as the side effects of "more jobs" as its manufacturers invariably insist that it is, but as evidence of good work *not* done by people able to do it. 7

THINKING ABOUT THE TEXT

1. Berry laments the presence of the many leftover and broken products that pollute our surroundings. To what causes does he attribute the effects of brimming landfills and rivers clogged with waste?
2. Explain, in your own words, what Berry means when he writes that "much of the litter that now defaces our country is fairly directly caused by the massive secession or exclusion of most of our people from active participation in the food economy."
3. How does Berry relate the problem of the destruction of the economies of "household, neighborhood, and community" to our "unemployment problem"? What does Berry mean by the "unemployment problem"?
4. Reread the last two paragraphs of Berry's essay until you understand the complicated cause-and-effect relationships that he perceives well enough to express his points in the form of a summary statement.
5. What sort of life do you think we all might have if Berry's view became an operating philosophy for everyone? List as many qualities of that life as you can imagine.
6. What is Berry's rhetorical strategy in cataloging so many objects that he finds on his roads and fields? What do you suspect is his intention?

WRITING FROM THE TEXT

1. Keep in a separate place all items that you would normally throw into your trash or recycling in the course of one week. Write an analysis of the objects to support or refute Berry's point that we have become "unwilling victims" or "perpetrators" of the "damned mess."

2. Write an analytical essay about your family or a family you know well that supports or refutes Berry's view that our homes do not employ children and old people in "viable household and local economies" to perform tasks that would be useful to themselves and others.
3. Imagine a life in which you and your friends decided to respect Wendell Berry's views and correct the many wastes that he describes in his essay. Write a description of that life, and project the corrections that would occur as a result of your living consciously, with a commitment to avoid waste.

CONNECTING WITH OTHER TEXTS

1. Connect H. Patricia Hynes' essay on waste (below) with Berry's essay. Focus your essay on the corrections that Hynes proposes to the problems that Berry cites.
2. If you are interested in Wendell Berry's views, find *What Are People For?* (North Point Press, 1990) in your bookstore or library and read the other essays in this collection. Write an essay that focuses on his ecological, social, and economic concerns. Beyond summarizing his views, *analyze* them.

SOLID WASTE: TREASURE IN TRASH

H. Patricia Hynes

Professor of Environmental Health at Boston University, H. Patricia Hynes (b. 1943) is an environmental engineer who has won awards and grants for her work in environmental policy. She is author of *The Recurring Silent Spring, Taking Population Out of the Equation,* and *EarthRight* (1990), from which a chapter is reprinted here. *A Patch of Eden,* published in 1996, documents how community gardens of inner cities have the potential for achieving social justice as well as an urban ecology. Hynes is the founder of Bread and Roses, a feminist restaurant and cultural center in Cambridge, Massachusetts. Hynes also designed and collaborated in building the passive solar home where she lives in Montague, Massachusetts.

> *Recycling is better than disposal, reuse is better than recycling, but reduction is the best of all.*
>
> *Donella H. Meadows, Dartmouth College (1989)*

1 In the verdant, seaward city of Seattle, I listened to Mayor Charles Royer describe the premier recycling program in the country. In less than two years, Seattle has achieved 30 percent recycling of household waste. The city's goal is 60 percent by 1994. Also in the audience were

more than 300 local officials from cities and counties that face common solid waste problems: a growing volume of trash; no more than a few years' additional capacity in existing landfills; active landfills shut down because they are leaching toxic materials; and organized citizen opposition to new landfills and incinerators. The participants came to this conference on recycling, sponsored by the National League of Cities, because recycling is no longer an issue of "if" and "when," as one speaker put it; it is a matter of "must" and "how."

Before I left for the conference, a friend confessed that when she hears the term "solid waste," she never knows whether it refers to shit or old tires. In the waste world, solid waste is whatever you put out in the trash for collection or take to the landfill. Solid waste encompasses paper, food and yard waste, disposable diapers, plastics, bottles and beverage containers, tires, metal, appliances, mattresses, and furniture. It includes commercial, office, and light industrial waste, the majority of which is corrugated cardboard, paper, and plastic. 2

Much solid waste can be recycled and reused for the same or new purposes; some can be composted for gardens and landscaping; some can be repaired and resold. Recycling and reuse are a kind of modern alchemy in which one person's scrap becomes another's valuable raw material. How much treasure is there in trash? The most optimistic estimate from government officials of how much of our waste can be recycled is about 60 percent. This calculation comes at a point when serious recycling programs are only two to three years old and the premier programs have so far achieved 30 percent. As recycling becomes a universal way of handling waste, as markets are aggressively developed for recycled products, and as people *demand* that new products and packaging be recyclable, the estimate of how much of our waste can be recycled will probably climb. **Some environmentalists contend that 70 to 90 percent of our waste can be reused and recycled.** 3

Recycling lends itself to anecdotes and stories—whether it is a proud city official talking about color-coded curbside containers or a personal story of reorganizing a space-tight kitchen for separate glass, metal, and paper containers. At the recycling conference a mayor from Kentucky asked the mayor of Seattle if it were true that the Seattle zoo composts the manure of herbivorous animals and offers it free to gardeners as "Zoo Doo." (It does.) Elsewhere a woman told of trying to fool the system when recycling was first introduced into her town. She has a small kitchen, and the notion of setting aside separate containers for newspapers, cans, bottles, and mixed paper other than newspaper was overwhelming. She felt she would be living in a garbage dump. To avoid recycling, she bought extra thick plastic bags so that the trash collector 4 wouldn't notice the newspapers crumpled up inside. She packed empty aluminum cans into milk cartons, then stuffed the cartons so they wouldn't rattle. After a few months she realized that it now took her more time to disguise the trash than it would to separate it for recycling, so she devised a recycling closet with separate storage bins for newspapers, glass, and cans. Not only has separating the trash become second nature for everyone in her household, but they have become more conscious of shopping and buying in an environmentally sound way. They purchase milk in paper cartons, not nonrecyclable plastic jugs. They avoid takeout food wrapped in styrofoam. They save brown paper bags and reuse them at the supermarket.

5 I called recycling "modern" alchemy. In fact, it is an old tradition that was abandoned more than thirty years ago. During World War I, the Depression, and World War II, recycling was commonplace for households, businesses, and garbage collectors in the United States. Children recycled bottles and scrap materials for their spending money. Until the early 1960s, "shirt hospitals" in New York City refit old collars to new shirts. One story has it that when Los Angeles mayor Sam Yorty ran for office in the late 1950s, he campaigned for an end to separating recyclables in garbage.

6 The roots of the current recycling movement, however, are firmly set in the late 1960s and early 1970s grassroots environmental movement. Within six months of Earth Day, April 22, 1970—a day of national consciousness awakening about pollution and the environment—more than 3,000 community-based recycling centers were created. Many of these centers closed during the recession of 1974–1975 because tax policies favored new materials over recycled ones. Leaders in the current recycling movement, however, "cut their teeth," as one puts it, in that early grassroots recycling movement. And extensive educational materials produced at that time for schools, communities, and media form the database for today's public awareness programs.

7 By 1980, local public officials began to feel the squeeze in waste as municipal landfills filled up and new ones became nearly impossible to site. Municipal solid waste managers turned to a combination of recycling and incineration, with low expectations, however, for recycling—20 to 30 percent of the waste stream—and great expectations for incinerators—all the rest of it. Environmentalists saw this strategy as one that favored incinerators, because recycling to separate out the nonburnables—glass and metal—merely smooths the way for incineration.

8 The later 1980s has witnessed a rapid, radical change in solid waste strategy and management plans. Citizen groups have arisen to stop incinerators from being planned or built until waste reduction, reuse, and recy-

cling are fully implemented to their maximum potential. In Sonoma County, California, the county waste management plan calls incineration unnecessary and politically unacceptable. Nor can incineration solve the problem of landfills with less than four to five years' operating capacity. A new incinerator will take at least that long to build *without* community protest and permit difficulties. On the other hand, a comprehensive community-based recycling program can be fully implemented in one year.

At the Seattle conference, regional solid waste planners talked nonchalantly about the goal of 60 percent recycling when many had accepted a 20 to 30 percent goal only a few years ago. By 1995, when front-running cities will be recycling more than half of their waste stream, what will the planners' new estimate be? 9

Recycling the materials we use—almost all of which come from the Earth as raw materials, and some of which are extremely polluting when disposed—is *living as if the Earth matters*. Every ton of material that is reused saves from 1.5 to 3 tons of new materials. Reusing finished products reduces industrial pollution from manufacturing and pollution from waste incineration. Recycling rather than landfilling or incinerating is also living as if people and local economies mattered. The Washington-based Institute for Local Self-Reliance calculates that recycling creates thirty-six jobs for every 10,000 tons of materials recycled compared to six jobs per 10,000 tons brought to a traditional disposal facility. On the average, it costs $30 per ton to recycle waste, $50 per ton to landfill waste, and $65 to $75 per ton to incinerate. Thus recycling can transform the local waste economy into a productive sector and save local governments enormous waste disposal costs. 10

In many cases, we are being brought to recycling by a crisis rather than by an ideal, which is what the Director of Seattle Solid Waste Utility says impelled her city to move so quickly. But the Chinese *kanji* for "crisis," Diana Gale told us, is made up of two characters, one meaning "danger" and the other meaning "opportunity." In Seattle, a crisis—existing landfills were placed on the EPA's national list of hazardous waste sites and shut down—was turned into an opportunity: an ambitious recycling program. For the people of Seattle who pay directly for garbage collection, abruptly rising garbage fees prompted enormous participation in the recycling program. To promote the program, Seattle restructured garbage rates and shared the savings from recycling with residents. In 1988, the city paid haulers $48 per ton for recycled materials, half the cost per ton Seattle would pay for new landfill space. That same year residents normally paid $18.55 a month to have two cans of refuse picked up by the city. If they separated out paper, glass, and aluminum cans from their garbage in containers pro- 11 vided by the city's contractors and reduced their garbage to one can, they paid $13.55. Superrecyclers are offered the option of an even cheaper minican. To minimize their weekly nonrecyclable garbage, Seattle officials said, people are inclined to buy soda in recyclable cans and to avoid unnecessary packaging in products they purchase. Built into this recycling program is the incentive to reduce waste before recycling it. With new programs to process yard waste into compost and recycle certain plastics, Seattle expects to attain its goal of 60 percent recycling by 1994.

12 Recycling, as many people testify, often brings about a change in consciousness. First, people begin to take note, then they resent how excessive packaging has become. They observe the "creep" in plastic replacing metal, glass, and paper containers as well as packaging materials. They reuse materials before throwing them away or recycling them. They avoid unnecessary waste and choose recyclable, returnable, and biodegradable products over disposable one. Surveys of households involved in curbside recycling show that once they recycle regularly, people reduce their waste by 20 percent above and beyond what they recycle. Whether they are brought to recycling by a crisis or an ideal, many agree that, once there, they enjoy a different kind of satisfaction—one that comes with "walking softly on this Earth."

THINKING ABOUT THE TEXT

1. How does Hynes define "solid waste" and what is her assertion about it?
2. What are the economic advantages of recycling that Hynes notes? What are the philosophical values? What are the behavior changes that she cites in people who start recycling?
3. How do the two Chinese characters that make the word *crisis* symbolize the reality of the recycling movement?
4. How do the anecdotes that Hynes incorporates into her essay contribute to her argument? How does the history of recycling contribute to Hynes' essay?
5. Is your response to Hynes' essay enthusiastic agreement, cautious approval, jaded boredom—what? How does your experience with recycling—participation or rejection—influence your reading of this essay?
6. What does the epigraph that precedes this essay mean?

WRITING FROM THE TEXT

1. In an essay, specify Hynes' thesis and analyze the effectiveness of her argument. Consider her opening, support, clarity, tone, and anticipation of objections from her reader.
2. Make a list of each of your purchases for a week, noting the types of packaging or container materials for each purchase. You might want to separate the items into categories such as grocery, toiletries, fast food, and clothing. Then write a paper in which you discuss the issue of packaging, analyzing the materials that have come into your life in one week.
3. Write an essay in which you analyze your own ability to "walk softly on this Earth." Discuss specifically how and why you have learned to recycle, reuse, or reduce.

CONNECTING WITH OTHER TEXTS

1. Connect Wendell Berry's essay "Waste" (p. 241) with this essay to argue that one must embrace the philosophy "to walk softly on this Earth" to make a significant change in the environment. Use ideas and statistics from both essays, as well as your own experience, in your essay.
2. Read other chapters in *EarthRight* to learn Hynes' other ecological ideas and plans. Write an essay in which you focus on and analyze two or three of her proposals.
3. Learn how your community—school or city—handles garbage, especially recycling. Use the data that you collect to write an approval or disapproval of your community's solid waste program.

■ COKE

Philip Dacey

A part-time college teacher at Southwest State University in Minnesota and a full-time poet, Philip Dacey (b. 1939) is widely published in anthologies and poetry journals. He coedited *Strong Measures: Contemporary American Poetry in Traditional Forms* (HarperCollins), and he is currently publishing his sixth book of poetry *The Deathbed Playboy* (Eastern Washington University Press). Dacey earned an M.A. in English from Stanford University and a M.F.A. in Creative Writing from Iowa State University. Dacey's writing and teaching now focus totally on poetry, but he reveals, "For many years I dreamed of writing fiction but came to my senses when I was about fifty" and decided to concentrate on only one genre. The following poem was first published in *Night Shift at the Crucifix Factory* (1991) and later in *Stand Up Poetry: The Anthology* (1994). Dacey has given numerous poetry readings and has recorded "Coke" and other poems set to music by his sons.

I was proud of the Coca-Cola stitched in red
on the pocket of my dad's shirt,
just above his heart.
Coca-Cola was America
and my dad drove its truck.

I loved the way the letters curved,
like handwriting, something personal,
a friendly offer of a drink
to a man in need. Bring me your poor,
your thirsty.

And on every road I went, faces
under the sign of Coke smiled down
out of billboards at me. We were all
brothers and sisters in the family
of man, our bottles to our lips,
tipping our heads back to the sun.

My dad lifted me up when he came home,
his arms strong from stacking
case after case of Coke all day. A couple of
cold ones always waited for us in the kitchen.

I believed our President and my dad
were partners. My dad said someday Coke
would be sold in every country in the world,
and when that happened there would be
no more wars. "Who can imagine," he asked,
"two people fighting while they swig their Cokes?"
I couldn't. And each night before sleep,
I thanked God for my favorite drink.

When I did, I imagined him tilting the bottle
up to his heavenly lips, a little Coke
dribbling down his great white beard.

And sometimes I even thought of his
son on the cross, getting vinegar

but wanting Coke. I knew that if I
had been there, I would have handed a Coke
up to him, who would have figured out
how to take it, even though his hands
were nailed down good, because he was God.
And I would have said when he took it,
"That's from America, Jesus. I hope
you like it." And then I'd have watched,
amidst the thunder and lightning
on that terrible hill, Jesus' Adam's apple
bob up and down as he drained that bottle
in one long divine swallow
like a sweaty player at a sandlot game
between innings, the crucial ninth
coming up next.

And then the dark, sweet flood
of American sleep,
sticky and full of tiny bubbles,
would pour over me.

THINKING ABOUT THE TEXT

1. The narrator's opening words "I was proud . . ." characterize his attitude as a young boy. Find phrases throughout the poem that reveal the numerous sources of his pride.
2. List the various characteristics of Coca-Cola in the poem. What does Coke represent?
3. Is the poet writing this as a young boy or as a man looking back to an earlier time? How can you tell? What was his vision of the world then? Find images to support your view.
4. Characterize the poet's tone. Is he innocent and hopeful? Smiling at his past naivete? Bitter and disillusioned? Support your interpretation.
5. A number of images are ironic or incongruous—they contradict our expectation of what seems appropriate, and in this poem the incongruities contribute to its humor. List the images that seem ironic or comical.
6. What is the poet implying about a young boy's world vision? What does America stand for here? Why does the narrator end the poem with this image: "the dark, sweet flood / of American

sleep, / sticky and full of tiny bubbles, / would pour over me"? What do these "tiny bubbles" suggest, and why does he emphasize that his "American sleep" was "dark" yet "sweet"?

WRITING FROM THE TEXT

1. Write an essay or poem focusing on a key image or symbol from your own childhood and show how your attitude toward this symbol has changed over the years.
2. Read the section on poetry analysis (pp. 443–452) and write an analysis of Coke as a critical symbol in this poem. (See item 2 in Thinking about the Text for help in brainstorming this topic.)
3. Write an analysis of what the poet is suggesting about American culture and values. Is he critical or supportive of what America represents? Is this poem to be read as a satire or to be read literally? How can you tell?
4. Compare and contrast the world of the young boy with the world of the adult narrator who seems nostalgic for this earlier time.

CONNECTING WITH OTHER TEXTS

1. Write an essay comparing and contrasting the narrator's attitude toward his father in "Coke" with the narrator's attitude toward his father and grandfather in "Digging" (p. 21).
2. Analyze the character of the father and of the adult narrator in terms of Cooper Thompson's "A New Vision of Masculinity" (p. 63). Do the father and son in "Coke" represent the same or different values and visions?

■ WHO'S NOT SUPPORTING WHOM?

Robert Moog

Credited with designing the first widely used electronic music synthesizers, Robert Moog (b. 1934) not only is president of his own music equipment company, but also continues to write and lecture on music technology. In spite of his extensive technical background—he has a Ph.D. in engineering physics from

Cornell—Moog believes *writing* is a critical skill, especially for those in science, business, and computers: "In this post-industrial era, it's easy to push buttons, but if you want to convey information or convince people of your views, you have to either talk or write well. I prefer to write." Drawing on his experience developing products, managing companies, and having his own business fold, Moog challenges the "buy American" trend. The following article appeared as a guest editorial in *Keyboard* magazine in September 1992.

Two years ago here in North Carolina, Harvey Gantt was running for the U.S. Senate against incumbent Jesse Helms. It was a heated campaign, with Helms, perhaps the most reactionary senator ever, accusing Gantt of favoring minorities, welfare cheaters, gays, and immoral musicians and artists at the expense of the moral white majority. Those of us who had Gantt bumper stickers on our cars could depend on hearing nasty remarks from some of our fellow citizens. 1

One day back then, I was filling the tank of my Toyota when another customer at the gas station came up to me and asked, "Why is it that all you Gantt people have Jap cars?" For an instant, the question made no sense to me, so I said to him, "I give up. Why is it that all us Gantt people have Jap cars?" With steam coming out of his ears, he sputtered, "Well, you're all so goddamn patriotic!" Then he turned, bolted to his shiny new Chevy, slammed the door, and varoomed off in a cloud of smoke. 2

If my mind was quicker, I could have told him why I have a "Jap" car. Since 1950 I'd been trying to buy a small, well-made car—one in which the gas mileage was good, the doors didn't leak, and the frequency-of-repair records were favorable. Such cars were simply not made in the United States. From my perspective it appeared that Detroit was so busy building land-going versions of the Queen Mary, changing model years, fighting with their unions, voting themselves obscene salaries, and making sure that their stockholders got their dividends every quarter, that they did not have time to find out what kinds of cars people like me wanted. And the automotive unions seemed to be too busy negotiating big fat wage and benefit packages for their members to worry about the unseemly number of "Monday cars" (*i.e.*, lemons) that were populating the highways of our country. 3

So I did what any good patriotic American would do. Believing in the free enterprise system and in the benefits of vigorous competition, I did the only thing that made sense—I bought a superior competitive product, one that met my needs. That, I thought, would certainly help stimulate some action in the marketing departments of the Detroit establishment. That's how progress happens in a free market. Companies 4 that are truly customer-oriented thrive, and the less able companies—those that are burdened with inflexible or incompetent management . . . well, too bad, that's how our system works.

5 During the past two decades, millions of Americans like me have opted for Japanese cars, and Detroit is beginning to get the message. American cars being made today are smaller, more reliable, and more fuel-efficient than the wheeled dream-boats of the '50s and '60s. Our free market system is working. In the meantime, I have my Toyota, which still gets 35 miles per gallon and runs like a top after seven years, and has cost me a total of $200 in repair bills. It's all part of our capitalist system; my car is an ongoing reminder to Detroit of what they have to do in order to get my business.

6 That's what I would have told the man with the Chevy at the gas station—if my mind had been quicker.

7 I remembered that gas station incident when I read Richard Marshall's letter in the June '92 issue of *Keyboard*. Like my Chevy-driver acquaintance, Marshall was off on a be-patriotic-and-buy-American rant. Marshall's nuggets of protectionist wisdom rang familiar: "Every time we purchase an instrument, we vote with our wallet, either to keep our neighbors employed and off welfare or to fill the bank accounts of those wonderful people who brought us Pearl Harbor. Going out of one's way to buy American is neither paranoid nor racist, as some have accused, but rather economic common sense," intoned Marshall, as if his logic were irrefutable.

8 Well, I, for one, don't buy any of this patriotism-through-purchase logic. I'll tell you why, from the perspective of a person who has been deep in the electronic musical instrument business for nearly 30 years.

9 Under the free market system, which is certainly a cornerstone of American capitalism, producers are free to make and sell any products they choose, and consumers are free to buy any products they choose. Under this system, producers who offer desirable products at the right prices thrive, and those who don't must either improve their products' desirability or fail. This system has been the engine of genuine economic progress in our society. Under this system, the United States has become the wealthiest and most powerful nation on Earth.

10 Now, when some foreign producers enter our free market and offer more desirable products than some domestic producers, how does it suddenly become the patriotic duty of consumers to abandon their role of free-market buyer and "go out of their way" to buy American? Buying a less desirable product in order to "help keep our neighbors employed and off welfare" is not "economic common sense" at all. It's charity. It's

short-term humanitarian aid, a form of middle-class welfare that subverts our cherished free-market economy and hurts our national strength in the long run.

So who's not being patriotic and supporting their fellow countrymen when American musicians buy Japanese instruments in ever-increasing numbers? I'll tell you who. It's us instrument builders whose instruments you're not buying, that's who! Somewhere along the line, each of us has neglected to build desirable instruments at the right price, or we've neglected to manage our businesses so they are profitable and financially sound. Many of us have faltered or failed, and in doing so we've taken a toll on our national economic vitality. 11

When I began studying electrical engineering at Columbia University, our Dean of Students gave us a definition of an engineer: "An engineer is someone who can do for two cents what any damn fool can do for three cents." This should be the golden rule of engineering. But we seemed to lose sight of this wisdom as we worked through courses in circuit theory, solid state electronics, and advanced mathematics. We were taken with how clever we were becoming, and sneered at those of our fellow students who were majoring in mere industrial engineering. Those were the guys who would be running the factories while we would be sitting in our air-conditioned offices, designing one clever circuit after another. By the time we graduated from Columbia, we'd forgotten about our Dean's advice to be better than a damn fool when it came to making things at the best price. 12

Thus, when I started Moog Music (called R. A. Moog, Inc. back then), I had little understanding of how to manage manufacturing. But what's worse, I had no understanding at all of how to manage a business. I hired several electrical engineers like me, and together we managed to build a lot of synthesizers in the 1960s. But we wasted a lot of effort and money, and when our market became saturated and the first serious competition came, we simply ran out of money. The company eventually became a division of Norlin Music and, after being mishandled by a string of managers with more testosterone than management smarts, dropped out of the musical instrument manufacturing business about eight years ago. 13

At its peak, Moog Music had about 300 employees. How many overpriced, underfeatured instruments would have to have been sold to well-meaning musicians who wanted to "keep our neighbors employed and off welfare," even for one year? Well, at an average salary of, say, \$15,000 a year (back then), and manufacturing labor being about 20% of an instrument's retail price, you musicians would have had to cough 14 up about $22 million just to keep Moog Music's employees off welfare for one year! For sure, everybody was better off with the forces of competition pushing my old company swiftly and mercifully into the ground.

15 An unusual story? Not at all. Moog's chief competitor, ARP Instruments, was riding high during the early '70s. But by the late '70s, a combination of mismanagement, bad product development decisions, and really nasty infighting in the front office propelled the company into involuntary bankruptcy (the worst kind). Lots of people were laid off. Should musicians have done their patriotic duty and come to ARP's rescue by buying carloads of poorly conceived, overpriced products? Are you kidding?

16 Another example is an Italian electronic keyboard manufacturer that I did some work for about ten years ago. It was a well-established company, originally an accordion manufacturer. But as electronic instruments increased in complexity, the sophistication of their management still remained geared to the labor-intensive practices of their earlier days. Shortly before its demise, the company was shipping instruments that had a mean time between failures of three weeks! Still, the head of the company would go on his daily rounds to turn out lights to save electricity, and to belittle the men and harass the women to remind everybody who was boss. So how many Italians do you think stepped forward to buy the company's instruments to "keep their neighbors off welfare"? None that I know of.

17 Space limitations prevent me from regaling you with more stories of instrument manufacturers who are no longer in business. Like Moog Music, most of these companies did enjoy a few years of successful, profitable operation, but then failed because of a combination of inadequate marketing, manufacturing control, and financing. Most had been founded by engineers who were not trained managers. And more to the point of this editorial, no amount of "going out of one's way to buy American" would have saved any of these companies.

18 To be sure, there are many American instrument companies that have operated successfully for many years, who have grown, and who have consistently offered successful, desirable products. My hat is off in admiration to Peavey, E-mu, and Ensoniq, to name three companies who are doing the right kind of job for their employees, their customers, and their country.

19 Let me put down a few words about global competitiveness. Much of what we buy and use in our daily lives comes from outside our borders, because the production capacity to meet our needs does not exist

here. Let's not get into why it doesn't exist, but merely note that if our supply of foreign petroleum, TV sets, sport shirts, computer printers, paper clips, rum, cheap shoes, expensive brandy, and thousands upon thousands of other items were to be cut off tomorrow, our domestic producers of these items could not keep up with our needs, and the conduct of our daily lives would be severely curtailed. To pay for all these foreign-made items, we have to export stuff that people in foreign countries want to buy. The more we export, the more foreign currency we have and the easier it is for us as a nation to afford the foreign goods that we need. This means that companies that make products that foreigners are willing to buy are helping us all to have foreign goods that we need.

Now, how do you help a company to be competitive in the world 20
market? By saying that you'll buy its products just because they're made in America? No way! Any time a company perceives that it has a captive, unquestioning market, it becomes less competitive. I've seen it happen many times, especially in the early days of synthesizers. To take an extreme case, look what happened in the former Soviet Union and the Eastern bloc countries. They went one step beyond asking their citizens to give preference to their domestic goods. Through their import restrictions, they made it virtually impossible for their citizens to buy foreign goods. The result: Has anybody ever seen a Soviet consumer product that's competitive in the world market (except maybe for vodka and caviar)? What Soviet car would you buy? How about a nice Soviet jacket or portable stereo? None of these things exist as world-marketable products, because the manufacturers of these products, having a captive domestic market, grew inefficient and unresponsive.

Here's my answer to how to help your fellow American instrument 21
builders: The next time you need an instrument, buy the best one for your needs that you can afford. If it happens to be an American product, great! Write to the marketing department of the instrument manufacturer, and tell them why you like their instrument. If they're on the ball (and they probably are if they got as far as making instruments that you like), they'll use your letter to fine-tune their product development program.

On the other hand, if you wind up buying a foreign-made instrument, 22
it's your patriotic duty to write to the American manufacturers whose products you didn't buy, tell them whose product you bought, and tell them why. If a company reads your letter and acts on it, then you have helped them to improve their product line, thereby helping them to be more competitive worldwide. The day's pay or so that you denied some

worker in that company because you bought a competitive product should be more than offset by the increased business that the company will enjoy because of the information you gave it. Or, if some company receives your letter and ignores it, then it won't last long anyhow, and the sooner its employees find employment elsewhere, the better it will be for them.

23 I'll close with a response to Marshall's crack about "the folks that gave us Pearl Harbor." Yes, Japan gave us Pearl Harbor, no doubt about it. They were able to do it because their country was under the control of an imperialist, warmongering regime. As it turns out, the Japanese people paid dearly for their military adventures. Today, the political climate in Japan is decidedly pacifist. The Japanese people have directed their energies and their intelligence to economic, rather than military, achievements.

24 In our free market economy, playing our free market game, the Japanese have made dramatic progress. In many cases, especially consumer electronics, they've gone far beyond us. They started out with the same technology that we had, but while we were keeping hundreds of thousands of people busy designing Star Wars Space Zappers and stockpiling nuclear weapons like so many bales of hay, Japanese engineers developed the technologies for portable DATs, professional-quality handheld video cameras, and, yes, digital keyboards. The Japanese nation has become wealthy by designing and making these things, and their products have given millions of people around the world great pleasure and enjoyment.

25 As a nation, we no longer need Space Zappers and thousands of nuclear weapons. We no longer need a military-industrial complex of the size that has developed over the past 40 years. Now, for our own safety as well as our own economic well-being, we have to put a stop to being the world's arms purveyor and start designing and building products that people at peace want to buy.

THINKING ABOUT THE TEXT

1. Moog opens his argument with a narrative about a time when he was criticized for supporting a liberal senatorial candidate (instead of Jesse Helms) and for driving a "Jap car." Discuss how this personal anecdote helps Moog identify his narrator, establish his focus, and build to his thesis. What is his thesis?
2. What does Moog believe is wrong with keeping neighbors off welfare by buying a less desirable product? Why is this not "eco-

nomic common sense"? How is this "patriotism-through-purchase" logic flawed?

3. How does the author's experience with Moog Music support his claims?
4. How can we help an American company be competitive in the world market? What should we do if we buy a foreign-made product?
5. What does Moog suggest that the American government can learn from the Japanese?

WRITING FROM THE TEXT

1. Focus on a Japanese-made product that you have purchased (for example, one made by Toyota, Honda, Mitsubishi, Nissan, Sony, Panasonic, Casio, Minolta, or Yamaha) and write a letter to the American competitor explaining whose product you bought and why. Be detailed, offer suggestions, and explain what it will take to get you to "buy American."
2. Moog identifies himself as a "good patriotic American." Write an essay focusing on Moog's implicit definition of "patriotism" and contrast it with the attitudes of the Chevy driver and Richard Marshall, whose letter triggered this article.
3. Write an analysis of Moog's argument. Consider his thesis, supporting points, tone, use of narrative, definition, and contrast. Where does he anticipate and counter possible objections? (See "Argument," pp. 413–422)

CONNECTING WITH OTHER TEXTS

1. Write an essay arguing that the "buy American" fervor reflects popular sentiment and is an indication of people's inability to think independently and question such trends. Connect Moog's essay to writings by Tavris (p. 274) and McCarthy (p. 277).
2. Focusing on a particular high-tech product (e.g., an automobile, VCR, CD player, or microwave), research the latest *Consumer Reports* evaluation of the various competitors. Then write a paper supporting or opposing the "buy American" trend, based on your findings. Be careful that the American products that you consider are indeed American and not just foreign products with American brand names on them.

THE SEINFELD SYNDROME

Elayne Rapping

A professor of communications at Adelphi University, Elayne Rapping (b. 1938) earned her M.A. and Ph.D. in English from the University of Pittsburgh. She notes, "My experience—as writer, teacher, parent and social activist—all contribute to my work." Her published books include *The Movie of the Week* (1992), *Media-tions: Forays into the Culture and Gender Wars* (1994), and *The Culture of Recovery* (1995). Rapping is currently writing *Cultural Politics*, scheduled for publication in 1998. "Writing is a way of figuring out who you are and what you think," Rapping insists. "If you can't explain it, you don't really own it." The following article was first published in the September 1995 issue of *The Progressive*, a journal that carries her columns every other month.

1 Am I the only left-leaning U.S. citizen who has not joined the cult of *Seinfeld?* I know it's hard to remain cult-less in these days of mass social anxiety and instability, when each day brings new waves of terror to our fast-shrinking global village: mad rightwing bombers; out-of-control viruses; contracts on America; the Invasion of the Body Snatchers at the White House; the sudden, nerve-wracking reappearance of the word "socialist" as a political swear word in public discourse.

2 It's all very stressful. And for those of us who can't quite get with the culture of crystals, or twelve steps, or cyberspace intimacy, or psychic healing, *Seinfeld* does seem a harmless enough way of getting our minds off our troubles. He and his costars are certainly funny, often hilarious. They're certainly intelligent and hip. They even hang out on the Upper West Side of Manhattan, one of the last bastions of intellectual, left-liberal culture.

3 But at the risk of alienating everyone I know, I must say that I find the show, and its fast multiplying gaggle of clones—*Mad About You*, *Ellen*, *Friends*—almost as scary as the social and political nightmares they serve to momentarily mask.

4 Call me a hopeless Puritan. But I see, in this airwave invasion of sitcoms about young Manhattanites with no real family or work responsibilities and nothing to do but hang out and talk about it, an insidious message about the future of Western civilization. It's not that I'm such a big fan of the way industrialism has structured our work and family lives. But these new sitcoms—which seem to be functioning as cheering squads for the end of work and family life as we, and the media heretofore, have known it—don't offer much in the way of replacement. In fact, what I see as I watch them is a scary commercial message on behalf of the new economic system, in which most of us will have little if any paid (never mind *meaningful*) work to do, and the family ties (remember that old show?)

that used to bind us, at least as economic units dependent on the wage of a bread-winner (remember that old term?), have become untenable.

"What, me worry?" ask these clever series, as mantras to get us 5
through our pointless postindustrial days. To which I answer, under my breath, "But I do, I do."

These shows function as an entirely new, yet logical—even in- 6
evitable—media development. On the one hand, they do indeed diverge radically from the classic professional career/family-based sitcom we have come to know and love/hate.

On the other hand, the TV sitcom, with its rigid work and gender 7
patterns, was always, at heart, propaganda for a radical and in many ways terrifying new economic order. For these were the years when the new corporate-driven economic order shepherded us, en masse, into suburban bedroom communities, where we learned to watch sitcoms and commercials—the classic genres—to find out how to adapt. Dad's job—so said the guys on the small screen—was to commute to an office-based job "in the city," while Mom's was to stay home with the new goodies prosperity had brought.

But even back then, when TV Dads were Dads and Moms were Moms 8
and their job descriptions were clear and unambiguous, the role of work in Sitcom Land was already problematic. After all, it was Mom who did most of the actual "work" upon which the system seemed to rest—the yearning for, purchasing, caring for, and replacing the consumer products that made the brave new world go round.

On *The Donna Reed Show*—where Dad rarely even appeared—and 9
even *Father Knows Best,* there was little attention paid to what Dad actually did to earn the (always invisible) paycheck upon which the whole structure stood. Up in the morning, dressed in business attire and that ubiquitous briefcase within which "work" was apparently brought home but never attended to, Mr. Gray Flannel Suit was the titular head of a household which, in truth, functioned almost entirely without his interference. His real (and generally marginal) role was dealing with household matters as a sort of assistant Mom.

Work itself, then, was already, even in the fifties, diminishing in the 10
representational world of mass culture, as the things men did for money became less and less dignified, less and less interesting, less and less autonomous, meaningful, and fulfilling. Nonetheless, the *idea* of work as a daily ritual was maintained as a central element in the structures and plots of these shows.

Even in those early days, an unusual number of Dads seemed to 11
hang around the house a lot and to make their livings not by dragging briefcases to out-of-frame urban offices, but—like Seinfeld himself—

within the entertainment industry. *Ozzie and Harriet* and *The Danny Thomas Show* were the first in a long tradition of family-business-as-show-business series in which Dad, and sometimes Mom and even the kids, got their paychecks from the media itself, doing work whose only product was laughter. Nonetheless, these happy-go-lucky Dads still were seen as bread-winners. In *I Love Lucy* and *The Dick Van Dyke Show,* they even went off to work each day, leaving Mom at home while they slaved away writing jokes or rehearsing songs at their show-biz offices.

12 And that has continued to be the work of choice for sitcom producers and writers, from *The Partridge Family* to *WKRP in Cincinnati* to *Home Improvement* to *Blossom* to *Frasier* to *Murphy Brown* to this season's new hits, *News Radio* and *Hope and Gloria.* Even *thirtysomething,* while not a sitcom, was a family show in which the Dads went off to work producing fantasies with which to sell products, while the Moms raised the kids, kept the men in line, bought great stuff, and tried to figure out what to do with themselves.

13 Indeed, it is hard to think of a sitcom, except *MASH* and the Norman Lear *oeuvre*—both produced in the wake of profound unrest and leftist protest—in which anyone does any work at all that actually resembles what most of us do each day, and in a way that resembles the way most of us do it. (The remarkable *Roseanne* and her imitators are also dramatic exceptions.)

14 Today, what passes on *Friends* and *Seinfeld* for an alternative—free at last from the oppression of corporate work and the father-dominated nuclear family—is a flat and empty vision indeed. In these shows we see a vision of daily life in which neither work nor parenting nor human relationships in general have much meaning or even staying power.

15 On *Seinfeld,* on *Mad About You,* on *Ellen,* on *Friends,* most of what fills the plot line and focuses the action, such as it is, are trivial "McGuffins" of small talk and mixed messages. What is the funny smell in the back of Seinfeld's car? How can we make a Thanksgiving dinner to suit each of our mismatched, variously weird, friends and relations? Who is right about the pronunciation of that polysyllabic word we heard on *Jeopardy!* or tried to get away with in Scrabble?

16 Characters do a lot of fussing about minor errands that turn out to be more time-consuming than you would imagine. Often the characters end up spending the entire show dealing with mishaps encountered in their endless errand-hopping hours. The cleaning dropped off last week gets mixed up with someone else's, for example, and the poor hero must attend a formal dinner in a tux five inches too long or short in the sleeves and pants. That sort of thing can go on for a whole segment, or

even longer, as "... To Be Continued" becomes an ever more common way to drag out the trivia of daily life into ever further threads of "you-know-the-feeling" humor.

The actual characters and relationships around which all these trivial pursuits revolve depart even more radically from the days of *I Love Lucy* and *Family Ties*. Unlike even the wacky Ricardos and Mertzes (or the Bundys of *Married With Children*, for that matter), these people rarely worry about deadlines and never have disciplinary problems—except with their pets, perhaps. None of these characters has anyone who depends upon them to come home. The *Mad About You* couple is married, but they have about as much stability as any college couple sharing an off-campus apartment for the term. Nothing in their lives is any more serious or future-oriented than the lives of the misfits and strays they hang out with. 17

People share apartments well into their thirties and hope their invisible jobs will hold up so they can pay their share of the rent for the next month. Date partners come and go with the speed and confusion of a Madonna video. Problems arise, get wittily chatted to death, and are offhandedly resolved and disposed of, like last night's Burger King wrappers to make way for tomorrow's pizza. 18

These people have the problems and attention spans of junior-high-school kids, and about the same amount of responsibility and maturity. "Who forgot to vacuum last week?" asks one roommate to the rest, and I feel I am back in an earlier age, when my own kids were in junior high and chores and homework and bringing dates home to meet the folks were the issues we argued about. Except that those issues were, even then, even for my white, middle-class kids, the easy ones. There were also worries about college boards, about whether someone, or someone's girlfriend, was pregnant, about drugs and sexually transmitted diseases, and—even in middle-class neighborhoods—the occasional hassle with racist, bullying police officers who were always particularly nasty to racially mixed groups of teenagers, no matter where they bought their shirts or what their parents did for a living. Nor were kids, then or now, oblivious to the issues—social, political, cultural—that kids have always had to worry about and plan for, as they hope the roof stays on for one more generation so they can look forward to some kind of meaningful work and personal life "when they grow up." 19

None of this ever comes up on these shows. What they present is a vision of the world and its future that I, for one, find terrifying. Forget education, forget long-term career plans, forget families and the responsibilities and stability they bring. Forget about growing up, period. It's not a good idea. There won't be any jobs worth having, you see. So 20 there won't be any point in planning to buy anything; to have kids that you see regularly and have some kind of influence on; to even count on long-term relationships of any kind with the people you do live with and see regularly.

21 Needless to say, politics is a nonexistent concept in the worldview that informs this scattershot existence. Indeed, the most offensive aspect of the trend may well be its adolescent way of mocking everything that has any meaning whatever. These shows make anyone who takes politics—or anything else—seriously seem like a schmuck.

22 On a recent episode of *Seinfeld,* for example, the topics that arose to fill the empty hours ranged from cancer to Congressional whips to a misunderstanding with an African-American cop, in which Kramer apparently called him a "pig." In each case, the idea that anything meaningful or tragic could possibly accrue to any of these topics was quickly bludgeoned to death. The Congressional reference became a "Stupid American History" joke. The cancer schtick involved a guy who pretended to be having chemotherapy so that he could acquire a toupee without embarrassment. And the cop plot was reduced to a silly riff in which Kramer affects an eyepatch and stumbles around in an effort to adjust his vision.

23 And these were just the serious topics. The rest of the twenty-two minutes was spent worrying about eyeglass frames, wondering whether a "hi" would be misunderstood, and trying to pick up a woman in a coffee shop. (The toupee, it turned out, was the turnon.)

24 When *Seinfeld* and *Ellen* and the gang of *Friends* do the silly things they do to compensate for this big empty abyss in the middle of their lives, it looks like great fun. After all, they have simply taken a lot of truly funny things we really do think about and talk about and laugh about—*in our spare time*—when we are finished with our real problems and responsibilities. But a world in which *all* time is spare and empty and free, in which all relationships and problems are trivial and transient and disposable, in which days and nights spread out before us in an endless line of pointless, silly, slap-happy conversations and activities—that, it seems to me, is anything but amusing or charming to contemplate.

25 Sure, it would be nice to think we could all just hang out in comfortable apartments (the *Seinfeld* and *Mad About You* pads, with their bicycles hung on walls and lines of breakfast cereals visible from the living room, are a far cry from the plush homes of the Cleavers and Huxtables, but they aren't refrigerator cartons under a bridge, either).

26 Sure, it would be nice to spend our days planning to go out to dinner or to ball games, or running around doing errands and then talking about them for hours with our equally leisured friends.

But that's not how most of us live. It's a fantasy. And after a short stretch, it's a fantasy that grates. The yuppie narcissisms, the shirking of responsibilities, the sneering at politics all get to be a bit much. 27

Yes, these shows are smarter and generally funnier than their white-bread, suburban predecessors. But do remind yourself every once in a while of how different these people really are from you and your real neighbors. I should know: I live just a block from the building in which *Mad About You* is supposed to take place. 28

THINKING ABOUT THE TEXT

1. After establishing, in her opening question, that she is one of the few who has not joined the "cult of *Seinfeld,*" Rapping proceeds to justify why *Seinfeld* is so successful. What are the reasons she offers?
2. How effective is this strategy of beginning with an apparent concession? What are some other concessions she makes throughout her argument?
3. Rapping finds *Seinfeld* and its "clones—*Mad About You, Ellen, Friends*—almost as scary as the social and political nightmares they serve to momentarily mask." What does she feel is "scary" about these sitcoms?
4. What are some very real issues that Rapping thinks *Seinfeld* and clones seem to ignore but that Rapping's own children have worried about? Do you believe that sitcoms need to deal with such issues in more serious ways?
5. Find examples that Rapping offers of the ways that *Seinfeld* and its clones trivialize real issues and problems.

WRITING FROM THE TEXT

1. Write an argument supporting your thesis that sitcoms should or should not be expected to deal seriously with important social and political problems and issues. You may want to include ideas not only from Rapping's essay but also from more hard-hitting sitcoms such as *Roseanne* (which Rapping mentions only in a parentheses as one of the "dramatic exceptions" to the *Seinfeld*-type sitcoms).
2. Focus on a particular episode of *Seinfeld, Friends,* or *Ellen* and analyze it thoroughly to support or refute Rapping's argument. (You will need to use tips from both summary, p. 379–382, and analysis, pp. 427–434, to provide adequate support for this essay.)

3. Rather than focusing on sitcoms, choose another type of television show that you know well (e.g., police shows, soap operas, young adult dramas, children's programs, or cartoons) and write an argument illustrating what you find to be disturbing or encouraging about these programs.

CONNECTING WITH OTHER TEXTS

1. Read "Is *Seinfeld* the Best Comedy Ever?" by Jay McInerney (below) and, using ideas from this essay and from Rapping's, write an argument supporting either Rapping or McInerney.
2. Using details from Rapping's essay, from *Seinfeld* or *Friends,* and from "In Groups We Shrink" (p. 274), write an argument that such programs seem to encourage or discourage conforming to the group.
3. Write an essay arguing that *Seinfeld* perpetuates or counters Cooper Thompson's "new vision of masculinity" (p. 63). Include supporting details from Thompson's essay and from the television shows.

IS *SEINFELD* THE BEST COMEDY EVER?

Jay McInerney

Longing to write fiction, Jay McInerney (b. 1955) worked as a newspaper reporter, editor for Random House and for Time-Life in Japan, and a fact checker for *The New Yorker* before he enrolled in Syracuse University's graduate writing program. He believes that although these jobs were writing-related, they distracted him from his own writing. After graduate school, he wrote the critically acclaimed *Bright Lights, Big City* (1984), which he also adapted for Columbia Pictures. Critics note that the strength of his work "lies in his humorous delivery and unexpected irreverances"—two traits that he seems to value in *Seinfeld.* McInerney's other novels include *Ransom* (1985), *Story of My Life* (1989), *Brightness Falls* (1992), and *The Last of the Savages* (1996). The following article was the cover story for the June 17, 1996 issue of *TV Guide.*

1 In the beginning was *The Honeymooners.* Then *I Love Lucy.* It's about time to elect *Seinfeld* to the sitcom Hall of Fame. Now that half the shows on prime time bear a striking familial resemblance to the show about Jerry and his friends, it behooves us to honor this "Citizen Kane" of situation comedies, and to propose that it may be—as Ralph Kramden would say—the greatest.

I wish to go on record as saying that the first time I saw *Seinfeld* I predicted that it would die a quick and quiet death. Not because I didn't think it was great; I just thought it was way too good to be on TV. I thought they'd cancel it. Generally, if I like a new television show, it's quickly devoured by a midseason replacement. And *Seinfeld* seemed too weird to survive on the tube. Or rather, too much like real life, which is actually far more peculiar than life in sitcom land. It was also outrageously funny, the humor arising out of mundane situations of failed communication and everyday embarrassment, like being caught picking your nose by your new girlfriend. *Seinfeld* pays homage to the fact that embarrassment is funny. Men probably laughed louder than women at the episode in which Elaine discovered that her nipple was exposed on her Christmas card photo, while women presumably had a huge laugh when George was caught with his pants down after a dip in a cold swimming pool. This stuff happens to all of us. And it's funny—particularly when it happens to someone else. But who ever thought they'd put it on TV? 2

It's easy to forget after seven seasons jut how strange *Seinfeld* seemed at first. Remember the show in which Jerry and George are trying to come up with an idea for a TV show to pitch to NBC? George suggests that they pitch a show about nothing: "no story, just talking." Kramer, on the other hand, proposes a show in which Jerry plays a circus manager. The characters will be circus freaks. "People love to watch freaks," says Kramer. Like the candy mint that is also a breath mint, *Seinfeld* is both of these things. It's a show about nothing in particular, which is to say, everyday life as we know it. And Jerry is the bemused ringmaster of a genuine freak show. 3

"We are all queer fish," F. Scott Fitzgerald once said. The revelation of *Seinfeld,* as distinct from most sitcoms, is that normal life is actually quite peculiar. Kramer, lurching around Jerry's apartment like a cross between Baby Huey and Frankenstein's monster, isn't the only freak; Newman, the Pillsbury Sourdoughboy, certainly qualifies. And George is neurotic enough to make Woody Allen seem positively serene and WASPy. I know people like this. But before *Seinfeld,* I don't recall seeing anyone like George or Elaine or even Jerry on TV. 4

Yankees owner George Steinbrenner, who will have a cameo on the show next season, declared recently: "George Costanza is a nice guy." He was also quoted as saying, "This Seinfeld is the nicest young man." Steinbrenner is wrong as usual. One of the nicest things about *Seinfeld* is its portrayal of George and Jerry and Elaine in their not-so-niceness. Unlike your average sitcom protagonists. George and Jerry are not especially nice to the women they date, or even to sweet little old ladies, like the one who 5 happens to have purchased the last loaf of rye bread from the bakery right before Jerry tries to buy one; Jerry knocks her over on the street and steals it. Mind you, he had a good reason, as we all do when we do something lousy. But let's not rob Jerry of his own obnoxious charm by calling him a nice guy. He'd sell Kramer down the river in a minute for a date with the buxom heiress to the O'Henry candy fortune. As would many of my closest friends. And George, in last month's season finale, doesn't see any harm in calling Marisa Tomei for a date just hours after learning that his fiancée has died.

6 As a New Yorker, I appreciate the fact that although it's filmed in L.A., *Seinfeld* actually has the lumpy texture of life in the city, the random looniness of the street, the idioms (Jerry waits *on* line, not in line) and speech inflections of Manhattan. But I don't necessarily expect the rest of the country to share my taste. Perhaps there is something inherently funny about the claustrophobia of New York apartment living, which is the backdrop that the three greatest sitcoms of all time—including *The Honeymonners* and *I Love Lucy*—have in common. (My only complaint vis-à-vis *Seinfeld*'s authenticity is the fact that all the characters seem to own and drive cars. This is nuts. No New Yorker in his right mind drives a car around the city. We ride around in foul-smelling yellow limos with bad shocks.)

7 Car quibbles aside, I still don't know how Jerry Seinfeld and cocreator Larry David managed to talk the network into a show about nothing except a bunch of neurotic New Yorkers. But from my own experience meeting with network types around the time *Seinfeld* was hatched, I can only assume they must have kidnapped an NBC executive and held him hostage until they got the green light. It presumably made things easier for the creators of subsequent quirky New York shows. *Mad Aboaut You?* No sweat—like *Seinfeld*, except Jerry and Elaine are married. *Friends?* Seinfeld with great-looking actors. *Caroline in the City?* Jerry Seinfeld with breasts.

8 However Jerry and Larry pitched the show, you have to hand it to the person who approved the *Seinfeld* pilot, which wasn't like *anything* on the tube. That's the most frightening concept in Hollywood—a genuine original.

THINKING ABOUT THE TEXT

1. Even though McInerney praises *Seinfeld* as the "'Citizen Kane' of situation comedies," a "genuine original," and perhaps "the greatest," to be elected to "the sitcom Hall of Fame," why did he initially predict that the show "would die a quick and quiet death"?

2. According to McInerney, does *Seinfeld* reflect reality and "normal life"? What is the key to its humor?
3. What does McInerney think is "one of the nicest things about *Seinfeld*"? Cite his specific examples.
4. Throughout this essay, what does McInerney imply about his evaluation of the quality of television programming today? Support your answer with quotations from the essay.

WRITING FROM THE TEXT

1. McInerney claims that "*Seinfeld* pays homage to the fact that embarrassment is funny" and that "normal life" is both peculiar and funny. Write an essay about an embarrassing event that happened to you or that you witnessed, discussing how it was handled in reality and then how it might have been handled differently if it were a part of a *Seinfeld* script.
2. Write an argument essay that supports or counters McInerney's assertion that many of the best television programs get cancelled or replaced by mediocre, predictable programs. Include examples of the television shows that you prefer and offer suggestions to improve the quality of other television programs.

CONNECTING WITH OTHER TEXTS

1. McInerney seems to praise *Seinfeld* for the very quality that Rapping (p. 260) faults it: *Seinfeld* is "a show about nothing in particular, which is to say, everyday life as we know it" (p. 267). Write an essay analyzing the reasons for the dramatic discrepancy between these two evaluations of *Seinfeld.*
2. Read the two essays about the "androgynous man" (p. 55 and p. 59). Then evaluate your favorite male character from *Seinfeld, Friends,* or another sitcom in terms of his androgyny.

DISCRIMINATING TASTES: THE PREJUDICE OF PERSONAL PREFERENCES

Victoria A. Sackett

The former deputy managing editor of *Public Opinion* magazine, Victoria A. Sackett (b. 1951) now writes for a public affairs firm in Washington, D.C. A graduate of Reed College, Sackett says she has always liked words—"putting them together in my head"—but she was "terrified" of writing. It was her great "revelation to discover that you can *learn* to be a writer, that it's not a given talent." She has had articles in the *New York Times*, the *Wall Street Journal*, *American Spectator*, and *Penthouse* and for four years was an editorial writer for *USA Today*. Sackett is a single woman who is exhilarated by her recent adoption of a Chinese baby.

1 The nation is suffering from a plague. It has nothing to do with our immune systems or cicadas or controlled substances or insider trading. But it is just as damaging to our individual well-being and our social fabric. We've developed a persistent low-grade fever of intolerance that's sapping our strength and making us all behave like cranky, spoiled brats.

2 This is not major-league prejudice, the kind we've seen in decades past leveled at ethnic groups and scary new ideas. This is a common, everyday strain of irritability whose target is Anyone who does Anything that we find vaguely Unpleasant.

3 The disease progresses in three distinct stages:

4 *Primary intolerance:* You begin to suspect that everyone else has the symptoms. You will be dismayed and irked by other people's impatience. Suddenly the world will seem to be populated with fast-food clerks who grow surly if a customer requests a napkin; cab drivers who shower invective upon riders going anyplace but the airport; friends who say, "Will you *please* get to the point?" instead of listening politely to your too-long stories; and women who smite stopped trucks with their umbrellas if the rear tires overlap a crosswalk.

5 *Secondary intolerance:* Behavior in others that never bothered you in the past begins to give you all the symptoms of a neurological or myocardial incident—muscles twitch, heart pounds, respiration rate accelerates, vision tunnels, head throbs. In the presence of whatever annoys you—gum-chewing, ice-crunching, high-pitched giggling, foot-shuffling, finger-drumming, toe-tapping—you will be unable to hear, see, smell, or think about anything but that which you would most like to avoid. You will take indirect action: glaring, sighing heavily, twisting in your seat, and glaring harder. You will begin to commit thought crimes—adrenaline-fed dreams of slapping, yelling, and smiting with your umbrella.

6 *Tertiary intolerance:* You give in to your fantasies and frustration and take direct action to ease your discomfort. You speak to the offender. "Would you mind not doing that? It bothers me," is the favored beginner's phrase. It means quite simply, "Stop doing things the way you want to and do them the way I want you to."

Once you've shushed your first talkative movie viewer, you know that the virus has entered your bloodstream. All the antibodies built up by your mother's fine teachings of patience have proven unequal to their task. This can be life-threatening. One young man at a recent Laurel, Maryland, showing of *The Untouchables*, for example, asked a noisy neighbor to be quiet once too often and was beaten unconscious by the talker and nine companions. 7

The cruelty of this particular ailment is that efforts to alleviate the symptoms make it worse. The more vexations that you attempt to control, the more easily you will be vexed. Victory over one provocation just lowers your resistance to another; once you begin to suspect that you *can* get people to behave according to your specifications, chances are you will be unwilling to let them get away with much of anything. We've hardly noticed it happening, but this is what has turned small-time intolerance into a countrywide epidemic. 8

The irony is that, as the nation has grown more tolerant and welcoming of all kinds of ethnic and other diversity, individuals succumbing to their petty prejudices now comprise veritable lynch mobs. Their targets are the newly beleaguered minorities: cholesterol eaters (watch what happens at a family dinner when you ask for butter *and* sour cream *and* bacon bits for your potato. Someone will describe for you in clinical detail just what saturated fat does to your innards), perfume wearers (Ann Landers published the seat number of a subscription ticket holder at the Arena stage who wore a scent that bothered someone near her), and smokers of any variety (I have one friend of otherwise saintly patience who can't *bear* the smell of fake logs burning. He was able to get his neighbors to stop). 9

Antismokers are the most contagious group. It begins in childhood. Every three-year-old holds his or her nose, waves a fat little arm in the air, and says "That stinks" when an adult lights up. It's always been this way, even before the surgeon general frightened us. But in the olden days, mothers and fathers used this behavior as an opportunity to teach one of life's most valuable lessons: It's rude to boss people around, and you can't always have everything the way you want it. 10

Now these children are congratulated for their wisdom and adults imitate *them*. It is true that both the small ones and the big ones have arguments in their favor. They can insist that it's their health and not their whim that is being indulged, but this is open to doubt. If smoking smelled good, chances are the investigations into its ill effects would have stopped with the damage it did to the smoker. 11

12 These days, smoke-haters are armed with a doctor's excuse for their own intolerance. There's no such thing as being rude to a smoker. And 90 percent of the people who are snarling at the addict, driving him out of restaurants, workplaces, and entire communities, throwing pitchers of water at him, and teaching their children to say "That's disgusting" to him are less concerned about being infected by his cigars or cigarettes than they are concerned with manifesting the symptoms of their own disease—final-stage intolerance.

13 Expanded to a global scale, tertiary intolerance could add up to something serious. Other than making each of us—the irritable as well as the irritating—less happy than we were when we could take things in stride, this plague of intolerance could threaten the fate of the world. What if our president, for instance, decided to take the advice of all the actresses and junior high school students who've been telling him that the Russians are just like us, so we should all lay down arms and be good friends? Then what if we found out that the Soviets were like us, but weren't what we liked—they smoke cigars, say, or shuffle their feet, or chew gum in movie theaters? Peace wouldn't have a chance.

14 Why have we become so testy? One explanation could well be the trend toward later marriage. People who live by themselves for prolonged periods tend to expect the world to be far more within their control than those who are constantly disrupted by the demands of spouses or offspring. Or, the other side of that, people who marry later tend to be those who enjoy the control they have over their own lives. Either way, there are more of them around, and they may be having their effect on the collective tolerance level.

15 The other culprit has to be assertiveness training. Since politeness came to be identified as meekness and repression, there have been no holds barred on expressing oneself. To avoid stating your wishes is to invite psychological damage, professional dead ends, and lack of respect from others. Few schools of thought have been swallowed so unquestioningly and with such exasperating results.

16 Widespread irritability may just be one more irritation that we have to deal with in late twentieth-century America. Maybe human nature requires a certain irreducible minimum of intolerance, the way the human body requires minute quantities of "trace minerals" that keep everything from going haywire. If we chase prejudice out of one part of our souls, it pops up somewhere else. Legislation and enlightenment have accustomed us to large-scale diversity, so now we fuss about petty differences. This is still an exhausting and unpleasant state of mind, but it may be as close as we can come to conquering intolerance altogether. We can't, after all, always have everything the way we want it.

THINKING ABOUT THE TEXT

1. What are the three stages of the "plague" that Sackett defines and describes in her essay?
2. What does Sackett mean when she writes that "efforts to alleviate the symptoms" of the disease only make it worse? Do you agree with her lack of hope?
3. Why does Sackett find it ironic that we today seem especially intolerant of petty prejudices? Do you agree that the intolerances that she cites are petty? What are your personal intolerances?
4. Why, according to Sackett, have we become so intolerant? Do you agree with her speculations about why we have become so "testy"? Do you have some theories of your own about the causes of our intolerance?

WRITING FROM THE TEXT

1. Write an essay in which you defend your personal preferences and frustration with behavior that you find insensitive or rude. In addition to citing your particular intolerances, describe and defend them by arguing their worth.
2. Write a response to Sackett that argues that she is correct, that people are intolerant and have prejudices about petty issues. Cite and describe the intolerances that you find most petty.
3. Write a response to Sackett that argues that she is wrong, that people are so impolite that they must be reminded not to talk in movie theaters or not to smoke in nonsmoking areas (add your own observations), and that only by speaking up will we rid the world of dreadful behavior.

CONNECTING WITH OTHER TEXTS

1. In "Discrimination at Large," (p. 207), Jennifer Coleman describes how others' intolerance of fat people has resulted in her being treated rudely. Connect Sackett's essay and Coleman's to your own observations to argue that intolerance of fat people is a prejudice that must be eliminated.
2. Connect the essays on androgyny (Gross, p. 55 and Perrin, p. 59) and masculinity (Thompson, p. 63) to Sackett's essay to argue that what it means to be a man is conditioned by petty prejudice.

IN GROUPS WE SHRINK

Carol Tavris

After studying sociology and comparative literature at Brandeis University, Carol Tavris (b. 1944) earned her Ph.D. in social psychology at the University of Michigan. Tavris has worked as a free-lance writer, taught in UCLA's psychology department, and served as both writer and editor for *Psychology Today.* She has published extensively in the field of psychology, with emphasis on emotions, anger, sexuality, and gender issues. Her most recent book, *The Mismeasure of Woman,* was published in 1992. The essay printed here appeared in the *Los Angeles Times* in 1991.

1 The ghost of Kitty Genovese would sympathize with Rodney King. Genovese, you may remember, is the symbol of bystander apathy in America. Screaming for help, she was stabbed repeatedly and killed in front of her New York apartment, and not one of the 38 neighbors who heard her, including those who came to their windows to watch, even called for help.

2 One of the things we find appalling in the videotape of King's assault is the image of at least 11 police officers watching four of their colleagues administer the savage beating and doing nothing to intervene. Whatever is the matter with them, we wonder.

3 Something happens to individuals when they collect in a group. They think and act differently than they would on their own. Most people, if they observe some disaster or danger on their own—a woman being stabbed, a pedestrian slammed by a hit-and-run driver—will at least call for help; many will even risk their own safety to intervene. But if they are in a group observing the same danger, they hold back. The reason is not necessarily that they are lazy, cowardly or have 50 other personality deficiencies; it has more to do with the nature of groups than the nature of individuals.

4 In one experiment in behavioral psychology, students were seated in a room, either alone or in groups of three, as a staged emergency occurred: Smoke began pouring through the vents. Students who were on their own usually hesitated a minute, got up, checked the vents and then went out to report what certainly seemed like fire. But the students who were sitting in groups of three did not move. They sat there for six minutes, with smoke so thick they could barely see, rubbing their eyes and coughing.

5 In another experiment, psychologists staged a situation in which people overheard a loud crash, a scream and a woman in pain, moaning that her ankle was broken. Seventy percent of those who were alone when the "accident" occurred went to her aid, compared with only 40% of those who heard her in the presence of another person.

For victims, obviously, there is no safety in numbers. Why? One reason is that if other people aren't doing anything, the individual assumes that nothing needs to be done. In the smoke-filled room study, the students in groups said they thought that the smoke was caused by "steam pipes," "truth gas" or "leaks in the air conditioning"; not one said what the students on their own did: "I thought it was fire." In the lady-in-distress study, some of those who failed to offer help said, "I didn't want to embarrass her." 6

Often, observers think nothing needs to be done because someone else has already taken care of it, and the more observers there are, the less likely any one person is to call for help. In Albuquerque, N.M., 30 people watched for an hour and a half as a building burned to the ground before they realized that no one had called the fire department. Psychologists call this process "diffusion of responsibility" or "social loafing": The more people in a group, the lazier each individual in it becomes. 7

But there was no mistaking what those officers were doing to Rodney King. There was no way for those observers to discount the severity of the beating King was getting. What kept them silent? 8

One explanation, of course, is that they approved. They may have identified with the abusers, vicariously participating in a beating they rationalized as justified. The widespread racism in the Los Angeles Police Department and the unprovoked abuse of black people is now undeniable. A friend who runs a trucking company told me recently that one of her drivers, a 50-year-old black man, is routinely pulled over by Los Angeles cops for the flimsiest of reasons "and made to lie down on the street like a dog." None of her white drivers has been treated this way. 9

Or the observers may have hated what was happening and been caught in the oldest of human dilemmas: Do the moral thing and be disliked, humiliated, embarrassed and rejected. Our nation, for all its celebration of the Lone Ranger and the independent pioneer, does not really value the individual—at least not when the person is behaving individually and standing up to the group. (We like dissenters, but only when they are dissenting in Russia or China.) Again and again, countless studies have shown that people will go along rather than risk the embarrassment of being disobedient, rude or disloyal. 10

And so the banality of evil is once again confirmed. Most people do not behave badly because they are inherently bad. They behave badly because they aren't paying attention, or they leave it to Harry, or they don't want to rock the boat, or they don't want to embarrass themselves or others if they're wrong. 11

12 Every time the news reports another story of a group that has behaved mindlessly, violently and stupidly, including the inevitable members who are just "going along," many people shake their heads in shock and anger at the failings of "human nature." But the findings of behavioral research can direct us instead to appreciate the conditions under which individuals in groups will behave morally or not. Once we know the conditions, we can begin to prescribe antidotes. By understanding the impulse to diffuse responsibility, perhaps as individuals we will be more likely to act. By understanding the social pressures that reward group-think, loyalty and obedience, we can foster those that reward whistle-blowing and moral courage. And, as a society, we can reinforce the belief that they also sin who only stand and watch.

THINKING ABOUT THE TEXT

1. What is Tavris' thesis? How does she support her position?
2. How does the psychologist's term for the behavior Tavris describes explain what actually happens?
3. How does Tavris imagine this condition will right itself?

WRITING FROM THE TEXT

1. Write about an incident that you observed or were a part of that confirms Carol Tavris' point.
2. Write about an incident that you observed or were a part of that shows an exception to Tavris' point.

CONNECTING WITH OTHER TEXTS

1. Read "Discrimination at Large" (p. 207) and argue that people's ridicule of fat people is often part of a group dynamic. Use Tavris' reasoning to show how people in groups sanction such ridicule. As part of your essay, consider Coleman's suggestion that the group can work as a whole to exert pressure on those who discriminate against the fat.
2. Write an essay that connects Tavris' ideas on group dynamics with the research reported by Sarah McCarthy (p. 277). You may want to focus on the causes and effects of group conformity.
3. Research the Rodney King incident of 1991 to find interviews and court testimony from the police officers who were participants in or observers of the beating. Do their own words and feelings confirm or refute Tavris' thesis?

■ WHY JOHNNY CAN'T DISOBEY

Sarah J. McCarthy

A graduate of Duquesne University, Sarah J. McCarthy (b. 1942) is an owner of Amel's Restaurant, in Pittsburgh, Pennsylvania, and a free-lance writer. McCarthy has written "Pornography, Rape, and The Cult of Macho" and "Cultural Fascism" for *Forbes* magazine. The essay reprinted here appeared first in *The Humanist* in 1979.

Few people are too concerned about whether Johnny can disobey. 1
There is no furor or frantic calls to the PTA, as when it is discovered that he can't read or does poorly on his S.A.T. scores. Even to consider the question is at first laughable. Parents and teachers, after all, are systematically working at developing the virtue of obedience. To my knowledge, no one as yet has opened a remedial disobedience school for overly compliant children, and probably no one ever will. And that in itself is a major problem.

Patricia Hearst recently said that the mindless state of obedience 2
which enveloped her at the hands of the Symbionese Liberation Army could happen to anyone. Jumping to a tentative conclusion from a tip-of-the-iceberg perspective, it looks as though it already has happened to many, and that it has required nothing so dramatic as a kidnapping to bring it about.

Given our experience with various malevolent authority figures 3
such as Adolph Hitler, Charles Manson, Lieutenant Calley, and Jim Jones, it is unfortunately no longer surprising that there are leaders who are capable of wholesale cruelty to the point of directing mass killings. What remains shocking, however, is that they are so often successful in recruiting followers. There seems to be no shortage of individuals who will offer their hearts and minds on a silver platter to feed the egos of the power-hungry. This becomes even more disturbing when one ponders the truism that society's neurotics are often its cultural caricatures, displaying exaggerated manifestations of its collective neuroses. There are enough examples of obedience to horrendous commands for us to ask if and how a particular culture sows the seeds of dangerous conformity.

Political platitudes and lip service to the contrary, obedience is 4
highly encouraged in matters petty as well as profound. Linda Eton, an Iowa firefighter, was suspended from her job and catapulted to national fame for the radical act of breast-feeding at work. A dehumanized, compartmentalized society finds little room for spontaneity, and a blatantly natural act like breast-feeding is viewed as a preposterous interruption of the status quo.

5 Pettiness abounds in our social relationships, ensuring compliance through peer pressure and disapproval, and enforced by economic sanctions at the workplace. A friend of mine, a construction worker, reported to his job one rainy day carrying an umbrella. The foreman was outraged by this break from the norm, and demanded that the guy never again carry an umbrella to the construction site, even if the umbrella was black, since it "caused his whole crew to look like a bunch of faggots."

6 Another friend, though less scandalizingly visible in his job as a security guard during the wee hours for a multinational corporation, was caught redhanded playing a harmonica. Mercifully, he was given another chance, only to be later fired for not wearing regulation shoes.

7 Ostensibly, such firings and threats are deemed necessary to prevent inefficiency and rampant chaos at the workplace. But if employers were merely concerned about productivity and efficiency, it certainly is disputable that "yes-people" are more productive and beneficial than "no-people." Harmonicas may even increase efficiency by keeping security guards sane, alert, and awake by staving off sensory deprivation. A dripping-wet construction worker could conceivably be less productive than a dry one. And the Adidas being worn by the errant security guard could certainly have contributed to his fleetness and agility as opposed to the cumbersome regulation shoes. The *real* issues here have nothing to do with productivity. What is really involved is an irrational fear of the mildly unusual, a pervasive attitude held by authorities that their subordinates are about to run amok and need constant control.

8 These little assaults on our freedom prepare us for the big ones. Having long suspected that a huge iceberg of mindless obedience existed beneath our cultural surface, I was not particularly surprised when I heard that nine hundred people followed their leader to mass suicide. For some time we have lived with the realization that people are capable of killing six million of their fellow citizens on command. Jonestown took us one step further. People will kill themselves on command.

9 In matters ridiculous and sublime, this culture and the world at large clearly exhibit symptoms of pathological obedience. Each time one of the more sensational incidents occurs—Jonestown, the Mai Lai massacre, Nazi Germany, the Manson murders—we attribute its occurrence to factors unique to it, trying to deny any similarities to anything close to us, tossing it about like a philosophical hot potato. We prefer to view such events as anomalies, isolated in time and space, associated with faraway jungles, exotic cults, drugged hippies, and outside agitators. However, as the frequency of such happenings increases, there is the realization that it is relatively easy to seduce some people into brainwashed states of obedience.

Too much energy and time have been spent on trying to understand the alleged compelling traits and mystical powers of charismatic leaders, and not enough in an attempt to understand their fellow travelers—the obedient ones. We need to look deeper into those who *elected* Hitler, and all those followers of Jim Jones who went to Guyana *voluntarily*. We must ask how many of us are also inclined toward hyperobedience. Are we significantly different, capable of resisting malevolent authority, or have we simply had the good fortune never to have met a Jim Jones of our own? 10

Social psychologist Stanley Milgram, in his book *Obedience to Authority*, is convinced that: 11

> In growing up, the normal individual has learned to check the expression of aggressive impulses. But the culture has failed, almost entirely, in inculcating internal controls on actions that have their origin in authority. For this reason, the latter constitutes a far greater danger to human survival.

Vince Bugliosi, prosecutor of Charles Manson and author of *Helter Skelter*, commented on the Jonestown suicides: 12

> Education of the public is the only answer. If young people could be taught what can happen to them—that they may be zombies a year after talking to that smiling person who stops them on a city street—they may be prepared.

Presumably, most young cult converts have spent most of their days in our educational system, yet are vulnerable to the beguiling smile or evil eye of a Charles Manson. If there is any lesson to be learned from the obedience-related holocausts, it must be that we can never underestimate the power of education and the socialization process.

Contrary to our belief that the survival instinct is predominant over all other drives, the Jonestown suicides offer testimony to the power of cultural indoctrination. Significantly, the greatest life force at the People's Temple came from the children. Acting on their survival instincts, they went kicking and screaming to their deaths in an "immature" display of disobedience. The adults, civilized and educated people that they were, lined up with "stiff upper lips" and took their medicine like the followers they were trained to be—a training that didn't begin at Jonestown. 13

When something so horrible as Jonestown happens, people draw metaphors about the nearness of the jungle and the beast that lurks within us. It seems that a more appropriate metaphor would be our prox- 14 imity to an Orwellian civilization with its antiseptic removal of our human rough edges and "animal" instincts. On close scrutiny, the beast within us looks suspiciously like a sheep.

15 Despite our rich literature of freedom, a pervasive value instilled in our society is obedience to authority. Unquestioning obedience is perceived to be in the best interests of the schools, churches, families, and political institutions. Nationalism, patriotism, and religious ardor are its psychological vehicles.

16 Disobedience is the original sin, as all of the religions have stated in one way or another. Given the obedience training in organized religions that claim to possess mystical powers and extrarational knowledge and extoll the glories of self-sacrifice, what is so bizarre about the teachings of Jim Jones? If we arm our children with the rationality and independent thought necessary to resist the cultist, can we be sure that our own creeds and proclamations will meet the criteria of reason? The spotlight of reason which exposes the charlatan may next shine on some glaring inconsistencies in the "legitimate" religions. Religions, which are often nothing more than cults that grew, set the stage for the credulity and gullibility required for membership in cults.

17 A witch hunt is now brewing to exorcise the exotic cults, but what is the dividing line between a cult and a legitimate religion? Is there a qualitative difference between the actions of some venerated Biblical saints and martyrs and the martyrs of Jonestown? If the Bible contained a Parable of Guyana, the churches would regularly extoll it as a courageous act of self-sacrifice. Evidently saints and martyrs are only palatable when separated by the chasm of a few centuries. To enforce their beliefs, the major religions use nothing so crass as automatic weapons, of course, but instead fall back on automatic sentences to eternal damnation.

18 Certainly there must be an optimal level of obedience and cooperation in a reasonable society, but obedience, as any other virtue that is carried to an extreme, may become a vice. It is obvious that Nazi Germany and Jonestown went too far on the obedience continuum. In more mundane times and places the appropriate level of obedience is more difficult to discover.

19 We must ask if our society is part of the problem, part of the solution, or wholly irrelevant to the incidents of over-obedience exhibited at Jonestown and Mai Lai. Reviewing social psychologists' attempts to take our psychic temperatures through empirical measurements of our conformity and obedience behavior in experimental situations, our vital signs do not look good.

20 In 1951 Solomon Asch conducted an experiment on conformity, which is similar to obedience behavior in that it subverts one's will to that of peers or an authority. This study, as reported in the textbook *So-*

cial Psychology by Freedman, Sears, and Carlsmith, involved college students who were asked to estimate lines of equal and differing lengths. Some of the lines were obviously equal, but if subjects heard others before them unanimously give the wrong answer, they would also answer incorrectly. Asch had reasoned that people would be rational enough to choose the evidence of their own eyes over the disagreeing "perceptions" of others. He found that he was wrong.

21 When subjects were asked to estimate the length of a line after confederates of the experimenter had given obviously wrong answers, the subjects gave wrong answers about 35 percent of the time. Authors Freedman, Sears, and Carlsmith stress:

> It is important to keep the unambiguousness of the situations in mind if we are to understand this phenomenon. There is a tendency to think that the conforming subjects are uncertain of the correct choice and therefore are swayed by the majority. This is not always the case. In many instances subjects are quite certain of the correct choice and, in the absence of group pressure, would choose correctly 100 percent of the time. When they conform, they are conforming despite the fact that they know the correct answer.

If 35 percent of those students conformed to group opinion in unambiguous matters and in direct contradiction of the evidence of their own eyes, how much more must we fear blind following in *ambiguous* circumstances or in circumstances where there exists a legitimate authority?

22 In the early sixties, Yale social psychologist Stanley Milgram devised an experiment to put acts of obedience and disobedience under close scrutiny. Milgram attempted to understand why thousands of "civilized" people had engaged in an extreme and immoral act—that of the wholesale extermination of Jews—in the name of obedience. He devised a learning task in which subjects of the experiment were instructed to act as teachers. They were told to "shock" learners for their mistakes. The learners were actually confederates of the experimenter and were feigning their reactions. When a mistake was made, the experimenter would instruct the teacher to administer an ever-increasing voltage from a shock machine which read "Extreme Danger," "Severe Shock," and "XXX." Although the machine was unconnected, the subject-teachers believed that they were actually giving shocks. They were themselves given a real sample shock before the experiment began.

23 Milgram asked his Yale colleagues to make a guess as to what proportion of subjects would proceed to shock all the way to the presumed lethal end of the shock-board. Their estimates hovered around 1 or 2 percent. No one was prepared for what happened. All were amazed that

twenty-six out of forty subjects obeyed the experimenter's instruction to press levers that supposedly administered severely dangerous levels of shock. After this, Milgram regularly obtained results showing that 62 to 65 percent of people would shock to the end of the board. He tried several variations on the experiment, one of which was to set it up outside of Yale University so that the prestige of the University would not be an overriding factor in causing subjects to obey. He found that people were just as likely to administer severe shock, whether the experiments occurred within the hallowed halls of Yale or in a three-room walk-up storefront in which the experimenters spoke of themselves as "scientific researchers."

24 In another variation of the experiment, Milgram found that aggression—latent or otherwise—was not a significant factor in causing the teacher-subjects to shock the learners. When the experimenter left the room, thus permitting the subjects to choose the level of shock themselves, almost none administered more than the lowest voltage. Milgram concluded that obedience, not aggression, was the problem. He states:

> I must conclude that [Hannah] Arendt's conception of the *banality of evil* comes closer to the truth than one might dare imagine. The ordinary person who shocked the victim did so out of a sense of obligation—a conception of his duties as a subject—and not from any peculiarly aggressive tendencies.
>
> This is, perhaps, the most fundamental lesson of our study: ordinary people, simply doing their jobs, and without any particular hostility on their part, can become agents in a terrible destructive process. Moreover, even when the destructive effects of their work become patently clear, and they are asked to carry out actions incompatible with fundamental standards of morality, relatively few people have the resources needed to resist authority. A variety of inhibitions against disobeying authority come into play and successfully keep the person in his place.

25 A lack of compassion was not a particularly salient personality factor in the acts of obedience performed by the follows of Hitler, Jim Jones, and the subjects in the Milgram experiments. Nazi soldiers were capable of decent human behavior toward their friends and family. Some, too, see an irony in that Hitler himself was a vegetarian. The People's Temple members seemed more compassionate and humanitarian than many, and yet they forced their own children to partake of a drink laced with cyanide. Those shocking the victims in the Milgram experiments exhibited signs of compassion both toward the experimenter and to the persons that they thought were receiving the shocks. In fact, Milgram finds that:

> It is a curious thing that a measure of compassion on the part of the subject, an unwillingness to "hurt" the experimenter's feelings, are part of those binding forces inhibiting disobedience . . . only obedience can preserve the experimenter's status and dignity.

Milgram's subjects showed signs of severe physiological tension and internal conflict when instructed to shock. Presumably, these signs of psychic pain and tortured indecision were a manifestation of an underlying attitude of compassion for the victim, but it was not sufficient to impel them to openly break with, and therefore embarrass, the experimenter, even though this experimenter had no real authority over them. One of Milgram's subjects expressed this dilemma succinctly: 26

> I'll go through with anything they tell me to do. . . . They know more than I do. . . . I know when I was in the service [if I was told] "You go over the hill and we're going to attack," we attacked. So I think it's all based on the way a man was brought up . . . in his background. Well, I faithfully believed the man [whom he thought he had shocked] was dead until we opened the door. When I saw him, I said: "Great, this is great!" But it didn't bother me even to find that he was dead. I did a job.

The experiments continued with thousands of people—students and nonstudents, here and abroad—often demonstrating obedience behavior in 60 to 65 percent of the subjects. When the experiments were done in Munich, obedience often reached 85 percent. Incidentally, Milgram found no sex differences in obedience behavior. Though his sample of women shockers was small, their level of obedience was identical to that of the men. But they did exhibit more symptoms of internal conflict. Milgram concluded that "there is probably nothing the victim can say that will uniformly generate disobedience," since it is not the victim who is controlling the shocker's behavior. Even when one of the experimental variations included a victim who cried out that he had a heart condition, this did not lead to significantly greater disobedience. In such situations, the experimenter-authority figure dominates the subject's social field, while the pleading cries of the victim are for the most part ignored. 27

Milgram found that the authority's power had to be somehow undermined before there was widespread disobedience, as when the experimenter was not physically present, when his orders came over the telephone, or when his orders were challenged by another authority. Most importantly, subjects became disobedient in large numbers only when others rebelled, dissented, or argued with the experimenter. When a 28 subject witnessed another subject defying or arguing with the experimenter, thirty-six out of forty also rebelled, demonstrating that peer rebellion was the most effective experimental variation in undercutting authority.

29 This social orientation in which the authority dominates one's psyche is attributed by Milgram to a state of mind which he terms "the agentic state." A person makes a critical shift from a relatively autonomous state into this agentic state when she or he enters a situation in which "he defines himself in a manner that renders him open to regulation by a person of higher status."

30 An extreme agentic state is a likely explanation for the scenario at Jonestown, where even the cries of their own children were not sufficient to dissuade parents from serving cyanide. Despite some ambiguity as to how many Jonestown residents were murdered and how many committed suicide, there remains the fact that these victims had participated in previous suicide rehearsals. Jim Jones, assured of their loyalty and of their critical shift into an agentic state, then had the power to orchestrate the real thing. The supreme irony, the likes of which could only be imagined as appearing in the *Tralfamadore Tribune* with a byline by Kurt Vonnegut, was the picture of the Guyana death scene. Bodies were strewn about beneath the throne of Jones and a banner which proclaimed that those who failed to learn from the lessons of history were doomed to repeat them.

31 How many of us have made the critical shift into an agentic state regarding international relations, assuming that our leaders know best, even though they have repeatedly demonstrated that they do not? Stanley Milgram predicts that "for the man who sits in front of the button that will release Armageddon, depressing it will have about the same emotional force as calling for an elevator . . . evolution has not had a chance to build inhibitors against such remote forms of aggression."

32 We should recognize that our human nature renders us somewhat vulnerable. For one thing, our own mortality and that of our loved ones is an unavoidable fact underlying our lives. In the face of it, we are powerless; and in our insecurity, many reach out for sure answers. Few choose to believe, along with Clarence Darrow, that not only are we not the captains of our fate, but that we are not even "deckhands on a rudderless dinghy." Or, as someone else has stated: "There are no answers. Be brave and face up to it." Most of us won't face up to it. We want our answers, solutions to our plight, and we want them now. Too often truth and rational thought are the first casualties of this desperate reach for security. We embrace answers from charlatans, false prophets, charismatic leaders, and assorted demagogues. Given these realities of our na-

ture, how can we avoid these authority traps to which we are so prone? By what criteria do we teach our children to distinguish between the charlatan and the prophet?

It seems that the best armor is the rational mind. We must insist 33
that all authorities account for themselves, and we need to be as wary of false prophets as we are of false advertising. Leaders, political and spiritual, must be subjected to intense scrutiny, and we must insist that their thought processes and proclamations measure up to reasonable standards of rational thought. Above all, we must become skilled in activating our inner resources toward rebellion and disobedience, when this seems reasonable.

The power of socialization can conceivably be harnessed so as to 34
develop individuals who are rational and skeptical, capable of independent thought, and who can disobey or disagree at the critical moment. Our society, however, continues systematically to instill exactly the opposite. The educational system pays considerable lip service to the development of self-reliance, and places huge emphasis on lofty concepts of individual differences. Little notice is taken of the legions of overly obedient children in the schools; yet, for every overly disobedient child, there are probably twenty who are obeying too much. There is little motivation to encourage the unsqueaky wheels to develop as noisy, creative, independent thinkers who may become bold enough to disagree. Conceivably, we could administer modified Milgram obedience tests in the schools which detect hyperobedience, just as we test for intelligence, visual function, vocational attributes and tuberculosis. When a child is found to be too obedient, the schools should mobilize against this psychological crippler with the zeal by which they would react to an epidemic of smallpox. In alcoholism and other mental disturbances, the first major step toward a reversal of the pathology is recognition of the severity of the problem. Obedience should be added to the list of emotional disturbances requiring therapy. Disobedience schools should be at least as common as military schools and reform schools.

The chains on us are not legal or political, but the invisible chains 35
of the agentic state. We have all gotten the message that it is dangerous and requires exceptional courage to be different.

If we are to gain control of our lives and minds, we must first ac- 36
knowledge the degree to which we are not now in control. We must become reasonable and skeptical. Reason is no panacea, but, at the moment, it is all that we have. Yet many in our society seem to have the same attitude about rationality and reason that they do about the poverty program—that is, we've tried it and it doesn't work.

37 Along with worrying about the S.A.T. scores and whether or not Johnny can read, we must begin to seriously question whether Johnny is capable of disobedience. The churches and cults, while retaining their constitutional right to free expression, must be more regularly criticized. The legitimate religions have been treated as sacred cows. Too often, criticism of them is met with accusations of religious bigotry, or the implications that one is taking candy from a baby or a crutch from a cripple. The concept of religious tolerance has been stretched to its outer limits, implying freedom from criticism and the nonpayment of taxes. Neither patriotism nor religion should be justification for the suspension of reason.

38 And, on a personal level, we must stop equating sanity with conformity, eccentricity with craziness, and normalcy with numbers. We must get in touch with our own liberating ludicrousness and practice being harmlessly deviant. We must, in fact, cease to use props or other people to affirm our normalcy. With sufficient practice, perhaps, when the need arises, we may have the strength to force a moment to its crisis.

THINKING ABOUT THE TEXT

1. What do the infamous authority figures such as Charles Manson and Jim Jones have to do with McCarthy's point in this essay?
2. What cases of failure to comply with workplace norms does McCarthy cite to support her assertion that we are petty in enforcing conformity? How does she anticipate and meet the reader's possible objections that regulations may increase efficiency?
3. McCarthy says that we spend too much time trying to figure out malevolent, charismatic leaders such as Hitler. Where, instead, should our contemplative energies be used?
4. Which institutions in our culture inculcate the need for obedience to authority? Give specific examples of expected conformity for each of the institutions that you discuss.
5. What psychology experiments does McCarthy cite to support her view that as a nation we lack "the resources needed to resist authority"?
6. If the subjects in the studies reflect social norms, how do people who comply with authority figures feel about their obedience? What are the reactions of both women and men during and after the test? Under what conditions *will* people resist authority?
7. What does the author predict as a possible reality for people who live in an "agentic state"? What does she insist we do to protect ourselves? How do you respond to her proposals for changes in the education of children?

WRITING FROM THE TEXT

1. Write an analysis of the conformity or obedience expectations of the institutions with which you have been identified. What was expected of you? What were your feelings then, and how do you feel now?
2. Write to persuade your reader that a particular authority figure you know expects specific obedience that is unnecessary or dangerous.

CONNECTING WITH OTHER TEXTS

1. Carol Tavris (p. 274) describes our shrinking from doing what we know is right when we are in groups. How does her analysis of human behavior relate to Milgram's findings, reported in McCarthy's essay? Write an essay that shows the relationship.
2. How would McCarthy's "disobedience school" influence some of the gender-related problems expressed in the essays in this text? Consider Brophy's analysis of women in "invisible cages" (p. 80), Cooper Thompson's reeducation program (p. 63), or Farrell's anger that men are expected to be "success objects" (p. 75). Propose a program for a disobedience school to liberate human beings from gender role conformity.

■ SECOND THOUGHTS ON THE INFORMATION HIGHWAY

Cliff Stoll

"An astronomer by training and a computer security expert by accident," Cliff Stoll (b. 1950) became a best-selling author with his first book, *The Cuckoo's Egg* (1989), which describes how he tracked and eventually caught a German spy ring operating over the Internet. Considering his computer expertise, many were surprised when he wrote his second book, *Silicon Snake Oil: Second Thoughts on the Information Highway* (1995), to express his "perplexed ambivalence toward computers, networks, and the culture that enshrines them." Further, Stoll argues that online living "directly threatens precious parts of our society, including schools, libraries and social institutions." A version of the following article was first published in *Newsweek* in 1995.

Surely you've heard the predictions of our future digital age: "Multimedia will revolutionize the classroom," "Interactive electronic information will make books obsolete," "Businesses will flock to the computer networks for instant, low cost information." Visionaries see a future of telecommuting office workers, interactive libraries, and multimedia classrooms. They speak of electronic town meetings and virtual 1 communities. Commerce and business will shift from offices and malls to networks and modems. Electronic mail will replace slow and inefficient snail mail. And thanks to the freedom of electronic networks, government will become profoundly democratic and efficient.

2 Such claims are utterly bogus. These glowing predictions of a digital nirvana make me wonder if some lemming-like madness has cursed our technologists. Do our computer pundits lack all common sense? I'm astonished at the wide gulf between their utopian dreams and the dreary reality that pours into my modem.

3 The truth is that no online database will replace your daily newspaper, no CD-ROM can take the place of a competent teacher, and no computer network will change the way government works. Work has never been easy; learning isn't painless, and bureaucracies have never been quick to change. The computer ain't gonna do it for you.

4 Consider today's online world. The Usenet, a worldwide bulletin board, allows anyone to post messages across the globe. Your word gets out, leapfrogging editors and publishers. Every voice can be heard cheaply and instantly. The result is that every voice *is* heard. The resultant cacophony more closely resembles Citizen Band Radio, complete with handles, harassment, and anonymous threats. When most everyone shouts, few listen.

5 How about electronic publishing? Try reading a book on your monitor. At best, it's an unpleasant chore: the myopic glow of a clunky computer replaces the friendly pages of a book. And you can't tote that laptop to the beach or leave it in your car—it'll get stolen. Yet Nicholas Negroponte, director of the MIT Media Center, predicts that we'll soon buy books straight over the Internet. Uh, sure.

6 What the Internet hucksters won't tell you is that the World Wide Web is an ocean of unedited data, without any pretense of completeness. Lacking editors, reporters, reviewers, or critics, the Internet has become a wasteland of unreviewed, unedited, unfiltered data. You don't know what to ignore and what's worth reading.

7 Logged onto the World Wide Web, I hunt for the date of the battle of Trafalgar. Hundreds of files show up, including Napoleon.txt, Trafalg.zip, and J41N32.gif. It takes fifteen minutes to unravel them—one's a biography written by an 8th grader, the second is a computer game that doesn't work, and the third is an image of a London monument. None answer my question, and my search is periodically interrupted by messages like, "Too many connections, try again later." This searching is a great way to waste time but hardly an efficient research tool.

Won't the Internet be useful in governing? Internet addicts clamor for government reports to be uploaded to the networks. But when Andy Speno ran for County Executive in Westchester County, NY, he put every press release and position paper onto a bulletin board. In that affluent county, with plenty of computer companies, how many voters logged in? Fewer than thirty did. This is hardly a good omen for the electronic democracy. 8

The strongest hype comes from those who are forcing computers into schools. We're told that multimedia and interactive video systems will make learning easy and schoolwork fun. Students will happily learn from animated characters while being taught by expertly tailored software. Teachers won't be as essential when we have computer-aided education. 9

Bah. These expensive toys are difficult to use in classrooms, require extensive teacher preparation, and waste what few dollars trickle into schools. Sure, kids love to play video games—but think of your own experience: Can you recall even one educational filmstrip of decades past? I'll bet you remember the two or three great teachers who made a difference in your life. 10

Cyberbusiness? We're promised instant catalog shopping—just point and click for great deals. We'll order airline tickets over the network, make restaurant reservations, and negotiate sales contracts. Stores will become obsolete. So how come my local mall does more business in an afternoon than the entire Internet handles in a month? Even if there were a trustworthy way to send money over the network—which there isn't—the networks are missing a most essential ingredient of capitalism: salespeople. Without the personal attention and human interactions of good salesfolk, the Internet can't blossom into an electronic shopping mall. 11

What's missing from this electronic wonderland? Human contact. Discount the fawning technoburble about virtual communities—computers and networks isolate us from each other. A network chat line is a limp substitute for meeting friends over coffee. No interactive multimedia display comes close to the excitement of a live concert. And who'd prefer cybersex to the real thing? 12

Is it likely that you can enjoy a rich online world and a plentiful personal life? Nope. Every hour that you spend linked through your modem is sixty minutes that you're not visiting with your friends or shagging fly balls with the kid down the block. While the Internet beckons brightly, seductively flashing an icon of knowledge-as-power, this non-place lures us to surrender our time on Earth. A poor substi- 13 tute it is, this virtual reality where frustration is legion and where—in the holy names of Education and Progress—important aspects of human interactions are relentlessly devalued.

THINKING ABOUT THE TEXT

1. Stoll's introduction reads like a list of promotions or "glowing predictions" of a computerized world. What are these predictions and how effective is Stoll's strategy to begin with these claims and then pronounce them "utterly bogus"?
2. According to Stoll, what are the disadvantages of electronic bulletin boards and electronic publishing?
3. What does Stoll imply by the term "Internet hucksters" and what does he think that computer service representatives don't tell about the World Wide Web? Consider his example of searching for the date of the battle of Trafalgar.
4. What does Stoll believe is the "strongest hype" about computers and how does he refute such predictions?
5. What evidence does Stoll offer for his claims that "electronic democracy" and "cyberbusiness" are not the success stories that promoters predicted? According to Stoll, what is missing?
6. Stoll's argument seems deliberately arranged to build to his conclusion, in which he goes beyond merely repeating his claims that glowing predictions about the computerized age are false and misleading. What is his actual thesis? What evidence can you find from his essay to support this assertion?

WRITING FROM THE TEXT

1. Using your own experience and details from the essay, write an argument supporting the claim that enjoying a "rich online world" does or does not steal valuable time from human interactions and real life.
2. Write an analysis of Stoll's argument and consider his supporting examples, logical reasoning, and ability to anticipate and counter objections.
3. Stoll criticizes the hype about multimedia and interactive video systems in the classrooms. Write an analysis of your own schooling before college and argue that Stoll is correct or incorrect about the value of computers in the classroom.

CONNECTING WITH OTHER TEXTS

1. Read "Get a Life?" (below) by Nicholas Negroponte. Using details from Negroponte's and Stoll's essays, as well as from your own observations, write an essay arguing either Stoll's position that a rich online life is a poor substitute for real life or Negroponte's stance that online living frees people to enjoy a richer life. Whichever argument you choose, make sure that you consider *and counter* the opposing claims made by the other author.
2. Write an analysis that compares and contrasts the writing style, use of language, and tone of the two opposed and very different authors, Cliff Stoll and Nicholas Negroponte. You may use the biographical information as well as precise details from both essays to help you analyze and evaluate the effectiveness of both writings.

■ GET A LIFE?

Nicholas Negroponte

Having studied architecture and computer-aided design as a graduate student at the Massachusetts Institute of Technology, Nicholas Negroponte (b. 1943) is a founder and the director of MIT's Media Laboratory, a research center devoted to exploring future forms of human communication. In addition to teaching at MIT, Negroponte has held visiting professorships at Yale, Michigan, and the University of California at Berkeley. He has delivered hundreds of presentations worldwide about the potential of technology for enhancing education. Author of *Being Digital,* Negroponte is senior columnist for *WIRED* magazine, which published the following essay in the September 1995 issue.

Any significant social phenomenon creates a backlash. The Net is no exception. It is odd, however, that the loudest complaints are shouts of "Get a life!"—suggesting that online living will dehumanize us, insulate us, and create a world of people who won't smell flowers, watch sunsets, or engage in face-to-face experiences. Out of this backlash comes a warning to parents that their children will "cocoon" and metamorphose into social invalids. 1

Experience tells us the opposite. So far, evidence gathered by those using the Net as a teaching tool indicates that kids who go online gain social skills rather than lose them. Since the distance between Athens, Georgia, and Athens, Greece, is just a mouse click away, children attain 2 a new kind of worldliness. Young people on the Net today will inevitably experience some of the sophistication of Europe. In earlier days, only children from élite families could afford to interact with European culture during their summer vacations abroad.

3 I know that visiting Web pages in Italy or interacting with Italians via e-mail isn't the same as ducking the pigeons or listening to music in Piazza San Marco—but it sure beats never going there at all. Take all the books in the world, and they won't offer the real-time global experience a kid can get on the Net: here a child becomes the driver of the intellectual vehicle, not the passenger.

4 Mitch Resnick of the MIT Media Lab recently told me of an autistic boy who has great difficulty interacting with people, often giving inappropriate visual cues (like strange facial expressions) and so forth. But this child has thrived on the Net. When he types, he gains control and becomes articulate. He's an active participant in chat rooms and newsgroups. He has developed strong online friendships, which have given him greater confidence in face-to-face situations.

5 It's an extreme case, but isn't it odd how parents grieve if their child spends six hours a day on the Net but delight if those same hours are spent reading books? With the exception of sleep, doing *anything* six hours a day, every day, is not good for a child.

6 Adults on the Net enjoy even greater opportunity, as more people discover they can work from almost anywhere. Granted, if you make pizzas you need to be close to the dough; if you're a surgeon you must be close to your patients (at least for the next two decades). But if your trade involves bits (not atoms), you probably don't need to be anywhere specific—at least most of the time. In fact, it might be beneficial all-around if you were in the Caribbean or Mediterranean—then your company wouldn't have to tie up capital in expensive downtown real estate.

7 Certain early users of the Net (bless them!) are now whining about its vulgarization, warning people of its hazards as if it were a cigarette. If only these whiners were more honest, they'd admit that it was they who didn't have much of a life and found solace on the Net, they who woke up one day with midlife crises and discovered there was more to living than what was waiting in their e-mail boxes. So, what took you guys so long? Of course there's more to life than e-mail, but don't project your empty existence onto others and suggest "being digital" is a form of virtual leprosy for which total abstinence is the only immunization.

8 My own lifestyle is totally enhanced by being online. I've been a compulsive e-mail user for more than 25 years; more often than not, it's allowed me to spend more time in scenic places with interesting people. Which would you prefer: two weeks' vacation totally offline or four to

six weeks online? This doesn't work for all professions, but it is a growing trend among so-called "knowledge workers."

Once, only the likes of Rupert Murdoch or Aga Khan could cut deals from their satellite-laden luxury yachts off the coast of Sardinia. Now all sorts of people from Tahoe to Telluride can work from the back seat of a Winnebago if they wish. 9

I don't know the statistics, but I'm willing to guess that the executives of corporate America spend 70 to 80 percent of their time in meetings. I *do* know that most of those meetings, often a canonical one hour long, are 70 to 80 percent posturing and leveling (bringing the others up to speed on a common subject). The posturing is gratuitous, and the leveling is better done elsewhere—online, for example. This alone would enhance US productivity far more than any trade agreement. 10

I am constantly astonished by just how offline corporate America is. Wouldn't you expect executives at computer and communications companies to be active online? Even household names of the high-tech industry are *offline* human beings, sometimes more so than execs in extremely low-tech fields. I guess this is a corollary to the shoemaker's children having no shoes. 11

Being online not only makes the inevitable face-to-face meetings so much easier—it allows you to look outward. Generally, large companies are so inwardly directed that staff memorandums about growing bureaucracy get more attention than the dwindling competitive advantage of being big in the first place. David, *who has a life*, needn't use a slingshot. Goliath, *who doesn't*, is too busy reading office memos. 12

In the mid-1700s, mechanical looms and other machines forced cottage industries out of business. Many people lost the opportunity to be their own bosses and to enjoy the profits of hard work. I'm sure I would have been a Luddite under those conditions. 13

But the current sweep of digital living is doing exactly the opposite. Parents of young children find exciting self-employment from home. The "virtual corporation" is an opportunity for tiny companies (with employees spread across the world) to work together in a global market and set up base wherever they choose. If you don't like centralist thinking, big companies, or job automation, what better place to go than the Net? Work for yourself *and* get a life. 14

THINKING ABOUT THE TEXT

1. According to Negroponte, what do people mean when they shout, "Get a life!" to those who spend time on the Net (that is, using a computerized network such as the Internet)?

2. What does Negroponte believe that experience has shown about using the Net as a teaching tool and what proof does he offer?

3. What does Negroponte claim are the advantages for adults of going online?

4. What is Negroponte's response to "certain early users of the Net" who "are now whining about its vulgarization, warning people about its hazards as if it were a cigarette"?

5. Negroponte claims that if he had been alive during the mid-1700s, he "would have been a Luddite under those conditions." Look up *Luddite* in a dictionary and explain what Negroponte means and what conditions he is referring to.

6. Why does Negroponte believe that "the current sweep of digital living is doing exactly the opposite" of what the Luddites feared?

WRITING FROM THE TEXT

1. Using your own experience and details from Negroponte's essay, write an argument supporting or countering his assertion that "online living" can enrich people's lives rather than consume their time or keep them from interacting with others.

2. Write an essay analyzing Negroponte's argument techniques such as supporting claims, using logical reasoning rather than merely emotional responses, and anticipating his opponents' objections and countering them.

CONNECTING WITH OTHER TEXTS

1. Read "Second Thoughts on the Information Highway" (p. 287). Does Stoll seem to be one of the "early users" that Negroponte thinks is "whining" about hazards of the computer? Write an essay using details from both essays and from your own experience to argue that the "hazards" of online living are or are not justified and valid.

2. The popular press—and Ann Landers' columns!—have been filled with laments from spouses abandoned as their husbands and wives nightly cruise the information highways. Find an article on this phenomenon in a popular newspaper or magazine and analyze the problem in terms of the arguments of Stoll or Negroponte.

THREE WAYS OF MEETING OPPRESSION
Martin Luther King, Jr.

A graduate of Morehouse College, Crozer Theological Seminary, Boston University, and Chicago Theological Seminary, Martin Luther King, Jr. (1929–1968) was the recipient of numerous awards for his literary work and leadership as well as the Nobel Prize for Peace in 1964. An ordained Baptist minister, King became well known as a national and international spokesperson for civil rights after his organization of the successful Montgomery, Alabama, bus boycott. In spite of threatening phone calls, being arrested, and having his home bombed, King continued to work with nonviolent resistance and argued eloquently for racial equality. He was assassinated on April 3, 1968. The following excerpt is from *Stride Toward Freedom,* published in 1958.

Oppressed people deal with their oppression in three characteristic ways. One way is acquiescence: the oppressed resign themselves to their doom. They tacitly adjust themselves to oppression, and thereby become conditioned to it. In every movement toward freedom some of the oppressed prefer to remain oppressed. Almost 2800 years ago Moses set out to lead the children of Israel from the slavery of Egypt to the freedom of the promised land. He soon discovered that slaves do not always welcome their deliverers. They become accustomed to being slaves. They would rather bear those ills they have, as Shakespeare pointed out, than flee to others that they know not of. They prefer the "fleshpots of Egypt" to the ordeals of emancipation. 1

There is such a thing as the freedom of exhaustion. Some people are so worn down by the yoke of oppression that they give up. A few years ago in the slum areas of Atlanta, a Negro guitarist used to sing almost daily: "Ben down so long that down don't bother me." This is the type of negative freedom and resignation that often engulfs the life of the oppressed. 2

But this is not the way out. To accept passively an unjust system is to cooperate with that system; thereby the oppressed become as evil as the oppressor. Noncooperation with evil is as much a moral obligation as is cooperation with good. The oppressed must never allow the conscience of the oppressor to slumber. Religion reminds every man that he is his brother's keeper. To accept injustice or segregation passively is to say to the oppressor that his actions are morally right. It is a way of allowing his conscience to fall asleep. At this moment the oppressed fails to be his brother's keeper. So acquiescence—while often the easier way—is not the moral way. It is the way of the coward. The Negro cannot win the respect of his oppressor by acquiescing; he merely increases the oppressor's 3 arrogance and contempt. Acquiescence is interpreted as proof of the Negro's inferiority. The Negro cannot win the respect of the white people of the South or the peoples of the world if he is willing to sell the future of his children for his personal and immediate comfort and safety.

4 A second way that oppressed people sometimes deal with oppression is to resort to physical violence and corroding hatred. Violence often brings about momentary results. Nations have frequently won their independence in battle. But in spite of temporary victories, violence never brings permanent peace. It solves no social problem; it merely creates new and more complicated ones.

5 Violence as a way of achieving racial justice is both impractical and immoral. It is impractical because it is a descending spiral ending in destruction for all. The old law of an eye for an eye leaves everybody blind. It is immoral because it seeks to humiliate the opponent rather than win his understanding; it seeks to annihilate rather than to convert. Violence is immoral because it thrives on hatred rather than love. It destroys community and makes brotherhood impossible. It leaves society in monologue rather than dialogue. Violence ends by defeating itself. It creates bitterness in the survivors and brutality in the destroyers. A voice echoes through time saying to every potential Peter, "Put up your sword." History is cluttered with the wreckage of nations that failed to follow this command.

6 If the American Negro and other victims of oppression succumb to the temptation of using violence in the struggle for freedom, future generations will be the recipients of a desolate night of bitterness, and our chief legacy to them will be an endless reign of meaningless chaos. Violence is not the way.

7 The third way open to oppressed people in their quest for freedom is the way of nonviolent resistance. Like the synthesis in Hegelian philosophy, the principle of nonviolent resistance seeks to reconcile the truths of two opposites—acquiescence and violence—while avoiding the extremes and immoralities of both. The nonviolent resister agrees with the person who acquiesces that one should not be physically aggressive toward his opponent but he balances the equation by agreeing with the person of violence that evil must be resisted. He avoids the nonresistance of the former and the violent resistance of the latter. With nonviolent resistance, no individual or group need submit to any wrong, nor need anyone resort to violence in order to right a wrong.

8 It seems to me that this is the method that must guide the actions of the Negro in the present crisis in race relations. Through nonviolent resistance the Negro will be able to rise to the noble height of opposing the unjust system while loving the perpetrators of the system. The Ne-

gro must work passionately and unrelentingly for full stature as a citizen, but he must not use inferior methods to gain it. He must never come to terms with falsehood, malice, hate, or destruction.

Nonviolent resistance makes it possible for the Negro to remain in the South and struggle for his rights. The Negro's problem will not be solved by running away. He cannot listen to the glib suggestion of those who would urge him to migrate en masse to other sections of the country. By grasping his great opportunity in the South he can make a lasting contribution to the moral strength of the nation and set a sublime example of courage for generations yet unborn. 9

By nonviolent resistance, the Negro can also enlist all men of good will in his struggle for equality. The problem is not a purely racial one, with Negroes set against whites. In the end, it is not a struggle between people at all, but a tension between justice and injustice. Nonviolent resistance is not aimed against oppressors but against oppression. Under its banner consciences, not racial groups, are enlisted. 10

If the Negro is to achieve the goal of integration, he must organize himself into a militant and nonviolent mass movement. All three elements are indispensable. The movement for equality and justice can only be a success if it has both a mass and militant character; the barriers to be overcome require both. Nonviolence is an imperative in order to bring about ultimate community. 11

THINKING ABOUT THE TEXT

1. What are the three ways that "oppressed people deal with their oppression"? Is the first method that King defines actually a way to "deal" with oppression?
2. What does King decide about each of the ways he defines and describes? What are the advantages of the method he prefers? Why does he prefer this method?
3. Cite the ways that King establishes that his argument is not only about the Negro struggling for rights.
4. King concludes that for "the Negro" to achieve civil rights and integration, "he must organize himself into a militant and nonviolent mass movement." Because King has ruled out violence as a means of meeting oppression, the word *militant* may seem inappropriate. What does the word actually mean?
5. This excerpt from a longer section of King's writing functions as an essay, but the section lacks an articulated thesis. What do you infer to be the central assertion for this excerpt?

6. This excerpt is filled with exemplary rhetorical devices. Be prepared to discuss the following in class:

   How does King organize this section of his writing?

   What are King's transitional devices?

   What are the lines that remind the reader that King was a minister who spoke meaningfully and memorably from the pulpit?

   Pronouns are often used as effective connecting devices within paragraphs. (See pp. 366–367 for a discussion of this device.) Examine King's use of the pronoun it in paragraph 5.

WRITING FROM THE TEXT

1. King concludes this section of his writing with the awareness that "nonviolence is an imperative in order to bring about ultimate community." Write an essay that describes an "ultimate community" of which King would approve.

2. Write an essay that shows your own experience or observations of specific moments of acquiescence, violence, or nonviolent resistance in response to oppression. Show in your essay what worked and what did not work. Does your experience confirm or refute King's position?

CONNECTING WITH OTHER TEXTS

1. Compare and/or contrast King's ideas in this essay published in 1958 with the ideas of a Black writer or speaker at the end of the twentieth century. Document the source of the ideas that you include as examples in your essay.

2. In an essay, show how Hazel Peoples ("My Man Bovanne," p. 46) has decided to create community. Integrate King's concepts with your discussion of Hazel's intentions.

3. Write to show how Brent Staples ("Black Men and Public Space," p. 219) exemplifies, in spite of conflicts, King's mandate. Beyond summary, analyze Staples' responses and methods.

4. Read "The Atlanta Riot" (p. 224) and analyze, in light of King's ideas, the father's response to the mob's threats on the cook's life and later on his home. Even though Walter White's family felt forced to buy guns, do you think that King would characterize their resistance as violent and wrong? Focus your essay on an assertion and justify your response.

II

THE RHETORIC

■ ■ ■

This rhetoric is designed for you to use easily and constantly, not only in class with your instructor but also at home when you are on your own. Therefore the instruction is deliberately focused and practical, with plenty of suggestions and illustrations. The rhetoric begins by demonstrating many prewriting techniques to help you move quickly beyond the blank page or computer screen. We are convinced that you will learn to write better only by actually writing, and our prewriting exercises prompt you to do just that. We guide you through the entire process, from discovering a topic and writing a draft to supporting a thesis and revising the essay.

To demonstrate the stages of an actual writing assignment, we trace one student's progress from prewriting and information gathering through organizing, outlining, drafting, revising, documenting, and editing the essay. This assignment typifies the writing that you will be asked to do in college; it begins with responses to readings and shows you how to meld your experience with other writers' ideas. This short project will also teach you how to paraphrase, quote, and document material responsibly.

Throughout this rhetoric, then, you will gain skills to craft the varied types of papers that you will need to write. We provide instruction, examples, and discussions of particular methods for developing essays, and we show you how to draft these essays, too. We offer opportunities for you to practice active reading, note taking, incorporating quotations, and interviewing—all important skills to help you write successful papers. We show how important it is to consider audience and style. In addition to the many shorter assignments, we provide instruction for all stages of a longer research paper, with guides to the most current MLA and APA documentation forms. In this edition we have added a brief glossary of terms related to the computer and have included illustrations of how to document electronic sources.

6

Prewriting as Discovery

■ ■ ■

Because writing involves discovery, we are eager to help you find ways to explore the ideas, experiences, and information that you bring to the composition class. We want you to understand the discovery process because that process has so much to do with your finished product.

Let's think for a few moments about how you will begin your assignments—about strategies that will encourage you to become involved in your subject and discover what you want to write about it. The practice exercises in this section are related to issues about family and generations, but even if you have not read the readings in Chapter 1, you can practice most of these prewriting exercises.

It seems paradoxical to suggest that you will discover what you want to write by writing. But students frequently tell us—and our own writing habits confirm—that the very act of working with words, ideas, or feelings on a page or computer screen will help you learn what you want to express about a topic.

Conversations with friends, too, can help you mull over your ideas. Sometimes a spirited exchange with a classmate or roommate will help you get going on a writing topic because you start to reconsider and refine your ideas as you discuss them, and you start to care whether your ideas have been communicated or accepted. If your perceptions are questioned, you may want to present your point more convincingly in written form. In fact, the best thing you can do when you are assigned a writing task is immediately to jot down any responses and ideas. Consider this initial, quick writing as a conversation with yourself, because that is what it is. It is also like the stretching exercises or warm-ups that runners, dancers, and musicians do.

To help you get moving, here are some prewriting exercises that come from the reading and writing topics in this book. Try these different methods; you may find a few that help you get beyond the blank page or screen.

FREEWRITING

As the term implies, *freewriting* involves jotting down uncensored thoughts as quickly as you can. Don't concern yourself with form or correctness. Write whatever comes into your mind without rejecting ideas because they may seem silly or irrelevant. In freewriting, one thought might trigger a more intriguing or significant one, so anything that comes into your head may be valuable. Here is one student's freewriting response to the topic of stereotyping:

Stereotyping? I don't think I stereotype—maybe I do. But I sure have had it done to me. When people see my tatoo they seem to think I'm in Hell's Angels or a skinhead. Talk about prejudgements! It's as if the snake coiling up my arm is going to get them, the way they look at it and pull back from me. I remember once, in a campground in Alaska, a bunch of us campers were stranded when the road washed out. As food and supplies dwindled, people started borrowing from each other. In the john one morning I asked this guy if I could borrow a razor blade and he jumped back. Not till he looked away from my arm and into my eyes did he relax. He gave me a blade, we talked, later shared some campfires together. . . . I could write about that experience, a good story. I wonder if people with tatooes have always been connected with trouble—pirates maybe, sailors and gang members today anyhow. It could be interesting to find out if the negative stereotypes about tatooes have always been there. Now that's some research I could get into.

Pete's response to the topic of stereotyping starts with his personal feeling that the subject doesn't really relate to him. But then he thinks about the fact that he has been stereotyped by others. As he considers how people react to his tattoo, he recalls an incident he thinks he could write about as a narrative. As he thinks more about the nature of tattoos, he finds an aspect of stereotyping that concerns him and that he might like to research. If he had not written down his feelings about stereotyping, he might have settled for a more predictable response to the assignment.

Notice that Pete's freewriting starts with a question that he asks himself about the topic—a perfect way to get himself warmed up and moving. He's not worried about checking his spelling. He can consult a dictionary when he is drafting his paper to learn that *tattoos* and *prejudgments* are the correct spellings. Pete also uses language in his prewriting that might not be appropriate in his essays: "guy," "bunch," "john," "anyhow," and "get into." Most important is that Pete got started on his assignment without procrastinating and that he explored his own unique thoughts and feelings. He found a personal experience he might relate and discovered research that he would like to do.

■ PRACTICING FREEWRITING

To help you see how freewriting can lead to discovery, write for fifteen minutes, without stopping, on one of the following topics. Do not worry about form and do not censor any idea, fact, picture, or feeling that comes to you.

1. One of your parents or one of your children
2. A time spent with a grandparent
3. A particular family occasion when you learned something
4. Your response to "Thanksgiving" (p. 4)
5. Your response to "The Ties That Bind" (p. 7)

Your freewriting may be written on a sheet of paper, composed at a computer, or jotted down in your journal.

JOURNAL WRITING

Journals may be used to record your feelings or respond to others' ideas, including material that you have read. As a conversation with yourself, journal writing may also help you warm up before writing a paper. It will give you another way to discover your ideas; in fact, many professional writers rely on journals to store ideas for future stories, articles, editorials, and poems.

Your professor may ask you to keep a journal just so that you will have additional writing practice while you are in a composition course. Nearly all of the "Thinking About the Text" questions and many of the "Writing from the Text" assignments in the reader make ideal topics for a journal. If you use your journal to write responses to assigned readings, you will:

- be better prepared for class discussions,
- retain more material from the readings, and
- gain more writing practice.

For your journal, you can use a notebook of any size. Some writers prefer notebooks that are thin enough to fit into a purse or a full backpack. That way, they can pull out their journals whenever the inspiration strikes them, such as on a bus or while waiting for someone. Others prefer binders so that they can add or delete loose-leaf pages as needed. It helps to date each entry so that you can trace the development of your thoughts and your writing.

Using a Journal for Active Reading

One type of assigned active reading is a *dialectical journal.* In this journal you write down specific phrases from your readings and then record thoughts that are evoked by these phrases—in effect, having a conversation with your reading material. You may find yourself jotting down questions you would like to ask the writer or words and terms you looked up in a dictionary. Include specific details that you want to interpret or analyze. You will find yourself discovering feelings about particular topics related to the reading.

Imagine Pete, the student who did freewriting about stereotypes, responding specifically to the essay "Don't Let Stereotypes Warp Your Judgments" (p. 428). His journal response to the essay might look like this:

"Are criminals more likely to be dark than blond?" That's a provocative question the author asks. It makes me think about all the bad guys in movies. Aren't they always dark? You never see Robert Redford playing a villain—or do you? I think some of our stereotyping comes from film, which is Heilbroner's point when he writes about "typecasts." Maybe only bad films use "types." I like what the author says about stereotypes making us "mentally lazy." I can see what he means when he says there are two people hurt in stereotyping—the person who is unjustly lumped into some category <u>and</u> the person who is "impoverished" by his laziness. Heilbroner says that a person can't "see the world in his own absolutely unique, inimitable and independent fashion." That makes sense about being independent. But I wonder what "inimitable" means?

Notice that Pete begins his journal entry with a question from the essay itself; he also might have started with his own question about the work. Pete jots down ideas that come to him as he responds to the assigned reading. It is important that he puts quotation marks around any words, phrases, or sentences from the text. In case he uses these later, Pete wants to remember that the ideas and language belong to the author of the essay.

In addition to moving Pete into his assigned topic, his journal writing lets him record his responses to parts of Heilbroner's essay. He is practicing finding the essence of the essay, as well as parts that he might want to quote in his own work. Further, if Pete reads "Proper Care and Maintenance" (p. 170) and "Black Men and Public Space" (p. 219), he will have relevant material in his journal that he can connect to these other readings, either for his own interest or for other writing assignments.

PRACTICING JOURNAL WRITING

Respond to any of the following topics by conversing with yourself in an uncensored dialog. Start with the question or topic, but permit your mind to wander around the block and down some alleys.

1. Sibling rivalry—does it relate to me?
2. How have my parents changed since I've been in college?
3. Do I agree with Ellen Goodman when she writes in "Thanksgiving" (p. 4), "We don't have to achieve to be accepted by our families. We just have to be."
4. Are any of the family conflicts in "The Ties That Bind" (p. 7) ones that I also have?

CLUSTERING

Clustering is a more visual grouping of ideas on a page. It is the perfect prewriting exercise for students who tend to see ideas or concepts in spatial relationships. We have found that many students use clustering for in-class writing assignments, including essay exams, where the object is not to discover a topic but to organize information that they already have. For these writers, clustering is the best way to see the assigned question in terms of main topics and subtopics, and thus the organization of content is quickly perceived.

One student used clustering in response to an assignment to discover some "between-worlds" topics in her own life. Rachel wrote the assignment as a question in the middle of the page. Then she drew lines from the topics to several subtopics, which she placed in boxes. As you can see, her subtopics are the chapter titles in the reader portion of this text. She placed "perceptions" and "genders" in the same box because, for her, these areas were closely related. Next to each subtopic, she then wrote down a brief phrase or reference to experiences and concerns that related to it. By clustering her responses, Rachel discovered topics that were important to her.

She was also able to group related issues—an immediate advantage of clustering. You may want to read the paper (p. 358) that came from this prewriting discovery work. But first look at Rachel's clustering exercise, which is reproduced below:

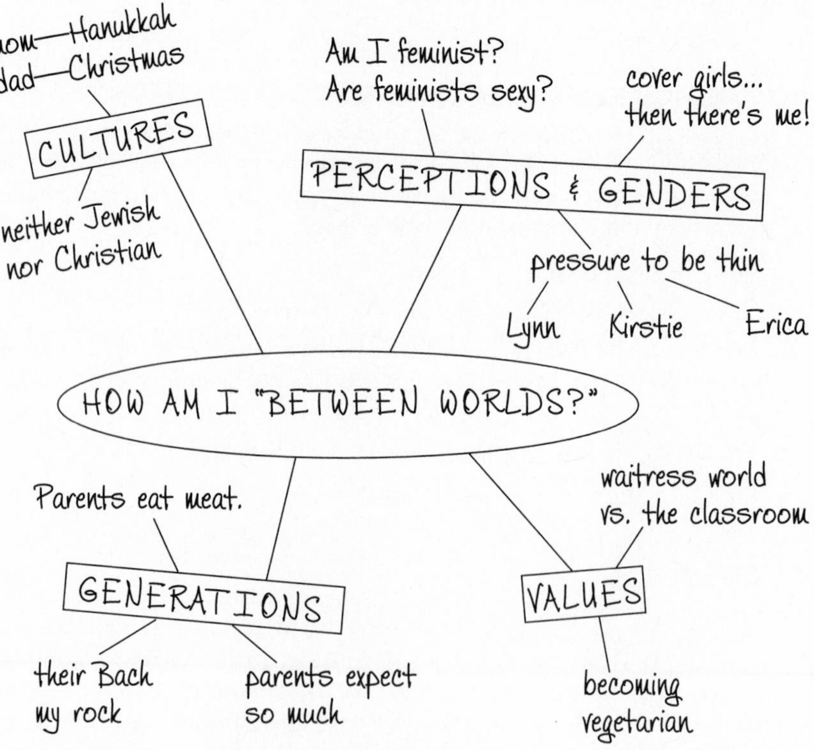

Notice that Rachel started with the assigned question of how she was "between worlds" and used that as a center or starting point for her personal inquiry into specific areas where she felt "betweenness." You can respond graphically to the topics below by clustering.

PRACTICING CLUSTERING

1. Write "self and family" in a box at the center of a page. As you cluster, consider how you are a part of your family and how you are apart from your family.
2. Write "incidents that united my family" in a box at the center of a page. Draw lines to other boxes that will include specific outings, celebrations, crises, customs, and events that have united your family. Don't forget the surprising or unlikely incidents that no one expected would draw you together.

Clustering may help you discover topics that interest you, as well as find relationships between ideas that you have written on your page.

LISTING

You can use listing as a way of making a quick inventory of thoughts, ideas, feelings, or facts about a topic. The object is to list everything, again without censoring any notion that comes to you. In addition to clustering her "between-worlds" experiences as shown (p. 306), Rachel listed her ideas after she discovered a topic for her paper. (You can see her listing on p. 328.)

If you are answering a specific question or know what your topic is, you can also use listing to collect from your reading the data that will be useful in your paper. Listing will help you see ways to group and to arrange the material that you have found.

For example, a student who is assigned a character analysis based on a particular reading may list details from the text that indicate the character's traits. To write a character analysis of Hazel Peoples, the speaker and central character in the short story "My Man Bovanne" (p. 46), student Tim Hogan wrote a list that you can see on page 437. Notice how Tim's list helps him find important details and then organize those details for his essay.

PRACTICING LISTING

1. Write a list of options or advantages your parents or grandparents had that you believe you do not have. List options or advantages you have that they did not.
2. List the tensions that occur between generations in your family.
3. List the customs, habits, and values in your family that are transmitted between generations.

4. List the behavior traits of the "senior" in "Senior-Teener: A New Hybrid" (p. 17).

ACTIVE READING

Active reading is an appropriate prewriting strategy when you are asked to write a specific response to something that you have read or when you know that your own experience and knowledge provide insufficient information for a meaningful essay. A great deal of college writing—in every course—fits these circumstances, so it is important that you either learn active reading or perfect the skills that you already have.

Active reading involves reading with a pen in your hand. *If* you are using your own book, you can read and mark directly in the copy. If you are using a library book, you will need to photocopy the pages you intend to read actively. As you read your own text or the photocopied pages, make the following markings:

- *Underline* key points and supporting details
- *Place checkmarks* and *asterisks* next to important lines
- *Jot* brief summary or commentary *notes* in the margins
- *Circle* unfamiliar words and references to look up later
- *Ask questions* as you read
- *Seek answers* to those questions
- *Question* the writer's *assumptions* and assertions as well as your own.

Reading actively allows you to enter into a conversation with your authors, to examine and challenge their ideas. Active reading will also help you find important lines more easily so that you don't have to reread the entire work each time that you refer to it during class discussions or in your essays. Don't underline or highlight *everything,* however, or you will defeat your purpose of finding just the important points.

If you have a writing assignment that requires you to use information from readings in addition to your own experience, you will profit from learning how to read actively and how to incorporate information that you have read into your own work. Rachel, the student who used clustering to discover her concern about the pressure among her friends to be thin, decided to do some reading about eating disorders. The excerpt on the facing page from "Bodily Harm" (p. 210), illustrates her active reading.

Recent media attention to the binge-purge and self-starvation disorders known as bulimia and anorexia—often detailing gruesome particulars of women's eating behaviors—may have exacerbated this serious problem on college campuses. But why would a woman who reads an article on eating disorders want to copy what she reads? Ruth Striegel-Moore, Ph.D., director of Yale University's Eating Disorders Clinic, suggests that eating disorders may be a way to be like other "special" women and at the same time strive to outdo them. "The pursuit of thinness is a way for women to compete with each other, a way that avoids being threatening to men," says Striegel-Moore. Eating disorders as a perverse sort of rivalry? In Carol's freshman year at SUNY-Binghamton, a roommate showed her how to make herself throw up. "Barf buddies" are notorious on many college campuses, especially in sororities and among sports teams. Eating disorders as negative bonding? Even self-help groups on campus can degenerate into the kinds of competitiveness and negative reinforcement that are among the roots of eating disorders in the first place.

check specific definitions

"special" =how to be unique?

How ironic!

Media may exacerbate the problem

general term

thinness as competition—without threatening men.

Self-help groups as negative reinforcement

This is not another article on how women do it. It is an article on how and why some women stopped. The decision to get help is not always an easy one. The shame and secrecy surrounding most eating disorders and the fear of being labeled "sick" may keep a woman from admitting even to herself that her behavior is hurting her. "We're not weirdos," says Nancy Gengler, a recovered bulimic and number two U.S. squash champion, who asked that I use her real name because "so much of this illness has to do with secrecy and embarrassment." In the first stages of therapy, says Nancy, much of getting better was a result of building up the strength to (literally) "sweat out" the desire to binge and to endure the discomfort of having overeaten rather than throwing up. "I learned to accept such 'failures' and moreover, that they would not make me fat."

the focus:

labeled "sick"

secrecy is part of the problem. Need to accept our "failures"

Writing notes in the margins helped Rachel to stay involved as she read and to remember details from the essay. Like Rachel, you can better understand and retain what you read if you practice active reading.

PRACTICING ACTIVE READING

1. Practice the steps listed on page 308 and actively read the next work that you have been assigned in this course. Do you feel better prepared for class discussion? Did you find the central point or thesis of the essay as a result of your active reading? Was the author's organization scheme apparent to you?
2. Actively read "The Only Child" (p. 11), "I Confess Some Envy" (p. 398), or "The Ties That Bind" (p. 7). After you have actively read one of these essays, join a small group of others who have read the same essay. Compare your active-reading notes with the markings of others in your group.

GROUP BRAINSTORMING—COLLABORATIVE LEARNING

Writing doesn't have to be a lonely activity, with the writer isolated from the world. In fact, much professional writing is a collaborative effort in which writers work together or consult editors. Corporations, educational institutes, and governmental organizations hold regular brainstorming sessions so that everyone can offer ideas, consider options, and exchange opinions. Reporters often work together on a story, business experts pool ideas to draft a proposal, and lawyers work as a team on a brief. Many of your textbooks—including this one—are the result of extensive collaboration.

Your college writing classes may offer you opportunities to work together in small groups, brainstorm for paper topics or supporting details, and critique and edit your classmates' writing. Just as freewriting is a conversation with yourself, group brainstorming provides a conversation with others. These small groups can provide new thoughts, multiple perspectives, and critical questions. Small-group discussion can prompt you to consider others' ideas, as well as help free you from the fear that you have nothing to say. You may find that you are more comfortable sharing ideas with a few classmates rather than the entire class.

In the classroom, groups of four or five work well, with each person recording the different comments and key ideas for an assigned question and then sharing these responses with the entire class. Students in your group can decide who will explain each response so that the burden for reporting the discussion does not fall on any one group member. Your instructor, however, may ask that someone from each group serve as group secretary, recording responses and then reading them. Either way, the goal is to generate as many different responses as possible to a given topic or question. Your group may need to be reminded that everyone's ideas are welcome and needed and that even seemingly farfetched comments can trigger very productive discussions. As in all of the prewriting activities, no idea or comment should be censored.

Let's assume that you have been assigned a paper about growing up with or without siblings. Each group can take a different aspect of this topic:

- The advantages of growing up with siblings
- The advantages of growing up as an only child
- The ways that only children find substitutes for siblings
- The reasons for sibling rivalry and competition and the solutions to these problems
- The unexpected bonds that develop between siblings
- The reasons that sibling friendships often outlast other friendships

After 10 to 15 minutes of discussion, each of you should make sure your group has recorded the key points so they can be shared with the class as a whole. After each report by a group, all students should be invited to add comments or insights on that topic. Students who are listening to a group should take notes to supplement their own essay ideas.

Group brainstorming is an ideal way to discuss reading assignments, and most of the "Thinking About the Text" questions in the reader are designed for collaborative work. Any of those questions may be used for this exercise. Following are brainstorming exercises for both general topics and specific readings.

PRACTICING BRAINSTORMING IN SMALL GROUPS

1. Brainstorm about the forces threatening the family unit today, and consider ways of preventing or solving particular conflicts. (All groups can do this, since the responses will be so varied.)
2. Discuss the extent to which grandparents are or are not valued by families. Support the discussion with your own experience.
3. Discuss the various types of families that are currently portrayed on television. One group can analyze the impact of the media on the family. Other groups can compare sitcoms with family dramas or PBS specials on the family. Another group can contrast portraits of more conventional families with those of less conventional ones. A final group can suggest programs that could help or support the family.

4. Read "The Ties That Bind" (p. 7) and "The Only Child" (p. 11) and discuss specific ways that two children in the same family can develop different values and habits. You may add your own experiences to this discussion.
5. Read "Fetal Alcohol Syndrome" (p. 23) and discuss children's rights and parents' responsibilities.

Brainstorming lets you see others' perspectives and consider their views in relation to your own—an awareness you will need when you are writing for an audience. Collaborative work gets you away from the isolation of your own desk or computer screen and into a social context.

INCUBATION

After you have done one or more of the prewriting responses to an assignment, allow yourself time to think about your topic before you begin to draft the paper. Rather than being a way to avoid the writing assignment, the incubation period lets you subconsciously make connections and respond to your focus. Students often comment on experiencing flashes of insight about their papers while in the shower, falling asleep, or doing some physical activity.

You, too, will find that your brain will continue to "work" on your paper if you are preoccupied with it, and productive insights can occur during this incubation period. If you do some prewriting on your paper when it is first assigned, your early thoughts and ideas may develop during incubation. Clearly, though, if you have waited until the night before the assignment is due, you aren't going to enjoy much of an incubation period!

The need for incubation continues throughout the drafting process. While you are away from your desk or computer screen, you can still be thinking about ways to hone your topic, increase support of your points, discover links between ideas in your paper, and recall words that will sharpen your meaning. This is also an ideal time to remind yourself that you are writing for readers and to consider their expectations.

CONSIDERING AUDIENCE

Identifying Your Audience

All writing is intended for an audience. Except for personal journal writers, who may be able to understand their own notes to themselves, writers have certain responsibilities to meet the needs and expectations of a reader. But who *is* the reader?

In some specific writing situations, you can easily define the audience for your work; for example, your reader may be a friend or family member who will receive your letter. You are surely aware that your writing tone—the voice that you use that affects your word choice and emphasis—will differ if you are writing to your lover, brother, elderly aunt, or mother. However, you may be less able to define the audience for other writing situations. You might assume that for papers assigned in your college classes, your reader is a classmate or an instructor, a thoughtful person who may know something about the subject of your writing and who is very willing (indeed, eager) to learn more.

In general, you should not assume that your only reader is your composition instructor, for that conclusion will prompt you to write for a very small audience. Further, your English teacher may be your easiest audience, because he or she is *required* to read what you have written, comment on your thinking and writing skills, and then perhaps place a grade on your work. In the real world, when you are writing for a boss, readers of a newspaper, or a community organization member, your easily distracted or unwilling reader may lack the empathy an academic instructor has for the effort you have put into your writing, which may be ignored or tossed into the trash rather than honored with comments or praise. The skills that you learn in your composition class, however, will prepare you for your broader college and real-world writing requirements.

Academic Audiences Academic readers (your instructors and classmates) will assume that you have carefully considered the assigned topic. This means that you understand what is expected of you and that you are writing to satisfy that assignment. This may require finding out what other people know or believe, collecting specific data, or sorting through your own thoughts and information on the subject. Your audience will expect a certain depth of response, even for a short paper. The reader will expect to learn specific facts, find actual examples, discover important insights, or see particular relationships that she or he was not aware of before reading your paper. The paper's required length may define how many dimensions of the subject you can explore to satisfy the assignment.

An academic audience will also expect you to have worked with integrity if you incorporate the ideas, facts, or words of another writer. (See the discussions of plagiarism on pp. 341 and 462–464.) Your reader will assume that you have understood any material that you have brought in from another source, that you have not distorted the material in any way, and that you have given credit to the writer whose words or ideas you have used.

An academic audience will expect you to make some point and to support that point logically and with sufficient details (of description, fact, or example) to be convincing. Such readers will expect that you know what you are writing about and that your work has not just been assembled from other people's work—that your treatment or perspective is fresh.

Academic readers will expect your material to be presented in an orderly way so that a lack of organization does not obscure the points you are making. They will expect your points to cohere. Finally, they will expect the language of your work to be appropriate: standard English and well-chosen words, edited to remove errors in grammar, spelling, and mechanics.

Nonacademic Audiences For writing outside the classroom—for example, a letter to the newspaper, a report for your boss, or an analysis for a community project—it is vital for you to engage an audience that is not required to read your writing. What are the expectations of this audience?

To start, you may need to convince those readers that your subject and the way you have treated it are worth their time. Depending on the attention span of your reader, you may have to establish the value of your subject and the quality of your writing in the first few sentences! Developing an engaging style will help keep your reader interested.

Voice Most instructors will tell you to "write in your own voice." That means that they want you to write using the vocabulary, sentence structure, and style that you use for communicating as an adult. You do not want to use pretentious words or artificial language, nor do you want to use diction that is more appropriate for talking with a friend. Often, your intention in writing and the position you take on your subject will help you to determine how emphatic your stance and your language will be. In any case, though, you will write in your own voice.

Stance and Tone To engage your audience quickly, you may want to assume a stance and tone that is positive for all readers, even those who are uninterested in or hostile to the topic you are writing about. You may want to anticipate possible objections, doubts, or lack of interest by writing in a tone that does not put off any reader. Consider these two opening sentences:

> Only someone ignorant of contract law will find ambiguity in the handling of surrogate parenting disputes.
>
> Surrogate parenting disputes may occur because the legal world has not yet determined how to judge these cases of ethical dilemma.

The tone of the first sentence is bold, the assertion straightforward. Some readers will be put off by the claim that "only someone ignorant of contract law will find ambiguity" because some of the audience may be ignorant of contract law, and the "will" suggests no room for consideration. The use of "ignorant" will be offensive to some readers and perhaps compelling to others. Some readers may continue to read in spite of the brash voice or even because of it. But others may conclude that the tone is too hostile to tolerate, and those readers will stop reading.

In contrast, the tone of the second sentence is cautious—"may occur"—and contemplative because the author recognizes that surrogate parenting disputes involve an "ethical dilemma." By suggesting that there is room for discussion, the writer may win the reader who is interested in an unbiased exploration of surrogate parenting disputes. The writer of the second sentence has tried to create a reasonable and informing relationship between writer and reader, one that should attract readers.

You will need to choose the tone that you want to use for your particular writing assignment. The subject matter of your work and the *audience* for whom you are writing will help you determine whether a neutral tone will keep your audience engaged.

Style *Style* is conscious use of language, and good style will help to ensure the attention of the audience. This means considering everything from your choice of words to your construction of sentences. Style includes the following elements:

- Word choice—precisely chosen words, wordplay, and level of diction (formal, conversational, or slang); see also pp. 558–561.
- Sentence structure—length, types, and variety
- Voice—real, rather than artificial or pretentious
- Tone—your intention, attitude, and relationship with the reader

Consider the following opening line from the *Harvard Health Letter.* The topic is controversial, and the reader may have opinions about the subject. Notice that the style of the author, Ruth Papazian, is apparent to the reader in her first sentence.

A Hot Issue

In January, 1992, when Florida shoppers bought strawberries that had been treated with gamma rays, food irradiation moved from the realm of theory to America's kitchen tables.

First, the author uses wit and wordplay in writing her title. There's nothing wrong with evoking a chuckle from a reader, even when the subject matter is serious or scientific. (An academic in the scientific fields may object to humor in formal papers. You will need to learn from your instructors the style requirements of specific disciplines.) Further, the writer creates an immediate and natural bond with any reader who has bought strawberries; that reader would wonder, "Hey! Do my strawberries get zapped?" The writer assures that bond by further noting that the issue moved from "theory"—which some readers may not care about—to "America's kitchen tables." Notice that the writer does not write "dining room tables." This writing is clearly directed toward general readers, because everyone eats, and the kitchen image evokes a folksiness that engages the audience.

In the rest of the article, the author uses sentences that further win the reader. For example, after establishing the topic, she writes in her seventh paragraph, "Since a caveperson first tossed a chunk of mastodon onto glowing embers, humans have been cooking with infrared radiation." Notice the gender-neutral *caveperson* instead of the sexist term *caveman,* and notice the diction of *chunk,* the humorous specificity of *mastodon,* and the effective imagery of *glowing embers.* Who wouldn't want to read this entire essay? (It's in the August 1992 issue, volume 17, number 10, if you're really engaged in the topic or want to see more of this author's style.)

An academic reader who is required to read your writing may not insist on lively style, wit, or exquisite word choice. And she or he may tolerate a brash tone or hostile stance. Nevertheless, ideas about engaging an audience are as applicable to writing done for academics as it is to the writing done for a nonacademic reader.

PRACTICING STYLE

1. Write two letters—one to your best friend and one to your parents or children—describing a party that you recently attended. (Your letters probably will vary in vocabulary, kinds of details, sentence structure, and tone.)
2. Write two memos—one to a co-worker who is a friend and one to your boss—arguing for a particular change at work.

Analyzing Audience Awareness

Clearly, professional writers have an understanding of audience when they direct their texts for publication. We can profit from a study of the techniques that they use to engage and hold their particular audiences.

Ellen Sweet In her informative essay on date rape, "Date Rape" (p. 89), Ellen Sweet begins her study of the epidemic with first-person accounts from women who have been raped by dates or acquaintances. Each woman's narrative has a similar theme: Because of her friendship with the rapist, she could not believe what was happening to her.

Sweet does not retreat from the burden of exposing shocking data—for example, the statistic that 60 to 80 percent of all rapes are committed by a person the victim knows. Sweet presents her data almost entirely through interviews, so her own voice is absent or controlled rather than inflammatory. The author wants her selected subjects' voices to reveal the problems of date rape: The victims reveal their shock that a friend would abuse them, the school officials reveal their refusal to acknowledge a pervasive campus problem, and the psychologists show the denial pattern of aggressive men who force women to have intercourse but believe that their behavior is acceptable. After quoting one school official who refused to involve his campus in the survey because he feared people would become "psychologically upset," Sweet coolly but pointedly writes, "One wonders just who are the 'people' who will get most psychologically upset: the students, or their parents who pay for their educations, or the administrators who are concerned about the school's image."

Sweet's intention is to stir her audience—originally, readers of *Ms.* magazine—to an awareness *and* a constructive course of action. Sweet wants readers to pressure their colleges' educators, administrators, and counselors to implement the sort of rape prevention programs that she discusses in her report. An audience that is merely angry will not do what the author wants done; hence her voice is modulated to inform and provide a course of action rather than to blame and enrage. Her conclusion is a controlled call to action: "Women clearly need to get more convincing, and men clearly need to believe them more. But until that ideal time, Montana State's Jan Strout warns, 'Because men have been socialized to hear yes when women say no, we have to scream it.'" Sweet lets her interviewed subjects "scream" for her. It is not surprising that this essay has been widely reprinted in the decade since its initial publication.

Example: Convincing an Audience

William F. Harrison Let's consider another essay that has been printed in a number of publications, including the *Los Angeles Times* on July 7, 1996. William F. Harrison is an obstetrician and gynecologist who practices in Fayetteville, Arkansas. A smoker of twenty years, Dr. Harrison saw the effects on his body of his addiction to cigarettes. For ten years he tried to stop smoking, and because he limited himself to a single cigarette a day, he thought he was not harming himself. Nevertheless, he had chronic bronchitis and laryngitis. After consulting with pulmonologists and pathologists, he learned that even a cigarette a day does irreparable harm to the body. He knew that he needed to stop entirely, and he did. He also knew that he needed to convince his patients to stop smoking. This essay reports the results of Dr. Harrison's research. Does the writer convince his reader?

■ WHY STOP SMOKING? LET'S GET CLINICAL

By William F. Harrison

Most of us in medicine now accept that tobacco is associated with major health consequences and constitutes the No. 1 health problem in this country.

What smokers have not yet come to terms with is that if they continue smoking, the probability of developing one or more of the major complications of smoking is 100%. It absolutely will happen. They will develop chronic bronchitis, laryngitis, pharyngitis, sinusitis and some degree of emphysema. It is also highly probable that they will develop serious disease in the arteries of all vital organs, including the brain and heart, markedly increasing their risk of heart attack and stroke. If they continue, they increase the probability of developing cancer of the lips, gums, tongue, pharynx, larynx, trachea, bronchi and lungs, of the bladder, cervix, gallbladder and other organs. Smoking contributes to rapid aging of the skin and connective tissues—women and men who smoke usually have the skin age of a person 10 to 20 years older than one who doesn't smoke, given the same degree of exposure to the sun.

About 415,000 people die prematurely each year in the U.S. as a result of smoking—the equivalent of 18 747s crashing every week with no survivors. Many of these victims die after long and excruciating illnesses, burdens to themselves, their families and society. The cost of this misery is incalculable, but we do know that the tobacco industry grosses about $50 billion a year from the agonies it inflicts.

How does all this damage come about?

In normal lungs, the trachea and bronchi—the large and small tubes leading to the alveoli (the tiny sacs that do the actual work of the lungs)—are lined with a film of tissue that is one cell layer thick. The surface of these cells is covered with tiny, finger-like structures called cilia. These cilia beat constantly in a waving motion, which moves small particles and toxic substances out of the lung and into the back of the throat where they are swallowed. In a smoker or someone like a coal miner, who constantly breathes in large amounts of toxic substances, many of the cilia soon disappear. If exposure continues, some ciliated cells die and are replaced by squamous cells, the same type that form the skin. Without the cleansing function of the ciliated cells, toxic materials and particles are breathed further into the lungs, staying longer in contact with all the tissue. Each group of ciliated cells killed and replaced by squamous cells decreases by a certain fraction the lungs' ability to cleanse themselves. As this occurs, the amount of damage done by each cigarette increases to a greater and greater degree. By the time one has been a pack-a-day smoker for 10 years or so, extensive damage has already been done. By 20 years, much of the damage is irreversible and progresses more rapidly. After 10 years of smoking, each cigarette may do as much damage to the body as three or more packs did when a smoker first started.

The longer one smokes, the harder it gets to quit. Smoking is one of the most addictive of human habits, perhaps as addicting as crack cocaine or heroin. One has to quit every day, and there are no magic pills or crutches that make stopping easy. It is tough to do. Only those who keep trying ever quit. And even those who have smoked for only a short time or a few cigarettes a day will probably find it difficult to stop. But the sooner a smoker makes this self-commitment, the more probable it is that he or she will quit before having done major damage to the body.

Clearly, William Harrison's purpose in writing is to convince readers who are smokers to stop smoking. His obligation as a writer is to produce plenty of research to answer the question "why stop smoking?" His intention also may be to prevent people from starting and to arm nonsmokers with specific evidence to help persuade a family member or a friend who smokes to stop.

Harrison begins his essay with a statement that seems matter-of-fact but provides a jolt even to readers who may think they have heard all the predictable sermons about not smoking. He states that the medical profession is now aware that the consequences of tobacco use create our country's primary health problem and that people who smoke are absolutely guaranteed to have at least one serious disease caused by smoking.

His opening engages the reader because he is straightforward in his presentation of facts. Harrison specifically cites those diseases that all smokers eventually *will* get—"chronic bronchitis, laryngitis, pharyngitis, sinusitis and some degree of emphysema"—and the diseases that smokers *probably* will get—"serious disease in the arteries of all vital organs, including the brain and heart" and "cancer of the lips, gums, tongue, pharynx, larynx, trachea, bronchi and lungs . . . bladder, cervix, gallbladder"—so that no one reading the list can feign ignorance or disinterest. No organ of the body remains untouched, and Harrison might have written just that statement. But because he actually cites the organs, the reader is almost overwhelmed by the catalog of specific details. Further, to catch the interest of the person who is indifferent to health, Harrison appeals to the reader's vanity by stating that smokers' skin ages ten to twenty years that of beyond nonsmokers.

When Harrison provides the statistics of people who die prematurely because they smoked—"415,000 per year"—he also gives an equivalent for this figure: "18 747s crashing every week with no survivors." The purpose of the equivalent is to shock us. We may be complacent about the number of smokers who die each year, but we all know the effect of a newspaper headline announcing the crash of a single plane. Imagine reading that eighteen planes crashed each week all year! Cleverly, Harrison admits that he doesn't know the cost of the "excruciating illnesses"—and the misery—that precede death from smoking-related diseases. But he knows and gives the profits of the tobacco industry: "$50 billion a year."

Harrison might have generalized what happens to the lungs when people smoke, but instead he credits his reader's intelligence by providing a highly specific and scientific account of how the cilia cells that normally cleanse the lungs disappear. In fact, his word choice is that the "ciliated cells die," a far more emphatic way to show that toxic material is no longer filtered out. By showing the human body as a mechanical organism, he convinces the reader that the smoker's body has no more chance to continue running well than a car would if it were deprived of oil or gasoline.

To drive home his point about the toxicity of smoking, Harrison equates the smoker with "a coal miner"; both breathe in "large amounts of toxic substances." He notes that after ten years of smoking, the lungs are so vulnerable that "each cigarette may do as much damage to the body as three or more packs did when a smoker first started." He uses this startling research to convince both the smoker who planned to stop after a few years and the smoker of ten years who cuts down to an occasional cigarette that profound harm is done to the body regardless of the smoker's intention.

Harrison's conclusion has to do with nicotine addiction, and he compares the addiction to quitting crack cocaine or heroin. In his frightening comparison he gives any young person who is considering smoking ample reason not to start, and he gives any person who loves a smoker the impetus to seek professional help to rid the smoker of this powerful and deadly addiction.

Finally, Harrison's title is an effective play on words. He's relying on the reader to hear "Let's Get Physical," lyrics of a popular song, in "Let's Get Clinical." His essay provides vivid clinical evidence of the physical damage that smokers will do to their bodies, information that is as far from a popular tune as it can be.

PRACTICING AUDIENCE AWARENESS

1. Write a letter to your college president or dean of student affairs to convince the administrator that your college needs better education, security, and counseling for rape prevention. Use the material in Sweet's essay for your letter.
2. Write a letter to a friend who smokes to convince that person to stop. Use the data in Harrison's essay for your letter.

A FINAL WORD ABOUT AUDIENCE

Both Ellen Sweet and William Harrison needed to make assumptions about their audience and to employ techniques to engage and hold their readers' attention. You, too, can do this by assuming a stance that will be attractive to your audience and by maintaining a voice that will keep your reader interested in your work. Good style—achieved with deliberately chosen vocabulary, sentence structure, and tone—can engage your reader immediately. Further, you will want to provide statistical data or details for support and give evidence that is meaningful to any reader.

With a realistic understanding of your audience in mind, you are ready to begin organizing and drafting your essay. You will gain an understanding of that aspect of the writing process in the next chapter of the rhetoric.

7

Organizing and Drafting an Essay

■ ■ ■

DISCOVERING A THESIS

From Prewriting to Working Thesis

The prewriting experiences described in the previous chapter should have helped you discover focus points and different ways in which you might respond to your writing assignment. You were also given some ideas about considering the audience for your writing. It is now important that you determine your specific approach for your paper. All essays require a focus—a controlling idea for both the writer and the reader. So after doing some prewriting activities, thinking about your topic, considering your audience, and writing an initial draft, you should be able to construct at least a tentative or working thesis that will help you direct your writing. That thesis may change a number of times as you draft and revise your paper. Let's think about how the controlling idea for your paper might be expressed.

Developing a Thesis

A thesis is an assertion about a limited subject that will be supported, proven, or described by the writer of the essay. Often, but not always, the view of the writer shows in the language of the thesis. Sometimes the writer constructs a thesis to forecast the plan or organization of the paper. The thesis will reflect the aim or intention of the paper.

Let's imagine that Pete is deciding from his prewriting experiences (pp. 302–303) how to respond to his assignment on stereotyping. His particular interest has to do with his tattoo and how he is stereotyped because of it, an awareness he gained in freewriting. Pete realized that he had a good focus for a story he could narrate. He also discovered that he was interested in doing some reading about the history of tattoos to learn whether they had always been regarded negatively.

If Pete's assignment had been to write about a personal experience involving stereotyping, he probably would have written about the incident in the Alaskan campground. Had he been asked to define stereotyping or show its consequences, Pete might have recalled his dialectical journal prewriting (p. 304) on the essay "Don't Let Stereotypes Warp Your Judgments," and he may have developed his paper in a different way. Pete may have used any of the following for a working thesis, depending on his purpose in writing the paper:

- An experience in Alaska showed me how uncomfortable stereotyping can be for the person being stereotyped.
- Stereotyping, or prejudgments based on standardized pictures in our heads, can create unnecessary anxiety and deprive us of worthwhile experiences.
- Because tattoos have been worn by the lower classes and fringe members of various cultures throughout history, there has been prejudice against them.
- Because prominent citizens of the world have started to wear tattoos, earlier prejudice against tattoos has diminished.

Each of these assertions requires Pete to develop his paper in a slightly different way. The first thesis can be supported with his own experience. The second statement requires some incorporation of definitive and appropriately documented material from Heilbroner's essay on stereotyping, as well as personal experience. The third and fourth thesis statements will require Pete to research material to support his assertions. Like Pete, your personal interests, as well as the aim of the assignment itself, will help you decide on a suitable thesis.

Recognizing a Thesis

If a thesis is a complete sentence that makes an assertion about a limited subject, which of the following are supportable thesis statements? Which are not? Which statements forecast a plan or direction for the paper?

1. Sexism in college courses.
2. Sexist language in college textbooks can be eliminated with the right attitude and language awareness.
3. I think the school's cafeteria should post a nutritional analysis of every meal it offers.
4. When grandparents live with two younger generations, everyone learns flexibility and new reasons to laugh.
5. Should Americans buy only American-made products?
6. Siblings can remind us of our family's history and values and can provide physical and emotional support as we age.

The first example may be a suitable subject or topic for an essay, but it is not a thesis. As the absence of a verb indicates, the example lacks an assertion that makes a claim about sexism. The second example does make a claim about sexist language and is a reasonable thesis. It has a limited subject (sexist language in college textbooks), and it forecasts that "attitude" and "language awareness" will be the subtopics discussed to support the thesis. Example three contains a clear assertion, but "I think" is unnecessary. The thesis should directly express this conviction: The school's cafeteria should post a nutritional analysis of every meal it offers. The fourth example is an effective thesis that forecasts two benefits of generations living together. A question like that in the fifth example may be a good way to engage a reader in an introduction, but it is not an assertion, so it is not a suitable thesis. The question encourages an unfocused, disorganized response. Contrast the direction implicit in the statements of examples two, four, or six with this question, and you will see why it is not effective. Example six is a very explicit thesis statement. It cites exactly the areas of support that will come in the paper: the "family's history and values" and "physical and emotional support." Writers who write from a strong thesis will know where they are going, and so will their readers.

Changing the Thesis

Before we discuss thesis statements any further, it is important to acknowledge some qualities about the thesis. For one thing, the thesis can undergo many changes in the course of drafting and rewriting a paper. Everyone has had the experience of finishing a draft only to discover that her or his feelings about the subject have changed. To reflect that new awareness in the paper, the writer will want to return to the thesis, revise it, and then reshape the points in the paper so that they will adequately support the new assertion. Perhaps it is best to consider any thesis as only a working thesis until you are about to edit your final draft. (See Rachel's work on developing a thesis, pp. 327–333.)

The "Missing" Thesis

Although the final draft of a well-written essay will be clearly focused and will support a central point, some writers do not explicitly state their thesis, and some instructors do not demand one. Sometimes the overt assertion may spoil the sense of discovery that the writer intends for the reader. But even if a thesis is implied rather than stated, in a well-structured essay you should be able to articulate the writer's fundamental assertion.

Positioning the Thesis

If you are going to state a thesis in your essay, you need to consider where you will place it. For many writers, and for many essays, placing the thesis at the conclusion of the introduction makes sense. The thesis follows logically from the introductory materials used to engage the audience, and the plan or direction of the paper is set forth so that the reader knows not only what is coming, but in what order the support will be presented. This forecasting also helps you, the writer of the essay, to stay organized and on target.

Although it may seem natural to place the thesis at the end of the introductory paragraph, not all writers do this. Essays that are tightly written, with very well-organized support, may conclude with the thesis to bring an inevitable (if not predictable) sense of closure. The reader will perceive where the writer is headed, so the assertion at the end of the paper will not come as a surprise.

Many writing instructors will require that you place your thesis within the first few paragraphs of your essay. Tired of wondering and writing "Where is all of this going?" in the margins of student papers, some instructors favor the clearly stated thesis that forecasts the subtopics and their order of presentation. In any case, a strong focus—whether stated in a thesis or implied—contributes to good writing, and you will want to perfect your ability to focus your work.

Sample Thesis Statements

The following chart shows how writers work from a limited subject to write a thesis that their experience or information can support.

Limited Subject	*Focus*	*Thesis*
College students	Commuting students	College students who live at home know the problems of living between worlds.
Native Americans	Popular depictions	The Native American is stereotyped and denigrated in American popular culture.
TV for children	Improved programming	In contrast to ten years ago, television programs designed for elementary-age children today are multicultural and interracial.
The men's movement	Is it necessary?	The men's movement is needed to create a social connection between men. The movement can rectify divorce and paternity inequities.

PRACTICING THESIS WRITING

Although seeing other writers' thesis statements will help you gain awareness of the thesis, you need to practice writing your own assertions for your own papers. You also need to have readers critique the thesis statements that you have written.

1. Return to one of your prewriting exercises or freewrite here on the subject of a parent's ability or inability to be open to new and possibly controversial ideas. Freewrite for fifteen minutes without censoring any thought that comes to you. Then reread what you have written. Find an aspect of that material that interests you. Limit your focus and write two or three different thesis statements that you can support with the ideas in your freewriting. Type or write these assertions neatly on a sheet of paper and make three copies before your next class session.
2. In the first few minutes of class time, work in groups of four students to comment on each other's assertions. Let each student in the group make comments about one thesis statement before you go on to look at each person's second assertion. Determine which statements are true assertions that can be supported. Then predict the type of support that is necessary (narrative of personal experience, definition, or examples from research material) for each thesis. If you are having trouble finding what is lacking in your thesis statements, talk with your instructor or writing assistant.

Critical Thinking and the "So What?" Response

After you have a tentative assertion toward which to direct your support, ask yourself, "So what?" A sure way to realize that your assumed assertion isn't headed anywhere meaningful is to discover yourself shrugging indifferently at your own claim. And as you jot down answers to this question, you will start to see what you are actually claiming. For example, imagine what would happen if you started with this assertion:

Thesis: Many people in the world are victims of stereotyping.

"So what?"

Some people have preconceived ideas about others.

"So what?"

It's unfair. People see them as types, not individuals.

"So what?"

These prejudgments limit the people who are stereotyped *and* the people doing the stereotyping.

As you continue to answer the "So what?" questions, you may discover a way to state your assertion that makes your reader more eager to read your paper. Compare the following assertion with the first one above. In what way is it better?

Thesis: Prejudgments limit the lives of the stereotyped individual and the person doing the stereotyping.

Notice how this statement conforms to the requirements of a thesis. It is a complete sentence, not a question or a phrase, and it articulates a definite opinion or assertion. Unlike the first attempt at a thesis, this statement establishes a definite focus on prejudgments (they "limit . . . lives"), and it suggests an order for the analysis ("the stereotyped individual" and "the person doing the stereotyping").

By asking yourself "So what?" *throughout* your writing, you will not only sharpen your thesis but also help yourself discover points and insights worth sharing with readers. If you continue to ask this question, you will prompt yourself to think more critically about each claim as you make it. You also will ensure that you are writing from a worthwhile assertion and that you are explaining your points to your reader.

SUPPORTING A THESIS

Drafting

Once you have done some prewriting, you are ready to begin the drafting process. No one writer drafts the same way; in fact, there are as many methods (and "nonmethods") for drafting as there are writers. But there are lots of strategies and approaches that help writers organize, develop, and support their ideas and assertions.

In the next pages we will trace how one student, Rachel, drafted her paper. Look back to page 306 to see Rachel's clustering exercise, where she discovered a topic related to living "between worlds." From this initial prewriting, she perceived that recurrent topics of interest were related to food: her vegetarianism, her friends' preoccupation with slimness, her awareness that her body does not fit the cover-girl mold, and even her job as a waitress.

Developing Support

Reviewing all of these food-related topics, Rachel realized that she was most interested in her friends' eating problems. She decided to pursue the topic. Because her instructor had required her to incorporate readings from this textbook in her paper, she started by actively reading "Bodily Harm." You can read an excerpt from this prewriting exercise on pages 308–310. This active reading helped to stimulate Rachel's thinking and helped her understand her friends' experiences.

Listing

After her prewriting activities, Rachel started to list more specific ideas and experiences that related to eating disorders:

- My friend, Lynn, hospitalized for anorexia, nearly died
- Another friend, Kirstie, was proud she could vomit automatically every time she ate
- My friend, Erica, in a treatment program, was shocked by the number of women over thirty still plagued by eating disorders
- Binge-and-purge syndrome
- Ads depict tall models in size 3 bikinis
- "Bodily Harm" examines psychological motives, "barf buddies," and "aerobic nervosa"
- "The Beauty Myth" continues to imprison women
- Jane Fonda, once bulimic, hooked so many on her "Work Out" videos
- Princess Di—bulimic and suicidal—the myth collapses
- My own insecurity about weight
- My cousin spent weeks in a hospital program for anorexics
- Weight loss—the ultimate "control" mechanism?
- Women's movement trying to free women from such images
- Young women torn between being feminist or sexy—why either/or?
- Sexy women are always pictured as thin
- Women competing without threatening men

Working Thesis

From this list, Rachel linked certain topics: friends' experiences, celebrities with serious eating disorders, advertising images of women, psychological motives, the women's movement, and dieting as a control mechanism. These groupings helped her draft a working thesis so that she could start planning her paper.

Working Thesis: Many women suffer from eating disorders.

Using this preliminary thesis as a guide, Rachel started to write.

First Draft

In this day and age many women suffer from eating disorders. Influenced by television commercials and movies, most women have been conditioned to believe they must be thin to be beautiful. Who wouldn't want to hear friends whisper, "What a body! She really knows how to stay in shape!" or "Don't you hate someone who looks that good?" Either way, the sense of envy is clear. A thin girl has something that others don't—and this gives her power and control. She can make herself in the image of the cover girls. "The pursuit of thinness is a way for women to compete with each other, a way that avoids being threatening to men" (Erens 211).

Unfortunately, this competition keeps women from seeking or obtaining the help they might otherwise get from close friends. Many bulimics keep their secret as guarded as they can. For example, my friend Kirstie did this. She waited for years before she told friends (and later, her family) that she was bulimic. At first, only her "barf buddy" (from Erens?) knew.

Kirstie seemed to have a good life with her family and friends. But years later, she revealed to me that her greatest pride was when she discovered that she was now vomiting automatically after eating, without needing to use a finger or spoon.

Erica was another friend who needed help. In fact, her situation was so bad that she needed to go into a hospital. And my friend Lynn would have died had she not entered the hospital when she did. She had to drop out of Berkeley immediately and get prolonged therapy for herself and her family. As Erens notes, "Family therapy considers the family itself, not the daughter with the eating disorder, to be the 'patient.' Often the daughter has taken on the role of diverting attention from unacknowledged conflicts within the family."

One problem Lynn had was conforming to her parents' expectations. Lynn decided to major in art even though her parents wanted her to get a degree in computer science so she would have a job when she graduated. There was so much stress in that house every time Lynn enrolled in another art class. Maybe she felt that the only thing she could control in her life was how thin she could get.

The message to be thin comes from popular role models. Actress Jane Fonda has sold many on the value of her "Work Out" and has helped spawn "aerobic nervosa" (Erens 211). Many women who admire her shape may not know that Fonda was once bulimic. And no one watching the televised spectacle of Prince Charles and Princess Diana's wedding could have predicted that years later biographers would be discussing "Di's bulimia."

Not just the superstars but all models seem incredibly thin today. Wolf contends: "the weight of fashion models plummeted to 23 percent below that of ordinary women, eating disorders rose exponentially, and a mass neurosis was promoted that used food and weight to strip women of that sense of control" (11). It seems that many women—celebrities, models, and my friends—have not escaped this curse.

Evaluating the First Draft

As Rachel was writing this draft, she found herself crossing out occasional words and adding phrases, but her main concern was getting her ideas down on the page. She remembered relevant ideas from some assigned readings in *Between Worlds,* and she put some of the quoted material in her draft. She didn't worry about the form of her quotes, but she was careful to copy the page numbers correctly so she wouldn't have to waste time searching for them later. Once she had written this rough draft, she reread it with a pen in hand, spotting weak areas and making quick notes to herself. Her critique of her first draft is shown on pages 331–332.

cliché? dull

In this day and age many women suffer from eating disorders. Influenced by television commercials and movies, most women have been conditioned to believe they must be thin to be beautiful. Who wouldn't want to hear friends whisper, "What a body! She really knows how to stay in shape!" or "Don't you hate someone who looks that good?" Either way, the sense of envy is clear. A thin girl has something that others don't--and this gives her power and control. She can make herself in the image of cover girls. "The pursuit of thinness is a way for women to compete with each other, a way that avoids being threatening to men" (Erens 211).

ybe ave. . . ut hesis here?

Unfortunately, this competition keeps women from seeking or obtaining the help they might otherwise get from close friends. Many bulimics keep their secret as guarded as they can. For example, my friend Kirstie did this. She waited for years before she told friends (and later, her family) that she was bulimic. At first, only her "barf buddy" (page? from Eren) knew.

Kirstie seemed to have a good life with her family and friends. illustrate But years later, she revealed to me that her greatest pride was when she discovered that she was now vomiting automatically after eating, without needing to use a finger or spoon. better link here? too gross? or OK?

develop

Erica was another friend who needed help. In fact, her situation was so bad that she needed to go into a hospital. And my friend Lynn would have died had she not entered the hospital when she did. She had to drop

develop

out of Berkeley immediately and get prolonged therapy for herself and her family. As Erens notes, "Family therapy considers the family itself, not the daughter with the eating disorder, to be the 'patient.' Often the daughter has taken on the role of diverting attention from unacknowledged conflicts within the family."

discuss & lir bette

One problem Lynn had was conforming to her parents' expectations. Lynn decided to major in art even though her parents wanted her to get a degree in computer science so she would have a job when she graduated. There was so much stress in that house every time Lynn enrolled in another art class. Maybe she felt that the only thing she could control in her life was how thin she could get. link?

Put earlier

The message to be thin comes from popular role models. Actress Jane Fonda has sold many on the value of her "Work Out" and has helped spawn "aerobic nervosa" (Erens 211). Many women who admire her shape may not know that Fonda was once bulimic. And no one watching the televised spectacle of Prince Charles and Princess Diana's wedding could have predicted that years later biographers would be discussing "Di's bulimia."

Not just the superstars but all models seem incredibly thin today. Wolf contends: lead in? "the weight of fashion models plummeted to 23 percent below that of ordinary women, eating disorders rose exponentially, and a mass neurosis was promoted that used food and weight to strip women of that sense of control" (11). It seems that many women--celebrities, models, and my friends--have not escaped this curse.

OK for thesis?

Revising the Thesis

Writing the draft helped Rachel realize the link between her friends' experiences and the influence of the media. She decided to revise her thesis to reflect this connection between the media and eating disorders.

> **New Working Thesis:** Magazine ads and commercials influence how women see themselves and how they behave.

Rachel felt that her material—both her personal experiences and readings—would support her new thesis. She also realized that this thesis helped her link the influence of the media on women's actions and behavior. Rachel showed her thesis to her instructor, who suggested she apply the "So what?" response to this assertion:

> Ads and commercials influence women's self-perceptions.
>
> "So what?"
>
> Women try to look like the skinny models.
>
> "So what?"
>
> It's dangerous! Women are starving themselves.
>
> "So what?"
>
> The media has to change—they are responsible for programming women this way.

After thinking about this conversation with herself, Rachel revised her working thesis again:

> **Revised Working Thesis:** The media must be forced to stop programming young women to believe that skeletal models are the ideal.

Rachel's revised thesis more accurately reflected her view that the media must change what they are doing to women. Her reference to the "skeletal models" would permit her to discuss her friends' experiences. A friend in her English class who knew her topic recommended she look at a book, *The Obsession: Reflections on the Tyranny of Slenderness* by Kim Chernin. Rachel found a few pages with pertinent information supporting her criticism of the media; she photocopied the pages in case she wanted to use them later.

WRITING AN OUTLINE

Organizing to Highlight Key Points

Excellent ideas and interesting information can get lost or buried in a paper that is not carefully arranged and organized. After collecting your thoughts and materials during the prewriting exercises, you need to present these materials in a logical and effective order. You may decide to arrange your thesis to reflect your organization scheme and help you draft your essay.

Notice how Rachel's thesis forecasts her essay's key points:

> The media must be forced to stop programming young women to believe that skeletal models are the ideal.

Rachel's thesis suggests that first she will look at how the media is "programming" women, and then she will show how specific women become "skeletal" victims of the advertising that they see. Further, her assertion that the media "must be forced to stop" this practice invites her to propose a solution. Although Rachel devised a general scheme for organizing her paper, she knew she needed a more detailed outline.

To Outline or Not to Outline

By helping you arrange your materials effectively, an outline can save you time and frustration. It can keep you from going around in circles and never arriving at your destination. Just as most drivers need a map to direct them through unfamiliar territory, most writers need outlines to draft their papers.

However, you probably have had the experience of being in a car without a map, when someone could intuit the right direction and get you where you needed to be. Some writers have that intuition and therefore find detailed outlines unnecessary. But these writers will still craft a strong thesis and rely on their intrinsic sense of organization to guide them as they write.

Most of us also have been in cars with drivers who were convinced they could manage without a map but couldn't. All that aimless driving and backtracking should prove the value of maps and directions! Such indirection or "backtracking" in papers prompts instructors to note in the margins: "Order?" "Repetitious," "Organization needs work," "Relevant?" "Transition needed," or "Where is this going?" If you see these indicators on your papers, you know your intuition is failing you. Outline before you write! Unless your instructor requires a particular outline form, your outline may be an informal "map" of key points and ideas in whatever order seems both logical and effective.

Ordering Ideas

You have a number of options for effective organization, and your purpose in writing will help you determine your arrangement. For example, Rachel's purpose was to convince readers that the media must stop promoting thinness as an ideal. Because this was the most important part of her argument, she saved it until the end, building support for it as she wrote. Rachel thus chose an emphatic arrangement scheme.

In an *emphatic* or *dramatic* organization, you arrange your material so that the most important, significant, worthy, or interesting material (for which you generally have the most information) is at the end of the paper. The virtue of this type of organization is that it permits you to end your paper in a dramatic way, using the most vital material or the bulk of your support for a concluding impression.

Some papers, however, invite a *spatial* arrangement. Often used in description, this kind of arrangement permits you to present your points in a systematic movement through space. Walter White uses a spatial arrangement in "The Atlanta Riot" (p. 224) when he initially describes from a distance the mob attacking victims. Then, like a zoom lens, he moves closer to each incident until he is inevitably involved.

Because White is narrating an episode, he also uses a *chronological* arrangement. White begins his story with an afternoon ride through town and ends with the evening attack on his house. Like White, you may use a chronological arrangement to narrate a story, tell historical detail, or contrast past and present. But variations in the chronology of a story add interest, especially when you can incorporate the values of *emphatic* ordering as White does.

After you have chosen a particular pattern of organization, you are ready to order your points further. Outlining can help.

An Informal Outline

Because Rachel found that it was difficult to focus her initial draft and order her supporting details, she decided to write an informal outline: a list of points, written in a logical order, that she planned to cover in her essay. She knew this outline would simply be a personal guide to help her stay focused and to make sure she included all relevant materials. Therefore she didn't spend hours on the outline or concern herself with its wording.

Rachel wrote her working thesis first and then listed her key points in the order she planned to cover them. She knew that she might add other points or modify this order as she wrote the paper, but at least she would have a map to help keep her on track.

Thesis: The media must be forced to stop programming young women to believe that skeletal models are the ideal.

Introduction
— Typical ad described: model in bikini
— Models as unhealthy and obsessed with being thin
— The horror: skinny models seem "right"
— Thesis
Anorexia and bulimia as epidemics
— Jane Fonda and her "Work Out"
— Princess Di, reputed bulimic
— Women competing with each other (use Erens)
My friend Kirstie, bulimic
— Kept this secret; only her "barf buddy" and I knew
— Obsessed with food
— Outpatient counseling didn't really work
— I didn't know how to help her
My friend Erica, anorexic
— Enrolled in an in-hospital program
— Shocked by number of older women in program
— Received nutritional and emotional help
My friend Lynn, anorexic, almost died
— Dropped out of Berkeley, enrolled in hospital
— Family received treatment too (use Erens)
— These friends felt programmed by the media to be thin
— Child models made to look like women (use Chernin)
— Model Christine Olman is only 12 (use Chernin)
— Ad photographer finds this deception disgusting
— Diet industry undermines women's control (use Wolf)
Conclusion
— A time for shock *and* action
— Refuse to support products that promote these images

In an informal outline like this, the ideas that you loosely group as information blocs may become paragraphs. In some cases your grouping or bloc may end up being split into two or more paragraphs. This outline includes supporting details, but the topic sentences are not written out; therefore the outline is still rather sketchy. In Rachel's case she didn't feel she needed more elaboration because she had already done some prewriting and initial drafting. Like Rachel, you may find that an outline will help you write stronger, more focused essays and ultimately save you time by organizing your ideas.

WRITING A PARAGRAPH

Focusing the Paragraph

Once you have done some prewriting and have written a working thesis, you are ready to draft your essay. Your thesis has made an assertion you need to support, and the body of your essay consists of paragraphs that build this support. Each of those paragraphs may include a *topic sentence*—a sentence that expresses the central idea of that paragraph. The topic sentences emerge naturally from the groupings discovered in prewriting and from the subtopics of the outline.

Not all paragraphs in an essay will have a topic sentence, but all paragraphs must have a focus. The value of a topic sentence is analogous to the value of a thesis: both of them keep the writer and reader on track. Again, like the thesis, the topic sentence should be deliberately placed to help the reader understand the focus of the paragraph.

Let's look at some short paragraphs that lack topic sentences.

Writing Topic Sentences

Practice writing your own topic sentence (the central idea) for each of these paragraphs:

1. Registration lines extend beyond the walls of the gymnasium. Because the health service requires proof of insurance, students wait in long lines to argue for exemptions. The financial aid office assigns appointment times, but invariably lines form there, too. At the bookstore, students wait 20 minutes at a register, and I need to have my out-of-state check verified in a separate line. Even before classes begin, I'm exhausted.
2. A great amount of corn is used as feed for cattle, poultry, and hogs. Corn is also distilled into ethanol—a fuel for cars and a component in bourbon. Corn is made into a sweetener used in snacks and soft drinks and a thickener for foods and industrial products. A small amount of corn is consumed at dining tables in kernel or processed form.

Although each paragraph is clearly focused, each would profit from an explicit assertion. Compare your topic sentences with your classmates' assertions before reading the possibilities below. Although topic sentences may be placed anywhere in the paragraph, the topic sentences here seem to be most effective as the first or last sentence in these paragraphs.

Some possibilities for the first example include the following:

- Going back to school means going back to lines.
- Lines are an inevitability at my college.
- Lines are the worst aspect of returning to school.

Some possibilities for the second example are as follows:

- Corn is used for extraordinarily diverse purposes.
- Humans, animals, and machines profit from products made of corn.
- Corn is a remarkably useful grain.

In addition to evaluating your classmates' topic sentences, it may be worthwhile to evaluate the relative strengths of the sentences above. Which are stronger, and why?

Analyzing an Effective Paragraph

In the following paragraph, notice how Rachel includes very good supporting details but lacks a topic sentence that expresses the central idea of the paragraph:

> During Kirstie's senior year in high school, she was dating a college guy, was enrolled in college prep classes, jogged religiously every morning and every evening, and loved to ski with her family and beat her brothers down the slope. She seemed to crave the compliments she received from her brothers and their friends because of her good looks, and she received plenty! But years later, she revealed to me that her greatest pride at that time was when she discovered that she could vomit automatically after eating, without needing to use a finger or spoon.

Rachel realized that she had not articulated the focus of her paragraph. She went back to clarify her point—that Kirstie had it all. But Rachel also realized that her perception of her friend was an illusion. Rachel brought the two ideas together to form a topic sentence:

> Few of us ever suspected that Kirstie was in trouble, because she seemed to have it all.

Rachel asserts that Kirstie "seemed to have it all," but was really "in trouble." First Rachel shows specific examples of Kirstie's seemingly happy life: "dating a college guy," being in "college prep classes," jogging "religiously," and skiing with her family. Then Rachel supports the fact that Kirstie was really a troubled young woman.

It is important that you use very specific examples to support your topic sentence. It would not have been enough for Rachel to claim that Kirstie had everything without showing specifically what that meant. She doesn't just mention that Kirstie had a boyfriend, but says that he was a "college guy." Kirstie doesn't simply have a close family; they go skiing together, and she spends time with her brothers and their friends. Rachel's support is vivid, visual, and specific. Her shocking last sentence is graphic and unforgettable because it is so detailed in its description.

Unifying the Paragraph

This last sentence also contributes to paragraph coherence and unity. Rachel's opening sentence suggests that Kirstie was in trouble, even though she did not appear to be. Subtle references to this trouble appear in the paragraph: Kirstie seems obsessed with exercise, and she craves compliments. Finally, after enumerating Kirstie's apparent successes—what she *should* be proud of—Rachel stuns the reader with the irony of Kirstie's "greatest pride," her ability to vomit automatically. Thus the concept of pride unites the paragraph. The key word in the topic sentence, "seemed," predicts the illusions that permeate and unite the paragraph. (For more on paragraph unity and coherence, see pp. 362–369.)

Developing a Paragraph

When you have a topic sentence or controlling idea for a paragraph, it is essential to support it with examples and any necessary explanation. Try to anticipate questions or objections that your reader may have; you can use the "So what?" response here to make sure the significance of your idea is clear. Support for your topic sentences can be drawn from your own ideas, experiences, and observations, as well as from your readings. If you are using material that does not belong to you, you may find it easier to photocopy pages so that you can mark comments directly on the source.

USING SOURCES FOR SUPPORT

Using Photocopied Pages

Although in a formal research paper you may be required (or prefer) to use note cards for recording data, for a short paper with few sources, you might choose to work from books or periodicals photocopied at the library. Here is Rachel's photocopied excerpt from *The Obsession* by Kim Chernin. Notice the quick notes she made as she read the photocopy:

Consider then the case of Christine Olman, one of the leading fashion models of our time. Her picture can be seen in *Vogue*, in *Bazaar*, in all the leading fashion magazines; she is photographed by the leading photographers, posing in the traditional seductive postures that sell consumer goods in our culture. Nothing unusual about all this we say? But then we look further. A newspaper article appears and then a television program, both talking about a new wave of young models. Suddenly, we are given a look behind the scenes, before the spotlights and cameras have begun to work. We are shown a room filled with people at work on the model, combing her, clothing her, making her up. But this time the labor of these illusion-makers is expended to its uttermost. For the model they are preparing is modeling clothes intended for mature women and she is twelve years old. This roomful of people is at work to transform a little girl into the illusion of a woman.

But what sort of figure in fact emerges when this labor of transformation has been accomplished? Is it a precociously full-bodied girl who actually looks like a mature woman? Not at all. What emerges is a preadolescent girl, with slender arms and shoulders, undeveloped breasts and hips and thighs, whose body has been covered in sexy clothes, whose face has been painted with a false allure and whose eyes imitate a sexuality she has, by her own confession, never experienced. And this, says fashion, is what a mature woman should attempt to look like.

"It's disgusting," says the photographer who makes his livelihood recording the ideal form of a woman in this land. "It's not necessary," he says, "to have a twelve-year-old look. But that's the look that's selling right now. And Christine is one of the hottest young models around."

It might be redundant to spell out the implicit message in all this, but it can't hurt to state, with all the literalness possible in language, the lesson we are meant to learn as women studying the fashions deemed appropriate for us. According to fashion, large size, maturity, voluptuousness, massiveness, strength, and power are not permitted if we wish to conform to our culture's ideal. Our bodies, which have knowledge of life, must undo this fullness of knowing and make themselves look like the body of a precocious child if we wish to win the approval of our culture.

from The Obsession p. 94

Giving Credit and Avoiding Plagiarism

No matter what method you use to record supporting material from readings—on note cards or photocopies—you must give proper credit for borrowed ideas and put quotation marks around the quoted words that you use in your paper. By including the author's name and a page number after every idea or quotation that she used, Rachel avoided *plagiarism:* using someone else's words or ideas without giving them credit.

Even if she *paraphrased* the material—put the ideas in her own words—Rachel knew she had to give the author credit for the idea or concept. Had she neglected to do this, she would have inadvertently plagiarized those ideas. (For more discussion of inadvertent plagiarism, see pp. 463–464.)

Rachel's instructor required her to use MLA documentation form. Therefore she gave credit either by citing the author's name before the material and then giving the source's page number in parentheses afterward or by including both the author and page citations in parentheses immediately following the quotation. Two popularly used documentation forms (MLA and APA) are described in detail on pages 488–507.

Remember, giving credit means the following:

- Using quotation marks around borrowed words or phrases
- Acknowledging the source and page number of any borrowed words or paraphrased ideas immediately afterward
- Including the complete source—author, title, and publishing information—in the list of works at the end of the paper.

Incorporating Quoted Material

Quoted material may support your ideas and may be a vital component of your paper. If the original material is particularly well written or precise, or if the material is bold or controversial, it makes sense to quote the author's words so you can examine them in detail.

All quoted material needs to be introduced in some way. It is a mistake to think that quoted material can stand on its own, no matter how incisive it is. Often, in fact, it is vital to introduce and also to comment on the quoted material. Let's look at an example from Rachel's paper:

Lynn's family became involved in her therapy, too. Erens emphasizes the importance of the family in any treatment plan: "Often, the daughter has taken on the role of diverting attention from unacknowledged conflicts within the family" (214). In therapy, Lynn and her family gradually learned that her parents' "unacknowledged conflicts" over Lynn's choice of art as a major instead of computer science contributed to Lynn's stress. Therapy involved acknowledging these internalized conflicts as well as seeing a relationship between her eating disorder and that stress.

In this passage, Rachel uses Lynn's experience to lead into the quoted material. The quote provides an explanation of family dynamics that reflects Lynn's situation. Rather than letting the quotation stand by itself, Rachel *uses* it by discussing the connection between the quoted material and her friend's specific experience.

The "Sandwich" as a Development Technique

If you have had instructors comment that your papers need more development, if you have trouble meeting the required length for an assignment, or if you find that you are merely padding your paper with strings of quotations, you will discover that the "sandwich" strategy is a solution to your problem. Even if your papers seem to satisfy the page requirement, but you are earning B's instead of A's on your papers, the problem may be that you have not critically thought about and *used* your supporting material. Because effective supporting material is often quoted from sources, you need to incorporate direct quotations effectively. The "sandwich" technique will help you write better developed and more convincing papers.

Just as bread holds the contents of a sandwich together, a writer needs to use the introduction and the discussion about the quotation to hold the quoted material together.

It may help to visualize the "sandwich" as consisting of the following:

- **The lead-in or introduction**—the top slice of bread—appeals to the reader and helps by providing enough of a context for the quoted material to make sense. Often you will want to include the title and author of the work and perhaps the author's credentials. The lead-in needs to be informative without duplicating the material in the quotation.
- **The direct quotation**—the "meat" of the sandwich—comes next.
- **The analysis or commentary**—that essential bottom slice of bread—provides a necessary line or two of clarification, interpretation, analysis, or discussion after the quotation. You may need to interpret or define the author's terms or discuss the signifi-

cance of the quotation to the work as a whole. Most important, your analysis demonstrates the necessity of the quoted material for the point you are making.

In the following example from the page Rachel photocopied (p. 340), notice how she leads in to her quote and then comments on it afterward without being redundant:

> In The Obsession Kim Chernin claims that today's ideal model excludes many women: "According to fashion, large size, maturity, voluptuousness, massiveness, strength, and power are not permitted if we wish to conform to our culture's ideal" (94). Such conformity spells self-destruction and is threatening to reduce women to mere skeletons.

In her lead-in, Rachel deliberately includes the title and author of her source so that she needs to give only the page number in parentheses after the quotation. Her lead-in prepares the reader to consider the fact that "many women" do not fit the "ideal" size. Her analytic comment after the quotation is a good example of critical thinking. Rachel deduces the consequences of conforming to the "culture's ideal." Her commentary drives her point home and convinces the reader of the severity of the problem: "self-destruction."

You will want to incorporate quotations smoothly and effectively into your own work. Practicing the "sandwich" will give you expertise.

PRACTICING THE "SANDWICH"

The following passage appears in Brent Staples' essay "Black Men and Public Space" (p. 219):

> I often witness that "hunch posture," from women after dark on the warrenlike streets of Brooklyn where I live. They seem to set their faces on neutral and, with their purse straps strung across their chests bandolier style, they forge ahead as though bracing themselves against being tackled.

Because the sentence that begins "They seem to set their faces on neutral . . ." has such memorable language to describe the women that Staples sees walking at night, students often choose to incorporate his description. Try writing a lead-in and analysis of that one sentence.

Lead-in:

"They seem to set their faces on neutral and, with their purse straps strung across their chests bandolier style, they forge ahead as though bracing themselves against being tackled" (221).

Analysis:

You might want to compare your "sandwich" with a classmate's. Determine whether you both managed to avoid the following problems in your lead-in. Can you identify the reasons that these lead-ins are weak?

1. **Brent Staples says,**"They seem to set their faces on neutral and, with their purse straps strung across their chests bandolier style, they forge ahead as though bracing themselves against being tackled" (221).
2. **In paragraph six, Brent Staples quotes,**"They seem to set their faces on neutral and, with their purse straps strung across their chests bandolier style, they forge ahead as though bracing themselves against being tackled" (221).
3. **Brent Staples feels like a criminal:** "They seem to set their faces on neutral and, with their purse straps strung across their chests bandolier style, they forge ahead as though bracing themselves against being tackled" (221).
4. **Recent statistics show that urban violence is epidemic:** "They seem to set their faces on neutral and, with their purse straps strung across their chests bandolier style, they forge ahead as though bracing themselves against being tackled" (221).
5. **Staples' essay shows that women who walk at night** "They seem to set their faces on neutral and, with their purse straps strung across their chests bandolier style, they forge ahead as though bracing themselves against being tackled" (221).

Explanation of the Errors

1. This lead-in effectively identifies the author, but it doesn't give a context for the quotation that follows. The reader cannot know who "they" are. (See "Pronoun Reference," p. 527–529, for an explanation of this error.) Further, the writer needs to prepare the reader for what is important in the quotation so that it makes sense to the reader.
2. This lead-in also identifies the author, but nothing is gained by starting with the paragraph number; in fact, this pointless information is distracting. Further, the writer does not prepare the

reader for this quotation. In addition, it is not accurate to write that "Brent Staples quotes" because Staples is not quoting anyone; he is the writer who is being quoted.

3. The writer seems to understand the discomfort that Brent Staples feels—"like a criminal"—but he has not shown how this feeling is a consequence of the women's posture. Moreover, there is no referent for "they."
4. This lead-in doesn't accurately anticipate the quotation. It may be true that "urban violence is epidemic," but this lead-in does not prepare the reader for the description of the women's posture.
5. This lead-in is effective because it identifies, before the reader is confused, that "they" are the "women who walk at night." However, the writer has a grammar error in the double subject—"women" and "they"—which prompts the reader to stumble between the lead-in and the quotation. The writer could easily correct this by starting the quotation with "seem" to avoid the double subject and moving smoothly from lead-in to quotation: "Staples' essay shows that women who walk at night 'seem to set their faces on neutral . . . .'"

Here is one example of an effective "sandwich"—good lead-in *and* analysis—using the quotation from Brent Staples:

In "Black Men and Public Space," Brent Staples describes the posture of women who walk at night: "They seem to set their faces on neutral and, with their purse straps strung across their chests bandolier style, they forge ahead as though bracing themselves against being tackled" (221). **Staples suggests that these women need to play multiple roles. They must appear to be indifferent to their environment and not make eye contact as they "set their faces on neutral." Further, they become soldiers with bandoliers and defensive football players guarding themselves against being attacked.**

Analyzing the Example

Notice that the lead-in identifies the title and author so that only a page reference will be necessary in the parenthetical citation. Further, the referent for the pronoun "they," which begins the quotation, is clarified in the lead-in—"women who walk at night."

Students often neglect the analysis portion of the sandwich, assuming that the quotation is self-explanatory. Many students neglect to interpret and analyze the quotation in some detail. However, the only way to convince your reader of your interpretation of the quoted material is to analyze it—to work with it.

Notice that the analysis above is quite complete. The first statement—"these women need to play multiple roles"—is a general assertion drawn from the specific images of women as soldiers with their bandoliers and as football players guarding "against being tackled." Because the women are on the defensive, the student explains, they don't make eye contact, and they "appear to be indifferent" as they "set their faces on neutral." The student has analyzed Staples' word choice and imagery so that he can convince the reader of his interpretation of Staples' description.

Paraphrasing

Paraphrasing a writer's ideas makes that information available to the reader in a condensed form. Sometimes you will want to put into your own words the essence of an entire piece that you have read; other times you will want to paraphrase just one section of the work. If the author's idea is useful but the material is wordy or filled with jargon or contains information you do not need, you will want to paraphrase rather than quote the text.

Here we will examine how to paraphrase one section of given works. Assume that you have been asked to write an essay in which you respond to Carol Tavris' "In Groups We Shrink" (p. 274) by comparing or contrasting Tavris' reported observations with experiences of your own. First, you may want to summarize the main point of her essay. Active reading of the piece probably will lead you to the third paragraph of Tavris' essay, where part of her focus is located.

> Something happens to individuals when they collect in a group. They think and act differently than they would on their own. Most people, if they observe some disaster or danger on their own—a woman being stabbed, a pedestrian slammed by a hit-and-run driver—will at least call for help; many will even risk their own safety to intervene. But if they are in a group observing the same danger, they hold back. The reason is not necessarily that they are lazy, cowardly or have 50 other personality deficiencies; it has more to do with the nature of groups than the nature of individuals.

The point of this section might be paraphrased like this:

> Although most individuals will help someone who is hurt or in danger, when they are in a group they think and act differently and may disregard a plea for assistance.

The important aspects of Tavris' original point are retained: that people alone act differently than they do when they are in groups. Notice that Tavris' finding that "most" people will help someone in need is part of the paraphrased thesis, an important detail that would be distorted if the summary writer indifferently wrote "some" or "many." Later in her essay, Tavris identifies the group's failure to respond to an emergency as "diffusion of responsibility" or "social loafing." In responding to her essay, it might be useful to quote those terms specifically to describe the apparent indifference of individuals in groups.

Analyzing Paraphrasing

Original from "Why Stop Smoking? Let's Get Clinical" (p. 318):

In normal lungs, the trachea and bronchi—the large and small tubes leading to the alveoli (the tiny sacs that do the actual work of the lungs)—are lined with a film of tissue that is one cell layer thick. The surface of these cells is covered with tiny, finger-like structures called cilia. These cilia beat constantly in a waving motion, which moves small particles and toxic substances out of the lung and into the back of the throat where they are swallowed. In a smoker or someone like a coal miner, who constantly breathes in large amounts of toxic substances, many of the cilia soon disappear. If exposure continues, some ciliated cells die and are replaced by squamous cells, the same type that form the skin. Without the cleansing function of the ciliated cells, toxic materials and particles are breathed into the lungs, staying longer in contact with all the tissue. Each group of ciliated cells killed and replaced by squamous cells decreases by a certain fraction the lungs' ability to cleanse themselves. As this occurs, the amount of damage done by each cigarette increases to a greater and greater degree.

Paraphrase:

Healthy lungs contain tiny sacs that are lined with cilia, hairlike structures that move poisons out of the lungs. In coal miners or smokers, these cilia are destroyed and are replaced by cells that can't do the cleansing, so the toxics touch more tissue longer. With the cleansing cells gone, the damage continues to increase each time smoke is inhaled.

Original from "Women: Invisible Cages" (p. 80):

The pressures society exerts to drive men out of the house are very nearly as irrational and unjust as those by which it keeps women in. The mistake of the early reformers was to assume that men were emancipated already and that therefore reform need ask only for the emancipation of women. What we ought to do now is go right back to scratch and demand the

> emancipation of both sexes. It is only because men are not free themselves that they have found it necessary to cheat women by the deception which makes them appear free when they are not.

Paraphrase:

> Society puts pressure on both men and women, so neither gender is actually free. We will have to rethink the irrational and unfair demands that are made on us if we really want to be emancipated.

The paraphrase condenses Brophy's point by removing what may be unnecessary information—that early reformers made mistakes in their analyses. Further, the paraphrase emphasizes the fact that neither gender is free.

Combining Paraphrase and Quotation

Most often, the material that you use to support your points will be a blend of paraphrase and direct quotation. You can capture the essence of an author's idea by paraphrasing it, but there will be well-crafted phrases and key ideas that need to be quoted to convey the flavor of the original work. When you combine paraphrase and direct quotation, you still need to be careful to give credit for both.

Rachel decided to paraphrase most of the material that she photocopied at the library (see p. 340), but then she found a choice quotation that succinctly expressed what she wanted to say. Here is how Rachel used the material from her photocopied page:

> In The Obsession Kim Chernin refers to the ideal model today as a "woman-child." She notes that one of the current top models, featured in Vogue and Bazaar, is twelve-year-old Christine Olman and that even professionals in the advertising industry are appalled by this: "'It's disgusting,' says the photographer who makes his livelihood recording the ideal form of a woman in this land. 'It's not necessary,' he says, 'to have a twelve-year-old look. But that's the look that's selling right now'" (Chernin 94).

Rachel introduces her quotation by referring to the title and author of this important study of women's eating habits. Rachel thus gains credibility by showing that she has consulted a respected writer on this subject. After identifying the source of her material, Rachel uses a key term from Chernin: "woman-child." This term must be quoted because it is from Chernin's book.

Rachel first summarizes Chernin's point about the current top models being children and then narrows her focus to the photographer, one of the "professionals" who is "appalled" by this practice. This serves as her lead-in to the specific quotation from the photographer in Chernin's text.

PRACTICING COMBINING PARAPHRASE AND QUOTATION

Practice incorporating choice quotations into your paraphrased versions of the following passages. In your lead-in, you may want to include the author's name and the source of the material. Compare your paraphrases with those written by your classmates. The page numbers given are from the essays as they appear in this textbook.

1. From "Women: Invisible Cages" (pp. 81–82): "That many women would be happier not pursuing careers or intellectual adventures is only part of the truth. The whole truth is that many *people* would be. If society had the clear sight to assure men as well as women that there is no shame in preferring to stay non-competitively and non-aggressively at home, many masculine neuroses and ulcers would be avoided, and many children would enjoy the benefit of being brought up by a father with a talent for the job instead of by a mother with no talent for it but a sense of guilt about the lack."
2. From "Why Stop Smoking? Let's Get Clinical" (p. 319): "By the time one has been a pack-a-day smoker for 10 years or so, extensive damage has already been done. By 20 years, much of the damage is irreversible and progresses more rapidly. After 10 years of smoking, each cigarette may do as much damage to the body as three or more packs did when a smoker first started."
3. From "Why Johnny Can't Disobey" (p. 285): "It seems that the best armor is the rational mind. We must insist that all authorities account for themselves, and we need to be as wary of false prophets as we are of false advertising. Leaders, political and spiritual, must be subjected to intense scrutiny, and we must insist that their thought processes and proclamations measure up to reasonable standards of rational thought. Above all, we must become skilled in activating our inner resources toward rebellion and disobedience, when this seems reasonable."

As you work on refining your incorporation of paraphrased and quoted material, you also will be revising your essay. Rewriting is such a critical activity in preparing an essay that we have devoted the entire next chapter to various aspects of revision.

8

Revising an Essay

■ ■ ■

REWRITING AND REWRITING

As we have already noted, rewriting may occur during all stages of the writing process. But it is essential that you give yourself time to reconsider your rough draft and make some necessary changes. Usually, these changes involve sharpening the thesis, reorganizing ideas, developing sketchy points, adding new material for support, removing irrelevant material, improving transitions between ideas, strengthening the introduction and conclusion, and editing for word choice, mechanics, and spelling.

Thinking Critically for an Audience

Every phase of the writing process involves thinking critically—reasoning, analyzing, and assessing so that your points are clear and your audience understands your points. The act of revision depends on good critical thinking.

Even during prewriting, which invites creativity and experimentation, you are evaluating your topic in relationship to your readers. In clustering and listing your ideas, you are discerning features in order to sort out your uncensored thoughts. In this way you are using critical thinking to group compatible ideas for presentation to a reader. In collaborative brainstorming, you have an opportunity to assess your ideas in light of your peers' views and to question others' assumptions as well as your own.

You use critical thinking to impose order on your material, and you assess your organization plan to ascertain whether your reader can follow your logic. Both logic and aesthetic considerations govern your judgment about which section of support belongs before another. Your decision to remove irrelevant details reflects your awareness that irrelevant points not only weaken your support but also confuse your readers.

The need for clarity and precision continues throughout drafting and revision. Even as you are revising, you continue to determine whether your depth of analysis has been sufficient and whether you have fully supported your assertions. You reconsider your focus, the logic of your organization, and the strength of your conclusion. As you edit, you scrutinize your word choice, sentence structure, grammar, and mechanics so that surface flaws do not frustrate your reader.

Thinking critically mandates that you recognize that your audience does not necessarily share your views. Thus the writing process forces you to challenge your own assertions and consider the readers' perspectives. Although it may appear that these stages of writing a paper involve a step-by-step process, all of these writing activities occur concurrently.

Revision may occur while you are drafting your paper, and editing may occur from the early drafts until the moment you hand the paper to your instructor. As was noted in the preceding chapter, Rachel started revising her draft as soon as she had a printout from her computer. Rachel thought critically about her aim in writing this essay—to persuade readers of the media's role in fostering eating disorders—and made substantial changes as she revised her rough draft.

Revising a Rough Draft

Working from her own evaluation of her rough draft (see pp. 331–332), Rachel rewrote her draft and, as required by the assignment, showed it to her instructor for comments. Rachel's paper had started out very rough, as most first drafts do, but she continued to develop her ideas and rearrange them. She believed that her second draft was stronger than the first but still could be improved. Her instructor helped her by identifying weak areas and suggesting improvements.

Example: Draft with Instructor's Comments

Eating Disorders and the Media *more striking or suggestive title?*

except for?

Bare, [with the exception of] a bikini, the deep-tanned model poses at a beach. She is surrounded by five adoring guys. She is sipping a frothy soda and inviting all of us to do the same . . . if we want to get the guys . . . if we want to be the envy of our friends. She is thin but tall. Viewers don't notice the bony ribs, [how hungry she is,] and all the "diet pills" she popped to stay that thin. A picture doesn't reveal the vomit on her breath or the spearmint gum used to mask it. In fact, our magazines and T.V. commercials present us with these ads until such girls don't seem skinny any more--they seem right. *✓clear point*

Tighten—avoid repeating "she is" *How thin?* *How tall?* *not //* *✓ very graphic* *stronger verb?*

It doesn't seem to matter that, for some years now, the media has been reporting the epidemic among college "coeds" of eating disorders, anorexia and bulimia. It doesn't seem to matter that the Women's Movement has tried to free women from being so caught up on the way they look. Despite the varied opportunities now available to women, "thirty-three thousand American women told researchers that they would rather lose ten to fifteen pounds than achieve any other goal" (Wolf 10) In the last decade, actress Jane Fonda has sold many on the value of her "Work Out" and has helped spawn "aerobic nervosa" (Erens 211). Many women who admire Jane Fonda's shape may not know that Fonda was once a bulimic. And no one watching the

diction (old-fashioned?) *briefly distinguish* *What is?*

televised spectacle of Prince Charles and Princess Diana's wedding could have predicted that years later, biographers would be discussing "Di's bulimia." [transition?]

[necessary?] Who wouldn't want to hear friends whisper, "What a body! She really knows how to stay in shape!" or "Don't you hate someone who looks that good?" Either way, the sense of admiration and affirmation is clear. A thin girl has something that others don't--and this gives her power and control. [specify what is wrong with this] She can make herself in the image of the cover girls. In "Bodily Harm," the author quotes Ruth Striegel: "The pursuit of thinness is a way for women to compete with each other, a way that avoids being threatening to men" (211). [You need Erens' name here or in your ( ) at end of this line.]

Unfortunately, this competition keeps women from seeking or obtaining the help they might otherwise get from close friends. Many bulimics keep their secret as guarded as their mothers might have kept their sex life. My friend Kirstie did this. She waited for years before she told her friends (and later, her family) that she was bulimic. [tighten] At first, only her "barf buddy" (Erens 211-- a cousin who had initially introduced her to this "great diet plan"-- knew. [awk split of subj/verb] Gradually, their friendship revolved exclusively around this dark secret and was eroded by their unacknowledged rivalry.

Few of us ever suspected Kirstie was in trouble: she seemed to have it all. [illustrate] But years later, she revealed to me that her greatest pride at that [develop] time was when she discovered that she was now vomiting automatically after eating, without needing to use a finger or spoon.

Even when Kirstie received out-patient counseling and her family thought she was "cured," she wasn't. *How could you tell?* For her it was either fasting or bingeing--there was no in-between. As her friend, I often felt trapped between either respecting her confidence or letting some adult know so she might get the help she needed. While encouraging her to find other interests and to be open with her therapist, I felt quite helpless. I didn't want to betray her confidence and tell her parents, but I worried that my silence was betraying our friendship.) *transition?*

According to another friend, many young women continue to have obsessions with food for years afterwards. My friend Erica was shocked by the number of women over thirty ~~who were~~ in her hospital treatment program for anorexics. She admitted that (this) is what made her decide she needed help ? while she was still in college. Unlike Kirstie, Erica decided she needed an in-hospital treatment program that cut her off from her old habits and helped her deal with her emotions and learn better nutritional habits. Erica managed to enter the program as soon as her finals were over and therefore she didn't jeopardize her schooling.) *good transition*

But some don't have that choice. My friend Lynn would have died had she not entered the hospital when she did. She had to drop out of

Berkeley immediately and get prolonged therapy before she could be released to her parents and begin her recovery. Her family became involved in her therapy too. As Erens notes, "Family therapy considers the family itself, not the daughter with the eating disorder, to be the 'patient.' Often, the daughter has taken on the role of diverting attention from unacknowledged conflicts within the family" (214). In therapy, Lynn and her family gradually learned that her parents' "unacknowledged conflicts" over her mother's return to work and over Lynn's choice of art instead of computer science as a major contributed to Lynn's stress. Therapy involved acknowledging these internalized conflicts as well as examining the pressure to be thin.

ghten this
scussion?

In addition to absorbing family conflicts, each of these friends felt that they were programmed by advertisers to accept and seek a lean look as the ideal. In *The Obsession* Kim Chernin refers to the ideal model today as a "woman-child." She points out that one of the current top models, featured in *Vogue* and *Bazaar*, is twelve-year-old Christine Olman and that even professionals in the advertising industry are appalled by this: "'It's disgusting,' says the photographer who makes his livelihood recording the ideal form of a woman in this land. 'It's not necessary,' he says, 'to have a twelve-year-old look. But that's the look that's selling right now'" (Chernin 94).

ective link
tween
rsonal
perience
reading

ideal
support
for
your
thesis!

better lead-in?

Chernin adds: "According to fashion, large size, maturity, voluptuousness, massiveness, strength, and power are not permitted if we wish to conform to our culture's ideal" (94). comment or expand

review "sandwich"

Such conformity threatens women today. It is ironic that this should happen at a time when women have more freedom to control their lives and their bodies. In "The Beauty Myth" Naomi Wolf notes that "the $33-billion-a-year diet industry" has undermined women's control over their bodies (17). "Reproductive rights gave Western women control over our own bodies; the weight of fashion models plummeted to 23 percent below that of ordinary women, eating disorders rose exponentially, and a mass neurosis was promoted that used food and weight to strip women of that sense of control" (11).

Be specific How?

Shorten quote or indent 10 spaces & delete " marks

It is time to let ourselves become shocked again. And then we need to move beyond shock and take action. Those who make the images will only change when those of us who support them stop buying products and tuning in on shows that continue to impose "bodily harm" on us. Return to your opening image, if you can, and sharpen your thesis. Don't forget "Works Cited"

Revising Can Make the Difference

Every paper can benefit from careful revision and editing, but many students do not have the opportunity to get their instructors' comments on their drafts before they revise. Occasionally, students can find trained tutors and willing peers who will provide feedback and make suggestions. The resulting comments may not be as thorough as those Rachel received, but they can help the writer see the essay from another perspective.

Some instructors may even spend time helping students serve as peer editors who critique each other's papers. A good peer editor need not excel at grammar or be an excellent writer. An effective editor needs to be a careful *reader,* one who is sensitive to the writer's main point and supporting details.

A Checklist for Revising and Editing Papers

Whether you are revising your own essay or commenting on a classmate's, the following checklist should help:

- *Focus:* Is the thesis clear? Provocative? Convincing?
- *Support:* Are all points illustrated and supported?
- *Organization:* Is the order logical? Are there smooth transitions?
- *Paragraphs:* Is each paragraph well focused? Well developed?
- *Sentences:* Are all sentences coherent? Are the sentences varied in type?
- *Wording:* Are there any unnecessary/confusing words? Diction problems?
- *Introduction:* Is it captivating? Developed? Does it set the right tone?
- *Conclusion:* Is there a sense of resolution? Does it return to the thesis?
- *Style:* Does the essay read well? Are there any stumbling blocks?
- *Mechanics:* Is the punctuation correct? The grammar? The spelling?

These questions will help you determine the strengths of the essay, as well as any areas that need improvement. If you are editing a classmate's essay, you do not have to be able to correct the errors. A peer editor only needs to point out areas that seem flawed or confusing; it is then the writer's responsibility to use a handbook (such as the one in this book) and correct the errors.

After studying the instructor's comments and corrections, Rachel continued modifying her draft. She rewrote certain phrases and paragraphs a number of times, shifted words and sentences, and found ways to tighten her prose by eliminating unnecessary words. Most of all, she tried to replace sluggish words with more precise and specific details. Notice below how her title gained more punch and how the opening is tighter and less repetitive. She also took the time to develop certain thoughts and paragraphs and to clarify her points. The following version is her final essay.

Student Example: Final Essay

Krell 1

Dieting Daze: No In-Between

Bare, except for a bikini, the deep-tanned model poses at a beach surrounded by five adoring and adorable guys. She is sipping a frothy diet drink and inviting us to do the same, if we want to get the guys and be the envy of our friends. She stands 5′10″ and wears a size 3. Viewers don't notice the bony ribs, the hunger pangs, and the "diet pills" she popped to stay that thin. A picture doesn't reveal the vomit on her breath or the spearmint gum used to mask it. In fact, our magazines and TV commercials bombard us with these ads until such girls don't seem skinny any more—they seem right.

It doesn't seem to matter that, for years now, the media has been reporting the epidemic among college women of eating disorders, anorexia (self-starvation) and bulimia (binge and purge). It doesn't seem to matter that the women's movement has tried to free women from bondage to their bodies. Despite the varied opportunities now available to women, "thirty-three thousand American women told researchers that they would rather lose ten to fifteen pounds than achieve any other goal" (Wolf 10). In the last decade, actress Jane Fonda has sold many on the value of her "Work Out" and has helped spawn "aerobic nervosa"—the excessive use of exercise to maintain an ideal weight (Erens

211). Many women who admire Jane Fonda's shape may not know that Fonda was once bulimic. And no one watching the televised spectacle of Prince Charles and Princess Diana's wedding could have predicted that years later, biographers would be discussing "Di's bulimia."

Such celebrities, and those females in the ads, are held up as models for all of us to mirror. A thin girl has something that others don't—and this gives her power and control. She can make her body resemble a cover girl's. In "Bodily Harm," Pamela Erens quotes Ruth Striegel, Ph.D., director of Yale University's Eating Disorders Clinic: "The pursuit of thinness is a way for women to compete with each other, a way that avoids being threatening to men" (211). But this competition threatens and endangers the women's well-being because it keeps women from seeking the help they might otherwise get from close friends.

In fact, many bulimics keep their secret as guarded as their mothers might have kept their sex life. My friend Kirstie waited for years before she told friends (and later, her family) that she was bulimic. At first the only one who knew about her bulimia was her cousin who had initially introduced her to "this great diet plan." This cousin became Kirstie's "barf buddy" (Erens 211). Gradually, their friendship revolved exclusively around this dark secret and was eroded by their unacknowledged rivalry.

Few of us ever suspected Kirstie was in trouble because she seemed to have it all. During her senior year in high school, she was dating a college guy, was enrolled in college prep classes, jogged religiously every morning and every evening, and loved to ski with her family and beat her brothers down the slope. She seemed to crave the compliments she received from her brothers and their friends because of her good looks—and she received plenty! But years later, she revealed to me that her greatest pride at that time was when she discovered she could vomit automatically after eating, without needing to use a finger or spoon.

Even when Kirstie received out-patient counseling and her family thought she was "cured," she would still binge and purge at will. Every conversation with Kirstie inevitably returned to the subject of food—fasting or bingeing—there was no in-between. As her close friend, I often felt helpless, trapped between either respecting her confidence and keeping her dark secret or letting an adult know and perhaps getting her more help. I didn't want to betray her confidence and tell her parents, but I worried that my silence was betraying our friendship. Even though we each went to different colleges and gradually lost touch, I find myself wondering if Kirstie ever got the help she needed.

According to another friend, even mature women continue to have obsessions with food. My friend Erica was shocked by the number of women over thirty in her hospital treatment program for anorexics. She admitted that seeing these older women is what convinced her she needed help while she was still in college. Unlike Kirstie, Erica decided she needed an in-hospital treatment program that cut her off from her old habits and helped her deal with her emotions and learn better nutritional habits. Erica managed to enter the program as soon as her finals were over, and therefore she didn't jeopardize her schooling.

But some don't have that choice. My friend Lynn would have died had she not entered the hospital when she did. She had to drop out of Berkeley immediately and get prolonged therapy before she could be released to her parents and begin her recovery. Lynn's family became involved in her therapy, too. Erens emphasizes the importance of the family in any treatment plan: "Often, the daughter has taken on the role of diverting attention from unacknowledged conflicts within the family" (214). In therapy Lynn and her family gradually learned that her parents' "unacknowledged conflicts" over Lynn's choice of art as a major instead of computer science contributed to her stress. Therapy involved acknowledging these internalized conflicts as well as seeing a relationship between her eating disorder and that stress.

In addition to absorbing family conflicts, each of these friends felt that she was programmed by advertisers to accept a lean look as the ideal. In <u>The Obsession</u>, Kim Chernin refers to the ideal model today as a "woman-child." She notes that one of the current top models, featured in <u>Vogue</u> and <u>Bazaar</u>, is twelve-year-old Christine Olman and that even professionals in the advertising industry are appalled by this: "'It's disgusting,' says the photographer who makes his livelihood recording the ideal form of a woman in this land. 'It's not necessary,' he says, 'to have a twelve-year-old look. But that's the look that's selling right now'" (Chernin 94). Chernin adds that this ideal excludes many women: "According to fashion, large size, maturity, voluptuousness, massiveness, strength, and power are not permitted if we wish to conform to our culture's ideal" (94). Such conformity spells self-destruction and is threatening to reduce women to mere skeletons.

It is ironic that this should happen at a time when women have more freedom to control their lives and their bodies. In *The Beauty Myth,* Naomi Wolf notes that the "$33-billion-a-year diet industry" has undermined women's control over their bodies (17). Within a generation, "the weight of fashion models plummeted to 23 percent below that of ordinary women, eating disorders rose exponentially, and a mass neurosis was promoted that used food and weight to strip women of that sense of control" (11). Stripped of control, many women feel compelled to diet constantly; images of emaciated models that were once so shocking have now become commonplace.

It is time to let ourselves become shocked again—shocked by an epidemic that is destroying women's lives. And then we need to move beyond shock and take action. Insisting

Krell 5

that our television sponsors, magazines, and video artists stop perpetrating such deadly images of women is something we can all do. A letter from one viewer carries clout because stations often assume that each letter represents many who didn't take the time to write. Ten letters from ten viewers wield even more power. It is time to protest the images of bikini-clad models parading before us and demand images that reflect the emotional and intellectual scope and diversity among women in our society. With some of our best and brightest dying among us, there is no in-between position any more. Those who make the images will only change when those of us who support them stop buying products and stop tuning in on programs that continue to impose "bodily harm" on us.

Works Cited

Bachmann, Susan and Melinda Barth, eds. Between Worlds: A Reader, Rhetoric, and Handbook. 2nd ed. New York: Longman, 1997.

Chernin, Kim. The Obsession: Reflections on the Tyranny of Slenderness. New York: Harper and Row, 1981.

Erens, Pamela. "Bodily Harm." Bachmann 210.

Wolf, Naomi. The Beauty Myth. New York: Doubleday, 1991.

REWRITING FOR COHERENCE

As you may have noticed, Rachel devoted considerable attention to the way she linked information and ideas within and between her paragraphs. The goal, of course, is to ensure that all parts of the paper cohere (that is, hold together).

To sustain your readers' interest and ensure their comprehension of your work, you will want to examine the drafts of your essays to determine whether your ideas hold together. Each idea should follow logically from the one before, and all of your points must support your focus. That logical connection must be clear to the reader—not just you, the writer of the essay, who may gloss over a link that is not obvious. All readers value clear connections between phrases, sentences, and paragraphs.

A Paragraph That Lacks Coherence

If the writing is carefully organized, the reader will not stumble over irrelevant chunks of material or hesitate at unbridged gaps. Let's examine an incoherent paragraph:

Students who commute to campus suffer indignities that dorm students can't imagine. Parking is expensive and lots are jammed. It is embarrassing to walk into class late. Often it takes over a half hour to find a spot. Commuters feel cut off from students who can return to the dorm to eat or rest. Commuters seldom have a telephone number to get missed lecture notes. Study groups readily form in dorms. Dorm students have a sense of independence and freedom. Commuters need to conform to old family rules and schedules, to say nothing of the need to babysit or cook for younger siblings and drive grandparents to the bank.

Although this paragraph has a clear focus and the ideas all belong, its coherence needs to be improved. You may sense that the information is out of order, the logic of the writer is not always obvious to the reader, sentences do not flow together, words are repeated, and emphasis is lost.

In the pages that follow, you will learn how to correct paragraphs like the one above and to avoid these problems in your own writing. You will also have the opportunity to correct this paragraph.

Using Transitions

Even when material is carefully organized, well-chosen transition words and devices will help you connect sentences and paragraphs and will help your points cohere. You are familiar with most of these words and expressions. But if you have been trying for more than five minutes to find a specific word to connect two ideas or sentences in your essay, the partial list of particular terms shown below may be useful. The principal organization or development method of your essay often will suggest the specific transition terms that will be useful to you for gaining unity in that essay. All will be useful at some time or another to help your reader see the connections that you intend.

Transition Terms

- *To show a time relationship:* first, second, before, then, next, meantime, meanwhile, finally, at last, eventually, later, afterwards, frequently, often, occasionally, during, now, subsequently, concurrently
- *To show a spatial relationship:* above, below, inside, outside, across, along, in front of, behind, beyond, there, here, in the distance, alongside, near, next to, close to, adjacent, within
- *To contrast:* in contrast, on the contrary, on the other hand, still, however, yet, but, nevertheless, despite, even so, even though, whereas
- *To compare:* similarly, in the same way
- *To give examples or illustrations:* for example, for instance, to illustrate, to show, in particular, specifically, that is, in addition, moreover
- *To show a cause or an effect:* as a result, accordingly, therefore, then, because, so, thus, consequently, hence, since
- *To conclude or to summarize:* in conclusion, finally, in summary, evidently, clearly, of course, to sum up, therefore

Noticing Transitions

If you are writing a narrative, some part of your essay—if not the entire work—probably will be arranged chronologically. Try to spot the *time signals* in the following excerpt from Bruce Halling's narrative "A Bully's Unjust Deserts" and underline them.

> One day as I crossed the street, I heard something hit the ground near me. Then I felt the sting of a dirt clod hitting me in the head. I stopped and looked in the direction of Ricky's house, but I couldn't see where he was hiding. I brushed most of the dirt out of my hair and kept walking, trying to ignore being hit several more times before I made it home.

Can you see how "one day," "then," and "before" are transitions that are used to help the reader connect the actions in the narrative?

With three or four of your classmates, read the next two paragraphs of Halling's narrative (which appears in complete form on pp. 386–388) and underline the transition words that have to do with the essay's chronological connections.

Chronological concepts may also be important for gaining transition and coherence in nonnarrative essays. Try to identify the time concept around which the following paragraph from "Discrimination at Large" (p. 207) is structured.

> Since the time I first ventured out to play with the neighborhood kids, I was told over and over that I was lazy and disgusting. Strangers, adults,

classmates offered gratuitous comments with such frequency and urgency that I started to believe them. Much later I needed to prove it wasn't so. I began a regimen of swimming, cycling and jogging that put all but the most compulsive to shame. I ate only cottage cheese, brown rice, fake butter and steamed everything. I really believed I could infiltrate the ranks of the nonfat and thereby establish my worth.

You may rightly perceive that "since the time I first," "I began" and "much later" are the three terms that denote the passage of time within this paragraph. But you may also note that the writer uses the past tense, as if what Jennifer Coleman "really believed" at one time is different from what she believes now. The chronological ordering of the essay emphasizes this fact. Read the rest of the essay to observe how Coleman uses these time-relationship transitions—"along the way," "for awhile," "still," "until," "until then," "now," and "finally"—to emphasize the history that led to her change in self-perception.

Essays that include description often require terms that connect sentences or paragraphs in *spatial relationship.* Notice the spatial concepts that connect the descriptions in this paragraph from "The Only Child." (The complete essay appears on p. 11.)

The room is a slum, and it stinks. It is wall-to-wall beer cans, hundreds of them, under a film of ash. He lights cigarettes and leaves them burning on the windowsill or the edge of the dresser or the lip of the sink, while he thinks of something else—Gupta sculpture, maybe, or the Sephiroth Tree of the Kabbalah. The sink is filthy, and so is the toilet. Holes have been burnt in the sheet on the bed, where he sits. He likes to crush the beer cans after he has emptied them, then toss them aside.

Do you see this paragraph, as we do, as a movement from the periphery to the interior? We sense that the author moves from broad description—"wall-to-wall beer cans" around the room—to smaller, interior descriptions—"holes [that] have been burnt in the sheet on the bed, where he sits." The outside-to-inside movement of this description parallels the author's description of elements outside of his brother (in his room) to his observation of what is closer and more central to him (his thoughts, his talk, his gestures). The arrangement also complements the author's argument that his brother's life and mind were destroyed by drugs—the external environment destroying the interior.

Using Transitions Effectively

The placement of the transition words listed on page 364 will seem contrived if you use them too often in any one essay or if you use the same ones in every essay you write. You also have other, more subtle ways to gain connections between sentences and paragraphs in your essays.

Key Word Repetition

In some cases you will want to repeat an important word, one that emphasizes the point that you are making. Its repetition will reinforce the focus point of your paragraph and essay.

In another paragraph from "The Only Child," the author emphasizes his disdain for his brother's living conditions by repeating his brother's explanation. Can you hear the irony or sarcasm in the author's repetition?

> He tells me that he is making a statement, that this room is a statement, that the landlord will understand the meaning of his statement. In a week or so, according to the pattern, they will evict him, and someone will find him another room, which he will turn into another statement, with the help of the welfare checks he receives on account of his disability, which is the static in his head.

Notice that the repetition of "statement" is very deliberate and strategic, rather than boring for the reader, because it emphasizes the nonreasoning to which the brother's mind has been reduced.

Synonyms or Key Word Substitutions

Synonyms are words that have the same or similar meanings. You can connect ideas or concepts within your paragraphs and throughout your essay by skillfully using synonyms—or key word substitutions—to emphasize your focus. Notice how Jennifer Coleman, in "Discrimination at Large," piles word substitutions into her sentences to simulate for her reader the effect of being assaulted, as fat people are, by denigrating words:

> It was confusing for awhile. How was it I was still lazy, weak, despised, a slug and a cow if I exercised every waking minute? This confusion persisted until I finally realized: it didn't matter what I did. I was and always would be the object of sport, derision, antipathy and hostility so long as I stayed in my body. I immediately signed up for a body transplant. I am still waiting for a donor.

How many substitutions for "lazy" did you find? How many implied substitutions for "contempt"? Coleman cites many specific terms for how she has been perceived and treated to make clear to the reader that these attacks come under many names, but the intention to denigrate is always the same.

Pronouns

Pronouns, words substituting for nouns that clearly precede or follow them, can effectively connect parts of a paragraph. By prompting the reader to mentally supply the missing noun or see the relationship the pronouns imply, the writer also has a way to engage the reader. To emphasize the contrast between people who are fat and those who are not, Coleman uses pronoun substitutions to unite her paragraphs:

> Things are less confusing now that I know that the nonfat are superior to me regardless of their personal habits, health, personalities, cholesterol levels or the time they log on the couch. And, as obviously superior to me as they are, it is their destiny to remark on my inferiority regardless of who I'm with, whether they know me, whether it hurts my feelings. I finally understand that the thin have a divine mandate to steal self-esteem from fat people, who have no right to it in the first place.
>
> Fat people aren't really jolly. Sometimes we act that way so you will leave us alone. We pay a price for this. But at least we get to hang on to what self-respect we smuggled out of grade school and adolescence.

In the first paragraph above, *I* and *me* contrast with *they* and *their* to emphasize the separation between the author and the "nonfat" and "superior" other people. In the second paragraph the author unites herself with "fat people," repeatedly saying "we" to emphasize their unity. Coleman's entire essay coheres because she skillfully employs numerous unifying devices in and between her paragraphs. Read the essay in its entirety to see how key word repetition, synonyms, and transitions between sentences and paragraphs create coherence within an essay. A discussion of transitions between paragraphs follows.

Transitions Between Paragraphs

Key word repetition is also one important way to achieve the important goal of *connection between paragraphs.* While your reader may be able to follow your movement and sustain your ideas within a paragraph, coherence within your essay as a whole requires transition sentences and, in longer essays, entire paragraphs of transitions.

One device that works well is to pick up a key concept or word from the end of the earlier paragraph and use it toward the beginning of the new paragraph. Notice the following excerpts from Shannon Paaske's research paper, which appears on pages 468–487. What moves the reader between paragraphs?

The Americans With Disabilities Act, signed in 1990, reinforced the legislation that was not earlier implemented. But because the law takes effect in gradual stages, the results of all of its provisions have not yet been fully realized. However, as each stipulation is introduced, its impact on the whole of American society is undeniable.

Equally undeniable is the fact that laws such as these, together with the flourishing of adaptive technology, have created greater awareness in our communities.

By repeating the key word "undeniable" and the concept of "laws," the author is able to connect the ideas in the earlier paragraph (the impact of laws) to her new material in the next paragraph (the impact of technology).

In another section of her research paper, Shannon uses a question to help her reader move from one paragraph to another:

Rebecca Acuirre, 16, who has cerebral palsy, says that she recently asked a stranger what time it was and he kept walking as though he didn't hear her. "Some people are prejudiced and ignore us. That makes me angry," she says.

How can these prejudices be abolished? "We need more exposure," says DeVries.

The repetition of the word "prejudice" helps these paragraphs to cohere. The question engages the reader because most of us feel obliged to think about answers to questions. And this rhetorical question does not merely repeat the word. Instead, it moves the reader beyond the previous aspect of prejudice to the solution Paaske will discuss in the next section.

Although all paragraphs in your essay should hold together, the device of repeating key words should not be overused or strained. If your technique is perceived as a formula, that awareness can irritate your reader. For example, let's imagine you have written a paragraph that ended with the sentence "These are rationalizations, not reasons." Avoid merely repeating the exact phrasing, such as "Although these are rationalizations, not reasons," at the start of your next paragraph. Instead, you might want to begin with something like this: "Such rationalizations are understandable if one considers the . . . ." With conscious practice of the technique, you'll improve your skills.

Avoiding Gaps

Transition terms and devices will help you achieve coherence in your work, but they can't fill in for gaps in logic—sentences or paragraphs that just don't go together or that are out of order. You can't expect your readers to move from one point to another if you have failed to write into your work the sense that you perceive. For example, in the incoherent paragraph on page 363, the writer places the following two sentences together:

```
   Parking is expensive and lots are jammed. It is embar-
rassing to walk into class late.
```

In the writer's mind there is a logical connection between these two thoughts. That link is not at all apparent to readers, and a transition term such as *and* or *therefore* will not bridge that gap. The writer must write something to express the connection between the two sentences so that there is no gap and there is no need for the readers to invent their own bridge.

PRACTICING COHERENCE

In small groups, return to the incoherent paragraph on page 363 and discuss its problems. As a group, rewrite the paragraph so that all information is included, but also so that the ideas are logically linked. As you fill in the gaps in logic, practice using the transition terms and devices that will ensure coherence in this paragraph. Here is one solution to improve the coherence of the paragraph:

> Students who commute to campus suffer indignities that dorm students can't imagine. Even before commuting students get to classes, they have a problem. Parking on campus is expensive and hard to find because the lots are jammed. Often it takes over half an hour to find a spot. By then class has started, and it is embarrassing to walk into class late. Commuters also feel cut off from those students who can return to the dorm to eat or rest. And while study groups readily form in dorms, commuting students seldom have even a telephone number to get missed lecture notes. Dorm students have a sense of independence and freedom from their families, but commuters need to conform to old family rules and schedules. Often the indignities of living at home include doing those tasks the students did through high school, like baby sitting or cooking for younger siblings, or driving grandparents to the bank.

In addition to considering the links between ideas in the body of your essay, you will want to refine your introduction and conclusion to frame your essay and to achieve coherence.

WRITING INTRODUCTIONS AND CONCLUSIONS

Introductions and Audience

Typically, a strong introduction hooks the reader and then expands on the hook while building to the thesis statement, which often concludes the introduction. The introduction to an essay has two obligations: to attract the reader to the subject of the essay and to establish for the reader the particular focus of the writer. The focus of the writer—the assertion he or she is making about a limited subject—is contained in the thesis statement. The thesis statement does not have to be at the end of the introduction, but that is often a natural place for it because both the writer and reader are then immediately aware of the key assertion that will be supported in the essay. The concept of the thesis is discussed in more detail on pages 323–327.

If you have not discovered in your prewriting activities a useful way to lead to your thesis, you may find the ideas below helpful. Some subjects will seem best introduced by one type of introduction rather than another, and it's a good idea to keep your audience in mind as you draft possible hooks to your topic. Clearly, a reader would be confused and find inappropriate an amusing anecdote used as an introduction to a study of AIDS, unemployment, or infant mortality in Third World countries. Your introduction should anticipate the intention and tone of the paper that will follow.

Often, you will have a working thesis before you write your first draft, but the idea for your introduction—the first words in the essay—will not come until you have worked extensively with your material. You may find that if you deliberately vary your introductions, perhaps trying each of the methods suggested here, you will not be intimidated by that blank sheet of paper or empty computer screen each time you start to write.

Types of Introductions

Direct Quotation An essay that begins with the words of another person, especially a well-known person, should help to convince your reader that you are a prepared writer who has researched others' views on the subject and found relevance in their words. When we were writing the introduction to Chapter 1 of the reader, we realized that one author in the chapter, Ellen Goodman, had incorporated into her essay a number of interesting comments from André Malraux. We found one of his comments so compelling that we used the quotation in our chapter introduction. André Malraux, a French novelist, political activist, and social and art critic, is not a noted authority on the sociology or psychology of family life. Nevertheless, his mildly philosophical statements about the family interested us, and we found his thoughts relevant for our introduction. Notice how we use Malraux's words throughout our introduction.

> In our opening essay, Ellen Goodman quotes André Malraux's belief that "without a family" the individual "alone in the world trembles with the cold" (qtd. in Goodman 5). The family often nurtures its members and tolerates differences and failings that friends and lovers cannot accept. But as

you may realize from your own experiences and observations, people also tremble with fear or anxiety even within the family unit. The writers in this chapter show the family as a source of both nurturing and trembling.

Description Whether it presents a vivid picture of nature or of a person, an introduction using description can appeal to the imagination and the senses simultaneously. The power of the opening can be enhanced if the writer also postpones specific identification of the subject, place, or person until the reader is engaged. In the following paragraph, notice that John Leonard does not reveal his subject. In fact, the reader of "The Only Child" (p. 11) does not know that he or she is reading about Leonard's brother until almost the last line of the essay.

> He is big. He always has been, over six feet, with that slump of the shoulders and tuck in the neck big men in the country often affect, as if to apologize for being above the democratic norm in size. (In high school and at college he played varsity basketball. In high school he was senior class president.) And he looks healthy enough, blue-eyed behind his beard, like a trapper or a mountain man, acquainted with silences. He also grins a lot.

Question The psychology behind a question probably lies in the fact that most of us feel obliged to at least *consider* answering when someone asks us something. If we don't have an immediate answer, we consider the subject and then continue with the reading—exactly what the writer wants us to do. But readers may find questions irritating if they seem silly or contrived, like "What is capital punishment?" Notice your own interest as you read the questions in the introduction to Robert Heilbroner's essay "Don't Let Stereotypes Warp Your Judgments" (p. 428).

> Is a girl called Gloria apt to be better-looking than one called Bertha? Are criminals more likely to be dark than blond? Can you tell a good deal about someone's personality from hearing his voice briefly over the phone? Can a person's nationality be pretty accurately guessed from his photograph? Does the fact that someone wears glasses imply that he is intelligent?

Anecdote or Illustration Just as listeners look up attentively when a speaker begins a speech with a story, all readers are engaged by an anecdote. If the story opens dramatically, the involvement of the reader is assured. In the following example, from Brent Staples' essay "Black Men and Public Space" (p. 220), the author initially misleads the reader into thinking the writer has malicious intentions—exactly the misconception that is the subject matter of his essay.

> My first victim was a woman—white, well dressed, probably in her early twenties. I came upon her late one evening on a deserted street in Hyde Park, a relatively affluent neighborhood in an otherwise mean, impoverished section of Chicago. As I swung onto the avenue behind

> her, there seemed to be a discreet, uninflammatory distance between us. Not so. She cast back a worried glance. To her, the youngish black man—a broad six feet two inches with a beard and billowing hair, both hands shoved into the pockets of a bulky military jacket—seemed menacingly close. After a few more quick glimpses, she picked up her pace and was soon running in earnest. Within seconds she disappeared into a cross street.

Definition Often the definition of a term is a necessary element of an essay, and a definition may interest the reader in the subject (if the writer does not resort to that boring and cliché opener, "According to Webster's Dictionary . . ."). Notice how Amy Gross uses her term, then gives many vivid examples before she gives an actual definition, in her essay "The Appeal of the Androgynous Man" (p. 55).

> James Dean was my first androgynous man. I figured I could talk to him. He was anguished and I was 12, so we had a lot in common. With only a few exceptions, all the men I have liked or loved have been a certain kind of man: a kind who doesn't play football or watch the games on Sunday, who doesn't tell dirty jokes featuring broads or chicks, who is not contemptuous of conversations that are philosophically speculative, introspective, or otherwise foolish according to the other kind of man. He is more self-amused, less inflated, more quirky, vulnerable and responsive than the other sort (the other sort, I'm visualizing as the guys on TV who advertise deodorant in the locker room). He is more like me than the other sort. He is what social scientists and feminists would call androgynous: having the characteristics of both male and female.

Deliberate Contradiction Sometimes the writer can start the paper with a view or statement that will be contradicted or contrasted with the subject matter of the essay. Brigid Brophy, in her essay "Women: Invisible Cages" (p. 80), does just that in her introduction:

> All right, nobody's disputing it. Women are free. At least, they look free. They even feel free. But in reality women in the western, industrialised world today are like the animals in a modern zoo. There are no bars. It appears that cages have been abolished. Yet in practice women are still kept in their place just as firmly as the animals are kept in their enclosures. The barriers which keep them in now are invisible.

Statistic or Startling Fact or Idea An essay that starts with a dramatic statistic or idea engages the reader at once. Notice how the following introduction from William F. Harrison's "Why Stop Smoking? Let's Get Clinical" (p. 318) uses statistics to engage (or frighten) the reader:

> Most of us in medicine now accept that tobacco is associated with major health consequences and constitutes the No. 1 health problem in this country.

> What smokers have not yet come to terms with is that if they continue smoking, the probability of developing one or more of the major complications of smoking is 100%. It absolutely will happen. They will develop chronic bronchitis, laryngitis, pharyngitis, sinusitis and some degree of emphysema.

Mixture of Methods Many enticing introductions will combine the approaches described above. For example, in her essay "In Rooms of Women" (p. 131), Kim Edwards employs narration, a statistic, description, illustration, and ironic contradiction to attract the reader to her account of being an outsider in Malaysia.

> When I lived on the East Coast of Malaysia, I used to do aerobics over a Chinese grocery store. I went there almost every afternoon, climbed up a tunnel of concrete stairs to a narrow room infused with the perfume of hair gel and perspiration, cosmetics and worn shoes. In Malaysia, where more than half the female population drifts through the tropical days beneath layers of concealing polyester, this room was an unusual domain of women. We were relaxed here, exposed in our leotards and shorts, our determination as strong as the situation was ironic. For an hour each day we stretched and ran and sweated, devoting ourselves entirely to the care of bodies which, in the outside world, we were encouraged to hide.

A Few Final Words on Introductions

In your prewriting activities, if you have not found a way to lead your reader into your paper, try one of the types of introductions defined and exemplified here. Those first few words can attract your reader, set the tone for your essay, and predict the focus of your study. Ideally, the introduction will also anticipate your conclusion.

WRITING CONCLUSIONS

The conclusion of an essay should bring closure to the reader, a feeling of completion or satisfaction. Ideally, the conclusion will fit like the lid on a box. You might return to your introduction and thesis, select key images or phrases that you used, and reflect them in your conclusion. This return to the start of the paper assures your reader that all aspects of your assertion have been met in the essay. An effective conclusion is one that echoes the tone of the introduction without merely repeating the exact words of the thesis (a type of closure that is contrived and dull). Although your conclusion may be weakened by tacking on a new topic or concept without sufficient explanation and development, you may want to suggest that there is some broader issue to think about or some additional goal that might be achieved if the situation that you have discussed were addressed.

For his conclusion to the essay "Don't Let Stereotypes Warp Your Judgments," Robert Heilbroner returns to the images of the pictures in our mind, the ideas stirred by the questions he uses in his introduction given on page 428:

> Most of the time, when we type-cast the world, we are not in fact generalizing about people at all. We are only revealing the embarrassing facts about the pictures that hang in the gallery of stereotypes in our own heads.

Another effective conclusion appears in Carol Tavris' essay "In Groups We Shrink" (p. 274). After describing specific real and test situations in which people in groups failed to respond to an obvious problem, Tavris concludes with a social psychologist's hope for improving behavior. She also plays with a line from the poet John Milton ("They also serve who only stand and wait"), a reference that the reader will enjoy if he or she knows Milton's poem "On His Blindness."

> By understanding the social pressures that reward groupthink, loyalty and obedience, we can foster those that reward whistle-blowing and moral courage. And, as a society, we can reinforce the belief that they also sin who only stand and watch.

The student papers in this book also show effective techniques in their conclusions. Rachel, who wrote the paper on eating disorders (pp. 358–362), was advised by her instructor to strengthen the conclusion of her rough draft (p. 356) by returning to the images and key words of her introduction. Rachel did this in her final paper. She also was able to echo the title of a source that she used in her essay. The part of her conclusion that mirrors her introduction looks like this:

> It is time to protest the images of bikini-clad models parading before us and demand images that reflect the emotional and intellectual scope and diversity among women in our society. With some of our best and brightest dying among us, there is no in-between position any more. Those who make the images will only change when those of us who support them stop buying products and stop tuning in on programs that continue to impose "bodily harm" on us.

Shannon Paaske also returned to her introduction to conclude her research paper on the disabled, "From Access to Acceptance: Enabling America's Largest Minority." Her thesis and conclusion are printed below, but you can read her entire essay on pages 468–487.

Thesis:

Although combinations of technological advances, equality-promoting legislation, and increasing media exposure have worked as a collective force in bringing about improvements in the lives of the people who make up what is sometimes termed "America's largest minority" (Davidson 61), ignorance and prejudice continue to plague the disabled.

Conclusion:

The legislation and technology that have developed at the end of this century will continue to make new worlds accessible to the disabled. Ideally, these developments will permit the disabled to be viewed in terms of their capabilities rather than their disabilities. In that climate, the disabled can gain acceptance in the worlds to which they have access. With the steps being taken by government, science, and the media, individuals alone are needed to make the dream of acceptance a reality for the disabled.

Notice that the title of Shannon's essay also is echoed in her conclusion.

Final Tips for Writing Conclusions

To draft a good conclusion, try the following:

- Return to your thesis and restate it in different words. Incorporate that restatement into your conclusion.
- Examine your introduction and try to incorporate the key words, images, description, anecdote, or response to the question into your conclusion.
- Consider your reader. Have you brought a sense of significant closure to your topic?

You have been considering your reader and the aim of your paper throughout as you have rewritten your rough drafts, verified the logic of your organization, strengthened the introduction and conclusion, and edited for surface errors. These essential revision strategies can help you with any paper that you write.

In the next chapter of the rhetoric we will show you ways to develop essays using specific methods or modes. Whether you are assigned a particular type of essay or you choose to use these methods of development within your papers, you will find the instructions, illustrations, and exercises pertinent for a variety of writing assignments.

9

Methods for Developing Essays

■ ■ ■

Your instructor may ask you to write a paper using a particular method of development for presenting your support. For example, your instructor may ask you to write a narrative or a comparison and/or contrast study. To help you understand how papers develop with one type of support or another, we have isolated these forms as models for discussion. In doing this, we do not mean to suggest that all paper topics will fit precisely into one of these categories. Nothing could be further from our experience as students, teachers, and publishing writers.

In fact, you may recall that our first student essay, Rachel's "Dieting Daze," incorporates narrative, definition, description, comparison-contrast and research in a problem analysis paper that argues for a change. These multiple approaches are ideal complements, and together they help the writer thoroughly address the topic.

Because you may be asked to develop a paper with a single and particular strategy, we have included in this chapter models of the methods most often assigned. But because we believe that most essays are developed with combined modes, we will start our analysis with an essay that combines multiple strategies. You will find "The Appeal of the Androgynous Man," by Amy Gross, on page 55. Please read or review the essay before you read the commentary below.

COMBINING MULTIPLE STRATEGIES

If you read "The Appeal of the Androgynous Man" with the intention of determining what kinds of support the author used, you may have noticed that Gross employs definitions, narration, comparison and contrast, characterization, and summary writing to argue her point and defend her thesis—that the androgynous man is more than an "all-man man."

Analyzing Mixed Methods

Definition and Characterization Through Comparison and Contrast The author's first obligation is to define *androgyny,* a word that might be unfamiliar to her reader. She does this through a *comparison-contrast* mode by first describing what the androgynous man is not. He is a man who "doesn't play football or watch the games on Sunday, who doesn't tell dirty jokes featuring broads or chicks, who is not contemptuous of conversations that are philosophically speculative, [or] introspective." She then describes what the androgynous man is—"more self amused, less inflated, more quirky, vulnerable and responsive" than the other type of man. Gross then gives an actual definition of androgyny: "having the characteristics of both male and female." The definition serves as a concluding sentence to the exemplifications in her comparison-contrast descriptions. This timely placement of a definition shows Gross' awareness of audience.

Audience Awareness In our discussion of audience (pp. 312–321) we noted that the writer must be aware of the reader's responses to the text. Gross is especially aware of her audience and even addresses the reader, something that is usually considered bad style in formal writing ("Now the first thing I want you to know . . ."). Gross must meet her reader's possible objections to the androgynous man in order to keep her audience. She states that the androgynous man is "neither effeminate nor hermaphroditic." After insisting that "all his primary and secondary sexual characteristics are in order," Gross notes that she would call the androgynous man "all-man," but that term wouldn't be correct because he is *more* than all-man. Her thesis comes as a natural assertion from the descriptions, characterizations, definitions, comparisons, and contrasts that started her essay.

Argument Strategy Gross' first goal after defining her terms is to disparage the opponent, the "all-man man." Our experience in teaching this work is that this section of her essay is the one that prompts the most bitter retorts from students. Gross is merciless in describing the all-man's grocery shopping habits, inspired only by the "little woman's" temporary absence from the kitchen. Our male students protest that they know how to cook and that their shopping is of necessity more than pretzels and a six-pack, steak and potatoes, and a "wad of cake or apple pie." Gross' word choice is both inflammatory and humorous. She creates a negative caricature of the "all-man man" because the negative image is an important part of her argument.

Narration Notice that part of the author's development includes a *narrative,* a very short but stinging anecdote to describe an evening she endured with an all-man man. Placed where it is, the humor in the narrative may soften the harshness of Gross' previous negativity. We all like stories, and a personal anecdote can't be too offensive; after all, the author might have reasoned, this nasty experience happened to *me!* In addition to supporting her points about this type of man, the narrative also contributes an additional aspect to her characterization of the androgynous man. He may be a hard-hat or well educated, but he will not be a "brute" with a "superman package" that includes an "imperialistic" ego. By showing that the androgynous man—as well as the "brute"—comes in varying social classes, she does not alienate any reader who is sensitive to class distinctions.

More Definition As part of her argument that the androgynous man is creative, Gross is compelled to *define* this term. She does this by insisting on what creativity is not—a cliché cartoon in beret and artist's smock. She contrasts this image with an actual definition: creativity is "a talent for freedom, associated with imagination, wit, empathy, unpredictability, and receptivity to new impressions and connections."

Expert Sources to Help an Argument To convince her reader that her personal preference for the androgynous man is more than "blind prejudice," Gross relies on experts to help her prove that the androgynous man really is more sensitive and creative. To do this, Gross uses a *summary* of two psychological studies of high masculinity in males and high femininity in females. Gross shows that the psychologists' findings support her "prejudice" that creative males—synonymous now with androgynous males—are more open "in their feelings and emotions" and have "a sensitive intellect and understanding self-awareness," as well as "wide-ranging interests." The androgynous man "shuns no behavior" because our culture would "label it as female," and even while he gets problems solved, he expresses concern for others. Gross uses a summary of another psychologist's findings to present a contrast with the androgynous man's characteristics, stating that highly masculine men lack "the ability to express warmth, playfulness and concern." Gross lets quoted summaries from the experts at reputable institutions help her convince any reader that nobody would want to try to have a relationship with an "all-man man."

More Audience Awareness Gross anticipates her reader's possible objection once again when she agrees that "gut appeal" and "chemistry" have something to do with a woman's selection of a partner. She again contrasts the qualities of the "all-man man"—described in her conclusion as a competitive jock whose idea of sex is to conquer—with the characteristics of the androgynous man. Her conclusion relies on a return to the terms that she has used throughout the essay to define androgyny. Gross reminds the reader of the androgynous man's "greater imagination, his wit and empathy, his unpredictability, and his receptivity to new impressions and connections." Because she has created a sexual scenario where these androgynous character traits would be played out, she has a suggestive, amusing, and cleverly emphatic recapitulation of her argument.

Why This Analysis?

The purpose of this analysis of "The Appeal of the Androgynous Man" is to encourage you to recognize the multiple modes and devices that professional writers use to engage and persuade their readers. This recognition can have a positive effect on your own writing. By practicing the single-development assignments given in the writing topics and described in the rhetoric—narration, definition, cause and effect, comparison and contrast, argument, and analysis (process, problem, subject)—you will learn to employ multiple methods confidently to write an engaging and convincing paper.

SUMMARY

If you are able to summarize what you have read, you are able to prove to yourself or an instructor that you understand both the content of the reading and the way the writer has arranged the material. Summarizing is therefore an important college skill, one that proves your ability to read, comprehend, and write. You may use summarizing as a personal learning tool, collecting summaries of assigned readings in any class as study guides for examinations. But you may be asked in some classes—from undergraduate through graduate studies—to submit summaries to show that you have read and understood journal articles or essays.

How to Write a Summary

The following steps will lead to a full summary appropriate for assignments in psychology, education, philosophy, political science, English, or any other class. These steps are also the first you will take if you are asked to summarize an essay and then evaluate it, an assignment that is frequently given in college courses.

1. Read the work *actively,* marking directly on the copy (if possible) the obvious divisions or sections within the text. *Underline the thesis,* if one is explicitly stated, as well as any key points or examples you see as you read.

2. Reread the text. On a separate sheet of paper, write a few sentences of summary (combining paraphrased and quoted material) for each section of the work that you have marked in the margins of the original.
3. Write the author's thesis or what you infer to be the central assertion of the entire essay. You may write a general thesis or one that forecasts the points the writer will use to support the assertion.
4. Write a draft that starts with the thesis, even if the writer delayed the central assertion of the work. Continue the draft with the sentence summaries that you wrote for each of the sections of the text. Use the full name of the author of the work once, then use only his or her last name in other places in your summary. It is important to use the writer's name so that your reader is reminded who had the ideas in the original text.
5. Reread your draft to be sure of the following:
   - Your thesis reflects the author's *full* point.
   - Each section of your summary has its own assertion (or topic sentence) and sufficient support from the original.
   - Your summary *parallels* the original in tone and order.
   - Your summary is both objective and complete. Objective means that none of your feelings about the text are reflected in statements or tone. Complete means that you have not left out any sections of the original.
6. Reread your summary to be certain that you use quotation marks around any key words or phrases that you have taken from the text. Most of the summary should be in your own words, but a particularly memorable phrase or expression will resist paraphrasing. You will want to include this memorable language in your summary within quotation marks. Check for spelling, mechanical errors, and sentence correctness. Insert necessary transition words and phrases prior to your final writing.
7. Unlike an essay you have written, a summary of someone else's work does not need a conclusion. End your summary with the author's final point.

Student Example: A Summary

The following is an example of one student's summary of the essay by Martin Luther King, Jr. that appears on p. 295.

A Summary of "Three Ways of Meeting Oppression"

Chris Thomas

In an excerpt from his book Stride Toward Freedom, Dr. Martin Luther King, Jr. shows that oppressed people deal with their oppression in three characteristic ways: with acquiescence, violence, or nonviolent resistance. King shows that only a mass movement committed to nonviolent resistance will bring a permanent peace and unite all people.

Although acquiescence—passive acceptance of an unjust system—is the easiest method of dealing with injustice, King insists that it is both morally wrong and the way of the coward. To acquiesce to unfair treatment is to passively condone the behavior of one's oppressors. King says, "Noncooperation with evil is as much a moral obligation as is cooperation with good. The oppressed must never allow the conscience of the oppressor to slumber" (295). King maintains that respect for Negros and their children will never be won if they do not actively stand against the system.

However, King contends that violence is no solution because it never concerns itself with changing the belief system of oppressors. "In spite of temporary victories, violence never brings permanent peace" (296). Thus King insists that violence is impractical as well as immoral: "The old law of an eye for an eye leaves everybody blind" (296). King states that bitterness and corruption become the legacy of this destructive method that "annihlates" rather than "converts." Thus violence destroys any possibility of brotherhood.

King's principle of nonviolent resistance is his answer to how one must deal with oppression. It is confrontational without resorting to physical aggression. Nonviolent resistance avoids "the extremes and immoralities" of the other two methods while integrating the positive aspects of each. The nonviolent resister, like the person who acquiesces, agrees that violence is wrong, but like the violent resister, he believes that "evil must be resisted" (296). King insists that this is the method that oppressed people must use to oppose oppression. It allows neither cowardice nor hatred. "Through nonviolent resistance the Negro will be able to rise to the noble height of opposing the unjust system while loving the perpetrators of the system" (296).

King states that by using nonviolent resistance, the American Negro and other oppressed people can "enlist all men of good will in [the] struggle for equality" (297). He maintains that the struggle is not between people or races but is "a tension between justice and injustice" (297). Only a mass movement of nonviolent resistance will unite people in a community.

Discussion of Student Summary

Chris begins his summary of the excerpt by identifying its source and the author's complete name. Although King does not state his thesis explicitly, Chris infers it from King's writing and then states it in the first paragraph. Chris' thesis and paragraphs reflect the three main points of King's essay, so Chris has organized his summary to parallel the original. The quoted material that he chose from King's essay reflects what Chris found most significant in language and specificity to support King's points. Although a different summary writer might choose other quotations to define and illustrate those points, the points and thesis would be nearly the same in each summary.

Summary as Part of a Larger Assignment

Chris' assignment was to write a complete and objective summary of another writer's work. Other assignments might require a response or evaluation of the content in addition to the summary. Still other assignments might use summary as a smaller, more abbreviated part of a larger essay. For example, a character analysis might have an introduction that summarizes the plot of the story in a few sentences. An argument essay might progress from a short summary of an experiment or survey. The act of summarizing will help you see what you do and don't understand about a reading. Your effective summary then can convince your reader that you comprehend the original well enough to use it to make your own points.

NARRATION

Everyone loves a good story, and most people enjoy telling them. Narration is telling a single story or several related ones. It is often associated with fiction—with myths, fairy tales, short stories, and novels—but writers of all types of essays use narrative strategies.

When to Use Narration

Narration can be used to argue a point, define a concept, or reveal a truth. Writers in all disciplines have discovered the power of the narrative. Journalists, historians, sociologists, and essayists often hook their readers by opening with a personal anecdote or a human interest story to capture the reader and illustrate points. In fact, many writers use narration to persuade their audiences to a course of action. For example, George Orwell's famous narrative "Shooting an Elephant" is a compelling indictment of imperialism.

Personal narratives can be powerful if they focus on a provocative insight and if the details are carefully selected and shaped. Therefore narratives are more than mere diary entries, because certain details may be omitted while others may be altered. Narratives may help the writer better understand the significance of an experience, and they help readers see for themselves. Typically narratives require no library research (our lives are rich with resources for this type of essay), but writers often choose to supplement personal narration with research and outside sources to move beyond their own experience.

How to Write a Narrative

Narratives typically focus on an incident involving a conflict, whether it is between opposing people, values, or perceptions. This incident is then dramatized so that the reader can picture what happened and can hear what was said. Such incidents often involve some aspect of change—a contrast between "before" and "after"—even though the change may be internal (a change in awareness) rather than external or physical.

Narratives do not have to feature life-shattering incidents; in fact, many of the best narratives involve profound changes that are not always obvious to others. In "Like Mexicans" (see p. 188) the narrator's preconception of his girlfriend's background changes. Initially, he is worried that she may come from a higher class because "she didn't look poor" and she wasn't Mexican, but after he visits her home and observes how her family lives, he realizes that her family's status is much like his own. In the narration he never articulates this change, but he leaves her house feeling reassured that they have more in common than he realized.

Brainstorming for a Subject Writers usually need to dig deep to find those buried experiences that have changed their attitudes and views. To help generate ideas, you will find specific narrative assignments at the end of many poems and essays in the "Writing from the Text" sections. If your assignment is more general—to write about any significant moment or change in your life—it will help to consider these questions.

WHAT ARE MY MOST VIVID MEMORIES OF:

Kindergarten? First grade? Second? Third? Fourth? Fifth? Sixth?

Junior high? High school? College?

Team sports? Living in another culture?

Staying with friends or relatives?

Getting a job or working?

WHEN DID I FIRST:

Feel ashamed (or proud) of myself

Stand up to my parents

Realize teachers make mistakes

Give in to peer pressure

Pressure another to go against authority

Wish I had different parents

Wish someone would disappear from my life

WHAT ONE INCIDENT SHOWED ME:

What living between two worlds really means

How it feels to be alone

Why conformity isn't always best

How stereotyping has affected me

How different I am from my sister/brother/friend

Why we have a certain law

How it feels to live with a physical disability

Additional Prewriting If you prefer a visual strategy, you might try clustering or mapping your ideas. One method is to write your topic—for example, "significant changes"—in a circle in the center of your page and then draw spokes outward from it. At the end of each spoke, write down a specific incident that triggered important changes in your life. Write the incident in a box and then use more spokes, radiating from the box, to specify all the changes that resulted. (For an illustration of clustering, see p. 306.)

After you have brainstormed about all possible changes, choose the incident that seems most vivid and worth narrating. Then use another sheet of paper and write about specific change in a circle at the center and write down all the details that relate to it. After you have lots of details, you are ready to focus these thoughts and draft your paper.

From Brainstorming to Drafting a Paper In a narrative essay the thesis is not always articulated in the essay itself because it can ruin the sense of surprise or discovery often associated with narratives. In fact, an explicit thesis can slow the momentum of the story or spoil the ending. Whether it is articulated or implied, however, a thesis is still essential to keep the writer focused and to ensure that the story has a point or insight to share.

Beginning with a Working Thesis For example, in the student essay that follows, Bruce Halling focuses on a time when he was intimidated by a bully, Ricky. At the start of his writing, Halling had only a topic. His idea of writing about being intimidated was not yet a thesis because the insight, focus, or assertion was not at first clear. But after he clustered or listed his details, he probably wrote a *working thesis*—a preliminary assertion that could be changed and refined as the narrative took shape.

> **Working Thesis:** Being plagued by a bully can make one yearn for revenge.

Discovering the Real Thesis Most writers aren't lucky enough to identify the thesis immediately. Often, particularly in a narrative, it takes considerable writing before the best thesis is discovered. Therefore writers typically continue sharpening their thesis throughout the writing process as they, too, discover the point of their story. As Bruce narrated this experience, it developed as a genuine "between worlds" experience.

> **Discovered Thesis:** As a child, I found myself caught between an intense wish for revenge and extreme guilt when this wish came true.

Once the thesis becomes clear to the writer, the rough draft needs to be revised so that all the details relate to this new thesis. Notice, however, that the thesis statement does not need to be specified in the actual essay.

Student Example: A Narrative

The following essay by student Bruce Halling demonstrates a narrative focusing on a significant change in the narrator's life:

A Bully's Unjust Deserts

Bruce Halling

A young boy sits alone, admiring his father's gun. Ricky knows he's not supposed to play with the gun, but his father never keeps it loaded, so Ricky isn't afraid. Perhaps he imagines he hears a strange noise in his house and wants to investigate. Perhaps he imagines he's a private detective or a criminal. He might have pointed the gun at himself as if he were captured by the enemy. Or he might have been looking down the barrel at the darkness inside. But we'll never know what Ricky was imagining.

Ricky was in my sixth grade class, and almost every day after lunch we would have to wait by the door to our room until the teacher returned. And almost every day Ricky would find some way to amuse himself, at my expense.

"Oops! Sorry, Bruce," Ricky lied after he bumped into me from behind. I turned and looked at him. Couldn't he see I wasn't going to be any fun? He slapped me in the face and then stuck his bottom lip out in an exaggerated pout. "Is Brucie gonna cry?"

"No," I said as I turned my back on him and walked a few steps away. I wanted so badly to knock him down on the ground and have the other kids laugh at him as they were laughing at me. Not all of the kids were laughing, though. My friends weren't laughing. They were admiring their shoes. I walked away from my friends to make it easier for them to ignore me. I didn't need their help, and I was glad they didn't offer it. I was prepared to take anything Ricky could give me, but no matter how much I wanted to, I could never bring myself to hit him. I always felt it was wrong to fight.

Ricky's house was on my street, and I had to pass it on my way home from school. Walking home from school should have been a nice stroll for a ten year old. I know that was what I had always wished my walks home would be. It wasn't a long walk—just three blocks, and the weather is always nice in the South Bay. But even in those few blocks, I had an obstacle, and it presented itself in the form of a young boy.

Some days I would stay after school to practice in the choir or to help the teacher. For my reward on those days, Ricky would be waiting for me on my way home. My house was on the other side of the street, and I always made sure to cross before I came to his house.

One day as I crossed the street, I heard something hit the ground near me. Then I felt the sting of a dirt clod hitting me in the head. I stopped and looked in the direction of Ricky's house, but I couldn't see where he was hiding. I brushed most of the dirt out of my hair and kept walking, trying to ignore being hit several more times before I made it home.

I stood in the shower, holding the valves to the hot and cold water as the dirt was washed out of my hair. Every time I thought about Ricky, I turned down the cold water until it was uncomfortably hot. As my skin turned red from the heat, I closed my eyes and wished for his death. I imagined it. Sometimes I would kill him. Other times he died in an accident. But always I was a witness. Always I would be free from his torment.

Unfortunately, later that year, my wish came true. I remember when I heard about Ricky's death. I was in an elevator with two of my friends who had also known Ricky. After I stepped into the elevator, I pushed the button for the third floor.

"Did you hear what happened to Ricky Liverpool?" one friend asked.

"Yeah," sighed the other friend as the door started closing.

"What happened?" I asked, feigning moderate interest.

"He shot himself in the head," one friend replied. The elevator gave a slight jerk upwards. I saw it in the way my friends bounced slightly, but I didn't feel it. I only felt the rigid walls of the elevator as my friends' polite lamentations seemed to punctuate my silence. The doors finally opened, and I followed my friends into the dim hallway.

I wasn't glad my wish came true. I wanted to feel happy. I wanted to feel freed. I could only feel sad. I felt sad because Ricky had died . . . and I had wanted it to happen. All of the hate I had built up inside for Ricky only brought me a tremendous amount of guilt. I realized then I had to be careful of what I wished for in the future. Because sometimes wishes do come true.

Analyzing Narrative Strategy: Show Rather Than Tell

When writers narrate a story, they try to recreate scenes so that the reader can experience the moment as they did. Rather than simply telling us what they felt, they try to *show* us. For example, in the student model, Halling could have simply told us that Ricky would often deliberately ridicule him. Instead, he lets us hear this, see it, and feel it with him as Ricky bumped him from behind:

> I turned around and looked at him. Couldn't he see I wasn't going to be any fun? He slapped me in the face and then stuck his bottom lip out in an exaggerated pout. "Is Brucie gonna cry?"

Such a scene draws in the reader because each of us can empathize with this moment of humiliation. The writer doesn't need to write, "I felt humiliated," because he has *shown* this more vividly than any claim he could make. Halling's use of dialogue, action, and vivid details (the exaggerated pout) makes Ricky seem real to the reader.

Selecting Telling Details The key to describing scenes and characters is to make sure each detail is revealing. It is not important to know the narrator's hair color or height, so such details would not be relevant or telling. But the fact that he is in the choir and stays after to help the teacher reveals that he is not a troublemaker, not one who would typically want to kill a classmate. Such details help us to understand better the narrator's character as well as the extent of his hatred of Ricky.

Similarly, the setting can be revealing. Although the weather is not always important in a story, here an afternoon stroll on a sunny day becomes darkened by the bully's attacks. In this scene the pleasant weather is juxtaposed against the narrator's pain as the clods of mud strike his head. The choice of setting itself can automatically reveal qualities about both character and conflict.

PRACTICING WRITING ESSAYS WITH NARRATION

Many of the topics in the "Writing from the Text" sections of the reader invite you to relate your own experience to the particular readings and to respond with a narrative. Here are some additional assignments:

1. Write an essay describing one school experience that taught you an unexpected lesson. Show us the incident as it happened, and describe what you learned and why it was unexpected.
2. Write an essay focusing on a time when you bullied or were bullied by someone else. Let us see what happened and what you discovered about yourself and others.
3. Write about a time when one of your peers, parents, or children embarrassed you. Was the situation funny, painful, or a little of both? Recreate the moment of embarrassment so that your reader sees and hears what happened.
4. Write about an incident when you felt that your cultural or family background was incorrectly prejudged. Describe what happened so that your reader can understand the event and your response to it. Did you make any discoveries as a result of this experience?
5. Write about an event that revealed that something you once believed or thought was important had lost its validity or importance. Dramatize the revelation as vividly as you can.

Readings in Part 1 That Use Narration

Examples of works in this text that are predominantly narration include the following:

"The Only Child," p. 11
"Ignorance Is Not Bliss," p. 14
"The Androgynous Man," p. 59
"Living in Two Worlds," p. 124
"In Rooms of Women," p. 130
"Like Mexicans," p. 188
"Living Under Circe's Spell," p. 198

"Black Men and Public Space," p. 219

"The Atlanta Riot," p. 224

"I Confess Some Envy," p. 398 (in the rhetoric)

Final Tips for a Narrative

- Focus your story on a provocative insight so that your story reflects some real thought.
- Continue sharpening your thesis as your narrative develops. Remember, the thesis does not need to be explicitly stated in the essay.
- Dramatize a scene or two, using action and dialogue. Don't just tell the reader; show the scene.
- Include telling details that reveal relevant character traits. Have your characters interact with each other.
- Rewrite sentences and revise paragraphs to eliminate wordiness and generalizations.
- Study other narratives in the text, looking for techniques and strategies. Experiment!

DEFINITION

Whether your entire essay is a definition or you have incorporated a definition into your essay to clarify a term or concept for your reader, explaining what a term means is an integral part of writing. Knowing your intended audience will help you determine which words you need to define. For example, in a paper for a psychology class, you would not need to define terms that are generally used in that field. But when you write for a general reader and use language unfamiliar to most people—a technical or foreign term or a word peculiar to an academic discipline—you will need to define the term so that your reader can understand it. Even if you are using a familiar word, you need to explain its meaning if you or an author you are quoting use it in a unique way.

Sometimes a brief definition is all that you need. In that case a few words of clarification, or even a synonym, may be incorporated into your text quite easily:

> *Los Vendidos,* or "The Sellouts," is the Spanish-language title of Luis Valdez's play.
>
> Achondroplasia—a type of dwarfism—may affect overall bone structure and cause arms and legs to be disproportionately smaller than the rest of the body.

A classic glaze for porcelain tea sets is celadon, a French name given in the seventeenth century to gray-green Chinese glazes.

Eating disorders include "bingeing, chronic dieting, and 'aerobic nervosa,' the excessive use of exercise to remain one's body ideal" (Erens 211).

Whenever possible, incorporate into your text the necessary clarification of a term. As the above examples show, such incorporation is unobtrusive and therefore superior to writing a separate sentence to define the term.

A formal definition may be required for some writing situations. In that case you will need to follow the dictionary model of establishing the term in a class and then distinguishing the term from its class by citing its difference, or *differentia:*

Haiku is a form of poetry composed of seventeen syllables in a 5–7–5 pattern of three lines.

A paring chisel is a woodworking tool with a knife-sharp edge, pushed by hand and used to finish a rough cut of wood.

When to Use Definition

You may be asked to write a definition essay, a paper that develops with the primary intention of increasing the reader's understanding of a term. This type of paper topic might be assigned in a psychology, sociology, history, philosophy, or English course. Usually, however, your goal will be something else. You may be attempting to convince your reader to consider the explained term in a positive light or to compare it—even to prefer it—to something else. Sometimes the persuasive aspect of the essay relies on the reader understanding the definition of a word.

Strategies for Incorporating Definitions

When an assignment calls for an extended definition of a concept or term, the following methods may be used alone or in combination:

- *Comparison-contrast:* You may want to contrast your definition of the word with the way it is typically used or with a more conventional definition of the term. If the term is unfamiliar, you might show how it is similar to another concept.
- *Description:* You can define a term by describing its characteristics: size, shape, texture, color, noise, and other telling traits.

- *Exemplification:* Giving examples and illustrations of a concept can help your reader to understand it better, but examples are rather specific and therefore should supplement a definition rather than be used by themselves.
- *Negation:* Understanding what something is *not* can help limit the definition and eliminate misconceptions.

Example: An In-Class Writing Assignment

The following definition reflects a brief in-class writing assignment in which the student was asked to explain Robert Moog's definition of a patriotic American in "Who's Not Supporting Whom?" (p. 252). The student, Ken Kiefer, had read Moog's article and had a time limit to write this response.

Patriotism Re-examined

Ken Kiefer

In "Who's Not Supporting Whom?" Robert Moog defies the prevalent definition of a patriotic American as one who only "buys American." Instead, he defines a "good patriotic American" as one who believes in the free enterprise system and in the benefits of vigorous competition. Convinced that such competition is best for America, Moog argues that patriotic Americans are those who buy the best product, no matter what country produces it. He feels that such competition is best for this country because it will force Americans to make a better product, one that is efficient and cost-effective.

In the long run, this alone will save American businesses and ensure employment for all—patriotic goals, for sure. Moreover, he claims that whenever Americans buy foreign-made products, it is their patriotic duty to write to American manufacturers and explain why. According to Moog, the patriotic American should not coddle American companies because ultimately this weakens and undermines the entire country and its economy.

Analysis of the Definition Essay

Because this essay had to be written during class, the time was limited. Therefore Ken immediately focused on a succinct definition of a "patriotic American"—one who believes in the free enterprise system and therefore buys the best product, not necessarily an American-made one. The remaining definition attempts to explain and justify this controversial definition. Ken used negation when he claimed that the patriotic American is not one who simply "buys American." He also supported his definition with some specific quotations from the article.

PRACTICING WRITING DEFINITION ESSAYS

1. In your college papers, you will most frequently incorporate short definitions to clarify terms. In small groups, armed with dictionaries, practice writing single sentences that define the following terms:
   a. schizophrenia
   b. satire
   c. Marxist
   d. interface
   e. Cubist
   f. picaresque
2. Although you will use definition most often as a component of your papers, it is useful to practice writing short definition essays. In small groups, collaborate with your classmates to write a short essay that defines one of the following:
   a. power
   b. "between worlds"
   c. artifice
   d. witty
   e. unconditional love
   f. disabled

Readings in Part 1 That Use Definition

Each of the following works requires definition to achieve its goal:

"The Appeal of the Androgynous Man," p. 55
"The Androgynous Man," p. 59
"Date Rape," p. 89

"When a Woman Says No," p. 98
"To live in the Borderlands means you . . . ," p. 127
"Crimes Against Humanity," p. 159
"An Open Letter to Jerry Lewis," p. 201
"Discrimination at Large," p. 207
"The Atlanta Riot," p. 224
"Mommy, What Does 'Nigger' Mean?" p. 230
"Passing," p. 234
"Who's Not Supporting Whom?" p. 252
"Three Ways of Meeting Oppression," p. 295
"Don't Let Stereotypes Warp Your Judgments," p. 428 (in the rhetoric)

Final Tips for Writing Definitions

- Consider your audience and define any terms that your readers can't be expected to know.
- Whenever possible, incorporate into your text the necessary clarification of a term. Avoid writing a separate sentence to define the term.
- For a formal definition, first establish the term in a class and then distinguish it from this class by citing its difference.
- Remember that definitions can also be developed by comparing and contrasting that word with other terms, by describing the characteristics of a term, by presenting examples, and by illustrating what the term is not.

CAUSE AND EFFECT

All your life you have been made aware of the consequences of your behavior: not getting your allowance because you didn't keep your room clean, winning a class election because you ran a vigorous campaign, getting a C on an exam because you didn't review all of the material, earning a friend's trust because you kept a confidence. In all of these cases a particular behavior seems to *cause* or result in a certain *effect*. In the case of the denied allowance, for example, your parents may have identified the cause: not keeping your room clean.

Causes are not always so easy to identify, however, for an action or inaction may have a number of indirect causes. For example, you may have won an election because of your reputation as a leader, your popularity, your opponent's inadequacies, your vigorous campaign, or even a cause that you may not have known about or been able to control. Effects usually are more evident: homeless families, few jobs for college graduates, small businesses failing, and houses remaining on the market for years are all obvious effects of a recession. What has caused the recession is typically more difficult to discern, but good critical thinking involves speculating about possible causes and their effects. And good writing can come from such cause-and-effect thinking.

When to Use Cause and Effect

Cause-and-effect development can be used in diverse writing situations. For example, you will use this strategy when you trace the reasons for a historical event, such as the causes for American entry into World War II and the results of that entry. You perceive cause-and-effect relationships when you analyze and write about broad social problems (such as runaway teens) or more personal concerns (such as why you and your siblings are risk takers). You may rely on cause-and-effect description to discuss a small town's abandoned shopping district or to compare the aspirations of college graduates in 1968 and those today. All of these thinking and writing tasks invite you to examine the apparent effects and to question what has caused them. This questioning inevitably involves speculation about causes rather than absolute answers, but this speculation can lead to fruitful analysis and provocative papers.

Brainstorming to Find Causes or Effects

To speculate about causes for an effect that you have perceived, you will want to brainstorm freely and let all of your hunches emerge. In fact, a lively prewriting session is the key to a lively cause-and-effect paper. To produce a paper that goes beyond predictable or obvious discussion, take time to think about diverse causes for an effect you have observed and to contemplate plausible effects of situations that you perceive.

For example, you may have noticed that your downtown area is no longer attracting people as it once did. Instead of stopping at the family-owned clothing store or the donut shop next to the downtown movie theater, you and your family and friends go out to suburban malls for shopping, dining, and movies. Consider the causes for this phenomenon.

You can brainstorm this perceived problem by writing a list of every possible cause that comes to you. After you have written your own list, you might look at this one:

WHY AREN'T WE GOING DOWNTOWN ANYMORE?

STORES

1. Limited stock—embarrassing, never have my size
2. Only carry expensive brands
3. Prices higher than the mall, too few sales
4. Old-fashioned, dull window displays, ugly mannequins
5. Clerks are old ladies who've been around forever

RESTAURANTS

6. Have boring menus: vegetable soup and bacon and eggs
7. Decorating is still very 1960s—pink and gray
8. Plastic plants
9. My favorite donut shop has closed
10. No inexpensive quick foods or snacks
11. Slow-moving waitresses

MOVIE THEATERS

12. Seats have broken springs and torn upholstery
13. Warped screen, bad sound system
14. Musty smell, no air conditioning
15. Same features play for weeks

OVERALL DOWNTOWN

16. Only old people shop downtown
17. I never meet any of my friends down there
18. Lots of homeless people, gangs
19. Dusty window-fronts of abandoned shops are demoralizing
20. Need to pay to park in city lots or need to feed meters

If you put some energy into the prewriting, you will undoubtedly come up with more causes than we have, and the paper that you write will have interesting explanations for a problem that threatens nearly every community. You might not have the sophistication of a city planner or the statistics and research of your city hall, but your insights are bound to create a provocative paper that is worth reading. And we think you will find that creative speculation is useful for any cause-and-effect brainstorming that you do.

Drafting a Paper

After you have listed causes and/or effects, your next drafting step is to discover ideas that logically connect. As you link points, evaluate them to make sure your reasoning is clear and that your points are plausible and logical.

For example, the fact that the donut shop has closed is not *why* you have stopped shopping for clothing in the downtown area. That point would seem illogical to your reader without your developing a connection—perhaps that empty shops are disheartening reminders of the economic recession or that a particular cruller the shop made provided a tasty, quick, and inexpensive snack during a shopping trip. Or you might see, as you draft, that some causes on your list are not worth developing.

In addition to developing plausible explanations for the points you do want to use, you need to consider organization. In your brainstorming, you may have perceived a natural grouping that worked well to get ideas down on paper. We answered our question about what was wrong with the downtown area by listing what was wrong with the stores, restaurants, movie theaters, and general atmosphere there. Suppose we realized that we could provide a better answer to the question if we organized around *issues* rather than grouped examples. Here is the revised list that might result:

WHY WE AREN'T GOING DOWNTOWN ANYMORE

ECONOMIC ISSUES:

1. points 2, 3, 10, 20

AESTHETIC ISSUES:

1. points 4, 6, 7, 8, 9, 12, 13, 14, 19

SOCIAL ISSUES:

1. points 1, 5, 11, 15, 16, 17, 18

You will also need to decide the order of the grouped points that you will include in your paper. We decided that the social causes of not going downtown were more significant than the aesthetic or economic issues, so we decided to conclude our paper by discussing social issues. (For more about ordering ideas, see pp. 334–335.)

Throughout your drafting, continue evaluating your points. Remove any points that are implausible or cannot be supported by the information you have, or do some research to find more convincing data. Continue to apply the "So what?" standard to ensure that you are developing a worthwhile paper. By this time in your drafting, it would help you to formulate a working thesis—in this case an assertion that establishes the cause and/or effect relationship that you perceive.

■ PRACTICING FINDING CAUSES AND EFFECTS

In small groups or individually, list multiple causes for the following effects:

1. Prevalence of two-income families
2. Increased number of comic book and sports card stores
3. Trend toward instructors assigning collaborative projects
4. Popularity of high-risk sports
5. Resurgence of rock music from the late 1950s and the 1960s

Now list the effects of these realities:

1. Prevalence of single-parent families
2. Increase in multicultural materials in education
3. More women in the professions
4. More people from all economic classes attending college
5. City-sponsored recycling projects

Any one of these brainstorming exercises could lead to a paper based on cause-and-effect development.

Example: Cause-and-Effect Essay

An analysis of a social issue is Robert McKelvey's goal in "I Confess Some Envy." In it, McKelvey, a Bronze Star recipient in Vietnam and now a child psychiatrist and professor at Baylor University, analyzes the causes of the envy he felt while watching the Desert Storm troops receive public acclaim. He cites the reasons that his generation of soldiers failed to gain support and the effects of this failure on him and his peers. This essay first appeared in the *Los Angeles Times* on June 16, 1991, shortly after the return of American troops from the Persian Gulf.

■ I CONFESS SOME ENVY

Robert McKelvey

Every year on the Marine Corps' birthday, the commandant sends a message to all Marine units world-wide commemorating the event. On Nov. 10, 1969, I was stationed with the 11th Marine Regiment northwest of Da Nang in Vietnam. It was my task to read the commandant's message to the Marines of our unit.

One sentence, in particular, caught my attention: "Here's to our wives and loved ones supporting us at home." Ironically, that week my wife had joined tens of thousands of others marching on the nation's capital to protest U.S. involvement in Vietnam.

It was a divisive, unhappy time. Few people believed the war could be won or that we had any right to interfere in Vietnam's internal affairs. However, for those of us "in country," there was a more pressing issue. Our lives were on the line. Even though our family and friends meant us no harm by protesting our efforts, and probably believed they were speeding our return, their actions had a demoralizing effect.

Couldn't they at least wait until we were safely home before expressing their distaste for what we were doing? But by then, the military had become scapegoats for the nation's loathing of its war, a war where draft dodgers were cast as heroes and soldiers as villains.

Watching the Desert Storm victory parades on television, I was struck by the contrast between this grand and glorious homecoming and the sad, silent and shameful return of so many of us 20-odd years ago. Disembarking from a troop ship in Long Beach, my contingent of Marines was greeted at the pier by a general and a brass band. There were no family, friends, well-wishers, representatives of the Veterans of Foreign Wars or children waving American flags.

We were bused to Camp Pendleton, quickly processed and sent our separate ways. After a two-week wait for my orders to be cut, during which time I spent most days at the San Diego Zoo, I was discharged from active duty. I packed up and flew home to begin pre-medical studies.

As the plane landed in Detroit, the on-board classical music channel happened to be playing Charles Ives' "America." The piece's ironic, teasing variations on the theme, "My Country 'Tis of Thee," seemed a fitting end to my military service.

My wife met me at the airport and drove me directly to Ann Arbor for a job interview. We were candidates for a job as house parents for the Religious Society of Friends (Quakers) International Co-op. Face to face with these sincere, fervent pacifists, I felt almost ashamed of the uniform I was still wearing with its ribbons and insignia.

I recalled stories of comrades who had been spat upon in airports and called "baby killers." The Friends, however, were exceptionally gentle and kind. They, at least, seemed able to see beyond the symbols of the war they hated to the individual human being beneath the paraphernalia. Much to my surprise, we got the job.

I took off my uniform that day, put it away and tried to resume the camouflage of student life. I seldom spoke of my service in Vietnam. It was somehow not a topic for polite conversation, and when it did come up the discussion seemed always to become angry and polarized.

Like many other Vietnam veterans, I began to feel as if I had done something terribly wrong in serving my country in Vietnam, and that I had better try to hush it up. I joined no veterans' organizations and, on those rare times when I encountered men who had served with me in Vietnam, I felt embarrassed and eager to get away. We never made plans to get together and reminisce. The past was buried deep within us, and that is where we wanted it to stay.

The feelings aroused in me by the sight of our victorious troops marching across the television screen are mixed and unsettling. There is pride, of course, at their stunning achievement. Certainly they deserve their victory parade. But there is also envy. Were we so much different from them?

Soldiers do not choose the wars they fight. Theirs happened to be short and sweet, ours long and bitter. Yet we were all young men and women doing what our country had asked us. Seeing my fellow Vietnam veterans marching with the Desert Storm troops, watching them try, at last, to be recognized and applauded for their now-distant sacrifices, is poignant and sad.

We have come out of hiding in recent years as the war's pain has receded. It has become almost fashionable to be a veteran and sport one's jungle fatigues. Still, a sense of hurt lingers and, with it, a touch of anger. Anger that the country we loved, and continue to love, could use us, abuse us, discard and then try to forget us, as if we were the authors of her misery rather than her loyal sons and daughters. It was our curious, sad fate to be blamed for the war we had not chosen to fight, when in reality we were among its victims.

Small-Group Discussion

1. After reading McKelvey's essay, meet in small groups to develop a list of the *causes* of the Vietnam soldiers' unhappiness during the war and afterwards. What are the *effects* of this unhappiness on McKelvey and his peers?
2. Discuss these questions in your small groups:
   a. What is the effect on McKelvey of his reading the commandant's message to the Marines in his unit?
   b. What is the effect the protesters at home intended by marching on the nation's capital? What may have been the effect of this march on the troops in Vietnam?

c. What caused McKelvey to refrain from discussing his service experience with friends or from joining veterans' organizations after he returned?

d. What has caused changes in attitudes toward Vietnam veterans?

PRACTICING WRITING ESSAYS ABOUT CAUSES AND EFFECTS

Write an essay that focuses on the causes and/or effects of one of the following:

1. Your having revealed an important truth about yourself to a member of your family
2. A friend or family member abusing alcohol or using drugs
3. Your family getting together for a holiday occasion
4. Your feeling trapped in the "invisible cages" described by Brigid Brophy (p. 80)
5. Your sense of being caught living between two worlds, as Marcus Mabry (p. 124), Kim Edwards (p. 130), and Joan Steinau Lester (p. 234) describe.
6. Your discovery that you are unwillingly intimidating others, as Brent Staples describes (p. 219)
7. Your need to conform to gender roles as discussed by Warren Farrell (p. 75), Brigid Brophy (p. 80), and Cooper Thompson (p. 63)

Readings in Part 1 That Use Cause and Effect

A number of essays in this textbook use cause and effect as a significant part of their development. You may be interested in reading some of these essays:

"An Open Letter to Jerry Lewis," p. 201
"Black Men and Public Space," p. 219
"The Atlanta Riot," p. 224
"Who's Not Supporting Whom?" p. 252
"In Groups We Shrink," p. 274
"Why Johnny Can't Disobey," p. 277
"Don't Let Stereotypes Warp Your Judgments," p. 428 (in the rhetoric)

Final Tips for Cause and Effect Development

- Brainstorm energetically to come up with every possible cause and/or effect for your particular topic.
- Go over your list of causes and effects to determine that each point is reasonable and supportable. Eliminate any that are illogical or for which you lack data. Do research if additional evidence is needed.
- Apply the "So what?" standard. Will this cause-and-effect analysis make worthwhile reading?
- Group ideas that belong together and order your evidence to conclude with your most emphatic and well-developed support.
- Develop your explanations fully so that your reader doesn't need to guess your assumptions or suppose your connection between points.
- Whether you have a stated or implied thesis, ensure that the assertion of your paper is both clear and worth supporting.
- Listen to the voice you have used throughout your essay. If your purpose in writing is to consider possible cause-and-effect relationships, don't feign a voice that purports to know all the answers.

COMPARISON AND CONTRAST

Whether you are examining your own experiences or responding to texts, you will inevitably rely on comparison and contrast thinking. To realize how two people, places, works of art, films, economic plans, laboratory procedures, or aspects of literature—or anything else—may be alike or different is to perceive important distinctions between them.

While we may start an analysis process believing that two subjects are remarkably different (how they *contrast*), after thoughtful scrutiny we may see that there are important similarities between them. Conversely, although we may have detected clear similarities in two subjects (how they *compare*), the complete analysis may reveal surprising differences. Therefore, while **comparison** implies similarity and **contrast** implies difference, these two thinking processes work together to enhance perception.

When to Use Comparison and Contrast Development

Subtle comparison-contrast cues are embedded in writing assignments, both in-class exams and out-of-class papers. For example, an economics instructor may ask for a study of prewar and postwar inflation; a philosophy instructor may want the student to show how one philosophical system departs from another; a psychology instructor may require an explanation of how two different psychologists interpret dreams; or a literature instructor may assign an analysis of how a character changes within a certain novel.

The prevalence of such assignments in all disciplines underscores the importance of comparison-contrast in many experiences and learning situations. Assignments that ask writers to explain the unfamiliar, evaluate certain choices, analyze how someone or something has changed, establish distinction, discover similarities, and propose a compromise all require some degree of comparison and contrast.

For example, a writer responding to the readings in Chapter 2 may initially believe that women and men have quite different complaints about their lives. Women feel that they need to be attractive; they feel limited in their choice of career, and restricted by the career heights and pay they may attain; and they feel obligated to be domestic (good mothers, cooks, and housekeepers). Men feel they need to be successful at work to be attractive to women; they feel burdened to select high-status, high-paying jobs regardless of their real interests, and they must work continuously; and they feel precluded from domestic life—cut off from their children and home life.

At first, the complaints of the two genders appear to be quite different. But the writer examining these complaints may perceive that they have something in common: that women *and* men suffer from "an invisible curriculum," a series of social expectations that deprive human beings of choice. A thesis for this study might look like this:

> **Thesis:** Although women and men seem to have different problems, both genders feel hampered by an "invisible curriculum" that affects their self-esteem and limits their choices at work and in their families.

How to Compare and Contrast

There are two basic methods for organizing data to compare or contrast. In the *block* method, the writer would organize the material for a study of conflicts affecting gender like this:

BLOCK 1. WOMEN

1. Need to feel attractive to be successful
2. Feel limited in workplace choices, level, pay
3. Feel obligated to be mothers, domestic successes

BLOCK 2. MEN

1. Need to feel successful at work to feel attractive
2. Feel burdened to achieve high position, work continuously
3. Feel cut off from children and domestic choices

In the *point-by-point* method, the writer would organize the material like this:

POINT 1. FACTORS THAT GOVERN SELF-ESTEEM

1. Women need to feel attractive
2. Men need to feel successful at work

POINT 2. RELATIONSHIP TO WORK

1. Women feel restricted in choice, level, pay
2. Men feel burdened to achieve high position, work continuously

POINT 3. RELATIONSHIP TO FAMILY

1. Women feel obligated to be mothers, domestic successes
2. Men feel cut off from children, domestic choices

Notice that in the block method, each point in the second block appears in the same order as the points in the first block. In the point-by-point method of arrangement the first subject (in this case, women) will precede the second in each point of comparative analysis.

Although you may be wise to follow one of these methods quite deliberately, professional writers do not always adhere to this somewhat rigid form. Consider, for example, the following essay by Ellen Goodman.

Example: Comparison and Contrast Essay

■ IN AMERICA, FOOD FOR THOUGHT

Ellen Goodman

I once knew a thin sociologist who believed that people were obsessed by food only when they were chronically hungry. Even Freud described "oral" as a stage that adults (and perhaps cultures) would grow out of, with no more than an occasional regression for, say, weddings or Thanksgiving.

But today we live in a country where most of us are on demand feeding. The average American doesn't have to stalk the wild hamburger or gather ice cream in the woods. But it seems that much of the time that we used to spend on the basic problem of food—getting enough—has simply been transferred to the more elaborate food problems.

Recently I read not only Julia Child's delightful new cookbook but also an intriguing group of articles in the latest *Psychology Today* magazine on the new food consciousness. These readings reminded me that we have developed two major alternatives to the meat-and-potatoes mainstream: the "gourmet-food" culture and the "health-food" culture.

On one level, the two food "regimens" seem wildly disparate. Gourmet food is a response to our fantasies about what tastes good, while health food is a response to our fears about what's bad for you. Moreover, as alternative menus to the burger bourgeoise, the first group offers Turkey Orloff, while the second group offers Tofu with bean sprouts. One group is "into" a fish mousse en croute, while the other is high on brown rice. It's a matter of vintage wine versus fresh carrot juice.

Yet I think they have more in common than meets the mouth. The most extreme devotees of both the sensible Julia Child and late Adelle Davis demonstrate, at times, a moral elitism that is both righteous and intimidating. Many of the gourmet set are convinced that anyone who doesn't make his or her own mayonnaise is hopelessly gauche. Others among the health contingents look on a beefeater with as much horror as if they'd caught him biting the left leg off their dog.

These two alternative groups often share another characteristic. They are the oral equivalent of joggers. Conversation among the most committed Cordon Bleu crowd runs the gamut from artichoke to zabaglione, with arguments about preserving the balance of the elusive hollandaise. Dinner among the food cultists concerns the organic growth of vegetables, and the best way to maintain harmony between the yin and the yang on the serving platter. No Twinkie would darken the lips of either group. Instant coffee is taboo, although for different reasons. And Wonder Bread is to both an unspeakable obscenity: the kidporn of the food fetishists.

But the appeal of both of these groups is enormous, for another reason. These advocates of the good life share something significant with the rest of us: the need to pay attention to food every day. The easy, fast-food mainstream of America, the simple three-meal culture, may satisfy our hunger pangs, but not some kind of innate need for allotting to food and eating an important place in our lives.

It may be that our current attraction to the alternative food cultures is more than the allure of the perfect paté or the sirens of guilt and sensible warnings of the natural-food advocates. It may be that part of our current fascination with analyzing and preparing "health foods" and concocting gourmet dinners is a rebellion against easy eating.

Analyzing Comparison and Contrast Strategy

In this essay, Goodman seems to be contrasting the "two major alternatives to the meat-and-potatoes mainstream: the 'gourmet-food' culture and the 'health-food' culture." Goodman acknowledges that these "two food 'regimens' seem wildly disparate." To show the apparent *contrasts* between the two eating habits, Goodman concentrates on one focal point at a time. Here she states why people are attracted to gourmet or health foods:

> Gourmet food is a response to our fantasies about what tastes good, while health food is a response to our fears about what's bad for you.

Then Goodman gives specific examples to support her point:

> [The] first group offers Turkey Orloff, while the second group offers Tofu with bean sprouts. One group is "into" a fish mousse en croute, while the other is high on brown rice. It's a matter of vintage wine versus fresh carrot juice.

But after establishing the obvious differences in what these groups eat, Goodman notes that they have similarities, that "they have more in common than meets the mouth." To emphasize what they share, she continues to use the *point-by-point method,* moving back and forth between the two eating preferences, treating one focus point at a time and specifically showing how each habit relates to the point that she has made:

- Both groups demonstrate "a moral elitism that is both righteous and intimidating":
  - — Gourmets insist that everyone make mayonnaise
  - — Health food eaters deplore beef eaters
- Both groups are preoccupied with and talk about foods:
  - — Gourmets' talk ranges from artichokes to zabaglione, how to maintain a hollandaise
  - — Health food eaters discuss organic vegetables, plan plates to preserve yin/yang
- Both groups share the same taboos, if for different reasons:

— Twinkies, instant coffee, Wonder Bread

Finally, Goodman concludes that these apparently different groups share something more significant than their differences: "the need to pay attention to food every day." The focus of Goodman's essay, then, turns out to be the *comparison* between the two food "regimens," and the essay develops with wonderful style and wit to show the author's subtle but significant perceptions.

Which Method to Use: Block or Point by Point?

Goodman used a point-by-point method to compare and contrast her two subjects. She might have chosen the block method, writing first on every aspect of the gourmet culture and then, in the second block, on every aspect of the health food regimen. Although the block method seems easier, it may let the writer ramble vaguely about each subject without concentrating on specific points of comparison or contrast. The resulting essay may resemble two separate discussions that could be cut apart with scissors. Imagine how much verve Goodman's essay would have lost had she looked first at the health food culture and then the gourmet culture. The dramatic speed of her delivery—"vintage wine versus fresh carrot juice"—would have been lost in the block method, and the *real* point of her essay (that the regimens share "a rebellion against easy eating" would have been buried in a conclusion following the two blocks of discussion of the different eating habits. Whenever it seems reasonable, use the point-by-point method to arrange your comparison and contrast material.

Ellen Goodman's essay is arranged *inductively;* that is, her thesis is "discovered" by the reader in the middle of her essay. If you place your thesis at the beginning of your essay—and many instructors in freshman composition courses prefer that you do—it may be important to forecast the way or ways in which the subjects compare or contrast. But remember that a weak thesis is worse than no thesis. For example, a weak thesis for the study of conflicts in the lives of women and men might be "Although women and men have different problems, they also share a social concern." Such a thesis is weak because it doesn't say anything specific. Furthermore, it doesn't help the writer focus on the basis for the study, and focus for the writer (as well as the reader) is one function of the thesis.

Writers do not always announce their intention to compare and contrast in their thesis, even though comparison and contrast elements predominate in the development of their thinking and writing. Consider the following essay, which James Seilsopour wrote when he was a student at Riverside City College in Riverside, California, in 1984.

Student Example: Comparison and Contrast Essay

I Forgot the Words to the National Anthem

James Seilsopour

The bumper sticker read, "Piss on Iran."

To me, a fourteen-year-old living in Teheran, the Iranian revolution was nothing more than an inconvenience. Although the riots were just around the corner, although the tanks lined the streets, although a stray bullet went through my sister's bedroom window, I was upset because I could not ride at the Royal Stable as often as I used to. In the summer of 1979 my family—father, mother, brothers, sister, aunt, and two cousins—were forced into exile. We came to Norco, California.

In Iran, I was an American citizen and considered myself an American, even though my father was Iranian. I loved baseball and apple pie and knew the words to the "Star-Spangled Banner." That summer before high school, I was like any other kid my age; I listened to rock'n'roll, liked fast cars, and thought Farrah Fawcett was a fox. Excited about going to high school, I was looking forward to football games and school dances. But I learned that it was not meant to be. I was not like other kids, and it was a long, painful road I traveled as I found this out.

The American embassy in Iran was seized the fall I started high school. I did not realize my life would be affected until I read that bumper sticker in the high school parking lot which read, "Piss on Iran." At that moment I knew there would be no football games or school dances. For me, Norco High consisted of the goat ropers, the dopers, the jocks, the brains, and one quiet Iranian.

I was sitting in my photography class after the hostages were taken. The photography teacher was fond of showing travel films. On this particular day, he decided to show a film about Iran, knowing full well that my father was Iranian and that I grew up in Iran. During the movie, this teacher encouraged the students to make comments. Around the room, I could hear "Drop the bomb" and "Deport the mothers." Those words hurt. I felt dirty, guilty. However, I managed to laugh and assure the students I realized they were just joking. I went home that afternoon and cried. I have long since forgiven those students, but I have not and can never forgive that teacher. Paranoia set in. From then on, every whisper was about me: "You see that lousy son of a bitch? He's Iranian." When I was not looking, I could feel their pointing fingers in my back like arrows. Because I was absent one day, the next day I brought a note to the attendance office. The secretary read the note, then looked at me. "So you're Jim Seilsopour?" I couldn't answer. As I walked away, I thought I heard her whisper to her co-worker, "You see that lousy son of a bitch? He's Iranian." I missed thirty-five days of school that year.

My problems were small compared to those of my parents. In Teheran, my mother had been a lady of society. We had a palatial house and a maid. Belonging to the women's club, she collected clothes for the poor and arranged Christmas parties for the young American kids. She and my father dined with high government officials. But back in the States, when my father could not find a job, she had to work at a fast-food restaurant. She was the proverbial pillar of strength. My mother worked seventy hours a week for two years. I never heard her complain. I could see the toll the entire situation was taking on her. One day my mother and I went grocery shopping at Stater Brothers Market. After an hour of carefully picking our food, we proceeded to the cashier. The cashier was friendly and began a conversation with my mother. They spoke briefly of the weather as my mother wrote the check. The cashier looked at the check and casually asked, "What kind of name is that?" My mother said, "Italian." We exchanged glances for just a second. I could see the pain in her eyes. She offered no excuses; I asked for none.

Because of my father's birthplace, he was unable to obtain a job. A naturalized American citizen with a master's degree in aircraft maintenance engineering from the Northrop Institute of Technology, he had never been out of work in his life. My father had worked for Bell Helicopter International, Flying Tigers, and McDonnell Douglas. Suddenly, a man who literally was at the top of his field was unemployable. There is one incident that haunts me even today. My mother had gone to work, and all the kids had gone to school except me. I was in the bathroom washing my face. The door was open, and I could see my father's reflection in the mirror. For no particular reason I watched him. He was glancing at a newspaper. He carefully folded the paper and set it aside. For several long moments he stared blankly into space. With a resigned sigh, he got up, went into the kitchen, and began doing the dishes. On that day, I know I watched a part of my father die.

My father did get a job. However, he was forced to leave the country. He is a quality control inspector for Saudi Arabian Airlines in Jeddah, Saudi Arabia. My mother works only forty hours a week now. My family has survived, financially and emotionally. I am not bitter, but the memories are. I have not recovered totally; I can never do that.

And no, I have never been to a high school football game or dance. The strike really turned me off to baseball. I have been on a diet for the last year, so I don't eat apple pie much anymore. And I have forgotten the words to the national anthem.

Discussing a Student's Comparison and Contrast Strategy

Seilsopour's intention is to contrast his expectations as a teenager with a reality imposed by political events. He develops his contrast by showing first his home life in Iran and his feelings about America at that time, then his family's way of life and his feelings about America after the family moved to the United States.

Seilsopour makes it clear that when he lived in Iran, he not only was an American citizen, but also had "typical" traits of an American teenager. He knew the words to the "Star-Spangled Banner"; he loved baseball, apple pie, rock music, fast cars, and Farrah Fawcett. He states that he anticipated starting high school and going to football games and dances. He also suggests atypical aspects of his life in Iran when he alludes to riding horses at "the Royal Stable," an activity that was curtailed by the revolution in Iran, which otherwise had little impact on his daily life there.

Seilsopour's move to the United States occurred shortly before the American embassy in Teheran was seized and hostages were taken. Seilsopour notes that seeing the bumper sticker—"Piss on Iran"—and feeling victimized by an insensitive high school teacher were the turning points in his perception of his life. He says, "I knew there would be no football games or school dances." The reality of his life at Norco High became isolation, paranoia, and absence from school—points that he develops as contrasts with his earlier anticipation.

Seilsopour also contrasts his family's past in Iran with their reality in the United States. His family had lived in a "palatial house" and had a maid, and his parents had associated with "high government officials." His mother may have been a typical woman of leisure, enjoying women's club activities and doing charity work. Because of anti-Iranian feelings, after Seilsopour's family moved to the United States, his Iranian father was unemployable in the defense industries where he had previously held good jobs. His mother supported the family by working 70 hours a week in a fast-food restaurant. The contrast between her former way of life and her life in the United States is *shown* rather than stated. Similarly, the contrast between his father's former high political status and his reduced self-esteem in the United States is *shown* rather than overtly summarized.

Seilsopour brings closure to his personal story by acknowledging his bitter memories and by specifically citing his former anticipations that were never met: "I have never been to a high school football game or dance." He notes that he has been "turned . . . off to baseball," and because of a diet he does not "eat apple pie much anymore." His conclusion pointedly sums up his attitude about being an American citizen whose youthful aspirations were crushed by political exigencies and adult insensitivity: "I have forgotten the words to the national anthem." Each point in his former catalog of preferences for American things is countered by his specific concluding denials.

Seilsopour's unstated thesis might have been something like this: "My expectations for being a typical American high school student were thwarted by the reality I met at Norco High." But Seilsopour's essay is much more dramatic and compelling because his essay *lacks* this obvious comparison-contrast set up. Notice that even though Seilsopour does not announce his intention of contrasting "expectations" with "reality," each of the points in his study is deliberately and specifically contrasted.

PRACTICING WRITING ESSAYS THAT USE COMPARISON AND CONTRAST

Select one of the following topics to write an essay that compares or contrasts:

1. A family member's response to an important decision with how you expected that person to respond
2. A perception of a family member that you held in your youth with a view of that person that you have today
3. Your understanding or interpretation of a particular movie, song, or event with a friend's view
4. Your concept of ideal employment with a job you have held or hold now
5. Brigid Brophy's understanding of the social climate that influences women with Cooper Thompson's view of what shapes men (p. 63)
6. Elayne Rapping's evaluation of *Seinfeld* (p. 260) with Jay McInerney's (p. 266)
7. Cliff Stoll's perception of the potential of computers (p. 287) with Negroponte's view (p. 291)

Readings in Part 1 That Use Comparison and Contrast

The works in this text that use comparison and/or contrast strategies for development include the following:

Final Tips for Comparison and Contrast

- Make sure that your thesis includes both of the subjects that are being compared and contrasted and that the wording is specific. *Avoid a thesis that simply claims they are both alike and different.*

- Consider using the *point-by-point* method of comparison-contrast for a more emphatic delivery of information.
- Continue *interrelating* the two subjects so that you never make a point about one without showing how it relates to the other.
- Search for *subtle links and distinctions* as well as for the obvious ones. Then analyze the *reasons* for those differences.

ARGUMENT

Convincing others that your beliefs and perspectives are worth understanding, and perhaps even supporting, can be a definite challenge. Sometimes one must counter both preconceptions and convictions to get readers to modify their beliefs or change their behavior. In fact, persuasion is a part of many writing situations, and to convince a reader that a certain assertion or opinion is supportable is the heart of argument.

Arguments and Proposals

A distinction can be made between two types of writing that attempt to convince readers to reconsider their views and beliefs:

> An *argument* employs logic to *reason* a point and get the reader to *think*
>
> A *proposal* employs logic to *influence* others and get the reader to *think and act*

Although these types of writing often overlap, some assignments seem to fit more in one category than the other. If you are asked to analyze an essay and argue for or against the writer's views, your essay will involve *argumentation.* You will be expected to focus on a thesis that can provoke the reader's thoughts and to use supporting evidence that is logically presented and carefully analyzed.

If you are asked to offer a solution to a problem or to persuade others to modify or change their behavior, your essay will need to include a *proposal* in addition to argumentation. You will be expected to focus on a thesis that provokes a response. Therefore you will also need to suggest a reasonable plan of action or activities for your reader.

Presenting a logical argument or proposal does not exclude appealing to your reader's emotions. For example, an essay may propose that the school district establish more bilingual education programs to help Hispanic students become assimilated into American culture. To appeal to readers emotionally, a Hispanic writer may decide to begin by illustrating the isolation she felt when she was enrolled in an English-speaking kindergarten but spoke no English. Another writer may start with research that demonstrates how bright Hispanic students are failing and dropping out before they finish high school. Both introductions would be designed to arouse an emotional response, yet both would need to be supported by logical evidence and analysis.

When and How to Use Argument

Argument strategies may be used in all types of essays. Whenever you are attempting to convince a reader that one course of action is superior to another (comparison-contrast), that a particular behavior caused a certain consequence (cause and effect), or that one interpretation of a reading has validity (analysis), you will need to employ argument strategies. Because you are attempting to convince readers of a view that may be different from their own, it often helps to begin by illustrating what is wrong with the current thinking or practice on this issue.

For example, if a writer is arguing that female students in the early grades need greater encouragement to succeed in math and science classes, then it would make sense to establish the need first. The introduction and part of the body of the essay might demonstrate how females are discouraged from pursuing math and science majors and how few women today excel in these fields, even though studies indicate that females are no less capable of succeeding in science and math than males are.

Audience and Argument It is critical to identify one's *audience* and to find an approach that would best appeal to them. Identification of the audience may include asking these questions:

- Is the reader aware that the problem exists?
- Will the reader find the problem sufficiently important?
- Is the reader affected by the problem?
- Do any readers have special interests or biases that will cause them to resist the information? The proposal? The essay?

If you are arguing for increased bilingual education programs, you may design your paper differently if your audience is predominantly Hispanic or Anglo than if it is predominantly educators or parents. If the writer can determine whether the audience is likely to be sympathetic, neutral, or hostile, the approach can then be designed with this in mind.

Organizing an Argument To keep the argument focused and organized, an outline can be critical. Often, this involves an informal list of points, written in a logical order, that the writer plans to cover. The outline functions as a map to keep the writer on track. It may also help your instructor to follow the argument and to detect any flaws or gaps before the essay is actually written. In such cases a more formal outline may be required. (For an illustration of an informal outline for an argument, see pp. 335–336.)

Avoiding Logical Fallacies

Just as the argument must be presented in logical order, the thinking and analysis must be logical, too. Name-calling and personal attacks only weaken an argument because they suggest that the writer is desperate and has no other support or logical reasoning to defend the argument. Moreover, such devices are *logical fallacies,* having no basis or foundation in reason. These tactics discredit the argument and erode the readers' trust.

Illogical claims, whether intentional or not, are often associated with advertisers and politicians, whose careers may depend on their power to manipulate and mislead the public. Calling someone a "liberal" or a "redneck" is intended to get the audience to respond emotionally to a prejudice rather than to think rationally about an issue. Often, these attacks are designed to divert attention from the issue to the opponent's personal traits or associates in order to cast doubt on his or her character or expertise.

Besides smearing or ridiculing the opponent, the following logical fallacies may involve manipulating the argument itself:

A *circular argument* does not prove anything; it simply restates the assertion ("Instructors who teach writing are better teachers because good instructors teach writing").

An *either/or* argument sets up a false black-and-white dilemma, assuming that a particular viewpoint or course of action can only have two diametrically opposed outcomes ("College professors either require writing assignments or are poor teachers").

A *hasty generalization* consists of drawing a broad conclusion from a few unrepresentative generalizations ("Math teachers use Scantron tests; math teachers don't teach students to think critically").

A *false analogy* compares two things that aren't really comparable and therefore results in a false conclusion ("If developmental math classes can be taught effectively in a large lecture hall, developmental English classes can be, too").

A *bandwagon* appeal suggests that "everyone is doing this-why don't you?" This pressures the reader to conform whether or not the view or action seems logical or right ("All good teachers are dividing students into small-group workshops in their classes today").

These are only some of the many logical fallacies that can weaken an argument. Instead of relying on illogical attacks and charges, writers must seek logical support for their positions and legitimate flaws in their opponent's argument.

Conceding and Refuting Rather than twisting facts or attacking the person, it is best to anticipate the opponent's objections and refute them, logically and directly, before the reader can even utter, "But . . . ." Overlooking or ignoring potential holes in an argument can render your argument vulnerable to attack. It doesn't necessarily weaken your argument to recognize what may appear to be a weakness in your plan, provided that you can refute it and show that it doesn't really undermine your argument.

Another effective strategy is to acknowledge conflicting viewpoints and perhaps even admit that they have merit but then show how your solution or viewpoint is still superior. Such a strategy suggests that you are informed, open-minded, and reasonable—qualities that will make the reader more receptive to your argument.

Evaluating an Argument Arguments and proposals written by students can be more than mere classroom exercises. They can be sent to newspapers, television stations, corporations, and government boards. Several of the argument assignments in the "Writing from the Text" and "Connecting with Other Texts" sections of the reader involve college-related issues and may be appropriate for the editorial or opinion page of your campus or local newspaper.

The following proposal was written by Joe Goodwin, a high school student, and printed in the "Campus Correspondence" section of the *Los Angeles Times* on August 9, 1992. As you read his argument, consider these questions in order to evaluate its effectiveness:

- Who is the targeted audience, and how does the writer appeal to this audience?
- What is the problem? What is the thesis?
- What are the supporting points?
- What are the strengths of the argument?
- What are the weaknesses? Are there any logical fallacies?
- How does the ending bring satisfying closure to the essay?

Student Example: An Argument Essay

My Favorite School Class: Involuntary Servitude

Joe Goodwin

Like most teen-agers, I hate to be told what to do. I chafe at curfews, refuse to patronize restaurants that tell me what to wear, and complain daily about the braces my parents and dentist want me to have.

Yet, I look forward to the "forced opportunity" for community service my high school requires. While criticism mounts against Maryland's action in becoming the first state to mandate students to perform 75 hours of community service over seven years, it is well to look at the experience of local school districts that have instituted similar programs.

For five years, every student at the Concord-Carlisle Regional High School in Massachusetts has been required to perform 40 hours of community service in order to graduate. Conventional wisdom would have us believe that this would be an especially burdensome task, perhaps an impossible one, for students who hold outside paying jobs. But the graduation requirement may be satisfied within the school by working as teacher's aides, library assistants or tutors. Outside school, the requirement may be met by working at hospitals, nursing homes, senior citizens' centers, soup kitchens or for the town's park service or recreational department.

To be sure, it would be wonderful if students volunteered such service. But the great benefit of the mandated program is the responsibility it places on the school to work with community leaders to locate the places where students can best make a solid contribution. It is unrealistic to expect students to roam from place to place in search of service opportunities. Once the arrangements for those opportunities are made, the student needs only to decide which kind of service best fits his or her personality.

Those who oppose the community-service mandate fear it will interfere with the regular school curriculum. But what more important class can a student take than one that teaches values and responsibility? Is it better to require students to listen to long lectures about the plight of the elderly and homeless, or to have them provide hours of warmth merely by reading the newspaper to a senior citizen?

Some say that schools should not be in the business of fostering civic concerns among its youth. But what more important role can a school play than in shaping values—respect for the elderly, patience for those younger, compassion for those less fortunate—among its young? These and related values used to be taught in the home. Now, they must be learned elsewhere, since we live in a world in which many families have two parents working long hours every day and many more have just a single parent.

There has been much talk about the decline of American society, about the disintegration of the American family. Yet, when those who find pleasure in lecturing about this decline are faced with a solution that would help strengthen society, they fall back on the past. It is this negative attitude toward change that has caused the country to reach the point of such neglect.

Today, the passion and commitment that marked my parents' generation—the 1960s—is gone, replaced by an ominous silence. I listen to my parents talk of their experiences with the civil-rights movement, the sit-ins, the war on poverty, and I am impatient for the time when my own generation is similarly involved in the great public events of our day. Though 40 hours of community service is not very much, it is a beginning.

My interest in community service was heightened last spring. While on a class trip to the Science Museum in Boston, a group of students in my 8th-grade class were involved in an altercation with another group of students from a largely black school in Roxbury, a neighborhood near downtown. Taunts were exchanged, a fight broke out. It was unsettling.

The following week, teachers from both schools arranged a daylong meeting of a representative sampling of students at each school. The discussion that resulted was an extraordinary experience. As I listened to black students describe their stereotypes of whites in the suburbs, as I heard one black girl say she cried herself to sleep the night of the fight in fear and frustration that racial relations would never improve, I realized how far America was from the ideals of equality and justice. If community service could help to bridge the gap between ideal and reality, I will feel happy indeed.

Analyzing Argument Strategy

Even as Goodwin begins his essay, he seems to be anticipating a possible objection against mandating community service for high school students. He admits that he, like most teenagers, "hate[s] to be told what to do," yet this is one "forced opportunity" that he supports. Then, one by one, he raises and refutes certain objections:

- Doing community service is a burden for students who hold outside paying jobs. (Students can choose to work on-campus or off.)
- Students should volunteer for such service. (He concedes that they should volunteer but believes that it is unrealistic to expect students to search for such opportunities on their own.)
- Community service will interfere with regular curriculum. (He believes that community service is as important as any class and that it teaches students to apply what they are learning in the classroom.)
- Schools should not be in the business of fostering civic concerns among students. (He argues that schools must help shape values, especially since many children are not getting such training at home.)

After anticipating and countering these objections, Goodwin notes that many critics relish *lecturing* about the decline of American society and the disintegration of the family but are not willing to implement the necessary changes. He contrasts their reluctance with the passion and commitment that characterized his parents' generation during the 1960s, and he asks for opportunities for his generation to become more involved and concerned.

Throughout his essay, Goodwin's tone is restrained and reasonable. His writing reflects a healthy balance between idealism (free choice) and realism (mandatory service). He might have been tempted to resort to name-calling or offensive attacks, but instead he relies on facts and evidence to support his case. Finally, he ends his argument with a brief narrative to remind us of the need to merge the realms of the inner city and the suburbs. He acknowledges that his proposal is only a beginning but suggests that it is long overdue.

PRACTICING WRITING ARGUMENT ESSAYS

Write an essay to convince your reader of one of the following assertions:

1. All college students, regardless of age, ethnicity, or status, are (or are not) caught "between worlds."
2. Graffiti taggers should (or should not) be prosecuted for leaving their marks around the community.
3. Year-round school is (or is not) a viable solution to overcrowding.
4. The lyrics in contemporary music reflect (or incite) societal tension.
5. Robert Moog (p. 252) is correct (or incorrect) in his position that "buying American" ultimately hurts American industry.
6. Ward Churchill (p. 159) is (or is not) correct that using Native American names for sport teams is a crime against the humanity of Native Americans.
7. Date rape (p. 89) is (or is not) a significant problem that warrants an education program on your campus.
8. Judy Scales-Trent (p. 184) is correct (or incorrect) about adding a "multiracial" designation to the next census.
9. Elayne Rapping (p. 260) is correct (or incorrect) in her perception of *Seinfeld*

Readings in Part 1 That Use Argument

Essays in this text that are primarily argumentative in their intention include the following:

Final Tips for Argument

- Recognize your purpose (argument or proposal).
- Identify your audience, consider the audience's perspective, and prepare your appeal. Avoid insulting or attacking your audience.
- Word your thesis carefully to provoke thought or action.

- Outline your argument so that it is focused and organized.
- Support all claims with convincing evidence and reasoned analysis.
- Anticipate objections and differing viewpoints, and show why your argument is stronger even if the others have some merit.
- Guard against logical fallacies; they weaken any argument.
- Make sure your conclusion brings satisfying closure to your argument. Avoid tacking on any new points.

ANALYSIS: PROCESS, PROBLEM, SUBJECT

When you analyze anything—a film, an instructor's performance, an experiment in a chemistry lab, or even your roommate's mysterious casserole—you are taking the whole apart to examine its components. This, in turn, lets you understand how the parts contribute to the entire work. The purpose of an analysis is not merely to take the process, problem, or subject apart, but to see the value of the individual parts and to appreciate their interaction in creating the whole.

When to Use Analysis

You analyze constantly, perhaps without knowing that you are going through any formal steps. For example, if you are giving a party, you may have an unconscious order or process. You will wait to hear who is coming before you shop for food, clean before you decorate, and stock the coolers before your friends arrive. The order of these steps is important. Further, you know that each individual step is important to achieving a successful whole—a great party—and that if any step is neglected (such as no ice for the cooler), the party may flop.

Written analysis involves the same attention to order and details, regardless of the academic field. In fact, you will find that written analysis is assigned in every academic discipline. Whether you are dissecting a frog in biology, interpreting a painting in art history, examining a poem in English, reviewing curriculum in education, exploring a management problem in business, or studying a discrimination problem in law, you will be expected to write analytical papers.

These papers will be specifically targeted to the subject you are studying, but three basic types of analytical assignments predominate: analysis of a process, a problem, or a subject. Sometimes these distinctions blur, depending on the writer's purpose and audience.

For example, you might write a set of directions about how to dissect a frog, describe how frogs are usually dissected, or write about the problems that students have in biology courses. All of these papers involve breaking the whole into parts and examining the parts to show a reader their importance to the whole.

Analysis of a Process

A paper that examines a process explains how to do something or how the process itself is done: for example, perform a swimming pool rescue, get a classmate to ask you out, train for a marathon, cook in a wok, avoid loaning your favorite jacket, tune up a 1957 Chevy, pay car insurance while earning minimum wage, or get a roommate's friend to move out.

Brainstorming for a Topic If a topic has not been assigned, brainstorm for possibilities. Consider what you know how to do that others don't (such as how to make a perfect quiche) or what you would like to learn in order to explain that process to a reader (such as how to create a bonsai arrangement). Don't overlook the unusual: how to wallpaper the inside of your car, how to chart a cross-country flight for the least amount of money, or how to get your little brother to do your chores. You might also want to research how other people do things: how communities implement recycling projects, how bills are passed in Congress, how a new course becomes part of your college's curriculum, or how marketing firms predict consumers' willingness to try new products. Remember that a process analysis paper doesn't need to be dull or tedious. These papers can be lively if you use ingenuity and a little prewriting energy.

How to Write a Process Analysis

If you are writing a paper that tells your reader how to do something, or one that describes how something happens, these tips will help:

1. Determine whether or not the chronology is important. For some processes the sequence of the steps is critical (performing a swimming pool rescue), while for others it isn't as important (getting a classmate to ask you out).
2. If the chronology is important, list the steps and reexamine your list to make sure any reader can follow the logic of your arrangement.
3. Write each step completely, including all of the necessary information and removing confusing or irrelevant details. Imagine yourself in your readers' position, trying to follow your instructions for something they have never done.

4. Write a thesis that clearly asserts your point:

   Thesis: Creating bonsai arrangements is satisfying and lucrative.

   Thesis: Following the proper sequence of steps will facilitate a swimming pool rescue.

5. Draft your essay by linking each step with appropriate transitions to move your reader smoothly through this process.
6. Rewrite and edit your essay so that the language is vivid and the directions are precise.

PRACTICING THE STEPS OF A PROCESS

In small groups, write down the steps explaining how to do the following:

1. Find summer employment
2. Balance a diet to achieve good nutrition
3. Prepare a 3-year-old for a romp in the snow
4. Stay awake in a dull lecture
5. Convince an unwilling landlord to make a repair
6. Use library computers to find a book or an article on immigrants seeking political asylum

Spend time reaching accord within your group to ensure that all steps follow logically and that no necessary steps are left out. Aim for clarity and precision; remove words that obscure your directions. Any one of these analyses could be drafted into a collaborative paper.

Throughout this textbook you will notice a number of sections that explain various processes such as how to conduct an interview; how to cluster, list, and read actively; how to incorporate quoted material; and how to write a thesis or an outline. These sections of this textbook may be useful to you as models of process analysis, and they also underscore how important process is to teaching and learning.

PRACTICING DESCRIBING A PROCESS

Select and describe a process that you know well from the following list:

1. How social cliques form
2. How a camera or videocamera works
3. How a college orients its freshmen
4. How glaciers form

5. How Olympic teams are created
6. How a batik is made
7. How pool, backgammon, or your favorite game or sport is played
8. How a music piece is practiced for performance

Write your description as precisely as you can so that a reader can learn the process. Does your interest in the topic show in your description?

Example: Process Analysis Essay

In the following essay, Walter Gajewski, Instructional Lab Coordinator of Academic Computing Services at California State University, Long Beach, describes the process of using electronic mail (or "e-mail," as it is popularly termed).

E PLURIBUS E-MAIL

Walter Gajewski

Communicating with colleagues worldwide is no longer the exclusive tool of the "mad hacker." Students and faculty at many colleges now have access to e-mail—electronic mail—which combines the capabilities of the computer with those of the telephone line. Text, sound, and video movies can be transmitted, by way of phone lines, from one computer address to another.

To contact colleagues at distant locations, you must either subscribe to a commercial service such as Compuserve, Genie, America Online, MCI Mail or Prodigy, or you need to have an account on a computer that is connected to the Internet. The Internet is a complex, worldwide network of thousands of computers that are accessible to university professors, government researchers, the military—and you, through your college or a commercial service. Over the Internet, talk is cheap. No matter how many messages you send or how far you send them, your college or university does not pay anything beyond the fixed amount required to maintain its own portion of the Internet.

When you use e-mail, you need to have a specific account name which is your e-mail "address." Before you can log on to your computer account, the computer will ask you to enter your secret password. (No one else should know or needs to know this password to send you mail.) Next, call up the mail utility software and wait to be asked for the "address" of the person or persons you are contacting. This could be one address or it could be a word (an "alias") that represents a mailing list of thousands of addresses that you compiled ahead of time. After you enter the address, the computer will request the subject of your communication, followed by the body of your message. This message may be any length.

When you are finished, you simply give the command that indicates you are done. (This command varies depending on your software package.) The computer will ask if you want to send copies to anyone else. The computer then sends off your message. In a matter of seconds, your mail arrives at its destination anywhere in the world.

As important as speed is the fact that documents traveling directly from computer to computer remain as computer files rather than as a fixed printed page. Therefore, this document can be immediately edited without needing to be retyped into the computer. The ease and versatility of this process has made e-mail very popular today. But the possibilities for e-mail are just emerging. If you are interested in the future of interpersonal communication, make sure you check in the mail—the e-mail, that is. :-)

Small-Group Discussion

In small groups, discuss Gajewski's strategy:

1. How does Gajewski attract the reader to his subject? Who is his intended audience?
2. Why does Gajewski incorporate definition in this analysis?
3. What is the process described? In what ways is chronology important to this analysis?
4. Cite specific details that Gajewski includes to encourage the reader to consider using e-mail.
5. If you are computer literate, can you follow the description of this process to use e-mail? Are there any steps that need to be expanded or removed?

Final Tips for Analyzing a Process

- Review the order of the steps you have written to determine that your reader can follow your instructions or description.
- Examine the details you have given to remove any confusing instructions or irrelevant details.
- Put yourself in your reader's position to determine whether you have defined necessary terms and provided necessary details.
- Reread your work to see whether appropriate transitions link the steps or the parts of your analysis.

Analysis of a Problem

Another kind of analysis paper describes a problem; it may or may not offer a solution. The writer may trace the history of the problem, but chronology is not as vital to this type of analysis as it is in a step-by-step process analysis. What is critical in this type of analysis is that the writer establishes the problem, examines its parts, and shows how the parts are related to the problem as a whole.

When to Use Problem Analysis

More than any other single type of writing, problem analysis appears in every academic field and profession. Our daily newspapers, weekly newsmagazines, monthly periodicals, and scholarly journals all feature essays analyzing issues. The writers of the readings in this textbook analyze a variety of problems: alcoholism, drug abuse, eating disorders, environmental waste, closeting homosexuals, living between two cultures, stereotyping, isolation of the disabled, group conformity, and racial, ethnic, and gender discrimination. In spite of the wide range of issues, writers of problem analysis share similar strategies when they examine an issue.

How to Write Problem Analysis

Your initial job in any writing situation is to engage your readers, and nowhere is this more important than in problem analysis. Why should your readers care about stereotypes, ethnic bias, the rights of the disabled, or any other subject that doesn't directly relate to them? It is your job to create reader interest, and you can do this in a number of ways. Sometimes historical review of the problem will intrigue readers. Startling statistics or a bold anecdote should jar complacent readers out of apathy. Sometimes posing a direct question to the readers prompts them to consider their responses and become involved in the topic—at least enough to read the work. After you have engaged your readers, decide how much background information they require to understand the problem. For example, if you are writing an analysis of changing interest rates, you will include less background material if you are writing the paper for your business class than for your English class.

Then, as in all analysis papers, you will need to decide the parts of the problem that you want to examine. You must describe the problem so that any reader can understand it. This might include a discussion of the severity of the problem, the numbers of people affected by it, which population is most affected, and the consequences if this problem is uncorrected. A detailed study about each aspect of the problem and how it relates to the other parts will constitute the body of your paper. If it is relevant to your analysis, you might speculate about the barriers to solving this problem (such as cost, social bias, frustration with earlier failures, indifference, or denial).

It is important that this analysis have a focus and a clear point or assertion. For example, if you are concerned about the fact that Americans are on the job more than workers in other countries, it is not enough merely to identify the number of hours that American employees work each week. Nor is it enough to show that they work more hours per week and more weeks per year than their European counterparts or that they are not routinely given flexible work schedules so that they can coordinate their family's needs with their work responsibilities. All of these important facts could support a point, but the point must be made.

You will need to clarify, in the form of a thesis or assertion, why the analysis of these facts is important: that American workers are overworked, that Americans have insufficient leisure time, that American children grow up deprived of their parents, or any other point that you deem significant as a result of your analysis. But without a point, you have no paper.

Once you have determined your assertion, you are ready to outline, draft, and revise your paper. (See the student example of a problem analysis on eating disorders, pp. 327–339, for specific suggestions about outlining, drafting, and revising.)

Example: Problem Analysis Essay

The following analysis was written by a Harvard-educated economist, Robert L. Heilbroner, who has written extensively on economics and business. This essay contains a unique perception of a common problem.

■ DON'T LET STEREOTYPES WARP YOUR JUDGMENTS

Robert L. Heilbroner

Is a girl called Gloria apt to be better-looking than one called Bertha? Are criminals more likely to be dark than blond? Can you tell a good deal about someone's personality from hearing his voice briefly over the phone? Can a person's nationality be pretty accurately guessed from his photograph? Does the fact that someone wears glasses imply that he is intelligent?

The answer to all these questions is obviously, "No."

Yet, from all the evidence at hand, most of us believe these things. Ask any college boy if he'd rather take his chances with a Gloria or a Bertha, or ask a college girl if she'd rather blind-date a Richard or a Cuthbert. In fact, you don't have to ask: college students in questionnaires have revealed that names conjure up the same images in their minds as they do in yours—and for as little reason.

Look into the favorite suspects of persons who report "suspicious characters" and you will find a large percentage of them to be "swarthy" or "dark and foreign-looking"—despite the testimony of criminologists that criminals do not tend to be dark, foreign or "wild-eyed." Delve into the main asset of a telephone stock swindler and you will find it to be a marvelously confidence-inspiring telephone "personality." And whereas we all think we know what an Italian or a Swede looks like, it is the sad fact that when a group of Nebraska students sought to match faces and nationalities of 15 European countries, they were scored wrong in 93 percent of their identifications. Finally, for all the fact that horn-rimmed glasses have now become the standard television sign of an "intellectual," optometrists know that the main thing that distinguishes people with glasses is just bad eyes.

Stereotypes are a kind of gossip about the world, a gossip that makes us prejudge people before we ever lay eyes on them. Hence it is not surprising that stereotypes have something to do with the dark world of prejudice. Explore most prejudices (note that the word means prejudgment) and you will find a cruel stereotype at the core of each one.

For it is the extraordinary fact that once we have typecast the world, we tend to see people in terms of our standardized pictures. In another demonstration of the power of stereotypes to affect our vision, a number of Columbia and Barnard students were shown 30 photographs of pretty but unidentified girls, and asked to rate each in terms of "general liking," "intelligence," "beauty" and so on. Two months later, the same group were shown the same photographs, this time with fictitious Irish, Italian, Jewish and "American" names attached to the pictures. Right away the ratings changed. Faces which were now seen as representing a national group went down in looks and still farther down in likability, while the "American" girls suddenly looked decidedly prettier and nicer.

Why is it that we stereotype the world in such irrational and harmful fashion? In part, we begin to type-cast people in our childhood years. Early in life, as every parent whose child has watched a TV Western knows, we learn to spot the Good Guys from the Bad Guys. Some years ago, a social psychologist showed very clearly how powerful these stereotypes of childhood vision are. He secretly asked the most popular youngsters in an elementary school to make errors in their morning gym exercises. Afterwards, he asked the class if anyone had noticed any mistakes during gym period. Oh, yes, said the children. But it was the unpopular members of the class—the "bad guys"—they remembered as being out of step.

We not only grow up with standardized pictures forming inside of us, but as grown-ups we are constantly having them thrust upon us. Some of them, like the half-joking, half-serious stereotypes of mothers-in-law, or country yokels, or psychiatrists, are dinned into us by the stock jokes we hear and repeat. In fact, without such stereotypes, there would be a lot fewer jokes. Still other stereotypes are perpetuated by the advertisements we read, the movies we see, the books we read.

And finally, we tend to stereotype because it helps us make sense out of a highly confusing world, a world which William James once described as "one great, blooming, buzzing confusion." It is a curious fact that if we don't know what we're looking at, we are often quite literally unable to see what we're looking at. People who recover their sight after a lifetime of blindness actually cannot at first tell a triangle from a square. A visitor to a factory sees only noisy chaos where the superintendent sees a perfectly synchronized flow of work. As Walter Lippmann has said, "For the most part we do not first see, and then define; we define first, and then we see."

Stereotypes are one way in which we "define" the world in order to see it. They classify the infinite variety of human beings into a convenient handful of "types" towards whom we learn to act in stereotyped fashion. Life would be a wearing process if we had to start from scratch with each and every human contact. Stereotypes economize on our mental effort by covering up the blooming, buzzing confusion with big recognizable cut-outs. They save us the "trouble" of finding out what the world is like—they give it its accustomed look.

Thus the trouble is that stereotypes make us mentally lazy. As S. I. Hayakawa, the authority on semantics, has written: "The danger of stereotypes lies not in their existence, but in the fact that they become for all people some of the time, and for some people all the time, substitutes for observation." Worse yet, stereotypes get in the way of our judgment, even when we do observe the world. Someone who has formed rigid preconceptions of all Latins as "excitable," or all teenagers as "wild," doesn't alter his point of view when he meets a calm and deliberate Genoese, or a serious-minded high school student. He brushes them aside as "exceptions that prove the rule." And, of course, if he meets someone true to type, he stands triumphantly vindicated. "They're all like that," he proclaims, having encountered an excited Latin, an ill-behaved adolescent.

Hence, quite aside from the injustice which stereotypes do to others, they impoverish ourselves. A person who lumps the world into simple categories, who type-casts all labor leaders as "racketeers," all businessmen as "reactionaries," all Harvard men as "snobs," and all Frenchmen as "sexy," is in danger of becoming a stereotype himself. He loses his capacity to be himself—which is to say, to see the world in his own absolutely unique, inimitable and independent fashion.

Instead, he votes for the man who fits his standardized picture of what a candidate "should" look like or sound like, buys the goods that someone in his "situation" in life "should" own, lives the life that others define for him. The mark of the stereotyped person is that he never surprises us, that we do indeed have him "typed." And no one fits this strait-jacket so perfectly as someone whose opinions about other people are fixed and inflexible.

Impoverishing as they are, stereotypes are not easy to get rid of. The world we type-cast may be no better than a Grade B movie, but at least we know what to expect of our stock characters. When we let them act for themselves in the strangely unpredictable way that people do act, who knows but that many of our fondest convictions will be proved wrong?

Nor do we suddenly drop our standardized pictures for a blinding vision of the Truth. Sharp swings of ideas about people often just substitute one stereotype for another. The true process of change is a slow one that adds bits and pieces of reality to the pictures in our heads, until gradually they take on some of the blurriness of life itself. Little by little, we learn not that Jews and Negroes and Catholics and Puerto Ricans are "just like everybody else"—for that, too, is a stereotype—but that each and every one of them is unique, special, different and individual. Often we do not even know that we have let a stereotype lapse until we hear someone saying, "all so-and-so's are like such-and-such," and we hear ourselves saying, "Well—maybe."

Can we speed the process along? Of course we can.

First, we can become aware of the standardized pictures in our heads, in other peoples' heads, in the world around us.

Second, we can become suspicious of all judgments that we allow exceptions to "prove." There is no more chastening thought than that in the vast intellectual adventure of science, it takes but one tiny exception to topple a whole edifice of ideas.

Third, we can learn to be chary of generalizations about people. As F. Scott Fitzgerald once wrote: "Begin with an individual, and before you know it you have created a type; begin with a type, and you find you have created—nothing."

Most of the time, when we type-cast the world, we are not in fact generalizing about people at all. We are only revealing the embarrassing facts about the pictures that hang in the gallery of stereotypes in our own heads.

Small-Group Discussion

In small groups, discuss Heilbroner's strategy:

1. How does Heilbroner attract the reader? What is his introduction technique?
2. What does Heilbroner perceive as the *real* problem of stereotyping? Where does his assertion appear? How does Heilbroner convince a reader that stereotyping is a problem if that person has never felt victimized by stereotyping?
3. How does Heilbroner analyze the severity of the problem? According to Heilbroner's analysis of the problem, which populations are engaged in stereotyping, and how widespread is this? Evaluate the quality of his support and how he uses it.
4. Explain why Heilbroner moves into a process analysis mode to propose a solution to the problem of stereotyping.

PRACTICING PROBLEM ANALYSIS

Problem analysis assignments appear after many of the works in the reader. In addition to those that reflect the theme of being "between worlds," you might write an analysis of any of these problems:

1. Limited inexpensive housing available for college students
2. Policies at work or school that seem poorly conceived
3. A family's inability to communicate
4. Athletes' use of drugs
5. Unnecessary packaging of everyday products
6. Overdrinking and overeating in our society

Readings in Part 1 That Use Problem Analysis

Essays in this book that are examples of a problem analysis include the following:

"The Ties That Bind," p. 7
"The Only Child," p. 11
"Ignorance Is Not Bliss," p. 14
"Senior-Teener: A New Hybrid," p. 17
"Fetal Alcohol Syndrome," p. 23
"The Appeal of the Androgynous Man," p. 55

Final Tips for Analyzing a Problem

- Engage your readers to convince them of the importance of the problem.
- Provide sufficient background information for your intended audience.

- Make sure that your thesis expresses why your analysis of the problem is important.
- Reread and revise to ascertain that you have adequately discussed the parts of the problem that require analysis and that you have related those parts to the problem as a whole.

Analysis of a Subject

Another type of analysis paper is one that examines a subject—a painting, poem, sculpture, car, contract, course, or short story. An analysis paper may also focus on a particular aspect of the subject—the composition of a painting, an image in a poem, the proportions of a sculpture, the motor of a car, the exceptions of a contract, the requirements of a course, or a character in a short story. These papers, too, involve breaking the subject into parts and closely examining its parts to show the reader their importance to the subject as a whole.

Brainstorming for a Topic If a topic has not been assigned, brainstorm to find a subject that interests you or on which you have some information. While it might not make sense for someone without mechanical aptitude to decide to analyze what is under the hood of a Volkswagen Jetta or for a mechanical engineering student to analyze "The Love Song of J. Alfred Prufrock," don't select a subject that is too familiar. The purpose of any writing assignment is discovery, and nothing will help you understand a subject better than careful analysis.

When to Use Subject Analysis

Instructors expect analysis when their assignments and exam questions contain words like *explain, interpret, describe, explore why, show how, explicate, discuss, relate,* or *trace.* If you have been asked to examine an art object, explain an economic plan, explicate a particular work of literature, explore why a company's health plan needs review, show how a historical treatise influenced a movement, trace a legal decision, analyze a candidate's platform, or describe a community's park system, you are required to examine the parts—or a part that has been assigned—and show how that part or those parts relate to the whole.

How to Write a Subject Analysis

Examine carefully the subject that you have selected or that has been assigned. Question the significance of the work, responding to it freshly. Don't assume that because it is a famous work of art or literature, it is therefore worthy of analysis. Determine for yourself why the subject is worth the time that you will devote to examining it.

If you have not been assigned a particular part to analyze, make a list of as many aspects or parts of the subject as you can. Then consider which parts are most significant and which you can most productively examine. In some cases, the success of your paper and how you will be evaluated will be determined by your ability to limit your selection to particularly provocative or relevant aspects. Ultimately, your job will be to show the significance of the parts or a particular part in relation to the entire work.

As introductory material, before you begin your analysis of the parts, describe the whole subject *briefly*. Remember that description is not the same thing as analysis, but realize also that your reader can't care about the parts without knowing something about the whole. Depending on the subject of your analysis, this introductory description might involve a historical context (of a treatise, bill, contract), an overall physical description (of a sculpture, painting, motor, person), or a summary (of a novel, short story, play, poem, bill, contract).

Write a description and detailed perception of the parts that you perceive to be the most significant for an understanding of the work. As you write an analysis of each part, keep your eye on the whole. Whether you are analyzing an art form, literary work, or object, you will need to return to your subject repeatedly to be sure that you are seeing or reading it thoroughly and carefully. You will not be able to write an analysis of a painting quickly glimpsed or a poem read only once.

Focus your paper with an assertion that shows your perception of the parts in relation to the subject that you are analyzing. Expressing your perception in the form of a thesis will keep both you and your reader on target.

Essay Assignments for Subject Analysis

Practice writing an analysis of one of the following topics:

1. A favorite painting or a photo from a magazine
2. The lyrics to a piece of music
3. A controversial campus policy
4. A piece of laboratory, electronic, or exercise equipment
5. The setting or music in a particular film
6. Mrs. Ardavi in "Your Place Is Empty" (p. 27)
7. Connie in "Where Are You Going, Where Have You Been?" (p. 101)
8. The multiple meanings of the word *artifice* in "A Work of Artifice" (p. 87)

9. The images in "The Blind Always Come as Such a Surprise" (p. 205)
10. The level of diction and word choice in "To Live in the Borderlands Means You" (p. 127)

Character and Poetry Analysis

Because literary analysis is frequently assigned in English courses and because narratives and short poems often are read in freshman composition classes, we include here a character analysis and a poem analysis to demonstrate the process of analyzing a subject. You will find that both narratives and poems are ideal for a focused subject analysis because the texts are short, yet there is plenty to analyze. Your thoughtful understanding of your life experiences will help you, as will a dictionary, but no research is needed, and all the details to be discusssed appear in the brief text.

What Is Character Analysis?

Character analysis can be used to study someone you know or someone in a text—a narrative, a poem, a short story, a novel, a play, or a biography. In history, psychology, art, and education courses you may be asked to analyze the traits of a particular person in order to understand the time period, the created work, or the behavior of important figures.

How to Write a Character Analysis Whether you are examining a subject from life or print, you will want to observe and record telling details—those that reveal something significant about the person. As you study a character, you will accumulate lots of facts, some that you will discard as irrelevant and others that you will decide are indicative of the person's character. From these facts you will be able to make assumptions about your subject's personality and character. In fact, the heart of your analysis will depend on inference—that is, a hypothesis that you formulate about character based on the facts that you have observed.

Prewriting for a Text-Based Character Study As you actively read the narrative or biography, list specific examples of speech, behavior, and thought that reveal the character. Read the text with an alert eye, pulling examples, important phrases, and key lines for your list. Mix facts and your responses or inferences about them as you go along. You do not need to evaluate each example as you write your list; you will sort, eliminate, and reword examples later.

Listing Information from a Book If you are keeping notes for a biographical study and are using a full-length book, you might find it useful to keep separate index cards for each character trait that you observe while you are reading. Record the page numbers each time you see that trait reappearing. By the time that you have completed a 300- or 400-page biography, you may have fifteen or twenty different inference cards, each with a different trait written at the top and each with many recorded page numbers. The cards that have similar traits can be grouped, the traits with few page numbers can be ignored, and the traits that look most useful for a character study can then be shaped into focus points for the paper. The page numbers on the cards that will form the focus points for the paper should be written into paraphrased and quoted note cards. These cards can then be arranged for a draft. This system of note taking, a variation of listing, is especially useful for longer texts.

Listing Information from a Short Story

If you are taking notes from a short text—a poem, play, or short story—you can use lined paper for your list. Here is how a list of character traits describing Hazel Peoples, the speaker and central character in Toni Cade Bambara's short story "My Man Bovanne" (p. 46), might look:

Plays checkers with a blind man—Shakey Bee

Dances close with a blind man—Bovanne

Talks late at night with men who call for "Mama comfort"

Laughs "real loud"

Argued with Elo about wigs

Sensitive—afraid she'll cry when children indict her dancing

Wears "short" dress

Wears "low-cut" dress

Thinks she can still wear sleeveless dresses

Gets loud when she drinks (her children's complaint)

Observant—notices Task's gesture is like his father's and grandfather's

Notices nobody got Bovanne a sandwich or talked with him

Outspoken—"You know what you all can kiss"

Hurt—when Elo's hand "landin light," like it didn't belong on her shoulder

"A chub-chub" and "not very pretty"—says about herself

Plans to buy Bovanne sunglasses—responsive to her children

Plans to make dinner for the family's organizational meeting

Plans to give Bovanne a bath, herb tea, massage

Will tell Bovanne he's needed to fix mailboxes and mimeo

Sees herself as a "hussy," as Elo always says she is

GROUPING AND ARRANGING

The grouping of like ideas on the list may be the next step in the prewriting of your character analysis. Find examples that belong together—usually because they support the trait that you have inferred about the person—and rewrite your list or number the examples on your list to reflect the commonality that prompts you to place the details together. If the reason the details belong together comes to you, or you realize that the details support a character inference, write down your idea.

Here is how the grouped list of details about Hazel Peoples might look:

Character Traits	*Inferences*
Wears short and low-cut dresses Wears sleeveless dresses w/o the "meat hangin" Outspoken—"You all know what you can kiss" Gets loud when she drinks Wears wigs	rebellious? brazen? vulgar? brash?
Plays checkers w/Shakey Bee Dances with Bovanne Talks late at night—"Mama comfort" Plans to give Bovanne a bath, massage, tea	caring
Plans to prepare dinner for the family Plans to help organize the community Plans to tell Bovanne he's needed to repair things	committed to community
Afraid she'll cry when her children criticize her	sensitive
Notices her son's gestures are like his father's Notices nobody is paying attention to Bovanne Feels Elo's hand landing too hesitantly on her Plans to buy Bovanne dark glasses	observant, knows feelings

Listing and grouping may take some time, but by listing the details of character that are important and by grouping items on the list that are analogous, you will have done a considerable amount of preparation for your paper.

Arranging and Thesis Construction Consider how you will arrange your character traits and the specific examples that support the traits. What do you want to emphasize in your analysis? Consider ending your character analysis with the trait that you find most significant or most indicative of character. By using your most emphatic point in the terminal spot in your paper, you will have a natural conclusion—one that gets at both the heart of your subject and the theme of the short story.

Perhaps the place to start is with the most obvious feature of the subject for analysis, because it will take less effort to convince your audience of your perception if your reader shares your perception. In the case of Hazel Peoples, her flamboyant exterior and behavior are probably the dramatic starting points for the analysis.

Determining a Thesis You need to have a thesis for your character study, whether or not you include it in your paper. You can determine one by using the character traits that you perceived during grouping. Remember that your thesis expresses a view about a limited subject, such as Hazel Peoples' character. If you have many observations on your prewriting list, you know you have good support ready.

Possible Thesis Statements Here are some possibilities for thesis statements for the character analysis of Hazel Peoples. Remember, each writer's perceptions and preferences will determine the thesis and the order in which the information will be presented.

1. Hazel Peoples is a sensitive woman whose caring commitment to her family and community is masked by her outrageous exterior.
2. Although Hazel Peoples seems to care about her family and friends, she is a vulgar woman whose behavior embarrasses her children.
3. In her speech, dress, and behavior, Hazel Peoples embodies the best and the worst of the 1960s and early 1970s.
4. Hazel Peoples' level of diction and word choice reveal her individuality and values.

Student Example: Character Analysis

As you read the following character analysis, notice that in addition to a thorough examination of the separate qualities of his subject's character, Hogan returns to the essence of the entire work to bring closure to his study.

Truth Beneath the Surface

Timothy Hogan

The old expression, "You can't judge a book by its cover," definitely applies to the character of Hazel Peoples in the short story "My Man Bovanne" by Toni Cade Bambara (46). Hazel Peoples dances with the blind man Bovanne, and then is scolded by her children because they judge her dress and manner as inappropriate and lewd. She is deeply hurt by her children's attack on her character, yet she still complies with their request to take charge of a political dinner the next night. However, Hazel plans on defying their wishes by bringing Bovanne to dinner. Although her exterior traits are viewed by her children as vile, Hazel Peoples is a truly liberated, empathetic and nurturing woman.

The picture of Hazel Peoples the reader sees is not at all flattering from an external point of view. She shows herself as a slightly inebriated, older woman who dances in an intimate way with a blind man—not just any blind man, but Bovanne, a man described by her children as a tom who "can smell a cracker a mile away" (49). Hazel's children criticize her manner of dress and her choice to wear a wig over her cornroll, something they had originally encouraged her to do. They chastize her for dancing so closely with Bovanne. Mrs. Peoples, at first glance and without further examination of her character, appears to be overtly flirtatious and in her children's view "a bitch in heat" (48). This brazen hussy most assuredly appears to be nothing more than a sleazy slut.

But then first impressions are often misleading, and it is on deeper exploration into her character that we realize Hazel is far more liberated than her apparently liberal children. Though her children are members of the Black Power Movement for civil rights, they choose to deny their mother the very right to be herself. Hazel Peoples is not at all a hussy; she is simply a sexually liberated woman. She has men folk calling her at night, for "mama comfort" she calls it, and when they get "messy," she changes the lock on her door. Her motivation for dancing with Bovanne has little to do with sexual advances; as she says, "Wasn't bout tits. Was bout vibrations" (47). Mrs. Peoples certainly understands the necessity to fight for liberties. And she defends her actions as her right to "enjoy [herself] cause [she's] a good woman" (50). Hazel intuitively understands the essence of what it is her children are striving for, even beyond their own comprehension of liberty and rights.

Hazel has a deep, empathetic understanding of human beings and their mannerisms, an ability to see beyond the surface of a person and into the truth of a person's character. Her account of the behavior of her blind friend Shakey Bee relates this empathy: "Blind people got a hummin jones if you notice. Which is understandable completely once you been around one and notice what no eyes will force you into to see people" (47). Hazel doesn't write off Shakey Bee because he is humming and grunting low. She has the compassion to adapt to this sound and even to grow to appreciate it—"it's like you in church"—except, of course, when she's playing checkers with him and wants to win! And while others forget about the goodness of Bovanne's nature, Hazel remembers and cares about this "nice man" who used to fix things for the very people who now cast discerning looks at him. Hazel sees Bovanne not as some old, useless blind man, but as someone who is overlooked despite all of his contributions to the community. Hazel relates her deep comprehension of human need when she comments to her children about the Reverend Trent. She says, "Reverend Trent a fool . . . the way he tore into the widow man up there on Edgecomb because he wouldn't take in three of them foster children and [his dead wife] not even comfy in the ground yet" (50). Hazel empathizes with people; she understands the need to look beyond surface impressions.

Hazel Peoples may not have the exterior qualities of the stereotypical mother, but her ability to nurture easily meets or exceeds expectation. Hazel cares; she is sensitive to the needs of people and meets needs where she can. Hazel chooses not to retaliate against her children's attacks on her. She organizes the family dinner for the political group because she realizes that others are in need of the benefits. This dinner can "get the breakfast program goin, and the school for the little kids," and she wants the older folk to know that they are still needed to "run the mimeo machine . . . and fix mailboxes" (52). Hazel's reason for asking Bovanne to dance comes out of her need to nurture, not because he is blind but because he is being overlooked and passed by. She plans on taking Bovanne home, to give him a bath and massage, and some herb tea. "Cause you gots to take care of the older folks. And let them know they still needed . . ." (51-52). Hazel values and understands people and their needs; she's a nurturing mother to more people than her ungrateful children.

Hazel Peoples reveals a truth that her children are unable to see: ". . . old folks is the nation" (52). The value of a person is not measured by something as superficial as age or dress. The value of a person is measured in terms of good character, an ability to empathize and nurture. Hazel Peoples has that character.

Work Cited

Bambara, Toni Cade. "My Man Bovanne." Between Worlds: A Reader, Rhetoric, and Handbook. 2nd ed. Susan Bachmann and Melinda Barth. New York: Longman, 1997. 46-52.

Small-Group Discussion

In small groups, discuss the strategies Hogan employs in his character analysis. Consider these questions:

1. What is the strategy of Hogan's introductory paragraph?
2. What is the thesis of this character study?
3. How does Hogan convince you that his character inferences are sound?
4. How is each paragraph individually focused? How is each paragraph related to the essay as a whole?
5. How does Hogan give his reader both an understanding of the parts of Hazel's character and their relationship to her as a whole? How does Hogan's character analysis contribute to your understanding of the short story as a whole?

PRACTICING CHARACTER ANALYSIS

In small groups, select one of these individuals and write a list of character traits: Darnell in "Proper Care and Maintenance" (p. 170), Matthew Soyster in "Living Under Circe's Spell," (p. 198), or Jennifer Coleman in "Discrimination at Large" (p. 207). Group the details that belong together, arrange the details, and write an assertion—a thesis—that would be workable for a character analysis.

What is Poetry Analysis?

When you are asked to write an essay about a poem, you will be expected to analyze it—that is, to study its parts and explain how they relate to the whole. This examination involves a closer scrutiny than an overview or summary. In a summary you relay what the poem is about or what happens in the poem. In an analysis you explain how certain elements function in the poem and why the poem is written as it is. While summary can't take the place of analysis, you might need to summarize as a part of analysis. But poetry analysis requires a close look at the elements of the poem.

Just as we can take apart a motor to see how the individual components work together, we can examine a poem to see how its elements contribute to the whole. The "whole" of the poem includes its meaning or the theme and insights that the poet wants us to gain from reading the work. Because poetry seems mysterious and unapproachable to some students, you might be intimidated by an assignment to analyze a poem. But if you realize that the elements of a poem are no scarier than the parts of a motor (and to some of us much less scary), you will be able to approach the poem and write about it, knowing that an examination of the parts will help you and your reader understand the poem as a whole.

What are the elements of a poem? Generally, in poetry analysis we focus on **key words, images,** and **figures of speech** (fewer parts than exist in a simple motor). The elements that you choose to analyze will depend on the poem you have chosen. We admit that you will need to read the poem several times before you can decide which element or elements to analyze, and you will need to know what these elements are. Have heart! Specific definitions, strategies, and examples follow.

Because poems are made up of words—interesting words or common words that may have obscure meanings—the dictionary is vital to the reader of poetry. In fact, an exploration of **key words** is a productive way to analyze a poem. Even though you may think that you know what a word means, the poet may be using a less known meaning of the word. Since most of us don't know the origin or obscure meanings of a word, a dictionary is indispensable in reading a poem. In addition to the **denotation,** or dictionary definition of a word, you should be aware of the **connotation,** or emotional association that the word conveys; the poet may be counting on your feelings about the word. Knowing the connotations, unusual definitions, or multiple meanings of a word is critical to understanding the poem.

For example, in Marge Piercy's "A Work of Artifice" (p. 87) the first association you may make with the word *artifice* is its connection with the word *artificial.* Confirm your hunch by checking a dictionary, where you will see that the word *artifice* comes from Latin words that mean "to make art." In fact, the poem does feature a gardener creating a bonsai tree, a work of art. You will also want to know the multiple denotations of the word *artifice* because they will help you understand the poem. Indeed, another meaning of the word *artifice* is a clever trick or strategem, and Piercy also shows that trickery and manipulation are related to the poem's theme. The word *artifice* has additional meanings, and each contributes to an understanding of the poem. Because words are the most basic element of any poem, the dictionary is a useful first step in analyzing poetry and helping you understand the other elements. Your knowledge of the multiple meanings of words can provide the focus for your analytic essay.

All poems consist of **images**—words that stir the senses: sight, sound, smell, touch, and taste. Because images are such vital elements of a poem, a productive analysis of a poem often involves examining particular images or patterns of images that seem to work together. In "On the Subway" (p. 168), Sharon Olds describes the passengers as "molecules stuck in a rod of light / rapidly moving through darkness." Olds creates an image—in this case a visual one—of passengers who seem insignificant, as tiny as molecules. These passengers are "stuck" on the subway car, which resembles a rod of light moving through the dark underground tunnels. The poet creates a visual picture of the entire subway world, and a close analysis of the imagery will help us understand that the poem is partially about being "stuck" and in the dark.

Images used suggestively rather than literally are called **figures of speech**, and a study of these figures can enhance your discussion of imagery. There are many kinds of figures of speech; the most common are metaphor, simile, and personification. A **metaphor** is an implied comparison between two unlike things. Poets aren't the only ones who use metaphors; you probably use them daily without realizing it. For example, when you say, "My boyfriend is a gem," you are comparing him to something that is valuable, dazzling, impressive, and maybe even sparkling. In Sharon Olds' image above, the poet implies a comparison between the subway car and a "rod of light." Part of your job in analyzing "On the Subway" might be to discuss the many comparisons between a subway car and a rod of light.

A **simile** is an explicit comparison using the words "like" or "as." In another poem, "Digging" (p. 21), the narrator claims that he holds his pen between his finger and thumb and the fit is "snug as a gun."

If you were focusing on the figures of speech in "Digging," you would want to analyze Seamus Heaney's comparison between the fit of a pen and the fit of a gun. You might also want to look at Heaney's use of personification: "the squat pen rests." **Personification** means giving human characteristics to an inanimate object, animal or abstraction. Heaney is creating the image of a pen that, like a human being, "rests," or lies tranquil.

You may hear people refer to a **symbol** or to **symbolism** when they are discussing poetry, and for that reason we will define and discuss the terms here. A symbol is something concrete that is used to represent or suggest something more abstract. For example, in Sharon Olds' poem "On the Subway" the narrator is carrying a briefcase, an object that suggests that she has a professional life. Her perception of how her life contrasts with the life of the boy sitting across from her encourages us to view her briefcase as a symbol. The briefcase does not just represent a job or profession. The briefcase suggests many abstractions: her social class, her affluence, her dignity, her power, and perhaps her control over her life. Like a stone tossed into water, a symbol sends out ripples of reverberating suggestions that contribute to our expanding notions of what the poet intends.

Words, images, and figures of speech are the basic elements of poems. In literature classes you may be asked to look at other elements when you write analytic papers. But these three elements will always be a part of your approach to a poem.

How to Actively Read a Poem

When you are assigned a poem to read, you need to read it through without worrying about what you don't understand. Then, in a second or third reading, read the poem aloud so that your ear catches connections that the poet intends. Just as you have been reading the essays in this book—actively—with a pen in hand, read the poem again and circle unfamiliar words, underline key words or lines, mark important ideas, and jot down comments in the margin. This is the time to use the dictionary to look up not only the words that may be new to you, but also words that may be used by the poet differently than you would expect. You need to write down the multiple meanings of each word as well as relevant origins of the word. Whether you prefer to write down these definitions on the page with the poem or on separate paper, it is important to record them for possible use later.

As you read, mark the examples of simile, metaphor, and personification, as well as images that relate to each other by similarity or contrast. Ask questions as you read: Why does the poet use a particular word? How do two images relate? Your responses to these questions provide notes that will help you choose the focus for your analysis.

Active Reading

Here is an example of active reading that a student, Jennifer Tabaldo, did to prepare for class discussion of Seamus Heaney's "Digging" (p. 21).

Digging

by Seamus Heaney

speaker holding pen

short & thick — *position of a digger*

Between my finger and my thumb
The squat pen rests; snug as a gun. — *surprising simile → aggressive*

Under my window, a clean rasping sound
When the spade sinks into gravelly ground:
My father, digging. I look down

Till his straining rump among the flowerbeds
Bends low, comes up twenty years away
Stooping in rhythm through potato drills — *strange word*
Where he was digging.

The coarse boot nested on the lug, the shaft
Against the inside knee was levered firmly. — *father holding spade*
He rooted out tall tops, buried the bright edge deep
To scatter new potatoes that we picked
Loving their cool hardness in our hands.

Proud!

By God, the old man could handle a spade.
Just like his old man.

My grandfather cut more turf in a day
Than any other man on Toner's bog.
Once I carried him milk in a bottle
Corked sloppily with paper. He straightened up
To drink it, then fell to right away
Nicking and slicing neatly, heaving sods — *grandfather holding spade*
Over his shoulder, going down and down
For the good turf. Digging.

harsh images: smell, sound, touch

The cold smell of potato mould, the squelch and slap
Of soggy peat, the curt cuts of an edge — *?*
Through living roots awaken in my head.
But I've no spade to follow men like them.

repeats opening

Between my finger and my thumb — *no gun simile*
The squat pen rests.
I'll dig with it. — *metaphor?*

Active Reading Discussed

You will notice that Jennifer circled key words, perhaps words that she needed to look up because she didn't know the meanings or thought the word might have an unusual meaning. She also blocked off words that were repeated, and she underlined similes and metaphors. She noted images and apparently discovered a pattern: narrator, father, and grandfather are all holding tools, whether spade or pen. She also marked images of harsh smells, sounds, and textures and commented on the narrator's "proud" tone as he praises his father's and grandfather's skills. Her active reading prepared her not only for class discussion but also for the essay that she was later assigned.

Although Jennifer and her classmates went through the poem line by line, questioning meanings and making observations about Heaney's word choices and imagery, Jennifer's instructor had warned the students that a written line-by-line explication could easily slip into mere summary. Therefore the instructor required that the students write an analysis that stems from a thesis. In a thesis-driven analysis the writer is controlling the organization of ideas rather than just following the lines of the poem.

The instructor also reminded students of the value of using the "sandwich" when incorporating quoted lines from the poem. You may want to review this technique (pp. 342–346). You will notice in Jennifer's paper that follows how skillfully she introduces the line she is quoting and how deliberately she explains and analyzes the words and images in each line that she includes. Notice that poetry lines are documented by line number in parentheses and that a break between two lines of a poem is indicated by a slash with a space on each side. (See pp. 554–555 for discussion of the slash.)

When Jennifer refers to the "narrator" of the poem, she means the speaker or "I" of the poem. In poetry analysis it is important not to assume that the poet and the speaker in a poem are always the same person. In this particular poem, Seamus Heaney may seem to be the speaker because he is a writer, but Jennifer avoids an unprovable assumption by using the word "narrator" or "speaker."

Jennifer used her active reading notes and ideas from class discussion to prepare the following analysis. Notice that she found the focus for her paper in the image patterns that she highlighted when she actively read the poem.

Student Example: Poetry Analysis

Digging Deep

Jennifer Tabaldo

Often a person is caught between his family's expectations for him and his own life choices. For some, this struggle results in frustration, rebellion, or a fear of inadequacy—of not measuring up to the family's standards. The fear of breaking tradition is the narrator's concern in Seamus Heaney's poem "Digging" (21). He reviews and comes to terms with his family's history as he discovers an acceptance of his own chosen career. In the poem, this acceptance is revealed in the images depicting the relationship between the family members and their tools.

The narrator's ambivalence toward his choice of writing as his life's labor becomes apparent in central images early in the poem. Although he depicts himself as a writer, a key simile reveals his discomfort in his relationship with his pen: "Between my finger and my thumb / The squat pen rests; snug as a gun" (1-2). Clearly, a writer's most valuable relationship should be that which exists between his pen and himself. The fit of the pen is so natural that it simply "rests" comfortably in his fingers. The pen's existance is so vital to him that his grasp is "snug," an image of him protecting the pen. The pen is warm and cozy in his grasp, but then the narrator shocks the reader with an unexpected simile: "snug as a gun" (2). Heaney's comparison between the pen and gun suggests the tension that the writer feels harboring a potentially powerful weapon or tool. The narrator seems insecure in his choice of writing as a career, and perhaps uses the gun simile defensively or rebelliously to protect himself from family criticism.

The narrator views his choice to become a writer as a choice not to become an actual digger and not to follow in his father's footsteps. His father was a potato farmer and spent a lifetime perfecting the art of digging. The son recalls his father at work, "the coarse boot nestled on the lug, the shaft / Against the inside knee was levered firmly" (10–11). These images of strength and skill illustrate the father's ease and comfort with his spade. The "coarse boot" is designed for heavy, fast, and rugged work and is "nestled on the lug" as if the two objects, the boot and lug, were meant to fit together, snuggly and comfortably. The shaft is "nestled" securely against the father's inside knee in a position that would exact the most efficient digging "rhythm." The son respects the competence and confidence that his father exhibits with his shovel.

This respect is apparent as he exclaims in awe, "By God, the old man could handle a spade. / Just like his old man" (15–16). It is obvious that the narrator's pride extends to his grandfather who "cut more turf in a day / Than any other man on Toner's bog" (17–18). The narrator's image shows the grandfather's efficiency and power "nicking and slicing neatly, heaving sods / Over his shoulder, going down and down / For the good turf" (22–24). Like the speaker's father, the grandfather developed an easy rhythm, "nicking and slicing neatly." His digging probably required even more physical energy than his son used in potato farming because "heaving sods / Over his shoulder" must have been back-breaking work.

Although the narrator admires his father and grandfather, he is also ambivalent, as we observe in the harsh images that attack our nose and ears: "the cold smell of potato mould, the squelch and slap / Of soggy peat" (25–26). Finally, it is the "curt cuts / Through living roots" that prompt the narrator to admit: "I've no spade to follow men like them" (28). Feeling apart from "them," he is unable to sever "living roots" as the men in his family do. But he is acutely aware of the patriarchal lineage that has existed in his family. He may sense his inability to excel at hard work as his father and grandfather did, and he sees that his failure to accept their physical, manly labor departs from the linear pattern and family tradition.

But he also must sense that the image of "going down and down for the good turf" is like the writer's search through layers of meaning to discover the truth. His forefathers' act of digging into the ground can be compared to the narrator's use of the pen to dig. Ultimately, the narrator must realize he can dig through many layers of experiences and family history—the living roots—to unearth the thoughts and feelings that he can put into words. He discovers that "digging" is a metaphor for his life's work, and we realize that he has found a common ground between the generations.

The narrator's epiphany is that he has carried on his family's tradition but with a different tool. Comfortable with this decision, he drops the opening simile that the pen is "snug as a gun"; it now simply "rests." The narrator hopes to attain, in his writing, the excellence that the grandfather achieved digging peat and that the father had digging potatoes. Ultimately, the narrator invites readers to experience the same epiphany: to discover that they, too, can admire their family's excellence and yet select their own life's work without conforming to family patterns and expectations.

Discussion of Essay

Jennifer's introduction opens with a few lines to capture audience interest in her topic—family expectations and children's fear of inadequacy—before she mentions the title and author of the poem she is analyzing. Then she builds a bridge to the thesis that she derived from her active reading notes. Her thesis sets up the organization for her paper because it requires that she examine "the relationship between family members and their tools." Thus she organizes her paper around a discussion of those images that show each family member—narrator, father, and grandfather—in relationship to tools.

The discussion of those images is the heart of her analysis. She not only incorporates the line smoothly, but also works with the language of the image. You may be surprised that her entire second paragraph is devoted exclusively to a discussion of the first two lines of the poem. Jennifer never expects the quoted line to stand on its own without her analyzing it. She also is careful to make sure that her interpretations of certain lines make sense in the context of the poem as a whole. Often, there is intentional ambiguity in a poem, and it is worthwhile to address it. For example, Jennifer speculates about the gun simile. She conjectures that "perhaps" the narrator "uses the gun simile defensively or rebelliously to protect himself from family criticism." Another reader of the poem might infer a different meaning in this simile. If you aren't sure about the poet's intention, you can soften your assertion with "perhaps" or "probably."

Without repeating herself, Jennifer's conclusion returns to her opening remarks about family patterns and expectations. She uses the word "epiphany," which undoubtedly came from class discussion. The word means a moment of sudden insight or revelation that is profound and possibly life-changing. Her entire paper, from the thesis on, anticipates the narrator's new awareness, even though she uses the term "epiphany" only in her conclusion.

PRACTICING POETRY ANALYSIS

In small groups, select one of the following poems and write a list of images that would be interesting to analyze: "A Work of Artifice," (p. 87), "On the Subway," (p. 168), or "Coke" (p. 249). Group the images that belong together, arrange the images in an order that makes sense, and write an assertion—a thesis—that would be workable for an analysis of the poem.

Poems in Part 1 for Analysis

Final Tips for Poetry Analysis

- Actively read the poem several times, marking key words, images, figures of speech, and your impressions.
- Note repetitions and image patterns that might help you find a focus for your analysis.
- Decide which elements provide the most productive approach to the poem and formulate a thesis based on that decision.

- Analyze the quoted words or lines that you have chosen to support your thesis. Remember to use the "sandwich."
- In your introduction, engage your audience and then briefly prepare your reader for your thesis. Give only enough summary of the poem that your reader has some context for your study.
- In your conclusion, return to your opening idea and your thesis without repeating yourself.

WRITING AN ESSAY EXAM

An in-class essay exam will require you to retrieve information that you know and to present it in an orderly way and with sufficient development that your instructor will be convinced that you know the material. Here is a six-step strategy that will help you present information that you know:

A Six-Step Strategy

1. Read the question more than once.
2. Determine what the question specifically requires you to do. Have you been asked to *define, list, summarize, compare or contrast, explain,* or *analyze?* See the list on page 453 for definitions of words that are commonly used on essay exams.
3. Briefly outline the material that will satisfy the question you were asked. Do not spend much time on this step; the outline can be brief, with only key words or phrases to remind you of material that you need to include.
4. Write a thesis that will focus your answer and possibly forecast the areas that you will develop in your response to the question.
5. Write the essay.
6. Reread your answer to correct errors in spelling and grammar. Use a dictionary if you are permitted to bring one to the exam. Do *not* plan to rewrite; you will seldom have sufficient time. If you recall material that would improve your essay, indicate that you have an insertion and write the added material on another sheet of paper.

It is most important that you understand exactly what the question requires you to do. For example, if the test question asks you to *list* the chemical elements that are commonly called salts, you are to enumerate—present in a list or outline form—the specific chemical elements called salts. An essay is not required, would be inappropriate, and might cost you points. If the question asks you to *compare and contrast* two subjects, and you show only how the subjects contrast, you have missed part of the question—how the subjects compare. The following chart will help you understand what is expected on exams.

Key Words Used on Exams

Word Used	*Meaning and Example*
analyze	Break into elements or parts and examine ("Analyze the job of the Attorney General of the United States," or "Analyze Piercy's use of 'artifice' in the poem 'A Work of Artifice' ").
compare	Look for and bring out points of similarity, qualities that resemble each other ("Compare the legislative branches of the state and national governments").
contrast	Stress the dissimilarities, differences ("Contrast the roles of Jim and the Duke and Dauphin as father figures for Huck Finn").
define	Give the meaning of a word or concept ("Define the term 'archetype' ").
describe	Give an account, word picture, or narration ("Describe the Aztec civilization at Teotihuacan," or "Describe the method for providing emergency first aid to an accident victim").
discuss	Examine, and consider from different points of view ("Discuss the use of pesticides in controlling mosquitoes").
explain	Make clear, interpret, tell the meaning of, tell how ("Explain how humans can, at times, trigger a rainstorm").
justify	Show good reason for, give evidence to support your position ("Justify the American bombing of Iraq").
relate	Show correlation, how things are connected ("Show the relationship of early childhood education to elementary school academic success").
summarize	Give the main points or facts in condensed form, omitting details ("Summarize the plot of *Othello*").
trace	In narrative form, describe the progress, development, or history of events ("Trace the opening of the American West through the development of wagon-train trails").

If you understand the meaning of words used in exams, you will not lose points or time by pursuing a direction that will fail to give you full credit for the information that you know.

An Outline for an In-Class Essay

Any of the practice assignments on page 454 could be posed as in-class essay exams. First we present a brief sample outline that would lead to a focused in-class essay. Try outlining answers to the practice assignments to improve your skills and as a study review of the essays that you have read.

Summarize and *discuss* the important issues raised in Ben Mattlin's "An Open Letter to Jerry Lewis" (p. 201).

1. Lewis' language is offensive
   —Stereotypes of "victims"
   ex. plight, curse, confined, bound
   ex. "dealt a bad hand" or "got in the wrong line"
   ex. needing help isn't an "indignity"
   ex. "kids"—offensive to adults!
   ex. "cripple" is in-group slang only
2. Lewis' inaccuracies are offensive, mislead, exploit
   ex. disabled kids aren't taunted by other kids
   ex. airports accommodate wheelchair passengers
   ex. life-expectancy is normal, not "if"
   —pity brings in money but depresses disabled
3. Dignity is needed, not pity
   —What is MDA really doing to help?
   employment?
   —Is MDA reducing obstacles: architectural, financial, attitudinal?
4. Show well-adjusted, active, normal disabled people

Each of the four areas contributes to the *summary* of Mattlin's issues. Each of the numbered points would be treated in a separate paragraph, with the key words noted in each section to become part of the specific development and exemplification in the *discussion* of Mattlin's grievances against Lewis and his telethons. Point number four would probably be an effective conclusion to the in-class essay. The thesis might forecast that *language, inaccuracies,* and *the question about what the MDA really does to help the disabled* are the central issues in Mattlin's letter to Jerry Lewis.

■ PRACTICING OUTLINING FOR IN-CLASS ESSAYS

1. Define irony and describe three specific examples of irony in Bambara's short story "My Man Bovanne" (p. 46).
2. Summarize and discuss Armin Brott's point in "Not All Men Are Sly Foxes" (p. 72).
3. Compare and contrast characteristics of the "senior" and "teener" in "Senior-Teener: A New Hybrid" (p. 17)
4. Using Martin Luther King's essay "Three Ways of Meeting Oppression" (p. 295), discuss how people meet oppression and explain why King favors one response over the others.

10

Writing the Research Paper

■ ■ ■

Assigned by most freshman composition instructors and loved by few freshman composition students, the research paper has a worse reputation than it deserves. Like most tasks that at first seem overwhelming, such as packing the car to go away to school or preparing for a party, the research paper needs time and organization. The steps suggested here and the model of a student paper in this section should help you handle the project.

PLANNING THE RESEARCH PAPER

Time Schedule for the Research Paper

Even if you had outstanding luck in high school and welded a research paper together in an amazing overnight session, your college professor probably won't be forgiving of the "solder drips" of hasty welding, and you may find your course grade threatened by a poorly prepared research paper. Instead, admit to yourself that the research paper requires your attention through a number of steps, all of which you can handle.

Further, the paper may allow you to experience the pleasure of discovering some new interest and information. If your instructor gives you some choice in your topic, take advantage of this opportunity to find out more about something that you really do want to learn more about. Instead of selecting a topic that is familiar or seems easy, pursue one that intrigues you, one that is worth the time and energy that you will devote to the investigation.

Some instructors assign due dates for the various stages of the paper. If yours does not, try dividing the time between the assigned date and the due date into four approximately equal parts. For example, if you have two months for the preparation of this paper, each stage will have two weeks. If you have one month, you can give each stage a week of your time.

STAGE 1

—*Determine the topic* that interests you and satisfies the requirements of the paper assigned. Allow a few days for this, but do not let yourself postpone that first decision for longer than a few days.

—Go to the library and begin your search for materials. Use the computers and *meet the reference room librarian*—the researcher's best friend. Ask the librarian whether your topic has additional subject headings that you should be aware of so that you can do a *complete* search while you are in the library. Make bibliography note cards for each source. (See the model note cards on pp. 461–462.)

STAGE 2

—*Read and take notes* on the material that you have found. If you take notes in the library on material that you do not intend to photocopy and take home with you, write direct quotations and paraphrase these later, when you know how much material you want to use. Keep accurate records of titles, authors, and page numbers so that you do not need to return to the sources to find information that you need for correct documentation. (This step will be discussed more completely on pp. 461–462.) As you take notes, think about how you might focus your paper.

STAGE 3

—*Determine a working thesis* and write an outline for the paper.

—*Write a draft* of your paper and meet with your instructor or writing center staff for feedback before you begin the revision.

—*Revise* your manuscript, strengthening the thesis, improving the arrangement, using more emphatic support, improving word choice and transitions, and clarifying any writing that your reader found ambiguous or weak.

STAGE 4

—*Type* your paper, the works-cited page, and, if your instructor prefers one, a cover sheet with the title and your name, section, professor's name, and date. (See the MLA model on p. 468.)

—*Proofread your manuscript* from cover page through the works-cited page. Neatly correct *all* typing and other errors that you discover. If you have a major correction—for example, an entire sentence omitted when you typed from your draft—you may need to retype the page or edit on your computer.

If you divide the research paper assignment into parts, you will not be overwhelmed by the task. You may discover that the time allotted for a certain stage is not realistic for you. For example, you may realize that you need longer to draft and revise your paper and less time for stage 4; this may be true if you are working on a word processor. But think how comfortable you will be if you still have 25 percent of your time for that final preparation of your manuscript.

GATHERING LIBRARY MATERIAL

Getting Started

Shannon Paaske's instructor required a research paper that was more developed and used more sources than the shorter documented papers that had been assigned in her composition course. In addition to the length and source requirements, Shannon's assignment was to respond more fully to one of the subjects included in the reader of *Between Worlds.* Shannon considered the topics that had been discussed in class, and she realized that she wanted to learn more about the world of the disabled.

Her initial response to the research paper may have been posed in the form of *questions:* What are the problems the disabled have in attending classes? In working? In their social lives? There appears to be interesting technology for the disabled on my campus; what *is* available to help the disabled? What kind of legislation exists to help the disabled? How do the disabled feel about their conditions? Are the attitudes of Mairs and Mattlin characteristic of the disabled? Have they written any other articles that aren't in this text?

With these questions in mind, Shannon went to her college library.

Meet the Librarian The week before the longer research paper was assigned, Shannon's composition instructor arranged a class library tour. The reference librarian showed the students how to use the computers and indexed guides for book and periodical searches.

The librarian will show you how to find books in the stacks and how to find and use the microfilm machines. All libraries have trained assistants whose job it is to show you how to find the microfilm reels and how to thread the film into the machine. You should never feel embarrassed to ask for help and instruction. Even professors who have used microfilm numerous times will ask for help when they haven't used the machines for a semester or two.

Finding Information

Before you begin your search for materials, ask a librarian for information about the library that you are using and anything about the computers that you do not understand. Each library has its own computer system with particular choices for you to make about the type of search that you can conduct (such as "keyword" or "browse"). Every time you use a new library or begin a different research project, ask the librarian which type of search he or she would recommend for the books that you need and which type of search for the periodicals. Many students leave libraries empty-handed or with few sources because they have not used the correct search or because they have not entered all of the appropriate headings.

The reference librarian should not be expected to do your work for you, but you will find that reference librarians know more ways to discover material than you can imagine. For example, a student's search for information on "Elephant Man's Disease" was thwarted when she used this term to find listings in the computer. But the reference librarian knew to consult the Library of Congress Subject Headings to find the correct search term: "neurofibromatosis" for the research project. Your library has information on just about every topic, so if you are not finding what you need, realize that you may be using an incorrect heading or misspelling a term. Computers are helpful, but it often takes a human being—a librarian—to show you how to access that help. Better than always giving you the answers, most librarians will also show you the process for finding the information for your research.

Electronic Sources Part of the research process has become computer-based, and students have found that electronic sources can help them locate materials easily and efficiently. When you go to the library, you are undoubtedly already using a computerized online catalogue to obtain the bibliographic information that you need to locate books and periodicals in your library system. In addition, you will discover that your college and community libraries have various other computerized services. In some cases the computer service will provide an abstract (or summary) of the text that you are seeking. In other cases, for certain periodicals the full text will appear on the screen. Your library may have the computer attached to a printer so that you can make your own copy of the abstract or article.

It is critical that you record the bibliographic information about the electronic sources that you use just as you record the information from printed sources. To fail to do this is plagiarism, using someone else's words or ideas without giving proper credit. This is a serious offense that may result in your being expelled from school or fired from a job. The form that you will use to document electronic sources is explained on pp. 499–501. You should look at this before you begin your search on the computer so that you will know what information to record.

Remember that reference librarians know the most recent electronic sources and how to use them. Never hesitate to ask questions of these highly skilled professionals—even computer buffs do!

Glossary of Computer-Related Terms Two terms that you will hear and use constantly are *hardware* and *software.* Hardware refers to the actual machinery, such as the computer, printer, keyboard, monitor, mouse, modem, and disk drive. Software consists of the programs that direct the operation of a computer or that process electronic data such as word processing programs, databases, and games.

The following glossary of terms is not comprehensive, but it will help you understand some of the vocabulary associated with computers.

CD-ROM (Compact Disk Read-Only Memory): a disk that stores text, data, graphics, and sound.

database: data such as bibliographies, abstracts (summaries), full texts, and spreadsheets that are stored electronically.

diskette or floppy disk: a portable storage medium (typically 3 ½ inches) used to save files and to move and retrieve information from machine to machine.

electronic mail (commonly called e-mail): a system for sending and receiving individual or organizational messages over the computer. (See essay on pp. 425–426.)

FAQ (rhymes with "back"—Frequently Asked Questions): common questions with answers posted at a Usenet news site or an online journal or report.

Gopher: a tool on the Internet that provides menus to help access information. The Gopher system is being replaced by the more appealing World Wide Web system.

hypertext: computerized documents that contain built-in special phrases that link to other documents, pictures, or sounds. These links are usually designated by being underlined or color-coded; clicking on a link (with a computer's mouse) causes the computer to access this new material.

Infotrac: an online service available at many public libraries and at some colleges that provides some full-text databases as well as databases with abstracts.

Internet: a global network of computer networks connecting universities, libraries, government offices, and corporations. Initially most users were educators, writers, scientists, and researchers, but now people use the Internet to bank, shop, chat with strangers or celebrities, play games, or catch up on news events. The Internet has an electronic mail system that lets users exchange e-mail with other subscribers.

Internet service providers: companies such as Netcom, AT&T Worldnet, and Earthlink that, for a fee, provide access to the Internet. Other providers, such as Compuserve, Prodigy, and America Online, offer online services in addition to access to the Internet.

modem: a device that converts material from a computer into tones that can be sent through telephone lines. Similarly, material from another computer can be converted into tones and received into a computer through a modem.

publication medium: the type of information source used such as a book, magazine, newspaper, film, videotape, CD-ROM, World Wide Web, and diskette.

Usenet news: a service that is available on the Internet. It includes postings and responses to the postings, all organized by topic. Newsnet can be compared to a global bulletin board system.

URL (Uniform Resource Locator): the address of a site on the Internet such as a World Wide Web page or Gopher site. You should be aware that occasionally a World Wide Web site or a Gopher site will cease to exist or may be changed to a new address.

Wilson Line: provides an electronic index (with some full-text sources available). Sources include the Readers Guide to Periodic Literature (a bibliography of popular magazines such as *Time* and *Newsweek*), the Humanities Index (a bibliography of scholarly journals in literature, history, and the arts), and the Social Sciences Abstracts Index (summaries of research on social issues).

World Wide Web (also called the Web, WWW, or W3): a service available on the Internet that provides global access to information in the form of texts, pictures, movies, and sounds by simply pointing and clicking. The World Wide Web is a hypertext-based system that allows the user to move from document to document by clicking on links that are underlined or color-coded.

Use and Abuse of Electronic Sources The value of doing an electronic search for materials is that you can locate materials that are not in your local libraries but may be in a library thousands of miles from your campus. Further, you can read material that may not yet be available in print, written as recently as the day of your search. You can also use certain computer services, such as Usenet news, to post questions about research materials and sources that readers around the world may help you answer. Also, using certain services, you can obtain maps, pictures, and graphics that can enhance your research.

Although you may find the ease of having instantly printed articles attractive, you won't want to rely exclusively on these ready sources for data in your papers. Remember that your classmates will have the same temptation, and you want your essay to give the reader unique information, not a clone of a classmate's paper. Also, you cannot always know the reliability of material from the Internet. Further, many superb materials are not available on a computer attached to a printer but are in conventional bound books on library shelves. So don't settle for fast-food take-out when there is an entire banquet in the library!

Evaluating Sources Your topic will determine the kinds of supporting material you will need in your paper. If your topic requires up-to-date information (news events, current legislation, technological or medical data, or recent statistics), you will want to consult periodicals. As the term implies, they are issued periodically, and therefore they are timely. If your writing does not require current information or if it necessitates an overview (or legislative changes, economic patterns, fashion trends, art, or political movements), you may want the depth and perspective that books provide. In addition to periodicals and books, don't neglect videos, films, and interviews as potential sources of information.

Sample Bibliography Cards

Shannon started by recording on index cards the bibliographic information that she would need to document her sources. Because she used cards instead of a sheet of paper, Shannon would be able to arrange the cards alphabetically when the time came to type her works-cited page. If your library provides you with a printed copy of the bibliographic information of books and periodicals that you are using for your essay, you may decide to use those sheets, arranging them in alphabetical order by author's last name when you write your works-cited page.

Here are *sample bibliography cards* for the note-taking phase:

For a book

PS	Nancy Mairs
508	"On Being a Cripple" from
P56	With Wings: An Anthology of Literature
W58	by and about Women with Disabilities.
1987	Ed. Marsha Saxon and Florence Howe.
	New York: Feminist Press,
	1987. 118-127.

For a periodical

Rab, Victoria Y. and Geraldine Youcha. "Body." <u>Omni</u>
June 1990: 22+.

Shannon began the reading and note-taking process after she had collected the books and had photocopied the pages of the periodical articles that were available and seemed most relevant to her subject. In earlier class assignments, Shannon had practiced summarizing and paraphrasing the main ideas of work that she used. She also had practiced finding and extracting the best parts of a writer's work to use in quoted form in her own writing. Because Shannon had worked with incorporating other writers' ideas and language into her material, she understood the problem of *plagiarism.*

Plagiarism

Using someone else's ideas or language as your own, accidentally or deliberately, is a serious offense that schools may punish with expulsion. If you are desperate to complete an assigned paper, using somebody else's work may seem like a good idea to you. *Don't do it.* Failing a course or risking expulsion from school cannot be a sensible decision. Talk to your instructor about your anxieties, then determine that you will do the work with integrity.

Plagiarism most often occurs inadvertently. Often, it occurs because of sloppy note taking, poor record keeping, or even ignorance. You can avoid this problem by assiduously recording, from your earliest notes on, the source of every idea—even in summary or paraphrased form—and of every key word or phrase of another writer that you are using. Plagiarism also occurs if you incorrectly begin or end the quotation marks that designate the quote you are incorporating into your text. Further, if you change or omit *anything* in the text that you are quoting, you need to use brackets (see p. 554) and ellipses (see pp. 552–553) to signify to your reader that you have made a change. Plagiarism also occurs if you incompletely or inaccurately cite the source of material that you have used. Make certain, even from the first note-taking sessions, that you have correctly recorded *all* of the information that you will need for your works-cited page. Examples of inadvertent plagiarism are shown below so that you can avoid this error in your own work.

Inadvertent Plagiarism Plagiarism occurs if a quotation is not used or documented correctly. Read the original, from Marcus Mabry's "Living in Two Worlds" (p. 124) and the incorrect uses of the quotation on page 463:

Original:

> Most students who travel between the universes of poverty and affluence during breaks experience similar conditions, as well as the guilt, the helplessness and, sometimes, the embarrassment associated with them. Our friends are willing to listen, but most of them are unable to imagine the pain of the impoverished lives that we see every six months. Each time I return home I feel further away from the realities of poverty in America and more ashamed that they are allowed to persist. What frightens me most is not that the American socioeconomic system permits poverty to continue, but that by participating in that system I share some of the blame.

Identify the incorrect uses of the material in each of the following examples:

1. Marcus Mabry talks about the student who travels between the universes of poverty and affluence during school breaks.
2. Mabry is frightened by the fact that "the American socioeconomic system permits poverty to continue" and that "by participating in that system" he shares some of the blame (124).
3. One student who was studying at Stanford describes the guilt, helplessness and the embarrassment that he and other students feel when they move between their school lives and their home lives when they return home for vacation.
4. Mabry is concerned not that "the American socioeconomic system permits poverty to continue, but that by participating in that system he shares some of the blame" (124).

Explanation of Errors

1. In his mistaken notion that he has "only paraphrased," this writer has failed to place quotation marks around Mabry's words "who travel between the universes of poverty and affluence." Additionally, the student has not documented with parenthetical information the source of the material that he has taken from

Marcus Mabry. Even if the student were to use only the image of the "universes of poverty and affluence," the image is Mabry's and must be documented.

2. This writer has misrepresented Mabry. The original expresses the idea that it is *not* America's "socioeconomic system" that frightens him but his fear that "by participating in that system" he "shares some of the blame." The writer has written a combination of paraphrase and quotation that does not correctly express Mabry's point.
3. The writer here has attempted a paraphrase of Mabry's words that stays too close to the original in repeating "guilt," "helplessness," and "embarrassment" without using quotation marks and that fails, in any case, to attribute and document the source of the idea.
4. This writer has made a change in Mabry's quoted material to merge her text smoothly with Mabry's words. But the writer has failed to use brackets to inform the reader that there is a change in the quoted material. This is how the quotation should look: "'the American socioeconomic system permits poverty to continue, but that by participating in that [he shares] some of the blame.'"

You may fear that there are too many ways for you to make mistakes when you use another writer's ideas or words in your essays. But if you carefully copy material from another source, double-check your paraphrases, and inspect your quoted material and compare it to the original to verify that you have been accurate in your sense as well as in the use of quotation marks, brackets, and parentheses, you will avoid the inadvertent plagiarism that threatens your integrity as a writer and flaws the writing that you produce.

With the goal in mind of paraphrasing and quoting carefully those relevant sections of her collected texts, Shannon began making note cards for her paper.

Sample Note Cards

The note cards that Shannon wrote during stage 2 of her paper preparation looked like these:

Original text:

"People without the use of their arms or legs can now rely on computerized 'sip and puff' machines. With light puffs into a plastic straw, users can switch on the TV and change its channels, telephone a friend and play computer games."

Paraphrased note card

"Machines — Miracles"
Ann Blackman p.70

Other developments include computerized "sip and puff" machines which enable peoplewithout the use of their arms or legs to change television channels, talk on the phone, and play computer games by inhaling or exhaling into a plastic straw.

Original text:

"We used to look at people who were disabled as shut-ins," [Jan Gavlin] says. "Not anymore. Computers, new materials and new attitudes have revolutionized our industry. If you can move one muscle in your body, wiggle a pinkie or twitch an eyebrow, we can design a switch to allow you to operate in your environment."

Quotation note card

"Machines — Miracles"
Ann Blackman p.71

According to Jan Gavlin, director of assistive technology at the National Rehabilitation Hospital in Washington, "If you can move one muscle in your body, wiggle a pinkie or twitch an eyebrow, we can design a switch to allow you to operate in your environment."

Developing a Working Thesis

While she read from her collection of materials and took notes, Shannon began to focus on her subject in a sharper way. She realized that there were a number of ways to approach the subject of the disabled, but that she was especially interested in three: technology that equips disabled people to leave home and enter the outside world, the media's recent interest in depicting the disabled, and the attitudes of the nondisabled person toward the disabled. Her working thesis looked something like this:

> Technology and the media have improved life for the disabled, but they still suffer social isolation and indignities.

Shannon talked with her instructor about her working thesis and the rough outline of the three parts that she planned to write. (For a complete discussion of outlining and for illustrations, see pp. 333–336.) After discussing her plan and what she had found in her research, Shannon and her instructor concluded that she did not have enough information about the social isolation of disabled people and that her own casual observations would be insufficient for a well-developed research paper. The instructor suggested that Shannon approach the special resources center on the campus to arrange interviews with disabled students who would be willing to talk about their social situations. Further, both the instructor and Shannon concluded that they knew very little about legislation that gave rights to the disabled, and both realized that any reader would want to know something about this legislation.

Gathering Additional Information, the Interview

Before she started the first draft of her paper, Shannon returned to the library to collect information on the legislation that gives disabled people access and ensures their rights. She made summary note cards of the legislation that had been passed. She discovered some old laws that were so ridiculous that they could provide a dramatic introduction for her paper.

Shannon also contacted the director of her campus special resources center and collected names and telephone numbers of students that he thought would enjoy talking with her. She needed an extra few days to arrange to meet and talk with these students. Shannon conducted three interviews with disabled individuals to use their experiences to support her research. More than reflecting their perspectives, she was able to catch their actual voices in print.

Preparing for the Interview To catch voices to use in your paper, you need to do some prior work. You will want to think through exactly what additional support you hope to gain from the interview. It helps to prepare an "icebreaker" question or two to put your interviewees at ease. If you suspect that they may be guarded or unwilling to reveal the information you need—particularly for an argument essay, in which they may represent the opposing position—you should order your questions so that the milder ones come first. Once the interviewees are engaged in conversation, it will be easier to get them to answer more hard-hitting questions.

Your questions should be written down in the order that you plan to ask them. If you number the questions, you can use these same numbers as you record the answers during the interview so that you don't have to rewrite the question, or even the topic, when you are taking notes.

Conducting the Interview Although you have prepared questions and ordered them, you may find that the answers cause you to skip to another question or to think up a question on the spot. Your ability to respond with follow-up questions and encouragement

("Why do you think that happened?" "How did you respond?") may determine the depth of the interview. Such follow-up questions may prompt the subjects to move from predictable responses to ones that are fresh and candid.

As you take notes, concentrate on getting down key phrases and controversial claims. Shannon recorded this from one of her interviewees: "Some people are prejudiced and ignore us. That makes me angry." Shannon put quotation marks around exact words so that she could remember which words were her subject's and which she added or paraphrased. As you interview your subjects, don't hesitate to ask them to clarify points or expand on ideas so you can get the necessary information.

Some interviewers use portable tape recorders as a backup to capture precise words, but tape recorders haven't replaced notebooks. Relying on tape recorders can be disastrous if the machine is malfunctioning or the tape turns out to be inaudible. Even if the tape is clear, it is tedious to sit through an hour or two of taped conversation to transcribe the key quotations. Before you leave, remember to ask about additional sources or reference materials (reading materials, brochures, and names of other specialists).

Because these people are giving you some valuable time for the interview, it is essential that you offer to meet where and when it is convenient for *them.* Prepare your questions before the meeting, arrive on time, and don't overstay your welcome. Remember to be exceptionally courteous and to show appreciation for their time and help.

Recording the Interview Immediately after the interview, write out or type up the questions and answers while the session is still fresh in your mind. If you discover that you have missed any important material or may have misunderstood a point, call your interviewee back immediately for a clarification.

When you integrate the interviewees' comments into your paper, be careful to quote exactly and to represent the context of the statement accurately. Misusing quotations or distorting their intended meaning destroys your integrity as a writer.

Shannon found that her conversations with disabled people provided insights that her readings could not. The strength of her argument, however, could not rely only on interviews and personal experiences. She used seven printed sources, including an article from *Scientific American,* to develop her argument.

Sample Student Paper

Shannon Paaske's full paper is included here. The numbers on the manuscript correspond to the numbers of the explanations on the facing page. These explanations will guide you through the rhetorical and form considerations for your own paper.

3.

1.

Paaske 1

Shannon Paaske
2. English 1A Sec. 6336
Prof. Douglas
November 17, 1996

From Access to Acceptance: Enabling America's Largest Minority 4.

In the early 1900's, a Chicago city ordinance stated that no "unsightly, deformed or
maimed person can appear on the public thor-
oughfares" (Davidson 62). A court case in Wis- 5.
consin in 1919 upheld the expulsion from
school of a twelve-year-old boy with cerebral
palsy because his teachers and fellow students
regarded him as "depressing and nauseating"
(62). In contrast to these limiting laws of
the first half of the 20th century, the second
half has drafted legislation and designed
equipment to improve life for the disabled. In 6.
1990, the Americans with Disabilities Act was passed by Congress. This enormous piece of legislation, among other things, requires both public buildings and private businesses to provide architectural access for disabled persons and it prohibits discrimination against them in the workplace. In 1991, a customized, computerized van allows a man paralyzed from the chest down to operate a motor vehicle by himself. And as this century concludes, major network television shows such as _Life Goes On_, _L.A. Law_, and _Star Trek: The Next Generation_ have regularly featured people with all types of disabilities.

Explanatory Notes for the Research Paper

The numbers on these explanatory notes correspond to the numbers in the margin of the research paper.

1. *Form.* Shannon types her last name and the page number of her manuscript in the upper right corner of *each* page of her paper. She leaves a one-inch margin on the sides, top, and bottom of each page of her paper.
2. *Heading.* According to the MLA, you do not need to use a separate sheet of paper for a title page. If your instructor prefers one, include the information required here and print it on the lower right corner or centered on a plain sheet of typing paper that will precede the first page of your manuscript.

   To follow the MLA form, begin your *heading* on the first page of your manuscript, one inch from the top of the first page and flush with the left margin. Include your name, the course number and section, your instructor's name, and the date on separate lines, double-spacing between them. Double-space again and center your title and then double-space between your title and the first line of your manuscript. Do *not* put quotation marks around or underline your title.
3. *Holding the paper together.* Secure the pages of your paper with *one* paper clip, as the MLA advises, or with a staple, as many instructors prefer. If you have the choice, use the staple because it will keep the pages together better than a paper clip. Either the staple or the paper clip is less expensive, more ecologically sound, and holds the manuscript together better than a plastic slide-on binder.
4. Your *title* should engage your reader by establishing an appropriate expectation for what the paper is about, and it should please your reader's ears as well as eyes. If your reader stumbles while reading your title, you need to work on it. Shannon establishes the focus of her paper, the disabled person's wish for "access" *and* "acceptance." Notice that she uses the strong verb "enabling," and she raises a possible question in her reader's mind about America's "largest minority." That question can be an effective way to engage the reader.
5. *Citations.* Shannon's opening sentence includes a quotation, so she must document the source. She ends her quotation and, without other punctuation, uses parentheses to enclose the last name of the author of the article and the number of the page on which she found the ordinance that she quotes. Any reader who wants more information about the article will find complete information on Shannon's works-cited page at the end of the manuscript. The second time that Shannon quotes material from Davidson's article, she uses only the page number; the reader understands that quoted language from the case study is also from Davidson, noted in the parenthetical citation above. Notice that the terminal punctuation, a period, appears outside the closing parenthesis.
6. *Introduction.* Shannon's introduction is a dramatic, abbreviated history of the legislation, equipment changes, and media responses to the disabled in this century. She cites two remarkable examples from the beginning of the century to engage her reader, and she concludes her first paragraph with the evidence of profound change in the last decade of the century. She chose to use the exact language of the ordinances, rather than paraphrasing their content, because the language is pointed and emphasizes the history that Shannon is writing about in her analysis.

Paaske 2

Clearly, America's institutions have come
a long way in acknowledging the 43 million 7.
people in this country with disabilities
(Blackman 70). Although combinations of technological advances, equality-promoting legis- 8.
lation, and increasing media exposure have
worked as a collective force in bringing
about improvements in the lives of the people
who make up what is sometimes termed
"America's largest minority" (Davidson 61), 9.
ignorance and prejudice continue to plague
the disabled.

Technological developments, almost exclusively computer-oriented, have revolutionized
the world of the disabled person. Citizens 10.
who were once confined to home, forbidden to
travel by air, and unable to attend classes
or enter businesses have been liberated by
recent inventions that encourage independence
as well as allow for enriching life experiences. Just how extensive is the new technology? According to Jan Gavlin, director of assistive technology at the National
Rehabilitation Hospital in Washington, "If
you can move one muscle in your body, wiggle a
pinkie or twitch an eyebrow, we can design a
switch to allow you to operate in your environment" (qtd. in Blackman 71). 11.

An example of one such device is the Eye-
gaze Response Interface Computer Aid (ERICA),
developed by biomedical engineer Thomas
Hutchinson at the University of Virginia. This
eye-controlled computer empowers severely
disabled yet bright people with the ability to

7. *Statistic acknowledgment.* Shannon notes that there are "43 million" disabled people in the United States. She documents this figure with a reference to her source, Blackman, and the page of the article on which she located this figure.
8. *Thesis.* Shannon's thesis, which begins with "although," prepares the reader for the problem that her paper will explore. Her intention is to forecast: to look at the technical and legislative changes and the increased media exposure as improvements for the disabled. But she will also examine the problems that "plague" the disabled and prevent their full acceptance.

9. *Uncommon knowledge quoted.* It is not common knowledge that the disabled are "America's largest minority," so Shannon documents the source of this statement with a parenthetical reference to Davidson's article and the page on which this statement was made.

10. *Summarized material.* In this section of her paper, Shannon summarizes the technological developments that illustrate positive steps that are being taken to enable the disabled. Shannon notes the previous limitations for the disabled before she cites specific equipment changes that have "revolutionized" their lives.

11. *Quotation within the article.* Shannon quotes a knowledgeable source, the director of assistive technology at the National Rehabilitation Hospital in Washington, Jan Gavlin, as he is quoted in Blackman's article. Because she wisely has used Gavlin's name in her paper, Shannon needs only to note that he is "quoted" in Blackman and give the page number on which his quoted comment appears. If she had not used Gavlin's name in her text, her in-text citation would have looked like this: (Gavlin qtd. in Blackman 71).

Paaske 3

learn and communicate. Ten years ago these people would have been misdiagnosed as mentally retarded by traditional tests that are unable to correctly measure their intelligence. Originally designed for children who previously might have been misdiagnosed, ERICA and other systems like it instead "create pathways for kids to express themselves and
for teachers to engage their minds" (Rab and 12.
Youcha 22).

Other developments include computerized "sip and puff" machines which enable people
who can't use their limbs to change television 13.
channels, talk on the phone, and play computer games simply by inhaling or exhaling into a plastic straw (Blackman 70). A system called DragonDictate is a computer program that prints dictation onto a monitor when the user speaks into a microphone (70). This type of program is especially useful to people who are unable to type because of poor muscle control (a characteristic of cerebral palsy) or who have various types of paralysis. The system even comes with a spell-check mode that responds to the incorrect word with an "oops."

Modern wheelchair designs also reflect the recent advancements that permit the disabled to leave home and enter the world. Robert Cushmac, 16, who was paralyzed from the neck down in a car accident when he was 10, gets from class to class at his Virginia high school, where he is an honors student, in a wheelchair activated by a chin-controlled joystick (Blackman 71). The Hi-Rider is a

12. *Two-author citation.* The quoted comment from an article written by two authors is used to conclude one section of the material on technological advancements. In the parenthetical reference is the last name of each author, connected with "and," and the page number of the article where the quotation appears.
13. *Paraphrased material.* Shannon describes in her own words how the "sip and puff" machine is used. She documents the source of her information, first with the author's last name and page number of the article where she found the information and then with the page number only. If Shannon had thought there would be any confusion in her reader's mind about the source of her information in this section of her paper, she would have repeated Blackman's name (as she does in the next paragraph) in addition to giving the page number of the article.

Paaske 4

"standing wheelchair" that was designed by Tom Houston who is paralyzed from the waist down. His design makes it possible for him to perform tasks previously impossible, such as reaching an object on an overhead shelf, or greeting someone face to face (Blackman 70).

As these examples show, the continuous
headway being made in adaptive technology has 14.
considerably altered the way of life for many
disabled people. However, it is highly unlikely that much of this progress could have been accomplished without the help of a sympathetic political climate. Federal Disability Laws passed by Congress since 1968 addressed the environmental needs of the disabled and particularly focused on independent living as a goal. This goal expressed the desire of people with disabilities to view themselves and be viewed "no longer as passive victims deserving of charitable intervention but as self-directed individuals seeking to remove environmental barriers that preclude their full participation in society" (DeJong and Lifchez 45).

Laws such as the Architectural Barriers Act of 1968 required buildings built with federal funds or leased by the federal government to be made accessible, and the Urban Mass
Transportation Act and Federal Aid Highway Act 15.
of 1970 and 1973 worked to make transportation a reality for the disabled (DeJong and Lifchez 42). Later laws were created to achieve the attitudinal changes implicit in the objectives of the independent living movement. One law is

14. *Transition.* Shannon moves from her review of the technological advancements designed to enhance the lives of the disabled to a review of legislation that has given them rights. Notice that her transition establishes that the technological advancements would not have occurred without the legislative changes. This is a more critically perceptive transition, showing a cause-and-effect relationship, than one that suggests merely that "another change for the disabled is in the area of legislation."

15. *Paraphrased and quoted material.* Shannon summarizes the various laws and acts and documents her source of information, the *Scientific American* article written by the two authors noted in her parenthetical references throughout this portion of her text. Her review of this legislation is historical, and it is chronologically arranged.

The Rehabilitation Act of 1973, which prohibits discrimination against disabled people in programs, services, and benefits that are federally funded. The Rehabilitation Comprehensive Services and Developmental Disability Amendments of 1978 established independent living as a priority for state vocational programs and provided federal funding for independent living centers (DeJong and Lifchez 42). The Social Security Disability Amendments of 1980 gave disabled people more incentives to work by letting them deduct independent-living expenses from their taxes (42). The Americans With Disabilities Act, signed in 1990, reinforced the legislation that was not earlier implemented. But because the law takes effect in gradual stages, the result of all of its provisions have not yet been fully realized. However, as each stipulation is introduced, its impact on the whole of American society will be undeniable. 16.

Equally undeniable is the fact that laws such as these, together with the flourishing of adaptive technology, have created greater awareness of the disabled in our
communities. The increasing number of dis- 17.
abled characters in movies and television reflect that awareness. Deaf actress Marlee Matlin, for example, has enjoyed success, starring in the Academy award-winning *Children of a Lesser God* in 1986, and in the television series *Reasonable Doubts*. In assessing Matlin's character in *Reasonable Doubts*,

16. *Conclusion to one section and transition to the next.* Shannon concludes her review of the legislation with a statement that the provisions of the most recent act for which she has information have not yet been fully implemented. She believes that the impact will be "undeniable" when the act is fully in effect.

17. *New focus point.* Again, Shannon relates the next section of her paper to the previous sections by asserting that technology and legislation have made the disabled visible citizens in our communities. The media have reflected this visibility by increasing the number of disabled people employed in film, television, and advertising.

Paaske 6

Ben Mattlin (no relation), a writer with a 18.
muscular dystrophy-related disease, says he
"can't say enough good things about working a
highly visible disability into a major character" (Mattlin 8). Ben Mattlin also finds it 19.
significant that this character was portrayed
as both intelligent and sexy. In addition, on
ABC's <u>Life Goes On,</u> Christopher Burke, an actor who has Down's Syndrome, played Corky, a
"competent, high-functioning integral part of
his family" (Mattlin 8). Because Matlin and
Burke are disabled actors who portray disabled characters—in contrast to the many
able-bodied actors who play disabled roles—
they have helped mark a path of new acceptance for the disabled.

Progressing along that path are retail
stores that employ the disabled to model in
their advertising. In 1991, retail store Kids
R Us hired disabled children from hospital pe-
diatric wards to work as professional models
for their catalogues and circulars. Some of
the store's executives got the idea while
watching these kids play. Vice President Ernie
Speranza reasoned, "They think of themselves
as average kids, so we decided we should too"
(Speranza qtd. in Yorks 1). Kids R Us was not 20.
the first retail store to make this move, and
since 1990, Target and Nordstrom's—representing both ends of the economic spectrum—have
hired disabled people of all ages as models in
an effort to better represent the diversity of
its clientele (Yorks 1).

Although efforts such as these indicate that the media have "started to get a broader

18. *Parenthetical explanation.* Shannon makes a point of noting that the media critic, Ben Mattlin, is no relation to Marlee Matlin. She is then free to use Mattlin's name in parenthetical documentation without concern that her reader will be perplexed.

19. *Summary and direct quotation.* In a combination of summarized information and direct quotation, Shannon uses Ben Mattlin's article about the depictions of disabled actors in various media. She was tempted to use Mattlin's critical comments about the "distorted images" of the disabled in particular films, but she realized that this digression would change the balance and focus of her paper. From Mattlin's article, she used only what was relevant to her essay—brief references to actual programs and actors and the appreciation of a disabled writer for positive portrayals of the disabled in film.

20. *Quotation within the article.* The vice president of a retail store is quoted within an article that Shannon read about the use of disabled people as models in advertising. She quotes him in her text and notes his name and the page of the quotation in her parenthetical reference.

perspective on real life" (Olson), people with 21.
disabilities have yet to enjoy full acceptance by American society. Nancy Mairs, a woman with multiple sclerosis who balances a college teaching and lecturing career with the demands of a marriage and motherhood, finds that while her family and the people she works with have accepted her disability, she still has had to endure an end-of-the-semester evaluation by a student who was perturbed by her disability
(122). 22.

While no longer blatantly discriminated against, the disabled often continue to suffer the burden of social bias. Even those remarkable individuals who are able to triumph over physical barriers have trouble surmounting social barriers. Post-polio actor Henry Holden relates his own experience with social discrimination:

> A guy with paralyzed legs is not 23.
> supposed to be able to sell insurance, but I did very well at it in New Jersey before I became an actor. A guy with paralyzed legs is not supposed to climb mountains, but I made the trek up the cliff at Masada in Israel at four o'clock in the morning. A guy with paralyzed legs is not supposed to ride horses, but I rode in an exhibition in Madison Square Garden. Yet I am not generally accepted by nondisabled people in social situations. The attitude in the country is that, if you have a disability, you should stay home. (Holden qtd. in Davidson 63)

21. *Quotation from an interview.* Because there are no page numbers associated with interviews, only the last name of the subject interviewed is enclosed in the parentheses. Shannon uses Steve Olson's comment about the value of images of the disabled in advertising as a transition to the final section of her paper. This section focuses on the feelings that disabled people have about nondisabled people's perceptions of them. Shannon gained these insights in interviews as well as readings.

22. *Paraphrased and summarized material.* An experience noted by an author in her essay is summarized and paraphrased by Shannon, and the source of the material is documented.

23. *Long quotations.* Because the experience of the actor Henry Holden is especially revealing, Shannon decided to include the long quotation in her paper. Because the quotation is longer than four typed lines, it cannot be incorporated within the manuscript. Instead, the longer quotation is set off from the rest of the paper with double-spacing at the top and bottom of the quotation, and it is indented ten spaces from the left margin. The quotation itself is double-spaced, and the final period *precedes* the parenthetical information.

Susan Rodde, who has cerebral palsy, confirms that in most social situations, "we,
the physically challenged, have to be the
icebreakers." At parties and social gatherings, the disabled person is often isolated
or ignored. Having used a wheelchair since a
surfing accident, Berkeley student Steve Olson confirms this experience: "Sometimes I
meet people at parties who feel uncomfortable
about [my disability]. I talk and tell jokes 24.
to break the ice, and soon no one realizes
there's a disabled person—me—sitting in the
room with them." Unfortunately, the "ice"
does need to be broken because many people
feel uncomfortable around disabled or disfig-
ured people, and so far, the responsibility
of making social contact lies with the disabled person.

But many of the disabled report that fully
abled people have a hard time "respecting the 25.
fact that we're the same as they are," says
Diane DeVries, who was born with no legs and
only partial arms. Perhaps because of ignorance or fear, our disabilities "remind people
of their own vulnerabilities" (DeVries). As 26.
Nancy Mairs says, "Society is no readier to
accept crippledness than to accept death, war,
sex, sweat, or wrinkles" (119). 27.

Because they may feel vulnerable, able-bodied people tend not to form close relationships with disabled people, and some even refuse casual contact. Rebecca Acuirre, 16, who has cerebral palsy, says that she recently asked a stranger what time it was and he kept

24. *Brackets.* Shannon has enclosed in brackets a change that she has made in material from an interview. It is possible that her subject used a pronoun that would have been ambiguous to the reader; Shannon substituted the noun and placed the clarifying term in brackets. The reader understands that the brackets are used to clarify or change tense or other language forms to permit easy reading of the quoted material as it is integrated with the writer's text. No changes may be made and put into brackets that would alter the meaning of the material quoted. (See p. 554 for more information about brackets.)

25. *Incorporating short quotations.* Shannon incorporates into her text the specific quoted material from her reading and interviews. When the subject of an interview is named in the text, there is no need for additional documentation.

26. *Interview subject quoted.* Because Shannon does not reuse Diane DeVries' name in her text, she documents the source of the quotation by using DeVries' last name in parentheses.

27. *Documentation from a book.* Nancy Mairs' name is used in Shannon's text, so only the page number of the book is cited in parentheses.

walking as though he didn't hear her. "Some people are prejudiced and ignore us. That makes me angry," she says.

How can these prejudices be abolished? "We need more exposure," says DeVries. Acuirre concurs, saying the media should do more to educate the public. On a personal level, Bill Davidson, in "Our Largest Minority, Americans 28.
with Handicaps," recommends the nondisabled public "help reverse centuries of discrimination" by getting to know disabled people "at work, in the marketplace, at school" and by making "contact that is real—not just casual" (63). Able-bodied people can help overcome their own preconceived notions and realize that if disabled people seem bitter, "it's not because of their disability . . . but because of society's attitude toward them." Prejudices can be stopped before they start by encouraging children "not to shun and fear" the disabled (63).

The legislation and technology that have
developed at the end of this century will 29.
continue to make new worlds accessible to the disabled. Ideally, these developments will permit the disabled to be viewed in terms of their capabilities rather than their disabilities. In that climate, the disabled can gain acceptance in the worlds to which they have access. With the steps being taken by government, science, and the media, individuals alone are needed to make the dream of acceptance a reality for the disabled.

28. *Incorporating summary and quotations.* Shannon introduces the author and title of the article in her text. This attribution within her text facilitates Shannon's documentation; she needs to note only the page number within the parentheses. Her citations document the specific quoted material as well as the paraphrased content of Davidson's article.

29. *Conclusion.* In her conclusion, Shannon reviews the relationship between the points she has made in her paper. She concludes by asserting that the advancements for the disabled lie in the hands of individuals, not only institutions. She uses the language of her title to bring a more dramatic closure to her analysis.

Paaske 10

Works Cited 30.

Acuirre, Rebecca. Personal interview. 23 Sept. 31.
1992.

Blackman, Ann. "Machines That Work Miracles." 32.
Time 18 Feb. 1991: 70-71.

Davidson, Bill. "Our Largest Minority: Americans 33.
with Handicaps." McCall's Sept. 1987: 61-68.

Dejong, Gerben and Raymond Lifchez. "Physical Dis- 34.
ability and Public Policy." Scientific American June 1983: 40-49.

DeVries, Diane. Telephone interview. 22 Sept. 1992. 35.

Mairs, Nancy. "On Being a Cripple." With Wings: 36.
An Anthology of Literature by and about
Women with Disabilities. Ed. Marsha Saxon
and Florence Howe. New York: Feminist Press,
1987. 118-127.

Mattlin, Ben. "Beyond Reasonable Doubts: The Me- 37.
dia and People with Disabilities."
Television and Families 13.3 (1991): 4-8.

Olson, Steve. Telephone interview. 18 Sept. 1992. 38.

Rab, Victoria Y. and Geraldine Youcha. "Body." 39.
Omni June 1990: 22+

Yorks, Cindy LaFavre. "Challenging Images." Los 40.
Angeles Times. 22 Nov. 1991 LA ed.: E12.

30. *The form for the list of sources used in the text.* The heading "Works Cited" is centered on the line that is one inch from the top of the page. The first cited work is typed two lines beneath the heading. The entire list is double-spaced. The list is alphabetically arranged by the author or speaker's last name or by the first word in the title of an unsigned article. The entry begins at the left margin. If it is longer than one line, its second line begins five spaces indented from the left margin. (More complete information on MLA form is on pp. 488–502.)

31. Entry for a personal interview. The date of the interview is noted.

32. Entry for a signed article in a weekly periodical.

33. Entry for a signed article in a monthly magazine.

34. Entry for a magazine article written by two authors.

35. Entry for a telephone interview. The date of the interview is noted.

36. Entry for a chapter within an anthology with two editors. Notice that the name of the author of the chapter Shannon used is listed first.

37. Entry for a signed article in a periodical with volume and number.

38. Entry for a telephone interview.

39. Entry for two authors of an article within a monthly periodical. Notice that the article started on page 22 but did not appear on continuous pages. The "+" symbol indicates that the pages were not consecutive.

40. Entry for a signed article in a daily newspaper. Notice the "E" preceding the page number to indicate the section of the newspaper in which the article appeared.

DOCUMENTING THE RESEARCH PAPER: MODERN LANGUAGE ASSOCIATION (MLA) STYLE

Whenever you use the words, information, or ideas of another writer—even in your own words as a summary or paraphrase—you must credit the source. Before 1984, writers gave credit to their sources by using numbers that referred to notes at the bottom of the page or at the end of the manuscript on a separate sheet of paper. In contrast to this older method, the new MLA style guide liberates the writer from hours of tedious work. Instead of using footnote numbers, you will place the necessary information in parentheses immediately following the quoted or paraphrased passage.

The forms illustrated below will show you exactly how to provide the necessary information for documenting your sources. The fourth edition (1995) of the *MLA Handbook for Writers of Research Papers* is the source of this guide, and it is certainly the form that your college English instructors will want you to use.

Writing Parenthetical Citations

Your in-text citation should give just enough information that your reader can find the origin of your material on the works-cited page (your bibliography) at the end of your paper. Here are sample parenthetical citations to illustrate MLA format:

Author Not Named in the Text When you haven't included the author's name in your text, you must note in parentheses the author's last name and the page or pages of your source.

"The first steps toward the mechanical measurement of time, the beginnings of the modern clock in Europe, came not from farmers or shepherds, nor from merchants or craftsmen, but from religious persons anxious to perform promptly and regularly their duties to God" (Boorstin 36).

Author Named in the Text It is often advantageous to introduce your paraphrased or quoted material by noting the author's name within your text, especially if your author is an authority on the subject. If you do include the author's name in the text, your parenthetical citation will be brief and less intrusive, containing only the page number by itself.

According to Daniel Boorstin, the senior historian of the Smithsonian Institute, "The first steps toward the mechanical measurement of time, the beginnings of the modern clock in Europe, came not from farmers or shepherds, nor from merchants or craftsmen, but from religious persons anxious to perform promptly and regularly their duties to God" (36).

Two Books by the Same Author If your paper contains two different works by the same author, your parenthetical reference will need to give an abbreviated form of the title, with the page number, so that your reader will know which work you are using in that particular section of your paper.

Ben Mattlin deplores the pity for the disabled that Jerry Lewis' yearly telethon evokes ("Open Letter" 6). Mattlin also exposes the hypocrisy in depicting the disabled as superheroes. His point is that "courage and determination are often necessary when living with a disability. But there's nothing special in that, because there's no choice. Flattering appraisals sound patronizing . . ." ("Beyond Reasonable Doubts" 5).

A Work with Two or Three Authors If the work was written by two or three authors, use each of their names in your text or in the parenthetical citations.

In their study of John Irving's The World According to Garp, Janice Doane and Devon Hodges analyze the author's attitude toward female authority: "Even novels that contain sympathetic female characters, as Irving's novel does, may still be oppressive to women" (11).

Critics have charged that John Irving's The World According to Garp doesn't really support female authority: "Even novels that contain sympathetic female characters, as Irving's does, may still be oppressive to women" (Doane and Hodges 11).

A Work with More Than Three Authors If your source was written by more than three authors, you may use only the first author's last name, followed by "et al." (which means "and others") and the page number, in parentheses or you may list all of the authors' last names in the text or with the page number in parentheses.

In Women's Ways of Knowing: The Development of Self, Voice, and Mind, the authors note that there are many women who "believed they were stupid and helpless. They had grown up either in actual physical danger or in such intimidating circumstances that they feared being wrong, revealing their ignorance, being laughed at" (Belenky et al. 57).

In Women's Ways of Knowing: The Development of Self, Voice, and Mind, the authors note that there are many women who "believed they were stupid and helpless. They had grown up either in actual physical danger or in such intimidating circumstances that they feared being wrong, revealing their ignorance, being laughed at" (Belenky, Clinchy, Goldberger, and Tarule 57).

In Women's Ways of Knowing: The Development of Self, Voice, and Mind, Belenky, Clinchy, Goldberger, and Tarule note that there are many women who "believed they were stupid and helpless. They had grown up either in actual physical danger or in such intimidating circumstances that they feared being wrong, revealing their ignorance, being laughed at" (57).

Author's Name Not Given If the author is anonymous, use the complete title in your text or an abbreviated form of the title with the page number in the parentheses.

The obituary for Allan Bloom in Newsweek describes him as the man who "ignited a national debate on higher education" and "defended the classics of Western Culture and excoriated what he saw as the intellectual and moral relativism of the modern academy" ("Transition" 73).

Corporate Author or Government Publication Either name the corporate author in your text or include an abbreviated form in the parentheses. If the name is long, try to work it into your text to avoid an intrusive citation.

Southern California Edison, in a reminder to customers to "Conserve and Recycle," gives the shocking statistic that "every hour, Americans go through 2.5 million plastic bottles, only a small percentage of which are now recycled" (Customer Update 4).

Literature: Novel, Play, Poem Because works appear in various editions, it is best to give the chapter number or part in addition to the page number to help your reader find the reference you are citing.

Novel

In the novel Invisible Man, Ralph Ellison uses a grotesque comparison to describe eyes: "A pair of eyes peered down through lenses as thick as the bottom of a Coca-Cola bottle, eyes protruding, luminous and veined, like an old biology specimen preserved in alcohol" (230; ch. 11).

Play

In William Shakespeare's Othello, Emilia sounds like a twentieth century feminist when she claims that "it is their husbands' faults" if their wives have affairs (4.3.89-90).

Poem

Poet Robert Hass, in "Misery and Splendor," describes the frustration of lovers longing to be completely united: "They are trying to become one creature, / and something will not have it" (13-14).

Indirect Source When you use the words of a writer who is quoted in another author's work, begin the citation with the abbreviation "qtd. in" and both writers' names if you have not used them in your text.

Women and men both cite increased "freedom" as a benefit of divorce. But Riessman discovered that women meant that they "gained independence and autonomy" while men meant that they felt "less confined" and "less claustrophobic" and had "fewer responsibilities" (Catherine Kohler Riessman qtd. in Tanner 40-41).

More Than One Work If you want to show that two works are the sources of your information, separate the references with a semicolon.

Two recent writers concerned with men's issues observe that many women have options to work full time or part time, stay at home, or combine staying at home with a career. On the other hand, men need to stay in the corporate world and provide for the family full time (Allis 81; Farrell 90).

Preparing the Works-Cited Page

Whenever you note in parentheses that you have used someone else's material, you will need to explain that source completely in the works-cited list (the bibliography) at the end of your manuscript. To see how this page will look, refer to the student research paper on page 486.

Because the complete source is listed only in the works cited, it is essential that each entry conform exactly to standard form so that the reader can easily locate your source. Most of the forms that you will need are illustrated below.

Elements of a Citation

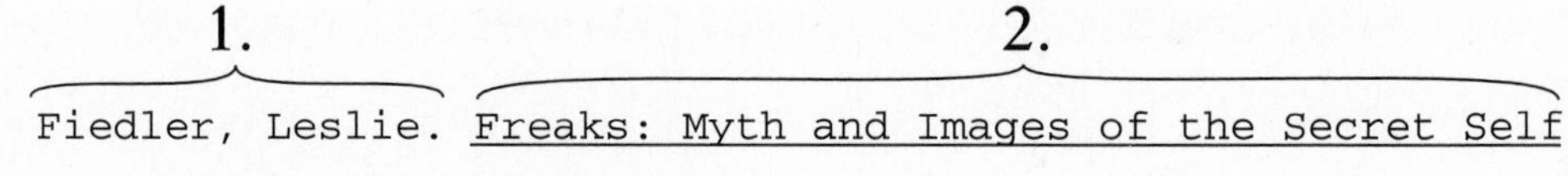

1.
2.
Fiedler, Leslie. Freaks: Myth and Images of the Secret Self.

6.{ New York: Simon, 1978.

3. 4. 5.

1. Use the author's full name—last name first—followed by a comma and then the first name and any middle name or initial. Omit any titles (Dr., Ph.D., Rev.). End with a period and one space.
2. Print the book's full title including any subtitles. Underline the title and capitalize the first letter of the first and last words as well as all important words. If there is a subtitle, separate the main title and the subtitle with a colon and one space. Place a period after the title and leave one space.
3. Type the publication information beginning with the city of publication, followed by a colon and one space.
4. Print the name of the publisher, followed by a comma. Shorten the name to remove "and Co." or "Inc." Abbreviate multiple names to include only the first name. (The "Simon" in the above example refers to Simon & Schuster.)
5. Include the date of publication and end with a period.
6. Any line after the first line is double-spaced and indented five spaces.

Sample MLA Entries

Books

One Author

Fiedler, Leslie. Freaks: Myths and the Images of the Secret Self. New York: Simon, 1978.

Two or Three Authors

Doane, Janice and Devon Hodges. Nostalgia and Sexual Difference: The Resistance to Contemporary Feminism. New York: Methuen, 1987.

Notice that any authors' names after the first author are written with the first name before the last name.

More Than Three Authors or Editors

Boardman, John et al., eds. The Oxford History of the Classical World. New York: Oxford UP, 1986.

or

Boardman, John, Jasper Griffin, and Oswyn Murray, eds. The Oxford History of the Classical World. New York: Oxford UP, 1986.

With more than three authors you have the choice of shortening the entry to provide only the first author's name, followed by the Latin abbreviation "et al." ("and others"), or you may provide all of the names.

Author with an Editor

Shakespeare, William. King Lear. Ed. Alfred Harbage. Baltimore: Penguin, 1969.

Cite the name of the author first and then, after the title of the work, give the editor's name, preceded by "Ed." (When "Ed." appears as a title before the name, it is capitalized. When "ed." appears after the name, as in the following example, it is in lower case.)

Book with an Editor and No Author Cited

Allen, Donald M., ed. The New American Poetry. New York: Grove, 1960.

If the book does not have an author, cite the editor's name, followed by "ed."

Selection from an Anthology or Collection

Roethke, Theodore. "I Knew A Woman." <u>The Collected Poems of Theodore Roethke</u>. New York: Doubleday, 1975. 122.

Mairs, Nancy. "On Being a Cripple." <u>With Wings: An Anthology of Literature by and about Women with Disabilities</u>. Ed. Marsha Saxton and Florence Howe. New York: Feminist P at City U NY, 1987. 118-27.

Give the author and title of the selection, using quotation marks around the title. Then give the underlined title of the anthology. If the anthology has an editor, note the name or names after the "Ed." Give the page numbers for the entire selection as shown above.

Two or More Selections from the Same Anthology

Anzaldúa, Gloria, "To live in the Borderlands means you . . . ," Bachmann 127.

Bachmann, Susan and Melinda Barth. <u>Between Worlds: A Reader, Rhetoric, and Handbook</u>. 2nd. ed. New York: Longman, 1997.

Olds, Sharon. "On the Subway." Bachmann 168.

To avoid repetition, give the full citation for the book once, under the editor's last name. Then all articles are listed under the individual authors' names, followed by the title of the work. After each title, put the editor's name as a cross-reference to the complete citation.

Two or More Books by the Same Author(s)

Olsen, Tillie. <u>Silences</u>. New York: Dell, 1979.

---. <u>Tell Me a Riddle</u>. New York: Dell, 1985.

Give the name(s) for the first entry only. After that, in place of the name(s), type three hyphens, followed by a period and one space and then the next title. The three hyphens always stand for exactly the same name(s) as in the preceding entry. The titles of the author's works should be listed alphabetically.

Corporate Author

National Council of Teachers of English. Guidelines for Nonsexist Use of Language in NCTE Publications. Urbana, Illinois: NCTE, 1975.

Use the name of the institution or corporation as the author even if it is also the name of the publisher.

Author Not Named

The Oxford Dictionary of Quotations. 2nd ed. New York: Oxford UP, 1964.

If a book has no author noted on the title page, begin the entry with the title and alphabetize according to the first word other than "a," "an," or "the."

Other Than First Edition

If you are citing an edition other than the first, place the edition number between the title and the publication information. (See above.)

Republication

Melville, Herman. Billy Budd, Sailor (An Inside Narrative). 1924. Chicago: U Chicago P, 1962.

If you are citing a work that has been published by different publishers, place the original date of publication (but not the place or publisher's name) after the title. Then provide the complete information for the source you are using.

Book Title Within the Title

Gilbert, Stuart. James Joyce's Ulysses. New York: Vintage, 1955.

If the title of the work that you are using contains another book title, do not underline or place the original book title in quotation marks.

Story or Poem Title Within the Title

Lessing, Doris. "The Temptation of Jack Orkney" and Other Stories. New York: Knopf, 1972.

If the title of the work that you are using contains a title that is normally enclosed in quotation marks (a short story or poem), keep the quotation marks and underline the entire title, extending the underlining to include the final period and closing quotation mark: Dare to Eat a Peach: A Study of "The Love Song of J. Alfred Prufrock."

Multivolume Work

Raine, Kathleen. Blake and Tradition. 2 vols. Princeton: Princeton UP, 1968.

If you have used two or more volumes of a multivolume work, state the total number of volumes in the work. Place this information ("2 vols.") between the title and publishing information.

Malone, Dumas. The Sage of Monticello. Boston: Little, Brown, 1981. Vol. 6 of Jefferson and His Time. 6 vols. 1943-1981.

If you are using only one volume of a multivolume work, give the title of that volume after the author's name and then give the publishing information. After the publishing date, note the volume number, the title, and the number of volumes in the collection. If the volumes were published over a period of years, indicate the dates.

Translation

Ibsen, Henrik. A Doll's House and Other Plays. Trans. Peter Watts. New York: Penguin, 1965.

When citing a work that has been translated, give the author's name. After the title, give the translator's name, preceded by "Trans."

Introduction, Preface, Foreword, or Afterword

Grumbach, Doris. Foreword. Aquaboogie. By Susan Straight. Minneapolis: Milkweed, 1990.

If you are citing material from an introduction, preface, foreword, or afterword written by someone other than the author of the book, give the name of the writer and designate the section that she or he wrote. Notice also that "Foreword" above is without underlining or quotation marks. After the title of the work, "By" precedes the author's name.

If the author of the introduction or preface is the same as the author of the book, give only the last name after the title:

Conrad, Joseph. Author's Note. Youth: A Narrative; and Two Other Stories. By Conrad. New York: Heinemann, 1917. 3-5.

Article in an Encyclopedia or Other Reference Books

Benet, William Rose. "Courtly Love." The Reader's Encyclopedia. 1948 ed.

"Hodgkin's Disease." The New Columbia Encyclopedia. 4th ed. 1975.

If there is an author of the edition or article, alphabetize by last name. Otherwise, alphabetize in the works-cited page by the title of the entry.

Periodicals: Journals, Magazines, and Newspapers

Journal with Continuous Pagination

Culp, Mary Beth. "Religion in the Poetry of Langston Hughes." Phylon 48 (1983): 240-45.

Journals sometimes paginate consecutively throughout a year. Each issue, after the first one, continues numbering from where the previous issue ended. After the title, give the volume number and the publication date in parentheses, followed by a colon and the page numbers.

Journal That Paginates Each Issue Separately

Hardwick, Julie. "Widowhood and Patriarchy in Seventeenth-Century France." Journal of Social History 26.1 (1992): 133-48.

If the journal numbers each issue separately, give the volume number, a period, and the issue number (as in "26.1" in previous example) after the title of the journal.

Monthly or Bimonthly Periodical

Mazzatenta, O. Louis. "A Chinese Emperor's Army for Eternity." National Geographic Aug. 1992: 114-30.

Notice that in a monthly or bimonthly periodical the month of publication is abbreviated, and no volume or issue numbers are given.

Weekly or Biweekly Periodical

Fotos, Christopher. "Right-to-Fly Law Spurs Operators to Provide Access for Disabled." Aviation Week & Space Technology 8 June 1992: 58-60.

Daily Newspaper, Signed Article

Soto, Onell R. "Putting the Tag on Graffiti-Smearers." Press Telegram 28 Jan. 1992: B3.

Daily Newspaper, Unsigned Article or Editorial

"Back to Future: The Nation's Cities." Editorial. Los Angeles Times 3 May 1992: M4.

If the newspaper is divided into numbered or lettered sections, give the section designation before the page number, as in "M4" above. If the article continues on a nonconsecutive page, write only the first page number followed immediately (no space) by a + and a period.

Rosenbaum, David E. "Budgetary Posturing." New York Times. 2 March 1995, late ed.: A1+.

If the newspaper has editions (late ed., natl ed.), include this item after the date and before the colon.

Titled Review

Ansa, Tina McElroy. "Taboo Territory." Rev. of Possessing the Secret of Joy, by Alice Walker. Los Angeles Times 5 July 1992: 4+.

The page number "4+" in the citation above indicates that the article starts on page 4 but does not continue on consecutive pages.

Untitled Review

Shore, Paul. Rev. of Backlash: The Undeclared War Against American Women, by Susan Faludi. The Humanist Sept.-Oct. 1992: 47-48.

Other Sources

Interview

Acuirre, Rebecca. Personal interview. 23 Sept. 1992.

Olson, Steve. Telephone interview. 18 Sept. 1992.

Film or Videotape

Children of a Lesser God. Dir. Randa Haines. With William Hurt, Marlee Matlin, Piper Laurie, and Phillip Bosco. Paramount, 1986.

If you want to refer to a particular individual involved with the film, cite that person's name first:

Matlin, Marlee, actress. Children of a Lesser God. Dir. Randa Haines. With William Hurt, Piper Laurie, and Phillip Bosco. Paramount, 1986.

Television or Radio Program

"Inspector Morse: Cherubim and Seraphim." 2 episodes. Mystery! Perf. John Thaw, Kevin Whateley. PBS. WNET, New York. 2 March 1995.

As in a film citation, if you wish to refer to a particular person in the program, cite that name first, followed by the rest of the listing. The episode is put in quotation marks; the program name is underlined. A series name (if any) is neither put in quotation marks nor underlined. Except for the comma between the local station and the city, a period follows every item. Narrators, directors, adapters, or performers can be listed if relevant.

Electronic Sources

Elements of an Electronic Citation When you use an electronic source such as an online database or the Internet, you need to let your reader know where you got your information. To cite an article, critical review, book or book excerpt, poem, Web page, or other material located online, you will include the standard elements of a citation (#1–6) as well as additional information for electronic sources (#7–11):

Ventura, Michael. "Shattered Illusions: Los Angeles Preparing for the Unknown." Los Angeles Times. 22 Jan. 1995, home ed.: M1. Los Angeles Times Online. Online. Internet. 14 Aug. 1996. Available WWW: http://www.lastimes.com/HOME/RESEARCH/.

1. Author (if given)
2. Title of the article (in quotation marks)
3. Title of the journal or newspaper (underlined)
4. Publication information: volume number, issue number, or other identifying number
5. Year or date of publication or posting (in parentheses)
6. Number of pages or paragraphs (if given) or n. pag. (to indicate "no pagination")
7. Title of the database (underlined) if your information is not in print form
8. Publication medium (Online)
9. Name of computer network (such as the Internet)
10. Date of access (Because electronic material is often changed or updated, you need to give the date when you obtained your information.)
11. Electronic address preceded by the word "Available" (e.g., "Available webkeeper@utne.com"). Important: Your citation will end with a final period, but this period is not part of the electronic address.

In Print and Online

Markels, Alex. "MCI Unit Finds Culture Shock After Relocating to Colorado." The Wall Street Journal Interactive Edition. (25 June 1996). 7 pp. Online. Internet. 28 June 1996. Available http://www.wsj.com/.

Because the pages of the online article were numbered and a total number of pages was given, the documentation includes "7 pp." The publication medium is "Online," and the computer service is "Internet." The article was accessed on June 28, three days after it was put online. The mailing address is given in this citation.

United States. CIA Publications and Handbooks. 1995 World Factbook. Washington, D.C.: Central Intelligence Agency, 1995. Online. 3 Jan. 1996. Available http://www.odci.gov/cia/publications/95fact/index.html.

If no author is given, as in a government publication, cite the institution or publishing agency.

Electronic Conference

Sagady, Alexander. "Mich 'Hands on' Family Law Workshop." 4 June 1996. Online. Newsgroup alt.dad's-rights. Usenet. 15 July 1996. Available asagady@sojournl.sojourn.com.

For electronic conferences, include the name of the computer network and any headings (as in "Newsgroup alt.dad's rights" above). Note that the posting date and the access date here are different.

Electronic Source Not in Print

Cardarelli, Luise. "Revenge of the Missing Girls: China May Come to Regret Its Preference for Boys." Online. The Utne Lens. 7 Feb. 1996. 3 pp. Available http://www.utne.com/lens/cs/16csgirls.html.

Nowviskie, Bethany. "John Keats: A Hypermedia Guide." Online. 10 May 1996. Available http://www.wfu.edu/~nowvibp4/keats.htm.

Source from Database

Abu-Haidar, Lamia. "Dole Bids Senate Farewell." Time Daily. (11 June 1996): n. pag. Pathfinder. Online. Internet. 11 June 1996. Available http://pathfinder.com/time/daily/.

Source Available Only on CD-ROM

Nehemiah, Marcia. "Nicholas Negroponte." Digit. Issue #8. CD-ROM. PC Carullo. pp. 55-60.

Many electronic sources are accessed through CD-ROM disks (or other electronic media such as diskettes or magnetic tape) instead of through online connections. To cite such sources, you need to provide the database and such basic information as the author, title, publication information, publication medium, publisher or distributor of the database, and date of electronic publication.

Organizing the Works Cited

The works cited are always arranged alphabetically, according to authors' last names. If no authors are named, then the works are listed according to title. If the title begins with "A" or "The," keep the article where it is but alphabetize the title according to the second word.

All sources—whether book or article—are arranged together in one list. Do not have a list of books and then a list of articles. Do not number the sources in your bibliography. Double-space between all lines; after the first line of each entry extends to the right-hand margin, the second line is indented five spaces. See the works-cited page in the model student research paper (p. 486).

DOCUMENTING THE RESEARCH PAPER: AMERICAN PSYCHOLOGICAL ASSOCIATION (APA) STYLE

Although most English instructors will require MLA form for documenting sources, instructors from other disciplines may prefer APA form. Check with your instructors to see which of the two forms they prefer. *These two styles are very different; don't confuse them.*

Writing Parenthetical Citations

The main difference between MLA and APA forms is that in APA parenthetical citations, the date of publication and sometimes the page number of the source are included. The punctuation, therefore, is also different.

Using APA form, if you introduce quoted material with the author's name, follow the author's name with the date of publication in parentheses. Then, at the end of the quotation, include the page number in parentheses.

> In Ben Mattlin's recent study (1991) of the media and people with disabilities, he approves Christopher Burke's role as a "competent, high-functioning, integral part of his family" (p. 8).

Notice that the date of the study is included within the introduction to the quotation, and then the page number is abbreviated as "p." within the final parentheses. (Note: The "p." is used in APA style but *not* in MLA style.)

If you do not use the author's name when you introduce the quoted material, place the author's name, the date, and the page number in parentheses at the end of the quoted material. Use commas between the items in the parentheses.

> One critic approves Christopher Burke's role as a "competent, high-functioning, integral part of his family" (Mattlin, 1991, p. 8).

If you paraphrase the material rather than quoting it specifically, include the author's last name and the date of publication either in your text or in the parentheses at the end of the summarized material. Do not include the page number.

According to Ben Mattlin (1991), disabled actors are playing important roles in television dramas. One writer who has examined the media's treatment of the disabled reports some positive changes in television (Mattlin, 1991).

Specific Examples of APA Form

Below are specific examples of common situations that you may need to document in APA form:

A Work with Two Authors If your material was written by two authors, name both in the introduction to the material or in the final parentheses each time you cite the work. In the parentheses, use "&" rather than "and."

DeJong and Lifchez (1983) examine state and federal funding for vocational programs and independent living centers provided for disabled citizens.

Two writers have reported on The Rehabilitation Comprehensive Services and Developmental Disability Amendments (DeJong & Lifchez, 1983).

Author's Name Not Given If the author of the material that you are using is not given, either use the complete title in your introduction to the material or use the first few words of the title in the parenthetical citation with the date.

Retired Supreme Court Justice Thurgood Marshall graduated first in his class at Howard Law School and then sued the University of Maryland Law School, which had rejected him because he was Black ("Milestones," 1993).

One obituary ("Milestones," 1993) noted that Thurgood Marshall graduated first in his class at Howard Law School and then sued the University of Maryland Law School, which had rejected him because he was Black.

Corporate Author If you are using a work with a corporate or group author that is particularly long, write out the full name the first time you use it, followed by an abbreviation in brackets. In later citations, use just the abbreviation.

The American Philosophical Association has prepared "Guidelines for Non-Sexist Use of Language" because philosophers are "attuned to the emotive force of words and to the ways in which language influences thought and behavior" (American Philosophical Association [APA], 1978).

Indirect Source If you use work that is borrowed from another source, you need to acknowledge that you did not use the original source.

Actor Henry Holden relates his own experience with social discrimination by noting that he is "not generally accepted by nondisabled people in social situations" (cited in Davidson, 1987).

Preparing the References Page

In APA form, the alphabetical listing of works used in the manuscript is entitled "References." (In MLA form, this listing is called the "Works Cited.") Here are some general guidelines for the references page:

- Double-space the entries. The first line should be indented five spaces, and all subsequent lines should start at the left margin. (This is the opposite of MLA style.)
- Alphabetize the list by the last name of the author or editor. If the work is anonymous, alphabetize by the first name of the title other than "a," "an," or "the."
- All authors' names should be listed last name first, with the parts of names separated with commas. Do not use "et al." Use initials for first and middle names. Use an ampersand ("&") rather than the word "and."
- For the titles of books and articles, capitalize only the first letter of the first word of the title and of the subtitle, as well as the first letter of all proper nouns.
- Underline the titles of books and journals. Do not underline or use quotations marks around the titles of articles. Capitalize the names of periodicals as they are normally written. Underline the volume number of periodicals.

- Give the full names of publishers, excluding "Inc." and "Co."
- Use the abbreviation "p." or "pp." before page numbers in books, magazines, and newspapers, but not for scholarly journals. For inclusive page numbers, include all figures ("365–370," not "365–70").

Sample APA Entries

Books

One Author

Fiedler, L. (1978). Freaks: Myths and images of the secret self. New York: Simon & Schuster.

Two or More Authors

Doane, J., & Hodges, D. (1987). Nostalgia and sexual difference: The resistance to contemporary feminism. New York: Methuen.

Editor

Allen, D. M. (Ed.). (1960). The new American poetry. New York: Grove Press.

Translator

Ibsen, H. (1965). A doll's house and other plays. (P. Watts, Trans.). New York: Penguin Books.

Author Not Named

The Oxford dictionary of quotations. (1964). New York: Oxford University Press.

Later Edition

Fowler, R. H., & Aaron, J. E. (1992). The Little, Brown handbook. (5th ed.). New York: HarperCollins Publishers.

Multivolume Work

Raine, K. (1968). Blake and tradition (Vol. 2). Princeton: Princeton University Press.

Malone, D. (1943-1981). Jefferson and his time (Vols. 1-6). Boston: Little, Brown.

Work in an Anthology

Mairs, N. On being a cripple. (1987). In M. Saxton & F. Howe (Eds.), With wings: An anthology of literature by and about women with disabilities (pp. 118-127). New York: Feminist Press at City University of New York.

Two or More Books by the Same Author

Olsen, T. (1979). Silences. New York: Dell Publishing.

Olsen, T. (1985). Tell me a riddle. New York: Dell Publishing.

Periodicals: Journals, Magazines, and Newspapers

Journal with Continuous Pagination

Culp, M. B. (1983). Religion in the poetry of Langston Hughes. Phylon, 48, 240-245.

Journal That Paginates Each Issue Separately

Hardwick, J. (1992). Widowhood and patriarchy in seventeenth-century France. Journal of Social History, 26(1), 133-148.

Article in a Magazine

Mazzatenta, O. L. (1992, August). A Chinese emperor's army for eternity. National Geographic, pp. 114-130.

Article in a Daily Newspaper, Signed

Soto, O. R. (1992, January 28). Putting the tag on graffiti-smearers. Press Telegram, sec. B, p. 3.

Article in a Daily Newspaper, Unsigned or Editorial

Back to Future. (1992, May 3). Los Angeles Times, p. M-4.

Titled Review

Ansa, T. M. (1992, July 5). Taboo territory [Review of Possessing the secret of joy]. Los Angeles Times Book Review, pp. 4, 8.

Personal Interview Interviews that you conduct yourself are not listed in APA references. Instead, use an in-text parenthetical citation. If the subject's name is in your text, use this form: "(personal communication, June 23, 1992)." If the subject's name is not in your text, use this form: "(S. Olson, personal communication, June 23, 1992)."

Electronic Sources The documentation form for electronic sources is still in flux, but the goal is to provide your reader with sufficient information to locate the material you have found. A typical citation will include the conventional APA form for the source, whether it is an article or book, then the electronic medium (online, CD-ROM), followed by the address.

Book in Print and Online

Austen, Jane. (1996). Pride and prejudice (Orig. pub. 1813). [Online]. Available http://uts.cc.utexas.edu/~churchh/ pridprej.html

Article in Print and Online

Markels, A. (1996). MCI unit finds culture shock after relocating to Colorado. [Online]. The Wall Street Journal Interactive Edition. 7 pp. Available http://www.wsj.com/

III

THE HANDBOOK

■ ■ ■

This handbook is designed to help you use words and control sentences to write convincing, error-free papers. You can use this handbook while you are drafting and revising your essays, as well as to understand the comments that your instructors write in the margins of your papers.

We do not believe that you need an extensive background in grammar to write clearly or well. But we are convinced that control of grammar and punctuation will give you power over both your ideas *and* your readers.

You may believe that you make numerous mistakes on your papers; indeed, the prevalence of circled words and margin notes on some may seem overwhelming. If you and your friends were to examine all of your papers, however, you would discover that you do not make a great number of *different* errors so much as you repeat the same kind of error many times. For that reason we have isolated those recurrent errors for discussion and correction.

This handbook begins with a short chapter entitled "Understanding How Sentences Work." This chapter is deliberately succinct; in it we try to meet your needs without telling you more than you ever wanted (or needed) to know about the elements of a sentence. The next chapter, "Understanding Common Errors," precisely identifies and describes those recurrent errors—the "terrible ten"—that typically appear in student papers. The following chapter, "Understanding Punctuation," will help you eliminate guesswork and punctuate accurately. In "Understanding Faulty Word Choice," you will learn how well-chosen words can strengthen your essays. To determine quickly whether your word choice is sound, you can use the alphabetical list of troublesome words in the last chapter, "Understanding Commonly Confused Words."

As you are revising your drafts, you can use this handbook whenever you feel uncertain about your grammar or mechanics. When your papers are returned, you can use it as a guide to error correction by matching your instructors margin notes to the symbols used in this book. Ultimately, this handbook is designed to empower you without overwhelming you.

Editing Symbols

The following symbols may be used by your instructor to indicate errors in your paper. You may also use these symbols when you proofread a paper to denote changes you will want to make in your drafts or to mark errors in your classmates' papers. It is important for you to ask your instructor for a clarification of a margin symbol if one is used that you do not understand.

^	insert (such as a missing word or punctuation
^,	insert comma
∼	reverse (such as letters or words)
ℓ	delete (such as punctuation or word)
#	add a space
⊂	close up space
¶	new paragraph
no¶	no paragraph
≡	capitalize
/	use lowercase

Sentence errors, discussed in Chapter 12, are commonly indicated by the following symbols:

frag	fragment
ros or r-o	run-on sentence
fs	fused sentence
cs	comma splice
ref	pronoun reference
agr	agreement

Symbols that are used to correct word choice errors, discussed in Chapters 14 and 15, and other symbols to designate common errors include the following:

cliché	cliché, an overused or trite expression
dialect	not standard English usage, or a regional, occupational, or ethnic word not appropriate in the context used
d or dic	diction, inappropriate level
id	idiomatic, not standard American usage; the problem often appears in preposition use
jarg	jargon, or an occupational word inappropriate for formal writing
nonst.	nonstandard; may indicate idiomatic use, jargon, or slang
sl or slang	the level of the word choice is inappropriate
trite	overused expression, as a cliché
wd ch	word choice; a general term that may indicate any of the more definitively marked errors on this list
w/w	wrong word; a general term that may indicate a word confused with another word, slang, jargon, improper word, or idiom
X	obvious error; may refer to any of the above
awk	awkward
coh	lacks coherence
?	confused meaning
red	redundant
sp	spelling error
trans	stronger transition needed
wdy	wordy

In addition to denoting errors, your instructor may indicate strong writing and good points by using this symbol:

√ excellent point and word choice

11

Understanding How Sentences Work

■ ■ ■

Understanding how sentences work will give you the vocabulary you need to discuss your writing as well as to correct errors that have been noted in your papers. Such knowledge will also increase your power and versatility as a writer. By eliminating some of the guesswork that can hamper student writers, this handbook can help give you the tools and confidence to write with conviction.

As you probably know, every sentence must contain a **subject** and a **verb.** This basic unit is called a **clause.** (For more on clauses, see pp. 519–520.) In key examples throughout this section, we often have underlined the subject once and the verb twice to help you identify them quickly.

SUBJECTS

A **subject** is who or what a clause is about:

`Ryan plays keyboard in a rock band.`

[Subjects may precede verbs.]

`There is a grin on Adam's face.`

[Subjects may follow verbs.]

Noun as Subject

The subject of the clause may be a **noun** or a **pronoun.** A **noun** can be a

person: athlete, Whitney Houston, veterinarian

place: Lake Erie, bike path, the Acropolis

thing: computer, hammock, Harley-Davidson
quality/idea/activity: wit, peace, dancing

Pronoun as Subject

A **pronoun** takes the place of a noun and can also function as the subject of a clause. Pronouns can be

personal: I, you, he, she, it, we, they

They reviewed their lecture notes.

indefinite: all, any, anybody, anything, each, either, everybody, everyone, neither, nobody, none, no one, nothing, one, some, somebody, someone, something

Everybody needs to recycle.

demonstrative: that, this, such, these, those

Those are the sale items.

relative: who, whom, whoever, whomever, whose, which, whichever, that, what, whatever

The order that is ready is the deluxe pizza.

[In this example, that is the subject of the dependent or relative clause. The subject of the independent clause is order.] (For more about clauses, see pp. 519–520.)

interrogative: who, whom, whoever, whomever, whose, which, that, what, whatever

Who recommended this awful film?

Compound Subject

Subjects may be *compound,* as in these sentences:

Julie and Joe restore old automobiles.

Books and papers collected on his desk.

Here are questions and assignments for each reading.

The dietician and nurses gave the patients new menus.

OBJECTS

Direct Object

Not all nouns function as the subject of a clause. A noun that receives the action of the verb is called a **direct object.** In the sentence "Julie and Joe restore old automobiles," the noun *automobiles,* answers the question, "What do Julie and Joe restore?" *Automobiles* is therefore the direct object of the verb *restore.*

Indirect Object

A noun that identifies to or for whom or what the action of the verb is performed is the **indirect object.** In the sentence "The dietician and nurses gave the patients new menus," the noun *patients* answers the question, "To whom were the menus given?"

Object of the Preposition

A noun that follows a preposition (see the list on p. 517) is called the **object of the preposition.** In the sentence "Books and papers collected on his desk," the noun *desk* is the object of the preposition *on.*

Objects may provide important information in a sentence, but they are not necessary in order to have a clause. *Verbs,* however, are essential.

VERBS

A **verb** is what the subject does, is, has, or has done to it. The verb may be more than one word (may be coming). The verb also changes form to agree with the subject (he drives; they drive) and to indicate time (he drove, he has driven). Regular verbs form their past tense by adding *-ed,* but there are a number of irregular forms such as *drive* that have special forms.

Action Verbs

An **action verb** specifies what the subject does, has, or has done to it. The action does not have to be physical in any sense: *meditate* is an action verb. Other action verbs include *dance, think, laugh, provoke, erupt,* and *suggest:*

```
Every Christmas Eve, Janine and Tim entertain their relatives with holiday tunes.

Dr. Sanders wrote an insightful study of Oates' work.
```

State-of-Being Verbs

A **state-of-being** or **linking verb** specifies what the subject is. State-of-being verbs include the following: *is, are, was, were, am, feel, seem, be, being, been, do, does, did, have, has, had.* These can be main verbs or helping verbs. For more on helping verbs, see the following section.

`Dylan is interested in American history.`

[is as main verb.]

`Evan is teaching math at Pinewood School.`

[is as a helping verb.]

Note: Words ending in *-ing* need a helping verb to function as the main verb of a sentence. The *-ing* form of the verb can also function as a noun: Playing is a form of learning for small children. Here *playing* is the subject, and *learning* is the object of the preposition *of.* Thus just because there is an *-ing* word in a word group, there is not necessarily a verb.

Helping Verbs

The **helping verb** is always used with a main verb. Helping verbs include *can, will, shall, should, could, would, may, might,* and *must.*

`The designated driver will get everyone home safely.`

`They should have requested assistance.`

ADJECTIVES AND ADVERBS

Many sentences contain modifying words that describe the nouns and verbs. **Adjectives** modify nouns (*corroded* pipes, *hectic* schedule) and pronouns (the *curious* one). **Adverbs** modify verbs (*cautiously* responded), adjectives (*truly* generous), adverbs (*very* slowly), and word groups (*Eventually,* he entered the room.) Adverbs answer the questions *how? when? where?* and *why?* They often end in *-ly,* but not always.

The following sentence contains both adjectives and adverbs. Can you identify each?

`According to Barbara Ehrenreich, angry young men often will vent their frustrations on vulnerable, weaker beings—typically children or women.`

The adjectives *angry* and *young* modify the noun *men;* the adjectives *vulnerable* and *weaker* modify the noun *beings.* The adverbs *often* and *typically* modify the verb *will vent.*

Adjectives and adverbs can provide valuable details, but they can be overused. Being descriptive doesn't require a string of adjectives and adverbs. Often a strong verb gives a more precise picture in fewer words:

`The drunken man walked unsteadily and unevenly from the bar.`

`The drunken man staggered from the bar.`

The verb *staggered* is vivid and precise. The pile-up of adverbs in the first sentence is wordy and imprecise. Such tightening often improves writing and saves space for more necessary depth and development.

PHRASES

Just as clauses do not necessarily have objects, adjectives, and adverbs, they also do not necessarily have any phrases therefore, typically, the subject and verb must be elsewhere in the sentence. This is particularly helpful to know to avoid fragments.

A **phrase** is a group of words forming part of a sentence. There are many types of phrases, but below we discuss two of the most common.

Prepositional Phrases

A **prepositional phrase** always starts with a **preposition** (a word that shows relationships in time and space) and ends with the **object** of the preposition. The most common prepositions are the following:

about	beside	from	outside	toward
above	besides	in	over	under
across	between	inside	past	underneath
after	beyond	into	plus	unlike
against	but	like	regarding	until
along	by	near	respecting	unto
among	concerning	next	round	up
around	considering	of	since	upon
as	despite	off	than	with
at	down	on	through	without
before	during	onto	throughout	
behind	except	opposite	till	
below	for	out	to	

Some prepositions, such as *along with, as well as, in addition to, next to,* and *up to* are more than one word long.

The object of the preposition is always a noun or pronoun:

Elaine assists the doctor **with his patients.**

During intermission, Becky and Joey went **for popcorn.**

For a few hours on Wednesday nights, Anne babysits **for her daughter.**

[In the last sentence, "for a few hours," "on Wednesday nights," and "for her daughter" are all prepositional phrases. Note how much easier it is to locate the subject and verb when the prepositional phrases are eliminated.]

Verbal Phrases

These phrases look like verbs, but they do not function as the main verb of the clause. Verbal phrases may serve as subjects, objects, adjectives, and adverbs. Two main types of verbal phrases are **infinitive phrases** and ***-ing* phrases.**

Infinitive Phrases If the verb is preceded by *to* (*to ski*), the verb is in the **infinitive** form. It helps to recognize infinitives because they cannot be the main verbs.

Most professors like **to challenge** students.

To think is **to question.**

[Infinitives can function as subjects.]

-ing Phrases A word ending in *-ing* may look like a verb, but it needs a helping verb or a main verb elsewhere in the sentence. Notice how *working* serves a different function in each of the following sentences (only in the first sentence is it part of the main verb):

Rïse Daniels is **working** as an art director.

Working as an art director requires overtime hours.

[When *-ing* words function as subjects, they are called **gerunds.**]

The **working** artist exhibited her paintings.

[When *-ing* words function as adjectives, they are called **participles.**]

-ing words and phrases can often lead writers to believe that they have a complete sentence—that is, at least one independent clause—when they may have only a fragment. For example, "In the evening after arriving home from work" is not an independent clause; it simply consists of three phrases.

One way to determine whether there is an independent clause, and therefore a sentence, is to draw a line through each phrase:

~~In the evening~~ ~~after arriving home~~ ~~from work,~~ Bill retreats ~~to his studio~~ ~~for hours~~ ~~to play piano~~ and ~~to compose new songs.~~

Now that you can recognize the most important parts of a sentence, you can better understand how clauses work and how they can be combined.

CLAUSES

A **clause** is a group of words with a subject and main verb. The two basic types of clauses are discussed below.

Independent (or Main) Clauses

The independent clause has a subject and main verb and can stand alone:

Dottie is receiving mail from fans each day.

Alyssa loves singing with Robert and Susie.

The poet invited Gigi and Keith backstage.

Dependent (or Subordinate) Clauses

The dependent clause has a subject and main verb but cannot stand alone. Dependent clauses begin with one of these subordinate conjunctions:

after	that, so that
although	unless
as, as if	until
because	what, whatever
before	when, whenever
how	whether
if, even if	which, whichever
in order that	while
since	who, whom, whose

Whenever a clause begins with one of these words (unless it is a question), it is a dependent clause. If we take an independent clause such as

We jogged

and put one of the subordinate conjunctions in front of it, it becomes dependent (and therefore a fragment):

```
After we jogged

Because we jogged
```

To make a complete sentence, we need to add an independent clause (or delete the subordinate conjunction):

```
After we jogged, we went for a swim.

Because we jogged, we justified eating brownies.

We jogged.
```

Every sentence must have at least one independent clause in it.

SENTENCE VARIATION

If you know how to control and combine clauses, you can vary your sentences for greater emphasis, more clarity, and less monotony. The four basic sentence types are illustrated below.

Simple Sentences

Simple sentences contain one independent clause:

```
Professor Hodges' students submitted fine critical analy-
ses of the textbook.
Despite his busy schedule, Walter spent hours with his
sons each night.
```

Compound Sentences

Compound sentences contain two independent clauses. There are only two ways to punctuate a compound sentence:

1. A **comma** followed by a coordinating conjunction (*and, but, for, or, nor, yet, so*):

   ```
   We arrived at the cabin, so they left.
   ```

2. A **semicolon** by itself (or it may be followed by a word such as *nevertheless* or *however*):

   ```
   We arrived; they left.

   We arrived; therefore, they left.
   ```

Notice that the writer's decision to use a coordinate conjunction or a semicolon is not arbitrary. If the writer wishes to clarify or emphasize the relationship between the two clauses, he or she will use a coordinate conjunction (such as *so*) or a conjunctive adverb (such as *therefore*). If the writer prefers not to define the relationship between the clauses, then the semicolon by itself is more appropriate.

Complex Sentences

Complex sentences contain one independent clause and one or more dependent clauses. Below, the dependent clauses are underscored with a broken underline:

> When the dependent clause comes first in the sentence, a comma is necessary.
>
> A comma isn't necessary when the dependent clause comes at the end.

Compound-Complex Sentences

Compound-complex sentences contain two or more independent clauses and one or more dependent clauses. The dependent clause or clauses may be at the beginning, at the end, or between the independent clauses. Here one dependent clause begins the sentence, and another ends the sentence:

> Although Jane is a senior citizen, she swims competitively, and we are all impressed that she has won so many medals.

In the following sentence, the dependent clause is between the two independent clauses:

> At work, Tammy cares for an elderly man who requires constant help, so she enjoys returning home each night to play with Jamie, Paul, and Duane.

Student Assignment

Using details from the most recent essay that you discussed in class, write your own sentences to illustrate each sentence type: simple, compound, complex, and compound-complex. Then underline all subjects once and all verbs twice to make sure you have the necessary clauses. Manipulating these sentence types will help you vary your sentences and combine your ideas more smoothly.

12

Understanding Common Errors

In the next three chapters, we examine the ten common errors that appear most frequently in student papers. These errors are listed below, with the symbols instructors use to note these errors in the margins of your papers:

frag	fragment
ros/fs	run-on sentence or fused sentence
ref	pronoun reference
agr	agreement
shift	inconsistency in text
mixed	mixed construction
mm	misplaced modifier
//	faulty parallelism
P	faulty punctuation
wd ch	faulty word choice

FRAGMENTS

Although sentence fragments are used frequently in fiction and advertising copy to simulate spoken English, the sentence fragment is considered nonstandard in formal writing. Fragments may confuse the reader, and they make your writing seem choppy and your ideas disconnected.

frag A **fragment** is a group of words that, for some reason, cannot stand alone as a complete sentence. The reason may be any one of the following.

1. The word group may lack a subject:

frag

While the students prepared their finals, they sunbathed at the same time. Became involved in discussions that distracted them from their studies.

[Add a subject.]

While the students prepared their finals, they sunbathed at the same time. Soon they became involved in discussions that distracted them from their studies.

2. The word group may lack a complete verb:

frag

Arriving before the concert began, we enjoyed the excitement in the air. The band tuning up before their opening song.

[Add a helping verb.]

Arriving before the concert began, we enjoyed the excitement in the air. The band was tuning up before their opening song.

3. The word group may lack both a subject and a verb:

frag

I value my piano teacher. A bright and patient woman. She encourages perfection even while she tolerates my mistakes.

[Attach the phrase *a bright and patient woman* to the independent clause before or after it.]

I value my piano teacher, a bright and patient woman. She encourages perfection even while she tolerates my mistakes.

or

I value my piano teacher. A bright and patient woman, she encourages perfection even while she tolerates my mistakes.

4. The word group may contain both a subject and a verb but be simply a dependent clause:

Native American music and dances are national treasures.

frag

Which is why our dance company performs them regularly.

[Avoid starting any sentence with *which* unless you are asking a question.]

Native American music and dances are national treasures.

This is why our dance company performs them regularly.

or

Because Native American music and dances are national treasures, our dance company performs them regularly.

Another example of such a fragment is the following:

frag Although rap music has been criticized for its violence and harsh language. Rap really reflects the tension in the cities rather than causes it.

Although rap music has been criticized for its violence and harsh language, rap really reflects the tension in the cities rather than causes it.

As was noted earlier, writers may deliberately use a fragment for emphasis or to mimic conversation, but these uses are always controlled and planned. Otherwise, fragments make an essay confusing or choppy. Sometimes the simplest solution is to connect the fragment to an independent clause that is either directly before or after it.

RUN-ON OR FUSED SENTENCES

ros fs cs **Run-on** or **fused sentences,** or sentences that are flawed with a **comma splice,** occur when a writer perceives that the thoughts in two complete sentences are related but fails to join the thoughts appropriately. Sometimes the writer makes the mistake of inserting a comma between the independent clauses, creating a comma splice. No punctuation at all between the independent clauses creates a run-on or fused sentence. Both errors occur because the writer sees a relationship between sentences and isn't sure what to do to show the relationship.

The "sentence" that follows is one that anyone might say and a writer might be tempted to write

ros It snowed for days the skiers were ecstatic.

The writer has clearly perceived a relationship between the joy of the skiers and the weather conditions. But the word group is incorrectly punctuated and is a run-on or fused sentence.

Comma Splice

The writer may decide to "correct" the error by inserting a comma between the two independent clauses:

cs It snowed for days, the skiers were ecstatic.

The comma is inadequate punctuation, however, for separating the independent clauses. That "correction" results in the sentence fault called a **comma splice,** which is noted as **"CS"** in the margin of a paper.

Correcting Run-on Sentences

The following methods illustrate alternatives for correcting run-on sentences. Notice that the five choices are all grammatically correct, but each places a different emphasis on the two clauses and may change the meaning of the sentence.

1. Separate each independent clause with a period:

   `It snowed for days. The skiers were ecstatic.`

2. Use a comma plus a coordinating conjunction (*and, but, for, or, nor, yet, so*) between the independent clauses:

   `It snowed for days, and the skiers were ecstatic.`

   or

   `It snowed for days, yet the skiers were ecstatic.`

   or

   `It snowed for days, so the skiers were ecstatic.`

3. Use a semicolon between the independent clauses:

   `It snowed for days; the skiers were ecstatic.`

4. Change one independent clause into a dependent clause:

   `Because it snowed for days, the skiers were ecstatic.`

   or

   `The skiers were ecstatic because it snowed for days.`

   Notice that when the dependent clause begins the sentence, a comma separates it from the main clause. Conversely, when the independent clause begins the sentence, there is no comma before the dependent clause that concludes the sentence. See page 519 for a list of words that begin dependent clauses.

5. Use a semicolon after the first independent clause and then a conjunctive adverb (see below) followed by a comma:

   `It snowed for days; consequently, the skiers were ecstatic.`

   or

   `It snowed for days; nevertheless, the skiers were ecstatic.`

Conjunctive Adverbs

Conjunctive adverbs include *accordingly, also, anyway, besides, certainly, consequently, conversely, finally, furthermore, hence, however, incidentally, indeed, instead, likewise, meanwhile, moreover, nevertheless, next, nonetheless, otherwise, similarly, specifically, still, subsequently, then, therefore,* and *thus.*

Style and Meaning

Grammatical correction of a run-on sentence is not the only concern of the writer. Style, emphasis, and meaning also should be considered when you are deciding which conjunction to use. Notice the difference in emphasis in the following examples:

```
It snowed for days. The skiers were ecstatic.
Because it snowed for days, the skiers were ecstatic.
```

In the first example the writer asks the reader to infer the relationship between the skiers' being "ecstatic" and the fact that "it snowed for days." In the second example the cause-and-effect relationship is defined clearly. Take the following simple sentences, also fused, and notice what happens to the meaning, emphasis, or relationship between the independent clauses when different corrections are employed:

ros Renée pitched the team won.

1. Renée pitched. The team won.

The writer has defined no relationship between the facts stated in the two sentences.

2. Renée pitched, and the team won.

A mild relationship is suggested by connecting the two events with *and.*

Renée pitched, so the team won.

The relationship between the team's victory and the person who pitched is defined in this construction by using *so.*

Renée pitched, yet the team won.

The use of *yet,* which signals something contrary to expectation, changes the relationship between the independent clauses in this example. The word *yet* tells the reader that in spite of the fact that Renée pitched, the team won.

3. Renée pitched; the team won.

The semicolon does not define the relationship between the two independent clauses although a subtle relationship *is* suggested by the writer's using a semicolon instead of a period. The semicolon is a compromise punctuation symbol. It is stronger than a comma, but it is not as complete a stop as a period.

4. `Whenever Renée pitched, the team won.`

   `The team won because Renée pitched.`

   `Although Renée pitched, the team won.`

   `The team won unless Renée pitched.`

The dependent clause, whether it begins or ends the sentence, defines the exact relationship between the two clauses in the sentence. Clearly, the subordinate conjunction that is chosen has everything to do with the meaning of the sentence.

5. `Renée pitched; therefore, the team won.`

   `Renée pitched; nevertheless, the team won.`

Again, the conjunctive adverb defines the precise relationship between the two clauses of the sentence. For the purpose of connecting two short independent clauses, most writers would find the combination of semicolon and conjunctive adverb and comma too cumbersome. A coordinating conjunction with a comma would probably be a better method of linking the two clauses.

PRONOUN REFERENCE

Pronouns are words that take the place of nouns. In most cases, pronouns are an advantage to the writer because they permit reference to nouns without the writers having to repeat the noun or finding a clear substitute (or synonym) for it. Ambiguity, vagueness, or confusion can result, however, if the writer has not used pronouns responsibly. The margin symbol **"ref"** indicates a problem with the pronoun reference.

ref

This chart shows the form personal pronouns take:

Singular

Subjective	*Possessive*	*Objective*
I	my, mine	me
you	your, yours	you
he	his	him
she	her, hers	her
it	its	it

	Plural	
we	our, ours	us
you	your, yours	you
they	their, theirs	them

Indefinite pronouns include *all, any, anybody, anything, each, either, everybody, everyone, everything, neither, nobody, none, no one, nothing, one, some, somebody, someone,* and *something.*

Pronoun problems occur when the reader does not know what noun is referred to by the noun substitute, the pronoun.

1. Sometimes the pronoun used could refer to either of two nouns:

ref

```
When Karen told Pat the news, she burst into tears.
```

She can refer to either Karen or Pat. The ambiguity must be resolved for the reader:

```
Pat burst into tears when Karen told her the news.
```

or

```
Karen burst into tears when she told Pat the news.
```

2. Sometimes the subject is implied by the writer but is not stated in the sentence. The pronoun does not clearly refer to any given noun, and confusion results for the reader:

ref

```
For years, Gabe carried rocks from the quarry, and it strained his back.
```

It cannot refer to the plural *rocks,* and the singular noun *quarry* didn't "strain his back." The writer probably means "this work" or "the constant hauling of heavy rocks." The writer needs to make that clarification in the sentence:

```
For years, Gabe carried rocks from the quarry, and this work strained his back.
```

3. Indefinite pronouns can also pose a problem for writer and reader if the singular form of the indefinite pronoun is inconsistent with the meaning of the sentence or the gender of the pronoun is assumed by the writer to be a generic *he.* Generally, a singular pronoun should be used with an indefinite pronoun:

Each boy on the football team has **his** own locker.

Anybody who has **her** doubts about the value of natural childbirth should take a Lamaze course.

If the writer is certain of the singular intention and gender of the subject, no problems arise in determining the form of the possessive pronoun and no reader will be offended. If the indefinite pronoun has a plural meaning, however, the grammatical necessity of a singular possessive pronoun may result in an inappropriate use of a generic *his,* an awkward, repetitive use of *his or her,* or the temptation to use the incorrect form *his/her.*

Here is an example of the problem:

ref Everybody running for class office should report to his counselor.

Everybody is a singular pronoun and requires a singular possessive pronoun: *his* or *her. Their* is plural and can't be used in this sentence. But should the writer assume the generic *his?* A reader might object that the implication of the sentence is that only males may run for class office. A similar misunderstanding would occur if the writer opted for *her* as the singular possessive pronoun. If this were a single-sentence statement, as in a school bulletin, the writer might choose *his or her* for a correct and clear mandate. But the repetitive use of *his or her* can be a burden in a lengthy manuscript.

Learn to find alternatives. A plural noun and plural possessive pronoun will take care of the problem, so rewrite the sentence:

All of the candidates for class office should report to their counselors.

You may also want to see "Sexist Language" (pp. 560–561) in Chapter 14 for further discussion of pronoun choices.

AGREEMENT

agr The margin note **"agr"** means that there is an agreement problem; the subject and the verb do not agree in number. Both subject and verb should be singular, or both should be plural. Speakers who are comfortable with standard English usually will not have trouble selecting the correct verb form for the subject of sentences. But some sentences, especially those that have groups of words separating the subject and verb, may offer a temporary problem for any writer. Some conditions to be aware of are listed below.

1. A prepositional phrase does not influence the verb of the sentence:

   The birds in the nest need food from the mother bird.

   Our first five days of vacation are going to be in New Orleans.

   Her secretary, in addition to her staff, prefers the new computer.

Notice that by removing the prepositional phrases from your consideration, you can easily determine the correct verb form for the subject of the sentence.

2. Subjects connected by *and* usually have a plural verb:

   The student's academic load and work time keep him busy.

   a. When the compound subject (nouns connected by *and*) is regarded as a unit, the subject is regarded as singular and has a singular verb.

      Peanut butter and jelly remains Raul's favorite lunch.

   b. If the double nouns refer to the same person or thing, the verb is singular:

      Danika's home and studio is 215 Thompson Street.

   c. When *each* or *every* precedes the multiple nouns, use a singular verb:

      Each instructor, student, and staff member prefers the new insurance plan.

   d. When nouns are connected by *or* or *nor,* the verb agrees with the noun closer to it:

      Your student ID or room key guarantees the loan of a beach chair.

      Your student ID or room keys guarantee the loan of a beach chair.

      Neither the police officer nor his cadets were attending the lecture.

      Either the band or the comedian provides the program notes.

3. Most indefinite pronouns have a singular verb, even if the pronoun seems to convey a plural sense. Indefinite pronouns include *anybody, anyone, each, either, everybody, everyone, everything, neither, none, no one, someone,* and *something.* Notice how each indefinite pronoun is used in the following sentences:

   Each of the band members has two free tickets.

   Everybody endures the stress of two finals a day.

   Everyone on the school board votes at each meeting.

   All, any, or *some,* however, may be singular or plural depending on what the pronoun refers to:

All of the pizza is gone.

All of the books are shelved.

4. Collective nouns (such as *band, family, committee, class, jury,* and *audience*) require a singular verb unless the meaning of the noun is plural or individuality is to be emphasized:

   The jury presents its decision today.

   The jury are undecided about a verdict.

5. Even when the subject follows the verb, the verb must be in the correct form:

   There remains too little time to organize the campaign.

6. Titles require singular verbs:

   Roots is the book we will read next.

   Jacoby and Associates is the law firm on the corner.

   Succulents is the section of the nursery Carlos prefers.

7. Nouns describing academic disciplines—such as *economics, statistics,* or *physics*—and diseases that end in an *s*—such as *mumps* and *measles*—and *news*—are treated as singular nouns:

   Physics challenges Maria, but she does well in the course.

   Measles usually attacks only the children who have not been inoculated.

SHIFTS

shift The margin note **"shift"** marks an inconsistency in the text in person, number, or verb tense.

Shifts in Person and Number

Shifts in person and number sometimes occur because you are not certain from what point of view to write or because you move from one perspective to another without being conscious of the change. You may begin with the idea of addressing a general audience—"someone"—and then decide to address the reader as "you." Or you may begin with a singular reader in mind and switch to a plural sense of "all readers." If you start to write from one perspective and switch to another, a distracting shift occurs:

shift If someone in the group writes a paper, they may present it.

Corrections:

If someone in the group writes a paper, that person may present it.

If a person writes a paper, he or she may present it.

or, better:

If people write papers, they may present them.

shift The vegetarian learns to prepare interesting and nutritious meals with vegetables and grains, but then you have to assure your friends that you're getting enough protein.

Corrections:

If you are a vegetarian, you learn to prepare interesting and nutritious meals with vegetables and grains, but then you have to assure your friends that you're getting enough protein.

or

Vegetarians learn to prepare interesting and nutritious meals with vegetables and grains, but then they have to assure their friends that they are getting enough protein.

Shifts in Verb Tense

Shifts in verb tense will confuse a reader about the time the action of your sentence takes place. You have probably heard oral story-tellers shift from one tense to another. Eventually, you may have figured out the course of the narration, perhaps by asking the speaker to clarify the time of the action. But a shift in tense is particularly distracting in writing because you can't ask a writer for a clarification of the text. Notice how the verb tense in the following example shifts from the past to the present:

shift Shortly after we arrived at the picnic site, it started to rain. So we pack up the bread, salami, and fruit and rush to the cars.

Correction for verb tense consistency:

Shortly after we arrived at the picnic site, it started to rain. So we packed up the bread, salami, and fruit and rushed to the cars.

Use the present tense throughout to write a summary or a description of a literary work:

shift Daisy Miller first meets Winterbourne in Geneva, and she later met him in Rome where she is dating the charming Giovanelli.

Winterbourne was furious that Daisy doesn't realize that Giovanelli wasn't a "real" gentleman.

Correction for verb tense consistency:

Daisy Miller first meets Winterbourne in Geneva, and she later meets him in Rome where she is dating the charming Giovanelli. Winterbourne is furious that Daisy doesn't realize that Giovanelli isn't a "real" gentleman.

Shifts in Voice

Just as a shift in number or tense can be distracting, a shift from one voice to another can confuse or distract your reader. Use the active voice or passive voice consistently.

When the subject of a sentence does the action, the sentence is in the **active voice:**

Lester brought the tossed salad.

When the subject *receives* the action, the verb is in the **passive voice.** Notice that the passive voice is less effective than the active voice because it is less direct:

The tossed salad was brought by Lester.

When the active and passive voice are combined, the sentence is inconsistent in voice and would be marked with a "shift" in the margin of the paper:

shift Lester brought the tossed salad, and the soft drinks were brought by Mike.

Correction:

Lester brought the tossed salad, and Mike brought the soft drinks.

In some cases, the passive voice is necessary because what might be the subject of the sentence is unknown or unimportant:

The car was hijacked last week.

Because the hijacker is apparently unknown, the sentence is in the passive voice, with the action being done to the car, the subject of the sentence.

```
NASA was granted additional funds to complete the study
for the space station.
```

The name of the agency that granted NASA the funds for the study may be unimportant to the writer of this sentence; the important point is that NASA has the funds for the project.

Passive voice constructions may create suspicion that the writer is deliberately hiding information:

```
The city council was voted unlimited travel funds.
```

Clearly, the city resident who reads that sentence in the local paper would want to know *who* did the voting and why the newspaper failed to name the subject of the verb *voted.* Use the active voice whenever you know and wish to identify the doer of a particular act.

MIXED SENTENCES

mixed The margin note **"mixed"** indicates that there are sentence parts that don't go together. The sentence may start with one subject and shift to another, or the verb may not fit the true subject of the sentence. The sentence also may begin with one grammatical construction and end with another. The problem, then, is a misfit in grammar or in logic, so the sentence is confusing to the reader:

mixed

```
Although he is active in the men's movement doesn't mean
he is a misogynist.
```

In this sentence the writer tries to make the dependent clause *Although he is active in the men's movement* the subject of the sentence. The writer probably intends *he* to be the subject of the sentence; rewriting the sentence to show this *and* selecting a correct verb for the subject will eliminate the confusion:

```
Although he is active in the men's movement, he is not a
misogynist.
```

Confused Sentence Parts

Each of the mixed sentences on page 535 contains a confusion between sentence parts. In some cases the writer has started with one subject in mind and has ended the sentence with a different or implied subject. In other cases the grammatical form of the first part of the sentence is inconsistent with the end of the sentence. Most often, the revision involves correct identification of the true subject of the sentence and then the selection of an appropriate verb.

mixed Among those women suffering with eating disorders, they are not always bulimic.

Not all women with eating disorders are bulimic.

mixed By prewriting, outlining, drafting, and revising is how he wrote good papers.

He wrote good papers by prewriting, outlining, drafting, and revising his work.

mixed The subject of ecology involves controversy.

Ecology involves controversy.

Faulty Verb Choice

In some sentences with mixed meaning, the fault occurs because the subject is said to do or to be something that is illogical.

mixed A realization between the academic senate and the dean would be the ideal policy on plagiarism.

The sentence says that "a realization" would be "the ideal policy," which is not exactly what the writer means. Correction of the faulty use of the verb *would be* will clarify the sentence.

Ideally, a policy on plagiarism would be decided between the academic senate and the dean.

or

Ideally, the academic senate and the dean would realize the necessity for a policy on plagiarism.

In speech, *is when* and *is where* are common constructions for defining words, but these are mixed constructions and should be corrected in writing.

mixed Acquiescence is when you give in to your oppressor.

Acquiescence means to give in to an oppressor.

mixed A final exam is where you show comprehensive knowledge.

On a final exam you show comprehensive knowledge.

MISPLACED (AND DANGLING) MODIFIERS

mm The margin note **"MM"** means misplaced modifier. A **modifier** is a word, phrase, or clause that is used to describe another word in the sentence. The modifier should be as close to that word as possible, or the meaning can be confusing or unintentionally humorous.

mm `Attacking our canary, I caught the cat.`

Written this way, *attacking the canary* refers to *I* rather than *cat.* Such a misplaced modifier can be easily corrected by rearranging the phrase so it describes *cat:*

`I caught the cat attacking our canary.`

Sometimes there may not be a word for the modifier to describe. In these cases, the sentence needs to be rewritten:

mm `At the age of 12, my family hiked into the Grand Canyon.`

Here the writer probably does not mean that his or her family was 12 years old, but this sentence does not contain a logical word for the opening phrase to describe. Therefore, *at the age of 12* is called a **dangling modifier** because it fails to refer logically to any word in the sentence. Dangling modifiers can be corrected by the following methods:

1. Keeping the modifier as it is and adding a word for the modifier to describe:

   `At the age of 12, I hiked into the Grand Canyon with my family.`

2. Turning the modifier into a dependent clause so that the meaning is clear:

   `When I was 12, my family hiked into the Grand Canyon.`

Often, the modifier is not simply "dangling" but is oddly placed in the sentence so that the meaning is absurd:

mm `You will value the difficult classes you took semesters from now.`

`Semesters from now, you will value the difficult classes you took.`

mm `Yuko's blind date was described as a six-foot-tall musician with a long ponytail weighing only 160 pounds.`

`Yuko's blind date was described as a 160-pound, six-foot-tall musician with a long ponytail.`

Misplaced words can turn even the most serious dissertation into a comedy of errors! Occasionally, an instructor may simply write "awk" (awkward) or "confusing" or "reword" in the margins when the error is actually a misplaced modifier. Becoming aware of the importance of the *placement* of each word or phrase in a sentence can help you detect and prevent such comical and confusing meanings before you type your final draft.

FAULTY PARALLELISM

To achieve clarity, emphasis, and harmony in writing, use **parallel construction** for parts of sentences that you repeat. The "parts" may be single words, phrases, or clauses. Therefore when you write any kind of list, put the items in similar grammatical form (all *-ing* words, all infinitives, and so on). Instead of writing "He likes hiking and to ski," you should write "He likes hiking and skiing" or "He likes to hike and to ski."

// If **faulty parallelism** is noted in the margin of your paper, you have not kept the parts of your sentence in the same grammatical form.

Single Words

// The movie entertained and was enlightening.

The movie was **entertaining** and **enlightening.**

Phrases

// Jane enjoys telling complicated jokes, performing the latest dances, and exotic food.

Jane enjoys **telling complicated jokes, performing the latest dances,** and **eating exotic food.**

Dependent Clauses

// The instructor reminded the students that papers must be submitted on time and to prepare reading assignments before class.

The instructor reminded the students **that papers must be submitted on time** and **that reading assignments must be prepared before class.**

Independent Clauses

// "I came, I did some learning, and I triumphed," announced the jubilant graduate.

"I came, I learned, and **I triumphed,"** announced the jubilant graduate.

You can also achieve greater clarity, emphasis, and balance by using parallel constructions with correlative conjunctions (paired terms such as *not only . . . but also; either . . . or;* and *neither . . . nor*):

// We discovered fast walking is good for health and also for friendship.

We discovered that fast walking is good **not only for health but also for friendship.**

// Fran doesn't work as a waitress any longer, and neither does Donna.

Neither Fran nor Donna works as a waitress any longer.

Mixture of Words and Phrases

The dancer was tall, graceful, and had a great sense of style.

The dancer **was tall and graceful** and **had a great sense of style.**

13

Understanding Punctuation

A **"P"** in the margin of an essay indicates some sort of error in punctuation. Because the comma is the most frequently used punctuation symbol, most errors occur in comma use. Commas usually function to separate elements within a sentence, but they also have standard uses in dates, addresses, and multiple-digit numbers. Below are models of the standard uses of the comma, with brief explanations to help you avoid comma errors.

THE COMMA

1. Use a comma *before a coordinating conjunction* joining independent clauses. (Coordinating conjunctions are *and, but, for, or, nor, yet,* and *so*. See also p. 520.)

   The school board has slashed the budget, so activity fees will increase this year.

   Many men want to take paternity leave when their babies are born, but most companies are not prepared for the requests.

   Short independent clauses may not need a comma with the conjunction, but if there is any doubt about the need or clarity, use the comma:

   He arrived so I left.

   He arrived, so I left.

2. Use a comma *to separate introductory elements* from the rest of the sentence:

   To register for classes, bring your advisor's signature card.

If elementary schools continue to close, increased bus service will be necessary.

Exhilarated, the climber reached the summit.

By the next century, most college graduates will be in service-related careers.

3. Use a comma *to separate items* in a series:

The campus bookstore has been criticized for selling cigarettes, sexist magazines, and greeting cards of questionable taste.

Triathlons require quick running, swimming, and cycling.

The requirements for ownership of the condominium include a bank-approved loan, a satisfactory security rating, and a willingness to comply with the homeowners' rules and procedures.

4. Use a comma *between coordinate adjectives* if there is not a conjunction. Coordinate adjectives are adjectives that modify the same word equally (and can be rearranged or joined with *and*).

The shady, blooming, fragrant garden welcomed the walkers.

A shady and fragrant garden welcomed the walkers.

For cumulative adjectives—those that don't modify the noun separately—do not use a comma because they can't be rearranged or joined with *and.*

That mansion features a beautiful white oak staircase.

Professor Pierce's exams require complicated mathematical computations.

5. Use commas *to set off nonrestrictive word groups.* Nonrestrictive elements describe nouns or pronouns by giving extra or nonessential information. The nonrestrictive element could be removed from the sentence without sacrificing the accuracy of the sentence.

Walden Pond, which is located outside of Concord, was the site of Thoreau's one-room shelter and bean field.

Amy Tan's first novel, The Joy Luck Club, was written in a few months.

```
The Rolls Royce, its silver hood ornament gleaming in
the sun, was completely out of gas.
```

6. Do *not* use commas with restrictive word groups. Restrictive elements limit the meaning of words or provide vital (or restricting) information.

   ```
   The entrees on the left side of the menu are suitable
   for diners who prefer low-cholesterol diets.
   ```

   The sentence gives the information that only the entrees on the left side of the menu are low in cholesterol. Presumably, the other items on the menu are not especially for clients who prefer low cholesterol.

   ```
   Our son who lived in Maryland studies American History.
   ```

   For a family with sons residing in different states, the restrictive clause is essential, and commas should not be used.

   ```
   Customers using credit cards collect free airline mileage.
   ```

   Again, the lack of commas shows that the information is restrictive. Only those customers who use credit cards will collect airline mileage; customers who pay by check or cash do not.

7. Use commas to separate transitional or parenthetical expressions, conjunctive adverbs, contrasting elements, and most phrases from the main part of the sentence:

   ```
   Silk, for example, can be washed by hand.
   ```

   ```
   Joseph Heller, as the story goes, wanted to call his
   novel Catch-18 instead of Catch-22.
   ```

   ```
   A medium avocado contains 324 calories; therefore, it is
   not an ideal fruit for people watching their weight.
   ```

   ```
   Darren, unlike his brother Stephen, can be reasonable.
   ```

   ```
   Her medical studies completed, Nancy started a practice
   in Fresno.
   ```

8. Use commas to set off expressions and questions of direct address, the words *yes* or *no,* and interjections:

   ```
   Sorry, Professor Doane, only two of those books are in
   the stacks.
   ```

   ```
   You will complete the immigration papers, won't you?
   ```

   ```
   Yes, most readers prefer the new MLA documentation form.
   ```

   ```
   Oh, I can't decide if we really need an attorney.
   ```

9. Use commas for dates, addresses, and titles:

    James Joyce was born on February 2, 1882, St. Bridget's Day and Groundhog Day, too.

    The special delivery letter was sent to 1010 Oak Street, Champaign, Illinois.

    Will Wood, Ph.D., begins his new research at Duke University.

10. Use commas to set off direct quotations:

    As Richard Ellman notes, "Stephen Dedalus said the family was a net which he would fly past."

    "I too believe in Taos, without having seen it. I also believe in Indians. But they must do half the believing: in me as well as in the sun," wrote D. H. Lawrence to Mabel Luhan.

11. Do *not* use a comma to separate a verb from its subject or object. The following examples all show **incorrect** uses of the comma:

    P Fast walking around a track, can be painless but effective exercise.

    P Christine explained to Mario, that law school studying had precedence over dining and dancing.

12. Do *not* use a comma between compound elements if the word groups are not independent clauses. The following examples show **incorrect** uses of the comma:

    P Frank can prepare a multi-course meal, and bake bread on the same day.

    P Sara understands that the conference is in June, and that she will need to grade finals while she is attending it.

13. A comma should not be used to separate an adjective from the noun that follows it. The following examples are **incorrect** uses of the comma:

    P It was a sunny, warm, and windless, day.

    P A massive, polished, ornately carved, buffet stood in the dining room.

THE APOSTROPHE

An **apostrophe** is used most frequently to form **contractions** and **possessives.**

Contractions

When two words are merged into one, the apostrophe takes the place of any missing letters:

does not	doesn't
it is	it's
should have	should've
I would	I'd

Contractions tend to make writing seem more conversational and informal; therefore, contractions are often avoided in formal writing and in research papers. Remember that the apostrophe takes the place of the missing letter and does not ever belong in the break between the two words:

couldn't [*not* could'nt]

Other instances in which apostrophes indicate a missing letter or letters are commonly found in informal writing and speech, particularly in dialogues from narratives and fiction:

around	'round
until	'til
1950s	'50s
playing	playin'

Again, such forms are typically reserved for writing that is intended to sound conversational.

Possessives

Possessive nouns indicate belonging or ownership and are typically placed immediately before whatever is owned. Rather than write "the trumpet of Jason" or "the office of his doctor," we eliminate the *of* and move the owner in front of the possession:

Jason's trumpet

his doctor's office

Sometimes such ownership is loosely implied:

tonight's party

Thursday's test

one day's sick leave

two weeks' vacation

But, in a sense, the party really does "belong" to tonight (not tomorrow) and the test "belongs" to Thursday (not Friday). Similarly, the sick leave is "of one day" and the vacation is "of two weeks." Clearly, the possessive form here makes the writing smoother and less wordy.

To indicate possession, obey the following guidelines:

1. Add *-'s* if the possessive noun does not end in *s* (whether it is singular or plural):

   Sarah's jokes

   Ben's request

   the men's movement

   the children's enthusiasm

2. Add an apostrophe at the end of the word if the possessive noun ends in an *s* (whether it is singular or plural):

   those actors' salaries

   five students' projects

   the Knights' generosity

   James' routine

   Yeats' poetry

You may find a variation of this second rule so that "Yeats' poetry" may be written "Yeats's poetry." It is correct either way.

Joint Possession When two or more people possess the same thing, show joint possession by using *-'s* (or *-s'*) with the last noun only:

We relaxed at Al and Helen's cabin.

Nate and Jess' help was appreciated.

Individual Possession When two or more people possess distinct things, show individual possession by using *-'s* (or *-s'*) with both nouns:

Andy's and Beth's summer projects aren't completed yet.

Luis' and Charles' questions were both fascinating.

Compound Nouns If a noun is compound, use *-'s* (or *-s'*) with the last component of that noun term:

My brother-in-law's woodworking is very professional.

Barbara and Joe took their sisters-in-law's advice.

Indefinite Pronouns Indefinite pronouns are those that refer to no specific person or thing: *everyone, anyone, no one,* and *something.* These pronouns also need an apostrophe to indicate possession:

We asked everybody's opinion of the film.

Is someone's safety in jeopardy?

Possessive Pronouns Possessive pronouns are already possessive and need no apostrophes:

my, mine
you, yours
her, hers
his
its
our, ours
their, theirs
whose

Whose car should we drive?

I would prefer to ride in **yours** rather than **theirs.**

Plurals of Numbers, Letters, Words, and Abbreviations Use *-'s* to pluralize numbers mentioned as numbers, letters mentioned as letters, words mentioned as words, and abbreviations. (Note: A number, letter, or word named as a word is usually italicized or underlined.)

They all marched in *two*'s.

He earned three *A*'s this term.

Their *hurray*'s were all we needed to hear.

All candidates must have earned their *B.A.*'s.

Exception: To indicate the years in a decade, simply add -s without an apostrophe.

The political demonstrations of the 1960s transformed the UB campus.

During the '90s, more schools have access to the Internet than they did in the '80s.

Some reminders:

1. Make sure a noun is possessive (and not merely plural) before you use an apostrophe. The noun *passengers* does not "own" anything in the following sentence; therefore it is a simple plural.

The ~~passenger's~~ passengers were not allowed to smoke.

2. Possessive pronouns need no apostrophes.

    The crowd expressed ~~it's~~ its pleasure.

    That responsibility is ~~her's~~ hers.

3. Many instructors prefer that their students not use contractions in formal writing and research papers.

THE PERIOD, QUESTION MARK, AND EXCLAMATION POINT

The most obvious use of the period is to mark the end of a sentence—unless the sentence is a direct question or needs an exclamation point:

Do you remember learning punctuation symbols in elementary school?

Yes, and it all seemed so easy then!

Because the exclamation point is used for strong commands and emphatic statements, it should not be overused. Further, an exclamation mark is never used with a period, a comma, or another exclamation point.

Don't use a question mark for an indirect or implied question:

I wonder if I ever had trouble with punctuation in elementary school.

Use the period for abbreviations:

Mr. Mrs. Ms.　　Dr. Rev. Capt.　　B.S. M.A. Ph.D.

B.C. A.D.　　A.M. P.M.　　i.e. e.g. etc.

Use only one period if the abbreviation falls at the end of a sentence:

Most archaeologists believe that Mayans were living in the area of Tikal by 600 B.C.

Notice that *no* period is used with postal abbreviations:

CA　NY　TX　IL

Do *not* use periods with acronyms (words that are made from the first letters of many words and are pronounced as words):

NATO　UNICEF

Usually no period is used in abbreviations of the names of organizations or schools:

NBC　NATO　UN　NBA　NYU

THE SEMICOLON

The semicolon is most often used to connect two independent clauses:

> Students with an advisor's signature card register in their division office; students without a signature must register in the gym.

Notice that the semicolon is used in place of a period to show that the two independent ideas—clauses that could stand alone as separate sentences—are *related.* The semicolon suggests the relationship without defining it.

The semicolon is also used after an independent clause and before some transitional phrases (such as *on the other hand* or *in contrast*) and after conjunctive adverbs (such as *therefore, however,* and *furthermore;* see the complete list on p. 526).

> Newcomers to the United States often enjoy material advantages that they lacked in their native lands; on the other hand, they often feel spiritually deprived in their new country.

> Professor Smiley will accept late papers; however, he reduces the grade for each day the paper is late.

The semicolon is used for separating items in a list if the punctuation within the list includes commas. Notice Naomi Wolf's use of the semicolon in this example from *The Beauty Myth:*

> In 1984, in the United States, "male lawyers aged 25-34 earn $27,563, but female lawyers the same age, $20,573; retail salesmen earn $13,002 to retail saleswomen's $7,479; male bus drivers make $15,611 and female bus drivers $9,903; female hairdressers earn $7,603 less than male hairdressers" (49).

THE COLON

A colon is used to introduce and call attention to a statement, rule or principle, and to introduce a direct quotation that is a complete sentence. Capitalize the first letter of a complete sentence if the sentence is a rule or principle or a quotation that begins with a capital letter.

> The candidates need to realize that women form a significant majority in this country: six million more potential votes.

In "Crimes Against Humanity," Ward Churchill cites shocking statistics relating to the American Indian: "The average life expectancy of a reservation-based Native American man is barely 45 years; women can expect to live less than three years longer" (165).

Dr. Blazer's policy is clear: United we soar—divided we stumble.

The colon is also used to introduce a list, to give bibliographic information, to report time, to separate main titles from subtitles, and to distinguish chapters from verses in the Bible.

The application form requires the following: a final transcript, a housing request, a medical report, and the first tuition check.

New York: Longman

Between Worlds: A Reader, Rhetoric, and Handbook

The train departs each morning at 5:30.

John 11:25

In some cases, a colon should not be used. For example, do *not* place a colon between a subject and a verb, between a verb and its complements, or between a preposition and its object:

The animals in that section of the zoo include: panthers, leopards, lions, and tigers.

The courses he needs to take are: biology, chemistry, physics, and calculus.

Don't put luggage on: the bed, the desk, or the reading chair.

THE DASH

The dash (which is sometimes created by typing two hyphens with no spaces around or between them) is used sparingly for dramatic emphasis, to call attention to material the dash sets off. Sometimes the dash is used in places where a colon could also be used, but the dash is considered more informal. Because the dash indicates a sudden shift in thought and is used for dramatic emphasis, it should not be overused. In formal writing, a comma, colon, or period may be more appropriate punctuation symbols.

We all believe that environmental protection is an obligation of our era—but we still use toxic cleaners in our homes.

Here the dash is used to emphasize the contrast between what "we all believe" and what we do. A comma could also be used in this sentence.

> Both successful women and less-successful women have the same goal—to "marry up"—so men still have a constant psychological need to be successful at work.

The dashes are used here to set off the definitive information, the "same goal" the writer believes women have. Commas could have been used, but the dashes achieve more emphasis.

The dash may also be used in the same manner as the colon to announce a dramatic point:

> The candidates need to realize that women form a significant majority in this country—six million more potential votes.

QUOTATION MARKS

Quotation marks are used to enclose direct quotations, some titles, and occasionally words defined or used in a special way. Quotation marks are used in pairs.

A *direct quotation* is noted with quotation marks. A direct quotation states in exact words what someone has said or written:

> Brigid Brophy insists, "If modern civilisation has invented methods of education which make it possible for men to feed babies and for women to think logically, we are betraying civilisation itself if we do not set both sexes free to make a free choice" (85).

Notice that Brophy's spelling of *civilisation* is British and that the writer quoting her is not permitted to change her spelling without indicating the change in brackets: "civili[z]ation." See more on brackets on page 554.

An *indirect quotation* notes what has been said in a paraphrased or indirect way. No quotation marks are needed:

> Brigid Brophy believes that men and women should be free to make the choices that education and technology have made possible (85).

A *quotation within a quotation* requires the use of standard quotation marks around the outside quotation and single quotation marks around the interior quotation:

According to Naomi Wolf, "Every generation since about 1830 has had to fight its version of the beauty myth. 'It is very little to me' said the suffragist Lucy Stone in 1855, 'to have the right to vote, to own property, etcetera, if I may not keep my body, and its uses, in my absolute right'" (11).

Commas and periods are placed inside quotation marks:

Brigid Brophy thinks that both genders should be "free to make a free choice" (85).

If we do not let men and women make choices, "we are betraying civilisation itself," believes Brigid Brophy (85).

Semicolons and colons are placed outside quotation marks:

Brophy says we are all "free to make a free choice"; in fact, we let convention limit our awareness of choice.

Brophy says we are all "free to make a free choice": about our educations, our careers, our domesticity.

Question marks go inside quotation marks if they are part of the quotation but belong outside of quotation marks if the quoted statement is being used as a question by the writer quoting the material:

The professor asked, "Who agrees with Brigid Brophy's thesis?"

Does Brophy think we "should be free to make a free choice"?

If you are quoting a conversation, begin a new paragraph for each speaker. Notice the punctuation of the quoted conversation in this excerpt from Bruce Halling's narrative, which appears on pages 386–388.

"Did you hear what happened to Ricky Liverpool?" one friend asked.

"Yeah," sighed the other friend as the door started closing.

"What happened?" I asked, feigning moderate interest.

If you are quoting poetry, integrate into your own text quoted single lines of poetry. Two or three lines of poetry may be brought into your text and enclosed in quotation marks, or they may be set off from your text without quotation marks but indented ten spaces from the left margin:

The gardener in Marge Piercy's poem "A Work of Artifice" "croons" to the plant as he "whittles" it into his desired shape. He says:

> It is your nature
> To be small and cozy
> domestic and weak;

or

The gardener in Marge Piercy's poem "A Work of Artifice" "croons" to the plant as he "whittles" it into his desired shape. He says, "It is your nature / To be small and cozy / domestic and weak."

The slash (/) is used when poetry lines are incorporated into a text to indicate the end of a poetry line. (The use of the slash is described further on pp. 554–555.) Set off poetry quotations of more than three lines and prose quotations of more than four lines.

Titles of short stories, songs, essays, poems, articles, parts of books, and the titles of episodes on television and radio are enclosed in quotation marks:

"My Man Bovanne"
"Chicago"
"Don't Let Stereotypes Warp Your Judgments"
"A Work of Artifice"
"Tracks" in *Aquaboogie*
"The Pool Guy" on *Seinfeld*

In special instances, quotation marks can be used to enclose words that are defined or used in a special way:

The "artifice" is not so much the "skill or ingenuity" used to shape women but the "trickery or craft" that keeps them dependent.

Do not use quotation marks around a word that you feel self-conscious about using. Instead, change the word:

The morning meeting is held to give the staff the "rundown" on the advertising goals for the day.

The morning meeting is held to explain that day's advertising goals to the staff.

THE ELLIPSIS

The ellipsis, a set of three spaced periods (. . .), informs the reader that something has been left out of a quotation. For example, a writer quoting material from Naomi Wolf's book *The Beauty Myth* might decide to leave out some material that is unnecessary to the text he or she is writing. Here Wolf writes about the phenomenon of eating disorders in countries other than the United States:

> It is spreading to other industrialized nations: The United Kingdom now has 3.5 million anorexics or bulimics (95 percent of them female), with 6,000 new cases yearly (183).

Here the passage is revised using an ellipsis:

> It is spreading to other industrialized nations: The United Kingdom now has 3.5 million anorexics or bulimics . . . with 6,000 new cases yearly (183).

The decision to remove material and use the ellipsis must be governed by the writer's intent. But the ellipsis may not be used to remove anything that would change the meaning of the section that the writer is quoting. The fact that 95 percent of the eating disorders in the United Kingdom are women may not be relevant to the writer of the revised text, so the ellipsis is used as a convenient tool to shorten the quoted material and keep the emphasis where the writer wants it. The missing words in this case do not change the meaning of the original.

If you remove material from the quoted material at the end of the sentence, use a period followed by the three spaced periods of the ellipsis. Notice this example of quoted material from H. Patricia Hynes' 1990 edition of *Earth Right:*

> The United States creates about 450,000 tons of residential and commercial solid waste every day. By the year 2000, this amount is expected to reach 530,000 tons per day. . . . The Environmental Protection Agency estimates that in the next five to ten years more than twenty-seven states and half of the country's cities will run out of landfill space (47).

If a parenthetical reference follows an ellipsis at the end of a sentence, use three spaced periods and then place the period to conclude the sentence after the final parenthesis:

> As Lisa Appignanesi records in her biography Simone de Beauvoir, Beauvoir believed that "the genuinely moral person can never have an easy conscience . . ." (79).

To avoid using the ellipsis too often, integrate carefully selected parts of quoted material into your text:

> As Carol Tavris notes, people respond "in shock and anger at the failings of 'human nature'" (276).

By paraphrasing part of the quotation and integrating the author's text with your own, you can avoid both using lengthy quotations *and* overusing the ellipsis.

PARENTHESES

Use parentheses to separate from the main material a digression or aside:

> Their house number (usually painted on the curb) was on the mail box.

> Because an increasing number of women (and men) are suffering from eating disorders, we must address the problem at our next NOW conference.

Rules govern the use of punctuation within and outside of parentheses. If a sentence requires a comma in addition to parentheses, use the comma after the second or closing parenthesis:

> During the Civil War (1861-65), African Americans were trained for active duty and fought in segregated units.

If the information within the parentheses is a complete sentence, the final punctuation is enclosed within the parentheses:

> More information on gardens that require little water appears throughout the book. (See the chapters on cactus and native plants, especially.)

Parentheses also are used in documentation to enclose the source of paraphrased or quoted information. In these cases the terminal punctuation appears outside the parentheses:

> As Virginia Woolf says in Orlando, "Clothes have . . . more important offices than merely to keep us warm. They change our view of the world and the world's view of us" (187).

(For a more complete discussion of how parentheses are used in MLA documentation, see pp. 488–502, and for their use in APA documentation, see pp. 502–507.)

BRACKETS

Use brackets to enclose words or phrases that you have added to a quotation, to show any changes that you have made in quoted material, or to record your own comments about quoted material:

> Today, more attention is being paid "to the relationship between eating disorders [anorexia and bulimia] and the compulsive eating of many women."

In the preceding example, the writer has clarified a point for the reader by defining within the quotation types of eating disorders. The brackets indicate that the words are not part of the original quotation.

> The Duke of Ferrara, in Robert Browning's poem "My Last Duchess," is disturbed that the Duchess "ranked [his] gift of a nine-hundred-years-old name / With anybody's gift."

In this example, the writer changed the original "my gift of a nine-hundred-years-old name" to fit into a text. To show the change from *my* to *his,* the writer placed brackets around the change. The diagonal line (or slash) between "name" and "With" indicates the end of the line in the poem.

> The "Poison Pen Letters" greeting card says, "Everything has it's [*sic*] price . . . but I didn't know you came so cheap!"

This use of the brackets is to enclose *sic,* a Latin word meaning "in this manner." The [*sic*] used after *it's* in the above example indicates that the error of not using *its* is in the original and is not an error written by the person quoting the original.

THE SLASH

The slash may be used sparingly to show options, as in pass/fail or Dean/Department Head. Notice that there is no space between the words and the slash when the slash is used to show options.

The slash is also used to define the end of a line of poetry if the line is incorporated into a text. For example, notice how the writer incorporates into a poetry explication some words from Kate Rushin's poem "The Bridge":

> The speaker in the poem observes that "Nobody / can talk to anybody," and the narrator resents the fact that she or he must function as a "connection to the rest of the world."

The slash indicates where the line ends in the original work (which appears on p. 195). Notice that a space appears on either side of the slash when it is used to indicate the end of a line of poetry.

In bulletins, reports, and some business correspondence, the slash is used in the form *he/she,* as in this sentence:

> The person who lost a ring in the library may claim it after he/she describes it to campus police.

In formal writing, you should avoid the form *he/she* by writing *he or she,* as in this sentence:

> The student who aspires to a law degree may attain it if he or she is willing to work hard.

Both *he/she* and *he or she* can be avoided by rewriting the sentence:

> The person who lost a ring in the library may claim it by describing it to campus police.

> The student who aspires to a law degree may attain it by working hard.

THE HYPHEN

The hyphen is used to divide a word or to form a compound word. To divide a word that will not fit on the typed or written line, separate the part of the word that will fit on the line with a hyphen at a syllable break, then conclude the word on the next line. The break must occur only between syllables and should not leave fewer than two letters at the end of the line or fewer than three letters at the beginning of the next line. The hyphen appears at the end of the first line, *not* at the beginning of the next line.

Notice how each error is corrected:

> Of all of the applicants for the job, she was the best te-
acher for the class.

> Of all of the applicants for the job, she was the best
teacher for the class.

A word can be broken between syllables if the break will leave at least two letters at the end of the line and three or more letters at the beginning of the next line. Because the syllables of *teach-* and *-er* will not fit that rule, the entire word must be moved to the next line.

P
```
After his paper was completed, the frustrated student fo-
und another critical article.
```

```
After his paper was completed, the frustrated student
found another critical article.
```

[A one-syllable word cannot be broken, so *found* must be moved to the next line.]

P
```
Since the 1993 Presidential inauguration, interest in the po-
-etry of Maya Angelou has increased.
```

```
Since the 1993 Presidential inauguration, interest in the po-
etry of Maya Angelou has increased.
```

[The hyphen is used *only* at the end of the first line.]

Divide compound words only where the hyphen already exists:

P
```
He gave the family heirloom to his sis-
ter-in-law.
```

```
He gave the family heirloom to his sister-
in-law.
```

P
```
Histories of popular music describe the heart-throb-
bing gestures of Elvis Presley.
```

```
Histories of popular music describe the heart-
throbbing gestures of Elvis Presley.
```

Hyphens are also used to form compound words that modify a noun if they precede the noun:

```
The grade-conscious students knew the best sequence for
the courses.
```

```
The award-winning play went on to Broadway.
```

If the modifiers follow the noun, the hyphens are usually left out.

```
The students are grade conscious.
```

```
The play was award winning and went on to Broadway.
```

Hyphens are used in spelled-out fractions and compound whole numbers from twenty-one to ninety-nine:

```
Over one-half of the voters will stay home election day.

Everyone hates that old school-bus song, "Ninety-Nine
Bottles of Beer on the Wall."
```

Hyphens are used to attach some prefixes and suffixes. Usually, prefixes are attached to a word without a hyphen: *preconceived, disinterested, unhappy.* But prefixes such as *ex-, self-,* and *all-,* prefixes that precede a capitalized word, or prefixes that are a capitalized letter usually require a hyphen; for example, *self-supporting, ex-champion, anti-European,* and *U-boat.* Sometimes, to prevent confusion, a hyphen is necessary to separate a prefix ending in a vowel and a main word that starts with a vowel; for example, *de-escalate, re-invent,* and *pre-advise.* A hyphen may also be necessary to avoid confusion between two words that have different meanings, such as *unionize* and *un-ionize.*

14

Understanding Faulty Word Choice

■ ■ ■

wd ch Poor word choice will weaken writing, and instructors will note these errors in the margins of papers. Specific examples are cited in the alphabetically arranged list of commonly confused words (pp. 562–571); the types of word choice problems are defined and exemplified here.

CLICHÉS

Clichés, or overused words or expressions, should be avoided because predictable language is stale. Expressions that were once novel and even colorful have lost their descriptive quality through overuse. Like a faded carpet, a cliché no longer adds color to the space it occupies. If you can complete the following expression automatically, you know that you have an example of a cliché:

> The bread was hard as a____________________.
>
> We searched all day, but it was like looking for a needle ____________________.

Good writing is clear, fresh, and vivid:

> The bread was as hard as aged camel dung and about as tasty.
>
> We searched all day, but it was like looking for a button in my mother's tool drawer.

SLANG, JARGON, AND COLLOQUIAL WORDS

Some of our most vivid language is considered **slang** (highly informal, often coined words that are used in speaking) or **jargon** (the special vocabulary of people who have the same job, interest, or way of life). In fact, in conversation, if pretentious language were substituted for some of the commonly used colloquial words—*intoxicated* for *drunk* or *children* for *kids*—our conversations would sound stuffy or silly. Slang is often vigorous and colorful, but it is nonstandard and therefore unacceptable in most formal writing. And the jargon that is acceptable in conversation or memos at work may be unintelligible to the general reader. If you think your "funky," "laid-back," or "awesome" word choice is going to influence negatively your reader's feelings about your integrity as a writer, elevate your language and remove the inappropriate word.

ARCHAIC WORDS, EUPHEMISMS, AND PRETENTIOUS WORDS

Some words that appear in literature, especially poetry, may not be appropriate for expository writing:

> Marcus Mabry was amongst the minority students accepted at Stanford.
>
> Marcus Mabry was among the minority students accepted at Stanford.

The word *amongst,* used in poetry, sounds inflated in expository texts.

Writers sometimes use **euphemisms**—substitutes for words that are perceived as offensive. One problem with euphemisms is they are often imprecise, as in this sentence: "We lost our grandmother last week." The reader might wonder whether she is still wandering in the parking lot of the local mall. Use direct and precise language to communicate accurately.

Pretentious language is used by writers who believe that it will make their work appear more refined or elegant. Avoid words such as *facilitate* or *utilize* when *help* and *use* are adequate. Some pretentious words have persisted and reached cliché status: *viable* and *parameters,* for example.

REDUNDANCIES

The legal profession has contributed some double-talk, such as *aid and abet,* to our language, and some other redundancies have persisted even though they are bulky or inane: *each and every, revert back, end result, temporary respite, exact same,* or *true fact.* You can see that *each* and *every* mean the same thing, so the words should not be used together. To revert means "to go back." And what is a fact if it isn't true? If you regard these redundancies as you would clichés—language that is predictable and imprecise—you will eliminate them from your writing.

SEXIST LANGUAGE

Language that demeans women or men is **sexist.** Most writers would know not to use *chick, broad, stud,* or *hunk* in papers. More subtle but equally insidious sexist language also needs to be avoided:

wd ch `The professor uses his wisdom to remain objective.`

wd ch `Each nurse is required to store her lunch in a locker.`

wd ch `A clever lawyer parks his car in the free lot.`

wd ch `The competent PTA president uses her gavel rarely.`

Even a superficial look at job and life-style choices in the last decades would confirm the necessity of unbiased language in print. Nurses and lawyers are both female and male; nowhere is it prescribed that only women will be PTA presidents. Consider the following choices for freeing your papers of sexist language:

`Professors use their wisdom to remain objective.`

`A professor uses wisdom to remain objective.`

`Nurses are required to store their lunches in lockers.`

`Each nurse is required to store his or her lunch in a locker.`

`Clever lawyers park their cars in the free lot.`

`A clever lawyer parks her or his car in the free lot.`

Vary using *his* or *her* pattern with *her or his,* but avoid this very awkward construction as often as possible by using a plural noun as the subject or by using the article instead of a possessive pronoun:

`Competent PTA presidents use their gavels rarely.`

`The competent PTA president uses the gavel rarely.`

Do not assume that any job is gender specific. *Fireman* should be *firefighter, clergyman* should be *minister* or *member of the clergy,* and *mailman* should be *letter carrier* or *mail carrier.* Do not add *lady* to job titles. "She is a lady doctor" is as inane as "He is a male artist."

You can further free your writing from sexism by eliminating the generic use of *man* in examples like the following:

> Mankind is more aware of stereotypes than it was a decade ago.
>
> Humanity is more aware of stereotypes than it was a decade ago.
>
> People are more aware of stereotypes than they were a decade ago.

15

Understanding Commonly Confused Words

■ ■ ■

There are a number of words that are often confused or misused by many writers, not just college students. Each of your authors learned something from the other about word choice as we compiled this list. Some words on this list are nonstandard, that is, words that are not considered acceptable for written work (for example, "should of" instead of "should have"). Certain words, called homonyms, are words that sound alike but have different meanings (for example, there/their/they're). You will find listed here a number of words that people misuse. Your audience and your intention will govern your word choice, but if you have an error noted in the margin of one of your papers, look here for an explanation in order to revise the language you used. Your instructor may use any one of the symbols listed on pp. 510–512 to denote your error.

COMMONLY CONFUSED WORDS

a, an Use *a* before words beginning with consonant sounds, including those spelled with an initial pronounced *h* (*a* horse) and those spelled with vowels that are sounded as consonants (*a* one-hour final, *a* university). Use *an* before words beginning with vowel sounds, including those spelled with an initial *h* (*an* igloo, *an* hour).

accept, except *Accept* is a verb meaning "to receive." *Except* is a preposition meaning "excluding" or "but."

I *accept* your plan to tour New York City *except* for the concert in Central Park.

advice, advise *Advice* is the noun meaning "opinion of what to do." *Advise* is the verb meaning "to give opinion or counsel."

I *advise* you to follow your counselor's *advice*.

affect, effect *Affect* is usually a verb meaning "to influence." *Effect* is a noun meaning "result." In psychology, *affect* is used as a noun meaning "a feeling or emotion." *Effect* can be used as a verb meaning "to implement, or to bring about."

The eyedrops do not *affect* his driving.

Candles create a romantic *effect* in the dining room.

An examination of *affect* is critical in understanding personality.

Congress must *effect* a change in the tax laws.

all ready, already *All ready* means "completely prepared." *Already* means "by now" or "before now."

We were *all ready* for the trip, but the bus had *already* left.

all right *All right* is standardly spelled as two words. (*Alright* appears in some dictionaries, but most readers still consider it a misspelling.)

all together, altogether *All together* means "in a common location," "in unison," or " as a group." *Altogether* means "completely" or "entirely."

We are *altogether* certain that caging the rabbits *all together* is a mistake.

allusion, illusion An *allusion* is an "indirect reference"; an *illusion* is "a deceptive appearance" or "a fantasy that may be confused with reality."

Mary Beth's use of biblical *allusions* gave the *illusion* that she was religious.

a lot *A lot* is always two words, never *alot.*

among, between Use *between* when referring to two; use *among* for three or more.

Between you and me, he is *among* the most creative students in the class.

amount, number *Amount* refers to a quantity of something that cannot be counted. *Number* refers to items that can be counted.

The *amount* of flour used depends on the *number* of cookies you want to bake.

anxious *Anxious* means "apprehensive" or "worried." Often it is confused with the word *eager,* which means "anticipating" or "looking forward to."

Yumiko was *anxious* about her tax refund because she was *eager* to buy a CD player.

a while, awhile *a while* is an article and a noun; *awhile* is an adverb.

We spoke for *a while* and then parted.

Wait *awhile* before you swim.

being as, being that These terms should not be used for *because* or *since.*

Because the lot is full, I parked on the street.

beside, besides *Beside* is a preposition meaning "next to." *Besides* is a preposition meaning "except" as well as an adverb meaning "in addition to."

The secretary sat *beside* his dean.

Everyone *besides* the team rides the school bus to each game.

Your expertise is needed; *besides,* you know how to have fun!

can, may *Can* means "is able to." "May" indicates permission.

You *can* talk on the telephone for three hours, but you *may* not in my house!

capital, capitol *Capital* refers to the city and is the word to describe an uppercase letter. *Capitol* indicates the building where government meets.

The *capital* is the destination for the class trip, but a visit to the *capitol* is impossible because the ceiling is under repair.

censor, censure *Censor* as a verb means "to suppress or remove objectionable material." *Censor* as a noun is "the person who suppresses the objectionable material." *Censure* means "to criticize severely."

The librarian refused to work with citizens who *censor* the classics.

The *censor* of a few decades ago *censored The Adventures of Huckleberry Finn!*

The city council needs to *censure* neon signs in "Old Town."

cite, site, sight *Cite* means "to quote by way of example, authority, or proof." *Site* is "the location of." *Sight* is a "spectacle or view."

The tourist *sights* were on the *site* of an ancient village as *cited* in the Fodor's Guide.

complement, compliment *Complement* means "to complete" or "something that completes or supplements another." *Compliment* is a noun or verb that means "to praise."

His sensitivity *complements* her assertiveness.

Most people see through false *compliments.*

conscience, conscious *Conscience* refers to one's sense of right and wrong. *Conscious* is an adjective that means "alert to or aware of."

The jury member was *conscious* of his nagging *conscience.*

could of, should of, would of These are incorrect forms for *could have, should have,* and *would have. Of* is a preposition, not a part of a verb.

The trainer *should have* exercised his horse today.

double negative Double negatives to emphasize negativity are nonstandard in English.

I didn't see anything [not *nothing*].

The child could hardly control [not *couldn't hardly control*] his tears.

due to *Due to* is used as an adjective to modify a noun, such as "injuries" in the following example, but is incorrectly used to modify a verb such as "canceled."

Most minor injuries during earthquakes are *due to* panic.

The beach party was canceled because of [not *due to*] rain.

due to the fact that Use *because* to avoid wordiness.

each *Each* is singular. (See also p. 530)

effect See **affect**

e.g. This is a Latin abbreviation meaning "for example." It is sometimes confused with *i.e.,* which means "that is." Neither of these abbreviations should be used in the text of a manuscript, but they can be used in parenthetical expressions.

either *Either* is singular. (See also p. 530).

elicit, illicit *Elicit* is a verb meaning "to evoke." *Illicit* is an adjective meaning "illegal or unlawful."

The attorney was unable to *elicit* any information from her client about *illicit* drug sales in the neighborhood.

emigrate from, immigrate to *Emigrate* means "to leave a country or region to settle elsewhere." *Immigrate* means "to enter another country and live there."

When Pano *emigrated* from Turkey, he missed living near the sea.

After the Revolution, many Cubans *immigrated* to the United States.

eminent, imminent *Eminent* means "celebrated" or "exalted." *Imminent* means "about to happen."

The *eminent* seismologist predicted that an earthquake was *imminent.*

especially, specially *Especially* means "particularly" or "more than other things." *Specially* means "for a specific reason."

Ryder *especially* values working on cabinets. He's known for *specially* ordered fine pieces of exotic woods.

etc. Avoid ending a list with the abbreviation *etc.* Writers often overuse it to suggest that they have more information than they do. The Latin expression is *et cetera,* which means "and others" or "and other things." The expression is best avoided because it is vague. It is also often misspelled as "ect."

everybody, everyone *Everybody* and *everyone* are singular. (See also p. 530).

except See **accept**

farther, further *Farther* refers to distance. *Further* implies quantity or degree. *Further* is now widely accepted for both meanings.

We drifted *farther* out to sea.

He is *further* along in his dissertation than his advisor expected.

fewer, less *Fewer* refers to items that can be counted. *Less* refers to measurable amounts.

Nathan does *fewer* chores and therefore earns *less* money than his brother.

firstly *Firstly* is pretentious. Use *first.*

fun *Fun* is colloquial when used as an adjective and should be avoided.

It was an amusing [not *fun*] movie.

further See **farther**

good, well *Good* is an adjective; *well* is usually an adverb.

Good work is almost always *well* rewarded.

hanged, hung *Hanged* refers to people. *Hung* refers to pictures and things that can be suspended.

The criminal was *hanged* from the tree.

The Walshes *hung* Debbie's recent paintings in the living room.

he, he/she, his/her The writer should no longer assume that *he* is an acceptable pronoun for all nouns. Further, *he/she* or *his/her* are awkward. To avoid this construction, use the plural or a specific noun instead of the pronoun. (See also pp. 528–529)

When a student works in a small group, he/she participates more.

When students work in small groups, they participate more.

hisself *Hisself* is nonstandard. Use *himself.*

hung See **hanged**

i.e. This Latin abbreviation should be replaced by the English *that is* in the text of a manuscript but may be used in parenthetical expressions.

illusion See **allusion**

imminent See **eminent**

imply, infer *Imply* means "to state indirectly or to suggest." *Infer* means "to come to a conclusion based on the evidence given."

By covering his ears, he *implied* that he no longer wanted to listen.

We can *infer* that the Duke of Ferrara is an arrogant man because he refused to "stoop" to speak to his wife.

irregardless *Irregardless* is nonstandard. Use *regardless.*

its, it's *Its* is the possessive form. *It's* is the contraction for *it is* or *it has* (see p. 545).

It's too bad that Dick and Jean's cat has injured *its* tail.

It's been a bad day for the Jacobys' cat.

later, latter *Later* refers to time. *Latter* refers to the second of two things named.

Initially, many southern European immigrants came to this country, but *later* the immigration policy restricted the numbers.

Both Diego Rivera and his wife Frida Kahlo painted, but the *latter* has gained more public recognition in the last few years.

lay, lie *Lay* means "to place or put" and requires an object. (The past tense is *laid.*) *Lie* means "to rest or recline." (The past tense of *lie* is *lay,* and so the two words are sometimes confused.)

Lay the piano music on the bench where Mrs. Main *laid* it yesterday.

The dog will *lie* down exactly where he *lay* yesterday.

lead, led The present tense of the verb is *lead,* and the past tense is *led.* However, *lead* is also used as a noun, meaning a grey metal, and confusion results because it is pronounced the same as *led.*

Lexa will *lead* the tour to Istanbul, and then it will be *led* by Barbara.

Usually plumbers replace *lead* pipes with copper.

loose, lose *Loose* is an adjective meaning "unrestrained or unfastened." *Lose* is a verb meaning "to misplace" or "to be defeated."

If his bathing suit is too *loose,* Lester will *lose* it in the next wave.

lots, lots of Avoid these constructions in formal writing. Elevate the diction to *many* or *much.*

mankind Avoid this term, as its sexism offends many readers. Use *humans, humanity,* or *humankind* instead.

It was one small step for the man who walked on the moon, but it was a giant step for *humanity.*

maybe, may be *Maybe* is an adverb that means "perhaps." *May be* is a verb.

Maybe the community will improve its social services, but that *may be* the only benefit of the turmoil.

may of, might of These are nonstandard forms of *may have* and *might have.* Avoid them.

media, medium *Media* is the plural of *medium.*

Pablo Picasso created clay forms and sculptures in wood and wire, but paint is the *medium* for which he is best known. Perhaps the *media* should review his other art forms.

myself *Myself* is a reflexive or intensive pronoun and, like the other *-self* pronouns, should not be used in place of personal pronouns.

I drove *myself* to the hospital because no one else was home.

"I can do it *myself!*" the toddler protested.

Juan ladled the chili for his father and me [not *myself*].

neither *Neither* is singular. (See also p. 530)

Neither of us is available to babysit tonight.

nohow *Nohow* is nonstandard for *in any way.*

none *None* may be singular or plural, depending on whether the noun or pronoun to which it refers is singular or plural.

None of the alternatives seems reasonable.

None of the students walk to campus. (all don't)

nowheres *Nowheres* is nonstandard for *nowhere.*

number See **amount**

of *Of* should not be used in constructions like *should have* or *would have. Of* is a preposition.

off of *Of* is not necessary with *off.* Use *off* alone or use *from.*

The marbles rolled *off* the table and continued rolling around Monahan's room.

O.K., OK, okay All three forms are acceptable, but in formal writing these expressions are inappropriate.

on account of A wordy way to write *because.*

only *Only* should directly precede the word or phrase to which it applies.

Only Vin cooked the dinner. (No one else cooked.)

Vin *only* cooked the dinner. (He didn't do the preparation or clean-up.)

Vin cooked *only* the dinner. (He didn't make the dessert or any other meals.)

owing to the fact that A wordy way to write *because.*

plus *Plus* is not appropriately used as a conjunction to join independent clauses. Use a standard coordinating or adverbial conjunction.

We celebrated the Fourth of July with hot dogs, corn on the cob, potato salad, and watermelon; in addition, [not *plus*] we enjoyed the firework display at Zaca Lake.

precede, proceed The verb *precede* means "come before" (note the prefix *pre-*). The verb *proceed* means "go forward" or "move on."

Spanish 4 *precedes* Spanish 5, "Literature of Mexico."

To *proceed* without a contract would be foolish.

prejudice, prejudiced *Prejudice* is a noun; *prejudiced* is an adjective. Do not leave out the *-d* from the adjective.

Prejudice that starts in childhood is difficult to obliterate, and he was distinctly *prejudiced* against working mothers.

principal, principle *Principal* is a noun for the "chief official" or, in finance, the "capital sum." As an adjective, "principal" means "major" or "most important." *Principle* is a noun meaning "a law or truth, rule, or axiom."

The school's *principal* uses two *principles* for deciding the graduation speakers: which students have the best grades and which students have the best *principles* to share with classmates.

The *principal* goal of the vacation is to relax.

proceed, precede See **precede**

raise, rise *Raise* is a verb meaning "to move or cause to move up," and it takes an object. *Rise* is a verb meaning "to go up," and it does not take a direct object.

The farmers who *raise* cows are concerned about the disease.

They *rise* early to attend to the livestock.

reason is because In speech, this expression is common. In formal writing, it is not appropriate. A clause using *that* is the preferred form:

The *reason* he paid his rent early was *that* [not *because*] he intended to be out of town on the first of the month.

reason why The expression *reason why* is redundant. *Reason* is sufficient.

The *reason* [not *reason why*] Jorge attends law school at night is not obvious to anyone but his family.

rise, raise See **raise, rise**

should of *Should of* is nonstandard; use *should have.*

He *should have* [not *should of*] known not to build a campfire on that windy hill.

since *Since* is sometimes used to mean *because,* but it is clear only as a conjunction in constructions having to do with time.

Andy has been waiting *since* January for his tax forms.

Since [or *because?*] you left, I've been dating others.

sit, set *Sit* means "to rest the weight of the body" as on a chair. *Set* means "to place."

Dorothy wants you to *sit* on the black leather sofa.

Tom would rather you not *set* stoneware dishes on his cherry-wood table.

site, cite, sight See **cite, site, sight**

somebody, someone *Somebody* and *someone* are singular. (see p. 530)

sometime, some time, sometimes *Sometime* means "at an indefinite time." *Some time* is the adjective *some* modifying the noun *time. Sometimes* means "now and then."

Sometime we should get together and play tennis.

Raul devoted *some time* to perfecting his pronunciation.

Sometimes Ken discards every yolk from the eggs as he prepares his omelette.

supposed to, used to Don't neglect to use the *-d* ending on these often used and often misspelled words!

He is *supposed to* [not *suppose to*] bring the wine for the dinner.

Ariane became *used to* [not *use to*] Dee's indifferent housekeeping.

than, then *Than* is used in comparisons. *Then* is an adverb denoting time.

There are many more calories in avocados *than* in apples.

First Sylvia Plath attended the school, and *then* she taught there.

their, there, they're *Their* is a possessive pronoun. *There* is an adverb denoting place. *They're* is a contraction meaning *they are.*

Their plans for hang gliding *there* in the park are apt to be postponed because *they're* not ready to pass the safety test.

then, than See **than, then.**

there is, there are The verb following the pronoun "there" is singular or plural according to the number of the subject that follows the verb. (See also p. 531)

There is a dictionary on the table. *There are* books and keys on the table.

this here, these here, that there, them there Nonstandard for *this, these, that,* or *those.*

thru *Thru* is a nonstandard spelling of *through* that should be avoided in all formal writing.

thusly Use *thus,* which is less pretentious.

till, until, 'til *Till* and *until* have the same meaning, and both are used. *'Til* is an unnecessary contraction of *until.*

to, too, two *To* is a preposition meaning "toward" and is part of the infinitive form of the verb (for example, to *run*). *Too* is an adverb meaning "overly." *Two* is a number.

Two trips *to* the market in one day are not *too* many for a fine cook like Mike.

toward, towards Either form is acceptable, but *toward* is preferred.

try and *Try and* is nonstandard; *try* to is preferred.

Try to [not *try and*] meet Mohammed before he locks up his bike.

unique *Unique* means "distinctively characteristic." It is an absolute adjective that shouldn't be modified by "most" or "very."

A tuxedo shirt and jacket, bow tie, and Bermuda shorts create a *unique* [not *most unique*] style for a hot-weather prom.

until See **till, until, 'til**

usage The noun *use* should be used whenever possible. *Usage* refers only to convention, as in *language usage.*

The *use* [not *usage*] of computers has facilitated essay writing, but papers with proper *usage* have not increased because of expensive equipment.

used to See **supposed to, used to**

weather, whether *Weather* is a noun that refers to the atmospheric conditions. *Whether* is a conjunction that indicates the possibility of alternatives.

Gail wasn't certain *whether* the stormy *weather* would keep John and Mark from jogging to Niagara Falls.

well See **good, well**

which, in which Writers occasionally use *in which* in places where *which* is sufficient. Read work carefully to eliminate the unnecessary preposition.

Salma grabbed the gray cape, *which* [not *in which*] had been left on the sofa.

which, who *Which* is used for a thing or things, not for people. Use *who* for people.

Martin Luther King, the American *who* defined civil disobedience for his generation, was a theologian as well as a political figure. His letter from Birmingham, *which* he wrote in jail, defines his position.

while Do not use *while* to mean *although* if there is a chance of confusion for the reader. Like *since, while* should be reserved for time sense. Unless the point is to show that the actions occur at the same time, *although* is the better word.

Nick begins cooking dinner *while* Chris drives home from Richmond.

Although [not *while*] Elizabeth continues to invest their savings, Bill never resists a rug sale.

who's, whose *Who's* is the contraction for *who is* or *who has*. *Whose* is a possessive pronoun.

Who's going to return the library books?

Who's been reading *Aquaboogie?*

That depends on *whose* book is due.

would of *would of* is nonstandard for the complete verb *would have.*

Los Vendidos would have [not *would of*] been a perfect theater experience for Cinco de Mayo.

you The indefinite use of *you,* or even its use to mean "you the reader," can be incongruous or offensive and can be avoided:

A decade ago, the fit hiker [rather than *you*] could camp on the beach with the seals at Pt. Sal, but now even the poor trail has eroded.

It is common practice in some African tribes for prepubescent females [rather than *you*] to be scarified.

your, you're *Your* is a possessive pronoun. *You're* is the contraction of *you are.*

Your savings will disappear if *you're* not careful.

Acknowledgments

■ ■ ■

Anzaldua, Gloria. "To live in the Borderlands means you..." reprinted from *Barrios and Borderlands* by Gloria Anzaldua. Copyright ©1994. Reprinted with permission of the publisher, Routledge.

Berry, Wendell. "Waste" from *What Are People for?* by Wendell Berry. Copyright © 1990 by Wendell Berry. Reprinted by permission of North Point Press, a division of Farrar, Straus & Giroux, Inc.

Brophy, Brigid. Excerpt from *Women: Invisible Cages* by Brigid Brophy. Reprinted by permission of Curtis Brown Group Ltd.

Brott, Armin. "Not All Men Are Sly Foxes" by Armin Brott from *Newsweek,* June 1, 1992. Reprinted by permission of the author.

Cade Bambara, Toni. "My Man Bovanne" from *Gorilla, My Love* by Toni Cade Bambara. Copyright © 1972 by Toni Cade Bambara. Reprinted by permission of Random House, Inc.

Churchill, Ward. "Crimes Against Humanity" by Ward Churchill. Reprinted by permission of the author.

Coleman, Jennifer A. "Discrimination at Large" by Jennifer A. Coleman from *Newsweek,* August 2, 1993. Reprinted by permission of the author.

Dacey, Philip. "Coke" reprinted from *Night Shift at the Crucifix Factory* by Philip Dacey by permission of the University of Iowa Press. Copyright © 1991 by Philip Dacey.

Dorris, Michael. "Fetal Alcohol Syndrome" from *Paper Trail* by Michael Dorris. Copyright © 1994 by Michael Dorris. Reprinted by permission of HarperCollins Publishers, Inc.

Edwards, Kim. "In Rooms of Women" by Kim Edwards. Reprinted by permission of the author.

Ehrenreich, Barbara. Excerpt from "Angry Young Men" by Barbara Ehrenreich as appeared in *New York Woman,* September 1989. Reprinted by permission of the author.

Erens, Pamela. "Bodily Harm" by Pamela Erens, originally appeared in *MS* Magazine, October 1985. Reprinted by permission of the author.

Farrell, Warren. "Men As Success Objects" by Warren Farrell from *Family Therapy Networker,* November/December 1988. Reprinted by permission of the author.

Goodman, Ellen. "Thanksgiving" and "When a Woman Says No" by Ellen Goodman. Copyright © 1996, The Boston Globe Newspaper Co./Washington Post Writers Group. Reprinted with permission.

Gross, Amy. "The Appeal of the Androgynous Man" by Amy Gross (appeared in *Mademoiselle,* May 1976). Copyright © 1976 by Amy Gross. Used by permission of the Wallace Literary Agency, Inc.

Harrison, Dr. William F. "Why Stop Smoking: Let's Get Clinical" by Dr. William F. Harrison. Reprinted by permission of the author.

Heaney, Seamus. "Digging" from *Selected Poems 1966-1987* by Seamus Heaney. Copyright © 1990 by Seamus Heaney. Reprinted by permission of Farrar, Straus & Giroux, Inc. and Faber and Faber Ltd.

Hynes, H. Patricia. "Solid Waste: Treasure in Trash" by H. Patricia Hynes from *Earthright.* Reprinted by permission of the author.

Kafka, Barbara. "The Myth of Thin" by Barbara Kafka as appeared in *Gourmet,* May 1996. Reprinted by permission of Barbara Kafka Associates.

King, Jr., Martin Luther. "Three Ways of Meeting Oppression" from *Stride Toward Freedom* by Martin Luther King, Jr. Copyright © 1958 by Martin Luther King, Jr., copyright renewed 1986 by Coretta Scott King. Reprinted by arrangement with The Heirs to the Estate of Martin Luther King, Jr., c/o Writers House Inc. as agent for the proprietor.

Kooser, Ted. "The Blind Always Com as Such a Surprise" by Ted Kooser from *Heartland II: Poets of the Midwest,* edited by Lucien Stryk. Copyright © 1975 by Northern Illinois University Press. Used by permission of the publisher.

Leonard, John. "The Only Child" by John Leonard from *Private Lives in the Imperial City* by John Leonard. Reprinted by permission of the author.

Lester, Joan Steinau. Excerpt from "The Old Images" from *The Future of White Men and Other Dilemmas* by Joan Steinau Lester. Reprinted by permission of the author.

Marby, Marcus. "Living in Two Worlds" by Marcus Marby *Newsweek on Campus.* All rights reserved. Reprinted by permission.

Marcus, Eric. "Ignorance Is Not Bliss" by Eric Marcus from *Newsweek,* July 5, 1993. All rights reserved. Reprinted by permission.

Mattlin, Ben. "An Open Letter to Jerry Lewis" by Ben Mattlin. Reprinted by permission of the author.

McCarthy, Sarah J. "Why Johnny Can't Disobey" by Sarah J. McCarthy as appeared in *The Humanist Magazine,* September/October 1979. Reprinted by permission of the author.

McInerney, Jay. "Is *Seinfeld* the Best Comedy Ever?" by Jay McInerney. Permission granted by International Creative Management Inc. Copyright © 1996 by Jay McInerney. Article first appeared in *TV Guide.*

Moog, Bob. "Who's Not Supporting Whom?" by Bob Moog from *Keyboard Magazine,* September 1992. Reprinted by permission of The GPI Group.

Naylor, Gloria. "Mommy, What Does Nigger Mean?" by Gloria Naylor as appeared in *The New York Times Magazine,* 1986. Reprinted by permission of Sterling Lord Literistic, Inc. Copyright © 1986 by Gloria Naylor.

Negroponte, Nicholas. "Get a Life?" by Nicholas Negroponte as appeared in *Wired* Magazine, September 1995. Rerpinted by permission of The Robbins Office, Inc.

Noyes, Dorothy. "Senior-Teener, A New Hybrid" by Dorothy Noyes from *Newsweek,* September 5, 1994. All rights reserved. Reprinted by permission.

Oates, Joyce Carol. "Where Are You Going, Where Have You Been?" by Joyce Carol Oates from *The Wheel of Love and Other Stories.* Copyright © 1970 by Joyce Carol Oates. Reprinted by permission of John Hawkins & Associates, Inc.

Olds, Sharon. "On the Subway" from *The Gold Cell* by Sharon Olds. Copyright © 1987 by Sharon Olds. Reprinted by permission of Alfred A. Knopf, Inc.

Perrin, Noel. "The Androgynous Man" by Noel Perrin from *The New York Times Magazine,* February 5, 1984. Copyright © 1984 by The New York Times Co. Reprinted by permission.

Piercy, Marge. "A Work of Artifice" from *Circles on the Water* by Marge Piercy. Copyright © 1982 by Marge Piercy. Reprinted by permission of Alfred A. Knopf, Inc.

Rapping, Elayne. "The Seinfeld Syndrome" by Elayne Rapping from *The Progressive,* September 1995, pp. 37-38. Reprinted by permission of *The Progressive,* 409 East Main Street, Madison, WI 53703.

Rushin, Kate. "The Bridge Poem" by Kate Rushin as appeared in *This Bridge Called My Back: Writings by Radical Women of Color.* Reprinted by permission of Kitchen Table: Women of Color Press and the author.

Sackett, Victoria. "Discriminating Tastes: The Prejudice of Personal Preferences" by Victoria Sackett as appeared in *Public Opinion,* July/August, 1987. Reprinted with the permission of The American Enterprise Institute for Public Policy Research, Washington, D.C.

Scales-Trent, Judy. "When the Government Decides Your Race" by Judy Scales-Trent as appeared in *The Los Angeles Times,* July 3, 1996. Reprinted by permission of the author.

Soto, Gary. "Like Mexicans", from *Small Faces* by Gary Soto. Copyright © 1986 by Gary Soto. Used by permission of Delacorte Press, a division of Bantam Doubleday Dell Publishing Group, Inc.

Soyster, Matthew. "Living Under Circe's Spell" by Matthew Soyster from *Newsweek,* October 11, 1993. All rights reserved. Reprinted by permission.

Staples, Brent. "Just Walk on By: Black Men in Public Space" by Brent Staples as appared in *MS Magazine.* Reprinted by permission of the author.

Stoll, Cliff. "Second Thoughts on the Information Highway" by Cliff Stoll. Reprinted by permission of the author.

Straight, Susan. "Proper Care and Maintenance" by Susan Straight as appeared in *The Los Angeles Times Magazine,* June 30,1 991. Reprinted by permission of The Richard Parks Agency. Copyright © 1991 by Susan Straight.

Sweet, Ellen. "Date Rape: The Story of an Epidemic and Those Who Deny It" by Ellen Sweet, originally appeared in *MS Magazine,* October 1985. Reprinted by permission of the author.

Tabaldo, Jennifer. Poetry analysis on the poem "Digging" by Seamus Heaney by Jennifer Tabaldo. Reprinted by permission of the author.

Tavris, Carol. "In Groups, We Shrink From Loner's Heroics" by Carol Tavris. Copyright © 1991 by Carol Tavris. Rerpinted by permnissin of Lescher & Lescher, Ltd.

Thomas, Chris. Summary of an excerpt from *Stride Toward Freedom* by Martin Luther King, Jr. by Chris Thomas. Reprinted by permission of the author.

Thompson, Cooper. "A New Vision of Masculinity" by Cooper Thompson as appeared in *Changing Men,* Volume 14, Spring 1985.

Tompkins, Jane. "Indians': Textualism, Morality, and the Problem of History" by Jane Tompkins. Copyright © 1986. Reprinted by permission of The University of Chicago Press and the author.

Tyler, Anne. "Your Place is Empty" by Anne Tyler as appeared in *The New Yorker,* November 22, 1976. Reprinted by permission of Russell & Volkening as agents for the author. Copyright © 1976 by Anne Tyler.

Ventura, Michael. "The Ties That Bind" by Michael Ventura as appeared in *The Los Angeles Times,* April 14, 1996. Reprinted by permission of the author.

White, Walter. From *A Man Called White* by Walter White. Copyright 1948 by Walter White, renewed © 1976 by the Estate of Walter White. Used by permission of Viking Penguin, a division of Penguin Books USA Inc.

Author Index

Note: Bold face indicates location of reading.

Subject and Title Index

■ ■ ■

Note: Bold face indicates location of reading.